THE FAR NORTHEAST

THE FAR NORTHEAST

3000 BP to Contact

**Edited by Kenneth R. Holyoke
and M. Gabriel Hrynick**

MERCURY SERIES
ARCHAEOLOGY PAPER 181
CANADIAN MUSEUM OF HISTORY
AND UNIVERSITY OF OTTAWA PRESS

Co-published by the **Canadian Museum of History** *and the* **University of Ottawa Press**
The University of Ottawa Press gratefully acknowledges the support extended to its publishing list by the Government of Canada, the Canada Council for the Arts, the Ontario Council for the Arts, the Federation for the Humanities and Social Sciences through the Awards to Scholarly Publications Program, and the University of Ottawa.

Copy editing	Robbie McCaw
Proofreading	James Warren
Typesetting	Nord Compo
Indexing	Tere Mullin
Cover design	Lefrançois agence marketing B2B
Cover image	*Wolastoqey: Pilick, Pihce,* Austin Paul

Legal Deposit: First Quarter 2022
Library and Archives Canada

**Library and Archives Canada
Cataloguing in Publication**

Title: The Far Northeast : 3000 BP to contact / edited by Kenneth R. Holyoke and M. Gabriel Hrynick.
Names: Holyoke, Kenneth R., editor. | Hrynick, M. Gabriel, 1988- editor.
Series: Mercury series.
Description: Series statement: Mercury series | Includes bibliographical references and index.
Identifiers: Canadiana (print) 20210222247 | Canadiana (ebook) 20210222425 | ISBN 9780776629650 (softcover) | ISBN 9780776629667 (PDF)
Subjects: LCSH: Woodland culture—Atlantic Provinces. | LCSH: Woodland culture—New England. | LCSH: Atlantic Provinces—Antiquities. | LCSH: New England—Antiquities.
Classification: LCC E99.W84 F37 2021 | DDC 971.5/00909—dc23

The Mercury Series

The best resource on the history, archaeology, and culture of Canada is proudly published by the Canadian Museum of History and the University of Ottawa Press.

La Collection Mercure

Le Musée canadien de l'histoire et les Presses de l'Université d'Ottawa publient avec fierté la meilleure ressource en ce qui a trait à l'histoire, à l'archéologie et à la culture canadiennes.

For this book/Pour ce livre

Series Editor/Direction de la collection:
Pierre M. Desrosiers

Editorial Committee/Comité éditorial:
Laura Sanchini, Janet Young, Karen Ryan, Gabriel Yanicki

Managing Editor/Responsable de l'édition: Robyn Jeffrey

Coordination: Lee Wyndham

How to Order

All trade orders must be directed to the University of Ottawa Press:
Web: www.press.uottawa.ca
Email: puo-uop@uottawa.ca
Phone: 613-562-5246

All other orders may be directed to either the University of Ottawa Press (as above) or to the Canadian Museum of History:

Web: www.historymuseum.ca/shop
Email: publications@historymuseum.ca
Phone: 1-800-555-5621 (toll-free) or 819-776-8387 (National Capital Region)
Mail: Mail Order Services
Canadian Museum of History
100 Laurier Street
Gatineau, QC, K1A 0M8

Pour commander

Les libraires et les autres détaillants doivent adresser leurs commandes aux Presses de l'Université d'Ottawa :
Web : www.presses.uottawa.ca
Courriel : puo-uop@uottawa.ca
Téléphone : 613-562-5246

Les particuliers doivent adresser leurs commandes soit aux Presses de l'Université d'Ottawa (voir plus haut), soit au Musée canadien de l'histoire :
Web : www.museedelhistoire.ca/magasiner
Courriel : publications@museedelhistoire.ca
Téléphone : 1-800-555-5621 (numéro sans frais) ou 819-776-8387 (région de la capitale nationale)
Poste : Service des commandes postales
Musée canadien de l'histoire
100, rue Laurier
Gatineau (Québec) K1A 0M8

ONTARIO ARTS COUNCIL
CONSEIL DES ARTS DE L'ONTARIO
An Ontario government agency
un organisme du gouvernement de l'Ontario

Canada Council for the Arts   Conseil des arts du Canada

Canada

uOttawa

Ken dedicates this volume to Carolyn,
Ruby, and Logan, whose love
and support make everything possible.

Gabe dedicates this volume to Nadine Byers,
his favourite person to be near in
the Far Northeast or anywhere else.

Table of Contents

List of Illustrations

TABLES

Wolastoqey: Pilick, Pihce

The People of the Beautiful and Bountiful River:
Kingsclear, A Long Time Ago

Artist Statement
The painting depicted on the cover of this book is based on a photograph in
the Provincial Archives of New Brunswick by George T. Taylor (photo P5-170).
It depicts a scene on the Wolastoq (Saint John River) in Pilick (Kingsclear First
Nation).

I grew up in the Kingsclear First Nation, on the banks of the Wolastoq,
paddling and fishing its waters since childhood, as my ancestors have done since
time immemorial. The painting is reminiscent of times past, when the air was
alive with sounds of salmon breaching the water's surface and smashing back
down into the Wolastoq; a time when the river valley echoed with the sounds
of paddles hitting canoe gunwales and the lingering smell of fish being smoked
in great hearths along the shoreline.

When looking at the painting, I am reminded of the creativity of my people.
The attire worn by the ancestors was painstakingly adorned with intricate bead
and quill work, each having their own unique patterns and motifs. I think of
the ancient ways of creating textiles and tanning hides for clothing; of creating

beads from clay, bone, stone, antler, shell, copper; and of the tools required to realize these aspects of culture and technology.

I think of the importance of the canoe: the exquisite product of the interaction of an environmentally savvy people and their surroundings. The canoe exemplifies the deep relationship the Wolastoqey have with their territory. Plant and animal resources are carefully sourced, processed, and combined into a functional artistic masterpiece that enables the people to become one with the water and wind. To construct a canoe, one would need an intimate knowledge of the characteristics of the materials that go into the craft, and of how to construct and wield the required tools. Safely and skillfully operating a canoe involves another vast body of knowledge, as does navigating the myriad of rivers, lakes, and streams that nourish the landscape. It is humbling to think that this knowledge was passed down through the millennia.

This painting also recalls the resilience and adaptability of the people, evident in the melding of Indigenous and European culture. Even after generations of external influences, the Wolastoqey retain their cultural identity and are proud of who they are: people of the beautiful and bountiful river.

Austin Paul
July 2021

Preface and Acknowledgements

This volume, *The Far Northeast: 3000 BP to Contact*, arises from a number of observations and suppositions about both the period and the related scholarship that have emerged in recent years. The first was, simply, a collection of papers about the Far Northeast—roughly northern New England, the Atlantic Canadian provinces, Quebec, and the nearby parts of Labrador—were published relatively recently, particularly about its Palaeoindian (see Chapdelaine 2012) and Archaic (see Sanger and Renouf 2006) periods. These publications offered an important culture-historical synthesis that did not exist for the Far Northeast after 3000 BP (cf. Deal and Blair 1991; Tuck 1976, 1984). For the Palaeoindian period, an abundance of recent research into the Northeast generally supports the notion of a shared cultural phenomenon across the Maine–Maritimes region (e.g., Singer 2017; Spiess and Wilson 1989). The Archaic period, in contrast, is characterized by overlapping cultural phenomena, some apparently shared over large areas of the Northeast (e.g., the Moorehead burial tradition) and elsewhere (e.g., Susquehanna River, the northeastern United States), and some locally defined but with more tenuous regional connections (e.g., the Gulf of Maine Archaic Tradition). In short, whether one takes a "lumper" or "splitter" view of the past 3,000 years, our impression was (and is) that we could benefit from a similar regional treatment to the more recent three millennia of pre-Contact history; that is, before the arrival of Europeans.

After spending much of the past few years talking about the possibility of a Woodland-period volume for the Far Northeast, and talking with each other, peers, mentors, and friends, we decided that it was time to bring together a cadre of researchers to talk about their perspectives on the period after ca. 3000 BP. When we called on authors to join us at the 52nd Annual Meeting of the Canadian Archaeological Association, in Québec City in 2019, we were struck by the immediate and positive response. We had endeavoured from the outset to produce a volume out of the eponymous session, and many authors in this volume joined us with draft manuscripts for two full days in a sunny room just off the side of the lobby at the Hilton Québec. Suffice it to say, we remain overwhelmed by the response, and by the quality of the scholarship contained herein.

While at the conference, we opted to group papers thematically; we discovered in reading the papers that many of the themes we highlighted throughout the two days—cultural continuity and discontinuity, diachronic change, material cultural conformity and nonconformity, intensification, place and place making, gender, identity, and the reality (or not) of archaeological boundaries—are scattered throughout each piece. Indeed, the volume itself is meant to be thematic for a particular period in a specific geography that encompasses much of northern New England, Quebec, and the Atlantic provinces. With that, the volume moves through the geography of the Far Northeast, from northern Vermont to Newfoundland and Labrador. In doing so, chapters jump back and forth through time (and space), crossing both of the titular, and quite arbitrary, temporal boundaries at 3,000 years and "Contact"—between Indigenous peoples and Europeans in North America, usually slotted at 500 BP, or 1500 CE— several times, highlighting the challenges of writing updated cultural histories in the antiquated frameworks of archaeology on this continent. The choice of Contact as a terminal point for this volume, and a rough estimate of 500 BP or 1500 CE, is arbitrary (see also Silliman's 2005 critiques of the term). Despite this, we think it is appropriate in the context of Indigenous histories in the Far Northeast; following Pauketat and Sassaman (2020:82), we note that "contacts are moments when people relate to and affect each other, not to mention the places and things entangled in the moment of engagement. Such moments can change the course of history." As chapters in this volume attest (see Anderson; Lelièvre et al.; Treyvaud) the histories of ancestral Indigenous groups and the non-Indigenous settler colonists with whom they interacted were intractably changed at, before, and after 500 BP.

The volume begins with an introductory and overview essay considering some of these frameworks, most particularly surrounding Woodland terminology, and its various uses and implications, linking continental terminology with its use in the Far Northeast (Holyoke and Hrynick, chapter 1). We then move to Newfoundland and Labrador, where Holly and colleagues (chapter 2) revisit the evidence for cultural discontinuity and demographic collapse (see also Holly 2011) among Indigenous groups in Newfoundland and Labrador after ca. 3500 BP, and the culturally specific causes and decisions made by groups leading to that collapse. Hutchings and Schwarz (chapter 3) describe the dearth of archaeological evidence for low-fired ceramics in Newfoundland and Labrador, and highlight recent excavations in the Labrador interior which have served to counter this narrative. Excavations along the lower Churchill River have revealed not only large concentrations of ceramics but in situ evidence of manufacturing and cultural connections with groups to the south and west.

Skipping across the Gulf of St. Lawrence, we encounter several chapters situated within the Maritime Peninsula sub-region (the Canadian Maritime provinces, the Bas-Saint-Laurent and Gaspésie regions of Quebec, and Maine east of the Kennebec River). Black (chapter 4) takes us back to Bliss Islands of Passamaquoddy Bay, in the Quoddy Region of southwestern New Brunswick, to analyze the ways lithic technological traditions and exchange relationships waxed and waned among the Ancestral Peskotomuhkati and their neighbours between 3500 BP and the eighteenth century. Blair and Rooney (chapter 5) build on nearly 50 years of modern, community-based archaeological work in the Mi'kmaq community of Metepenagiag in eastern New Brunswick and explore the ways that the archaeological and cultural landscape between the Early and Middle Maritime Woodland periods (ca. 3000–1900 BP) help situate the deep historical connections to the landscape that exist for that community. Burke's (chapter 6) contribution brings together data from across the region to offer a projectile-point counterpart to the Petersen and Sanger (1991) sequence for ceramic technologies during the Woodland/Ceramic period (ca. 3000–500 BP). The chapter builds a reliable chronology for changing styles of projectile points while contextualizing those stylistic changes as part of larger technological manifestations through time. Hanley and colleagues (chapter 7) also pull a large regional data set together, in this case providing a comprehensive sourcing study of natural and artifactual copper on the Maritime Peninsula using laser ablation techniques. The chapter suggests ancestral Indigenous groups in the region sought out local sources for making copper implements. It also asks important questions about the reasons known local varieties were sought, and draws attention to the likelihood of undiscovered source locations in the region. Hrynick and Betts (chapter 8) examine expressions of gender in archaeological data at various scales during the Maritime Woodland period in the Port Joli Harbour area of southern Nova Scotia. Building upon a decade of research in that region (see Betts 2019, among others), and weaving archaeological and ethnohistorical data, they argue that among Ancestral Wabanaki, gender informed both ritual and quotidian activities, revealing a dualistic structuring of social spaces that suggests differing notions of place for women and men in Wabanaki society. Lelièvre and colleagues (chapter 9) describe recent archaeological work on two sites in Mi'kma'ki, on the Chignecto Peninsula of northern coastal Nova Scotia and the role that archaeology is playing in situating L'nuk—Mi'kmaq people (lit. the people)—on their lands through the deep past, ca. 3500 BP, to present day. Weaving oral histories, archaeological data, and the perspectives of both Indigenous and non-Indigenous researchers, the authors demonstrate the many ways that actions in the landscape make and remake places. Newsom (chapter 10) examines manufacturing choices made by potters during the Early Woodland period in the Penobscot River Valley, Maine. Focusing on Vinette or CP1 ceramics, Newsom observes that contrasting technological decisions in fabric, rim eversion, and exterior design indicate individual potter's decisions or preferences expressed within a broader, shared cultural framework for ceramic design during that period. We then return to Peskotomuhkatihkuk (the Quoddy Region), as Patton and colleagues (chapter 11) examine changing settlement patterns on the "cusp of Contact" during the later Late Maritime Woodland (ca. 900–450 BP). Employing data from shellfish and shell-bearing sites, the authors challenge how archaeologists on the Maritime Peninsula have envisioned the spatial and cultural boundaries of sites, and offer that flexibility in settlement type and subsistence base indicates shifting ways Peskotomuhkati households and communities were gathering foodstuff, moving on the land, and interacting with one another. Woolsey (chapter 12) examines the changing role that ceramic technology played in the lives of ancestral Indigenous groups on the Maritime Peninsula by integrating data from across the region. Building a technological chronology that extends from the introduction of ceramics ca. 3000 BP to the disappearance from the archaeological record after about 500 BP, Woolsey uses evidence from the manufacture and abandonment of vessels to argue that diachronic changes from utilitarian to ritual purposes coincide with dynamic social changes among ancestral Wabanaki groups.

Leaving the Maritime Peninsula, we move into adjacent Quebec with Chapdelaine's (chapter 13) chapter providing the first culture-historical synthesis of the Woodland period (ca. 3000–400 BP) for Quebec's Eastern Townships—an area encompassing the region east of Montréal, south of the St. Lawrence River, and abutting the United States border. Chapdelaine integrates decades of research and highlights the changing relationships groups occupying that region had with Iroquoian and Algonquian neighbours to the west, south, north, and east. Treyvaud (chapter 14) explores the role that archaeology has played in affirming W8banaki presence in Ndakina—our territory—throughout the pre- and post-Contact periods, and the role that colonization has played in disenfranchising and dislocating ancestral Indigenous occupants. Drawing from recent archaeological and community projects, Treyvaud presents the ways W8banaki are documenting and describing their ancestral and contemporary knowledge and experiences on Ndakina.

Jumping back to Maine, this time west of the Kennebec River, Anderson (chapter 15) inquires broadly about the conceptualization of villages and early horticulture in the Far Northeast, and specifically the cartographic and historical representations of people on the land during the early Contact period at the mouth of the Saco River in southwest Maine. Using Champlain's 1605 map and drawing on recent archaeological work on the Biddeford campus of the University of New England, Anderson questions the depiction or reality of Chouacoët as a village, where the so-called northern boundary of horticultural villages may lie, and precisely what we mean when we describe late pre-Contact villages. Tremblay and colleagues (chapter 16) draw on data from the Penobscot River in central Maine, the St. Lawrence River Valley near the modern cities of Québec and Montréal, and the Lake Champlain and Connecticut River areas of northern Vermont to explore the relationships between late pre-Contact Iroquoian and Algonquian groups, most specifically the St. Lawrence Iroquoians. Using neutron-activation analysis on ceramics and clays from throughout the region, the authors demonstrate the migrations of St. Lawrence Iroquoian groups into northern Vermont and Maine, with evidence to suggest the continuation of stylistic traditions even after access to clay sources ended. Finally, we end in northern Vermont, with Cowie and colleagues (chapter 17) analyzing changing subsistence practices among groups living on the Missisquoi River between the Late Archaic and Late Woodland/early Contact period (ca. 4700–400 BP). Drawing on data from lipid, macrofauna, and floral residues, the authors describe cultural responses and adaptation to a dynamic riverine environment and resource base, and how hunting and fishing practices demonstrate a persistence of activity at this place, even following the widespread adoption of maize horticulture.

Throughout this work, differing local orthographies for Indigenous groups (e.g., Wabanaki, W8banaki) and their ancestors (or Ancestors) are used. We have taken this approach acknowledging both the diversity of groups and engagements between descendent communities and archaeologists, and the way those relationships inform our writing.

The production of this volume occurred during a truly unique moment in the history of the world, highlighted by the descent into a pandemic and the response to it. We applaud the authors, reviewers, and readers; Pierre Desrosiers, Lee Wyndham, and the editorial staff at the Canadian Museum of History; and the University of Ottawa Press—we sincerely thank them all for their attention to detail and their remarkably timely responses to requests, clarifications, and revisions, despite the times. We want to thank M. Alexandre Pelletier-Michaud for his translation of several of the abstracts included herein, and the translation of one of the articles, and the generosity of the University of New Brunswick's Busteed Publication Fund and the University of Toronto's Archaeology Centre—specifically Director Ed Swenson and Administrator Annette Chan—for their financial support for translation services. We would also like to thank the Grand Conseil de la Nation Waban-Aki for sponsorship of the Canadian Archaeological Association session in 2019, and the presenters who joined us for those two days, many of whom produced the scholarship contained herein. Finally, a thanks to the many reviewers whose attention to detail and insightful comments guided and improved the volume manuscript and its many parts (presented here alphabetically): Jennifer Birch, David Black, Jamie Brake, Claude Chapdelaine, Gary Coupland, Michael Deal, Steven Dorland, Bill Farley, Donald Holly Jr., Gregory Lattanzi, Moira McCaffrey, Bonnie Newsom, Jess Robinson, David Sanger, Kenneth Sassaman, Arthur Spiess, Karine Taché, and Cora Woolsey, and two anonymous reviewers that undertook a thorough and thoughtful review of the entire volume.

References Cited

Betts, Matthew (editor)
2019   *Place-making in the Pretty Harbour: The Archaeology of Port Joli, Nova Scotia.* Mercury Series Archaeology Paper No. 180. Canadian Museum of History and University of Ottawa Press, Gatineau.

Chapdelaine, Claude (editor)
2012   *Late Pleistocene Archaeology & Ecology in the Far Northeast.* Texas A&M University Press, College Station.

Deal, Michael, and Susan Blair
1991   *Prehistoric Archaeology in the Maritime Provinces: Past and Present Research.* New Brunswick Archaeological Services, Fredericton.

Holly, Donald H., Jr.
2011   When Foragers Fail: In the Eastern Subarctic, for Example. In *Hunter-Gatherer Archaeology as Historical Process*, edited by K. E. Sassaman and D. H. Holly Jr., pp. 79–92. University of Arizona Press, Tucson.

Pauketat, Timothy R., and Kenneth E. Sassaman
2020   *The Archaeology of Ancient North America.* Cambridge University Press, New York.

Petersen, James B., and David Sanger
1991   An Aboriginal Ceramic Sequence for Maine and the Maritime Provinces. In *Prehistoric Archaeology in the Maritime Provinces: Past and Present Research*, edited by Michael Deal and Susan Blair, pp. 113–170. New Brunswick Archaeological Services, Fredericton.

Sanger, David, and M. A. P. Renouf
2006   *The Archaic of the Far Northeast.* University of Maine Press, Orono.

Silliman, Stephen W.
2005   Culture Contact or Colonialism? Challenges in the Archaeology of Native North America. *American Antiquity* 70(1):55–74.

Singer, Zachary
2017   The Palaeoindian Occupation of Southern New England: Evaluating Sub-Regional Variation in Palaeoindian Lifeways in the New England-Maritimes Region. PhD dissertation, Department of Anthropology, University of Connecticut, Mansfield.

Spiess, Arthur, and Deborah B. Wilson
1989   Palaeoindian Lithic Distribution in the New England-Maritimes Region. In *Eastern Palaeoindian Lithic Resource Use*, edited by C. J. Ellis and J. C. Lothrop, pp. 75–97. Westview Press, Boulder.

Tuck, James A.
1976   *Newfoundland and Labrador Prehistory.* Archaeological Survey of Canada, National Museum of Man. Van Nostrand Reinhold, Toronto.
1984   *Maritime Provinces Prehistory.* Canada Prehistory Series. Archaeological Survey of Canada, National Museum of Man, Ottawa.

1

CONTINENTAL THOUGHTS, (MARITIME) PENINSULAR PERSPECTIVE

What Can the Far Northeast Say about "the Woodland"?

Kenneth R. Holyoke[1] and M. Gabriel Hrynick[2]

Abstract

In this chapter, we introduce some of the themes that led to this volume, *The Far Northeast: 3000 BP to Contact*, and the session that preceded it at the 2019 Canadian Archaeological Association Annual Meeting. We briefly review the Woodland concept in the Far Northeast in terms of taxonomy and offer two examples from the Maritime Peninsula relating to projectile-point morphology and dwelling structure as ways of thinking through our central question: What can the archaeology of this region say about the Woodland? We suggest that Woodland-period archaeology of the Far Northeast is indicative of problems in the evolutionary scheme of hunter-gatherer culture change throughout the Northeast broadly, and argue for a model of the Far Northeast in which the region was culturally more integrated than sometimes conceived, both within the Far Northeast and northeastern North America more broadly.

Résumé

Dans ce chapitre nous présentons certains des thèmes ayant mené à ce recueil, *The Far Northeast: 3000 BP to Contact*, et à la session qui l'a précédé à la conférence annuelle de l'Association canadienne d'archéologie de 2019. Après une brève revue des implications taxono-miques du concept de période Sylvicole dans l'extrême Nord-Est (*Far Northeast*), nous abordons la question centrale de cet ouvrage : que peut nous apprendre l'archéologie sur « le Sylvicole » dans la péninsule des Maritimes ? Nous proposons comme pistes de réflexions deux exemples régionaux touchant à la morphologie des pointes de projectiles et aux structures d'habitation. À notre sens, l'archéologie du Sylvicole dans l'extrême Nord-Est révèle des failles dans le modèle évolutif utilisé pour expliquer les changements culturels chez les peuples chasseurs-cueilleurs du Nord-Est. Nous proposons plutôt un modèle basé sur une plus grande cohésion culturelle, tant à l'interne dans la région de l'extrême Nord-Est que plus largement avec le nord-est de l'Amérique du Nord.

Affiliations
1. Department of Anthropology, University of Toronto, Ontario, Canada
2. Department of Anthropology, University of New Brunswick, New Brunswick, Canada

In recent decades, archaeologists working in the Far Northeast of North America (see figure 1.1) have produced synthesis volumes that have clarified what the concept of Palaeoindian and Archaic mean as regional taxonomic units (Chapdelaine 2012; Sanger and Renouf 2006). As with any culture-historical task, grappling with time also means grappling with space. The edges of cultural phenomena seem to depend in large part on where models for them are first developed, or on the serendipity of research agendas. The past 3,000 years in the Far Northeast have thus long been imagined in comparison to a global Neolithic, a continental Formative, and an Eastern Woodland (Willey and Phillips 1958; cf. Ramsden 2008), all of which build upon an evolutionary model of hunter-gatherer improvement punctuated by "revolutions" in development (e.g., Price and Brown 1985; see also Pauketat and Sassaman 2020:1–7).

However, much as Sassaman (e.g., 2008) has argued for a new understanding of the Archaic period in eastern North America, we have a nagging feeling that the unilinear evolutionary models through which archaeologists have long been imagining the Far Northeast no longer hold much potency. This is a challenge for the region we work in—the Maritime Peninsula—because the period beginning about 3,000 years ago and ending with European contact has often explicitly been defined in terms of difference from an external, and seemingly better understood, Woodland. In brief, ceramic technology adopted by mobile hunter-gatherers here could be contrasted with village formation, burial elaboration, and the development of horticulture elsewhere in the Northeast. Archaeologists on the Maritime Peninsula now find themselves grappling with the distinct impression that, to the extent those developments in the broader Northeast occurred, they were not part of a tidy concurrent package.

The concept of Woodland and its anthropological implications describe an evolutionary process that envisioned Archaic-period foragers becoming Woodland-period horticulturalists. Horticulture was perceived as driving change, and concomitant with increasingly complex social behaviours. Archaeologists

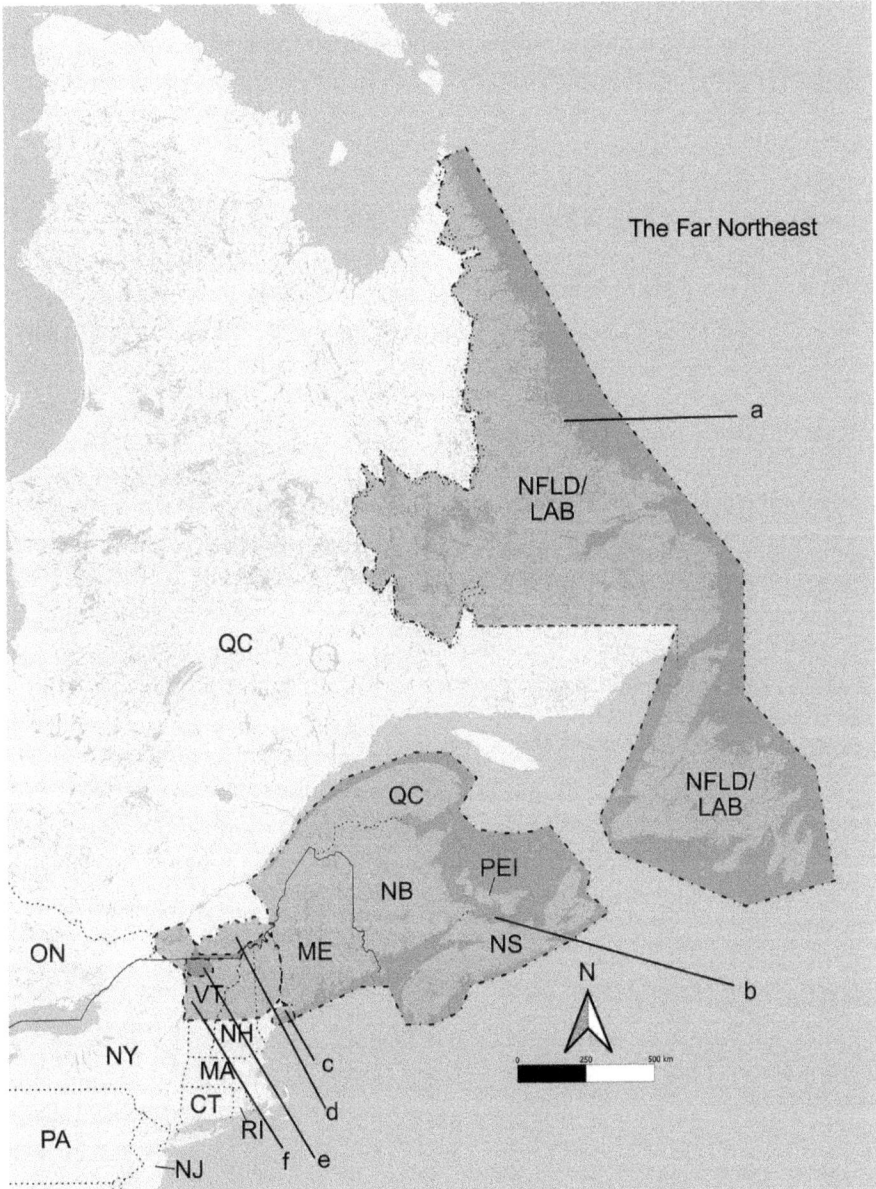

Figure 1.1. Showing the Far Northeast and geographies/regions/site areas described in this volume, showing (A) Newfoundland and Labrador area (Holly et al.; Hutchings and Schwarz); (B) Maritime Peninsula region (Black; Blair and Rooney; Burke; Hanley et al.; Holyoke and Hrynick; Hrynick and Betts; Lelièvre et al.; Newsom; Patton et al.; Treyvaud; Woolsey); (C) area around Casco Bay, Maine (Anderson); (D) Eastern Townships area, Quebec (Chapdelaine); (E) area around Swanton and the Missisquoi River (Cowie et al.); (F) portion of northern New England and southwest Quebec (Tremblay et al.).

Source: Map created by K. Holyoke using Esri Light Gray Canvas basemap; data sources: Esri, HERE, Garmin, © OpenStreetMap contributors, and the GIS User Community.

have had to reckon with the recognition that the global archaeological record shows that hunting-and-gathering societies exhibit tremendous social and economic diversity—even complexity (e.g., Price and Brown 1985; Sassaman 2004)—and the Woodland period was no exception. In the Far Northeast, the Maritime Archaic (Betts and Hrynick 2021), preceding the "onset" of the Woodland, suggests enough hunter-gatherer complexity to stand as an illustrative example (e.g., Bourque 2012). It, along with a number of other Archaic-period examples (e.g., Anderson 2004; Custer 1994; Gibson and Carr 2004; Randall 2015; Thompson and Pluckhahn 2010; Versaggi et al. 2001) in eastern North America, suggests to us that it is increasingly difficult to sustain evolutionary models of hunter-gatherer behaviour. While the Archaic and Woodland labels are convenient mnemonics for complex history, the concept of a stepwise evolution of groups in the Far Northeast is illusory at best (e.g., Sanger 1974).

We think it is worth asking, then: Is the Woodland a model that facilitates interpretive progress, or is it a cumbersome taxon requiring so many caveats as to be essentially a temporal designator only? We suspect the latter. To explore this question in this introductory chapter, we attempt the following: We invite the reader to imagine with us a pre-Contact time when the Far Northeast was culturally central, rather than peripheral; was historically dynamic; was regionally integrated and extra-regionally influential; and that can be more readily understood through in situ historical explanation than by external comparison. We downplay ecological contrasts insomuch as environmental marginality is explanatory only insofar as it is addressed by people with historically and culturally created tools. For our case in this chapter, we use the Maritime Woodland period on the Maritime Peninsula, where we both primarily work, and which, we argue, offers a particularly useful way to think about the narrative construction of "Woodland" and about what that means. As a taxonomic matter, it seems apt that *peninsularity* suggests a narrowness of perspective and isolation. (This view, we think, is alive and well; for instance, a recent review [Holland-Lulewicz 2020] focused on interactions in eastern North America excluded the Maritime Peninsula from eastern North America.)

Our examples, which are not an exhaustive treatment of the Woodland concept in the Far Northeast, culture-historically, do fit well, we think, with some of the themes of this volume, namely:

(1) The onset of Woodland cultural manifestations in the Far Northeast may not lag behind Early Woodland elsewhere (Blair et al., chapter 5, this volume; Holly et al., chapter 2, this volume; Taché 2011).

(2) Raw material and cultural influence in the last 3,000 years are manifest by material moving from the region elsewhere (Black,

chapter 14, this volume; Burke, chapter 6, this volume; Chapdelaine, chapter 13, this volume; Cowie et al., chapter 17, this volume; Hanley et al., chapter 7, this volume; Tremblay et al., chapter 16, this volume) and by shared artifact forms, respectively (Burke, chapter 6, this volume; Hutchings and Schwarz, chapter 3, this volume; Newsom, chapter 10, this volume).

(3) Changes occur at similar times throughout the Far Northeast. Moreover, these often align with those of horticultural neighbours (Hrynick and Betts, chapter 8, this volume; Patton et al., chapter 11, this volume; Woolsey, chapter 12, this volume).

(4) Archaeological boundary areas defining the Far Northeast and its sub-regions are blurry, and shifted through time (Anderson, this volume; Lelièvre et al., chapter 9, this volume; Treyvaud, chapter 14, this volume).

The Woodland Concept as a Contrasting or Guiding Model

The Maritime Peninsula is the traditional homeland of the Wabanaki, comprised of the Canadian Maritime provinces, the Bas-Saint-Laurent and Gaspésie regions of Quebec, and the state of Maine east of the Kennebec River (Hoffman 1955). The Maritime Peninsula serves as a gateway to the coastal Far Northeast in many ways. Practically, it frames archaeological research in a space that today is crossed by international and interprovincial borders, and delineates the Algonquian-speaking world from Iroquoian groups of the Great Lakes and southern interior New England and New York to the west and south, and Eskimo–Aleut/Eskaleut groups and Beothuk farther northeast. And while Wabanaki never adopted sustained maize horticultural practices prior to European contact, the Wabanaki people—comprised of Wolastoqiyik (Maliseet) along the Saint John River in New Brunswick, Quebec, and Maine; Mi'kmaq in eastern New Brunswick, Nova Scotia, and Prince Edward Island; Peskotomuhkatiyik (Passamaquoddy) in the Canadian and American Passamaquoddy Bay area; and Penobscot in interior and central coastal Maine—lived in a borderland and, in all likelihood, frequently interacted with groups to the north, west, and south, probably over expansive interior and coastal water routes (e.g., Sanger 2009; Sanger et al. 2001).

Snow (1994) noted the importance of an in situ model for the development of Iroquoian cultures from Middle Woodland, rather than an emphasis on migration, going so far as to term it a "controlling model." In his view, archaeologists in New England and the Maritime Provinces, for better or for worse, lacked similar controlling models. On the Maritime Peninsula, at least, archaeologists seem to have regarded discontinuity (e.g., migration, depopulation) as controlling models against which regional culture histories are developed (see Black and Hrynick 2016 for further discussion). In contrast, David Black (pers. comm. 2020) has pointed out that, regionally, evolutionary models should at their core be about "descent with modification" and, by definition, require continuity. Regardless, culture-historical narratives have been approached differently in the Far Northeast than in Iroquoia. In this chapter, we focus narrowly on the Maritime Peninsula because it is the region we know best, but it seems to us that Newfoundland and Labrador's controlling model is also discontinuity (see Holly, chapter 2, this volume). (It is worth noting here that in our reading of Snow, "controlling models" are not necessarily right or wrong, they are simply the narratives archaeologists generally employ.)

Taxonomy stands in for guiding culture-historical models and explanation whether implicitly or explicitly; in this way, taxonomy may function as what Snow described as a controlling model. Our work is no exception, in that we view many of the chapters in this volume as contrasting with the notion of a Ceramic period on the Maritime Peninsula, which is distinct from the Woodland period in neighbouring regions (e.g., Blair et al., chapter 4, this volume; Lelièvre et al., chapter 9, this volume; Patton et al., chapter 11, this volume; Woolsey, chapter 12, this volume). Indeed, this is part of the reason why Keenlyside (1983), Black (e.g., 2004), and others (e.g., Leonard 1995) advanced the "Maritime" Woodland taxon, embracing connections to the wider Northeast, while acknowledging the close relationship ancestral Indigenous groups on the Maritime Peninsula had with their coastal world and waterscapes (*sensu* Pawling 2017). That the terminology did not make its way across the Gulf of St. Lawrence to Newfoundland and Labrador is both a matter of history, owing to the perceived absence of characteristic "markers" of Woodland innovation and economics: low-fired ceramics and horticulture (Tuck 1976), and a resultant archaeology of "traditions" that acknowledges the arrivals and departures of multiple genetically distinct ancestral Indigenous groups on the island and mainland (Holly Jr. 2011, 2013; Tuck 1976).

We also question if the abundance of taxonomy dealing with space has much meaning. Not all of the divisions archaeologists employ seem to describe archaeological difference, and many seem to reflect divisions among where archaeologists are located rather than what they study: one archaeologist's Daniel Rattle complex is another's Middle Maritime Woodland period (figure 1.2). For the 2019 Canadian Archaeological Association (CAA) session which developed into this edited volume, we opened the two-day discussion about current and future research in the Far Northeast by invoking a threadbare debate about the futility of finding cohesive taxonomic units in the broader Northeast of North America. We drew attention to the many different terms used to describe the period between 3000 BP and Contact (ca. 500 BP) in the Far Northeast alone—some of which are found herein and consolidated in figure 1.2—and made jest by bringing them together into a bingo game (figure 1.3). In pulling on those threads, however, we found that the debates about taxonomy, borne out in writing for the Far Northeast alone (e.g., Black 2004; Blair 2004; Chapdelaine 2012; Leonard 1995, 1996; Sanger 1974), forced us to think about what we mean when we talk about, for the sake of simplicity, "the Woodland," and how "Woodland" as a traditional culture-historical paradigm has shaped the way archaeologists think and write about the period 3000 BP to Contact in the Far Northeast. The Woodland-period concept is under revision in adjacent regions (e.g., Anderson, chapter 15, this volume; Leveillee et al. 2006), and has been abandoned almost entirely elsewhere (e.g., Pauketat and Sassaman 2020; Sassaman, pers. comm. 2020). In Newfoundland and Labrador, Woodland terminology was not adopted. When we use the term "the Woodland," we are most frequently using it as a temporal noun referring to the period of time between 3000 BP and Contact (ca. 500 BP, give or take). Breaking that 2,500-year period into an early, middle, and late follows culture-historical conventions, but are also predicated on economic and technological shifts among groups in the region that are not always starkly evident. We also use the term "Woodland" adjectively, to refer to "patterns" (*sensu* McKern 1939) that we (and we suspect others) have consciously, or unconsciously, conceived of as being distinctly "Woodland." Thus, we acknowledge the cavalier way "the Woodland" is invoked throughout this chapter, but we also suspect this lends credence to the frustration expressed with the taxon.

The standard concept of the Woodland is that, sometime around 3,000 years ago, a "new age" began with the end of the Archaic and ended when, about 500 years ago, a group of French explorers endeavoured to search farther along the St. Lawrence River than any European before them. But the Woodland in the Northeast did not start "with a bang" (cf. Holly 2013:62), nor is it simply the "Archaic with pottery" (Willey and Phillips 1958:119). Indeed, in many ways, archaeologists have tended to conceive of the Woodland as a package of things and behaviours: elaborate and widespread burial ceremonialism, low-fired ceramics, horticulture, and monumental architecture. Some of these are unique to the post-3000 BP world, and some of them are presaged by and built upon the histories and structures of the preceding Archaic period (e.g., Petersen 1995; Sanger 2008; Sassaman 2008, 2010). We think, however, that this version of the Woodland concept has been stretched well beyond its original Midwestern and culture-historical origins (e.g., Griffin 1952, 1967; Ford and Willey 1941; McKern 1939; Willey 1966; Willey and Philips 1958).

The simplified history of the Woodland is as a geographically circumscribed taxonomic system. By 1952, in his *Archeology of Eastern United States*, Griffin had introduced the most widespread taxonomic subdivisions of Early, Middle, and Late Woodland. The Early and Middle Woodland periods were characterized by cord-marked pottery (Vinette 1 [Ritchie and MacNeish 1949], or Ceramic

Region	Maine/Maritimes (Quoddy Region)	Maine/Maritimes	Mi'kma'ki	Penobscot Bay	Newfoundland	Vermont	Lower North Shore of Quebec	Labrador	Quebec	Newfoundland, Labrador, & Quebec Lower North Shore
BP	Historic	Contact (CP-7)								
500	Protohistoric	later Late Ceramic (CP-6)	Kiskuke'k L'nu'k	Historic Contact	Beothuk	Historic			Sylvicole supérieur (or Sylvicole terminal)	Beothuk
	Later Late Maritime Woodland	early Late Ceramic (CP-5)		Salt Pond Phase (Grindle Ware)	Little Passage Complex Recent Indian	Late Woodland	Anse Morel complex	Point Revenge Complex		Late Boreal Woodland
1000	Earlier Late Maritime Woodland	late Middle Ceramic (CP-4)	Kejikawe'k L'nu'k	Oak Point Phase (Eaton Ware)	Beaches Complex Recent Indian	Middle Woodland	Anse Lazy complex / Longe Point complex / Petite Hauve complex	Daniel Rattle Complex	Sylvicole moyen tardif	
1500	Middle Maritime Woodland	middle Middle Ceramic (CP-3)			Cow Head Complex Recent Indian		Flèche Littorale complex		Sylvicole moyen ancien	
2000		early Middle Ceramic (CP-2)		Whitmore Phase (Wiesenthal Ware)						
				(Vinette I)				Intermediate Indian		
2500	Early Maritime Woodland	Early Ceramic (CP-1)				Early Woodland				
							Ruisseau Manius complex		Sylvicole inférieur	Early Boreal Woodland
3000										

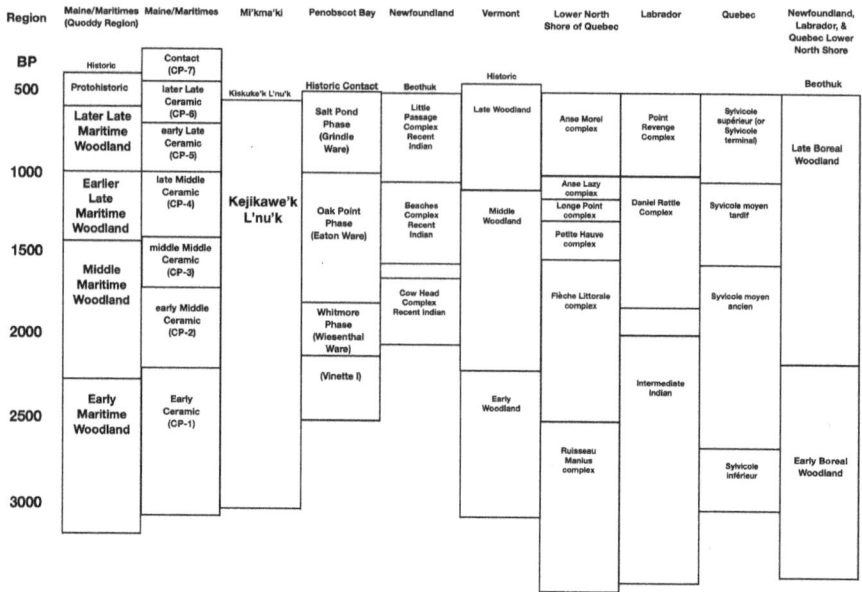

Figure 1.2. Table roughly collating a variety of temporal schemes for the Far Northeast for taxa between the last 3,000 years and contact by Europeans. Note that the timeline is in approximate years before present and may not reflect universal use of the particular terms within a particular area. Inclusion here reflects neither an attempt to be critical of a particular culture-history scheme nor to endorse one, but rather to highlight the large number of non-equivalent, equivalent, and semi-equivalent taxa scholars use to describe time in the Far Northeast. The chart conflates a variety of archaeological units (e.g., periods, complexes, phases) but reflects ambiguities of local use.

Source: Non-exhaustive table compiled from a variety of sources and the authors' interpretations of them including Betts and Hrynick (2021), Black (2002), Bourque (1971), Chapdelaine (1990), Confederacy of Mainland Mi'kmaq (2007), Holly (2013), Kristensen (2011), Loring (1989), Pintal (1998), and Thomas (2001).

period 1 [Petersen and Sanger 1991]), semi-sedentary group mobility, and a variety of stemmed and side-notched points. The Late Woodland was characterized by sedentary group mobility, incised pottery, and small triangular points. In addition to settlement mobility, projectile-point types, and ceramics, widespread mortuary ceremonialism and ritual exchange systems became synonymous with Early Woodland (Meadowood/Adena/Middlesex) and Middle Woodland (Hopewellian) periods, and maize horticulture became synonymous with the Late Woodland.

The Woodland in the Far Northeast

While Woodland as a cultural-historical paradigm historically implied a notion of cultural completeness or apogee (*sensu* Fagan 2011), in which the Northeast's version of the Neolithic revolution formed the waiting room for European contact, in the Far Northeast a variety of factors contributed to a static economic and cultural model of the last ca. 3,000 years. Among them is the

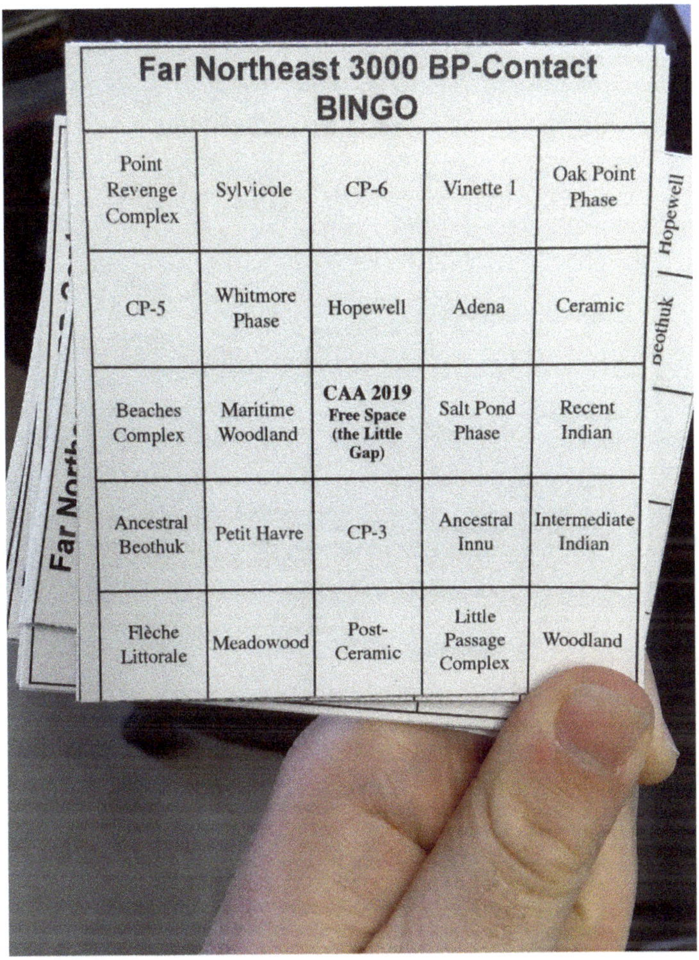

Figure 1.3. Far Northeast typology bingo.

ethnographic tendency, historically, to conflate place and time. By this we mean the explicit or implicit goals of ethnographers to be interested in the Far Northeast because its isolation would preserve a purer form of the Indigenous past (see Holly 2011, 2013; Smith 2011). Speck (1997 [1940]:4) introduced *Penobscot Man* with this assertion: "Despite considerable advancement in civilization of the rural American stamp, an undercurrent of conservatism resulting from insular location and the wilderness at their backs lurks in the minds of these Indians." While directed at the changes after European contact, the implications of statements such as Speck's are of a sort of essential conservatism such that technological and economic change was slower in the Far Northeast than elsewhere, permitting access to an otherwise elusive Algonquian past.

Ultimately, the original conception of the Woodland, its division from the Archaic, and its internal subdivisions were predicated on the visibility of specific (sometimes singular) material culture traits. The absence of many of these index fossils (or simply superficial stylistic differences in them) in the Far Northeast, coupled with the staggered development of professional archaeology—an early florescence of research in the late 1960s and early 1970s (e.g., Turnbull 1977; Spiess 1985) was followed by a relative dearth until sustained multi-year projects in the Canadian Maritimes accelerated in the 1990s and 2000s (e.g., Black 2004; Blair 2004)—in the region helped to construct the narrative of a marginal Woodland period on the Maritime Peninsula and the broader Far Northeastern world.

We return to two examples here that we frequently considered as we devised the CAA session. First, why are projectile-point typologies across the Northeast so similar through time, generally speaking, to those outside of the region, and second, why does settlement change seem to resemble those of horticultural southerly neighbours? These examples are limited, but we think highlight the need for this volume.

A Point About Projectile Points

At the CAA conference we proposed a superficial but, we think, illustrative example of the challenges with working with a longstanding culture-historical unit such as the Woodland: projectile-point types have been invoked both as "index fossils" and as devices to indicate technological conformities and differences between the Maritime Peninsula and the wider Northeast. Reliance on external-point typologies (e.g., Boudreau 2008; Ritchie 1961) has historically tended to work insofar as the point forms seem coarsely to match associated radiocarbon dates, and as a result painted a picture of relative Northeast technological conformity during the Woodland period; on the Maritime Peninsula, a lack of projectile points from good stratigraphic or dated contexts contributed to this perception (see Burke, chapter 6, this volume). Projectile points, then, are one technology that illustrates the way that archaeologists in this region have tended to rely on external explanations for cultural change— shaving or adding 100–200 years on the adoption of particular styles could be accounted for in the diffusion of styles from the Northeast "core" to the peninsular "periphery."

That one can look at a lanceolate biface with a short stem or a small triangular point with a concave base almost anywhere between the Ohio River and the Gulf of St. Lawrence and fairly confidently assign them to a 500–1,000-year range of dates within the period 3000 BP to Contact is useful. Notably, these similarities in projectile-point forms are mirrored by some other broadly coeval Northeast phenomena, from technological innovations or shifts (e.g., the development of low-fired ceramics [Petersen and Sanger 1991], the decreasing size of stone projectiles, and the steep increase in frequency of tools particularly well suited to bark working and stripping; see, e.g., Austin 1980; Black 2002, 2004, chapter 4, this volume; Blair 2004; Bourque 1971; Burke, chapter 6, this volume; Deal 2002, 2016; Snow 1980), the participation in burial ceremonialism and mortuary architectural phenomena (e.g., Adena/Middlesex mound building; see, e.g., Blair et al., chapter 5, this volume; Taché 2011; Turnbull 1976), and the construction of features (e.g., shell middens and wigwams; see, e.g., Black 2004; Hrynick and Black 2016). Combined, this evidence builds on what we already assume were sustained social and economic relationships within and outside the Maritime Peninsula during the (Maritime) Woodland (for the Archaic, see also Sanger 1991, 2009).

How do archaeologists begin moving past projectile points (and lithic technology more generally) as a convenient Woodland time-stamp to understanding them as intentional acts of culture making and culture change on the Maritime Peninsula (e.g., Pauketat and Alt 2005)? Technological processes that result in certain projectile-point forms are embedded in a wide range of choices, perhaps most visible by studying the distribution of specific materials from the source, or quarry, out through their various social and economic networks (cf. Burke, chapter 6, this volume; Eid 2017; Tomasso and Porraz 2016). It stands to reason that within hunter-gatherer societies, quarries are significant places in their social landscapes, "special places [...] permanent fixtures on the landscape linking generation after generation of hunter-fisher-gatherers that sought knappable stone for the manufacture of tools that were critical to their survival" (Burke 2007:64). The circulation of stone from those quarries is also integral to mediating, maintaining, and reifying social relationships, passing along information about people and the larger world, and communicating and reproducing social mores (e.g., Bradley 2000; Gero 1989; Jones 1990; Jones and White 1988; MacKenzie 1983; McBryde 1978, 1984; Paton 1994; Taçon 1990, 1991), even the maintenance of cosmological and lived worlds (Brumm 2010).

In the case of Washademoak multicoloured chert, the distribution and preparation of the material suggests changing interactions with a quarry over time, mostly situated within the Maritime Woodland. For example, there are very few extant projectile points made of Washademoak chert. Despite this, the most elaborate of them appear to be associated with Late Maritime Woodland sites, including important aggregation and meeting places at some distance from the source (e.g., Bourque and Cox 1981; Holyoke and Black 2018; Leonard 1995, 2002). Procurement practices shifted and appear to have intensified over time, even within the "source area" for Washademoak chert, and indicate that collecting stone was embedded in the quotidian lives of highly mobile peoples (e.g., Blair 2010; Holyoke 2012; Holyoke and Black 2018; Holyoke and

Hrynick 2015). It may even indicate cultural preferences expressed as colours, textures, and qualities of stone sought at different times in different places (e.g., Black 2018, chapter 4, this volume; Blair 2004, 2010; Holyoke et al. 2020; Sanger 1991)—patterns repeated throughout the Far Northeastern world for materials like Ramah chert (e.g., Loring 2017) and Mistassini quartzite (e.g., LeBlanc et al. 2010; Holly Jr. 2013).

Projectile points are the end product of vast networks of social and economic exchanges, technological processes, and cultural and personal preferences that situate Wabanaki technological choices in historical, lived practices (Black, chapter 4, this volume; Burke, chapter 6, this volume). Recent work has also highlighted that where recognizable forms—the distinctive lanceolate among them—suggest participation in larger ritual and ideological systems, Ancestral Wabanaki reinterpreted them (e.g., Pelletier-Michaud 2017). That a distinct local (and extra local) flavour permeates the relationship with technology beyond just making projectile points (e.g., Blair 2004; Blair et al., chapter 5, this volume; Burke, chapter 6, this volume; Hanley et al., chapter 7, this volume; Woolsey, chapter 12, this volume) might demonstrate the "adaptability" of these broad cultural systems (Deal 2016:95) but also the ideological agency of Wabanaki themselves, one that requires situating explanations for these practices using data from this region.

Gimme Shelter

Among the most important papers about the Far Northeast's Woodland period is Black's (2002) identification in economic and subsistence terms of a shift in subsistence, ca. 1400 BP, that could be glossed in rough terms as a shift toward "collecting" rather than "foraging" (*sensu* Binford 1980). This Middle to Late Woodland transition occurred among hunter-gatherers throughout the Maritime Peninsula (Betts 2019), much like it did elsewhere.

The questions this realization raised are analogous to the "village problem" in southern New England in which the proliferation of maize horticulture ca. 1000 BP did not correspond to a clear archaeological manifestation of village life around that time (Kerber 1988). As southern New England archaeologists have shifted away from models of villages, *sensu stricto*, "as a restricted geographic place where some portion of the population lived year-round" (Thompson and Birch 2019:1) to models of dispersed villages, mobile farmers, or other more spatially expansive units that apply typical "tribal"-level social organization to more geographically flexible and expansive settlements (e.g., Chilton 2005; Leveillee et al. 2006). It is tempting to overemphasize the similarities, but archaeological interpretations of Far Northeast communities in the Late Woodland increasingly resemble the kinds of communities New England archaeologists purport for horticulturalists.

Studying houses themselves offers one way to begin to approach the question, because they are ubiquitous and comparable. Tentatively, there is a trend in the Late Woodland toward an increase in house floor size in both the horticultural and non-horticultural worlds (Farley et al. 2019), and evidence to suggest increasingly larger and more internally complex features in some interior regions leading up to the Late Woodland (Blair 2004). Houses also force archaeologists to acknowledge some differences, such as the apparent trend toward longhouses as a primarily horticultural phenomenon, although a possible longhouse is reported at the Goddard site in Maine (Bourque and Cox 1981; Cox 2021). But the architectural data suggest—in a preliminary way, for now—roughly coeval patterns of settlement change among horticulturalists and hunter-gatherers alike in much of the Northeast.

There are other similarities in settlement change that raise more questions than answers about the relationship between horticulture and village life in New England and delayed-return hunter-gatherer lifeways. These include evidence for year-round occupation of coastal areas on the Maritime Peninsula (e.g., Betts 2019; Black 2002), a series of plausible village or aggregation sites (e.g., Goddard, Melanson, End of Dyke), and the intensification of a variety of foraged and hunted plant and animal resources (Leonard 1996; Webb 2018).

Overall, much of these data suggest that one of the major themes that characterizes the late pre-Contact throughout the region is increasing sedentism (e.g., Patton et al., chapter 11, this volume) and subsistence intensification, even in the absence of horticulture (cf. Leonard 1996). It has long been asserted that with increasingly sedentary behaviours or the adoption of a more village-focused way of life, hunter-gatherers will begin to establish or demarcate territories or boundaries (e.g., Dyson-Hudson and Smith 1978; Lee and DeVore 1968), and while within the Maritime Peninsula this has not been strongly demonstrated prior to European contact (e.g., Bourque 1989), it is evident in adjacent horticultural regions (e.g., Mulholland 1988). It would seem that the Far Northeast is a crucial place to think anthropologically about economy, history, and the transitions to sedentism.

Discussion and Conclusion

Shared projectile typology and settlement are admittedly cursory examples; the form of projectiles and models of hunter-gatherer settlement along a forager-collector continuum are often taken nearly for granted in a general sense, with most academic attention focusing on their local or temporal nuances. This is precisely why these two cases have most intrigued us: it seems that there are fundamental questions surrounding these in our region that speak to questions of hunter-gatherer cultural change generally. Moreover, there seems to be a substantial degree of integration across the region such that localization (of Early

Woodland technological forms on local materials, for instance [Deal 2016]) and local ecological and economic explanations may often be tenuous.

With that in mind, it is unclear how much our perception of what Woodland is or should be shapes or has shaped what we know now. Have Woodland questions (or perhaps the search for Woodland answers) served to elucidate or mask continuities or variabilities at the intra-regional, regional, and inter-regional level? The papers in this volume challenge themes that have operationalized Woodland scholarship more generally, and present new ones: change through time, continuity (or discontinuity); local responses to global events (e.g., relating to technological change and burial ceremonialism); the expansion and contraction (and expansion again) of exchange relationships within and outside the region; changing relationships with technology; lack of radiocarbon dates and decreasing (or not) typological conformity as one moves east; the importance of place; and questioning the importance or reality of boundaries and margins. In doing so, the research herein addresses lacunae in the regional archaeological understanding of cultural change, frequently pointing to a number of complex and coeval changes enacted and experienced by pre-Contact groups in the Far Northeast.

Where we focus most of our work, the ca. 2,500-year period that we refer to as the Maritime Woodland is characterized by both a surprising uniformity with neighbours to the south, west, and north, and at the same time an intra-regional diversity that is both under-explored and under-explained. Operating at this broad regional and temporal scale can help us evaluate how a Woodland framework has counterintuitively served to both integrate the Far Northeast into the Northeast and eastern North America while at the same marginalizing it by masking regional and sub-regional diversity, and shaping regional discourse and research objectives.

The Algonquian past—with its clear linkages to contemporary Indigenous communities—is as much of the Woodland period in the Far Northeast as in the rest of the Northeast. The problem we face is that evolutionary models for that change can no longer be sustained, nor can ethnographic boundary areas be conflated with archaeological ones unless attempts are also made to account for extensive pre-Contact interaction. Returning to our opening theme for this essay, while we have traditionally conceived of the period 3000 BP to Contact in comparison to external events, these may not be entirely misapplied, especially, we think, if an emphasis is placed on interaction. If archaeologists conceive of the global Neolithic, the continental Formative, and the Eastern Woodland as dynamic periods of cultural and technological change, ones which include increasing social complexity, sedentism, and inter-regional interactions, then the Maritime Peninsula and the wider Far Northeast 3000 BP to Contact may be all three.

The essays in this volume offer an opportunity to begin to approach the regional and extra-regional questions of Woodland-period culture change as archaeologists confront longstanding notions of Palaeoindian, Archaic, and Woodland that are resistant to explanatory utility. Problematic, conflicting, and inconsistent taxa may remain; however, the maturity of archaeological research in this region is demonstrated throughout this volume. The essays in this volume emphasize that dichotomies between horticulturalists and hunter-gatherers are too reliant on generalizations about the latter, generalizations usually based on foraging economic strategies that archaeology has played a crucial role in nuancing. Strict environmental adaptations and uniform technological and cultural progressions are replaced with historically contingent processes of being and becoming, making, learning, and relearning. Both archaeologists and Indigenous communities are increasingly questioning past understandings of the geographic origins and tempos of social practices, in ways that increasingly include Indigenous voices. That these critical anthropological conversations are taking place in a region once thought so removed that its geography (Northeast) was qualified by a distant adverb—"Far"—stands to reckon we may be more central than we've been given credit.

Acknowledgements

We would like to thank all of the participants in the 2019 CAA session on which this volume is based for a series of insightful papers and discussions, and the Grand Conseil de la Nation Waban-Aki for sponsorship of the session. Gary Coupland, David Sanger, and Kenneth Sassaman generously read drafts of this chapter, and we are grateful for their insights, many of which are incorporated here. We would like to thank David Black in particular for comments on this essay as part of an ongoing conversation we have had with him over the past decade about Woodland-period culture change; many of his insights—and parenthetical dashes—are reflected here.

References Cited

Anderson, David G.

2004   Archaic Mounds and the Archaeology of Southeastern Tribal Societies. In *Signs of Power: The Rise of Cultural Complexity in the Southeast*, edited by L. Gibson and P. J. Carr, pp. 270–299. University of Alabama Press, Tuscaloosa.

Austin, Shaun J.

1980   Cape Cove Beach (DhAi-5, 6, 7), Newfoundland Prehistoric Cultures. Master's thesis, Department of Anthropology, Memorial University of Newfoundland, St. John's.

Betts, Matthew W.

2019   *Place-Making in the Pretty Harbour: The Archaeology of Port Joli Harbour, Nova Scotia.* Mercury Series, Volume 180. Canadian Museum of History and University of Ottawa Press, Ottawa.

Betts, Matthew W., and M. Gabriel Hrynick
2021   *The Archaeology of the Atlantic Northeast*. University of Toronto Press, Toronto.

Binford, Lewis R.
1980   Willow Smoke and Dogs' Tails: Hunter-Gatherer Settlement Systems and Archaeological Site Formation. *American Antiquity* 45(1):4–20.

Black, David. W.
2002   Out of the Blue and into the Black: The Middle-Late Maritime Woodland Transition in the Quoddy Region, New Brunswick, Canada. In *Northeast Settlement-Subsistence Change, A.D. 700–1300*, edited by J. P. Hart and C. B. Rieth, pp. 301–320, New York State Museum Bulletin #496. University of the State of New York/State Education Department, Albany.

2004   Living Close to the Ledge: Prehistoric Human Ecology of the Bliss Islands, Quoddy Region, New Brunswick, Canada. Publications in Northeast Archaeology No. 6. Copetown Press, St. John's.

Blair, Susan E.
2004   Aliwitahsik, Litahuswagon: Terminology and the Conceptual Framework. In *Wolastoqiyik Ajemseg, The People of the Beautiful River at Jemseg, Volume 2: Archaeological Results*, edited by Susan E. Blair, pp. 133–140. New Brunswick Manuscripts in Archaeology 36E. Archaeological Services, Heritage Branch, New Brunswick Culture and Sport Secretariat, Fredericton.

2010   Missing the Boat in Lithic Procurement: Watercraft and the Bulk Procurement of Tool-Stone on the Maritime Peninsula. *Journal of Anthropological Archaeology* 29:33–46.

Boudreau, Jeff
2008   *A New England Typology of Native American Projectile Points: Expanded Edition*. Massachusetts Archaeological Society, Middleborough, Massachusetts.

Bourque, Bruce
1971   Prehistory of the Central Maine Coast. PhD dissertation, Department of Anthropology, Harvard University.

1989   Ethnicity on the Maritime Peninsula, 1600-1759. *Ethnohistory* 36(3): 257–284.

2012   *The Swordfish Hunters: The History and Ecology of an Ancient American Sea People*. Bunker Hill Publishing, Piermont, New York.

Bourque, Bruce. J., and Steven Cox
1981   Maine State Museum Investigations at the Goddard Site. *Man in the Northeast* 22:3–27.

Bradley, Richard
2000   *An Archaeology of Natural Places*. Routledge, New York.

Brumm, Adam
2010   "The Falling Sky": Symbolic and Cosmological Associations of the Mt. William Greenstone Axe Quarry, Central Victoria, Australia. *Cambridge Archaeological Journal* 20(2):179–196.

Burke, Adrian L.
2007   Quarry Source Areas and the Organization of Stone Tool Technology: A View from Quebec. *Archaeology of Eastern North America* 35:63-80.

Chapdelaine, Claude

1990 Le concept de sylvicole ou l'hegemonie de la poterie. *Recherches Amérindiennes au Québec* 20(1):2–4.

Chapdelaine, Claude (editor)

2012 *Late Pleistocene Archaeology & Ecology in the Far Northeast.* Texas A&M University Press, College Station.

Chilton, Elizabeth S.

2005 Farming and Social Complexity in New England: AD 1000–1660. In *North American Archaeology*, edited by Timothy R. Pauketat and Diana Loren, pp. 138–160. Wiley-Blackwell, Malden, Washington.

Confederacy of Mainland Mi'kmaq

2007 *Kekina'muek: Learning about the Mi'kmaq of Nova Scotia.* Published for The Confederacy of Mainland Mi'kmaq by Eastern Woodland Print Communication, Truro, Nova Scotia.

Cox, Steven L.

2021 *Goddard: A Prehistoric Village Site on Blue Hill Bay, Maine.* Occasional Publications in Maine Archaeology No. 16. Maine Archaeological Society, Augusta.

Custer, Jay F.

1994 Current Archaeological Research in the Middle Atlantic Region of the Eastern United States. *Journal of Archaeological Research* 2(4):329–360.

Deal, Michael

2002 Aboriginal Land and Resource Use in New Brunswick During the Late Prehistoric and Early Contact Periods. In *Northeast Settlement-Subsistence Change, A.D. 700–1300*, edited by J. P. Hart and C. B. Rieth, pp. 321–344. The New York State Education Department, Albany.

2016 *The Collection of Ages: Precontact Archaeology of the Maritime Provinces.* Memorial University of Newfoundland Printing Services, St. John's.

Dyson-Hudson, Rada, and Eric Alden Smith

1978 Human Territoriality: An Ecological Reassessment. *American Anthropologist* 80:21–41.

Eid, Patrick

2017 Analyse techno-économique des chaînes opératoires lithiques du Témiscouata (Québec), durant le Sylvicole et la période de Contact. PhD dissertation, Départment d'Anthropologie, Université de Montréal.

Fagan, Brian

2011 *The First North Americans: An Archaeological Journey.* Thames and Hudson, London.

Farley, William A., Amy N. Fox, and M. Gabriel Hrynick

2019 A Quantitative Dwelling-Scale Approach to the Social Implications of Maize Horticulture in New England. *American Antiquity* 84(2):274–291.

Ford, James A., and Gordon R. Willey

1941 An Interpretation of the Prehistory of Eastern United States. *American Anthropologist* 43:325–363.

Gero, Joan M.

1989   Assessing Social Information in Material Objects: How Well Do Lithics Measure Pp? In *Time, Energy and Stone Tools*, edited by R. Torrence, pp. 92–105. Cambridge University Press, New York.

Gibson, Jon L, and Philip J. Carr (editors)

2004   *Signs of Power: The Rise of Cultural Complexity in the Southeast*. University of Alabama Press, Tuscaloosa.

Griffin, James B.

1952   *Archeology of Eastern United States*. University of Chicago Press, Chicago.

1967   Eastern North American Archaeology: A Summary. *Science, New Series* 156(3772):175–191.

Hoffman, Bernard G.

1955   The Historical Ethnography of the Micmac of the Sixteenth and Seventeenth Centuries. PhD dissertation, Department of Anthropology, University of California, Berkeley.

Holland-Lulewicz, Jacob

2021   From Categories to Connections in the Archaeology of Eastern North America. *Journal of Archaeological Research*. https://doi.org/10.1007/s10814-020-09154-w.

Holyoke, Kenneth R., and M. Gabriel Hrynick

2015   Portages and Lithic Procurement in the Northeastern Interior: A Case Study from the Mill Brook Stream Site, Lower Saint John River Valley, New Brunswick, Canada. *Canadian Journal of Archaeology* 39(2):213–240.

Holyoke, Kenneth R., Susan E. Blair, and Cliff S. J. Shaw

2020   Aesthetics or Function in Heat-Treating? The Influence of Colour Preference in Lithic Preparation on the Maritime Peninsula. *Journal of Anthropological Archaeology* 60. https://doi.org/10.1016/j.jaa.2020.101229.

Holly, Donald H., Jr.

2011   When Foragers Fail: In the Eastern Subarctic, for Example. In *Hunter-Gatherer Archaeology as Historical Process*, edited by K. E. Sassaman and D. H. Holly Jr., pp. 79–92. University of Arizona Press, Tucson.

2013   *History in the Making: The Archaeology of the Eastern Subarctic*. Altamira Press, Lanham, Maryland.

Hrynick, M. Gabriel, and David W. Black

2016   Cultural Continuity in Maritime Woodland Period Domestic Architecture in the Quoddy Region. *Canadian Journal of Archaeology* 40:23–67.

Jones, Rhys

1990   Hunters of the Dreaming: Some Ideational, Economic and Ecological Parameters of the Australian Aboriginal Productive System. In *Pacific Production Systems: Approaches to Economic Prehistory*, edited by D. E. Yen and J. M. J. Mummery, pp. 25–53. Australian National University, ANU Printing Service, Canberra.

Jones, Rhys, and N. White.

1988   Point Blank: Stone Tool Manufacture at the Ngilipitji Quarry, Arnhem Land, 1981. In *Archaeology with Ethnography: An Australian Perspective*, edited by

B. Meehan and R. Jones, pp. 51–87. Australian National University, Highland Press, Canberra.

Kerber, Jordan (editor).

1988   Where Are the Woodland Villages? *Massachusetts Archaeological Society Bulletin* 49(2):44–45.

Kristensen, Todd J.

2011   Seasonal Bird Exploitation by Recent Indian and Beothuk Hunter-Gatherers of Newfoundland. *Canadian Journal of Archaeology* 35(2):292–322.

LeBlanc, David, Isabelle Duval, and Jean-François Moreau.

2010   Geochemical Signature of Mistassini Quartzite and Ramah Chert Artefacts and Quarries, Québec/Labrador, Canada. In *Ancient Mines and Quarries: A Trans-Atlantic Perspective*, edited by Margaret Brewer-LaPorta, Adrian Burke, and David Field, pp. 67–84. Oxbow Books, Oxford, UK.

Lee, Richard B., and Irven DeVore

1968   Problems in the Study of Hunters and Gatherers. In *Man the Hunter: The First Intensive Survey of a Single, Crucial Stage of Human Development—Man's Once Universal Hunting Way of Life*, edited by Richard B. Lee and Irven DeVore, pp. 3–12. Aldine Transaction Publishers, New Brunswick, New Jersey.

Leonard, Kevin

1995   Woodland or Ceramic? A Theoretical Problem. *Northeast Anthropology* 50:19–30.

1996   Mi'kmaq Culture During the Late Woodland and Early Historic Periods. PhD dissertation, Department of Anthropology, University of Toronto, Toronto.

2002   Jedaik (Shediac, NB): A Nexus Through Time. Unpublished report, prepared for the Shediac Bay Watershed Association, Shediac Bridge, New Brunswick.

Leveillee, Alan, Joseph Waller Jr., and Donna Ingham

2006   Dispersed Villages in Late Woodland Period South-Coastal Rhode Island. *Archaeology of Eastern North America* 34:71–89.

Loring, Stephen A.

1989   Tikkoatokak (HdCl-1): A Late Prehistoric Indian Site near Nain. In *Archaeology in Newfoundland and Labrador 1986*, edited by C. Thomson and J. S. Thomson, pp. 52–71. Newfoundland Museum and Historic Resources Division, Department of Municipal and Provincial Affairs, St. John's.

2017   To the Uttermost Ends of the Earth… Ramah Chert in Time and Space. In *Ramah Chert: A Lithic Odyssey*, edited by Jenneth E. Curtis, and Pierre M. Desrosiers, pp. 169–219. Parks Canada and Avataq Cultural Institute, Inukjuak.

MacKenzie, Kim (Producer/Director)

1983   *Spear in the Stone* [Documentary]. Worldwide: Ronin Films.

McBryde, Isabel

1978   Wil-im-ee moor-ring' or, Where Do Axes Come From? *Mankind* 11(3): 354–382.

1984   Kulin Greenstone Quarries: The Social Contexts of Production and Distribution for the Mt William Site. *World Archaeology* 16(2):267–285.

McKern, Willam. C.

1939   The Midwestern Taxonomic Method as an Aid to Archaeological Culture Study. *American Antiquity* 4(4):301–313.

Mulholland, Mitchell T.

1988   Territoriality and Horticulture. In *Holocene Human Ecology in Northeastern North America*, edited by George P. Nicholas, pp. 137–166. Interdisciplinary Contributions to Archaeology. Springer, Boston.

Pauketat, Timothy R., and Susan M. Alt

2005   Agency in a Postmold? Physicality and the Archaeology of Culture-Making. *Journal of Archaeological Method and Theory* 12(5):213–236.

Pauketat, Timothy R., and Kenneth E. Sassaman

2020   *The Archaeology of Ancient North America*. Cambridge University Press, New York.

Paton, Robert

1994   Speaking through Stones: A Study from Northern Australia. *World Archaeology* 26(2):172–184.

Pawling, Micah A.

2017   *Wəlastəkwey* (Maliseet) Homeland: Waterscapes and Continuity within the Lower St. John River Valley, 1784–1900. *Acadiensis* 46(2):5–34.

Pelletier-Michaud, Alexandre

2017   The Bristol-Shiktehawk Bifaces and Early Woodland Ceremonialism in the Middle St. John Valley, New Brunswick. Master's thesis, Department of Anthropology, University of New Brunswick, Fredericton.

Petersen, James B.

1995   Preceramic Archaeological Manifestations in the Far Northeast: A Review of Current Research. *Archaeology of Eastern North America* 23:207–230.

Petersen, James B., and David Sanger

1991   An Aboriginal Ceramic Sequence for Maine and the Maritimes. In *Prehistoric Archaeology in the Maritimes: Past and Present Research*, edited by Susan E. Blair and Michael Deal, pp. 113–170. Council of Maritime Premiers, Maritime Committee on Archaeological Cooperation, Fredericton, New Brunswick.

Pintal, Jean-Yves

1998   *Aux Frontières de la Mer: La Préhistoire de Blanc-Sablon*. Ministère de la Culture et des Communications du Québec, Québec City.

Price, T. Douglas, and James A. Brown

1985   Aspects of Hunter-Gatherer Complexity. In *Prehistoric Hunter-Gatherers: The Emergence of Cultural Complexity*, edited by T. Douglas Price and James A. Brown, pp. 3–20. Academic Press, Toronto.

Ramsden, Peter

2008   Is There a North Atlantic Prehistory? The Case of the Neolithic and the Archaic. *North Atlantic Archaeology* 1:63–87.

Randall, Asa R.

2015   *Constructing Histories: Archaic Freshwater Shell Mounds and Social Landscapes of the St. Johns River, Florida*. University Press of Florida, Gainesville.

Ritchie, William A.

1961   *A Typology and Nomenclature for New York Projectile Points*. New York State Museum and Science Service Bulletin no 384. University of the State of New York and State Education Department, Albany.

Ritchie, William A., and Richard S. MacNeish
1949   The Pre-Iroquoian Pottery of New York State. *American Antiquity* 15:97–124.

Sanger, David
1974   Recent Meetings on Maine–Maritimes Archaeology: A Synthesis. *Man in the Northeast* 7:128–129.
1991   Five Thousand Years of Contact between Maine and Nova Scotia. *The Maine Archaeological Society Bulletin* 31(2):55–61.
2008   Discerning Regional Variation: The Terminal Archaic Period in the Quoddy Region of the Maritime Peninsula. *Canadian Journal of Archaeology* 32:1–42.
2009   Birchbark Canoes, Dugouts, and Gouges: Is There Any Logical Relationship? *The Maine Archaeological Society Bulletin* 49(2):17–34.

Sanger, David and M. A. P. Renouf
2006   *The Archaic of the Far Northeast*. University of Maine Press, Orono.

Sanger, David, Alice R. Kelley, and Henry N. Berry IV
2001   Geoarchaeology at Gilman Falls: An Archaic Quarry and Manufacturing Site in Central Maine, USA. *Geoarchaeology* 16(6):633–665.

Sassaman, Kenneth E.
2004   Complex Hunter-Gatherers in Evolution and History: A North American Perspective. *Journal of Archaeological Research* 12(3):227–280.
2008   The New Archaic: It Ain't What it Used to Be. *The SAA Archaeological Record* 8(5):6–8.
2010   *The Eastern Archaic, historicized*. Issues in Eastern Woodlands Archaeology. AltaMira Press, Lanham, MD.

Smith, Nicholas N.
2011   *Three Hundred Years in Thirty: Memoir of Transition with the Cree Indians of Lake Mistassini*. Polar Bear & Co, Solon, Maine.

Snow, Dean
1980   *The Archaeology of New England*. Academic Press, New York.

Speck, Frank G.
1997 [1940]   *Penobscot Man: The Life History of a Forest Tribe in Maine*. University of Maine Press, Orono.

Spiess, Arthur E.
1985   Wild Maine and the Rusticating Scientist: A History of Anthropological Archaeology in Maine. *Man in the Northeast* 30:101–129.

Taché, Karine
2011   New Perspectives on Meadowood Trade Items. *American Antiquity* 76(1): 41–80.

Taçon, Paul S. C.
1990   The Power of Place: Cross-Cultural Responses to Natural and Cultural Landscapes of Stone and Earth. In *Perspectives of Canadian Landscape: Native Traditions*, edited by J. Vastokas, pp. 11–43. Robarts Centre for Canadians Studies, North York, Ontario.
1991   The Power of Stone: Symbolic Aspects of Stone Use and Tool Development in Western Arnhem Land, Australia. *Antiquity* 65:192–207.

Thomas, P. A.

1994 Vermont Archaeology Comes of Age: A Perspective on Vermont's Prehistoric Past. *Journal of Vermont Archaeology* 1:38–91.

Thompson, Victor D., and Jennifer Birch

2019 The Power of Villages. In *The Archaeology of Villages in Eastern North America,* edited by Jennifer Birch and Victor Thompson, pp. 1–19. University of Florida Press, Gainesville.

Thompson, Victor D., and Thomas J. Pluckhahn

2010 History, Complex Hunter-Gatherers, and the Mounds and Monuments of Crystal River, Florida, USA: A Geophysical Perspective. *Journal of Island & Coastal* Archaeology 5(1):33–51.

Tomasso, Antonin, and Guillaume Porraz

2016 Hunter-Gatherer Mobility and Embedded Raw-Material Procurement Strategies in the Mediterranean Upper Paleolithic. *Evolutionary Anthropology* 25:164–174.

Turnbull, Christopher

1976 The Augustine Site: A Mound for the Maritimes. *Archaeology of Eastern North America* 4:50–62.

1977 Of Backdirt and Bureaucracy: The Role of Government in Canadian Archaeology. In *New Perspectives in Canadian Archaeology: Proceedings of a Symposium Sponsored by the Royal Society of Canada,* edited by A. G. McKay, pp. 119–136. Royal Society of Canada, Royal Ontario Museum, National Museum of Man, Toronto.

Versaggi, Nina, LouAnn Wurst, T. Cregg Madrigal, and Andrea Lain

2001 Adding Complexity to Late Archaic Research in the Northeastern Appalachians. In *Archaeology of the Appalachian Highlands,* edited by L. Sullivan and S. Prezzano, pp. 121–136. University of Tennessee Press, Knoxville.

Webb, W. Jesse

2018 A Late Maritime Woodland Peskotomuhkati Fishery from The Mainland Quoddy Region, Southwestern New Brunswick, Canada. Master's thesis, Department of Anthropology, University of New Brunswick, Fredericton.

Willey, Gordon R.

1966 *An Introduction to American Archaeology, Volume I: North and Middle America.* Prentice-Hall, Englewood Cliffs, New Jersey.

Willey, Gordon R., and Philip Phillips

1958 *Method and Theory in American Archaeology.* University of Chicago Press, Chicago.

THE STRUGGLE WAS REAL

On the End of the Archaic on the Island of Newfoundland and Labrador

2

DONALD H. HOLLY, JR.,[1] CHRISTOPHER B. WOLFF,[2] AND STEPHEN H. HULL[3]

Abstract

The transition between the end of the Maritime Archaic and the so-called Intermediate Indian period on the island of Newfoundland and Labrador was marked by significant changes in just about all dimensions of life for First Nations peoples living in the region at the time: cemeteries stop being used, longhouses are no longer erected, an exquisite ground-stone-tool technological tradition comes to an end, long-distance exchange networks contract, and vast areas of the region are abandoned. These changes, which coincide with a relative reduction in the number of archaeological site components, a contraction in land-use area, a detrimental shift in settlement strategy, and a steep decline in radiocarbon dates suggest that a demographic collapse put an end to the Archaic period on the island of Newfoundland and Labrador.

Résumé

La transition entre la fin de l'Archaïque Maritime et la période dite *Intermediate Indian* sur l'île de Terre-Neuve et au Labrador fut marquée par des changements considérables touchant presque tous les aspects de la vie des Premières Nations qui habitaient la région à l'époque : les cimetières cessèrent d'être utilisés, les maisons longues cessèrent d'être construites, une riche tradition technique de la pierre taillée disparut, les réseaux d'échanges étendus se contractèrent, et de vastes pans du territoire furent abandonnés. Ces changements coïncident avec une baisse relative du nombre de composantes des sites archéologiques, une diminution de la superficie du territoire utilisée, un passage vers des modes d'occupation du territoire désavantageux et une baisse abrupte du nombre de dates radiocarbones. Ces données suggèrent qu'un effondrement démographique a marqué la fin de la période Archaïque à Terre-Neuve et au Labrador.

Affiliations

1. Department of Sociology, Anthropology, and Criminology, Eastern Illinois University, Illinois, United States (corresponding author: dhholly@eiu.edu)
2. Department of Anthropology, University at Albany, New York, United States
3. Provincial Archaeology Office, Government of Newfoundland and Labrador, Newfoundland and Labrador, Canada

Since the ecological turn in anthropology in the 1960s, which included a newfound appreciation for hunter-gatherers' ability to mitigate risk and respond to resource fluctuations, there has been a tendency to interpret changes in hunter-gatherer prehistory as seamless cultural adjustments through which people became re-suited to their natural environments. Support for making such claims draws on an ethnographic literature replete with examples of how hunter-gatherers strategically employ cultural institutions and customs—such as sharing, the extension of kinship obligations, trade relationships, group fission and fusion, technological ingenuity, mobility, and an intimate knowledge of the natural environment—to buffer against resource shortfalls and adjust to new environmental and resource realities (Gould 1982; Jarvenpa 2004; Kelly 1983; Lee and Devore 1968; Minc and Smith 1989; Ridington 1982; Stopp 2002).

Notwithstanding cultural adaptations that might make hunter-gatherers better able to respond to changes in their natural environment than, say, sedentary farmers (see Berbesque et al. 2014), hunter-gatherers are not impervious to struggle or even collapse; nor, when it occurs, is the natural environment solely to blame. Hunter-gatherers, like all people, have culturally constituted ways of living, worldviews, and social aspirations that might make them more or less vulnerable to failure (Bar-Yosef 1998:173; Friesen 2004; Holly 2011; Holly et al. 2018; Hood 1993:179; Schwarz 1994). The demise of the Dorset on the island of Newfoundland around 1200 BP, for instance, was not only due to warming conditions that reduced sea ice and access to their staple food, harp seal (Bell and Renouf 2008; Renouf and Bell 2009), but also to a Dorset reluctance, or inability, to restructure their way of life in the face of these changes (Holly 2011, 2013:107-108). That other Indigenous people (the predecessors of the Beothuk) living on the island at the same time persisted when the Dorset abandoned it tells us that environmental accommodation was certainly possible.

Here we look at what appears to be another challenging period in eastern subarctic prehistory: the transition from the Maritime Archaic (MA) to what has been called the Intermediate Indian period, hereafter referred to as the

Intermediate Indigenous (II) period,[1] around 3500 BP. On the eve of this transition, the First Nations peoples of the island and Labrador lived primarily on the coast and enjoyed a maritime food economy; they produced stone tools fashioned from Ramah chert quarried in northern Labrador, and exquisite slate bayonets, adzes, gouges, and other implements; they lived part of the year in longhouses; they buried some of their dead in cemeteries and under mounds; they exchanged exotic raw materials and objects, and shared mortuary traditions and ceremonial practices with distant peoples; and they competed with one another for access to prestige items and status (see Fitzhugh 1978a, 2006; Holly 2013:40–45; Hood 1993, 1995; Spiess 1992; Wolff 2008). On the other side of this transition, the island of Newfoundland is completely abandoned, along with long stretches of the Labrador coast, and the interior of the Labrador Peninsula becomes a major area of activity; exchange networks sharply contract and stone tools are more often than not fashioned from local materials; the longhouses are replaced by smaller dwellings, often delineated only by the sharp edges of lithic scatters; and people are no longer interred in cemeteries—indeed, we do not know where the dead are buried (see Brake 2006; Fitzhugh 1974; Loring and Jenkinson 2018; Madden 1976; Nagle 1978; Neilsen 2006; Schwarz et al. 2016, 2018; Stassinu Stantec 2019).

Not much of this is disputed, but explanations for why these changes occurred and what they mean are. Explanations for why the Archaic ended include disruption caused by the usurpation of traditional subsistence grounds by PaleoInuit descending out of the Arctic, the influx of Susquehanna-tradition peoples and ideas on the southern frontier, increased activity in the interior of Labrador, and the reconstitution of social allegiances, but perhaps most significantly, climatic cooling and instability caused in part by changes to the track of the Labrador Current (see Fitzhugh 1978a:92; Fiedel 2001; Holly 2013; Hood 1993, 2000; Sanger 2006). And as to what these changes might mean, some archaeologists suggest not very much at all—emphasizing adjustment and continuity through the MA/II transition—while others see radical reorganization and discontinuities (Arbour et al. 2018; Beaton and Renouf 2014:35; Brake 2009:39–40; Fitzhugh 1978a:91; Holly 2013; Loring 1989; Loring and Jenkinson 2018; Luckenbach et al. 1987; Madden 1976; Nagle 1978; Tuck 1975).

In this chapter, we take a close look at what happened then, with a focus on the difficult matter of charting demographic changes across this transition.

---

1. It is high time to revisit the region's archaeological terminology (Arbour et al. 2018; Friesen 2015; Loring and Jenkinson 2018; Neilsen 2016; Stopp 2008:97–99). Until this is accomplished and there is consensus, we offer the Intermediate Indigenous period as a temporary substitute for the Intermediate Indian period. Note that by "Indigenous" we are referring to the First Nations, or Amerindian people of the region, not the PaleoInuit, who were also on the landscape at the time.

We focus on paleodemography, since cultural changes are already evident and could be interpreted as adjustments of the rather seamless sort. If a concurrent decline in population occurred then, however, it would suggest that the transition was less seamless than it was cataclysmic. A significant population decline at this juncture would have significant implications for our understanding of the region's prehistory. It would lend some support to the notion that the Algonquian-language family arrived later in the region (Denny 1994; Fiedel 1991; Luckenbach et al. 1987; Pentland 1985), along with its speakers, rather than developing in situ out of the Archaic (Tuck 1975), as the landscape then would have been effectively cleared (or nearly so) of populations that might have otherwise worked to thwart their spread (see Fiedel 1991:22–26). It could also inspire a broader rethinking of hunter-gatherer adaptations: namely, that however flexible and resilient hunter-gatherer lifeways may be, there are social and cultural limitations to (even) how far they may be willing or able to change—to say nothing of that, seemingly, universal human capacity for error.

Newfoundland and Labrador Paleodemography: Issues

Paleodemography is a challenge—hunter-gatherer paleodemography much more so. Calculating population size and density for hunter-gatherers in pre-history is greatly complicated by the often-ephemeral nature of the hunter-gatherer archaeological record. This is especially a problem in Newfoundland and Labrador, where lithic scatters and spot finds are the norm, dense forests conceal sites inland and an active shoreline erases those on the coast, and a frequently thin and deflated stratigraphy makes it difficult to precisely delineate and date occupations. Quite simply, the fine-grained temporal data needed to adequately chart population changes over time is not available. Furthermore, many areas of the province remain sparsely, or selectively, surveyed. Radiocarbon dates, necessary for generating summed probability distributions, are uncommon, and, as is the case elsewhere (see Palmisano et al. 2017:60; Peros et al. 2010), are disproportionately associated with long-running and well-funded excavations or those that focus on questions of particular popular or scholarly interest. To wit, more than a third of all the "prehistoric" radiocarbon dates on the island of Newfoundland (n=541) come from just two sites: the famous Norse site at L'Anse aux Meadows (n=136) and the spectacular Dorset site at Phillip's Garden (n=57).

Traditionally, anthropological interest in hunter-gatherer demography has centred on understanding the factors that might have kept population levels low: high residential mobility, child mortality, nutritional/fat deficiencies, suppressed ovulation from extended breast-feeding, violence, infanticide, STD-induced sterility, and even suicide (Howell 1979; Keckler 1997; Konner and Worthman 1980; Pennington 2001; Steegmann 1983). It can be tempting to generalize these processes to all hunter-gatherers—and many have succumbed—but one should keep in mind that good demographic data on foragers is hard to come by, and what is available is largely limited to the few groups that can be studied today. As these are typically groups that inhabit similar (challenging) environments and share similar adaptations (i.e., high residential mobility), it would be unwise to assume that they are representative of the entirety of the foraging spectrum. The processes that shaped the populations of complex or sedentary hunter-gatherers may have been very different (Howell 1979:3; Keckler 1997).

There has been a tendency to envision hunter-gatherer population trajectories in prehistory as glacially slow-growing, or even static, although that is beginning to change (see Bocquet-Appel and Demars 2000; Gamble et al. 2005; Glassow and Johnson 2019; Hull 2011; Maschner et al. 2009), and for these trajectories to have been rigidly curtailed by the environment or narrowly determined by biological impetuses beyond people's control or even recognition (Cannon 2011; Hull 2011). The role of social conditions in hunter-gatherer demography, such as relations with other peoples, is likewise undertheorized, with the only exceptions to this being of the extraordinary sort—population crashes and demographic swamping caused by colonial-era conquests, Neolithic advances, and disease epidemics (Bellwood 2005; Shennan 2015:150; Ubelaker 1988:291).

Population estimates for hunter-gatherers occupying a given area in antiquity are often educated guesses based on early historical records, analogies with people occupying similar environments, and expectations of the carrying capacity of the environment. The overall impression is one of stasis, in the sense that past groups are assumed to have numbered about the same as those observed at the dawn of the Colonial period. They tend to be environmentally deterministic too, as they are based on the presumption that the carrying capacity was met by historically observed peoples. Archaeologists working in Newfoundland and Labrador, however, have long asserted that people experienced periodic population crashes as a result of environmental fluctuations (Fitzhugh 1972, 1973; Tuck and Pastore 1985). Some of these events, or at least their severity, have been challenged (Renouf 1999), but if any of them occurred it would mean that there were times in the past when there were more people living in the region and times when there were less. Indeed, there is evidence to suggest that this was the case (see Holly 2005), which should give one pause in assuming that Colonial period population sizes mirrored those in the past.

Scholarly estimates suggest that the Beothuk of the island of Newfoundland numbered between 500 and 2,000 persons at the beginning of the Colonial period. This is based on population estimates by early observers, analogies with other groups inhabiting similar environments, and expectations of the carrying capacity of the boreal forest (see Kroeber 1947:171; Marshall 1977, 1996:278–284; Mooney 1928:24; Upton 1977:134). Estimates for the Indigenous populations of Labrador, which include the Inuit, Innu, and Naskapi, follow a similar logic. The Labrador Inuit are estimated to have numbered about 3,600 persons, and the Innu (known historically as Montagnais), Naskapi, and neighbouring Atikamekw of Quebec 5,500 (Kroeber 1947:134, 141; Mooney 1928:24), which translates to a population density of 1.73 people per 100 km^2 (Inuit) to 0.44 people per 100 km^2 (Innu, Naskapi, and Atikamekw) (cf. Rogers and Leacock 1981:173). Notwithstanding that these estimates include populations that do not neatly align with modern political boundaries, a total population of 11,000 for Labrador and Newfoundland—encompassing some 405,000 km^2—is a reasonable approximation of scholarly estimates for the province, and is in line with estimates that the Subarctic region as a whole had the lowest population density in North America (Ubelaker 1988).

Archaeological efforts at paleodemography frequently aim for relative, as opposed to absolute, population estimates. Relative estimates are accomplished by assuming that larger populations will have a stronger archaeological signal—that they will leave more things behind (Palmisano et al. 2017; Powell 1988; Ross 1985; Tallavaara et al. 2014). This is a reasonable expectation, but one should consider that the average North American owns far more stuff today than anyone had in antiquity (see Arnold et al. 2012) and generates as much trash in their lifetime as thousands once did. And while this might be an exceptional example, it is likely that some hunter-gatherer groups (perhaps mobility-dependent) produced more or less stuff than others. There is apt to be cultural variation in technology too, which together with taphonomic processes, could also affect the archaeological "signal." People who made stone tools that are not easily identified to a tradition, or that used material that does not preserve, for example, might appear less numerous than those that fashioned clearly diagnostic tool types out of stone (see Le Blanc 2009:547; Robinson and Ort 2011). Even population estimates derived from dwelling size are complicated by cultural variation in the use of household space (Webster and Freter 1990:49), provided one can even identify house features in the archaeological record, control for contemporaneity, and account for seasonal variation in settlement patterns (Powell 1988:169–171).

Archaeologists have been increasingly using summed probability distributions of radiocarbon dates to assess prehistoric population sizes (Filios 1989; Gamble et al. 2005; Glassow and Johnson 2019; Orton et al. 2017; Palmisano et al. 2017; Peros et al. 2010; Williams 2012). The logic of doing so draws on the aforementioned premise that more stuff equals more people, but this approach is even more problematic than counting arrowheads since the existence of radiocarbon dates depends, at least in part, on a decision made by an archaeologist. Thus, while no archaeologist would neglect to record an arrow-head, there are many radiocarbon samples that are never collected or dated due to budget constraints, excavation strategies, or even interest (Filios 1989:8; Palmisano et al. 2017; Peros et al. 2010:661; Surovell and Brantingham 2007; cf. Gamble et al. 2005). More recent sites, for instance, may not be radiocarbon dated as often as older sites because of the availability of better or cheaper means of dating (ceramic styles, coins, tin cans), or because one deems them to be less extraordinary. This could give the impression of a population crash at the moment that people start minting coins, for instance (Palmisano et al. 2017:66). Inversely, because older sites and material are less likely to survive in the archaeological record than recent ones, a summed probability distribution of radiocarbon dates could convey the impression of population growth over time, when what it is really tracking are taphonomic processes (Surovell and Brantingham 2007). It is worth noting that in Newfoundland and Labrador, isostatic uplift has sometimes worked to preserve older sites, formerly on the coast, by lifting them away from a site-destroying active shoreline. Thus, in contrast to other regions, older sites might stand a better chance of surviving than more recent sites that are located closer to the modern shoreline. Finally, studies indicate that summed probability distributions should be based on a sample size of at least 500 radiocarbon dates (Williams 2012), but we only have 213 dates to work with. In short, summed radiocarbon probability distributions constitute a sample (preserved) of a sample (found) of a sample (dated).

Accordingly, summed radiocarbon probability distributions work best when combined with other population proxies such as raw counts of sites and artifacts, and site-size estimates (Hull 2011; Palmisano et al. 2017; Tallavaara et al. 2014; Williams 2012). In Newfoundland and Labrador, however, the size of occupations is difficult to assess from site-record forms maintained at the Province's Archaeology Office (PAO) since archaeologists often estimate (to the extent this is even possible) the total area of a site and not the extent of individual occupations within it. This makes it a challenge, for instance, to parse the small MA component at Hebron-1 out from the massive (150,000 m^2) historic Moravian mission that overlays it. Likewise, artifact counts are not always broken down by "tradition" or "complex" in reports on multi-component sites and, even if they were, uneven precision in identifying the formal tools of some traditions and complexes could skew artifact counts in favour of one or another cultural occupation. Finally, assemblages are often (and often only can be) attributed to cultural traditions and not to more spatially and chronologically "precise" taxonomic units, such as complexes or phases. Of the 569 MA site components considered in this study, for instance, only 55 have a more precise taxonomic resolution than Tradition listed on the site-record form; and even if more precise taxonomic classifications were provided, there would still be some dispute over the contours, duration, and utility of them (Nagle 1978; Neilsen 2006).

With all the aforementioned caveats in mind, we attempt a comparative analysis of relative population size across the MA and II periods by tracking changes in component frequencies, effective land-use area, settlement strategies, and summed probability distributions of radiocarbon dates. We also offer some broad observations of trends in the archaeological record of the terminal Archaic, which include the end of a cemetery-burial tradition, a contraction in exchange networks, and the disappearance of longhouses.

Newfoundland and Labrador Paleodemography: Analysis

Components

PAO records indicate that there are 416 sites in Labrador and 153 sites on the island of Newfoundland with an MA component, and 184 sites in Labrador and just one site on the island with an II component. Our sample does not include any components in which cultural affiliation was questioned by the observer. Note that we use the term "component" here, since a single site could contain both an MA and II component.

A simple raw count indicates that there was a 67% decline in components between the MA and the II periods across the study area. On the island of Newfoundland, the decline was near total (99%), with only one site yielding any II artifacts (Beaton and Renouf 2014). Labrador witnessed a loss of 232 components, representing a 56% decline across the MA-II transition. Such simple calculations are belied, of course, by the different time depths of each period. The MA period begins with the arrival, some 8,500 years ago, of people moving into southern Labrador from the lower north shore of Quebec, and ends shortly after the abandonment of the island of Newfoundland, around 3200 BP. The II period is short by comparison. It begins as early as 3,500 years ago in Labrador and ends ca. 2,000 years later (1500 BP) in what archaeologists have alternatively deemed the Recent Indian (Tuck 1971), Late Prehistoric (Fitzhugh 1978b), Late Precontact Amerindian (Stopp 2008), Late phase (Madden 1976:129), and ancestral Innu/Beothuk period (Arbour et al. 2018; Loring and Jenkinson 2018).

The different time depths of the MA and II periods make it difficult to make a simple reckoning of components since, if the population size had remained the same, one might reasonably expect people to generate more components if they had more time to do so. If we were instead counting projectile points, and we found 100 of those in a 500-year time frame, for example, we might reasonably expect to find 200 projectile points in a 1,000-year period (see Anderson et al. 2008:108; Hull 2011). However, there is no easy way to tighten the chronology to make the analysis more precise. In an ideal scenario, we would want to compare the archaeological record from a sliver of time at the very end of the Archaic with a similarly narrow sliver of time at the beginning of the II period—in the same way that a historical demographer interested in the effect of the Irish famine on the population might compare the 1840 census with the 1850 census. But, as already mentioned, the great majority of components are attributed only to "tradition," which means we can only compare two very long and unwieldy blocks of time. Nonetheless, it's a start.

Dividing the total number of components (n=569) by the maximum extent of the MA period, 5500 years (8500 BP to 3000 BP), yields an average component per year (CPY) of 0.103. Or, to put it another way, if we assume a uniform rate of component production (unlikely) it could be said that archaeologists have about one MA component for every 10 years of the tradition. The CPY for the II period is slightly less (.092), meaning that we have one II component for about every 11 years of the tradition. All things being equal (mobility, preservation, etc.), a larger population should produce a higher CPY. And if so, one could say that the MA were slightly more populous than the II (see figure 2.1, model one).

It is highly unlikely, however, that the MA population remained the same size throughout the entire 5,500-year tradition. Many of the earliest MA sites are little more than lithic scatters and spot finds. Moreover, it appears to have taken these first peoples of the tradition some 2,000 years to fully explore and fill in the contours of the province. The island of Newfoundland, for instance, was not settled until nearly 3,000 years after the adjacent shores of southern Labrador were. Accordingly, it is reasonable to assume that the pioneering population of the region was very small, and that it remained so for a long time.

In comparison, the population at the dawn of the II period should, in theory (if there were not a population crash), have been about the same size as the MA population that immediately preceded it. And there is good evidence, in the form of longhouses, cemeteries, the dense clustering and wide distribution of sites, and in the quantity of radiocarbon dates (discussed later), to indicate that MA populations were quite large near the end of the Archaic.

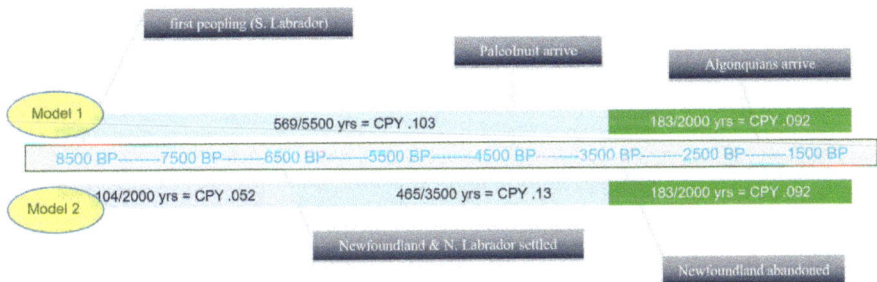

Figure 2.1. Components per year, per tradition, two models.

Accordingly, we are probably grossly underestimating the size of the MA population prior to the transition by averaging components across the entire tradition, since it assumes that components were being generated at the same rate for 5,500 years. But how to account for these demographic changes without finer chronological control?

If we reasonably assume that the MA generated half the average number of components of the tradition during the first 2,000 years in which these people were pioneering the land (25.9 components per 500 years, or 104 in 2,000 years), and just considered the last 3,500 years of the MA tradition (66.4 components per 500 years, or 465 in 3,500 years), we arrive at CPY of 0.13, or one component for every 7.5 years of the last two thirds of the tradition (see figure 2.1, model two). This is considerably more components than what was generated during the subsequent II period, and suggests that a sharp population decline occurred at the transition.

Settlement Area

MA sites extend all along the coast from Labrador's southernmost border with Quebec to its northern tip, dot the circumference of the island of Newfoundland, and are present in small quantities throughout the interior of Labrador (figure 2.2). The distribution of II sites on the Labrador coast is broadly similar, albeit with less clustering of sites (see northern Labrador) and some pronounced gaps in settlement (see southern Labrador). Far more significant differences between the two periods are evident on the island of Newfoundland, where there is just one II site, and in the interior of Labrador, where there is a proliferation of activity in the II period, especially in the Lake Melville area (figure 2.3).

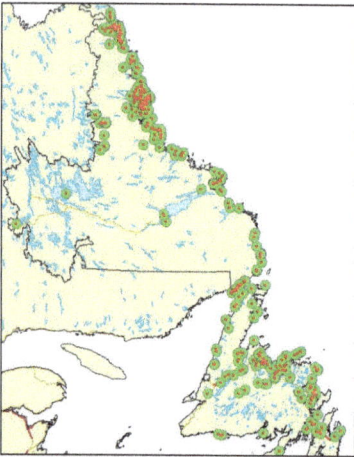

Figure 2.2. Maritime Archaic sites in Newfoundland and Labrador, with 15-k foraging radius.

In an effort to assess differences in settlement area and land use between the two periods, we imposed a 15 km foraging radius around each site. This is based on ethnographic evidence suggesting that non-equestrian hunter-gatherer daily foraging trips (round-trip) rarely exceeded 30 km, and typically averaged half that (see Binford 2001:235–238; Conolly 2018; Ellis 2011; Kelly 1995:133; Politis 2007:171–174). We did not account for terrain or technology (the possibility that greater distances may have been possible with sleds or watercraft) and allowed radii to overlap. We also realize that the actual land-use area for each group must have been far larger than our calculations indicate below, as there must be many sites that have been lost to time, or remain undiscovered (not surveyed and/or buried), or are undiscoverable (left no archaeological evidence). Nonetheless, we assume that there is a relative equivalence between foraging radius and overall land use, so while II populations probably made greater use of the island of Newfoundland than is indicated by the one known site, it was far less than what was used by the MA, who left 153 sites. Our aim here is simply to get a workable sense of operating space.

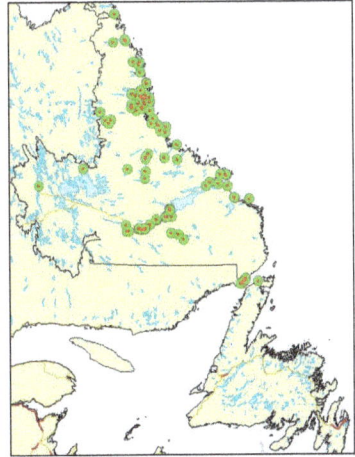

Figure 2.3. Intermediate Indigenous sites in Newfoundland and Labrador, with 15-k foraging radius.

Using a 15 km radius around each site, we calculated a total use area of 402,202 km^2 for the MA period and 129,355 km^2 for the II period. The difference between the two represents a loss of 68% of the land-use area. Most of this occurred with the abandonment of the island of Newfoundland; the MA occupation there totalled 108,149 km^2, and for the II, a mere 706.86 km^2—a decline in land-use area of 99%. Labrador, however, still saw a decline of 56%, from 294,053 km^2 during the MA period to 128,648 km^2 in the II period (figure 2.4).

In theory, shifts in land use need not coincide with a reduction in population. The last few centuries have witnessed a global population shift from rural to urban areas, and similar shifts are apparent in antiquity too—in the ballooning of city states in Mesopotamia (Pollock 1999:64) and the coalescing of villages in Iroquoia (Birch and Williamson 2013). But there is little evidence for anything akin to this in the eastern Subarctic. Formal cemeteries, a plausible reflection of increased population densities and the associated need to make claims to land tenure (Fitzhugh 2006:62; Renouf and Bell 2011), end with the Archaic. The longhouses do too. Longhouses are large, segmented structures thought to be the remnants of conjoined-tent features. The largest of these features encompass a dozen or so "apartments," extend over 70 metres, and may have housed 100 individuals (Fitzhugh 2006; Hood 1993, 1995; Wolff 2008). They are replaced with lithic scatters and cobble hearths (Brake 2006:18), although some structural features have been identified recently in the II archaeological record (Schwarz et al. 2018; Stassinu Stantec 2019). Not one burial feature of any kind is known from the II period. Accordingly, the overall impression is that there was a sharp reduction in land-use area that was not offset by concomitant increased sedentism and population packing. This too points to a population decline.

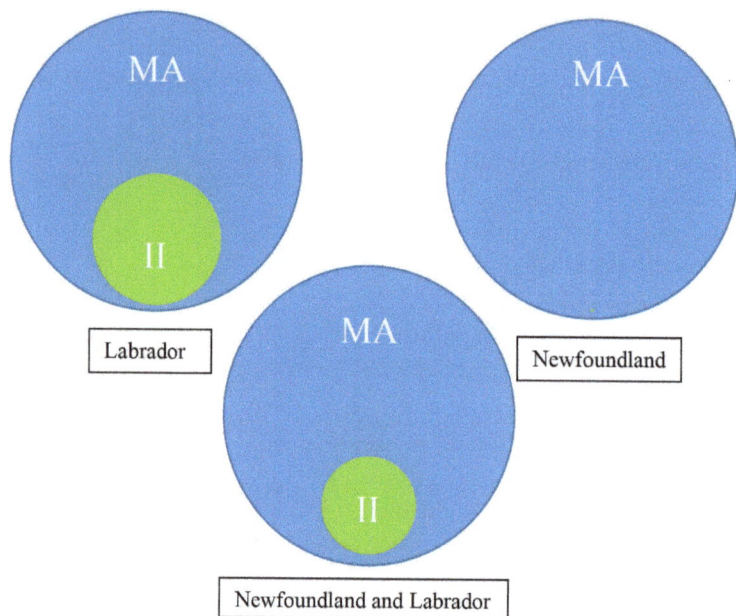

Figure 2.4. Visualization of Maritime Archaic and Intermediate Indigenous land-use areas.

There is also a clear shift away from the coast with the end of the MA (Brake 2006). This includes the abandonment of the entire island of Newfoundland, and its 10,000 km of shoreline. It is hard to square this with the interpretation that this was an adaptive shift. While the interior has been unjustly portrayed as impoverished (Neilsen 2016:8–11, 64), it is difficult to imagine a scenario in which the interior would have been more attractive, from a purely subsistence-resource perspective, than the coast (Fitzhugh 1972). The interior offers far less food variety. Caribou, arguably its most significant food resource, are mostly a seasonal bounty, and they, like bear, beaver, and partridge, can be found near the coast. The inverse, however, is not true—people cannot readily access coastal resources if they are living far inland. Coastal or near coastal locations thus offer people access to the greatest variety of resources. This may explain why 85% of MA sites in Labrador and 83% of MA sites on the island of Newfoundland are located within one kilometre of the coast, and 92% and 89%, respectively, are within 15 km (see also Brake 2006); the former indicates a clear commitment to coastal resources, and the latter the option to pursue them. Indeed, that many coastal MA sites on the island of Newfoundland are situated in places that offered easy access to the interior (Renouf and Bell 2006) suggests a settlement strategy that emphasized such flexibility. In comparison, just 44% of II sites in Labrador are directly on the coast, and only 63% within

15 km of it (the one II site on the island is located on the coast)[2] (figure 2.5). It suggests a narrow—dangerously so—commitment to interior/lacustrine resources. Accordingly, the shift to the interior in the II period appears to have come with diminished resource variety—and if variety means options, and options mean food security, then this shift was clearly not adaptive.

The turn to the interior also hints at population loss, since there is no indication that the coast became unproductive at this time (cf. Brake 2006). For centuries prior to the end of the Archaic, MA peoples shared northern Labrador with PaleoInuit peoples, who had arrived on the scene around 4300 BP. But when the Archaic ended and their II descendants shifted inland nearly a thousand years later, PaleoInuit peoples remained on the coast—indeed, they proliferated there. PaleoInuit sites contemporaneous with the II occupation dot the length of the Labrador coast, extend to the lower north shore of Quebec, and are common on the island of Newfoundland. Their presence in these places indicates that a maritime-based food economy was viable at this time. Moreover, that the PaleoInuit could be so prolific then, even going so far as to occupy Newfoundland, suggests that II peoples might have been absent from the island, not because they did not want to be there, but because they couldn't. Maybe they simply did not have enough people to be everywhere.

Summed Probability Distribution of Radiocarbon Dates

Summed probability distributions of radiocarbon dates is an increasingly popular way to assess demographic change in the archaeological record. To do our analysis, we created arbitrary time slices of 500 years. To minimize errors resulting from bad data we discarded dates with very large error ranges (>100 years) and those associated with the Gakushuin Laboratory in Japan, which Spriggs and Anderson (1993) found to be unreliable. Similar chronometric hygiene protocols are commonly employed elsewhere (see Fitzpatrick 2006; Taché and Hart 2013), although they are not as strict as some would prescribe (Spriggs and Anderson 1993). We also discarded dates that were not clearly associated with an MA or II occupation. This left us with 213 radiocarbon dates. We then measured how much of the remaining radiocarbon-date-error ranges fell into each time slice, or bin. For instance, if the entire date fell within one 500-year bin, then that bin would add the value of 1.0, or 100 percent. If half fell into one bin and the other in another bin, each bin would add a value of 0.5, or 50 percent. These values are summed for each 500-year bin for both the MA and the II periods. The higher the value for any given bin, the higher the probability for a larger population during that period.

---

2. We counted II sites on the shores of Lake Melville as coastal locations since this is a saltwater tidal extension of Hamilton Bay.

Maritime Archaic (Newfoundland)

Proximity to coast	# of components
< 1 km	127
1-15 km	9
>15 km	15

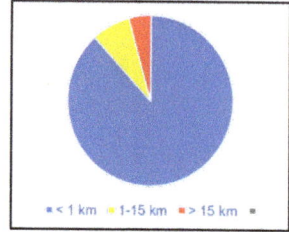

Maritime Archaic (Labrador)

Proximity to coast	# of components
< 1 km	352
1-15 km	30
>15 km	34

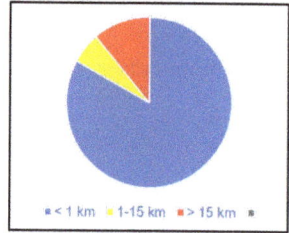

Intermediate Indigenous (Newfoundland)

Proximity to coast	# of components
< 1 km	1
1-15 km	0
>15 km	0

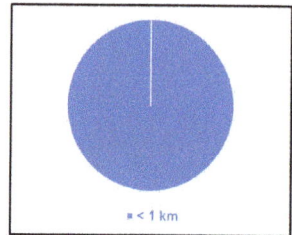

Intermediate Indigenous (Labrador)

Proximity to coast	# of components
< 1 km	82
1-15 km	35
>15 km	67

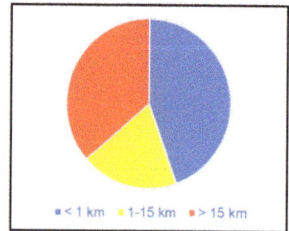

Figure 2.5. Proximity to the coast.

If radiocarbon dates can be used as a population proxy, our analysis (see figure 2.6) points to a slow-growing, if not stagnant, population trend for the first several thousand years of the MA period. Even accounting for the expected loss of early sites due to taphonomic factors (Surovell and Brantingham 2007), the small number of dated MA components in this earliest period is somewhat remarkable from the standpoint that the earliest MA components should be expected to receive an inordinate amount of research attention and effort to date them. In light of this, that there are so few early dated sites from Labrador

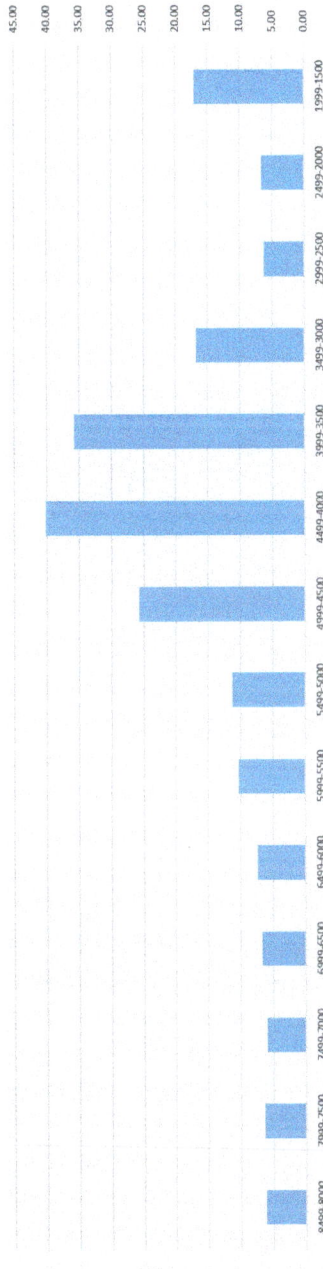

Figure 2.6. Summed probability distribution of radiocarbon dates associated with First Nation sites in Newfoundland and Labrador.

and none from the island of Newfoundland suggests that the pioneering population was indeed very small. Dated components increase slightly around the time of the first settlement of Newfoundland, but the first real increase occurs around 5000 BP, representing a doubling of dated components. Then, dated components double again at 4500 BP. As much of this increase occurs on the island of Newfoundland, it suggests that the bulk of the population growth during this period was made possible by the opening of the island to settlement. That this is when the size of the longhouses increase, subsurface cemeteries appear, and exotic raw materials circulate throughout the region, suggests that population growth was also tied to broader social and cultural phenomenon.

All of this ends after 3500 BP, coincident with a precipitous drop in radiocarbon dates. The decline is so steep that within a thousand years—and probably less in real time—First Nations groups are only producing about as many dated components as they had 5,000 years earlier. Such a sharp decline in radiocarbon dates in so little time suggests a spectacular population crash. Moreover, there is little evidence of a recovery from this until after 2000 BP, when the number of radiocarbon dates finally starts to climb again. Some of this, we suspect, is signalling the arrival of Algonquian-speaking populations to the region.

Conclusion

We suggest that the transition from the Maritime Archaic to the Intermediate Indigenous period was a radical restructuring event in Newfoundland and Labrador prehistory that was marked by major cultural changes and a significant population crash. These findings challenge conventional thinking about hunter-gatherers. Since the ecological turn in anthropology in the 1960s, there has been a tendency to view hunter-gatherer societies as impervious to failure on account of cultural adaptations and institutions that seemingly would have prevented this from happening, or, alternatively, to attribute failures to environmental circumstances beyond their control. Yet, as the demise of the Dorset on the island of Newfoundland shows us, there is good reason to think that hunter-gatherers are neither impervious to failure, nor when it occurs, that are they blameless (Holly 2011); that the Ancestral Beothuk were able to weather changes to the resource environment when the Dorset did not tells us as much. With this in mind, we might ask if cultural and social factors had some part to play in putting an end to the MA too.

It is possible that no one could have weathered the storm of colder temperatures and climatic instability that set into the region after 3500 BP. That the island of Newfoundland was completely abandoned and uninhabited for four centuries may indicate that the island was absolutely inhospitable to human occupation at this time. On the other hand, we do not have another group on the island when the MA vanish from it—as we do for the Dorset—against which to fully assess the island's inhospitableness at this time. We might wonder, for instance, if PaleoInuit peoples who were then living farther north on the Labrador coast, might have fared better than the MA had they been on the island with them when the climate took a turn for the worse. We know, for instance, that PaleoInuit people were able to outmaneuver and displace MA groups in northern Labrador centuries earlier, probably owing to the fact that the PaleoInuit moved in smaller groups, and more often, than the MA (Fitzhugh 2006; Hood 2000). This presumably allowed them to exploit less productive areas and more quickly adapt to changes in the resource environment. In contrast, the MA seem to have been beholden to more productive and resource-dense areas because of a desire to maintain large social groups (see Hood 2008:342). We also know that PaleoInuit people were very successful in the centuries following the end of the Archaic (see Holly 2013:67). They managed to remain and flourish on the Labrador coast when the MA could not, and they would be the first people to recolonize the island of Newfoundland. Their success suggests that the environment may have been only relatively inhospitable (to a particular lifeway), not absolutely so (to all lifeways).

Indeed, the success of PaleoInuit people at this time would seem to offer further proof of an MA population crash, since, if it had not occurred, we might ask why post-Archaic (II) peoples did not remain on a coast that was clearly productive enough to support other people living there? And, if there was not a crash, why did it take so long—over 1,200 years—for First Nations peoples to resettle the island of Newfoundland? Maybe the answer to both questions is that there were simply not enough II period people to do so. If a society needs a certain number and concentration of people in order to reproduce itself (Wobst 1974), it stands to reason that post-Archaic/II populations might have been only able to accomplish this by surrendering large portions of the coast and region so that they could coalesce in central Labrador.

The end-of-the-Archaic population crash we have outlined here has implications for our understanding of Newfoundland and Labrador prehistory, and, more broadly, the way we think about hunter-gatherer adaptations. With regard to the former, it now seems reasonable to assume that the low population density of II peoples might have helped facilitate the movement of Algonquian speakers into Newfoundland and Labrador after 2000 BP. Although the timing, nature, and origin of Algonquian speakers/language in the region remains a matter of debate, a major depopulation event would at least clear one hurdle to migration—an entrenched resident population. The timing of the arrival of the Algonquian language in the region, as currently calculated to about the first millennium AD (Denny 1994; Fiedel 1991; Luckenbach et al. 1987; Pentland 1985), also fits well within this window of opportunity. Of course, an influx of Algonquian speakers does not require that there was a complete break in the cultural sequence; there might have well been absorption and cultural exchange, especially in central Labrador, where post-Archaic populations were densest.

With regard to the latter, the struggles of transitional MA/II peoples in the region add further support to the notion that forager lifeways were not simply conditioned by the natural environment but were also informed by the precedent of tradition and extant social relations, and by how people attempted to navigate both. That this might occasionally result in failure should not come as a surprise, as it acknowledges hunter-gatherers as part of a common humanity that shares an all-too-human capacity to err.

Acknowledgements

We would like to thank Ken Holyoke and Gabe Hrynick for inviting us to participate in the CAA session that gave rise to this volume. We would also like to thank several anonymous reviewers and the copyeditors for a close and critical reading of our manuscript. Wolff and Holly's work at Stock Cove, which generated a number of radiocarbon dates for this project, was generously supported by the Arctic Social Science program of the National Science Foundation.

References Cited

Anderson, David G., Scott C. Meeks, Albert C. Goodyear, and D. Shane Miller
2008   Southeastern Data Inconsistent with Palaeoindian Demographic Reconstruction. *PNAS* 105(50):108.

Arbour, Chelsee, Napes Ashini, Anthony Jenkinson, and Stephen Loring
2018   Pour ramener l'été: À la recherché d'une concordance entre l'histoire innue et l'archéologie. *Recherches Amérindiennes au Québec* 48(3):31–44.

Arnold, Jeanne E., Anthony P. Graesch, Enzo Ragazzini, and Elinor Ochs
2012   *Life at Home in the Twenty-First Century*. Cotsen Institute of Archaeology Press, Los Angeles.

Bar-Yosef, Ofer
1998   The Natufian Culture in the Levant, Threshold to the Origins of Agriculture. *Evolutionary Anthropology* 6:159–177.

Beaton, Gregory, and M. A. P. Renouf
2014   The Big Brook 2 Site (EjBa-2) in Northwestern Newfoundland: Evidence of Southern Branch Maritime Archaic Culture from a Lithic Workshop/Quarry Site. *North Atlantic Archaeology* 3:25–45.

Bell, Trevor, and M. A. P. Renouf
2008   The Domino Effect: Culture Change and Environmental Change in Newfoundland, 1500-1100 cal BP. *The Northern Review* 28(Winter):72–94.

Bellwood, Peter
2005   *First Farmers: The Origins of Agricultural Societies*. Blackwell, Malden, Massachusetts.

Berbesque, J. Colette, Frank W. Marlowe, Peter Shaw, and Peter Thompson
2014   Hunter-Gatherers Have Less Famine than Agriculturalists. *Biology Letters* 10:1–4.

Binford, Lewis

2001   *Constructing Frames of Reference: An Analytical Method for Archaeological Theory Building Using Hunter-Gatherer and Environmental Data Sets*. University of California Press, Berkeley.

Birch, Jennifer, and Ron F. Williamson

2013   Organizational Complexity in Ancestral Wendat Communities. In *From Prehistoric Villages to Cities: Settlement Aggregation and Community Transformation*, edited by Jennifer Birch, pp. 153–178. Routledge, New York.

Bocquet-Appel, Jean-Pierre, and Pierre Yves Demars

2000   Population Kinetics in the Upper Paleolithic in Western Europe. *Journal of Archaeological Science* 27:551–570.

Brake, Jamie

2006   A Comparison of Maritime Archaic Indian and Intermediate Indian Site Distribution in Labrador. *Nexus* 19:8–31.

2009   *The Ferguson Bay 1 Site and the Culture History of Western Labrador*. Occasional Papers in Northeastern Archaeology No. 18. Copetown Press, St. John's, Newfoundland and Labrador.

Cannon, Aubrey

2011   Cosmology and Everyday Perception in Northwest Coast Production, Reproduction, and Settlement. In *Structured Worlds: The Archaeology of Hunter-Gatherer Thought and Action*, edited by Aubrey Cannon, pp. 54–68. Equinox, Sheffield.

Conolly, James

2018   Hunter-Gatherer Mobility, Territoriality, and Placemaking in the Kawartha Lakes Region, Ontario. *Canadian Journal of Archaeology* 42:185–209

Denny, Peter J.

1994   Archaeological Correlates of Algonquian Languages in Quebec–Labrador. In *Actes du Vingt-Cinquième Congrès des Algonquinistes*, edited by William Cowan, pp. 83–105. Carleton University Press, Ottawa.

Ellis, Christopher

2011   Measuring Palaeoindian Range Mobility and Land-Use in the Great Lakes/Northeast. *Journal of Anthropological Archaeology* 30:385–401.

Fiedel, Stuart

1991   Correlating Archaeology and Linguistics: The Algonquian Case. *Man in the Northeast* 41(Spring):9–32.

2001   What Happened in the Early Woodland? *Archaeology of Eastern North America* 29:101–142.

Filios, Elena

1989   The End of the Beginning or the Beginning of the End: The Third Millennium B. P. in Southern New England. *Man in the Northeast* 37:79–93.

Fitzhugh, William

1972   *Environmental Archaeology and Cultural Systems in Hamilton Inlet, Labrador: A Survey of the Central Labrador Coast from 3000 B.C. to the Present*. Smithsonian Institution Press, Washington, DC.

1973   Environmental Approaches to the Prehistory of the North. *Journal of the Washington Academy of Sciences* 63(2):39–53.

1974   Hound Pond 4: A Charles Complex Site in Groswater Bay, Labrador. *Man in the Northeast* 7(Spring):87–103.

1978a   Maritime Archaic Cultures of the Central and Northern Labrador Coast. *Arctic Anthropology* 15(2):61–95.

1978b   Winter Cove 4 and the Point Revenge Occupation of the Central Labrador Coast. *Arctic Anthropology* 15(2):146–174.

2006   Settlement, Social and Ceremonial Change in the Labrador Maritime Archaic. In *The Archaic of the Far Northeast*, edited by David Sanger and M. A. P. Renouf, pp. 47–81. University of Maine Press, Orono.

Fitzpatrick, Scott M.

2006   A Critical Approach to ^{14}C Dating in the Caribbean: Using Chronometric Hygiene to Evaluate Chronological Control and Prehistoric Settlement. *Latin American Antiquity* 17:389–418.

Friesen, T. Max

2004   A Tale of Two Settlement Patterns: Environmental and Cultural Determinants of Inuit and Dene Site Distributions. In *Hunters and Gatherers in Theory and Archaeology*, edited by George M. Crothers, pp. 299–315. Center for Archaeological Investigations, Carbondale, Illinois.

2015   On the Naming of Arctic Archaeological Traditions: The Case for Paleo-Inuit. *Arctic* 68(3):iii–iv.

Gamble, Clive, William Davis, Paul Pettitt, Lee Hazelwood, and Martin Richards

2005   The Archaeological and Genetic Foundations of the European Population during the Late Glacial: Implications for "Agricultural Thinking." *Cambridge Archaeological Journal* 15:193–223.

Glassow, Michael A., and John R. Johnson

2019   Differences in Human Population Density between the California Islands and the Coastal Mainland. In *An Archaeology of Abundance: Reevaluating the Marginality of California's Islands*, edited by Kristina M. Gill, Mikael Fauvelle, and Jon M. Erlandson, pp. 226–247. University Press of Florida, Gainesville.

Gould, Richard

1982   To Have and Have Not: The Ecology of Sharing among Hunters-Gatherers. In *Resource Managers: North American and Australian Hunter-Gatherers*, edited by Nancy M. William and Eugene S. Hunn, pp. 69–91. Westview Press, Boulder, Colorado.

Holly, Donald H. Jr.

2005   The Place of "Others" in Hunter-Gatherer Intensification. *American Anthropologist* 107:207–220.

2011   When Foragers Fail: In the Eastern Subarctic, for Example. In *Hunter-Gatherer Archaeology as Historical Process*, edited by Kenneth E. Sassaman and Donald H. Holly Jr., pp. 79–92. University of Arizona Press, Tucson.

2013   History in the Making: The Archaeology of the Eastern Subarctic. Altamira Press, Lanham, Maryland.

Holly, Donald H. Jr., Paul Prince, and John C. Erwin
2018   Bad Year Economics at Birchy Lake. *Journal of Anthropological Research* 74:201–231.

Hood, Bryan C.
1993   The Maritime Archaic Indians of Labrador: Investigating Prehistoric Social Organization. *Newfoundland Studies* 9:163–184.
1995   Circumpolar Comparison Revisited: Hunter-Gatherer Complexity in the North Norwegian Stone Age and the Labrador Maritime Archaic. *Arctic Anthropology* 32:75–105.
2000   Pre-Dorset/Maritime Archaic Social Boundaries in Labrador. In *Identities and Cultural Contacts in the Arctic*, edited by Martin Appelt, Joel Berglund, and Hans Christian Gulløv, pp. 120–128. Danish National Museum and Danish Polar Center, Copenhagen.
2008   *Toward an Archaeology of the Nain Region, Labrador*. Arctic Studies Center, Smithsonian Institution, Washington.

Howell, Nancy
1979   *The Demography of the Dobe !Kung*. Population and Social Structure. Academic Press, New York.

Hull, Kathleen L.
2011   Hunter-Gatherer Demography and Culture Change. In *Hunter-Gatherer Archaeology as Historical Process*, edited by Kenneth E. Sassaman and Donald H. Holly Jr., pp. 34–54. University of Arizona Press, Tucson.

Jarvenpa, Robert
2004   *Silot'ine*: An Insurance Perspective on Northern Dene Kinship Networks in Recent History. *Journal of Anthropological Research* 60:153–178.

Keckler, Charles N. W.
1997   Catastrophic Mortality in Simulations of Forager Age-at-Death: Where Did the Humans Go? In *Integrating Archaeological Demography: Multidisciplinary Approaches to Prehistoric Population*, Center for Archaeological Investigations, Occasional Paper No. 24, edited by Richard R. Paine, pp. 205–228. Center for Archaeological Investigations, Carbondale, Illinois.

Kelly, Robert L.
1983   Hunter-Gatherer Mobility Strategies. *Journal of Anthropological Research* 39:277–306.
1995   *The Foraging Spectrum: Diversity in Hunter-Gatherer Lifeways*. Smithsonian Institution Press, Washington, DC.

Konner, Melvin, and Carol Worthman
1980   Nursing Frequency, Gonadal Function, and Birth Spacing Among !Kung Hunter-Gatherers. *Science* 207:788–791.

Kroeber, Alfred L.
1947   *Cultural and Natural Areas of Native North America*. University of California Press, Berkeley.

Le Blanc, Raymond J.
2009   Some Implications of High-Latitude Osseous Technologies for Forager Technological Organization. In *Painting the Past with a Broad Brush: Papers in*

Honour of James Valliere Wright, Mercury Series, Paper No. 170, edited by David L. Keenlyside and Jean-Luc Pilon, pp. 529–554. Canadian Museum of Civilization, Gatineau, Quebec.

Lee, Richard B., and Irven Devore (editors)
1968   *Man the Hunter.* Aldine de Gruyter, New York.

Loring, Stephen
1989   Une réserve d'outils de la période Intermédiaire sur la côte du Labrador. *Recherches amérindiennes au Québec* 19(2–3):45–57.

Loring, Stephen, and Anthony Jenkinson
2018   The Toad-Man's Estate: An Archaeological Reconnaissance of the Shapeiau (Shapio) Lake Region, Nitassinan. *Provincial Archaeology Office 2017 Archaeology Review* 16:168–183.

Luckenbach, Alvin H., Wayne E. Clark, and Richard S. Levy
1987   Rethinking Cultural Stability in Eastern North American Prehistory: Linguistic Evidence from Eastern Algonquian. *Journal of Middle Atlantic Archaeology* 3:1–33.

Madden, Marcie M.
1976   A Late Maritime Archaic Sequence in Southern Labrador. Master's thesis, Department of Anthropology, Memorial University, St. John's, Newfoundland.

Marshall, Ingeborg
1977   An Unpublished Map Made by John Cartwright between 1768 and 1773 Showing Beothuck Indian Settlements and Artifacts and Allowing a New Population Estimate. *Ethnohistory* 24:223–249.

1996   *A History and Ethnography of the Beothuk.* McGill-Queen's University Press, Montréal.

Maschner, Herbert, Bruce Finney, James Jordan, Nicole Misarti, Amber Tews, and Garrett Knudsen
2009   Did the North Pacific Ecosystem Collapse in AD 1250? In *The Northern World AD 900–1400*, edited by Herbert Maschner, Owen Mason, and Richard McGhee, pp. 263–278. University of Utah Press, Salt Lake City.

Minc, Leah, and Kevin Smith
1989   The Spirit of Survival: Cultural Responses to Resource Variability in North Alaska. In *Bad Year Economics: Cultural Responses to Risk and Uncertainty*, edited by Paul Halstead and John O'Shea, pp. 8–39. Cambridge University Press, Cambridge.

Mooney, James
1928   The Aboriginal Population of America North of Mexico. *Smithsonian Miscellaneous Collections*, No. 80. Smithsonian Institution, Washington, DC.

Nagle, Christopher
1978   Indian Occupations of the Intermediate Period of the Central Labrador Coast: A Preliminary Synthesis. *Arctic Anthropology* 15:119–145.

Neilsen, Scott W.
2006   Intermediate Indians: The View from Ushpitun 2 and Pmiusik[u] 1. Master's thesis, Department of Anthropology, Memorial University, St. John's, Newfoundland.

2016   An Archaeological History of Ashuanipi, Labrador. PhD dissertation, Department of Anthropology, Memorial University, St. John's, Newfoundland.

Orton, David, James Morris, and Alan Pipe

2017   Catch Per Unit Research Effort: Sampling Intensity, Chronological Uncertainty, and the Onset of Marine Fish Consumption in Historic London. *Open Quaternary* 3:1–20.

Palmisano, Alessio, Andrew Bevan, and Stephen Shennan

2017   Comparing Archaeological Proxies for Long-Term Population Patterns: An Example from Central Italy. *Journal of Archaeological Science* 87:59–72.

Pennington, Renee

2001   Hunter-gatherer Demography. In *Hunter-Gatherers: An Interdisciplinary Perspective*, edited by Catherine Panter-Brick, Robert H. Layton, and Peter Rowley-Conwy, pp. 170–204. Cambridge University Press, Cambridge.

Pentland, David H.

1985   The Linguistic Background of Cree-Montagnais. In *La synthèse archéologique et ethnohistorique du complexe La Grande*, pp. 592–604. La Société d'énergie de la Baie James, Montréal.

Peros, Matthew S., Samuel E. Munoz, Konrad Gajewski, and André E. Viau

2010   Prehistoric Demography of North America Inferred from Radiocarbon Data. *Journal of Archaeological Science* 37:656–664.

Politis, Gustavo G.

2007   *Nukak: Ethnoarchaeology of an Amazonian People*. Translated by Benjamin Alberti. Left Coast Press, Walnut Creek, California.

Pollock, Susan

1999   *Ancient Mesopotamia*. Cambridge University Press, Cambridge.

Powell, Shirley

1988   Anasazi Demographic Patterns and Organizational Responses: Assumptions and Interpretive Difficulties. In *The Anasazi in a Changing Environment*, edited by George J. Gumerman, pp. 168–191. Cambridge University Press, Cambridge.

Renouf, M. A. P.

1999   Prehistory of Newfoundland Hunter-Gatherers: Extinctions or Adaptations? *World Archaeology* 30:403–420.

Renouf, M. A. P., and Trevor Bell

2006   Maritime Archaic Site Locations on the Island of Newfoundland. In *The Archaic of the Far Northeast*, edited by David Sanger and M. A. P. Renouf, pp. 1–46. University of Maine Press, Orono.

2009   Contraction and Expansion in Newfoundland Prehistory, AD 900–1500. In *The Northern World AD 900–1400*, edited by Herbert Maschner, Owen Mason, and Robert McGhee, pp. 263–278. University of Utah Press, Salt Lake City.

2011   Across the Tickle: The Gould Site, Port au Choix-3 and the Maritime Archaic Indian Mortuary Landscape. In *The Cultural Landscape of Port au Choix*, edited by M. A. P. Renouf, pp. 43–63. Springer, New York.

Ridington, Robin

1982   Technology, World View, and Adaptive Strategy in a Northern Hunting Society. *The Canadian Review of Sociology and Anthropology* 19:469–481.

Robinson, Brian S., and Jennifer C. Ort
2011 Palaeoindian and Archaic Period Traditions: Particular Explanations from New England. In *Hunter-Gatherer Archaeology as Historical Process*, edited by Kenneth E. Sassaman and Donald H. Holly Jr., pp. 209–226. University of Arizona Press, Tucson.

Rogers, Edward S., and Eleanor Leacock
1981 Montagnais-Naskapi. In *Handbook of North American Indians: Subarctic, vol. 6*, edited by June Helm, pp. 169–189. Smithsonian Institution Press, Washington, DC.

Ross, Anne
1985 Archaeological Evidence for Population Change in the Middle to Late Holocene in Southeastern Australia. *Archaeology in Oceania* 20:81–89.

Sanger, David
2006 An Introduction to the Archaic of the Maritime Peninsula: The View from Central Maine. In *The Archaic of the Far Northeast*, edited by David Sanger and M. A. P. Renouf, pp. 221–252. University of Maine Press, Orono.

Schwarz, Fred
1994 Paleo-Eskimo and Recent Indian Subsistence and Settlement Patterns on the Island of Newfoundland. *Northeast Anthropology* 47 (Spring):55–70.

Schwarz, Fred, Corey Hutchings, and Vincent Bourgeois
2018 Historic Resources Management Program Lower Churchill Project, Central Labrador 2017. *Provincial Archaeology Office 2017 Archaeology Review* 16:222–231.

Schwarz, Fred, Roy Skanes, Sara Beanlands, and Corey Hutchings
2016 Historic Resources Management Program Lower Churchill Project, Central Labrador. *Provincial Archaeology Office 2015 Archaeology Review* 14:199–210.

Shennan, Stephen
2015 Language, Genes, and Cultural Interaction. In *The Oxford Handbook of Neolithic Europe*, edited by Chris Fowler, Jan Harding, and Daniela Hofmann, pp. 139–154. Oxford University Press, Oxford.

Spiess, Arthur E.
1992 Archaic Period Subsistence in New England and the Atlantic Provinces. In *Early Holocene Occupation in Northern New England*, edited by Brian S. Robinson, James B. Petersen, and Ann K. Robinson, pp. 163–185. Occasional Publications in Maine Archaeology, No. 9. Maine Historic Preservation Commission, Augusta, Maine.

Spriggs, Matthew, and Atholl Anderson
1993 Late Colonization of East Polynesia. *Antiquity* 67:200–217.

Stassinu Stantec
2019 *Lower Churchill Hydroelectric Development Project 2017 Historic Resources Assessment and Recovery Program*. Report on file at the Provincial Archaeology Office, Government of Newfoundland and Labrador, St. John's.

Steegmann, A. Theodore Jr.
1983 Boreal Forest Hazards and Adaptations: The Past. In *Boreal Forest Adaptations: The Northern Algonkians*, edited by A. Theodore Steegmann, pp. 243–267. Plenum Press, New York.

Stopp, Marianne

2002   Ethnohistoric Analogues for Storage as an Adaptive Strategy in Northeastern Subarctic Prehistory. *Journal of Anthropological Archaeology* 21:301–328.

2008   FbAx-01: A Daniel Rattle Hearth in Southern Labrador. *Canadian Journal of Archaeology* 32:96–127.

Surovell, Todd A., and P. Jeffrey Brantingham

2007   A Note on the Use of Temporal Frequency Distributions in Studies of Prehistoric Demography. *Journal of Archaeological Science* 34:1868–1877.

Taché, Karine, and John P. Hart

2013   Chronometric Hygiene of Radiocarbon Databases for Early Durable Cooking Vessel Technologies in Northeastern North America. *American Antiquity* 78:359–372.

Tallavaara, Miika, Petro Pesonen, Markku Oinonen, and Heikki Seppä

2014   The Mere Possibility of Biases Does Not Invalidate Archaeological Population Proxies—Response to Teemu Mökkönen. *Fennoscandia archaeologica* 31:135–140.

Tuck, James A.

1971   Newfoundland Prehistory Since 1950: Some Answers and More Questions. *Man in the Northeast* 1(Spring):27–33.

1975   The Northeastern Maritime Continuum: 8000 years of Cultural Development in the Far Northeast. *Arctic Anthropology* 12:139–147.

Tuck, James A., and Ralph T. Pastore

1985   A Nice Place to Visit, But… Prehistoric Human Extinctions on the Island of Newfoundland. *Canadian Journal of Archaeology* 9:69–80.

Ubelaker, Douglas H.

1988   North American Indian Population Size, AD 1500 to 1985. *American Journal of Physical Anthropology* 77:189–294.

Upton, Leslie F.

1977   The Extermination of the Beothucks of Newfoundland. *The Canadian Historical Review* 58:133–153.

Webster, David, and Ann Corrine Freter

1990   The Demography of Late Classic Copan. In *Precolumbian Population History in the Maya Lowlands*, edited by T. Patrick Culbert and Don S. Rice, pp. 37–61. University of New Mexico Press, Albuquerque.

Williams, Alan N.

2012   The Use of Summed Radiocarbon Probability Distributions in Archaeology: A Review of Methods. *Journal of Archaeological Science* 39:578–589.

Wobst, H. Martin

1974   Boundary Conditions for Paleolithic Social Systems: A Simulation Approach. *American Antiquity* 39:147–178.

Wolff, Christopher B.

2008   A Study of the Evolution of Maritime Archaic Households in Northern Labrador. PhD dissertation, Department of Anthropology, Southern Methodist University, Dallas, Texas.

3

PRE-CONTACT CERAMIC ASSEMBLAGES FROM THE CHURCHILL RIVER, CENTRAL LABRADOR

COREY HUTCHINGS[1] AND FRED SCHWARZ[2]

Abstract

Until recently, pre-Contact ceramics appeared to be relatively scarce in the archaeological record for Newfoundland and Labrador. Occasional sherds had been recovered from archaeological sites on the island and in Labrador, and a few sites, such as the Gould site in Newfoundland, yielded significant ceramic assemblages. Nevertheless, pre-Contact sites containing ceramics remain extremely rare, and no periods or occupations have been defined that commonly or consistently contain evidence for their use. Consequently, it has been generally accepted that there is no Ceramic period in Newfoundland and Labrador prehistory.

Between 2012 and 2017, archaeologists from Stantec Consulting excavated 50 pre-Contact sites along the lower Churchill River as part of the historic resources management program for the Lower Churchill hydroelectric project. Most pertain to the North West River Phase (Intermediate/early Late pre-Contact in central Labrador). Unexpectedly, 10 of these sites (20% of the total) yielded pre-Contact ceramic sherds; three yielded sizeable collections, and two showed possible evidence for local manufacture of ceramic vessels. In contrast with coastal Labrador and the island of Newfoundland, ceramics do appear to be a common and consistent element in pre-Contact assemblages in the Churchill Valley, at least during this period.

This chapter will describe the attributes, distribution, dating, and possible functions of the ceramics recovered from the Churchill Valley, and will explore the implications for understanding the cultural relationships between the North West River Phase in central Labrador and other cultural complexes along the north shore of the St. Lawrence River, the Labrador coast, and the island of Newfoundland.

Résumé

La céramique précontact demeurait jusqu'à récemment relativement rare dans l'archéologie de Terre-Neuve-et-Labrador. Des tessons épars ont bien été trouvés sur des sites archéologiques tant au Labrador qu'à Terre-Neuve, et quelques sites (notamment le site Gould, à Terre-Neuve) ont même produit des assemblages céramiques considérables. Néanmoins, les sites contenant des céramiques précontact demeurent extrêmement rares, et leur utilisation généralisée n'est attestée pour aucune période ou occupation particulière. Il est par conséquent généralement accepté qu'il n'y a pas eu de «période céramique» dans la préhistoire de Terre-Neuve-et-Labrador.

De 2012 à 2017, des archéologues employés par Stantec ont fouillé 50 sites précontact le long du fleuve Churchill dans le cadre du programme de prévention archéologique du projet hydroélectrique du Bas-Churchill. La majorité de ces sites est associée à la phase *North West River* (phase ancienne à intermédiaire de la période précontact récente du centre du Labrador). À la surprise des archéologues, 10 de ces sites (20 % du total) ont livré des tessons de céramiques précontact; trois de ces sites ont produit des assemblages céramiques considérables, et deux d'entre eux pourraient contenir des éléments indiquant la fabrication locale de récipients en céramique.

Contrairement à la côte du Labrador et l'île de Terre-Neuve, la céramique semble donc être un élément commun et fréquent des assemblages archéologiques de la vallée du fleuve Churchill, du moins pour cette période. Cet article présente les attributs, la distribution, les datations et les fonctions possibles des céramiques de la vallée du Churchill, et explore ce qu'elles pourraient impliquer pour notre compréhension des relations culturelles entre la phase *North West River* du centre du Labrador et les différents complexes culturels de la Côte-Nord du Saint-Laurent, la côte du Labrador et l'île de Terre-Neuve.

Affiliations

1. Independent Consultant, Newfoundland and Labrador, Canada (corresponding author: coreyhutchings@gmail.com)
2. Independent Consultant, Newfoundland and Labrador/Nova Scotia/Prince Edward Island, Canada

For archaeologists working in the greater Northeast (and, for that matter, those working in the Subarctic and eastern Arctic), Newfoundland and Labrador sometimes seems to occupy a strange, liminal space. It is certainly part of the greater Northeastern culture area; historical, material culture, and ethnographic connections are indisputable, perhaps most exemplified by the distribution of Ramah Chert, a lithic resource derived from Labrador but encountered in Newfoundland, New Brunswick, and even further afield, indicating that these connections have great antiquity. But, culture-historically, Newfoundland and Labrador are too complex, too ambiguous. The Arctic and Subarctic environment, and the repeated occupation by pre-Inuit (Paleo-Eskimo) peoples, sets the region apart from the rest of the greater Northeast. The region is arguably a part of the Northeast, and yet a part apart, as it were: an outlier in the Northeast, an outlier in the Arctic, and even an outlier in the Subarctic. One manifestation of this liminality is that archaeologists do not traditionally consider the region to have had a Ceramic or Woodland period, such as is commonly defined in other parts of this culture area, including the Maritimes and the north shore of the St. Lawrence. This is not to say that pre-Contact ceramics have not previously been encountered on sites in Newfoundland and Labrador; they have. And yet ceramics, seen as a diagnostic element of material culture in the Late pre-Contact period elsewhere in the greater Northeast, have previously appeared in Newfoundland and Labrador as isolated objects, encountered in sites where they "do not belong." Even in those very rare sites where pre-Contact ceramics have been recovered in quantity (e.g., Teal 2001), they do not appear to be part of a widespread pattern. Their presence is a curiosity and an anomaly.

However, a recent (2012–2017) program of intensive and extensive recovery of archaeological sites associated with the Crown-owned Nalcor Energy's Lower Churchill hydroelectric project (LCP) has now led to the recovery of pre-Contact archaeological data from interior Labrador on an unprecedented scale. Among the many insights provided by these data is a new understanding of the place of pre-Contact ceramics in the province's past. Of the 45 pre-Contact sites excavated during this project, 10 returned some number of pre-Contact ceramic sherds. In other words, on the lower Churchill River, over 20% of pre-Contact sites contained evidence for ceramic use. More broadly, this doubles the total number of pre-Contact ceramic sites province-wide. These discoveries in the Churchill Valley, along with other recent finds elsewhere in Labrador, not only dispel the myth that pre-Contact use of ceramics was isolated or sporadic but hint at more profound connections between Labrador and the greater Northeast than previously thought. This chapter will provide a review of pre-Contact ceramics recovered in the province to date, an overview of the Nalcor historic resources management program, a review of the Lower Churchill ceramic assemblages, a discussion of evidence pointing to local ceramic production, and, finally, it will discuss the implications and questions arising from these new finds.

Pre-Contact Ceramics in Newfoundland and Labrador

The apparent lack of pre-Contact ceramics in Newfoundland and Labrador is often cited as one of the reasons for the divisions and differences seen in the nomenclature of pre-Contact cultures between Newfoundland and Labrador and the greater Northeast region. This disconnect is most noticeable between the well-known Woodland period seen extensively throughout the greater Northeast, defined at least in part by the appearance of ceramics, and the Late pre-Contact (or so-called Recent period) of Newfoundland and Labrador. The Recent period is represented on both the island and mainland area of the province, commencing approximately 2000 BP and extending to European contact (although no early Contact-period sites have been distinctly identified in Labrador).

Earliest Finds

The majority of the early ceramic finds in the province came from Labrador, and for the most part were uncollected or have left the province. Despite this, three distinct reports of pre-Contact ceramics from Labrador exist, with one artifact in the collection of the American Museum of Natural History.

The first instance of pre-Contact ceramics in the province was recorded by Junius Bird in 1934 at Avertok (Hopedale), Labrador (Bird 1945:142-143). During his excavations of Inuit houses, he encountered "a small grit-tempered potsherd of Indian manufacture" (142). It was encountered lying directly on the paving stones at the inner entrance tunnel to an Inuit winter house. Bird makes note that the nearest reported location for similar pottery is south of Forteau Bay, Quebec, at Anse au Dune, as found by William Wintemberg, and suggests that the piece may have been transported to the area by the Inuit. The Wintemberg find, for which no photos could be found, is described by William Duncan Strong (1930:133): "At about the same place sherds of pottery with roulette decorations and similar in type to those from Algonkian sites in Ontario and Maritime provinces were found. According to Wintemberg, the potsherds were associated with the workshop sites." Stephen Loring (1992:279-280) instead speculates that a small pre-Contact/late Recent period component near this site, which predated Inuit occupation, was likely the source for the ceramic. Loring does note, though, that this fragment is significantly different than the sherds he recovered from Kamarsuk (discussed below), and we can now also say that it differs significantly from most subsequent finds in Labrador.

The two other early reports of ceramics from Labrador both lack photos, collected artifacts, or formal site records. James Pendergast communicated to Loring that he found several small, grit-tempered ceramic sherds from a site he discovered near the oil tank farm at the Royal Canadian Air Force airport at Terrington Basin in Goose Bay (Loring 1992:279).

In 1975, near the community of Pinware, Labrador, James Tuck and Robert McGhee found a small sherd of dentate-stamped pottery at a construction site

(Tuck and McGhee 1975). In a later paper, Gerald Penney (1981:172) describes the fragment as a Point Peninsula rim sherd, but it is unclear where this information came from. No other information on this site was recorded. Stephen Hull suggests that a nearby component of this site produced a hearth in association with flakes of Ramah chert, an end scraper, and charcoal. Based on current knowledge, it is possible this site was occupied by Labrador Recent-period peoples who relied heavily on Ramah chert (Hull 2014), but this is based on limited information.

First Excavations from Newfoundland

The first pre-Contact ceramic sherd from the island portion of the province came from the L'Anse à Flamme site, located on the south coast (figure 3.1). L'Anse à Flamme was a multi-component site with evidence of Maritime Archaic, pre-Inuit, Recent period (Little Passage complex) and European occupations. Penney (1981:171) reported a rim sherd (figure 3.2) that was later identified as a Point Peninsula pot that was excavated in situ 35 cm below the surface in a secure Dorset pre-Inuit context: "Wright describes the sherd as being decorated with a sloppy form of dentate stamp that approaches a pseudo-scallop shell impression even though it superficially looks like cord wrapped stick. It has an incipent [*sic*] collar with an exterior chevron motif." (Penney 1981:171)

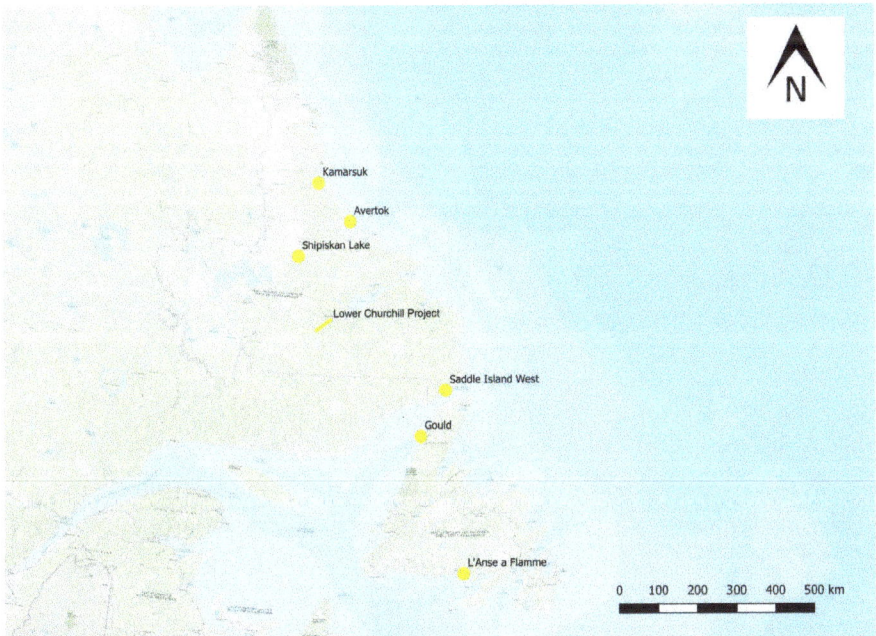

Figure 3.1. Locations for all sites with recovered precontact ceramics recovered in the province.

Figure 3.2. Pre-Contact ceramic rimsherd collected at L'Anse à Flamme (CjAx-1).

Both Penney and, later, Loring (1992:280) saw similarities between this object and that found at Avertok, as well as with the Wintemberg finds at Anse au Dune. These three examples stand in contrast to later recovered ceramics from Labrador.

Later Finds from Labrador

The first undisturbed pre-Contact ceramics from Labrador (figure 3.1) were recovered in 1982 by Stephen Loring at the late Recent-period site of Kamarsuk (HbCj-01) (Loring 1985, 1988, 1992). While excavating, Loring (1985:128) noted "a half-dozen small undecorated grit tempered earthenware sherds found in a refuse deposit immediately adjacent to the northeast wall of the structure." The sherds all appeared to be from a single vessel and, though undecorated, allowed for the first description of a vessel form: a small conical-based pot with smooth steep walls (Loring 1992:271). "The maximum thickness of the body sherds is 140 mm; at the rim the vessel's walls have thinned to 88 mm" (Loring 1985:128).

The initial find of six fragments were likely unstable, as a later photograph (Loring 1992:Plate 6.6) shows many more small fragments. Upon recent viewing of the artifacts, the number of pieces now stands at 41 undecorated fragments and it is likely that the under-fired fragments have since degraded (figure 3.3). Another significant ceramic find made during this period was at the Basque site at Saddle Island, Red Bay, in the Strait of Belle Isle. In the 1980s, a member of James Tuck's crew recovered a piece of Indigenous ceramic between the roof fall and drain of a Basque structure (figure 3.4A). Tuck (2005:17) described the piece as a castellation with "corn ear" motif and assigned it an Iroquoian cultural affiliation. Tuck took care to separate it from other ceramics in the region, remarking: "It is quite unlike the poorly fired ceramics rarely produced by Recent Indians in Labrador" (2005:17). This is noteworthy in that Tuck at this point clearly believed that not only were ceramics being produced in Labrador but he also assigned the production to a cultural phase.

Tuck's impression of the sherd seems to have further support when the piece was examined in depth by Claude Chapdelaine and Gregory G. Kennedy. In a description of the sherd's style, they state that it "is undoubtedly of Late Woodland style and it looks more like a Saint Lawrence Iroquoian vessel than any other Iroquoian ceramic tradition" (Chapdelaine and Kennedy 1990:42-43). In a first for the province, they established the chemical composition of the piece and compared it to local clay sources in Labrador and selected samples from Saint Lawrence Iroquoian sites of the Québec City area. From these studies, they determined that the clay of the sherd was likely local. With this evidence, two suggested possibilities have been forwarded: the artifact was either made by an Algonquian potter imitating an Iroquoian style or an Iroquoian potter using unusual clay (Hull 2014).

A second recovery of pre-Contact ceramics was made at Saddle Island, in 1987. In this instance, Tuck's archaeology crew recovered pre-Contact ceramic fragments in direct association with Recent-period hearths (Tuck 2005:31). The general appearance and production of these sherds appear to have more in common with the Kamarsuk examples than the other fragment from the site. Tuck (1987:7) highlighted the grit temper, thick paste, and under-fired nature of the sherds as being similar to those recovered by Loring. Tuck's interpretation that the vessel forms "pertain to small, thick vessels, possibly with conical bases" also matches Loring's examples. The most significant difference with Saddle Island examples is that they were decorated (figure 3.4B).

> The more complete of the two has a castellated rim with exterior deco-
> ration consisting of three rows of horizontal impressed (?) lines on an
> incipient collar set off from the neck by a horizontal row of oblique
> impressions. The neck is decorated by oblique plaits of cord-wrapped
> paddle (?) impressions. [...] The second vessel has a row of oblique impres-
> sions below the rim, and oblique, cris-cross [sic] and horizontal incised lines
> on the neck. (Tuck 1987:7)

Tuck suggested (1987:7-8) that this divide between the Saddle Island and Kamarsuk sherds cast doubt on whether the Saddle Island examples were locally produced or were another example of imported objects or technology from the St. Lawrence.

Changing Views

The understanding of pre-Contact ceramics in this province has continued to evolve through small and large finds. The discovery by Ponius Nuk of Sheshatshiu of plain, grit-tempered ceramics with dentate and cord decoration associated with Ramah chert debitage from a shallow, ephemeral camp spot near his cabin at Shipiskan Lake in the north-central Labrador interior (Loring 2013) served to bridge the supposed gap between the undecorated assemblages of Kamarsuk and the similar but decorated examples from Saddle Island. This small assemblage also serves as the closest visual match to the newly recovered ceramics from the LCP (see below). Dentate-stamped ceramics were also recovered from the Gould site at Port au Choix in western Newfoundland, which contained a Recent-period Cow Head Complex component (Stapelfeldt 2009:60, 2013).

The question of whether ceramics in Newfoundland and Labrador pre-Contact sites were locally produced or imported arose again when the single largest concentration of ceramics recovered to date was identified at the Recent-period component at the Gould site. Excavations in 1999 produced 290 pottery sherds estimated to be from seven different pots in two areas, near a charcoal concentration and near a large depression (Teal 2001). Teal reports that all ceramic sherds are composed of grit-tempered clay and the condition of the sherds ranges from highly friable to solid (figure 3.5). Additionally, the sherds collected were the first undisturbed artifacts that appear to have adhered residues (Teal 2001:52).

The high number of large fragments allowed for the identification of 61 of the 290 sherds to type. Identified types included 15 rim sherds, 10 neck sherds, and 36 body sherds (Teal 2001:54). This information is used to interpret both vessel form and minimum number of vessels—another first for the province. A comparison of the vessels' rim shapes (squared, rounded, in-sloping, concave, and collared) and decoration styles (dentate stamping, dentate rocker-stamping, and incised linear lines) were used to determine a minimum number of vessels of seven (Teal 2001:54).

The completeness of the Gould-site collection allowed for some of the first complex comparisons of ceramics from Newfoundland with those from the wider Atlantic region. Direct similarities with Ceramic period 3 (as per a seriation popularized by Petersen and Sanger [1991]) were suggested by Teal (2001), but with provisions that they were not exactly the same and more likely hinted at direct or indirect contact between groups rather than a shared cultural identity across both areas.

Figure 3.3. Pre-Contact ceramic assemblage from Kamarsuk (HbCj-1).

Figure 3.4. Sherds recovered from Saddle Island West 16 (EkBc-16): (A) fragment recovered from a Basque context; (B) fragments recovered from a Late pre-Contact hearth.

The Lower Churchill Hydroelectric Project

The LCP includes development of a large hydroelectric dam, reservoir, and associated infrastructure at Muskrat Falls on the lower reaches of the Churchill River, the largest river in Labrador (figure 3.6). Starting in 1998, an associated and extensive historic resources assessment was conducted to identify archae-ological sites within the project footprint, including the reservoir and

Figure 3.5. Selected pre-Contact ceramic fragments from the Gould site (EeBi-42).

associated transmission infrastructure (see, e.g., IED/JWEL 2000). Directed survey identified numerous pre-Contact sites clustered in three specific zones spaced approximately 25 km–30 km apart: a dense cluster of sites on both the north and south sides of Muskrat Falls itself (23 on the south side of Muskrat Falls, nine on the north), another significant cluster of nine sites at Gull Lake at the western end of the Muskrat Falls reservoir area, and a third cluster of eight sites at Sandy Banks, midway between Muskrat Falls and Gull Lake (figure 3.1). A total of 45 of these sites contained pre-Contact components recovered by archaeological excavation between 2012 and 2017. Most of these pre-Contact sites consist of small, discrete occupation areas or clusters of campsites; the majority appear to date between 2000 and 1400 BP and pertain typologically to what is known as the North West River Phase of the central Labrador pre-Contact period (Fitzhugh 1972). A small number of sites appear typologically or by absolute dating to pertain to earlier phases of the Intermediate period (3000–2500 BP). A limited number of artifacts (but no radiocarbon dates) suggest occupation continuing into the later pre-Contact period, ca. 1000 BP.

The first of the pre-Contact ceramics recovered on the Churchill River came from four sites on the south side of Muskrat Falls. Two sites in the Sandy Banks cluster contained pre-Contact ceramics: a single sherd from one of the small single-component sites on the south side of the river, and a small collection of ceramic sherds from Locus A at FgCg-01, the Sandy Banks site (Stantec 2015). Finally, three sites in the Gull Lake cluster yielded pre-Contact ceramics. These include FgCh-02 (which contained only a single sherd) and the very large assemblages at FfCh-02 and FfCi-02 (discussed below).

It is perhaps noteworthy that no previous excavation of sites of the North West River Phase (including the type sites at North West River; Fitzhugh 1972) has yielded evidence for pre-Contact ceramics in this time period. It is possible that the recovery of this previously rare artifact type is in part a function of the sheer number of sites recovered during the LCP, and the large areal extent of excavations in comparison to previous excavation effort. In this regard, it should be noted that during stage-one and stage-two assessments in the Churchill Valley, conducted between 1998 and 2012, none of the sites now known to contain pre-Contact ceramics initially indicated any evidence for ceramic use.

Churchill River Ceramic Assemblages

With the purported rarity of pre-Contact ceramics in the province and the absence of recovered ceramics during stage-one and -two assessments, the eventual recovery of ceramics from over 20% of the excavated pre-Contact sites from the LCP area was unexpected. A total of 10 sites with pre-Contact ceramics were recorded, with examples from each of the three site clusters discussed above (figure 3.1). Collections varied from sites with single examples to assemblages with hundreds of sherds and/or sherdlets. Some variation in decoration, firing temperature, and temper were encountered, along with evidence of burning and residues. Finally, spatial patterning was observed at a number of sites, relating variously to ceramics use (and possibly production) and/or discard. The weight of this evidence implies that ceramics comprised an integral element in the material culture of people travelling on the Churchill River during the Late pre-Contact period.

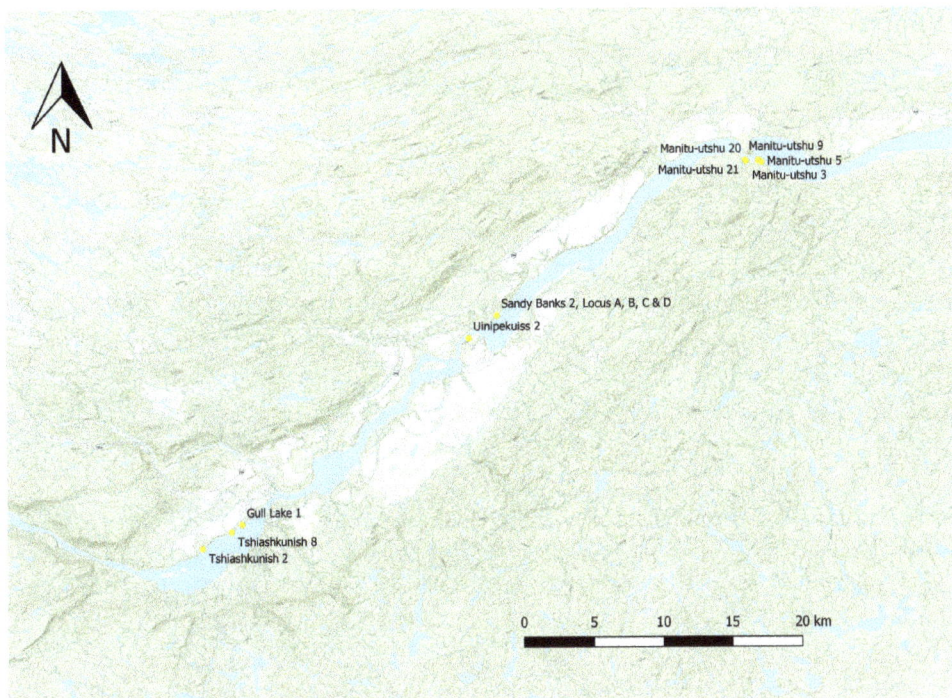

Figure 3.6. Sites with precontact ceramics excavated during the Lower Churchill Project.

Muskrat Falls Site Cluster

Five sites with pre-ceramic sherds were recorded from this cluster. All of these sites were located on the south side of the river and all appear to be related to a historically known portage route skirting the south side of Muskrat Falls.

Manitu-utshu 3, FhCe-15

This site was recorded in 2012 after a single quartzite flake was collected from a test pit excavated on the terrace edge (Stantec 2014a). During subsequent excavation, a total of 16 m^2 was excavated at Manitu-utshu 3 (FhCe-15) on a very narrow strip of terrace between the historic portage trail to the south and the terrace edge to the north. FhCe-15 yielded a small collection of 299 pieces of lithic debitage, primarily quartzite. A single crude plain rim sherd of sparsely grit-tempered ceramic with a distinctive fine, terracotta-coloured paste was recovered (figure 3.7B). No decoration is present, and only the convex interior face of the object is intact. No radio carbon dates are available for this site, and none of the four finished quartzite artifacts are suggestive of a cultural affiliation. The quartzite-dominated artifact and debitage collection is consistent with a North West River Phase affiliation (dating approximately 1800 BP [Fitzhugh 1972]).

Manitu-utshu 5, FhCe-17

A total of 36 m² was excavated at FhCe-17 (Stantec 2014a), between the portage trail and the terrace edge. FhCe-17 yielded a large collection of 1,978 pieces of lithic debitage. The majority of pieces were of quartzite (53%), with rhyolite (24%), quartz (11.9%) and Saunders chert (11%) also represented.

A collection of pre-Contact ceramics consisting of four small sherds and two very small fragments of a thick, coarse, sparsely grit-tempered ware was recovered (figure 3.7C). Exterior surfaces of sherds where present, noticeably blackened, and the collection is free from decoration with the exception of one sherd exhibiting an exterior ridge, which may be from a collar corner or a shoulder carination.

A date of 1900 ± 30 BP (Beta-373499) from a single cultural feature is consistent with a North West River Phase occupation dating to the terminal Intermediate/early Late pre-Contact period.

Manitu-utshu 9, FhCe-21

Manitu-utshu 9 (FhCe-21) was situated north of the portage trail, on the terrace edge 200 m south of the lower falls. Excavation of 92 m² at the site (Stantec 2014a) yielded a large collection of 1,268 pieces of lithic debitage. Quartzite was the dominant lithic material (37.5%), but rhyolite (29.7%) and Saunders chert (26.2%) were almost equally well represented in the collection. Quartz comprised 6.4% of the debitage assemblage.

FhCe-21 yielded a relatively large sample of pre-Contact ceramics, numbering 27 distinct sherds, along with 23 g of crumbled clay fragments (figure 3.8). All sherds are of a low-fired, thick-walled, grit-tempered ware. Many sherds do not show a complete cross-section and have only interior or exterior surfaces, and most were collected from a single feature, discussed below. Where clear interior surfaces are evident, these are often blackened. Exterior surfaces show no evidence of decoration.

The quartzite-rhyolite-chert assemblage is broadly consistent with a North West River Phase date in the Intermediate period, while a radiocarbon date of 1950 ± 30 BP (Beta-373501) is also consistent with the North West River Phase as traditionally dated.

Manitu-utshu 20, FhCe-32

FhCe-32 was situated north of the portage trail on a terrace edge. During recovery work in 2013 (Stantec 2014b), a total of 196 m² was excavated.

The site yielded a large collection of 2,486 pieces of lithic debitage; a slight plurality of these (42.7%) was of rhyolite, although quartzite was almost equally well represented (41.6% of the debitage). Ramah represented a relatively high 10.2% of the debitage assemblage, while other materials were found in only trace frequencies.

A single sherd of pre-Contact grit-tempered ceramic sherd—a small, relatively thin undecorated body sherd (figure 3.7D)—was recovered from the site. The yellow-tan paste exterior and a grey interior of this sherd are significantly different from those recovered at nearby sites and from elsewhere in the project area.

Manitu-utshu 21, FhCe-33

The site was situated overlooking the crescent-shaped sandy cove immediately downstream of the upper falls at Muskrat Falls. A total of 248 m^2 was excavated during recovery work (Stantec 2014b), yielding a large collection of 9,791 pieces of lithic artifacts and debitage. More than half of the debitage (54.5%) consisted of rhyolite, and more than a third was quartzite (37.7%). A relatively small percentage of the debitage was chert (3.4%), and quartz and Ramah chert were present in significant but lesser quantities (2.4% and 1.9%, respectively). The lithic assemblage was diverse in terms of both raw material use and artifact typologies, and may represent a palimpsest of occupations over a prolonged period.

Two sherds of pre-Contact ceramic along with a collection of finished tools were recovered from an irregular lens of charcoal-stained sediment measuring approximately 2 m by 0.5 m, which is interpreted as the remains of a small hearth. The recovered ceramics are relatively thin undecorated body sherds with grey-tan grit-tempered paste, tan exterior surfaces, and grey-black interior surfaces (figure 3.7C).

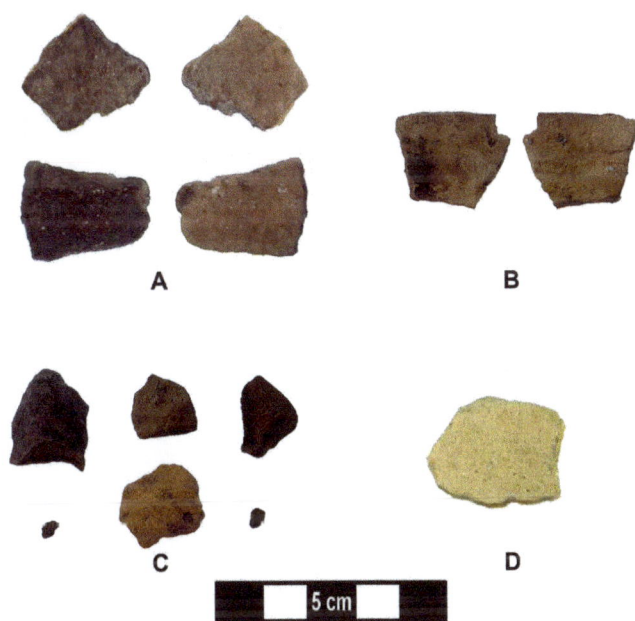

Figure 3.7. Small precontact ceramic assemblages from sites on the southside of Muskrat Falls. A: Manitu-utshu 21 (FhCe-33). B: Manitu-utshu 3 (FhCe-15). C: Manitu-utshu 5 (FhCe-17). D: Manitu-utshu 9 (FhCe-32).

Figure 3.8. Pre-Contact ceramic assemblage from Manitu-utshu 9(FhCe-21).

Sandy Banks Site Cluster

Two sites in this cluster had evidence of pre-Contact ceramics. Unlike the cluster of small-to-medium Historic-period and pre-Contact sites in the Muskrat Falls cluster, the sites clustered in the Sandy Banks area are dominated by a single, large, multi-component site at Sandy Banks (FgCg-01).

Sandy Banks 1, FgCg-01

This large multi-component site consisted of four loci, with evidence for both pre-Contact and Historic occupations. Two of these, Locus A and Locus B, contained pre-Contact components with collections of pre-Contact ceramics (Stantec 2015, 2016).

FgCg-01 Locus A

FgCg-01 Locus A is situated near the edge of a relatively level and well-drained terrace 6–8 m above the river. Six cultural features were exposed in the 132 m² excavation, the majority pertaining to a nineteenth-century occupation. Pre-Contact materials from Locus A were associated with two somewhat diffuse cobble-hearth features (Feature 1 and Feature 2), which yielded small lithic assemblages as well as 15 sherds of grit-tempered pre-Contact ceramic (figure 3.9A). These sherds are all relatively thick-walled with a grey, low-fired paste, grit temper, and smoothed (but not burnished) interior and exterior surfaces. They all appear to be undecorated body sherds.

FgCg-01 Locus B

In all, 168 m² was excavated at Locus B, located along the edge of the terrace east of Locus A. Locus B yielded a total of 17,038 lithic pieces consisting almost entirely of quartzite, although cherts, quartz, rhyolite, and Ramah (233 pieces, or 1.4% of the collection) were present in smaller frequencies.

One feature in Locus B yielded pre-Contact ceramics: Feature 7, a linear, diffuse boulder and cobble hearth, was associated with quartzite debitage, and included lithic debris and artifacts, charcoal, and calcined bone fragments, along with a collection of grit-tempered ceramics. The 11 sherds of ceramics are mostly fragmentary, with worn edges (figure 3.9B). They are nearly identical in production to those recovered from Locus A: undecorated, thick-walled with a grey, low-fired paste, grit temper, and smoothed interiors and exterior surfaces. Mineral liberation analyzer–scanning electron microscope (MLA-SEM) analysis of two sherds from FgCg-01 (Wilton 2016) indicated that the precursor material for the clay fabric of these sherds potentially derived from central Labrador, but differed significantly from comparative samples specifically recovered from the Churchill Valley to date. A date of 1900 ± 39 radiocarbon years BP (UOC-1134) was obtained on a charcoal sample taken from Feature 7.

Uinipekuiss 2, FgCg-06

FgCg-06 was located on the east side of the mouth of a small brook, on the south bank of the Churchill River. Recovery work included the excavation of a total of 58 m² at the site (Stantec 2015).

FgCg-06 yielded a large collection of 4,180 pieces of lithic debitage. The majority of lithic debitage pieces (84.7%) consisted of quartzite, with various cherts making up 11.1% and rhyolite accounting for 3.6%, with trace numbers (n=21) of quartz accounting for 0.5%. Four sherds of low-fired, grit-tempered, undecorated body sherds were also recovered at the site (figure 3.9C). The fragments are quite friable and small in size and no evidence of burned surfaces or residue was noted.

Figure 3.9. Small ceramic assemblages from sites excavated in the reservoir. A: Sandy Banks 1 (FgCg-1), Locus A. B: Sandy Banks 1 (FgCg-1), Locus B. C: Uinipekuiss 2 (FgCg-06). D: Gull Lake 1 (FgCh-02).

Gull Island Cluster

Three sites in this cluster on Gull Lake, along the north banks of the Churchill River, contained evidence of pre-Contact ceramics, with two of these being multi-locus sites that are among the largest excavated in the project. All of the sites yielded quartzite-dominated lithic collections.

Gull Lake 1, FgCh-02

FgCh-02 is one of a pair of adjacent sites (the other being FgCh-03) situated on the northern shore of Gull Lake, approximately 800 m above the outflow. In all, 176 m² were excavated at FgCh-02 (Stantec 2018), revealing two discrete lithic scatters.

FgCh-02 contained a large collection of 11,538 pieces of lithic debitage, dominated by quartzite (99%), with chert (n=83), and quartz (n=5) recovered in trace amounts. A single ceramic sherd was recovered in the western portion of the site, from within Feature 1. The sherd is a thin, undecorated, grit-tempered rim sherd (figure 3.9D).

Tshiashkunish 8, FfCh-02

FfCh-02 was located on a point of land projecting from the north shore of Gull Lake. Recovery work at FfCh-02 in 2017 (Stantec 2018) led to the excavation of 269 m^2 at three discrete loci on the site. One of these (Locus B) yielded a single sherd of pre-Contact ceramic, a thick-bodied, low-fired, grit-tempered, undecorated sherd. Locus A, on the other hand, contained a large collection of pre-Contact ceramics, many decorated, and most associated with a specific feature (figure 3.10).

Excavation of 141 m^2 at FfCh-02 Locus A (Stantec 2018) revealed three discrete lithic scatters, yielding a large collection of 20,019 lithic pieces, consisting almost entirely of quartzite, with only low numbers of rhyolite (42 pieces), chert (31 pieces), and Ramah (41 pieces). The near-exclusive use of local quartzites (99.43%), along with the biface forms, are broadly compatible with the North West River Phase (Fitzhugh 1972).

Associated with the lithic assemblage from FfCh-02 Locus A was a large collection of 276 sherds of pre-Contact ceramic. All but two of these fragments were recovered from Feature 2, a small, 1.5 m × 0.75 m × 25 cm ochre-stained mound and surrounding ochre/charcoal stained deposit spread over 1.5 m^2 and containing a high density of quartzite debitage and tool fragments but little fire-cracked rock. Ceramic sherds recovered from this feature vary in thickness, from approximately 2 mm to 6.5 mm, and exhibit a grey-to-brown low-fired paste, grit temper, and smooth interior and exterior surface treatment (figure 3.11). Several of the sherds also display convincing coil breaks. While most of the body sherds tend to be thicker and undecorated, the assemblage does include several thin rim and neck sherds exhibiting exterior decoration. The decoration consists exclusively of linear dentate stamps applied in a simple horizontal fashion along the exterior surface. The few decorated rim sherds that were recovered show a series of slightly diagonal notches along the lip of the rim. These notches were likely applied with the dentate tool used on the exterior surface. No decoration was observed on the interior surfaces of any of the sherds, but some sherds have burnt residues preserved on the interior. A radiocarbon date of 1770+/-30 BP (Beta-539697) was obtained on charcoal from FfCh-02 Locus A Feature 2.

The substantial decorated ceramic collection from Locus A allowed for more precise stylistic comparison of the collection to other ceramic traditions. There are few dated samples within the region with which to compare them, although dentate-stamped ceramics from the Gould site in Port au Choix on the island of Newfoundland (see Stapelfeldt 2009) have been dated to 1500 ± 40 BP (Beta-134156). Similar dentate-decorated ceramics have also been collected from the above mentioned Shipiskan Lake in the north-central Labrador interior (Loring 2013). The combination of coil-built manufacture, grit temper, smoothed interior, and dentate-stamped exterior surfaces would normally suggest a date broadly in the Middle Woodland period (2200-1800 BP) (Côté and Inksetter 2001), or more specifically, Ceramic periods 2–4 (Bourgeois 1999; Petersen and Sanger 1991), at least partly contemporary with the North West River Phase in central Labrador or the Daniel Rattle complex on the north-central Labrador coast.

Tshiashkunish 8, FfCi-02 (Locus D)

FfCi-02 is situated approximately midway along the north shore of Gull Lake, on the eastern side of a small, sheltered cove. Recovery work in 2015 (Stantec 2016) led to the excavation of 553 m^2 at the site and the identification of six discrete occupation loci. Of these loci, only one, Locus D, contained evidence of pre-Contact ceramics.

The pre-Contact component of FfCi-02 Locus D contained a large collection of lithics, with 30,788 lithic pieces recovered. The lithic collection consists almost exclusively of quartzite, with minimal traces of rhyolite (29 pieces), chert (2 pieces) and quartz (1 piece). The placement of the lithic assemblage from Locus D within the regional-type sequence from North West River (Fitzhugh 1972) is somewhat problematic. The near-exclusive use of local quartzites, along with the biface forms, is compatible with the North West River Phase, while the stemmed projectile points are more suggestive of the David Michelin component, and the formal teardrop-shaped endscrapers are normally diagnostic of the early Intermediate-period Charles complex (Fitzhugh 1972).

Locus D contained the largest collection of pre-Contact ceramics recovered from any site within the project area. A total of 1,414 sherds and sherdlets of grit-tempered ceramics (weighing a total of 914 g) were recovered. The vast majority (1,346 sherds) were collected from within, or immediately adjacent to, Feature 4, a localized pit deposit of sand and ceramic sherdlets. The remaining 68 sherds were recovered from discrete scatters situated several metres to the south, northeast, and northwest of Feature 4. Charcoal associated with this feature was radiocarbon dated to 1580+/-30 BP (Beta-539699).

Two distinct ware types can be distinguished within this collection. One ware type is represented by a group of five moderately large body sherds of a relatively high-fired, dark-grey-bodied ware (figure 3.12E). The wall thickness ranges from 8.3 mm to 8.9 mm, and the fabric contains considerable quantities of very coarse grit. These sherds have unsmoothed exterior surfaces, while their interior surfaces are smoothed and coated with a distinctive whitish deposit. When refitted, several of these sherds display a compound curve, suggesting that the original vessel had a neck.

The second ware is represented by virtually all the remaining sherds in the assemblage, collected from within and around Feature 4 (figure 3.12A–D). The majority of these are small, often with worn, rounded corners, and composed of a fine, soft, tan-coloured paste containing relatively little grit. Even the largest sherds are quite small, but a few are large enough to reveal some vessel characteristics. Full-section rim sherds and near-rim body sherds range in thickness from 6.5 mm to 8.8 mm, although most sherds are considerably thicker (10.3 mm–12.1 mm) and appear to derive from the lower body or base of a vessel. All sherds with identifiable exterior and/or interior surfaces have clearly been smoothed, although not enough to obscure evidence for coiling or ring-building on some larger sherds. Rims appear to have a simple, sometimes slightly-flattened lip.

In contrast to the other ware type all of the sherds associated with Feature 4 display unusual, soft paste. When first exposed during excavation and still damp, these sherds and sherdlets were soft enough to be shaved with a trowel. Initially, these sherds appeared to be only leather-hard and were so fragile it became necessary to excavate Feature 4 in a series of block-lifts. The sherds eventually hardened after slow drying. The consistency in the field, as well as the worn character of pieces, suggests that the vessel from which they derived may never have been truly fired, merely "fire-hardened," and that it shattered in an early stage of firing before achieving the temperatures required for ceramic change (normally ca. 550°C–600°C).

Because of the generally small size of all pieces, clear evidence for the decorative techniques employed is limited. Most sherds show no evidence for surface decoration at all, while some display isolated fingernail depressions that may not be intentionally decorative, or short, fine incisions that may result from temper particles being dragged across the vessel surface during smoothing. A few sherds have larger individual punctations or folds, but again the small size of the sherds makes it difficult to confirm whether these were intended to be decorative. However, there are four sherds that are clearly decorated. One is a flattened-lip rim sherd decorated with a row of upward-jabbed punctations on the vessel exterior, just below the rim; these appear to have been executed with a reed or flat, slender stick (figure 3.12A). Another sherd, although tiny, clearly evidences two parallel, wide incised grooves (figure 3.12B), while another has two wide incised grooves that converge to form a chevron (figure 3.12D). The final decorated piece is a body sherd with a slightly corrugated surface, formed by partial smoothing of the coils with which the vessel was built. This is not the only sherd to retain evidence for coil construction, but in this instance, the "troughs" between the coils are enhanced by rows of very fine punctations (figure 3.12C). Once again, the combination of coil-built manufacture, grit temper, and smoothed interior and exterior surfaces would normally suggest a dating broadly in the Middle Woodland period (Côté and Inksetter 2001), more specifically, Ceramic periods 2–4 (Petersen and Sanger 1991).

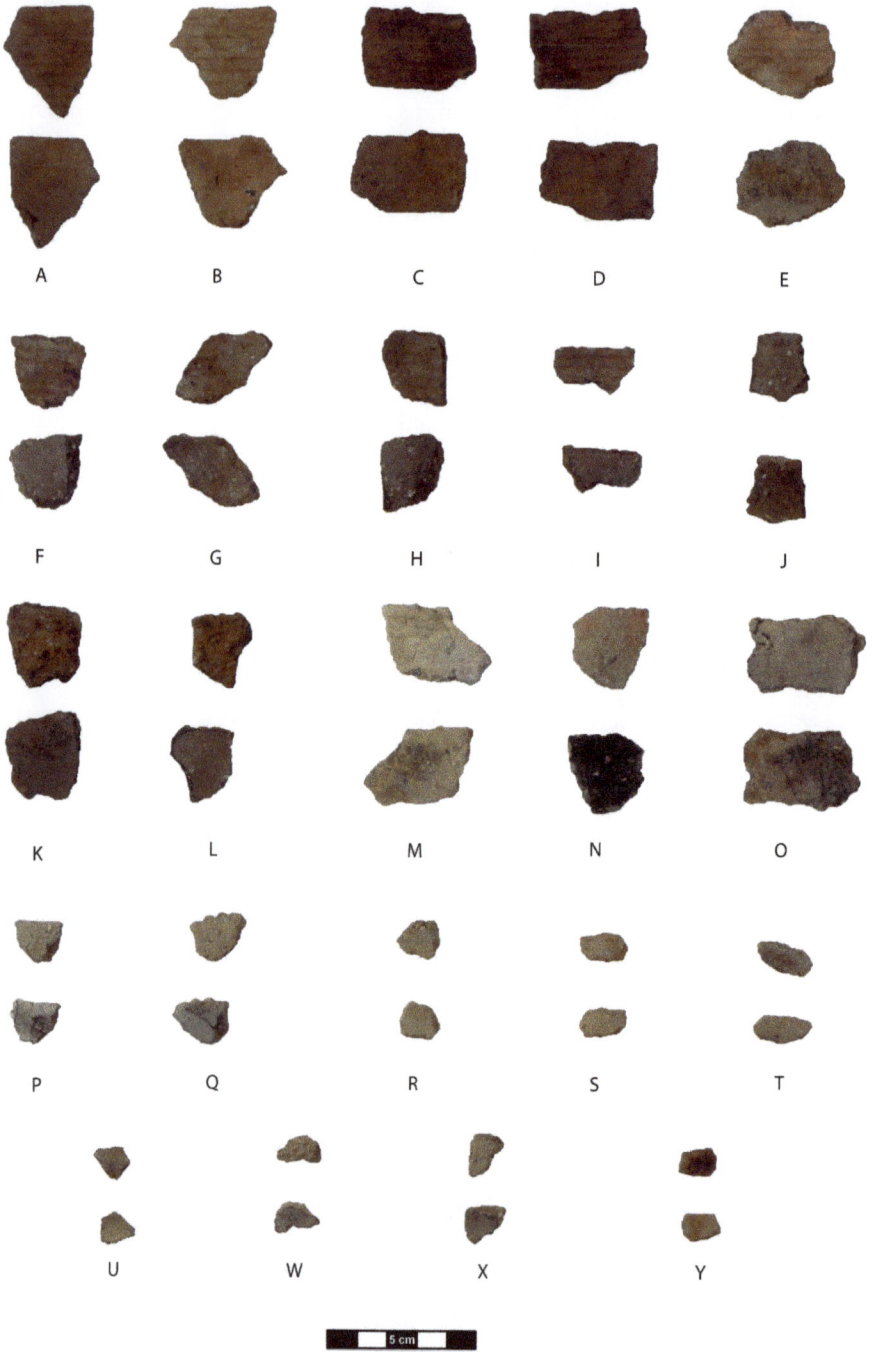

Figure 3.10. Selected precontact ceramic sherds from Tshiashkunish 8 (FfCh-02).

Figure 3.11. Detail of decoration and residue of selected sherds from Tshiashkunish 8 (FfCh-02).

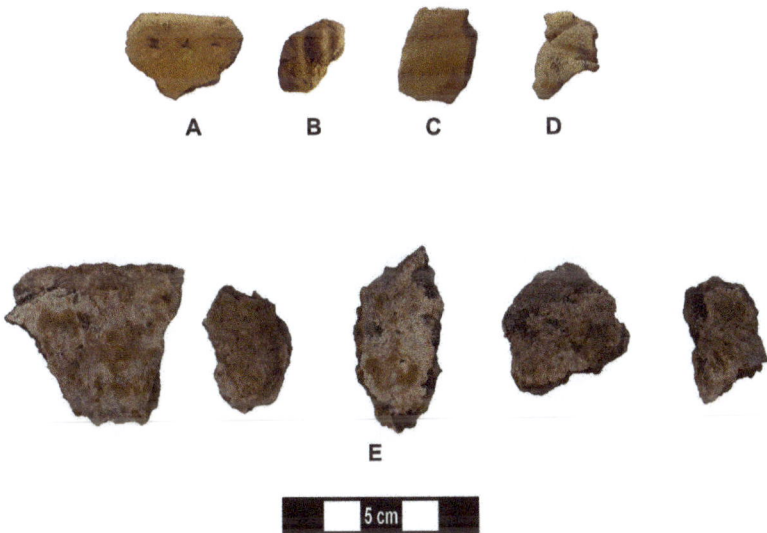

Figure 3.12. Selected fragments from Tshiashkunish 8 (FfCi-02). A-D: Decorated fragments. E: second recovered ware type.

Evidence for Local Ceramic Production

Review of the recovered ceramics from 10 pre-Contact sites on the Churchill River demonstrates that ceramics may actually have been a more common artifact class in central Labrador, and at least in the period from ca. 2000 to 1500 BP, than previously believed. Also significant is that two of these sites yielded potential evidence for the local production of ceramics.

FhCe-21 Feature 1

Feature 1 at FhCe-21, on the south side of Muskrat Falls (figure 3.13), is a long, narrow, and deep-pit feature, roughly kidney-shaped, measuring approximately 50 cm–75 cm wide, nearly 1.5 m long, and 30 cm–50 cm deep. This pit yielded lithic debitage and artifacts, including dozens of fragments of a white heat-shattered biface, along with charcoal and fire-cracked rock. The flanks of the pit appear to have slumped inward, but to have been originally steep-sided. Associated with this pit was an assemblage of 27 distinct sherds of grit-tempered ceramic, along with 23 g of crumbled clay fragments and sherdlets. While the precise function of this pit is unclear, the degraded condition of many of the sherdlets raises the possibility that it was a kiln for firing locally made ceramics. In some respects, this feature resembles the suspected ceramic-production features recorded by Teal (2001) at the Gould site.

FfCi-02 Feature 4

As described above, the majority of the ceramic collection from FfCi-02 was recovered from Feature 4. The feature manifested as a small pit and adjacent mound of intermixed sand from the A and B Horizons representing the occupation level and underlying sterile level respectively. In cross-section, Feature 4 is recognized as an in-filled pit with a band of fire-reddened sand mirroring the floor of the pit (figure 3.14). The majority of this feature was removed as a series of two block lifts, but excavation prior to lifting revealed a scatter of ceramic sherds that extended to the south of the pit. Feature 4 appears to be a pit feature and adjacent mound of spoil formed in antiquity when a pit containing ceramic was excavated and distributed to the south in a fan of spoil (which also contained hundreds of ceramic sherds and sherdlets). Feature 4 is interpreted as the remains of a sand "kiln," a pit for firing pottery, from which fire-cracked rock has been removed (creating Feature 2) and the fill redistributed as spoil. Given the highly fragmented and remarkably low-fired nature of the sherds recovered from Feature 4, it appears that the firing process was not successful (perhaps not surprising, given the low levels of temper in the sherds).

Figure 3.13. Feature 1, Manitu-utshu 9(FhCe-21) interpreted as a potential ceramic firing pit.

Figure 3.14. Tshiashkunish 8 (FfCi-02), Locus D, Feature 4. The source of the majority of under fired ceramic sherds. Fire-reddened soil is visible tracing base of pit.

Discussion and Conclusions

Previous recovery of ceramics from archaeological sites in Newfoundland and Labrador has generally consisted of perplexing, isolated stray finds of individual sherds, or (equally perplexing) finds of larger ceramic assemblages that appear to be unique in their regions. However, in the Churchill Valley of central Labrador, an unusually large-scale program of archaeological recovery work at 45 pre-Contact sites associated with Nalcor's LCP at Muskrat Falls has led to the recovery of ceramics at 10 of these sites (over 20% of the total). The vast majority of these sites are dateable to the period 2000–1500 BP, and their quartzite-dominated lithic assemblages are generally compatible with the North West River Phase of the late Intermediate/early Late pre-Contact period.

The ceramic sherds associated with these sites consist primarily of undecorated grit-tempered body sherds of coil-built vessels with smoothed interior and exterior surfaces, broadly consistent with Middle Woodland-Period manufacture, while the assemblage of decorated (dentate-stamped) ceramics from FfCh-02 is also consistent with this period (specifically with Ceramic periods 2–4; Petersen and Sanger 1991). Associated radiocarbon dates, including three dates derived specifically from ceramic-bearing features, range between 1950 and 1580 BP and are also consistent with this dating. Preliminary analysis suggests the possibility of both local manufacture (as at FfCi-02 and possibly FhCe-21) and importation from elsewhere in central Labrador or the rest of the Ungava peninsula (as for the sherds recovered from FgCg-01).

For the first time in Newfoundland and Labrador, the results of archaeological recovery work on the lower Churchill River have yielded evidence that, at least within this part of central Labrador, pre-Contact ceramics are not just an isolated or occasional find but, rather, a consistently present, integral part of the local toolkit. In this context, it is unclear why such ceramics have not been more widely recovered, either elsewhere in central Labrador (e.g., at North West River), or further afield in Labrador or Newfoundland; however, it is worth noting that the areal extent of the recovery work for the LCP vastly exceeds any previous archaeological excavation program undertaken in the region.

The implications of these results are numerous. The most intensive pre-Contact occupation of the lower Churchill Valley clearly occurs in the period ca. 2000–1500 BP. It may be neither useful nor accurate to refer to this as a Ceramic period or Middle Woodland occupation, but the widespread occurrence of ceramics with Middle Woodland attributes in these sites does suggest some greater degree of interaction with the greater Northeast, perhaps specifically with the north shore of the St. Lawrence, or even with the Maritimes, in this time period than in preceding or subsequent centuries. In terms of broader relationships across Newfoundland and Labrador, it may be significant that, with the exception of the enigmatic "Iroquoian" sherd from Saddle Island in the Strait of Belle Isle, the majority of the pre-Contact ceramic finds from both Labrador and Newfoundland, most notably the large ceramic assemblage from the Gould site in western Newfoundland, also appear to show Middle Woodland attributes or to be otherwise datable to this same period.

In any event, the ceramics recovered from North West River Phase sites on the Churchill River indicate that, at least within this region and at least within this time period, ceramic use was not a sporadic phenomenon but rather played an integral part in local food preparation and/or storage. Researchers in the region must be aware that the potential to recover pre-Contact ceramics is greater than previously imagined. Further ceramic analysis, including residue analysis to determine vessel functions, analysis of clay and temper sources, and stylistic analysis to clarify regional and inter-regional relationships, may not be a matter of explaining a curious stray find or unusual local assemblage but rather may provide insights of broad regional significance. The pre-Contact period in Newfoundland and Labrador may be "apart" from the greater Northeast, but it is also "a part" of the greater Northeast, and further analysis of the role of pre-Contact ceramics offers opportunities to explore how the region is both a part of, and apart from, the region as a whole.

References Cited

Bird, Junius B.

1945   *Archaeology of the Hopedale Area, Labrador.* Anthropological Papers of the American Museum of Natural History, Vol. 39, Pt. 2. American Museum of Natural History, New York.

Bourgeois, Vincent

1999   A Regional Pre-Contact Ceramic Sequence for the Saint John River Valley. Master's thesis, Department of Anthropology, University of New Brunswick, Fredericton.

Chapdelaine, Claude, and Gregory G. Kennedy

1990   The Origin of the Iroquoian Rim Sherd from Red Bay. *Man in the Northeast* 40:41–43.

Côté, Marc, and Leila Inksetter

2001   Ceramics and Chronology of the Late Prehistoric Period: The Abitibi-Témiscamingue Case. In *A Collection of Papers Presented at the 33rd Annual Meeting of the Canadian Archaeological Association*, edited by Jean-Luc Pilon, Michael W. Kirby and Caroline Thériault, pp. 111–127. Ontario Archaeological Society, Ottawa.

Fitzhugh, William

1972   Environmental Archaeology and Cultural Systems in Hamilton Inlet, Labrador: A Survey of the Central Labrador Coast from 3000 B.C. to the Present. *Smithsonian Contributions to Anthropology*, No. 16. Smithsonian Institution Press, Washington, DC.

Hull, Stephen

2014   Potsherds. *Inside Newfoundland and Labrador Archaeology* (blog), May 9, 2014. https://nlarchaeology.wordpress.com/2014/05/09/potsherds/, accessed January 20, 2020.

IEDE/JWEL (Innu Economic Development Enterprises/Jacques Whitford Environment, Ltd.)

2000   Churchill River Power Project, 1998 Environmental Studies. Historic Resources Overview Assessment, Labrador Component. Manuscript on file, Newfoundland and Labrador Hydro, St. John's.

Loring, Stephen

1985   Archaeological Investigations into the Nature of the Late Prehistoric Indian Occupation in Labrador: A Report of the 1984 Field Season. *Archaeology in Newfoundland and Labrador* 5:122–153.

1988   Keeping Things Whole: Nearly Two Thousand Years of Indian (Innu) Occupation in Northern Labrador. In *Boreal Forest and Sub-Arctic Archaeology,* edited by C. S. Paddy Reid, pp. 157–182. Occasional Publications of the London Chapter, Ontario Archaeological Society No. 6, London, Ontario.

1992   Princes and Princesses of Ragged Fame: Innu Archaeology and Ethnohistory in Labrador. PhD dissertation, Department of Anthropology, University of Massachusetts, Amherst.

2013   Pottery from the North: Addendum to Stapelfeldt. *Arctic Studies Center Newsletter* 20:31–32.

Penney, Gerald

1981   A Point Peninsula Rim Sherd from L'Anse a Flamme, Newfoundland. *Canadian Journal of Archaeology* 5:171–173.

Petersen, James B., and David Sanger

1991   An Aboriginal Ceramic Sequence for Maine and the Maritime Provinces. In *Prehistoric Archaeology in the Maritime Provinces: Past and Present Research, Reports in Archaeology,* No. 8, edited by Michael Deal and Susan Blair, pp. 133–170. The Council of Maritime Premiers, Fredericton, New Brunswick.

Stantec Consulting Limited (Stantec)

2014a   2012 Historic Resources Assessment and Recovery Field Program. Manuscript on file, Nalcor Energy and Provincial Archaeology Office of Newfoundland and Labrador, St. John's.

2014b   2013 Lower Churchill Hydroelectric Development Project 2013 Historic Resources Assessment and Recovery Program. Manuscript on file, Nalcor Energy and Provincial Archaeology Office of Newfoundland and Labrador, St. John's.

2015   Nalcor Energy Lower Churchill Project - 2014 Historic Resources Management Program. Manuscript on file, Nalcor Energy and Provincial Archaeology Office of Newfoundland and Labrador, St. John's.

2016   Lower Churchill Hydroelectric Development Project 2015 Historic Resources Assessment and Recovery Program. Manuscript on file, Nalcor Energy and Provincial Archaeology Office of Newfoundland and Labrador, St. John's.

2018 Lower Churchill Hydroelectric Development Project 2017 Historic Resources Assessment and Recovery Program. Manuscript on file, Nalcor Energy and Provincial Archaeology Office of Newfoundland and Labrador, St. John's.

Stapelfeldt, Kora.

2009 A Form and Function Study of Precontact Pottery from Atlantic Canada. Master's thesis, Department of Archaeology, Memorial University, St. John's, Newfoundland and Labrador.

2013 Pottery in Motion: Towards Cultural Interaction Studies in Newfoundland and Labrador. *Arctic Studies Center Newsletter* 20:29–30.

Strong, William Duncan

1930 A Stone Culture from Labrador and its Relation to the Eskimo-Like Cultures of the Northeast. *American Anthropologist* 32:126–144.

Teal, Michael

2001 An Archaeological Investigation of the Gould Site (EeBi-42) in Port au Choix, Northwestern Newfoundland: New Insight into the Recent Period Cow Head Complex. Master's thesis, Department of Archaeology, Memorial University, St. John's, Newfoundland and Labrador.

Tuck, James A.

1987 European-Native Contacts in the Strait of Belle Isle, Labrador. In *Between Greenland and America: Cross-Cultural Contacts and the Environment in the Baffin Bay Area*, edited by L. Hacquebord and R. Vaughan, pp. 61–74. Arctic Center, Groningen, Netherlands.

2005 Archaeology at Red Bay, Labrador: 1978-1992. Manuscript on file, Provincial Archaeology Office of Newfoundland and Labrador, St. John's.

Tuck, James A., and Robert McGhee

1975 Belle Isle Archaeological Project, 1975. Manuscript on file, Provincial Archaeology Office of Newfoundland and Labrador, St. John's.

Wilton, Derek

2016 Report on the MLA-SEM Examination of Two Precontact-Period Pottery Shards and Three Mud Samples from the Churchill Valley, Central Labrador. *Provincial Archaeology Office 2015 Archaeology Review* 14:229–239.

4

FAR NORTHEASTERN FLAKED-LITHIC MATERIAL ACQUISITION AND EXCHANGE

Looking Through the Bliss Islands Lens

DAVID W. BLACK

Abstract

During the past several decades, exploring patterns of lithic material acquisition and exchange has become a significant focus of archaeological research in the Far Northeast. Studies have determined sources of specific lithic materials, traced distributions of distinctive exotic materials, and defined suites of materials characteristic of particular periods and subregions. Indigenous people acquired locally available materials for making flaked-stone tools and accessed exotic lithic materials through travel and exchange. This chapter examines variability in the lithic material assemblages of a single point in the Maritimes landscape—the Bliss Islands group, Quoddy Region, New Brunswick—resulting from the participation of Ancestral Peskotomuhkatiyik and others in lithic material acquisition and exchange systems over a period of about 3,500 years.

While the Bliss Islands assemblages are dominated by locally acquired lithic materials, four times are identified—the Terminal Archaic-Early Maritime Woodland transition, the Early-Middle Maritime Woodland transition, the earlier part of the Late Maritime Woodland period, and the early Loyalist period—when distinctive suites of exotic lithic materials were acquired and used by inhabitants of the islands. Variations in lithic material usage among the subperiods of the Maritime Woodland appear to be as dramatic as among the larger-scale culture-historic periods of the entire pre-Contact sequence.

Résumé

Au cours des deux dernières décennies, l'étude des schèmes d'acquisition et d'échange de matériaux lithiques est devenue un aspect important de la recherche archéologique de la Péninsule maritime. Des études on permit de déterminer des sources spécifiques de matériaux lithiques, des témoins de distribution de matériaux lithiques exotiques particuliers, ainsi que des ensembles de caractéristiques matérielles de périodes et sous-régions particulières. Les autochtones se procuraient des matériaux disponibles localement afin de fabriquer des outils de pierre taillée. Ils participèrent aussi à des pratiques d'acquisition et d'échange qui leur permit d'obtenir des matériaux lithiques exotiques. J'examine ici la variabilité des assemblages de matériaux lithiques d'une seule pointe du territoire de la Péninsule maritime – le groupe des îles Bliss, Région de Quoddy, Nouveau-Brunswick – résultant de la participation des Peskotomuhkatiyik et autres dans les systèmes d'acquisition et d'échange de matériaux lithiques sur une période de 3500 ans.

Alors que les assemblages des îles Bliss sont dominés par des matériaux lithiques acquis localement, cette analyse identifie quatre périodes – la transition entre l'Archaïque récent et le Sylvicole inférieur, la partie la plus tardive du Sylvicole inférieur, la partie la plus récente du Sylvicole Supérieur, et le début de la période loyalist – pendant lesquelles des ensembles distincts de matériaux lithiques exotiques étaient acquis et utilisés par les habitants des îles. Lors de la transition entre l'Archaïque récent et le Sylvicole inférieur, des artéfacts fabriqués à partir de matériaux lithiques du Maine, comme le porphyre de Kineo–Traveler Mountain, étaient acquis, alors que, durant les parties plus tardives du Sylvicole inférieur, de la rhyolite de Tobique était acquise de l'intérieure des terres du Nouveau-Brunswick. Lors de la partie la plus récente du Sylvicole supérieur, une variété de matériaux lithiques exotiques – porphyre de Kineo–Traveler Mountain et chert rouge et vert de Munsungun, au Maine, du chert multicolore de Washademoak à l'intérieur des terres du Nouveau-Brunswick, et diverses variétés de cherts et roches volcaniques siliceuses de la région de Mina Basin/North Mountain en Nouvelle-Écosse – étaient utilisés par les Peskotomuhkatiyik ancestraux vivant sur les îles Bliss. Lors du début de la période loyaliste, la famille Bliss amena à leurs demeures sur l'île des pierres à fusil fabriquées à partir de silex européen.

Affiliation

– Department of Anthropology, University of New Brunswick, New Brunswick, Canada

During the past several decades, exploring patterns of pre-Contact lithic material acquisition and exchange has become a significant focus in the burgeoning field of geoarchaeological research in the Far Northeast (e.g., Black 2011; S. E. Blair 2010; Burke 2007). The ultimate aims of such studies are to reconstruct now-intangible past human activities, meanings, and cultural systems (Reimer 2018:141). The proximate aims are to reveal and measure the still-tangible lithic traces and imprints of those past systems on the archaeological record. These aims are particularly difficult to achieve in the Far Northeast, where bedrock geology is varied and complex (Dincauze 1976), and where potential tool stones have been distributed from their original sources to secondary bedrock and surficial geological contexts by multiple environmental processes in episodes spanning hundreds of millions of years (AGS 2001). Researchers have identified and documented sources of specific lithic materials (e.g., Black and Wilson 1999; Bourque et al. 1984; Pollock et al. 1999; Pollock et al. 2008a), traced distributions of distinctive exotic lithic materials (e.g., Burke 2000:255-261, 2007; Pelletier and Robinson 2005; Pollock et al. 1999; Pollock et al. 2008b), and defined suites of lithic materials that characterize particular periods and sub-regions (e.g., Black 2011; S. E. Blair 1999; Burke 2006; Doyle 1995:299-316; Gilbert 2011:177-179; Rosenmeier 2011:363-407). It appears that, through time, Indigenous people developed various strategies for acquiring and working locally and regionally available lithic materials, while also participating in macro-regional interaction and exchange systems that varied in scale, orientation, intensity, and duration (e.g., S. E. Blair 2004; Bourque 1994; Taché 2011; Wright 1999:598-602).

The study presented here is a first approximation of what Burke (2011) refers to as a community-scale approach to lithic material sourcing. It documents variations among the lithic material assemblages of a single point in the Far Northeastern landscape—the Bliss Islands group, Quoddy Region, New Brunswick—produced through the activities of Ancestral Peskotomuhkatiyik and others in lithic material acquisition from the Terminal Archaic through the Maritime Woodland to the Historic periods. The emphasis here is on the presence and significance of exotic lithic materials.

The purpose of this chapter is to present a more nuanced view of pre-Contact lithic material procurement in the Quoddy Region than has been previously available, in light of recently accumulated knowledge about Far Northeastern lithic material sources, and to address issues raised by previous studies. This analysis has been simplified by considering only flaked-lithic materials from the Bliss Islands sites, by omitting consideration of intra-assemblage spatial organization of lithic materials, and by presenting data in terms of a single quantitative measurement: mass. Various types of visual presentations are employed to underline two methodological points: (1) that much can be accomplished in archaeological lithic material studies through visual techniques employing hand-specimen descriptions, low-power stereo-microscopic examinations, and digital photography (Black 2011; Gilbert et al. 2006a, 2006b; Pollock et al. 1999; Pollock et al. 2008a); and (2) that while lithic material identification and sourcing are inherently probabilistic, and while many archaeological assemblages are not amenable to analysis using inferential statistics, comparisons may be facilitated and interpretations reinforced or challenged through descriptive statistical techniques.

Lithic Material Analyses in Quoddy Region Archaeology

In the Quoddy Region (QR), interest in the materials from which stone tools were made extends back to the beginnings of scientific archaeology (Matthew 1884:21). However, before the 1980s, lithic artifacts were considered mainly from formal, functional, and culture-historical perspectives; the materials from which flaked-stone tools were made received little systematic attention. During the early 1980s, analyses of lithic materials in QR assemblages were pioneered in two theses: Wilson (1983) identified lithic materials from five sites in New Brunswick under Christopher J. Turnbull's supervision, and Crotts (1984) studied lithic materials in six assemblages from the QR under David Sanger's supervision.

Two of the sites Wilson (1983) considered are located in the QR: Holt's Point (BgDr9; Sanger 1987:100-102) on the northern shore of Passamaquoddy Bay, and Partridge Island (BgDr48; Bishop and Black 1988) in the insular QR. Wilson analyzed both formal tools and debitage from the assemblages, quantifying them by piece count. She found that the assemblages were dominated by aphanitic volcanics, and that virtually all of the lithic materials represented could have been acquired from bedrock or secondary sources within eight kilometres of the sites (assuming that the small amounts of "chalcedony" identified were associated geologically with local volcanic formations). She inferred that there was little evidence for long-distance acquisition or exchange of lithic materials.

Crotts (1984) focussed on analyzing lithic materials used to make formal tools from the Passamaquoddy Bay sites (Sanger 1971a, 1987), quantifying them by piece count. She identified two classes of materials, "indigenous" and "foreign" (corresponding, roughly, to *local* and *exotic*, as used in the analysis below). Crotts's indigenous materials included quartz, quartzites, porphyritic tuffs, rhyolites, black siltstone and black volcanics. Her foreign materials included cryptocrystalline quartz, red and green mudstone, green volcanic, ferromanganese metasediment, and white-spotted metasediment.

Crotts was cautious about ascribing sources to foreign lithic materials. However, her cryptocrystalline quartz category probably corresponds to several of the brightly coloured, variegated-chert types distinguished in the analysis below. Crotts speculated that these materials might have been acquired from sources in Nova Scotia, on the Grand Manan archipelago, and/or in the Washademoak Lake area of southern interior New Brunswick. She recognized similarities between the red and green mudstone from the Passamaquoddy Bay sites and radiolarian cherts (Gauthier et al. 2012; Jones and Murchey 1986) from the Munsungun Lake area of Maine (Brockman and Keegan 2016:46), and between some green volcanics in the Passamaquoddy Bay sites and porphyritic volcanics from the Mount Kineo–Traveler Mountain area of Maine (Brockman and Keegan 2016:37). Crotts's description of the ferromanganese metasediment resembles Tobique rhyolite (TOBR; Gilbert et al. 2006b), and she recognized the central Saint John River valley as a potential source for this material.[1] Finally, Crotts identified the white-spotted metasediment as coming from the Hinkley Point area of Cobscook Bay, Maine. She considered it foreign, while, by the criteria employed here, it would be classified as local (Gilbert 2011:166; Gilbert et al. 2006a).

Crotts (1984:69) found that substantial proportions of the stone tools she examined were made from foreign lithic materials, ranging from ca. 30% at the Orr's Point site (BgDr7) to ca. 50% at the Carson site (BgDr5). Further, Crotts (1984:2) concluded that there was no evidence for changes in lithic material usage during the ca. 2,400 years of occupation represented in the sites she studied. Her interpretations were echoed by Sanger (1987), who reported comparable findings for additional Late Ceramic period (approximately Late Maritime Woodland) assemblages. In terms of identifying specific sources of foreign materials, Sanger (1987:78) emphasized the nascent state of relevant geological information in New Brunswick and adjacent areas. Nevertheless, although it remained largely implicit, an implication of Crotts's work is that pre-Contact residents of the QR acquired lithic materials and/or numerous finished artifacts from sources outside the region.

A preliminary analysis of lithic materials recovered from eight Bliss Islands (BI) components between 1981 and 1986 was presented in Black's (1989) dissertation on insular QR human ecology; that analysis was reproduced unchanged in published versions of the dissertation (e.g., Black 2004). This was a first attempt to consider lithic material use in the QR from a stratigraphic perspective. Both debitage and formal artifacts were considered, as were the

---

1. Tobique rhyolite (Burke 2000:388)—Tobique chert/rhyolite (Brockman and Keegan 2016:96)—occurs as cobbles in a part of the Tobique River basin underlain by Carboniferous-aged bedrocks (Potter et al. 1979). Some variants of TOBR could be described as cherty rhyolite (Gilbert et al. 2006b), exhibiting blebs of bright-red chert within the rhyolitic groundmass. Cobbles of translucent chert, somewhat similar to the Carboniferous-associated cherts found further south in New Brunswick, are associated (Gauthier et al. 2012:2438).

products of both flaked- and ground-stone technologies; the materials were quantified by piece count and by mass. Source interpretations largely followed Crotts (1984). Although lithic material analysis was not a focus of the BI research at that time, Black (2004:141-144) reported chronological variations in lithic material use, and suggested that such variations might form an aspect of subsequent culture-historic formulations. In a thesis written under D. W. Black's supervision, MacDonald (1994) pursued this avenue of research by comparing the stratigraphic patterning of lithic materials in the Partridge Island and Weir (BgDq6) sites (including lithic artifacts recovered during the 1993 excavation at the Weir site).

Bliss Islands Site Inventory

The Bliss Islands are located offshore from Blacks Harbour, New Brunswick, in the traditional territory of the Peskotomuhkatiyik (the Passamaquoddy people). Designations, locations, and descriptions of the BI sites, and the chronological relationships among them, have been presented in a series of publications (e.g., Black 1985, 1988, 1989, 2000, 2002, 2004, 2013, 2018). The BI site inventory is representative of much of the known range of littoral archaeological sites in the QR as a whole (Black 2004:70-71, 2018).

Flaked-stone artifacts have been recovered from nine sites, representing twelve culture-historical components (table 4.1). These sites are, from oldest to most recent, Seebeskook (BgDq33), Rum Beach (BgDq24), Pocket Beach (BgDq27), Weir, Northeast Point (BgDq7), Camp (BgDq4), Lighthouse Cove (BgDr60), Pintlowes Cove (BgDr61), and Loyalist (BgDr66). The Weir site contains four stratified components; each of the other sites is treated here as a single component. The Rum Beach assemblage appears to date largely to the later part of the Terminal Archaic period (TA; ca. 3600−3000 BP). The Seebeskook site also probably is TA in age. The Pocket Beach site probably dates to the earlier part of the Early Maritime Woodland period (EMW; ca. 3000−2600 BP). Together, these sites represent the TA−EMW transition (Black 2018:40, 53, 55). The Weir-site components range from the later part of the EMW (ca. 2600−2200 BP) through the Middle Maritime Woodland (MMW; ca. 2200−1400 BP) to the earlier part of the Late Maritime Woodland (eLMW; ca. 1400−1000 BP). The Northeast Point site also dates to the eLMW, as does much of the material from the Camp site. The Lighthouse Cove and Pintlowes Cove sites date to the later part of the Late Maritime Woodland (lLMW; ca. 1000−400 BP). The Loyalist site is Historic period.

Table 4.1. Bliss Islands site inventory, cultural components and quantities of flaked lithics.

Borden Number	Site Name— Component Designation	Cultural Component	Amount of Flaked Stone (g)	Weir Site Flaked Stone (g)	Proportion of Weir site assemblage (%)	Proportion of site complex assemblage (%)
BgDq33	Seebeskook	Terminal Archaic	779.4			6.04
BgDq24	Rum Beach	Terminal Archaic	3297.1			25.56
BgDq27	Pocket Beach	earlier Early Maritime Woodland	279.1			2.16
BgDq6	Weir site— stratified assemblages	Early–Late Maritime Woodland	1534.8			11.90
	Weir site sc1	later Early Maritime Woodland		110.6	7.21	† [0.86]
	Weir site sc2	Early–Middle Maritime Woodland		99.5	6.48	[0.77]
	Weir site sc3	later Middle Maritime Woodland		249.7	16.27	[1.94]
	Weir site sc4	earlier Late Maritime Woodland		1075.0	70.04	[8.33]
BgDq7	Northeast Point	earlier Late Maritime Woodland	1567.2			12.15
BgDq4	Camp site	Early–Late Maritime Woodland	5289.0			41.00
BgDr60	Lighthouse Cove	later Late Maritime Woodland	42.1			0.33
BgDr61	Pintlowes Cove	later Late Maritime Woodland	69.7			0.54
BgDq5	Ledge	later Late Maritime Woodland	0.0			0.00
BgDr66	Loyalist site	Historic–Early Loyalist	41.8			0.32
		Totals	12,900.2	1534.8	100.00	100.00

† In the column at the right, the proportions shown in brackets are not summed to produce the total because these proportions are redundant on the proportion for the Weir site as a whole.

Lithic Material Assemblages

The amounts of flaked lithics from each of the analytical units on the BI are presented in table 4.1. A total of ca. 14.0 kg of flaked stone has been recovered, of which ca. 12.9 kg are analyzed here. This total includes both formal and expedient flaked-stone tools and flaked-lithic debitage. For each site, the total mass of flaked lithics recovered is shown, as well as the proportion each site assemblage represents of the total from the site inventory.[2] The BI assemblages vary substantially in the amount of flaked lithics each contains. About 61.5% of the lithic material comes from three components—Camp, Northeast Point, and Weir-site stratigraphic component 4 (or sc4)—dating largely to the eLMW.

The earlier assemblages were surface-collected from intertidal zones (Black 2018); the later assemblages were mostly excavated from land-based deposits, but some include surface-collected pieces. Excavation units were placed judgementally, usually to salvage areas most threatened by coastal erosion. Excavated areas and volumes vary considerably from site to site, both absolutely and as proportions of estimated extant site areas and volumes (Black 2004:24). On average, piece sizes are larger in the intertidal assemblages; this may reflect actual differences between earlier and later technologies (Black 2000; Sanger 2008) but also probably reflects lower rates of recovery of small pieces of lithic debitage from intertidal contexts (Black 2018:47). Variations among the assemblages are further complicated by factors influencing the preservation and characterization of lithic materials. For example, many felsic volcanics and some cherts are better preserved in shell-bearing deposits and less well preserved in peat and humic soil deposits.[3]

Thus, the lithic assemblages described here are not random samples of lithic assemblages on the BI. Moreover, some assemblages are too small to allow random sampling from within the assemblages for statistical purposes. For these reasons, the assemblages are not amenable to inferential statistical analyses. Descriptive analyses follow.

Predictably, the number of lithic material types identified in analytical units is positively correlated with the amounts of flaked lithics in the units, whether the lithics are quantified by piece count or by mass. The mass of lithic materials

---

2. A total of ca. 1.8 kg of flaked lithics has been catalogued from the Weir site; however, some lithics were recovered from erosional surfaces adjacent to the site and during preparation of site margins prior to formal excavation (Black 2004:27). Here, only the ca. 1.5 kg of flaked lithics recovered from formally excavated units, and thus assignable to stratified sub-assemblages, are considered.

3. Acidic soil environments, groundwater, and exposure to sunlight degrade unstable cryptocrystalline silica and other elements in the groundmasses of some volcanics and bleach the colour from them, producing chalky appearance and texture (Black 2011:114, 2018:46-48). Some cherts also are sensitive to exposure and acidity (Bouras and Evans 2006), and to intentional or accidental exposure to heat (Holyoke 2012:143-152), which produce surface sheen, hydration rinds, paler colours, and opaque white variegations. Gauthier and Burke (2011; Gauthier et al. 2012) explored the chemical effects of such weathering; their work suggests it may be possible to use non-destructive geochemical techniques to refine characterizations of bleached archaeological lithics.

from each component is only weakly correlated with the number of pieces recovered. This reflects the larger average size of artifacts recovered from the earlier components.

More surprising is the negative correlation between the amounts of flaked stone recovered and the volumes of material excavated for each component. This relates to the fact that, in the QR, flaked lithics are most frequently found associated with black-soil-dominated deposits. Black-soil deposits—which may incorporate dwelling floors (Hrynick and Black 2016)—are sometimes extensive in area, but usually are only a few centimetres in depth. In contrast, flaked lithics are rarely found associated with shell-dominated layers and features, which generally are more voluminous than black-soil deposits. These observations could partly be explained as reflecting differing functions of the two classes of deposits. However, a culture-historical phenomenon also is involved, since substantial gravel-based dwelling floors, associated with substantial shell middens in the MMW components, also contain few flaked lithics.

Historic Flaked Lithics

Only one Historic-period assemblage includes flaked lithics. The Loyalist site is interpreted as the homestead of Samuel Bliss (dating 1783–1803 CE), after whom the islands are currently named (Black and Blair 2000; C. R. Blair 2013). The flaked lithics consist of 12 gunflints made from European flint (e.g., Luedtke 1992:28-29, 121). While Historic-period lithic artifacts are not considered further here, the Loyalist gunflints illustrate two important points: (1) flaked-stone technology was important, not just for Indigenous people but for European newcomers as well, until as recently as two centuries ago; and (2) this specialized flaked-lithic assemblage, brought to the BI through an uncontroversial episode of migration, illustrates an extreme—100% exotic lithic material—never approached among the pre-Contact lithic assemblages.

Pre-Contact Flaked Lithics

Identification and sourcing of lithic materials have been approached conservatively. No non-arbitrary or completely unambiguous distinction between "local" and "exotic" lithic materials was possible. MacDonald (1994:3) introduced a distinction between the geological and anthropological meanings of the term "exotic," differentiating "geologically exotic" lithic materials (those brought into the QR by geological processes) from "culturally exotic" lithic materials (defined as those that can be inferred to have come from geological sources outside the QR, and to have been brought into the region through human activities). The focus has been to distinguish local from exotic materials and to source both local and culturally exotic materials. To add flexibility to the analytical system, MacDonald (1994:73) developed a sliding scale of exoticness, represented by five categories: local, probably local, possibly exotic, probably exotic, and exotic materials.

Lithic distribution data including all 54 types proved to be too unwieldy for graphic presentation. As a result, these types have been compressed to the 22 lithic material classes by amalgamating some similar types. Grouping has been focussed on local and probably local materials. Materials for which there are indications of exotic sources, materials which are inferred to be exotic, and materials sufficiently distinctive as to make sourcing feasible are retained as individual types.[4]

Figures 4.1 to 4.5 show a series of bar graphs presenting lithic material distributions for the eight more recent pre-Contact components (comparable graphs for the three earlier components are presented in Black 2018:42, 80, 81). The graphs are constructed using the same template for each in order to enhance comparability of data from component to component. The 22 lithic material classes are shown on the x axis of each graph, identified using the abbreviations introduced in the caption to figure 4.1. The materials are arranged to extend from local materials at the left to exotic materials at the right. Labels within the graphs show the division of the 22 lithic classes along the sliding scale of exoticness.

The y axis of each graph is calibrated to show mass in grams. The height of each bar in the graphs shows the amount of lithic material for the material type represented by the abbreviation below the bar. Because of the considerable disparity in total amounts per component and per material, the y axis scale varies from graph to graph. However, within each figure, graphs are shown with their y axes calibrated to the same scale.

Assemblages from Intertidal Sites

The lithic material distributions for the three intertidal assemblages are dominated by local and probably local materials, especially dark-coloured aphanitic volcanics, but include substantial amounts of light-coloured aphanitic volcanics, bleached volcanics and cherts, dull-coloured quartzites, and bull quartz (Black 2000, 2018:41-45, 80–81). Kineo-Traveler Mountain porphyry (KTMP) from central interior Maine is the only exotic material definitely associated with TA-style tools. In fact, the Rum Beach assemblage contains more KTMP than any other component on the islands.

Rum Beach also contains several artifacts made of flow-banded rhyolite. Initially, this distinctive volcanic was tentatively identified as the material that Doyle (1995:303; Bourque et al. 1984; Burke 2000:387) called banded-spherulitic

---

4. For additional information about the development of the BIPS, and for detailed descriptions of each of the 22 lithic classes graphed in figures 4.1–4.5, see the Appendix.

rhyolite, which outcrops on Vinalhaven Island in the Penobscot estuary and which is strongly associated with Turner Farm Occupation 3 (Bourque 1995:97-162; Doyle 1995:313) and other TA components in Maine (Bourque et al. 2006:322). It also bears some resemblance to Mount Jasper rhyolite from New Hampshire (Pollock et al. 2008b). However, the flow-banded rhyolite from Rum Beach is not completely consistent with hand specimens of either of those materials. Thus, it is referred to here as brown-grey flow-banded rhyolite and is classified as a possibly exotic material. It may be a non-spherulitic, flow-banded variant of the Vinalhaven material (Newton 1999:104), or it may have been acquired from one of the other flow-banded rhyolite sources noted by Doyle (1995:203), Rosenmeier (2011:362), and Pollock et al. (2008b), or from an undocumented source. Although it has not been identified in other BI assemblages, it has been identified in other QR intertidal assemblages.[5]

Assemblages from Excavated Sites

Weir Site

Figure 4.1 shows the entire flaked-lithic material assemblage from the Weir site. This assemblage is dominated by local and by probably local materials, such as bull quartz, quartzites, and aphanitic volcanics. There are few bleached lithics because the site is largely comprised of shell middens and other shell-bearing deposits. The Weir site contains several definitely exotic lithic materials, including KTMP, TOBR, and Minas Basin multicoloured chert (MBMC), as well as a diverse suite of other potentially exotic lithic materials.

When the lithic materials from the Weir site are considered as stratified sub-assemblages (figure 4.2), interesting patterns emerge. The earlier sub-assemblages, from sc1 and sc2, are dominated by local materials, especially volcanics. The sub-assemblage from sc2, representing the EMW−MMW transition (Black 2004:76-77), is the only assemblage on the BI in which TOBR is present. TOBR has been reported from Maine−Maritimes assemblages dating to the TA−EMW transition (S. E. Blair 2010:38-40; Burke 2006:423, 430; Gilbert 2011:139; Kingsbury and Hadlock 1951:25; Sanger 1971b, 2008:17-18, 33). It has not been reported from QR assemblages dating to the later parts of the Maritime Woodland. The sub-assemblage from sc3 (MMW) apparently contains only local and probably local lithic materials.[6]

---

5. Black (2018:44), Gilbert (2011:176, 225), and Gilbert et al. (2006a) present additional information about flow-banded rhyolites in QR assemblages, suggesting that some were acquired from local sources.

6. The small amounts of KTMP and POS-EMCC in the sc3 sub-assemblage (figure 4.2, lower left) almost certainly are intrusive because the same materials were found in sc4 in larger amounts immediately above where they occurred in sc3.

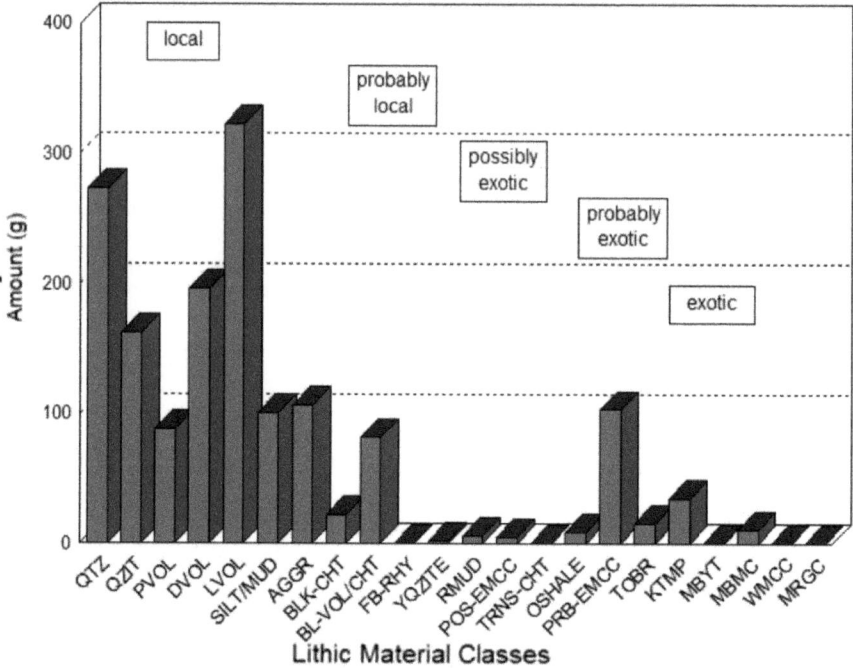

Figure 4.1. Weir site flaked lithic material distribution. Lithic Material Classes: Bull Quartz (QTZ), Quartzites (QZIT), Porphyritic Volcanics (PVOL), Dark Aphanitic Volcanics (DVOL), Light Aphanitic Volcanics (LVOL), Siltstones and Mudstones (SILT/MUD), Apple-green Glassy Rhyolite (AGGR), Mottled Black Chert (BLK-CHT), Bleached Volcanics and Cherts (BL-VOL/CHT), Brown-Grey Flow-banded Rhyolite (FB-RHY), Yellow Quartzite (YQZITE), Red Mudstone (RMUD), Possibly Exotic Multicoloured Cherts (POSS-EMCC), White-spotted Translucent Chert (TRNS-CHT), Orange Siliceous Shale (OSHALE), Probably Exotic Multicoloured Cherts (PRB-EMCC), Tobique Rhyolite/Chert (TOBR), Kineo-Traveler Mountain Porphyry (KTMP), Minas Basin Yellow Tuff (MBYT), Minas Basin Multicoloured Chert (MBMC), Washademoak Multicoloured Chert (WMCC), Munsungun Red and Green Chert (MRGC).

Both the amount and the density of lithics are much greater in the sc4 sub-assemblage than in the earlier sub-assemblages; about 70% of the Weir-site flaked-lithic assemblage is associated with sc4. There are two definite exotic lithic materials present: KTMP and MBMC. There is also a substantial proportion of material classified as probably exotic multicoloured chert, including some artifacts made from red and white moss agates and variegated cherts that may be MBMC variants. Several other potentially exotic lithic materials represented by single artifacts are considered in greater detail below.

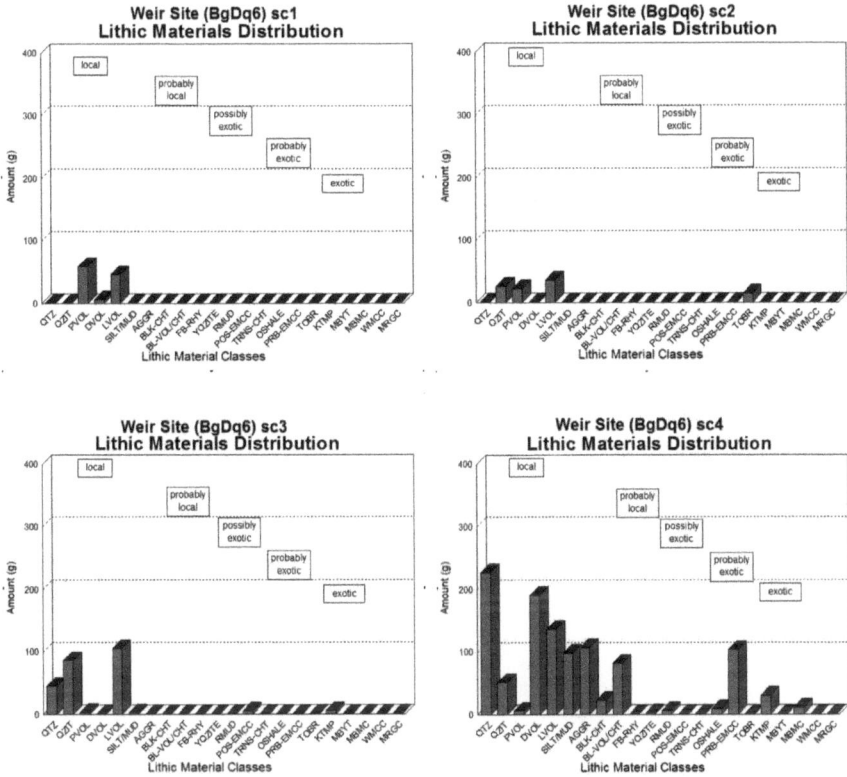

Figure 4.2. Weir site flaked lithic material distributions by stratigraphic component: *upper left,* sc1 (EMW); *upper right,* sc2 (EMW−MMW transition); *lower left,* sc3 (MMW); *lower right,* sc4 (eLMW).

Northeast Point Site

The Northeast Point lithic material distribution, shown in figure 4.3, is dominated by bleached volcanics and cherts because the assemblage was embedded in shell-free black soil and overlain by acidic peat. Despite its comparatively small volume and inferred brief period of occupation, Northeast Point yielded the most diverse assemblage of exotic and potentially exotic lithic materials on the BI.

Exotic materials include Munsungun red and green chert (MRGC), MBMC, and Minas Basin yellow tuff (MBYT)—a distinctive material associated with geological sources on the north shore of Minas Basin (Black 2011:116). Several scrapers made from brightly coloured red, white, and grey-blue variegated cherts, classified as possibly or probably exotic, may represent MBMC variants. The assemblage includes a single flake of KTMP and two artifacts made of Washademoak multicoloured chert (WMCC). The assemblage also includes several scrapers and flakes made of a material referred to as white-spotted translucent chert (TRNS-CHT), considered in more detail below.

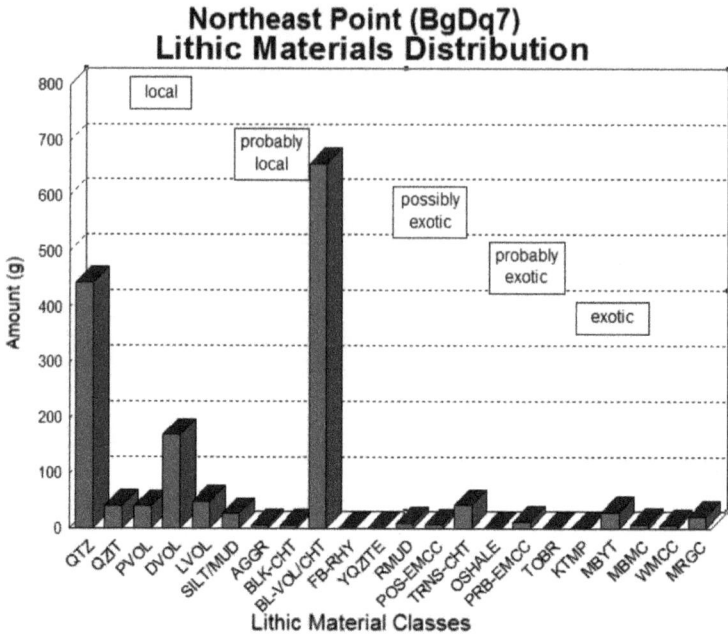

Figure 4.3. Northeast Point site flaked lithic material distribution.

Camp Site

The Camp site has yielded the largest lithic assemblage from the BI; diagnostic artifacts indicate that this site contains material contemporaneous with the Middle Woodland components at the Weir site, and material dating to the later part of the Historic period. However, the majority of the flaked-lithic artifacts from the Camp site are morphologically and technologically consistent with those from the eLMW components at Northeast Point and Weir sc4. The lithic material assemblage (figure 4.4) is dominated by local and probably local materials: quartz, quartzites, aphanitic volcanics, and mudstones. Bleached lithics are present due to surface exposure and humic soil.

The total amount of exotic lithic materials in the Camp site is greater than at either Weir or Northeast Point; however, their diversity is lower. While there are a few pieces of WMCC, most of the exotic material is MBMC and MBYT, including pieces consistent with variegated chert from the Davidson Cove quarry site (Deal 2001) near Scots Bay. In contrast to Northeast Point and Weir site sc4, no MRGC and no KTMP have been identified in the Camp site assemblage.

Camp Site (BgDq4)
Lithic Materials Distribution

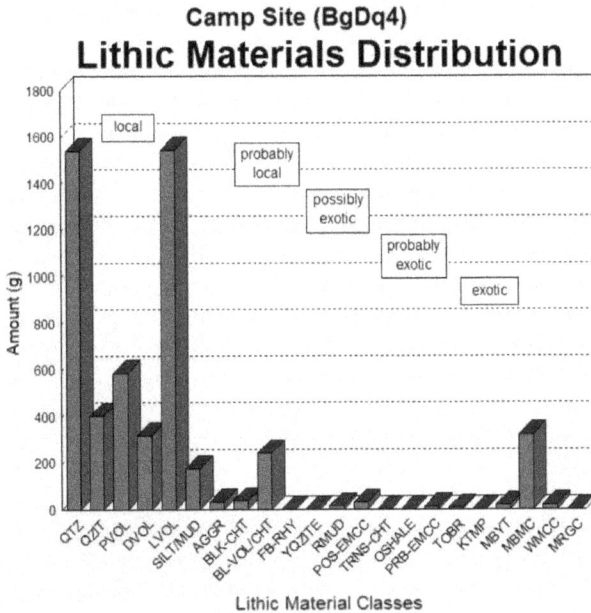

Figure 4.4. Camp site flaked lithic material distribution.

Lighthouse Cove and Pintlowes Cove Sites

Small numbers of lithics were recovered from two sites, Lighthouse Cove and Pintlowes Cove, dating to the lLMW. These are much smaller in extent and in volume than the eLMW components, and contain lower densities of artifacts. The lithic material distributions for these sites are shown in figure 4.5; only local and probably local materials are represented. There is one additional lLMW site on the BI, the Ledge site (BgDq5; Black 2004:41-42), from which no lithic artifacts have been recovered.

While the BI data indicate no use of exotic lithics during the centuries immediately before European contact, other assemblages dating to this time include exotic lithics. For example, MBMC, WMCC, and MRGC have been identified at Devil's Head site on the American side of the QR (Shaw 2016). And the BI assemblages do not exhaust exotic lithic types known from the QR; for example, despite their absence from the BI, Ramah chert artifacts have been recovered from Late Woodland components elsewhere (Gilbert 2011:183-185; Hrynick et al. 2017:96).

Some Cautionary Tales

Hand-specimen and low-power stereomicroscopic examinations of lithic materials have great potential for expanding knowledge of past human behaviour with respect to material choice and acquisition, manufacture and technology,

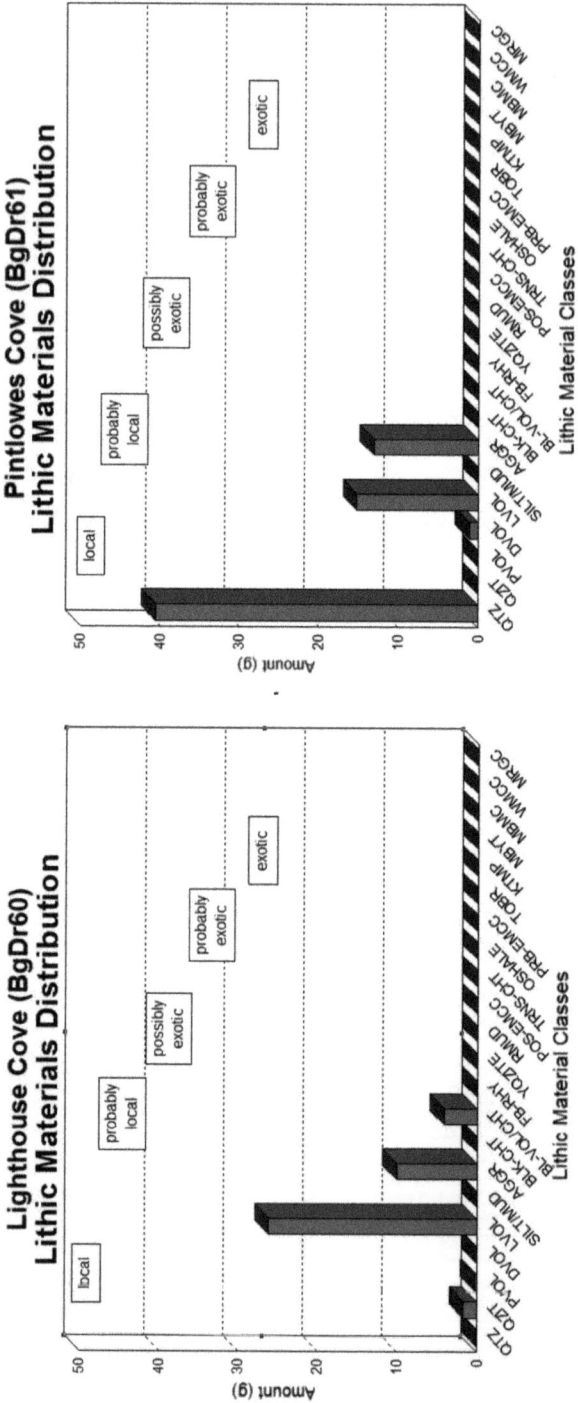

Figure 4.5. Lghthouse Cove site and Pintlowes Cove site flaked lithic material distributions.

and social interaction and exchange. Visual examinations are the essential initial steps in characterizing and identifying lithic materials. These techniques are non-destructive, and they are the only techniques that can be applied to every piece of lithic material recovered from the archaeological record. Recent advances in digital photography and web-based research dissemination have enhanced the ability of archaeologists to communicate the results of such studies and research tools based on them. These technical advances also may obviate some of the effort and expense involved in accumulating lithic comparative collections (Dincauze 1976) and have the potential to ameliorate some concerns about visual characterization techniques (Calogero 1992; Odell 2000:272-273). However, visual techniques have technical and empirical limitations (Reimer 2018:139). The examples below illustrate some analytical conundrums encountered among the BI assemblages.

There is Sometimes Only One

Finds of single formal tools or tool fragments made of unusual lithic materials, without associated debitage of the same material, are problematic in terms of material identification and sourcing. Such artifacts themselves reveal little about intra-material variability, and unique artifacts frequently are the least acceptable candidates for destructive analytical techniques. It is tempting to consider such artifacts to be culturally exotic—acquired as finished tools manufactured at a distance—a priori. Three examples of such finds, all from Weir site sc4 (figure 4.2, lower right), are illustrated in figures 4.6–4.8.

A biface tip (figure 4.6a–b) made of distinctive quartzite (figure 4.6c) was found on the west mound at the Weir site. Pebbles and cobbles of quartzite are common on QR shorelines and in adjacent areas. However, the yellow quartzite tool lacks cortex and, in colour and texture, is unlike local quartzites (Gilbert 2011:138, 227; Gilbert et al. 2006a). This material bears some resemblance to White Rock quartzite from southern Nova Scotia (Colwell and Ferguson 1992); similar quartzites ostensibly are present as cobbles on Prince Edward Island and on the Gulf of St. Lawrence shores of New Brunswick (MacDonald 1994:167), and as artifacts in some Nova Scotia sites (Rosenmeier 2011:40). Its association with other exotic lithic materials increases the likelihood that this artifact was brought from a distant source; however, this has not been determined definitively.

A scraper made of orange siliceous shale (figure 4.7a–b) also was found in the west mound at the Weir site. This material is orange-red, cryptocrystalline, opaque, and waxy, with occasional quartz micro-veins (figure 4.7c). The orange material is variegated at a fine scale by occasional patches of megaquartz and translucent grey chert, small irregular light-coloured spots, and very fine black dendrites. Although the material has been characterized as siliceous shale, in several respects it resembles red-hued radiolarian cherts from the Munsungun

Figure 4.6. Yellow Quartzite biface tip (BgDq6:2511): a) obverse face; b) reverse face; c) photomicrographs.

area (e.g., Category 1A; Pollock et al. 1999:275).[7] This artifact may represent an extreme of regional variations among radiolarian cherts, and may have been obtained from an unreported source of such materials. Again, the lack of debitage of similar material, the fact that scrapers from LMW contexts are frequently made from exotic materials, and the association of the artifact with those made of other unusual lithic materials increase the likelihood that it was brought from a distant source.

A side-notched projectile point (figure 4.8a–b) was found immediately beneath the peat soil on the central mound of the Weir site. Initially, the material was identified as black siltstone, and, following Crotts (1984:44-46), was categorized as local (Black 1989:478). Subsequently, Wilson (1991) noted some characteristics that suggest a volcanic origin for this material, referred to here as mottled black chert. It is indistinguishable in hand specimen from some variants of Touladie chert outcropping in the Lake Témiscouata area of Quebec (Burke 2000:385; Chalifoux and Burke 1995:252-254; Chalifoux et al. 1998:38; MacDonald 1994:142). However, for reasons discussed below, it cannot be identified as an exotic lithic material in the BI context.

Figure 4.7. Orange Siliceous Shale scraper (BgDq6:2643): a) ventral face; b) dorsal face; c) photomicrographs.

---

7. Siliceous shales and mudstones often are associated with, or intergrade into, radiolarian cherts (Gauthier et al. 2012; Jones and Murchey 1986).

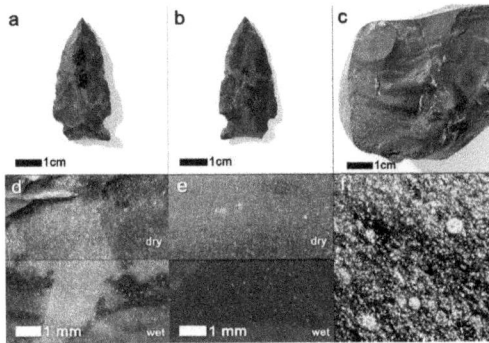

Figure 4.8. Mottled Black Chert side-notched projectile point (BgDq6:1901): a) obverse face; b) reverse face; c) Cobble 19, interior exposed; d) photomicrographs of projectile point; e) photomicrographs of Cobble 19; f) photomicrograph of a thin section from Cobble 19 (ca. 25 diameters magnification).

Beware the Look-Alikes

It is not always possible to determine whether a lithic material is local or exotic, much less specify a source for it, based on visual characteristics alone. Photographs and descriptions of lithic materials from the Touladie chert source in the upper Saint John drainage indicated (e.g., Burke and Chalifoux 1998; Chalifoux et al. 1998) that the mottled-black-chert projectile point (figure 4.8a–b) might be made of an exotic lithic material from that source. However, subsequent research revealed that macroscopically similar, geologically related, radiolarian cherts outcrop in Ordovician-aged formations in the Munsungun source area (e.g., on Norway Bluff; Pollock et al. 1999:274-276, 280; Burke 2000:387), on the Gaspé Peninsula (Chalifoux 1999; Gauthier et al. 2012) and on the west coast of Newfoundland (e.g., Coniglio 1987; James et al. 1987). Geologically related Ordovician-aged bedrocks also outcrop in northern New Brunswick (Potter et al. 1979), and these contain macroscopically similar radiolarian cherts (Thériault 2012). Moreover, Ordovician bedrocks, including chert, outcrop in the Oak Bay/St. Stephen area (Potter et al. 1979), the extreme northwestern portion of the QR (the Cookson Group, see McLeod et al. 1994), suggesting the possibility of a local source for this material.

Specifying a source for the mottled black chert was further complicated when a cobble of macroscopically similar material (figure 4.8c) was recovered from an intertidal context on the BI (Cobble 19, see MacDonald 1994:70). Like the projectile point, the material in this cobble is indistinguishable in hand specimen from some variants of Touladie chert (MacDonald 1994:142). Photomicrographs (figure 4.8d–e) indicate that while similar, the materials in the projectile point and the cobble are not identical in appearance; the projectile point is blacker and more vitreous, while the cobble is greener and waxier. A thin section from Cobble 19 (figure 4.8f) shows that the material is a fossiliferous chert, structurally similar to radiolarian cherts from the Munsungun source area.

Although nothing about Cobble 19 suggests it is culturally exotic, the possibility that it is a curated cobble of raw material that eroded from an archaeological context cannot be dismissed. However, it seems more likely that the cobble was geologically transported to the location where it was found. If so, it probably is derived from a nearby bedrock source, such as the Cookson Group.

Thus, the material from which the projectile point shown in figure 4.8a was made cannot be definitely identified as exotic. If it is an exotic material, the potential source areas are numerous and disparate, spanning ca. 1,500 km, at distances ranging from tens to hundreds of kilometres away. Largely because of the presence of Cobble 19, mottled black chert is categorized as probably local in this analysis. This projectile point represents a case where material sourcing may be resolvable only through the application of relatively non-destructive geochemical techniques (Reimer 2018:138); for example, laser ablation–inductively coupled plasma–mass spectrometry (Lavers 2010) or energy-dispersive X-ray fluorescence (Gauthier et al. 2012).

In the Right Ballpark

In the past, brightly coloured, high-quality cherts (agates, jaspers, chalcedonies, and carnelians) found in Maritime archaeological sites were sometimes ascribed to the relatively well-known Minas Basin/North Mountain source area in Nova Scotia in a rather off-hand manner (Burke 2000:229; Sanger 1987:78). Subsequent research has illuminated a wider range of potential sources for such materials within the Maritimes region (Black and Wilson 1999; S. E. Blair 1999; Burke 2000; Thériault 2013). Gilbert et al. (2005) proposed criteria for distinguishing between Mesozoic-associated cherts from Nova Scotia sources and Carboniferous-associated cherts from New Brunswick sources. The TRNS-CHT artifacts shown in figure 4.9 illustrate a case where such criteria can be used to roughly ascribe a lithic material to a source without specifying a particular source location.

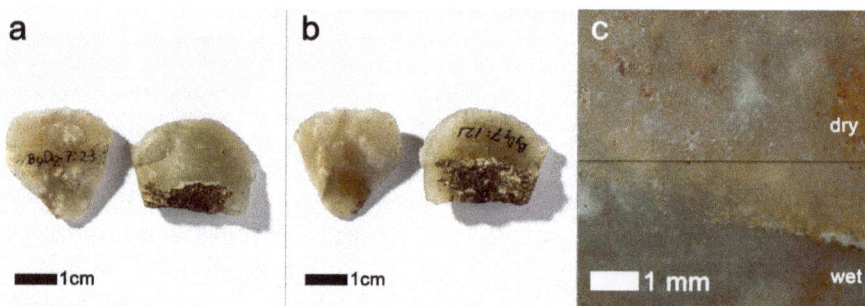

Figure 4.9. White-spotted Translucent Chert scrapers (BgDq7:23, 121a): a) dorsal faces; b) ventral faces; c) photomicrographs.

White-spotted translucent chert (TRNS-CHT) is a cryptocrystalline material that exhibits light pinkish, brownish, and greyish translucent areas (figure 4.9a–b), interspersed with amorphous, more opaque white spots (figure 4.9c). Some exterior surfaces consist of thin opaque white bands, which may represent either cortex or partial infillings of cavities in the parent material. The surfaces of these white bands often are stained brown, probably by contact with soil.

At the Northeast Point site, TRNS-CHT occurs as both formal unifacial tools and as debitage. However, this material was first identified in debitage recovered from Unit 1 at the Partridge Island site, the only excavated portion of that site dominated by black-soil midden (Bishop 1994:22-23; MacDonald 1994:96 -101). This debitage assumed increased significance when MacDonald (1994:46-48; Black 2002:307) recognized that Partridge Island Unit 1 represents an eLMW component comparable to the Northeast Point site and Weir site sc4. TRNS-CHT was subsequently identified in other lithic assemblages in the QR: Deer Island Point (Gilbert 2011:235-236) and Devil's Head (Shaw 2016:38). It has not been identified in archaeological assemblages elsewhere in New Brunswick or further afield.

With respect to sourcing, Wilson (1983) adopted the conservative position that this material was geologically associated with local volcanics. MacDonald (1994:144) speculated that it might come from a Minas Basin/North Mountain or Grand Manan basalt-associated source. Subsequently, Wilson (1994) detected evidence indicating this material is a carbonate-hosted chert. This interpretation was reinforced when Black and Wilson (1999) conducted research on Carboniferous-associated chert outcropping around the edges of the New Brunswick Lowlands.

Several characteristics of TRNS-CHT—overall translucency, colour range, and vague variegation—are more consistent with Carboniferous-associated cherts than Mesozoic-associated ones, although it does not exhibit some characteristics common in cherts from the Belyeas Cove source on Washademoak Lake (Black and Wilson 1999), such as carnelian colouring, strain fracturing, and botryoidal chalcedony silica fabrics (Gilbert et al. 2005). At both Northeast Point (figure 4.3) and Deer Island Point (Gilbert 2011:71), TRNS-CHT is associated with WMCC completely consistent with materials observed at the Belyeas Cove source. However, no consistent association between these two material types can be demonstrated. No material similar to TRNS-CHT has been observed at Belyeas Cove, and it is not associated with WMCC in the Camp site (figure 4.4). Moreover, when a substantial amount of WMCC was identified in the Wallace Cove (BgDq29) Unit E1 assemblage (Black 2003b), from an eLMW feature structurally and contextually similar to those at Northeast Point (located 2 km distant), no TRNS-CHT was identified.

Thus, for this analysis, TRNS-CHT is classified as possibly exotic. However, the most parsimonious explication of the material, considering its expression, its distribution, and its characteristics, is that it is geologically exotic to the QR—originating from an unknown source in the Carboniferous bedrocks of the New Brunswick Lowlands, located glacially and fluvially upstream from the QR shores—but culturally local, in that Indigenous people used it only in small amounts when they encountered it in secondary geological deposits.

Patience Pays

Sourcing lithic materials based on visual characteristics often is dependent on the intersection of detailed source information and appropriate technical capabilities for examining archaeological specimens. The flakes shown in figure 4.10, part of a cluster of lithic debitage recovered from the Northeast Point site, illustrate such a case. The material from which these flakes are made exhibits dusky red opaque and green semi-translucent bands, separated by a complex irregular transitional band, light brown in colour, speckled with green (figure 4.10a–b). Initially, because of the green portion, this material was thought to be a variant of the green chert defined by MacDonald (1994:159–160) and was categorized as possibly exotic.

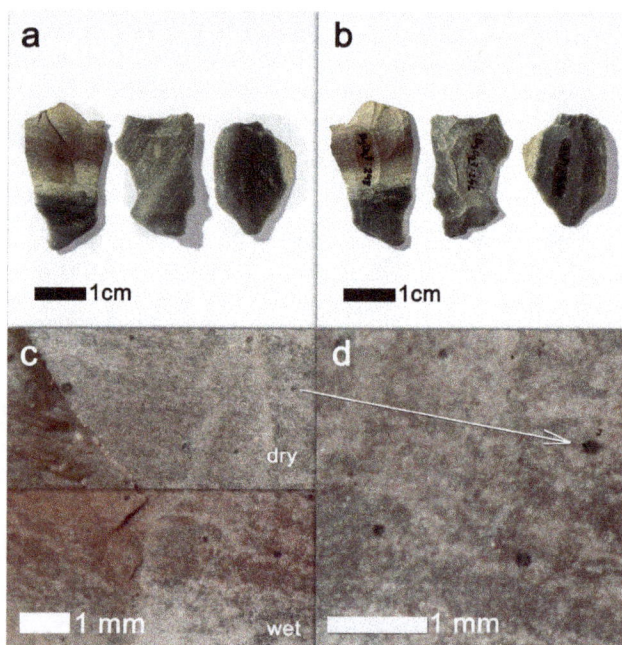

Figure 4.10. Munsungun Red and Green Chert biface reduction flakes (BgDq7:248, 246a and b): a) dorsal faces; b) ventral faces; c) photomicrographs (BgDq7:248); d) photomicrograph of probable chlorite-replaced radiolarian fossils.

However, artifacts and debitage made from green-hued translucent, semi-translucent, and opaque lithic materials of varying qualities are common in QR assemblages. Moreover, cobbles of such materials have been recovered from intertidal deposits on the BI, and elsewhere in the QR. These green lithic materials have been variously identified as cherts, felsic volcanics, or very fine-grained quartzites, and primary and secondary sources of such materials are widely distributed in New Brunswick. The relationships among these materials and their ultimate bedrock sources have not been worked out in any detail. As a provisional approach, a variety of such materials have been lumped together as apple-green glassy rhyolite and categorized as probably local. The debitage cluster from Northeast Point does not fit comfortably in this category.

When C. D. Gilbert photographed the Bliss Islands Petrographic Series for digital data-basing, he had access to a broader range of detailed material descriptions in the published literature than was available during the earlier BI analyses. And he was able to take high-quality photomicrographs of the archaeological type specimens using a Nikon stereo-microscope. Gilbert recognized similarities among the Northeast Point banded flakes and radiolarian cherts from the Munsungun source area (Burke 2000:387). While taking the photomicrographs (figure 4.10c), he observed small circular green features in the brown transitional bands (figure 4.10d), resembling the chlorite-replaced radiolarian microfossils illustrated by Pollock et al. (1999:280-281). As a result, the debitage cluster from Northeast Point can be identified confidently as an exotic lithic material—MRGC (cf. Category 1D, see Pollock et al. 1999:275).

Refitted overlapping flakes indicate that the banded debitage from Northeast Point results from the manufacture of a bifacial tool; however, no formal artifact made from MRGC was recovered. In this case, material from a distant source was identified from debitage alone, reinforcing the importance of analyzing debitage as well as formal tools.

Discussion and Conclusions

Lithic material assemblages are one of several dimensions—including site structures, subsistence practices, settlement patterns, lithic and ceramic technologies—changes in which reflect the dynamic adaptations of Ancestral Peskotomuhkatiyik to the Quoddy Region. The Bliss Islands analysis goes some way toward achieving the proximate goals of lithic material studies by revealing the imprint of past lithic acquisition practices on the archaeological record over about 3,500 years. It has been apparent for some time that pre-Contact lithic material acquisition and exchange patterns in the Maine–Maritimes area varied among macro-scale culture-historic periods. During the Paleo-American period, flaked-stone tools were frequently made from brightly coloured, cryptocrystalline cherts, often obtained from distant sources through direct acquisition. During the Archaic period, and particularly during the Terminal Archaic, most flaked-stone tools were made from dull-coloured, somewhat intractable, porphyritic or flow-banded rhyolites; these materials usually were obtained locally or through short-distance transport and exchange. During the Maritime Woodland period, preferences shifted again to include cryptocrystalline cherts and other brightly coloured lithic materials, acquired both locally and from further afield. The results of the Bliss Islands study are consistent with this macro-scale diachronic patterning. However, the data presented here indicate that smaller-scale variations in lithic material preferences within the Maritime Woodland period were equally dramatic.

Wilson and Crotts came to different conclusions about the prevalence of exotic lithics in QR sites because, while the former analyzed both Middle and Late Maritime Woodland components and considered both formal tools and debitage, the latter analyzed largely Late Maritime Woodland components and considered only formal tools. Crotts inferred little temporal variation in usage of local and exotic lithic materials, and Sanger generalized this interpretation in his formulation of the Quoddy Tradition, because earlier Late Maritime Woodland lithic assemblages dominated the sites they investigated. Quantifying lithic materials by mass, analyzing both formal tools and debitage, and distinguishing stratified subsamples indicates lower proportions of exotics than estimated by Crotts and Sanger, but larger amounts than estimated by Wilson, and reveals that exotic lithic materials are unevenly distributed both temporally and spatially.

All pre-Contact lithic material assemblages on the Bliss Islands are predominated by locally available quartz, quartzites, and aphanitic volcanics acquired from exposed bedrocks and surficial deposits. The proportions of these materials vary from assemblage to assemblage; dark-coloured volcanics are more common in the earlier assemblages, while lighter-coloured materials are more common in the later ones. The Indigenous inhabitants of the QR lived adjacent to the littoral zone. They crossed the littoral every time they launched a boat and whenever they hunted, fished, and collected intertidal and subtidal foodstuffs. Local lithic materials were available to them at virtually all times, from a few steps away to a few minutes away, either on foot or by boat. They presumably procured local lithic materials during routine subsistence activities and travel, in close proximity to the habitation sites where they reduced those materials and manufactured artifacts from them.

Thus, distributions of local lithic materials can be understood as part of the resource catchment of the QR's inhabitants. In contrast, to understand the presence of exotic lithic materials in these assemblages and to approach the ultimate aims of lithic material sourcing involves considering the social catchment—in Rosenmeier's (2011:101) terms—of pre-Contact peoples. Indigenous inhabitants of the Bliss Islands and other places in the QR acquired and used exotic lithic materials during three periods: the Terminal Archaic-Early Maritime Woodland transition, the Early−Middle Maritime Woodland transition, and the Late Maritime Woodland period. Exotic lithic assemblages suggest that their patterns of social relationships changed through time.

During the Terminal Archaic−Early Maritime Woodland transition, Indigenous people acquired KTMP from Maine. They also may have acquired exotic flow-banded rhyolites from coastal New England, or used local rhyolites in imitation of materials used further to the south. Their social catchment appears to have been oriented to the south and west, perhaps to connect with neighbouring groups using Broadpoint technologies (e.g., Black 2018).

During the Early Woodland period, and the Early−Middle Maritime Woodland transition, Ancestral Peskotomuhkatiyik acquired small amounts of exotic lithics—cryptocrystalline cherts and TOBR—from traditional Wolastoqey and Mi'kmaq territories in central and eastern New Brunswick. Their social catchment apparently was oriented to the north and east, opposite in direction to the previous period, perhaps because nodes of Early Maritime Woodland habitation and ceremonialism developed then on the Saint John (S. E. Blair 2003; Pelletier-Michaud 2017; Turnbull 1990) and Miramichi (Blair and Ward 2013) river systems.

At least from the point of view of lithic material distributions, the social catchment of Ancestral Peskotomuhkatiyik appears to have reached its greatest extent during the Late Maritime Woodland period. During that time, they acquired exotic lithics from sources in coastal Nova Scotia, interior Maine, and interior New Brunswick. In contrast to earlier times, exotics were predominantly brightly coloured, variegated cherts, the most common from sources on the shores of the Minas Basin/North Mountain area of Nova Scotia. The social catchment of people living in the QR included the inhabitants of much of the Wabanaki homeland, and there is occasional evidence (e.g., Ramah chert) for connections to groups as far away as Labrador. At the same time, materials local to the QR appear in assemblages some distance away (e.g., scrapers made of Perry Formation grey quartzite in the Late Maritime Woodland Goddard-site assemblage, at the mouth of the Penobscot River, in Maine).

Evidence of exotic lithic use is most common in components dating to the earlier part of the Late Maritime Woodland. On the Bliss Islands there are at least three cultural components dating between ca. 1500 BP and ca. 1000 BP, each containing a qualitatively and quantitatively distinctive suite of exotics. In well-preserved components (e.g., Northeast Point and Weir site sc4), lithic material assemblages appear to vary from feature to feature. These components plausibly represent a series of distinct occupations of the islands by small groups of people over several centuries.

While some evidence of later Late Maritime Woodland activities may be occulted in mixed components spanning considerable periods (e.g., the Camp site), separate components containing exotic lithic materials from that time are absent from the Bliss Islands and remain relatively elusive elsewhere in the QR. This may in part result from changes in settlement patterns between the earlier and later parts of the Late Maritime Woodland (Blair et al. 2017). However, Hrynick et al. (2017) have recently presented evidence that Ancestral Peskotomuhkatiyik continued to acquire exotic lithics through the Late Maritime Woodland and into the Protohistoric period, as did their contemporaries elsewhere in the Maritimes (e.g., Betts and Holyoke 2019:233-238).

Acquisition of exotics was more important in some periods than in others. In contrast to the Late Maritime Woodland period, there is little evidence for use of exotic lithic materials during the Middle Maritime Woodland; rather, Ancestral Peskotomuhkatiyik continued to make flaked-stone tools from volcanics similar to those favoured in earlier periods, and began to use more quartz. This lack of exotic materials does not mean that their social catchment was restricted within the boundaries of the QR. The lack does, however, suggest that if the social catchment of the Middle Maritime Woodland was embodied materially, it was embodied in some other artifactual medium (ceramics, for example).[8]

A community-scale study like the one reported here contributes to the ultimate goals of lithic material analyses but can only hint at the shapes that larger-scale interpretations eventually will take. Since the bulk of lithic materials evidence, on the Bliss Islands and elsewhere in the QR, dates to the earlier part of the Late Maritime Woodland, those assemblages currently present the most rewarding evidence with which to approach questions of the cultural practices through which Ancestral Peskotomuhkatiyik acquired exotic materials and the meanings those materials held for them.

Exotic lithics have been recovered in small amounts; however, their acquisition during the earlier Late Maritime Woodland appears to have been pervasive and persistent. Ancestral Peskotomuhkatiyik invested time, effort, and thought into acquiring exotics. And, as S. E. Blair (2010) and Shaw (2016) have emphasized, the acquisition and movement of these materials must be understood in the context of boat-based transportation.

8. A reviewer of this chapter pointed out that "some of the temporal/cultural changes in stone raw material use patterns seen in the Bliss Islands might be highly local, rather than more broadly applicable to the Maritimes/Far Northeast." While the details of raw material use can be expected to vary from site to site and from area to area, the overall pattern of changes may be broadly detectable in the coastal Northeast (e.g., Black 2002:314). Note, in particular, the pattern of pre-Contact lithic material use recently reported from Port Joli Harbour, Nova Scotia (see Betts and Holyoke 2019, esp. figure 7.47).

The exotic lithic materials that Ancestral Peskotomuhkatiyik acquired during the Late Maritime Woodland period are not obviously technologically superior to the local materials that they used. Moreover, they worked exotic materials similarly to local materials. They did not use them to manufacture technologically distinctive projectile points (as Paleo-Americans did with comparable materials); in fact, during the Late Maritime Woodland, exotics and brightly coloured local lithics were used most frequently to make small formal and informal scraping and cutting tools. Nor did they use exotics to make artifacts for incorporation into ceremonial features and caches (as their Archaic and Early Woodland predecessors sometimes did). Nevertheless, ancestral Peskotomuhkati motivations for acquiring exotics must have transcended the merely utilitarian. At the resolution afforded by the archaeological record, it appears that Peskotomuhkati aesthetics with respect to lithic materials changed abruptly and dramatically at the Middle-Late Maritime Woodland transition. Exotic materials apparently held value and conveyed meaning in Late Maritime Woodland culture.

There are several ways that exotic lithics might have come to the QR. First, they could have been transported directly: Ancestral Peskotomuhkatiyik could have acquired exotic lithics by, for example, canoeing across the Bay of Fundy to places like Scots Bay and Davidson Cove, bringing chert back to the QR. On the other hand, Ancestral Mi'kmaq could have travelled across the Bay of Fundy bringing chert artifacts and raw materials with them. Direct access would have required long-distance travel and formal inter-ethnic social and economic relationships between Ancestral Peskotomuhkatiyik and neighbouring groups.

Second, exotic lithics could have been acquired indirectly through circulatory/exchange practices: At one extreme, exotic lithic assemblages may be the imprint left on the archaeological record by the cumulative results of socially prescribed, but rather informal, hand-to-hand gifts and exchanges of artifacts and materials between individuals over several centuries. At the other extreme, Ancestral Peskotomuhkatiyik may have participated in a formally structured, ritualized, seasonally constrained, circulatory/exchange system that provided regular access to exotic lithics and other valuables. In either case, exotic lithics may have held intrinsic value, or they may have functioned as catalysts for the exchange of other goods, and as symbolic reinforcements for various types of social relationships.

The practices and meanings outlined above are not mutually exclusive. Late Maritime Woodland exotic lithic assemblages, as currently known in the QR, may be consistent with any or all of them. Many more community-scale studies of lithic material assemblages from the Quoddy Region and adjacent areas must be compared and contrasted to produce better substantiated understandings of lithic material acquisition, and more nuanced interpretations of interactions among the Maritime Woodland peoples of the Far Northeast.

Acknowledgements

The Bliss Islands Archaeology Project's fieldwork and analyses have been funded by the Social Sciences and Humanities Research Council of Canada, Government of New Brunswick Archaeological Services, and the University of New Brunswick. I thank Susan Blair, Chris Blair, Bob Bosien, Adrian Burke, Éric Chalifoux, Drew Gilbert, Ken Holyoke, Al Honsinger, Gabe Hrynick, David Keenlyside, Philip LaPorta, Shianne MacDonald, Leah Rosenmeier, David Sanger, Christian Thériault, Chris Turnbull, and Lucy Wilson for their assistance, inspiration, and encouragement. Anita Crotts provided copies of colour plates from her thesis. Steven Cox provided hand specimens of Vinalhaven banded-spherulitic rhyolite and insights into the Goddard assemblage. Chris Brouillette provided hand specimens of Mount Jasper rhyolite, and Brent Murphy several Newfoundland cherts. Steve Powell provided access to specimens of White Rock quartzite. The photographs in figures 4.6–4.10 were taken by Drew Gilbert, using techniques developed by him (e.g., Gilbert 2011), with the exception of figure 4.8f, photographed by Lucy Wilson. Christian Thériault translated the abstract.

Appendix. The Bliss Islands Petrographic Series: Identification and Classification.

Purpose

The purposes of this typology are to facilitate measuring variability among Quoddy Region pre-Contact lithic material assemblages and to identify potential sources for the material types specified.

History

Understandings of the lithic materials recovered from the Bliss Islands (BI) sites have developed incrementally over the past three decades. The following is a brief summary of the development of the BI Petrographic Series (BIPS), including 54 lithic material types identified in the BI assemblages. Lucy Wilson (1991, 1994) worked with Shianne MacDonald (1994:140-169) to develop the first iteration of the BIPS, which has been modified and extended in the years since (e.g., Gilbert and Black 2006). Initial interpretations were established through participation in three lithic material workshops: Chalifoux and Burke (1993), Sanger (1994), and Black and Keenlyside (1996). Descriptions in the published literature, lithic specimens held by various institutions, and the opinions of colleagues have informed interpretations of material identities and potential source locations. Petrographic series subsequently developed for various nearby areas (e.g., Black 2003a; S. E. Blair 1999; Gilbert 2011; Shaw 2016) have been patterned on the model developed then.

Characterization

Lithic types were defined by examining each lithic artifact in sequence and using the first piece of each material type encountered as a type specimen. If the next piece examined could be convincingly included in a material type already defined, it was identified as belonging to that type, and the description of the type was modified as necessary. If the next piece examined could not be included in a type already described, a new material type was defined, and that piece became the type specimen. Thus, as the analysis progressed and as the number of lithic material types increased, the variability within types and the distinctions among types became more evident.

Lithics were examined in hand specimens, using magnifying devices and stereo-microscopes of various strengths. Rock type, mineralogy, colours and colour variegation, translucency and patterning in translucency, fracturing characteristics and fracture-surface appearance, presence/absence and characteristics of cortex, jointing, weathering, flaws, inclusions, and other salient characteristics were assessed and described. Petrographic thin-section analysis was employed to supplement visual characterizations for a few types (e.g., Black 2011:116-117).

Source Identification

Identification and sourcing of lithic materials have been approached conservatively. It became clear early in the research process that no non-arbitrary or completely unambiguous distinction between "local" and "exotic" lithic materials was possible. MacDonald (1994:3) introduced a crucial distinction between the geological and anthropological meanings of the term "exotic." She distinguished between "geologically exotic" lithic materials (those brought into the Quoddy Region [QR] by geological processes) and "culturally exotic" lithic materials (those brought into the QR by people).

The focus of the research was to distinguish local from exotic materials and to source both local and culturally exotic materials. To facilitate this, and to add flexibility to the analytical system, MacDonald (1994:73) developed a sliding scale of exoticness represented by five categories: local, probably local, possibly exotic, probably exotic, and exotic materials.

At one end of this scale are local lithic materials, designated using these criteria:

- similarity to materials occurring in QR bedrocks and surficial geological deposits;
- presence of cobble cortex on some specimens;

- red-stained cortex indicating the material is derived from clasts in locally outcropping conglomerates (e.g., the Perry Formation, see Schluger 1973);
- presence in relatively larger amounts in several assemblages; and/or
- occurrence in a range of artifact types—cores, blocks and shatter, reduction flakes, utilized flakes, and formal unifacial and/or bifacial tools.

Several series of bedrocks that outcrop in the QR contain lithic materials with properties appropriate for the manufacture of flaked-stone tools. These include silt/mudstones, quartzites and cherts from the Perry Formation, and bull quartz and aphanitic volcanics from the Mascarene Group (see McLeod et al. 1994). The presence of cortex and other features indicate that local lithic materials were frequently obtained from cobbles collected in the intertidal zones (cf. Pearson 1970:184).

MacDonald (1994) sampled 95 cobbles, derived from eroded bedrock and glacial deposits, from three intertidal zones on the BI. The cobbles were not randomly selected; fine-grained materials that might have been used to make flaked-stone tools were specifically targeted. This cobble collection is dominated by bull quartz, quartzites, light- and dark-coloured aphanitic volcanics, siltstones, and mudstones. This range of materials facilitated determining which archaeological materials were categorized as local and probably local (MacDonald 1994:70). Only two among the 95 specimens collected are materials that might be confused with suspected exotic materials observed in the archaeological assemblages. One of these, a small clast of variegated chert, is somewhat different in appearance from the cherts observed in the flaked-stone assemblages. Small clasts of chert have been reported from some QR conglomerates and surficial deposits on both the Canadian (Sabina 1972:27) and American (Brockman and Keegan 2016:49) sides of the QR. The other, a cobble of black and grey mottled chert, referred to here as mottled black chert, might be confused with exotic chert/mudstones from distant sources.

At the opposite end of the scale, lithic materials are suspected of being exotic based on these criteria:

- absence of visually similar materials in QR bedrocks and surficial geological deposits;
- presence in relatively small amounts, in relatively few assemblages;
- presence as a single formal tool, or a few tools, and/or as spatially or technologically restricted clusters of debitage; and/or
- association with other materials suspected of being exotic.

Particular material types were confirmed as being exotic when it was determined that they are consistent with lithic materials that are (arguably) available only from specific source locations at a distance from the QR. Between the two extremes are a series of materials categorized as to the likelihood of their being exotic based on current information. Various materials have been shifted from one category to another as the analysis has progressed; further revisions will become necessary as additional information accumulates.

Aspiration

The BIPS is an etic classification of pre-Contact lithic materials; the study has been conducted within a Western scientific framework and based in Western geological conceptions, understandings, and classifications of rocks and minerals. One of the aspirations of the study is that this etic framework may elicit emic understandings of Indigenous lithic materials use.

Table A.1. Flaked-Lithic Materials Identified in the Bliss Islands Prehistoric Assemblages.

Lithic Material	Abbreviation (illustrations)	Description (structure; texture; colours; transparency; lustre; fracture; features/inclusions; type; common names)	Source Category (source locations)	Relevant Sources
Bull Quartz	QTZ (Black 2018:11; Gilbert et al. 2006a)	Massive; inter-grown crystals; opaque milk-white, translucent light grey and/or transparent; vitreous to greasy; conchoidal, sub-conchoidal, blocky; occasional veins and inclusions of dark-coloured minerals; occasional cobble cortex, sometimes stained red; volcanic, hydrothermal precipitates	LOCAL (vein fills in volcanic bedrocks; clasts in sedimentary bedrocks and surficial deposits)	Brockman and Keegan 2016:40; MacDonald 1994:141, 169
Quartzites	QZIT (Black 2018:29, 79, 81; Gilbert et al. 2006a)	Massive; medium- to fine-grained interlocking crystals, sugary; greys, light browns, salmon pink; opaque or semi-translucent; vitreous; conchoidal, sub-conchoidal; occasional cobble cortex, sometimes stained red; metamorphic, non-foliated	LOCAL (clasts in sedimentary bedrocks and surficial deposits)	MacDonald 1994:146-147

Lithic Material	Abbreviation (illustrations)	Description (structure; texture; colours; transparency; lustre; fracture; features/inclusions; type; common names)	Source Category (source locations)	Relevant Sources
Porphyritic Volcanics	PVOL (Black 2018:77)	Massive or flow-banded; porphyritic/aphanitic; light green, light grey, dark brown, black; mostly opaque; vitreous to dull; conchoidal, sub-conchoidal; phenocrysts predominantly feldspars and micas, varying in size and colour; occasionally pitted from weathering of phenocrysts; occasional vugs; occasional cobble cortex; volcanics, felsic to intermediate	LOCAL (volcanic bedrocks; clasts in sedimentary bedrocks and surficial deposits)	MacDonald 1994:141, 157–158
Dark Fine-Grained Volcanics	DVOL (Black 2018:2, 31, 32, 43)	Massive or flow-banded; aphanitic; dark greens, dark greys, black; mostly opaque; vitreous to dull; conchoidal, sub-conchoidal; occasional surface bleaching to light green or grey; occasional cobble cortex, sometimes stained red; volcanics, intermediate to mafic	LOCAL (volcanic bedrocks; clasts in sedimentary bedrocks and surficial deposits)	MacDonald 1994:162, 167–169
Light Fine-Grained Volcanics	LVOL (Black 2018:31, 38)	Massive or flow-banded; aphanitic; light greens, blues, greys, light browns; mostly opaque; vitreous to dull; conchoidal, sub-conchoidal; sometimes porphyritic at micro-scale; occasional vugs; occasional surface bleaching to white or pink; occasional cobble cortex; volcanics, felsic to intermediate	LOCAL (volcanic bedrocks; clasts in sedimentary bedrocks and surficial deposits)	MacDonald 1994:142, 147, 159
Siltstones and Mudstones	SILT/MUD	Layered (and/or laminated); fine-grained; light greens, dark greys, red-browns, purple; opaque; waxy to dull; conchoidal, sub-conchoidal, splintery; occasional striped or banded variegation; occasional silica veins; occasional cobble cortex, sometimes stained red; sedimentary, detrital	LOCAL (clasts in sedimentary bedrocks and surficial deposits)	MacDonald 1994:157–158, 162

Lithic Material	Abbreviation (illustrations)	Description (structure; texture; colours; transparency; lustre; fracture; features/inclusions; type; common names)	Source Category (source locations)	Relevant Sources
Apple-Green Glassy Rhyolite	AGGR (Black 2018:30, 31, 37; Gilbert et al. 2006a)	Massive or flow-banded; fine-grained; light to dark grey-green; semi-translucent to opaque; vitreous; conchoidal, sub-conchoidal; occasional white spots; occasional vugs; some surface bleaching to light green or white; probable felsic volcanic, but may be chert or very fine-grained quartzite (category may include all of these)	PROBABLY LOCAL (volcanic bedrocks; clasts in sedimentary bedrocks and surficial deposits)	MacDonald 1994:159–160
Mottled Black Chert	BLK-CHT (figure 4.8, this chapter)	Massive or layered; fine-grained; light greys, dark greys; opaque; waxy to dull; conchoidal; mottled variegation; sedimentary, chert-mudstone	PROBABLY LOCAL (Ordovician-aged bedrocks; clasts in surficial deposits; widespread potential exotic sources)	Burke 2000: 169–185; Chalifoux and Burke 1993; Pollock 1987; Thériault 2012
Bleached Volcanics and Cherts	BL-VOL/CHT (Black 2018:20, 40, 46, 52)	Massive, flow-banded or layered; fine-grained to cryptocrystalline; white to light grey; opaque; waxy to dull; conchoidal, sub-conchoidal; materials bleached to chalky white (so cannot be further identified using visual techniques); most probably local volcanics, some may be bleached cherts	PROBABLY LOCAL (volcanic bedrocks; clasts in sedimentary bedrocks and surficial deposits)	MacDonald 1994:154
Brown-Grey Flow-Banded Rhyolite	FB-RHY (Black 2018:18, 24, 39, 47; Gilbert et al. 2006a)	Flow-banded; aphanitic; dark browns and grey-blues; mostly opaque, occasional translucency; vitreous to dull; conchoidal, sub-conchoidal, splintery; frequent weathered joint surfaces; volcanic, intermediate	POSSIBLY EXOTIC (volcanic bedrocks; clasts in sedimentary bedrocks and surficial deposits)	Bourque et al. 1984; Doyle 1995; Pollock et al. 2008
Yellow Quartzite	YQZITE (figure 4.6, this chapter)	Massive; medium- to fine-grained interlocking crystals, sugary; yellow-gold; translucent; vitreous; conchoidal; metamorphic, non-foliated	POSSIBLY EXOTIC (possible sources in Nova Scotia and Prince Edward Island)	Colwell and Ferguson 1992; MacDonald 1994:167

Lithic Material	Abbreviation (illustrations)	Description (structure; texture; colours; transparency; lustre; fracture; features/inclusions; type; common names)	Source Category (source locations)	Relevant Sources
Red Mudstone	RMUD (Clarke 2016:64, 66	Layered (and/or laminated); fine-grained; dusky red; opaque; waxy to dull; conchoidal, sub-conchoidal, splintery; occasional fine white specks; occasional fine linear fractures filled with silica; sedimentary, detrital; siliceous shale, mudstone	POSSIBLY EXOTIC (Ordovician-aged sedimentary bedrocks; clasts in surficial deposits)	Clarke 2015:52; MacDonald 1994:152-153; Pollock et al. 1999
Possibly Exotic Multi-Coloured Cherts	POSS-EMCC (Black 2018:45)	Layered; micro- to crypto-crystalline; white, reds, blues, greys; opaque or patchy translucency; waxy to dull; conchoidal, sub-conchoidal; distinct, minute variegation; volcanic or sedimentary, hydrothermal precipitates; jasper, agate, chalcedony	POSSIBLY EXOTIC (volcanic bedrocks; clasts in sedimentary bedrocks and surficial deposits)	Booth 2003:92–99; MacDonald 1994:154, 165–166
White-Spotted Translucent Chert	TRNS-CHT (figure 4.9, this chapter)	Nodular (or layered); micro- to crypto-crystalline; opaque white, translucent light grey and pink-brown; waxy to dull; conchoidal, sub-conchoidal; vague, cloudy variegation; amorphous white patches; dark-brown cortex with thin white subcortical band; volcanic or sedimentary, chemical precipitates; agate, chalcedony	POSSIBLY EXOTIC (clasts in sedimentary bedrocks and surficial deposits)	Bishop 1994:22–23; Gilbert et al. 2006a; MacDonald 1994:144–145
Orange Siliceous Shale	OSHALE (figure 4.7, this chapter)	Massive; crypto-crystalline; orange-red; opaque; waxy; conchoidal; fine linear fractures filled with silica; finely variegated with small patches of megaquartz, grey chert, white spots and black dendrites; sedimentary; siliceous shale, chert mudstone, jasper	PROBABLY EXOTIC (Ordovician-aged sedimentary bedrocks)	MacDonald 1994:167–168
Probably Exotic Multi-Coloured Cherts	PRB-EMCC (Black 2018:45, 53)	Layered; micro- to crypto-crystalline; white, reds, blues, greys; mostly opaque; waxy to dull; conchoidal, sub-conchoidal; distinct, minute variegation; volcanic or sedimentary, hydrothermal precipitates; jasper, agate, chalcedony	PROBABLY EXOTIC (volcanic bedrocks; clasts in sedimentary bedrocks and surficial deposits)	Booth 2003:92–99; MacDonald 1994:148–151

Lithic Material	Abbreviation (illustrations)	Description (structure; texture; colours; transparency; lustre; fracture; features/inclusions; type; common names)	Source Category (source locations)	Relevant Sources
Tobique Rhyolite/Chert	TOBR (Gilbert et al. 2006b)	Flow-banded; aphanitic; opaque dark red and dark grey, translucent red; vitreous to dull; conchoidal, sub-conchoidal, splintery; variegation ranges from sublinear to swirled; occasional surface bleaching to paler colours; chert blebs within volcanic groundmass; occasional larger pieces of chert; intermediate volcanic, hydrothermal alteration; jasper	EXOTIC (Tobique River, near junction with Saint John River, central interior New Brunswick)	Burke 2000:198–210; Sanger 197b1; Clarke 2016:111, 150, 171, 173; Thériault 2013
Kineo-Traveler Mountain Porphyry	KTMP (Black 2018:21–22, 25, 48; Gilbert et al. 2006b)	Massive or flow-banded; porphyritic/aphanitic; dark green, blue-green; mostly opaque, some thin-edge translucency; vitreous; conchoidal, sub-conchoidal; macroscopic quartz and feldspar phenocrysts; quartz phenocrysts vary from blebs to euhedral grains to angular fragments; quartz phenocrysts act as windows; frequent surface bleaching to chalky white; occasional surface pitting from weathered phenocrysts; volcanic, felsic; Kineo felsite, Kineo flint	EXOTIC (Mount Kineo-Traveler Mountain area, central interior Maine)	Black et al. 1998; Brockman and Keegan 2016:37; Caldwell 1998: 239–241; Doyle 1995; MacDonald 1994:163–164
Minas Basin Yellow Tuff	MBYT (Black 2011:116)	Layered; micro- to crypto-crystalline; yellows, browns, greys; mostly opaque, patchy translucency, waxy to vitreous; conchoidal, sub-conchoidal; distinct, minute variegation; patches of megaquartz; silica windows; dendritic structures; patchy transitions to basalt host rock; silica replacement "ghosts" of volcanic phenocrysts; volcanic, hydrothermal precipitates; siliceous tuff; moss agate	EXOTIC (Economy Mountain–Parrsboro area, north shore of Minas Basin, Nova Scotia)	Black 2011:117; Booth 2003:93; Burke 2000:390

Lithic Material	Abbreviation (illustrations)	Description (structure; texture; colours; transparency; lustre; fracture; features/inclusions; type; common names)	Source Category (source locations)	Relevant Sources
Minas Basin Multi-Coloured Chert	MBMC (Gilbert et al. 2005; Gilbert et al. 2006b)	Layered; micro- to crypto-crystalline; white, dusky reds, bright reds, blues, greys, yellow-browns; mostly opaque, patchy translucency; waxy to dull; conchoidal, sub-conchoidal; distinct, minute variegation; patches of megaquartz; macroscopic geode and fortification structures; bands of fibrous silica; silica windows; patchy transitions to host rock; volcanic, hydrothermal precipitates; jasper, agate, chalcedony	EXOTIC (Minas Basin and North Mountain shorelines, central-western Nova Scotia)	Black 2011:112–116; Booth 2003:92–99; Brockman and Keegan 2016:91; Deal 2001
Washademoak Multi-Coloured Chert	WMCC (Gilbert et al. 2005; Gilbert et al. 2006b)	Layered; micro- to crypto-crystalline; bright red-orange, grey-black, brown-gold; mostly highly translucent, occasional opaque bands and layers; vitreous to waxy; conchoidal, sub-conchoidal; vague, cloudy variegation; occasional patches of megaquartz; barite inclusions; opaque transitions to host rock; macro- and micro-scale strain fractures; vugs lined with botryoidal chalcedony; occasional small-scale fortification structures; sedimentary, hydrothermal precipitates; carnelian, chalcedony	EXOTIC (Washademoak Lake area, lower Saint John River, interior New Brunswick)	Black 2011:117–118; Black and Wilson 1999; Brockman and Keegan 2016:97
Munsungun Red and Green Chert	MRGC (figure 4.10, this chapter)	Massive, layered or laminated; fine-grained to micro-crystalline; reds, greens, yellow-browns; mostly opaque, sometimes semi-translucent; waxy to dull; conchoidal; sometimes banded, sometimes mottled, occasionally speckled; bleaching enhances banding and colour variegation; occasional radiolarian microfossils; fine linear fractures filled with silica; sedimentary, detrital; chert-mudstone	EXOTIC (Munsungun Lake area, central–eastern interior Maine)	Brockman and Keegan 2016:46; Burke 2000:186–197; Gilbert et al. 2006b; Pollock et al. 1999

References Cited

AGS (Atlantic Geoscience Society)
2001   *The Last Billion Years: A Geological History of the Maritime Provinces of Canada.* Nimbus Publishing, Halifax, Nova Scotia.

Betts, Matthew W., and Kenneth R. Holyoke
2019   Lithic Technology and Other Artifacts. In *Place-Making in the Pretty Harbour: The Archaeology of Port Joli, Nova Scotia,* edited by M. W. Betts, pp. 217–324. Mercury Series 180. Canadian Museum of History and University of Ottawa Press, Ottawa.

Bishop, Jennifer C.
1994   *The Partridge Island Site: Early and Middle Woodland-Related Sites in the Quoddy Region,* edited by D. W. Black. New Brunswick Archaeology 28. Department of Municipalities, Culture and Housing, Fredericton.

Bishop, Jennifer C., and David W. Black
1988   The Lands Edge Also: Culture History and Seasonality at the Partridge Island Shell Midden Site. *Canadian Journal of Archaeology* 12:17–37.

Black, David W.
1985   Living in Bliss: An Introduction to the Archaeology of the Bliss Islands Group, Charlotte County, New Brunswick. New Brunswick Archaeology 8. Historical and Cultural Resources, Fredericton.

1988   *Bliss Revisited: Preliminary Accounts of the Bliss Islands Archaeology Project, Phase II.* New Brunswick Archaeology 24. Tourism, Recreation and Heritage, Fredericton.

1989   Living Close to the Ledge: Prehistory and Human Ecology of the Bliss Islands, Quoddy Region, New Brunswick, Canada. PhD dissertation, Department of Anthropology, McMaster University, Hamilton, Ontario.

2000   Rum Beach and the Susquehanna Tradition in the Quoddy Region, Charlotte County, New Brunswick. *Canadian Journal of Archaeology* 24:89–104.

2002   Out of the Blue and Into the Black: The Middle-Late Maritime Woodland Transition in the Quoddy Region, New Brunswick, Canada. In *Northeast Subsistence–Settlement Change: A.D. 700–1300,* edited by John P. Hart and Christina B. Rieth, pp. 301–320. New York State Museum Bulletin 496. The University of the State of New York and State Education Department, Albany.

2003a   Ponapsqey: Jemseg Crossing Petrographic Series and Preliminary Evaluations of Flaked Lithic Materials from the Jemseg Assemblage. In *Wolastoqiyik Ajemseg. The People of the Beautiful River of Jemseg,* vol. 2: *Archaeological Results,* edited by Susan E. Blair, pp. 89–116. New Brunswick Archaeology Series 31. Culture and Sport Secretariat, Fredericton.

2003b   The Wallace Cove Site (BgDq29): Analysis of Lithic Artifacts. Manuscript on file, AMEC Earth & Environmental Ltd., Fredericton.

2004   *Living Close to the Ledge: Prehistoric Human Ecology of the Bliss Islands, Insular Quoddy Region, New Brunswick, Canada.* 2nd ed. Occasional Papers in Northeastern Archaeology No. 6. Copetown Press, St. John's, Newfoundland.

2011   Background, Discussion and Recommendations for Extending the Analysis of Lithic Materials used by Palaeoindians at the Debert and Belmont sites. In *Ta'n Wetapeksi'k: Understanding from Where We Came: Proceedings of the 2005 Debert Research Workshop*, edited by Tim Bernard, Leah M. Rosenmeier, and Sharon L. Farrell, pp. 111–128. Confederacy of Mainland Mi'kmaq and Eastern Woodlands Print Communications, Truro, Nova Scotia.

2013   "Some Clams in Those Days": Shell Midden Archaeology on the Bliss Islands. In *Underground New Brunswick: Stories of Archaeology*, edited by Paul Erickson and Jonathan Fowler, pp. 27–36. Nimbus Publishing, Nova Scoria.

2018   "...gathering pebbles on a boundless shore..."—The Rum Beach Site and Intertidal Archaeology in the Canadian Quoddy Region. UNB Libraries, Scholar Research Repository. Electronic document, https://unbscholar.lib.unb.ca/islandora/object/unbscholar%3A9409, accessed January 22, 2020.

Black, David W., and Christopher R. Blair
2000   Faunal Remains from the Loyalist Occupation of the Bliss Islands, New Brunswick. In *Studies in Canadian Zooarchaeology: Papers in Honour of Howard G. Savage*, edited by T. Max Friesen. *Ontario Archaeology* 69:39–54.

Black, David W., and David L. Keenlyside
1996   Northeastern Lithic Sourcing. Workshop held at the 29th Annual Meeting of the Canadian Archaeological Association, Halifax.

Black, David W., Joanna E. Reading, and Howard G. Savage
1998   Archaeological Records of the Extinct Sea Mink, *Mustela macrodon* (Carnivora: Mustelidae), from Canada. *Canadian Field-Naturalist* 112(2):45–49.

Black, David W., and Lucy A. Wilson
1999   The Washademoak Lake Chert Source, Queens County, New Brunswick, Canada. *Archaeology of Eastern North America* 27:81–108.

Blair, Christopher R.
2013   Looking for Bliss: An Early Loyalist Family in Passamaquoddy Bay. In *Underground New Brunswick: Stories of Archaeology*, edited by Paul Erickson and Jonathan Fowler, pp. 107–116. Nimbus Publishing, Halifax.

Blair, Susan E.
1999   The Prehistoric Archaeology of the Grand Manan Archipelago: Cultural History and Regional Integration. New Brunswick Archaeology 29. Heritage Branch, Culture and Sport Secretariat, Fredericton.

2003   Pihcesis Ajemseg: The Maritime Woodland Period at Jemseg. In *Wolastoqiyik Ajemseg. The People of the Beautiful River of Jemseg*, vol. 2: *Archaeological Results*, edited by Susan E. Blair, pp. 251–276. New Brunswick Archaeology Series 31. Heritage Branch, Culture and Sport Secretariat, Fredericton.

2004   Ancient Wolastoq'kew Landscapes: Settlement and Technology in the Lower Saint John River Valley, Canada. PhD dissertation, Department of Anthropology, University of Toronto, Toronto.

2010   Missing the Boat in Lithic Procurement: Watercraft and the Bulk Procurement of Tool-Stone on the Maritime Peninsula. *Journal of Anthropological Archaeology* 29:33–46.

Blair, Susan E., Margaret Horne, Katherine Patton, and W. Jesse Webb

2017   Birch Cove and the Protohistoric Period the Northern Quoddy Region, New Brunswick, Canada. *Journal of the North Atlantic* (Special Volume) 10:59–69.

Blair, Susan E., and Pamela Ward

2013   The Metepenagiag Site Complex. In *Underground New Brunswick: Stories of Archaeology*, edited by Paul Erickson and Jonathan Fowler, pp. 7–16. Nimbus Publishing, Halifax.

Booth, Ian

2003   *Fundy Mineral Collecting.* Privately published, Nova Scotia.

Bouras, E., and G. Evans

2006   A New Look at Munsungan: Excavations at the Ray Carter Site. *Maine Archaeological Society Bulletin* 46(1):25–56.

Bourque, Bruce J.

1994   Evidence for Prehistoric Exchange on the Maritime Peninsula. In *Prehistoric Exchange Systems in North America*, edited by Timothy Baugh and Jonathan E. Ericson, pp. 17–46. Plenum Press, New York.

1995   *Diversity and Complexity in Prehistoric Maritime Cultures: A Gulf of Maine Perspective.* Plenum Press, New York.

Bourque, Bruce J., Steven L. Cox, and Robert A. Lewis

2006   The Archaic Period of the Merrymeeting Bay Region, South Central Maine. In *The Archaic of the Far Northeast*, edited by David Sanger and M. A. Priscilla Renouf, pp. 307–340. University of Maine Press, Orono.

Bourque, Bruce J., Robert G. Doyle, and Stephen L. White

1984   The Archaeological Distribution of Banded Spherulitic Rhyolite in Maine. *Man in the Northeast* 28:111–119.

Brockman, Mark, and Barry Keegan

2016   *Indigenous Lithic Sources of Northeastern North America.* Franklin Publishing, Farmington, Maine.

Burke, Adrian L.

2000   Lithic Procurement and Ceramic Period Occupation of the Interior of the Maritime Peninsula. PhD dissertation, Department of Anthropology, State University of New York, Albany.

2006   Stone Tool Raw Materials and Sources of the Archaic Period in the Northeast. In *The Archaic of the Far Northeast*, edited by David Sanger and M. A. Priscilla Renouf, pp. 411–438. University of Maine Press, Orono.

2007   Quarry Source Areas and the Organization of Stone Tool Technology: A View from Quebec. *Archaeology of Eastern North America* 35:63–80.

2011   Lithic Sourcing and Lithic Technology. In *Ta'n Wetapeksi'k: Understanding from Where We Came: Proceedings of the 2005 Debert Research Workshop*, edited by Tim Bernard, Leah M. Rosenmeier, and Sharon L. Farrell, pp. 129–131. Confederacy of Mainland Mi'kmaq and Eastern Woodlands Print Communications, Truro.

Burke, Adrian L., and Éric Chalifoux

1998   Stratégie d'acquisition du chert Touladi et production lithique durant la période du Sylvicole au Témiscouata. In *L'éveilleur et l'ambassadeur: Textes en honneur de*

Charles A. Martijn, edited by Roland Tremblay, pp. 33–51. Paléo-Québec No. 27. Recherches amérindiennes au Québec, Montréal.

Caldwell, D. W.
1998   *Roadside Geology of Maine*. Mountain Press Publishing, Missoula.

Calogero, Barbara L. A.
1992   Lithic Misidentification. *Man in the Northeast* 43:87–90.

Chalifoux, Éric
1999   Late Palaeoindian Occupation in a Coastal Environment: A Perspective from La Marte, Gaspe, Quebec. *Northeast Anthropology* 57:69–79.

Chalifoux, Éric, and Adrian L. Burke
1993   Northeastern Lithic Material Sourcing. Workshop held at the 26th Annual Meeting of the Canadian Archaeological Association, Montréal, Québec.

1995   L'occupation préhistorique du Témiscouata (est du Québec), un lieu de portage entre deux grandes voies de circulation. In *Archéologies québécoises*, edited by Anne-Marie Balac, Claude Chapdelaine, Norman Clermont, and Françoise Duguay, pp. 237–270. Paléo-Québec No. 23. Recherches amérindiennes au Québec, Montréal.

Chalifoux, Éric, Adrian L. Burke, and Claude Chapdelaine
1998   *La préhistoire du Temiscouata: Occupation d'amérindiennes dans la haute vallée de Wolastokuk*. Paléo-Québec No. 26. Recherches amérindiennes au Québec, Montréal.

Clarke, George F.
2015   *Six Salmon Rivers and Another*. Edited by Mary Bernard. Brunswick Press, Fredericton.

2016   *Someone Before Us: Buried History in Central New Brunswick*. Edited by Mary Bernard. 4th ed. Chapel Street Editions, Woodstock, New Brunswick.

Colwell, J. A., and S. A. Ferguson
1992   Geology and Scenery of the White Rock Area. Electronic document, http://ees.acadiau.ca/ft2.html, accessed January 22, 2020.

Coniglio, M.
1987   Biogenic Chert in the Cow Head Group (Cambro–Ordovician), Western Newfoundland. *Sedimentology* 34:813–823.

Crotts, Anita L.
1984   Pattern and Variation in Prehistoric Lithic Resource Exploitation in the Passamaquoddy Bay Region, New Brunswick. Master's thesis, Quaternary Studies Institute, University of Maine, Orono.

Deal, Michael
2001   Vignette: Distribution and Utilization of Scots Bay Chalcedony. Electronic document, http://www.ucs.mun.ca/~mdeal/Anth3291/DavidsonCove.htm, accessed January 22, 2020.

Dincauze, Dena F.
1976   Lithic Analysis in the Northeast: Resume and Prospect. *Man in the Northeast* 11:31–37.

Doyle, Robert G.

1995   Appendix 6: Lithic Materials. In *Diversity and Complexity in Prehistoric Maritime Cultures: A Gulf of Maine Perspective*, by Bruce J. Bourque, pp. 297–316. Plenum Press, New York.

Gauthier, Gilles, and Adrian L. Burke

2011   The Effects of Surface Weathering on the Geochemical Analysis of Archaeological Lithic Samples Using Non-Destructive Polarized Energy Dispersive XRF. *Geoarchaeology* 26:269–291.

Gauthier, Gilles, Adrian L. Burke, and Mathieu Leclerc

2012   Assessing XRF for the Geochemical Characterization of Radiolarian Chert Artifacts from Northeastern North America. *Journal of Archaeological Science* 39:2436–2451.

Gilbert, C. Drew

2011   The Archaeology of the Deer Island Point Site (BfDr5), Charlotte County, NB. Master's thesis, Department of Anthropology, University of New Brunswick, Fredericton.

Gilbert, C. Drew, and David W. Black

2006   The Bliss Islands Petrographic Series. FileMaker Pro 7 database on file, Department of Anthropology, University of New Brunswick, Fredericton.

Gilbert, C. Drew, Michael J. Gallant, and David W. Black

2005   Distinguishing Carboniferous- from Mesozoic-Associated Chert Toolstones in the Canadian Maritimes. Electronic document, https://www.unb.ca /fredericton/arts/_assets/documents/anthro-mesozoicchert.pdf, accessed January 22, 2020.

Gilbert, C. Drew, Patrick M. Gamblin, and David W. Black

2006a   The Usual Suspects: Local Lithic Materials in Quoddy Region Archaeological Assemblages. Electronic document, https://www.unb.ca/fredericton/arts /_assets/documents/anth/locallithics.pdf, accessed January 22, 2020.

2006b   The Usual Suspects: Exotic Lithic Materials in Quoddy Region Archaeological Assemblages. Electronic document, https://www.unb.ca/fredericton/arts /_assets/documents/anth/exoticlithics.pdf, accessed January 22, 2020.

Hrynick, M. Gabriel, and David W. Black

2016   Cultural Continuity in Maritime Woodland Period Domestic Architecture in the Quoddy Region. *Canadian Journal of Archaeology* 40:23–67.

Hrynick, M. Gabriel, W. Jesse Webb, Christopher E. Shaw, and Taylor C. Testa

2017   Late Maritime Woodland to Protohistoric Culture Change and Continuity at the Devil's Head Site, Calais, Maine. *Archaeology of Eastern North America* 45:85–108.

Holyoke, Kenneth R.

2012   Late Maritime Woodland Lithic Technology in the Lower Saint John River Valley. Master's thesis, Department of Anthropology, University of New Brunswick, Fredericton.

James, Noel P., Jack W. Botsford, and S. Henry Williams

1987   Allochthonous Slope Sequence at Lobster Cove Head: Evidence for a Middle Ordovician Platform Margin in Western Newfoundland. *Canadian Journal of Earth Sciences* 24:1199–1211.

Jones, David L., and Benita Murchey
1986   Geologic Significance of Paleozoic and Mesozoic Radiolarian Chert. *Annual Review of Earth and Planetary Sciences* 14:455–492.

Kingsbury, Isaac W., and Wendell S. Hadlock
1951   An Early Occupation Site, Eastport, Maine. *Massachusetts Archaeological Society Bulletin* 12(2):22–26.

Lavers, Dominique
2010   The Recent Indian Cow Head Complex Occupation of the Northern Peninsula, Newfoundland: A Geochemical Investigation of Cow Head Chert Acquisition. Master's thesis, Department of Archaeology, Memorial University, St. John's, Newfoundland.

Luedtke, Barbara
1992   *An Archaeologist's Guide to Chert and Flint.* Archaeological Research Tools 7. Institute of Archaeology, University of California, Los Angeles.

MacDonald, Shianne L.
1994   Exploring Patterns of Prehistoric Lithic Material Use in the Insular Quoddy Region, New Brunswick. Master's thesis, Department of Anthropology, University of New Brunswick, Fredericton.

Matthew, George F.
1984   Discoveries at a Village of the Stone Age at Bocabec, New Brunswick. *Bulletin of the Natural History Society of New Brunswick* 3:6–29.

McLeod, Malcolm J., Susan C. Johnson, and Arie A. Ruitenberg
1994   Geological Map of Southwestern New Brunswick. Map NR–5. New Brunswick Department of Natural Resources and Energy, Fredericton.

Newton, Jennifer L.
1999   The Vinalhaven Rhyolite and Perry Creek Formations: Felsic Volcanics and Volcaniclastic Rocks of Vinalhaven Island, Maine. Electronic document, https://keckgeology.org/files/pdf/symvol/12th/Maine/newton.pdf, accessed January 22, 2020.

Odell, George H.
2000   Stone Tool Research at the End of the Millennium: Procurement and Technology. *Journal of Archaeological Research* 8(4):269–331.

Pearson, Richard J.
1970   Archaeological Investigations in the St. Andrews Area, New Brunswick. *Anthropologica* 12:181–190.

Pelletier-Michaud, Alexandre
2017   The Bristol–Shiktehawk Bifaces and Early Woodland Ceremonialism in the Middle St. John Valley, New Brunswick. Master's thesis, Department of Anthropology, University of New Brunswick, Fredericton.

Pelletier, Bertram G., and Brian S. Robinson
2005   Tundra, Ice and a Pleistocene Cape on the Gulf of Maine: A Case of Palaeoindian Transhumance. *Archaeology of Eastern North America* 33:163–176.

Pollock, Stephen G.
1987   Chert Formation in an Ordovician Volcanic Arc. *Journal of Sedimentary Petrology* 57(1):75–87.

Pollock, Stephen G., Nathan D. Hamilton, and Robson Bonnichsen

1999   Chert from the Munsungun Lake Formation (Maine) in Palaeoamerican Archaeological Sites in Northeastern North America: Recognition of its Occurrence and Distribution. *Journal of Archaeological Science* 26(3):269–293.

Pollock, Stephen G., Nathan D. Hamilton, and Richard A. Boisvert

2008a   Archaeological Geology of Two Flow-banded Spherulitic Rhyolites in New England, USA: Their History, Exploitation and Criteria for Recognition. *Journal of Archaeological Science* 35(3):688–703.

2008b   Prehistoric Utilization of Spherulitic and Flow Banded Rhyolites from Northern New Hampshire. *Archaeology of Eastern North America* 36:91–118.

Potter, R. R., J. B. Hamilton, and J. L. Davies

1979   Geological Map of New Brunswick. 2nd ed. Map NR–1. New Brunswick Department of Natural Resources, Fredericton.

Reimer, Rudy

2018   Lithic Sourcing in Canada. *Canadian Journal of Archaeology* 42:137–143.

Rosenmeier, Leah M.

2011   Towards an Archaeology of Descent: Spatial Practice and Communities of Shared Experience in Mi'kma'ki. PhD dissertation, Department of Anthropology, Brown University, Providence, Rhode Island.

Sabina, Ann P.

1972   *Rock and Mineral Collecting in Canada.* Vol. 3. Miscellaneous Report 8. Geological Survey of Canada, Ottawa.

Sanger, David

1971a   Prehistory of Passamaquoddy Bay: A Summary. *Maine Archaeological Society Bulletin* 11(2):14–19.

1971b   Deadman's Pool, a Tobique Complex Site in Northern New Brunswick. *Man in the Northeast* 2:5–22.

1987   *The Carson Site and the Late Ceramic Period in Passamaquoddy Bay.* Mercury Series 135. Archaeological Survey of Canada, National Museum of Man, Ottawa.

1994   Geoarchaeological Approaches to Lithic Sourcing in the Northeast. University of Maine at Orono workshop held at Smyrna Mills, Maine.

2008   Discerning Regional Variation: The Terminal Archaic of the Quoddy Region of the Maritime Peninsula. *Canadian Journal of Archaeology* 32:1–42.

Schluger, P. R.

1973   Stratigraphy and Sedimentary Environments of the Devonian Perry Formation, New Brunswick, Canada, and Maine, U.S.A. *Geological Society of America Bulletin* 84(8):2533–2548.

Shaw, Christopher E.

2016   An Analysis of Lithic Materials and Morphology from the Late Maritime Woodland and Historic Periods at the Devil's Head Site in the Maine Quoddy Region. Bachelor's thesis, Department of Anthropology, Bates College, Lewiston, Maine.

Taché, Karine

2011   New Perspectives on Meadowood Trade Items. *American Antiquity* 76:41–79.

Thériault, Christian C. L.
2012   The Potential Significance of Selected New Brunswick Ordovician Cherts in the Regional Archaeological Record. Paper presented at the 45th Annual Meeting of the Canadian Archaeological Association, Montréal, Quebec.
2013   Sampling Past *Milieux*: The Upsalquitch River Forks Area Geoarchaeological Survey. Master's thesis, Department of Anthropology, University of New Brunswick, Fredericton.

Turnbull, Christopher J.
1990   *The Bernard Collection: A Tobique Complex Site from the Mid-St. John River Valley, New Brunswick.* New Brunswick Archaeology 25. Tourism, Recreation and Heritage, Fredericton.

Wilson, Lucy
1983   Lithic Analysis of Selected New Brunswick Archaeological Sites. Bachelor's thesis, Department of Anthropology, University of New Brunswick, Fredericton.
1991   Examination of Archaeological Lithics from the Bliss Islands Archaeology Project, Phases I and II. Manuscript on file, Department of Anthropology, University of New Brunswick, Fredericton.
1994   Examination of Archaeological Lithics from the Bliss Islands Archaeology Project, Phase III. Manuscript on file, Department of Anthropology, University of New Brunswick, Fredericton.

Wright, James V.
1999   *A History of the Native People of Canada*, Vol. 2. Mercury Series 152. Canadian Museum of Civilization, Hull, Quebec.

5

CULTURAL PATTERNING THROUGH THE EARLY MARITIME WOODLAND IN THE FAR NORTHEAST

A Perspective from the Archaeological Landscape of Metepenagiag, Mi'kmaqi

SUSAN E. BLAIR[1] AND MICHAEL P. ROONEY[2]

Abstract

The modern Mi'kmaq First Nation of Metepenagiag, in northeastern New Brunswick, is located at the confluence of the Northwest and Little Southwest Miramichi Rivers. This landscape contains an archaeological record that includes habitation components in deep alluvial deposits, food processing and storage pits, tool-production areas, and ceremonial and mortuary sites. While these sites span the entire Maritime Woodland period, many of them date to or contain components from the Early and early Middle Maritime Woodland (ca. 3000–1900 BP). Some of these components reflect local materials and approaches to tool production, while some contain features that signal an affiliation with archaeological entities better known outside the Far Northeast, including Adena/Middlesex and Meadowood. These patterns have fractured community histories and have emphasized the role of external influence in this cultural landscape. In this paper, we synthesize the evidence that is currently available, including information not readily available in published literature, and integrate recent research. By emphasizing community-based approaches and historical process, we demonstrate how these broad patterns are interwoven with threads of continuity that tangibly connect the Early Woodland inhabitants of Metepenagiag with modern Mi'kmaq through community memory, human-animal relationships, and landscape use spanning millennia.

Résumé

La Première Nation Mi'kmaq de Metepenagiag est située à la confluence des branches *Northwest* et *Little Southwest* de la rivière Miramichi, dans le nord-est du Nouveau-Brunswick, au Canada. Ce paysage renferme un riche patrimoine archéologique, incluant des structures d'habitation profondément enfouies dans les dépôts alluviaux, des fosses associées à la préparation et au stockage des aliments, des stations de production d'outils, ainsi que des sites cérémoniaux et mortuaires. Bien que ces sites couvrent toute la période du Sylvicole Maritime, plusieurs ont produit des dates ou des composantes associées aux périodes du Sylvicole Maritime inférieur et moyen ancien (ca. 3000–1900 AA). Certaines de ces composantes renferment des outils produits à partir de matériaux locaux et selon des approches locales, alors que d'autres présentent des structures témoignant d'une affiliation avec des unités archéologiques mieux connues en dehors de la région de l'extrême Nord-Est (*Far Northeast*), incluant Adena/Middlesex et Meadowood. Ces associations ont encouragé la fragmentation de l'histoire des communautés, en mettant l'emphase sur des influences extérieures au paysage culturel de Metepenagiag. Dans cet article nous présentons une synthèse des connaissances actuelles, en intégrant des données non publiées et des travaux récents. En mettant de l'avant des approches communautaires et les processus historiques, nous démontrons l'existence à l'intérieur de cette trame temporelle de fils conducteurs reliant directement les occupants de Metepenagiag du Sylvicole inférieur aux Mi'kmaq contemporains à travers la mémoire communautaire, les interactions humains–animaux et l'occupation continue d'un paysage sur plusieurs millénaires.

Affiliations

1. Department of Anthropology, University of New Brunswick, New Brunswick, Canada
2. Stantec Consulting Ltd./Department of Anthropology, University of New Brunswick, New Brunswick, Canada

As the de facto earliest portion of the Maritime Woodland, the Early Maritime Woodland (EMW) represents the establishment of a broad pattern in the Far Northeast, one that shares many elements with developments occurring elsewhere in eastern North America. The more visible aspects of this pattern appear as changes in technology from the preceding Late Archaic at a point slightly before 3,000 years ago. Further, the Late Archaic period itself is largely viewed as the culmination of longstanding regional traditions extending back over 8,000 years ago (Robinson 1992, 1996). Whether this change is a gradual transition (Petersen 1995:221; Robinson 2016; Rutherford 1989, 1991:112; Sanger 1974:129) or a sharp break from the Archaic pattern (Fiedel 2001; Taché 2011a; Tuck 1991:65) has been the source of debate. However, time and continuity are configured in this shift, and most agree that it includes a reduction in a technological focus on heavy ground-stone tools (Wright 1999:574), changes in bifacial tools and projectile points (Petersen 1995:221; Blair 2004a), and the development of unifacial scraper and ceramic-based technologies (Blair 2004a, 2004b; Bourque 1971; Sanger 1974; Taché 2005, 2011b).

Within the Far Northeast, our understanding of the EMW (as is the case with other broad chronological periods in the Maritime Peninsula) has been influenced by a gap in professional research occurring in the early to mid-twentieth century. This regional gap coincides with an expansion of archaeological research in other parts of eastern North America. As a result, perspectives on typological and cultural patterning in the Far Northeast often integrate phenomena first described in more central and southern portions of northeastern North America. In other words, regional archaeological cultures have often (but not always) been defined and characterized in the archaeological literature of elsewhere (Leonard 1995). Indeed, the construction of the Woodland itself operates at a subcontinental level, and first emerged as a culture-historical model that explicitly sought to integrate local variability into a unified, macroregional culture area (Kroeber 1948; McKern 1937; see Braun 1980).

The tension between broadly defined culture-historical units and local and regional variability is strongly evident in the EMW. In many parts of eastern North America, the Early Woodland or its equivalent has been associated with broad trends of increasing cultural complexity, interregional interaction, and, in some parts, incipient horticulture (Bourque 1994; Crawford et al. 2019; Fiedel 2001; Johanson et al. 2020; Kidder et al. 2010; Levine et al. 1999; Lewis 1996; Mainfort 1989; McCord 2008; Mueller 2018; Pauketat and Sassaman 2020; Railey 1996; Redmond 2016; Ritchie 1955; Robinson 2016; Stothers and Abel 1993; Taché 2011a, 2011b; Wright and Henry 2013; but see Braun 1980). Historically, these developments were connected to a series of Early Woodland manifestations centred in the Great Lakes Basin (i.e., Meadowood, Glacial Kame, Red Ochre) and in the American Midwest (i.e., Adena, Middlesex, Robbins) (Cudmore 2016; Cochran 1996; Conolly 2018; Dragoo 1963, 1976; Granger 1978, 1981; Greenman 1932; Griffin 1942; Henry and Barrier 2016; Henry 2017; Otto and Redmond 2008; Ritchie and Dragoo 1960; Swartz 1971; Taché 2011a). Based primarily on tool morphology and style, at least three EMW manifestations have been identified in the Maritime Peninsula, two of which correspond to developments occurring in the broader Northeast: Meadowood, Adena/Middlesex, and a locally developed tradition (e.g., Allen 1980; Belcher 1989; Blair 2004a, 2004b; Black 1992). In this paper, we explore these tensions and perspectives through an examination of an EMW landscape in the Maritime Peninsula, located in and around the contemporary community of Metepenagiag (Red Bank) in the unceded and unsurrendered lands of the Metepenagiag Mi'kmaq Nation (see figure 5.1).

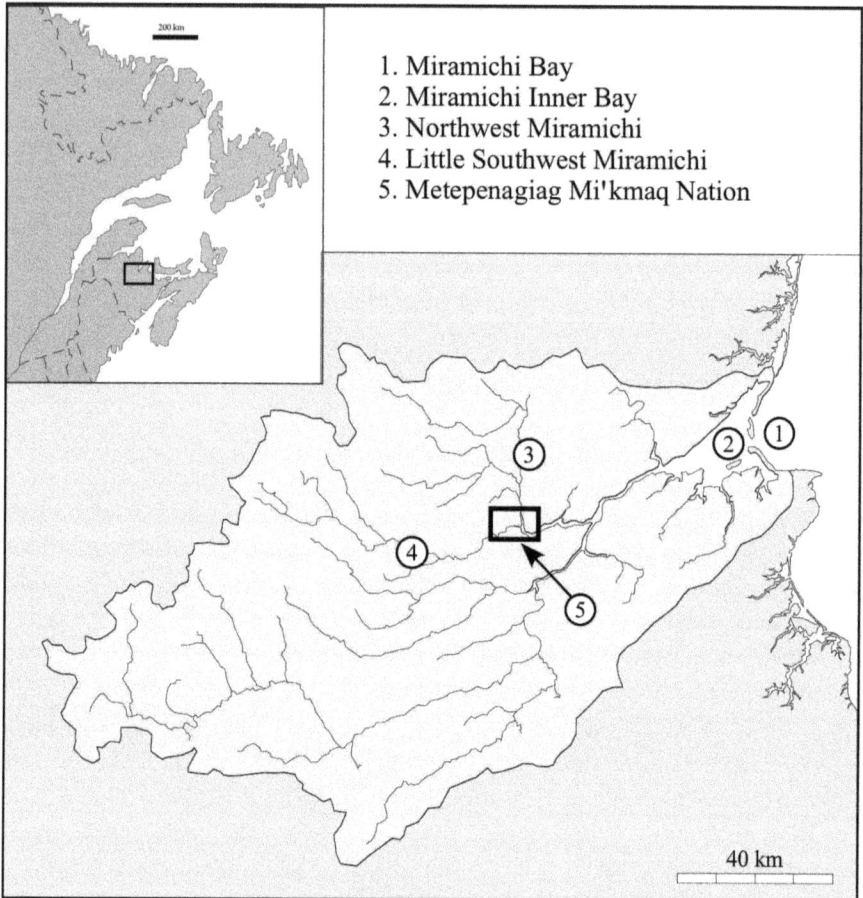

Figure 5.1. The Miramichi River drainage in the Northeast, showing the location (in the rectangle) of the Metepenagiag Mi'kmaq Nation and the archaeological landscape.

The Early Woodland in Eastern North America

In the Midwest, the Great Lakes Basin, and the Mid-Atlantic, the Woodland emerged from Late Archaic traditions that were characterized by widely distributed, logistically organized settlements that participated in large-scale exchange systems, ceremonial expressions that involved segregation of spaces and objects for the dead from those of the living, and increasing use of monumentality to express ecological, sociological, and cosmological relationships (Claassen 2015; Redmond 2017; Sassaman 2005, 2010; Sanger et al. 2019). These patterns were expanded on and intensified in the Early Woodland through a growing focus on monumental constructions of earth, earthen mounds constructed on pre-existing ritual spaces, ritual activities involving the use of smoking pipes, elaborate mortuary complexes, and increased social differences manifested as in the circulation of prestige items in exchange networks (Bollwerk and Tushingham; Clay 1983, 1986, 1987, 2005, 2014; Hays 2010; Henry 2018; Levine et al. 1999; Lowery 2012; Monaghan and Herrmann 2019; Mueller 2018; Pauketat and Sassaman 2020; Purtill et al. 2014; Rafferty 2001, 2004, 2006; Robinson 2016; Taché 2011a, 2011b; Tushingham and Eerkens 2016; Whittaker and Green 2010). While there is evidence in some areas of small-scale horticulture in the Early Woodland (Crawford et al. 2019; Hart et al. 2007), in much of the Northeast these patterns were based around a hunter-gatherer adaptation, although in some places changes in technology and settlement patterning may indicate increasing sedentism. In these contexts, archaeological patterns are linked to several distinct cultural manifestations, including Middlesex/Adena and Meadowood. While early formulations of these emphasized mortuary components, later investigations explicated the whole cultural system, describing hunter-gatherer societies that were semi-sedentary, organized around a base-camp model, with evidence of early social ranking (Curry 2018; Levine et al. 1999; Mueller 2018, 2018; Redmond 2016; Taché 2011a, 2011b). In their mid-twentieth-century formulations, Middlesex/Adena and Meadowood were modelled as distinctive, distributed in space and time (in effect, narrowing their potential time span through asserting sequentiality), a formulation that persists despite evidence of overlap in both regards (Heckenberger et al. 1990; Loring 1985; Robinson 2016).

The confusion arising from taxonomic diversity is accentuated by what appears to have been, on the part of Early Woodland peoples, a sharp separation between mortuary sites and non-mortuary places. Many of the elements that might be considered diagnostic of culture-historical entities such as Adena are not found in more diverse habitation sites, making it difficult to make correlations between kinds of sites within Adena (Clay 1998; Grantz 1986; Waldron and Abrams 1999). This is further complicated by the presence of a major plateau in the radiocarbon calibration curve; when radiocarbon age is plotted relative to calendar age, the relationship is expressed as an undulating or wobbling slope (Bowman 1990; Suess 1970). At particular points in time, a wide range of radiocarbon years may represent fewer calendrical years (a steep slope in the curve), or a small range of radiocarbon years may represent a broad range of calendrical years (a plateau in the curve). The Early Woodland falls on a broad plateau that extends from 2,700 to 2,300 years ago, a plateau delimited by two steep slopes (see the difference between uncalibrated dates and calibrated dates, below).

In the Maritime Peninsula, this taxonomic confusion is amplified. In part, this is because the view that clustering of particular material traits is an indicator of cultural affiliation has required us to turn ourselves inside out to explain how, when, and why Adena and Meadowood culture came here (and, in some cases, this is extended to Adena and Meadowood people), and once it/they got here, how it/they integrated into a local population, or whether, in fact, they replaced a local population or entered a somehow depopulated Archaic landscape (Allen 1980:143; McEachen 1996;Tuck 1984;Wright 1999). Put another way, attempts to reconcile the local archaeological evidence from the Maritime Peninsula with better known taxonomies from elsewhere have led to an assumption that the relationship between these regions is hierarchical, with people, ideas, and/or objects flowing from a core in the Midwest or Great Lakes to a periphery in the Far Northeast, and this, in turn, has shaped expectations about the EMW itself. When artifacts and places are encountered that correspond to Early Woodland phenomena like Adena, Middlesex, and Meadowood on the Maritime Peninsula, it is often assumed that they came from somewhere else, leading to conjectures about temporality (such components must be later and restricted in duration) and cultural expression (such phenomena, whatever they represent, are only partially expressed versions of the "original" phenomena). Further, the great distances between the presumed core and peripheries can lead us to assume that the processes of transmission are not ongoing but rather reflect short-term (albeit, long distance) movements, such as migrations, rather than long-term relationships. This leads to inferences that the initial appearance of Adena, Middlesex, or Meadowood traits are in some way "purer" expressions, with devolution and localization of both forms and materials over time. Underpinning these assumptions is a Western epistemology that envisages human interactions as hierarchical and structured around centres and edges, with phenomena emanating from a core (Escobar 2008). We will return to these assumptions and expectations below, after an examination of archaeological evidence from Metepenagiag provides a basis for evaluation.

This interplay between local evidence and regional and macroregional frameworks for the Early Woodland is relevant to the archaeological landscape of Metepenagiag because it contains abundant evidence from the period between 3,000 and 2,000 years ago at places that are both interconnected and distributed. While the people of Metepenagiag see these as continuous places of cultural life, archaeologists have delimited them into a series of sites, including Augustine Mound, McKinlay, Tozer, Oxbow, Mejipkei and Tabougel Mejipki, Lukuwakn, Mitchell, Howe, Hogan-Mullin, and Wilson (figure 5.2). We refer to these below as the Metepenagiag Site Complex (Blair and Ward 2013). These sites contain evidence of local practices and lifeways that are both densely concentrated in the areas in and around the community and continuous through time, but also particular places that produced artifacts that exhibit either Middlesex/Adena or Meadowood traits and forms. We discuss these below, with particular attention to evidence that may have long resided in reports and notes that have had limited dissemination.

The Archaeological History of Metepenagiag

The modern community of Metepenagiag (or Red Bank), located on the Miramichi River in northeast New Brunswick is a part of the Metepenagiag Mi'kmaq Nation and unceded and unsurrendered Mi'kma'ki. The Miramichi River is a broad, multibranched river that drains an area of 13,000 km² into the Gulf of Saint Lawrence; it has a large estuary, and it is tidal between 70 km and 130 km in from the mouth. Metepenagiag is located near one of the modern heads of tide, at the confluence of the Northwest and the Little Southwest Miramichi Rivers (see figure 5.2). The major tributaries of the Miramichi River are a key part of the community landscape, both past and present.

The archaeological history of Metepenagiag extends to the late nineteenth and early twentieth century (Wintemberg 1937; see Turnbull 1986), but most of this work was incidental and short-term until the 1970s, when the community initiated a series of active, community-driven archaeological programs. These involved a set of collaborative relationships, initiated by former chief and Elder Joe Augustine almost 50 years ago (Augustine et al. 2006; Blair et al. 2014; Blair and Ward 2013), among researchers from the Metepenagiag community, the provincial government, and local universities. These culminated in the community creating Metepenagiag Heritage Park, a major community tourism project and interpretation centre. The resulting community research projects integrated a body of independent, detailed, local traditional knowledge, including information about the location and use of key archaeological places (Augustine et al. 2006; Blair et al. 2014), as well as previous archaeological research in the area (notably Wintemberg 1937), and focused on identifying, mapping, and in some cases excavating portions of dozens of archaeological sites, including large habitation sites, ceremonial and/or mortuary sites, tool-production areas, and pit features related to food processing and consumption (see figure 5.2; Allen 1980, 1981, 2005; Augustine et al. 2006; Blair and Ward 2013; McEachen et al. 1999; Suttie 2006; Turnbull 1976, 1980; Webb et al. 2013). The local culture-historical sequence, developed through careful excavation of deeply stratified sites supplemented by radiometric dating, reveals a pattern of regular and persistent activity over a period from before 3,000 years ago to the present (Allen 1994). These longstanding community-driven research collaborations were renewed in 2006, through a memorandum of understanding between Metepenagiag Heritage Park, Metepenagiag Mi'kmaq Nation, and the University of New Brunswick, resulting in reanalysis of archaeological data from the community; it is research that occurred under this agreement between community and academic researchers that is reported herein.

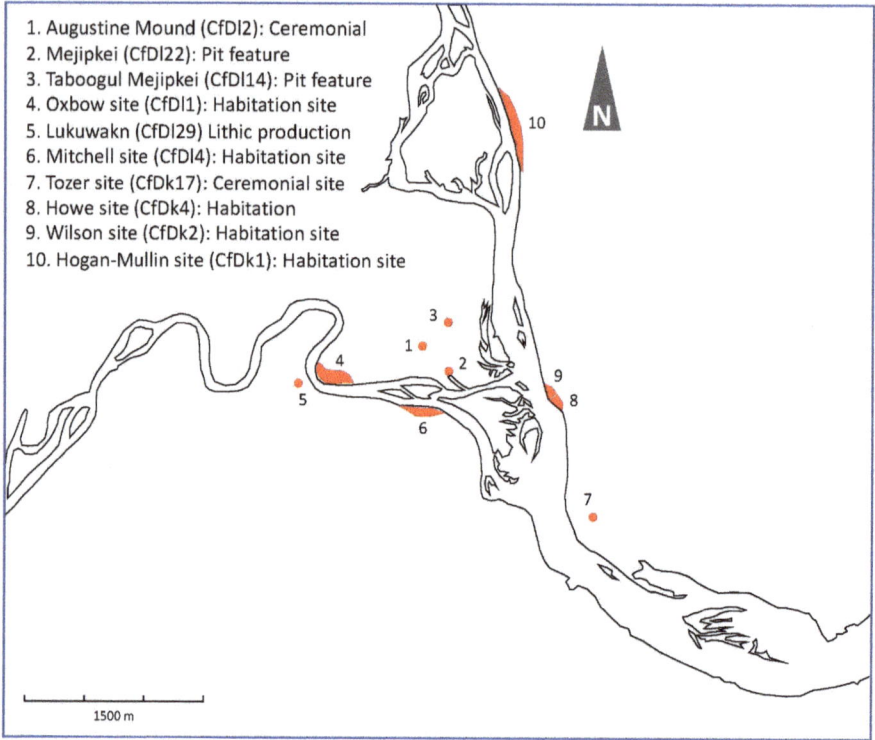

1. Augustine Mound (CfDl2): Ceremonial
2. Mejipkei (CfDl22): Pit feature
3. Taboogul Mejipkei (CfDl14): Pit feature
4. Oxbow site (CfDl1): Habitation site
5. Lukuwakn (CfDl29) Lithic production
6. Mitchell site (CfDl4): Habitation site
7. Tozer site (CfDk17): Ceremonial site
8. Howe site (CfDk4): Habitation
9. Wilson site (CfDk2): Habitation site
10. Hogan-Mullin site (CfDk1): Habitation site

Figure 5.2. Metepenagiag Mi'kmaq Nation and area archaeological sites.

Localities and Places in the Metepenagiag Landscape

The area in and around Metepenagiag Mi'kmaq Nation has a particular concentration of places that were in use during the EMW. From an archaeological perspective, these represent a range of site types that are distributed in the area in a way that leads us to integrate them into a larger EMW site complex, the Metepenagiag Site Complex (see Blair and Ward 2013). These are summarized and located on figure 5.2. Below, we review sites in each of these categories, ending with a detailed discussion of the Augustine Mound and our recent work contextualizing ceremonialism at Metepenagiag through radiometric dating.

As Allen (2005:70-71) states: "Maritime Woodland Period occupation sites, measuring anywhere from 10 to 500 metres in length, line the river shores near the best fishing pools, where the river channels cut close to the banks and at the head of tide on both branches, where the rivers are narrower and shallower. For the most part [...] it is difficult to determine where one site ends and another begins." While many of these places can be observed in debris exposed by erosion on river banks and shorelines around the community, some of them have been subject to formal excavation (Oxbow, Mitchell, Lukuwakn), while others have been examined after having been exposed and damaged by development and agricultural activity (Wilson, Hogan-Mullin, Howe, and Tozer).

The Oxbow Site

The Oxbow site (CfDl1) was the focus of several seasons of archaeological fieldwork directed by Allen in the late 1970s and early '80s (Allen 1980, 1981, 1994, 2005). Due to highly acidic soils, the Oxbow assemblage is dominated by inorganic materials (stone and pottery), with hearths and living surfaces containing calcined and charred food remains. This deposit was between 1.68 m and 2.2 m deep (at which point the excavations encountered the water table; Allen 1980:28), and included 22 distinct cultural layers containing complexly patterned surfaces, with workshops, food-processing areas, and dwelling floors, as well as hearths containing abundant sturgeon dermal bones and spines (Allen 2005; Stewart 1981; Webb et al. 2013). While a few of the formal tools from the site are made from regionally available volcanic toolstones, between 95% and 98% of the flaked-stone assemblage is made from the local cobble quartz (Allen 1980:30, 2005). The evidence from Oxbow indicates that the area was regularly occupied for thousands of years, through the period of time when the ceremonial sites in the area, including Augustine Mound, McKinley, and Tozer were created and used. Despite this, with the exception of two flaked-and-ground-stone axes from the lower portions (layer 19) of the site (Allen 2005:42, 53), the Oxbow assemblage lacks any definitive evidence of Adena- or Meadowood-like material culture.

The excavations at Oxbow were halted at the water table, at a level below the latest radiometric-dated layers. These layers contained several small projectile points of local forms made of regionally available materials; low-fired decorated and undecorated ceramics; biface fragments; large, steep-edged unifacial scrapers; flaking debris and cores; two flaked-and-ground stone axes (figure 5.3); as well as large quantities of sturgeon dermal bones and spines. While material recovered during the 1984 excavation produced dates that are more

Figure 5.3. Flaked-and-ground celt from the lower layers of the Oxbow site.
Source: Photo by C. Drew Gilbert.

typical of the Middle Maritime Woodland (1745 ± 95 BP, S-2551, 1760 ± 90 BP, Beta-10512, and 2070 ± 60 BP, Beta-10513), the 1978–1979 excavations indicated that these layers were associated and slightly below material radiometrically dated to 2,640 ± 50 BP and 2,600 ± 60 BP (Allen 1980:141, 2006:51; Webb et al. 2013). The attribution to the EMW is supported by similarities between the small, stemmed points from lower layers of Oxbow, and the small, stemmed points from the mound fill of the Augustine Mound (see below). The presence of sturgeon, as we will discuss below, is a unifying feature of activity throughout this sequence and in most (if not all) parts of the Metepenagiag Site Complex.

Other "Habitation" Sites in and around Metepenagiag

The material recovered from Oxbow represents an important baseline for all other archaeological work in that it was undertaken by archaeologists using modern techniques, and its deeply stratified nature both precluded modern agricultural disturbance and allowed for the emergence of a temporal framework. This is unlike other archaeological locales with EMW components elsewhere in the area, which were more shallowly deposited and have been impacted heavily by recent agricultural and infrastructural developments (Turnbull 1986). These latter locales include the Howe (CfDk4), Wilson (CfDk2), and Hogan-Mullin (CfDk1) sites (Allen 1981, 1986); the first two are located in close proximity to each other on the east banks of the Northwest Miramichi River, upstream from where it meets the Little Southwest, while the last is located on the same bank, some 2 km upstream (see figure 5.2). Like Oxbow, these sites produced very large lithic assemblages overwhelmingly dominated by quartz and local tool forms; they also contained small numbers of artifacts that are reminiscent of Meadowood forms (see Granger 1978), including thin side-notched point base fragments, cache blade fragments, and double-ended and triangular bifacial scrapers and side-notched drills (Allen 1980:140; McEachen 1996; McEachen et al. 1999:48–50). These shallow, disturbed sites are different from the Oxbow site in that disturbance precludes us from determining the kinds of features that might be associated with these materials. As a result, the impression that Meadowood-like material on these sites are related to habitation-related (non-mortuary) spaces might be incorrect. At best, these sites indicate an ambient Meadowood-like EMW presence but give us little opportunity to address issues of chronology and social and material relationships.

Lukuwakn

In 2005, the community broke ground for the interpretation centre for Metepenagiag Heritage Park on a terrace 10 m above the Little Southwest Miramichi, across the river from and overlooking the Oxbow site (figure 5.2). As a part of this work, they encountered a dense concentration of quartz flakes and artifacts in the 25 cm to 30 cm layer of sandy soil that overlay the glacially derived outwash that formed the terrace (Blair 2007). These were restricted to a roughly oval area that was 5 m by 6 m in size, but within this area they were densely deposited and accompanied by a seemly random distribution of 61 small post molds (wedge-shaped reddish stains that resulted from topsoil being carried down into voids in the subsoil). We were unable to determine the original function of the post molds, but in the absence of an associated hearth, suggested they might be related to temporary structures, such as drying racks or rain shelters. In all, 15,862 artifacts were recovered; 99.5% of these were quartz shatter and debris resulting from tool production. In addition to these, the assemblage produced four broad, leaf-shaped quartz bifaces that were similar to those from the submound features of Augustine Mound (see below), two small, stemmed points that were similar to those from the mound fill of Augustine Mound and lower layers of the Oxbow site, and a single large flaked-and-ground-stone axe (figure 5.4). Given the shallow nature of the deposit and the lack of associated habitation features (such as hearths that might contain wood charcoal and date-able organic material), we were unable to acquire a radiometric assay. The presence of formal tools and, in particular, small stemmed points and a flaked-and-ground axe led us to infer an EMW age for the site (Blair 2007).

The Mitchell Site

The Mitchell site is located on the opposite shore and just downstream from the Oxbow site on the banks of the Little Southwest Miramichi River (figure 5.2; Emin 1978; Bourgeois and Allen 2005). Excavation undertaken by community members and provincial archaeologists in 1978 revealed a small lens of charcoal-rich soil and a small lithic assemblage, including bifaces (8), scrapers (6), retouched flakes (5), and hundreds of pieces of flaking debris and shatter. Like other sites in the area, the assemblage is overwhelmingly made of quartz (98% by piece count). In addition, two small fragments of undecorated, low-fired ceramic were recovered (Emin 1978). The site was re-examined in 1998, resulting in the recovery of additional lithic debris similar to that recovered in 1978. Based on the only projectile point, a small, stemmed point of the kind found in the deepest layers of the Oxbow site and in the mound fill of the Augustine Mound, the site is considered to date to the EMW, at some point between 2600 and 2100 BP (Emin 1978; Bourgeois and Allen 2005).

Mound Terrace Pit Features

Mejipkei, Taboogul Mejipkei, and Others

Community-based survey and excavation identified a large number of anthropogenic depressions, or "pits," not directly associated with larger sites. These were scattered on the terrace around the Augustine Mound and on the tops of adjacent raised banks. While estimates vary, somewhere between 60 and 120 of these pit features have been identified in the area of Metepenagiag (Allen 2005; Suttie 2006). Of these, only two, subsequently named Mejipkei and Taboogul Mejipkei, have been excavated (figure 5.2). While wood charcoal and bark fragments from Mejipkei have been radiocarbon dated to the Late Maritime Woodland (1490±110 BP, Beta-8223, and 1060±190 BP, Beta 8224; Suttie 2006:17), the total assemblage of pits may represent repeated activities over a much longer period of time. These features range in size and shape, but Mejipkei was around 2 m in diameter and 1-m deep, containing greasy organic layers, calcined animal bones, evidence of burning, and occasionally, toolmaking debris (Suttie 2006).

Allen initially suggested that these features were storage pits (Allen 2005:71). Suttie (2006) undertook isotope analysis of samples from the greasy organic layers from Taboogul Mejipkei through the Stable Isotopes in Nature Laboratory, or SINLAB, at the University of New Brunswick. While the samples produced "negligible nitrogen content," he reports d13C results of -22.65 and -22.92 and indicates that "the d13C values are consistent and allow for a narrowing of the spectrum of possible organic sources for this residue," suggesting that it "originated either from migratory birds, anadromous fish or a mixture of various other organic compounds" (Suttie 2006:56). Most of the identifiable animal remains from the features were large numbers of sturgeon dermal bones and spines. Based on this, Suttie has suggested a more complex use-life involving smoking or roasting of food, possibly followed by storage. While none of these pit features have been definitively associated with the EMW, their distribution and their association with sturgeon (a species that is persistently emphasized in archaeological deposits extending to the beginning of the EMW) suggests that at least some of them may date to this period. As we speculate below, given their position on the mound terrace and their strong association with sturgeon remains, it seems possible that the pits result from people gathering to undertake ceremonial activities and feasting, serving as a link among places like Oxbow and Augustine and an ancient sturgeon fishery.

Ceremonial Places

The McKinlay Collection
In 1908, an archaeological assemblage from the banks of the Northwest Miramichi just upstream across from the mound terrace were sent to the British Museum. Although Turnbull (1986) was able through historical research to narrow the source of these materials to a property in Sunny Corner (on the other side of the river from the modern community of Metepenagiag), their

precise provenience is unknown. Turnbull convincingly argues that the assemblage is not from the Augustine Mound itself but from a different (apparently non-mound) mortuary site. In general terms, they appear to be from an area close to the Howe and Wilson sites, discussed above (see figure 5.2). Turnbull visited the British Museum and reported his observations (Turnbull 1986). The assemblage includes four stemmed points (two made of the local white quartz), unstemmed bifaces (18), scrapers (2), flaked-and-ground-stone celts (5), gorgets (2), block-end tubular stone pipes (4), pre-Contact, low-fired pottery sherds (5), and a boatstone (a conical slate object with three holes drilled into it, one at the tip of the cone and one on each side of the object). In addition, there were numerous copper beads and fragments of textiles (Turnbull 1986:37). It was also clear from the correspondence, and from an account recorded in Wallis and Wallis (1955:259), that the site had had human remains interred in it. Turnbull observed that: (1) most of the artifacts themselves were well within the range of artifact shapes and materials from the Augustine Mound (in other words, exhibiting a very high morphological and material consistency), (2) like at Augustine Mound, the artifacts were strongly similar to Adena-related objects from elsewhere in eastern North America, and (3) additional Adena-related classes of artifacts were present, such as the boatstone, an artifact class not encountered at Augustine Mound. An additional object of note is a fragment of pottery with a triangular motif trail onto the area below the lip edge. This motif is very similar to one recorded for the Adena/Middlesex-related Boucher cemetery in Vermont (Turnbull 1986; Heckenberger et al. 1990; Robinson 2016).

The Tozer Site

The Tozer site, located on a terrace back from the east bank of the river just downstream from the confluence of the Northwest and Little Southwest Miramichi (figure 5.2), was discovered during road construction in 1928, and subsequently investigated by Wintemberg (1937; see McEachen et al. 1999). The site was distributed over 8 m and consisted of two circular deposits of red ochre containing "17 ochre-coated cache blade-like bifaces, one lanceolate biface, one stemmed biface, a copper awl, a nearly complete ground slate gorget" (McEachen et al. 1999:157; see also Wintemberg 1937). The bifaces themselves are thin, triangular, with polished flake ridges; McEachen et al. (1999:164) affiliate them with Meadowood-style tools, and present instrumental neutron activation analysis data to suggest that while they look similar to grey materials from the Great Lakes region, they are made from fine-grained felsic rocks likely from northeastern New Brunswick.

The Tozer site differs from other ceremonial sites in the area in several ways. First, it did not include quartz artifacts. Second, many of its artifacts were morphologically different from those found in other ceremonial sites in the area, with the exception of the gorget. In other words, the Tozer site is convincingly "Meadowood-like" just as the Augustine Mound is convincingly "Adena-like," at least in terms of their mid-twentieth-century conceptualizations. Elsewhere, Loring (1985) has pointed to the dual nature of Meadowood and Middlesex/ Adena sites, emphasizing several key features: they often co-occur in close proximity to each other, they cannot be demonstrated to be temporally distinct, and they often contain distinctive assemblages. To explain this, he suggests we consider intra-societal relationships, a suggestion we return to below.

The Augustine Mound

The Augustine Mound is a low earthen mound containing mortuary features, located on the terrace that has formed between the Northwest and Little Southwest Miramichi Rivers. While it has been a primary component of conceptions of archaeological heritage in the community (see Augustine et al. 2006), it is poorly reported in the published literature (primarily described in Turnbull 1976) and is the focus of the remainder of this chapter.

History of Research
and Structure of the Augustine Mound

In 1972, Elder Joe Augustine became concerned about the potential impact of local development on a broad terrace of land (the "mound terrace") that currently sits 15 m above summer water levels (figure 5.2). In particular, he was aware of a small raised mound of earth; his grandfather had passed down to him that it was a place of importance to the Ancestors, where they used to gather and dance (Augustine et al. 2006; Turnbull 1980). Based on these concerns and informed by public accounts of archaeology elsewhere, he undertook a small excavation into the top of what would later be called Augustine Mound (CfDl2). The material that he recovered was from one of ten mortuary features under the mound fill. While the features were highly variable in form and content, the overall assemblage had two broad characteristics that have significantly shaped subsequent archaeological interpretations. First, the presence of large volumes of copper, mostly in the form of 4,000 rolled copper strips and beads, rendered the soil toxic to microorganism that would normally destroy organic materials, leading to the preservation of a remarkable assemblage of baskets, bags, tassels, hides and pelts, and woven fabrics (Blair et al. 2014; Gorman and Blair 2008; Jarratt 2015; Turnbull 1976, 1980). Second, the assemblage contained stone tools, shell and copper beads, and blocked-end tubular pipes and slate gorgets that had a high degree of stylistic similarity to Adena forms.

After a preliminary publication (Turnbull 1976) and an initial phase of active community-based field research, the community re-evaluated the project, leading Turnbull to delay dissemination of a more complete description of the assemblage, notwithstanding an almost complete final report (Turnbull 1980, pers. comm. 2003). At this very time, the preliminary publication of results led to a great deal of archaeological interest outside of the region, and in the absence of access to critical details about the site and the assemblage, the site became contextualized through the better understood Midwestern phenomena, and the partial analysis in the preliminary report became integrated into regional syntheses (Tuck 1984; Rutherford 1991; Wright 1999). As a result, the site became widely viewed as a single event involving exotic (essentially Adena) materials imported into the Maritimes from the south as a "package"; furthermore, this event is considered to take place in the Early Woodland proper—some 2,400 years ago (Allen 1980; McEachen 1996; see Wright 1999). In 2007, with the creation of the Metepenagiag Heritage Park, the analysis and dissemination of results was renewed (Augustine and McLaughlin 2006), including a reassessment of the assemblage and undertaking additional radiometric dating, which is reported on here.

Field Methods

The mound itself was circular in plan, approximately 11.5 m in diameter and 1 m high. The material that composed the mound itself, the "mound fill" (Turnbull 1976), contained archaeological materials (in particular, stone tools and toolmaking debris), indicating that that particular part of the mound terrace was in use prior to construction of the mound. The mound was excavated in quarters (or quadrants), with a 1-m baulk left between each. As indicated by Turnbull (1980:10-11):

> The excavations were conducted in the mound fill of each quadrant in succession. [...] The mound fill was excavated in 20 cm arbitrary levels to the top of the premound surface. There was not much discernable difference in the mound fill but the top of the premound surface was readily identifiable in the excavations [...] The one metre strip between the quadrants was left as balks for control over mound stratigraphy and construction. Once the mound fill was removed the burial pits were evident as discolourations in the premound surface.

All excavated soil was screened through quarter-inch mesh, and pit features were excavated by hand with trowels and small tools. In cases where fragile perishable materials were encountered in masses, they were encased in wrappings and plaster, block-lifted and excavated in the laboratory (Turnbull 1980:11-12). Based on this approach, Turnbull (1980:25) determined that "all the material in the mound fill is at least older than the burials." Further, he was not able to discern episodes of mound construction based the even distribution of mound fill materials; "they [artifacts] are scattered generally evenly through the fill by level and by quadrant" (26). However, he noted that the mound fill also contained historic artifacts, leading him to infer that the surface of the mound was impacted on by various activities on the mound terrace in recent times.

Features

In his 1976 report, Turnbull indicates that there were 11 burial pits excavated into the subsoil and discusses the six that had been analyzed at the time of his report (Features 10, 11, 12, 14, 15, and the "central pit"). Some of these, however, are partially adjoined, while others contained very little material. For our analysis, we consider the site to represent 10 distinct burial units (submound features numbered Features 5, 9, 10, 11, 12, 14, 15, 18, 20, 27; see figure 5.5). In almost all cases, these were distinctive, clearly evident, and separate from the subsoil and the mound fill. The exception to this, however, was Feature 14. This was the largest pit feature in the site, both in size and in number of artifacts, and was also the most stratigraphically complex. While Elder Joe Augustine excavated portions of Feature 14 in his 1972 work, there is some evidence that it may have been previously intruded on from above:

> The beads in the fill and [lack of] beads at the "burial" level seem to suggest that the burial had been disturbed. [...] The slight hollow in the mound centre is probably indicative of this disturbance too. There is nothing in the fill or site to suggest an age for this reopening of the pit. The multiple layers of sod in the mound centre suggest a certain amount of time had taken place between the opening and the present. Possibly it was done in the last century when the 19th century artifacts were deposited at the site, possibly it was done thousands of years ago during the mound use or just after its construction. (Turnbull 1980:220)

Further, it appears that the excavation of parts of the pit itself may have predated mound construction: "Before the mound and main burial pit fill was brought to the site, there was more material—heavy with charcoal and rocks (probably from sterile gravels)—piled on top of the stratum that extends into the pit. It is tenuous evidence but possibly the central pit was used before the mound was constructed" (Turnbull 1980:218). Feature 14 remains enigmatic and is the subject of forthcoming further study. For the purpose of this chapter, however, we treat the contents of Feature 14 separately from other categorizations (both functional and temporal).

Although it represents a different kind of depositional event, we also recognize that the mound fill itself is an archaeologically distinct unit, and we present the material recovered from the mound fill accordingly. The features themselves contained offerings and human remains. The offerings are summarized in table 5.1.

Table 5.1. Number of artifacts by feature from Augustine Mound.

Feature	fill	F5	F9	F10	F11	F12	F14	F15	F18	F20	F27
Projectile Points	14	7		5		5	9		1		
Unstemmed Bifaces	7	11	18	3	4	3		1			
Biface fragments	16		0				27				
Tubular stone pipe	6	2*					2*				
Gorgets and gorget blanks				3			1				
Copper projectile point		1									
Copper beads	xx	xxx	-	xxx	x	xxx	xxx	x	x	x	-
Shell columella beads		24			1						
Hafted beaver incisor tool		1					1				
Modified beaver incisors				2							
Carnivore mandible				1							
Shell and copper bead strand						2					
Shell pendants							8				
Steep-edge scrapers	33		1	1			6		1		
Cores	59						10				
Flakes	1573	4	8	3	5	2	25	1	3		
Flaked & ground celts	1	1		5			1				
Pecked & ground celts	1										
Abrasive stone	2			1			5				
Hammerstone		1		2							
Fossil plant segment				1							
Precontact Pottery sherds	6						20				

*broken but all fragments present; these have likely been ceremonially broken
Estimates of copper bead numbers: - = 0, x = under 10, xx = 11 to 300, xxx = more than 300

The Mound Fill

The mound fill contained materials typical of local habitation sites, including small, stemmed projectile points; unstemmed bifaces; unifacial and bifacial scrapers; large volumes of stone-tool-making debris (of which over 95% are local quartz); abraders; sherds of low-fired, undecorated pottery; and both a flaked-and-ground- and pecked-and-ground-stone celt. The mound fill also produced a number of fragments of tubular stone pipe and several hundred loose tubular copper beads (Jarratt 2015; table 5.1 here). These latter materials are almost certainly related to the mortuary features, but the faunal materials (Stewart 1982) and flaked lithic and pottery assemblages are much more similar to habitation material from the deepest excavated components of the nearby Oxbow site (see above). Some of the incorporation of burial feature material into the mound fill may have happened as a result of later intrusion and admixture, as noted by Turnbull (1980). The mound fill also contains a range of historic materials of the kind typical of eighteenth- and nineteenth-century debris, including buttons, flat glass, iron nails, scrap iron, European clay tobacco-pipe fragments, and pieces of refined earthenware. Three quarters of these historic materials were in the upper levels of the mound fill (levels 2 and 3), while one earthenware fragment and one nail were found in level 4 or 5. Pre-Contact materials were distributed more randomly by level or quadrant, as noted above (Turnbull 1980:26). In some cases, the material that comprised the mound itself infilled the burial pits; these cases are noted below.

Feature 5

This pit was oval, 108 cm to 124 cm wide by 65 cm deep, and had steep upper sides tapering to a rounded bottom. No artifacts were recovered from the feature fill, but instead were found on the pit bottom and sloping sides. These include a number of projectile points and bifaces, a flaked-and-ground-stone celt, and two blocked-end tubular pipes. Of the 18 bifacial tools, 13 were of local quartz, while the remainder were various non-local materials (figure 5.6).[1] In addition to stone tools, Feature 5 contained a flattened copper projectile point with a split-wood and sinew-bound haft still attached, several long coils of leather with crimped copper beads, shell columella beads, a hafted, double-ended beaver-incisor tool, and at least 17 different textile fragments, all covered in birchbark sheets. The hafted beaver-incisor tool consisted of two beaver incisors with the blade ends curving in opposite directions, and with the material holding them together wrapped in a bark tube. Two radiometric assays submitted on bark from Feature 5 returned uncalibrated dates of 1920±70 BP (TO12920) and 2160±40 BP (Beta-236517) (see discussion below).

Feature 9

This pit was oval in shape, 120 cm by 80 cm by 65 cm deep. The feature itself lacked copper beads, and thus produced almost no organic material. Clustered at the very bottom of the pit on a small patch of red ochre was a cluster of 18

---

1. Formal raw material analysis of the non-quartz lithic assemblage has not yet been completed; however, these artifacts are generally made of fine-grained to cryptocrystalline materials that are grey, black, brown, and dark red, and are typically banded, mottled, and variegated; materials that are significant in later Maritime Woodland–period procurement and/or exchange in the region, such as brightly coloured, variegated, and translucent materials such as Minas Basin chert and Washademoak chert (Black and Wilson 1999), are rare or absent.

unstemmed bifaces, eight flakes, and a scraper, all made of quartz. One radio-metric assay returned a result of 2625±50 BP (S1634).

Feature 10

This pit was 100 cm by 80 cm by 80 cm deep, with steeply sloping sides.

Grave offerings were placed in three concentrations, all accompanied by red ochre (figure 5.7). Concentration One was a dense cluster of artifacts, including flaked and ground celts, an elliptical gorget, a fossil, modified beaver incisors, a carnivore mandible, and a few copper beads. Concentration Two contained abundant charcoal and red ochre, as well as stemmed and unstemmed quartz bifaces, a gorget blank, and two coils of copper beads in a hide wrap-ping, with the coils containing over 159 beads (table 5.1). Concentration Three included a large flaked-and-ground-stone celt, parts of a wood-splint basket, masses of coils of copper beads, various fragments of woven textile, two hair tassels, quantities of acorn and hazelnut shells, and, remarkably, a reel-shaped gorget with a wooden haft (see discussion below). Radiometric assays on bark returned dates of 2420±40 BP (Beta-236518) and 2950±75 BP (S1655). Turnbull (1980) considered this date to be consistent with his hunch that there were traces of earlier mortuary activity at the site, including, possibly, Feature 10.

Feature 11

This pit was oval in shape, 56 cm to 63 cm wide by 73 cm deep. It is connected to Feature 14 (the main, central pit) by a low "saddle," as is Feature 15, reinforcing the similar radiometric results below. This saddle consists of an area of inter-connecting subsoil, such that Features 11, 14, and 15 are deeper pits within a shared, shallow depression, suggested that the three features were constructed at the same time. The bottom of the pit, designated as Feature 11, held two concentrations of offerings, one at each end of the pit, with an area of red ochre between them. Concentration One consisted of a small area (25 cm by 28 cm, and 2 cm to 3 cm deep) containing large sheets of partially burnt wood, several tiny fabric fragments, four loose copper beads, and several quartz bifaces (table 5.1). Concentration Two was associated with few artifacts, consisting of a few strands of copper beads, a small section of fabric, one shell columella bead, and an animal pelt. Three radiometric assays returned results of 2350±60 BP (S1656), 2490±55 BP (S1657), and 2550±80 BP (TO12921).

Feature 12

This pit was shallow with flaring walls and was 96 cm by 66 cm by 40 cm deep. Infilling material contained a small stemmed projectile point and two small quartz flakes. This pit is the furthest from the mound centre, "part of the pit laying outside the actual extent of the mound" (Turnbull 1980:188). Artifacts on the pit floor were found in two concentrations. Concentration One was a large area (30 cm by 60 cm), containing birchbark, large unstemmed bifaces and stemmed points, one of which still retained a split-wood and sinew haft, and an object consisting of many interconnected strands of copper beads (possibly a headdress; Turnbull 1980). As well, there were many fragments of fabric and basketry, and several matted and poorly preserved animal pelts. Concentration Two consisted of a small area (9 cm in diameter) containing a string of copper beads—not of the type that are typical of other features in the mound (copper beads crimped on leather), but rather several strands of a two-ply plant cord (Z-twist). One is strung with alternating shell disc beads and shell columella beads, while a second string consists of conical copper beads "strung small end of the cone into the large end. Although they are corroded together now, they may have been jinglers—noisy beads" (Turnbull 1980:196). This is the only feature containing this kind of stringing and these kinds of beads. Three radiometric assays returned dates of 2210 ± 70 BP (TO12922), 2290 ± 30 BP (Beta-369128), and 2670 ± 50 BP (S1635).

Feature 14

This was the feature first identified in 1972 by Elder Joe Augustine. It was also very complex, and the infilling material was difficult to distinguish from interred material. It was located at the very centre of the mound and was connected to Features 11 and 15 by a shallow depression. Its original dimensions are difficult to reconstruct; minimally, it was greater than 150 cm by 160 cm, and possibly more than 200 cm in diameter. The infilling material produced numerous loose copper beads (at least 63) and small pockets of red ochre. In the lower part of the feature, there are a number of exceptional artifacts of Adena forms (figure 5.8), including stemmed points (one of which retained its wooden haft), unstemmed bifaces, a beautifully made slate, reel-shaped gorget, two broken blocked-end tubular stone pipes, a flaked-and-ground-stone celt, a double-ended beaver-incisor tool, a shell pendant (consisting of the curving surface of a bivalve or very large snail, shaped and pierced), various fragments of braiding and matting, as well as many lumps and concentrations of red and yellow ochre. In addition to these offerings, Feature 14 also produced material more like the mound fill, including scrapers, cores, and flakes, abrasive stones, and fragments of low-fired, pre-Contact pottery (table 5.1). Further, small numbers of historic artifacts (clay tobacco-pipe fragments, iron, earthenwares) were scattered in Feature 14, reinforcing the impression of overall disturbance. In an effort to sort out some of the internal complexities of Feature 14, five radiometric assays were submitted for analysis, resulting in the following dates: 1970 ± 30 BP (Beta-369127), 2140 ± 30 BP (Beta-369134), 2160 ± 30 BP

(Beta-369132), 2330±110 BP (RL344), and 2350±30 BP (Beta-369131) (see discussion below).

Feature 15
This feature was irregular, roughly sub-oval in outline, 115 cm by 50 cm in size. As noted above, it was connected to Feature 14 and Feature 11 by a single shallow depression and these features were likely constructed at the same time. It produced very few copper beads, as well as a single brown quartzite biface, a quartz flake, and scattered pieces of red ochre. As single radiometric assay returned a date of 2350±30 BP (Beta-369138).

Feature 18
This pit had a complex shape—it had an initial diameter of 150 cm, tapering at a 50 cm depth to a diameter of 70 cm, then expanding again to 80 cm toward a dish-shaped bottom, at 119 cm below surface. The infilling material was unusually stratified, consisting of layers of sand and gravel. This was the deepest feature on the site and contained a single stemmed biface with a "turkey tail" base, stylistically different from other bifaces recovered from the site. Based on this, Turnbull (1980:262) suggested that Feature 18 might be older than other features. In addition, the feature also produced a quartz scraper, some highly fragmented copper, and thin bark sheets and strips. Two radiometric dates, 2080±40 BP (Beta-236519) 2260±70 BP (TO12924), were obtained from bark; neither of these dates support the inference of an older age for this feature.

Feature 20
This shallow convex basin is the shallowest feature from the site, being 75 cm by 60 cm wide by 8 cm deep. It contained a few copper beads, a layer of birch-bark, and hide and matted material. A single radiocarbon date of 2100±30 BP (Beta-369130) was obtained from bark.

Feature 27
This feature was located near the margin of the mound. It contained charcoal and bark fragments but no artifacts. In an effort to date construction events and the distribution of features in the mound, a single assay was run on charcoal from Feature 27, returning a date of 2170±30 BP (Beta-369129).

Augustine Mound Artifact Classes

Stone Artifacts
Collectively, the mortuary features in the Augustine Mound contained a range of stemmed (27) and unstemmed bifaces (67), chiefly consisting of large

straight and lobate stemmed points in forms typologically associated with Midwestern manifestations of Adena. Most of the broad, unstemmed bifaces were similar in shape and form to the stemmed points. While the majority (60%) of the bifaces are made of local quartz, the non-quartz bifaces are of unusual materials, consisting of a wide range of waxy, chert-like materials of anonymous but likely nonlocal sources (table 5.2). While some have speculated that these materials may originate in places like the Great Lakes Basin and the Ohio Valley (Tuck 1984), they have yet to be subjected to a rigorous provenancing study. Although it was difficult to discern traces of wear on the quartz objects, almost all of the non-quartz bifaces had polish on the flake ridges and arrises consistent with patterns of wear produced by long periods of carrying and wrapping (Pelletier-Michaud 2017). The presence of some preserved hafts suggests that at least some of them were hafted as spear ends. The site also produced reel-shaped, diamond-shaped, and rectangular gorgets, one of which, remarkably, is also hafted (see description in the organic artifact section, below). The assemblage also contained blocked-end tubular stone-pipe fragments of Ohio Valley pipestone representing at least four pipes, all of which had been ceremonially broken. The forms and materials of the bifaces, pipes, and gorgets all appear in restricted contexts in the Canadian Maritimes (in particular, in mortuary or ceremonial contexts). The mortuary features also produce seven flaked-and-ground-stone celts or axes. This type of artifact appears to be particularly associated with the EMW but is distributed more broadly than most of the other artifact classes from mortuary features. They are found in a range of contexts (including several from the lower layers of the Oxbow site and one from the Lukuwakn site). Indeed, flake-and-ground-stone axes, often of fine-grained, waxy materials, are one of the few artifact classes that link habitation and mortuary components, and as such warrant further attention as items that may be able to bridge these two otherwise carefully separated settings.

Table 5.2. Number of flaked-stone tool by type from Augustine Mound (brackets indicate number made of local white quartz).

Feature	fill	F5	F9	F10	F11	F12	F14	F15	F18	F20	F27
Bifacial tools	37 (17)	18 (13)	18 (18)	8 (8)	4 (3)	8 (4)	36 (12)	1 (0)	2 (2)		
Steep-edge scrapers	33 (30)		1	1			6 (5)		1 (1)		
Cores	59 (59)						10 (10)				
Flakes	1573 (1555)	4 (4)	7 (7)	3 (3)	5 (5)	2 (2)	25 (24)	1 (1)			

Copper Artifacts

The mound contained many copper beads that consist of strips of copper formed into tubes or rings, sometimes occurring loose, and other times crimped around leather strips (Jarratt 2015). The original number of beads is difficult to determine due to corrosion that in some cases has reduced them to dust. In other cases, the beads represent part of larger, composite objects that are folded and massed in a way that makes extricating elements for the purposes of counting not only difficult but problematic from a conservation point of view. The current estimate for the number of these beads is over 4,000, and given these factors, this undoubtedly represents an underestimation (Jarratt 2015). Because of these difficulties, table 5.1 does not provide a bead count. The presence of these beads is directly correlated with the preservation of organic material (see below). In some cases, these strings of copper beads crimped on leather appear to be part of a larger object. For example, in Feature 12, these appears to be attached to each other in the form of a headdress (Turnbull 1980). The copper from Augustine Mound has yet to be provenanced, although a preliminary sample was examined with a University of New Brunswick microprobe to evaluate trace elements; a comparison with samples from Lake Superior and the Minas Basin area of Nova Scotia indicated a correlation with the Nova Scotia samples (Evans 2006).

In addition to crimped or rolled copper beads, the mound produced conical beads that were strung in a nesting fashion, likely with the goal of jingling (see Feature 12; Turnbull 1980:196). In addition to beads and objects containing beads, the site also produced a few singular forms, in particular, a flat leaf-shaped copper point that still retained a fragment of a split-wood haft (figure 5.9) and some of the sinew bindings.

Organic Artifacts

Approximately 300 textile fragments were preserved, including fabric, basketry, matting, and bag fragments (Gorman and Blair 2008; figure 5.10 here). A preliminary analysis of this material was undertaken by Gorman in 2008. The textile artifacts represent a number of different structural types, including plaited basketry or matting, S-twined basketry, S-twining of paired and wrapped cordage elements, S-twining of three-element braids of twisted cordage, obliquely braided fabric, interlaced fabric, three-element braids, two- and four-ply, Z-spun S-twisted cordage, and moose-hair tassels.

The textiles included fine, complex, cloth-like materials that Gordon has convincingly argued were made through the twining of paired and wrapped cordage elements on a simple frame (Gordon, pers. comm. 2007). In every textile made with spun or twisted cordage, the spin and twist of the yarns was consistently Z/S. That is, they were spun either on a spindle whorl in a clockwise direction or downwards on the thigh if right-handed (Gorman and Blair 2008). Turnbull suggested that some of the basketry fragments might be made of wood, an interpretation supported by Gorman's analysis; as such, they are the oldest known wood-splint basketry in the Northeast, resolving the debate as to whether wood-splint basketry was introduced as a result of European contact (Gordon 1990, 2002; Lester 1987; McMullen 1992; Whitehead 1980). In most cases, Gorman's analysis was not able to determine materials used to make these textiles. However, fibers from obliquely braided textile fragments and from two yarns were submitted in the late 1970s by Turnbull to the Royal Canadian Mounted Police's crime-detection laboratory in Sackville, New Brunswick, where the hairs were identified as *Bovidae* (Donahue 1978:27).[2] The weaving of bison-wool textiles was documented across parts of the Northeast during the historic period (Amsden 1932). The presence in the Augustine Mound of spun wool textiles refute previous assertions that wool-yarn manufacture was introduced to the Mi'kmaq from the French (Wallis and Wallis 1955:87). In addition to textiles, there were also a number of hide pieces with fur attached that appear to represent animal pelts. These (and many of the textiles) occurred as masses of fused material, impeding analysis and identification.

The assemblage also contains pendants made from the flat outer portions of a large shellfish shell, and beads made of the inner columella of a large whelk (see table 5.1). In addition, a number of objects (both inorganic and organic) retained fragments of hafts. For example, there were several loose, modified beaver incisors, but also a complete double-ended beaver-incisor knife (as described above, see figure 5.10). Some of the projectile points (two stone and one copper) retained hafts and handles. In the case of projectile points, these included short segments of shafts of split wood wrapped in sinew. The most unexpected and exceptional hafted stone tool, however, was a gorget attached with its flat surface parallel to a short section of wood (see figure 5.11). This configuration upends many of our assumptions about gorgets; while it remains unclear what this indicates in terms of function, Suttie (pers. comm. 2009) has suggested it may have been a counterweight, such as for an atlatl or spear thrower.

Finally, the mortuary features also contained abundant birchbark. Many of the inhumations were wrapped in bark, and bark was used to line surfaces in preparation for the inhumation. We considered the possibility that birchbark may have been also modified as tools, including the possibility that the bark placed with the dead ancestors might represent containers or canoe parts, but we were unable to document evidence to support this idea due to the fragmentary nature of the bark itself.

---

2. *Bovidae* is the taxonomic classification for bison, domesticated cow, sheep, and goat (Donahue 1978:27).

Figure 5.4. Artifacts from the Lukuwakn Site: (A) small stemmed points and point fragments; (B) quartz bifaces and biface preforms; (C) quartz cores; (D) flaked-and-ground stone axe.
Source: Photo by S. Blair.

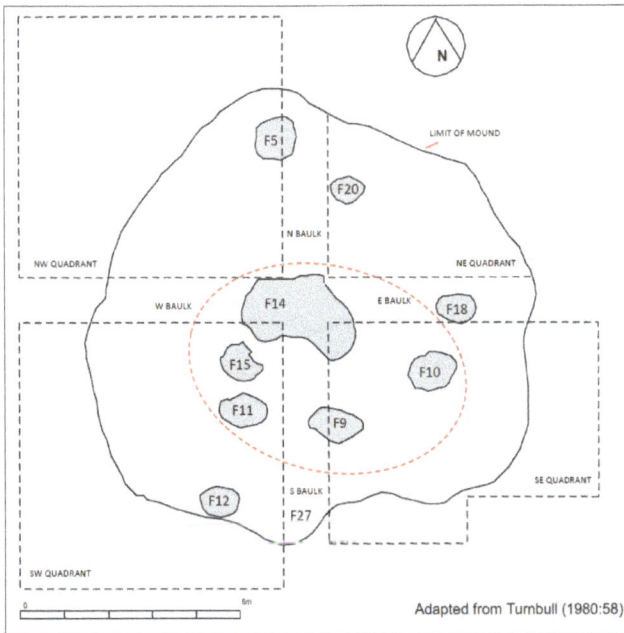

Figure 5.5. Features in the mound fill; the features inside the dotted line date to between 2700 and 2300 BP, while those outside date to between 2300 and 2000 BP.

Figure 5.6. A selection of stemmed and unstemmed bifaces from Feature 5 of the Augustine Mound. *Source:* Photo by C. Drew Gilbert.

Figure 5.7. A selection of artifacts from Feature 10 of the Augustine Mound: (A) gorget (also shown in Plate 8 with haft attached); (B) gorget; (C) gorget blank; (D)–(F) flaked-and-ground stone axes; and (G)–(J) quartz stemmed projectile points.
Source: Photo by C. Drew Gilbert.

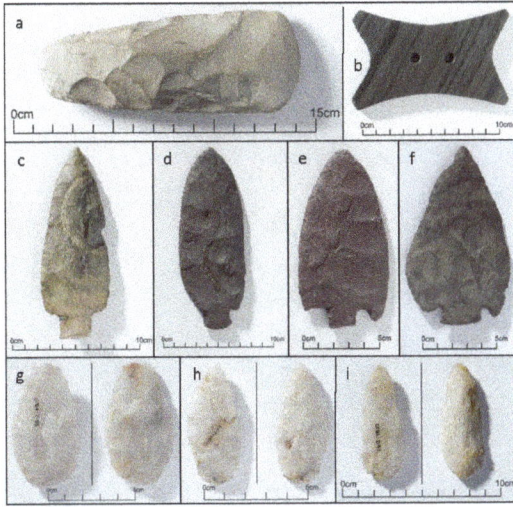

Figure 5.8. A selection of lithic artifacts from Feature 14 from the Augustine Mound: (A) flaked-and-ground stone axe; (B) ground slate gorget; (C)–(F) stemmed bifaces; and (G)–(I) unstemmed quartz bifaces showing both obverse and reverse.
Source: Photo by C. Drew Gilbert.

Figure 5.9. Hafted copper point from Feature 5 of the Augustine Mound.
Source: Courtesy of C. Turnbull, Archaeological Services, Government of New Brunswick. Photo by C. Turnbull.

Figure 5.10. A selection of organic artifacts from the Augustine Mound: (A) a band of 2/2 obliquely braided fabric (or cloth) on two-ply yard with both edges present (Gorman and Blair 2008); (B) basketry containing strands of copper beads crimped on leather; (C) double-ended beaver-incisor tool; and (D) fabric made with weft-twined wrapped warps.
Source: Photo by E. Gorman.

Figure 5.11. Hafted gorget from Feature 10 of the Augustine Mound site.
Source: Courtesy of C. Turnbull, Archaeological Services, Government of New Brunswick. Photo by C. Turnbull.

Dating the Augustine Mound

At the time of the 1976 article, Turnbull reported on a single radiometric date of 2330±110 BP (RL344); subsequently, he ran five additional radiometric assays. We have supplemented this with 15 additional assays (figure 5.12, table 5.5). The pattern that has emerged through radiometric dating indicates that older materials were consistently from features near the centre of the mound footprint, while more recent samples were consistently from features closer to the edge (figure 5.5). In particular, Features 9, 10, 11, 14, and 15 are within a loosely defined inner circle, while Features 5, 12, 18, 20, and 27 occur outside of this central area. An outlier to this pattern is Feature 14, the feature that Elder Joe Augustine initially identified. This is the feature first dated by Turnbull and is at the very centre of the mound. In his initial notes, Turnbull suggested that there may have been repeated intrusion into the top of the mound prior to Augustine's work. As we describe below, this may explain the fact that this feature, unlike the others in the inner circle of the mound, returned a number of later radio-metric dates.

Based on this research, we consider there to be a series of episodes of activity at the mound.

(1) Pre-mound: activity prior to mound construction, represented by material in the mound fill, that occurred prior to 2,700 years ago.

(2) Early mound activity: activity concentrated in the more centrally located parts of the mound that dates to between 2,700 and 2,300 years ago.

(3) Late mound activity: through expansion of the mound, additional burial pits that date to between 2,300 and 2,000 years ago.

(4) Post-mound construction: activities that did not result in evident mortuary features, which occurred after 2,000 years ago.

Tables 5.3 and 5.4 indicate the distribution of materials and material types in earlier (and most archaeological evident) episodes, with Feature 14 separated from the chronology, as it may have its own use-life that extends through this sequence. In general, the pre-mound activity is similar to material from nearby habitation sites. While the small sample precludes statistical analysis, this organization of material suggests several aspects: many of the diagnostic Adena elements (including stemmed point forms, blocked-end tubular pipes, shell artifacts) occur late in the life of the mound, during late mound activity, and the use of local quartz to make objects in Adena forms for interment in the mound is more evident in the early mound activity, and relatively less in the late mound activity.

Table 5.3. Distribution of material classes by age from Augustine Mound.

Period	Pre-mound	EARLY					LATE						F14
Feature	fill	F9	F10	F11	F15	Subt	F5	F12	F18	F20	F27	Subt	F14
Projectile Points	14		5			5	7	5	1			13	9
Unstemmed Bifaces	7	18	3	4	1	26	11	3				14	
Biface fragments	16					0						0	27
Tubular stone pipe	6					0	2*					2	2*
Gorgets			3			3						0	1
Shell beads & pendants				1		1	24	2	1			27	8
Steep-edge scrapers	33	1	1			2			1			1	6
Cores	59					0						0	10
Flakes	1573	8	3	5	1	17	4	2	3			9	25
Flaked & ground celts	1		5			5	1					1	1
Pecked & ground celts	1					0						0	
Abrasive stone	2		1			1						0	5
Hammerstone			2			2	1					1	
Precontact Pottery sherds	6					0						0	20

Table 5.4. Distribution of quartz flaked-stone artifacts from Augustine Mound.

Period	Pre-Mound (Fill)		EARLY		LATE		F14	
	Total #	% QTZ	Total #	% QTZ	Total #	% QTZ	Total #	% QTZ
Bifacial tools	37	46%	31	94%	28	68%	36	33%
Scrapers	33	91%	2	100%	1	100%	6	83%
Cores	59	100%	-	-	-	-	10	100%
Flakes	1573	99%	16	100%	6	100%	25	96%
Total	1702	98%	49	96%	35	74%	67	76%

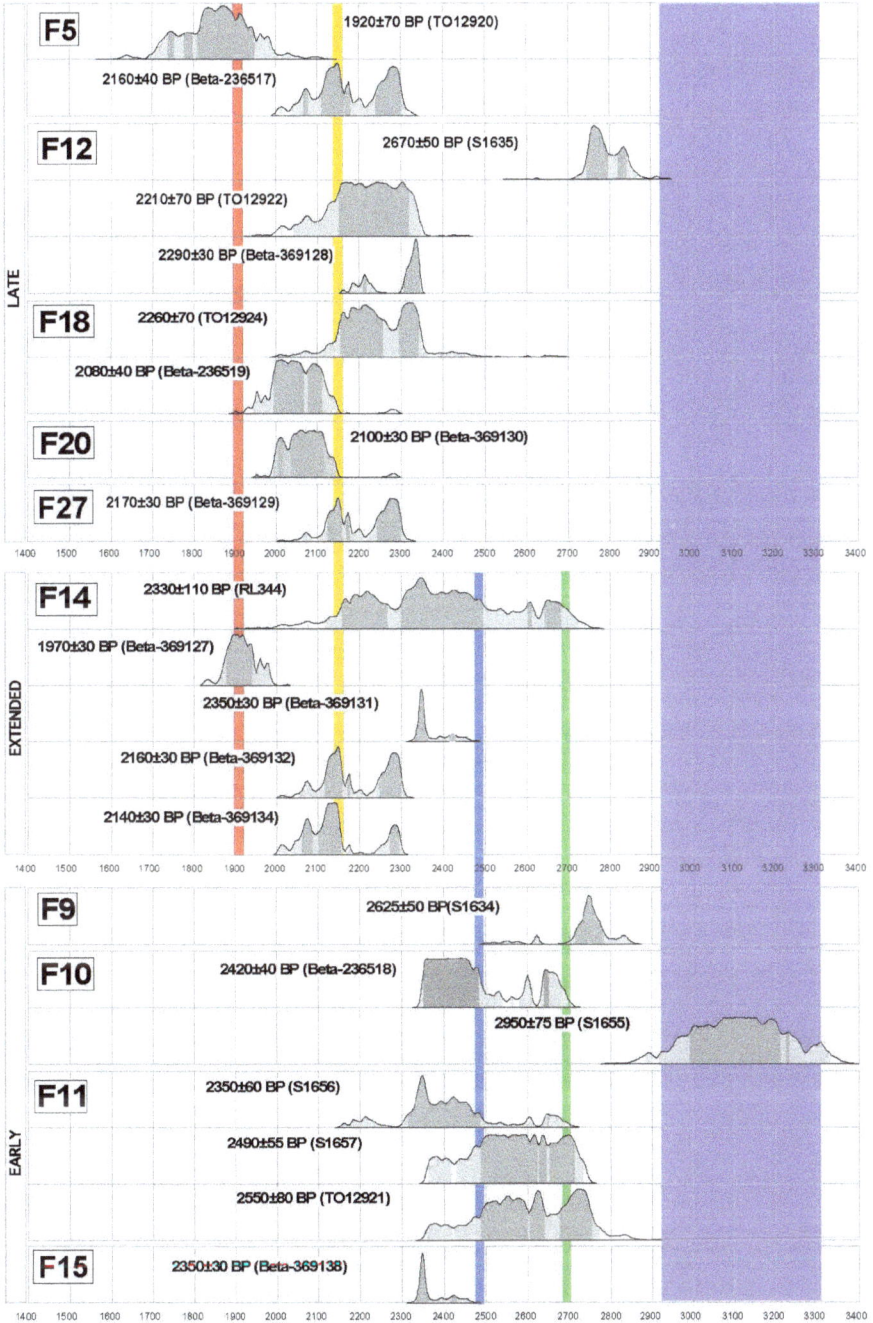

Figure 5.12. Calibrated radiometric dates from the Augustine Mound, with coloured bars indicating shared areas of high probability between features.

Analysis and Integration

Despite the accumulation of evidence about EMW settlement and ceremonialism from different sites and locations within the modern community of Metepenagiag, their integration into coherent landscape which successfully contextualizes broad, macroregional patterns into deep local traditions has remained a challenge. We attempt here to use the refined chronology afforded by our recent research, integrated into the previously obtained radiocarbon sequence (table 5.5, figure 5.12) as a mechanism to integrate disparate localities into the Metepenagiag Site Complex.

Table 5.5. Radiometric dates from Metepenagiag Site Complex.

Uncal Date	Lab No.	Context	Reference
1060±190	Beta8224	Mejipkei, burned bark	Allen 2006
1080±90	S1823	Oxbow, wood charcoal from Unit 79-14 Level 6	Allen 2006
1490±110	Beta8223	Mejipkei, wood charcoal	Suttie 2006
1675±50	S1607	Oxbow, wood charcoal from Feature 35 (hearth), Unit 78-11	Allen 1980
1675±85	S2550	Oxbow, Unit 84-4, Layer 8	Allen 2006
1745±70	S1651	Oxbow, Feature 61 (hearth) Unit 78-10,Level 7	Allen 1980
1745±95	S2551	Oxbow, wood charcoal from Unit 84-6, Level 19	Allen 2006
1760±90	Beta10512	Oxbow, wood charcoal from Unit 84-6, Layer 19	Allen 2006
1770±30	Beta369135	Feature adjacent to Augustine Mound, wood charcoal	
1920±70	TO12920	Augustine Mound, bark from Feature 5	
1970±30	Beta369127	Augustine Mound, Feature 14	
1995±50	S1636	Oxbow, wood charcoal from Feature 45 (hearth), Unit 78-11	Allen 1980
2060±100	S1804	Oxbow, wood charcoal from Unit 79-14	Allen 1980
2070±60	Beta 10513	Oxbow, wood charcoal, Unit 84-6, Layer 19	Allen 2006
2080±60	S1806	Oxbow, wood charcoal (hearth) Unit 78-12, Levels 15/16	Allen 1980
2080±40	Beta236519	Augustine Mound, bark from Feature 18	
2100±30	Beta369130	Augustine Mound, Feature 20	
2120±65	S1652	Oxbow, wood charcoal from Feature 67 (hearth), Unit 78A	Allen 1980
2140±30	Beta369134	Augustine Mound, Feature 14	
2145±65	S1606	Oxbow, wood charcoal (hearth) Unit 78-12	Allen 1980
2160±30	Beta369132	Augustine Mound, Feature 14	

2160±40	Beta236517	Augustine Mound, bark from Feature 5	
2170±30	Beta369129	Augustine Mound, Feature 27	
2210±70	TO12922	Augustine Mound, wood charcoal from Feature 12	
2260±70	TO12924	Augustine Mound, wood charcoal from Feature 18	
2290±30	Beta369128	Augustine Mound, Feature 12	
2330±110	RL344	Augustine Mound, wood charcoal from Feature 14	Tumbull 1976
2350±30	Beta369131	Augustine Mound, Feature 14	
2350±30	Beta369138	Augustine Mound, Feature 15	
2350±60	S1656	Augustine Mound, wood charcoal from Feature 11	Tumbull 1980
2420±40	Beta236518	Augustine Mound, bark from Feature 10	
2480±110	S1805	Oxbow, wood charcoal, Unit 78-12 Level 14	Allen 1980
2490±55	S1657	Augustine Mound, wood charcoal from Feature 11	Tumbull 1980
2550±80	TO12921	Augustine Mound, bark from Feature 11	
2600±60	S1653	Oxbow, wood charcoal, Feature 49 (charcoal stain), Unit 78-11	Allen 1980
2625±50	S1634	Augustine Mound, wood charcoal from Feature 9	Tumbull 1980
2640±50	S1605	Oxbow, wood charcoal from Feature 50 (hearth), Unit 78-11	Allen 1980
2670±50	S1635	Augustine Mound, wood charcoal from Feature 12	Tumbull 1980
2950±75	S1655	Augustine Mound, wood charcoal from Feature 10	Tumbull 1980
2980±80	S1654	Oxbow, wood charcoal, Unit 78-10	Allen 1980

Prior to 3,000 years ago

The earliest period of activity yet identified in the community began prior to 3,000 years ago. While this period remains poorly understood, there are hints and traces of activity. For example, it remains possible that some of the undated pit features on the mound terrace may extend back prior to 3000 BP. Also, the earliest components at Oxbow were below the water table and were inaccessible to standard archaeological methods. Just above this level were small quantities of lithic debris, and several larger projectile points made from regionally available materials. These were not associated with dateable material, but Allen (1981) speculated a Late Archaic age for them.

3,000 to 2,700 years ago

The period between 3,000 and 2,700 years ago is one of increased archaeological visibility. Turnbull (1980) suggests that some mortuary activity at the location of the Augustine Mound may have taken place prior to mound construction. In addition, the mound fill, created from material from around what would become the mound, contained small stemmed points, large ovoid scrapers, knapping tools, and debris, mostly (more than 98%) made of local quartz (table 5.4). These are similar to artifacts that date to before 2,600 years ago at the Oxbow site. Further, localities such as Tozer, Wilson, Hogan-Mullin, and Howe contain materials that reflect what might be called a Meadowood sensibility (McEachen 1996; McEachen et al. 1999; Allen 1988). While Meadowood-like technologies (including the production of thin, triangular unstemmed bifaces) are distributed among ceremonial sites (and, in particular, the Tozer site) and what are ostensibly habitation sites (Wilson, Hogan-Mullin, and Howe), the widespread focus on small, thin bifacial tools in this period made on local materials indicates a degree of integration into otherwise local expressions, as is reflected in material from the lowest layers of the Oxbow site. On the other hand, the unified nature of the assemblage at Tozer, and its consistency in form with Meadowood, may represents early evidence of engagement of local people in broader networks and exchanges, and, in this sense, presage the activity in the subsequent period. Future radiometric dating of these "Meadowood-related" materials may reveal patterns similar to those evident in other parts of the Maritime Peninsula, where some have suggested technical expressions of externally linked manifestations like Meadowood are integrated into local technical practices and persist throughout the EMW, until as late as 2200 BP (Blair 2004a, 2004b). If this is the case here, then some of these Meadowood-like materials might be coeval with the whole range of EMW activities at the mound (see Heckenberger et al. 1990; Loring 1985; Robinson 2016).

2700 to 2300 BP

The creation of the mound and its first major period of use occurred between 2,700 and 2,300 years ago. This activity is related to mortuary practices and involves the integration of existing toolmaking strategies and materials into objects obtained from afar. During this period, people produced large bifaces and stemmed points in local quartz at sites such as Lukuwakn, often echoing the style of Adena tools from elsewhere. In some cases, as with the quartz bifaces from Features 5 and 9, these forms were similar to styles being made in the Midwest (see figures 5.4 and 5.6), carefully produced of local quartz expressly for placement in mortuary contexts, while other forms, such as flaked-and-ground-stone celts, were more ubiquitous in a range of sites, and were similar morphologically, technologically, and in terms of raw material choices to tools from sites elsewhere in the Northeast. Copper beads, ground slate objects, and a wide array of woven objects were also procured and interred at the Augustine Mound. While large Adena-like points were placed in burials, they stand in sharp distinction from material found in and around hearths, living surfaces, and lithic reduction areas at places such as Oxbow, the Mitchell site, and Lukuwakn, where people produced an array of small points that are similar to those made in the preceding period. At the Oxbow site, layers from this period also produced evidence of some of the earliest pottery from the region, and continued evidence of an active sturgeon fishery. Although this link is unsubstantiated, the emphasis on sturgeon within these layers suggests the possibility that some of the many pit features containing sturgeon remains that occur in and around the surrounding areas may also date to this period.

2,300 to 2,000 Years Ago

At some point between 2,300 and 2,000 years ago, there were additions to the mound in the form of new mortuary features. At some time during this period, we speculate that a second mortuary site with strong Adena characteristics was established—resulting in the McKinley collection. These features and assemblages continue many of the patterns evident in the earlier parts of the mound, including ongoing inclusion of copper beads and organic objects, the use of local materials for production of mortuary objects, and the use of distinctive (Adena) forms as grave inclusions. However, these latter patterns appear to intensify—non-local materials become proportionally more important, and, based on "transport" wear on their flake ridges and arrises, many of the lithic objects made from non-local materials appear to have been either transported into the region as finished objects and/or curated for long periods of time before interment. It is of note that, in terms of style, material, and assemblage consistency, this period contains some of the most distinctively Adena objects but is comparatively late in terms of our general understanding of the Adena phenomenon elsewhere. While this might normally be interpreted as a late echo of events to the south and west, the Adena-like objects in this period are an intensification of longstanding local interpretations of whatever "Adena" represented.

The distinction between mortuary assemblages and nearby non-mortuary places, such as Oxbow, becomes more marked as well—there is no blurring of the lines between bifaces destined for burials at the Augustine Mound and those used and discarded or lost around hearths and in living surfaces; the non-local materials used to make flaked-stone objects for inclusion as grave offerings do not show up in any of the local habitation sites as debris or tools. While neither was apparently appropriate for the placement in graves, both pottery and sturgeon remains become more visible away from mortuary components in this period, again with the likely correlation with some of the pit features in the community.

After 2,000 Years Ago

The time after 2,000 years ago contains a record of ongoing adaption, adjustment, and change. While the Augustine Mound was no longer being actively expanded, it continued to be a place that is known and set aside in the community memory. It became in this time the place "where the Ancestors used to dance." The presence of pit features in the nearby area, and the scatter of later artifacts near the mound and on the mound surface, hint at these later uses. In this long period, people continued to live and carry out their ceremonial and social lives, and evidence to stone-tool production, pottery making, and sturgeon consumption appears on many shores and terraces. This continued until the community was transformed by colonial forces and settlement to become reconstituted as a federally recognized First Nation. The sturgeon, so vital to the deep history of the community, disappeared—a victim to by-catch and active persecution as an impediment to an intensive eighteenth- and nineteenth-century net fishery for salmon (Blair et al. 2013). However, the relationship of people to the land and its places continued. The most recent engagement of the community in the life of the mound saw it once again transformed through community efforts into a living tool for education, engagement, and resistance. Both the Augustine Mound and the Oxbow site have been recognized as national historic sites, ensuring the perpetuation of community memory into the future.

Patterns and Continuities

There are several key elements of this community history that are relevant to our efforts to situate EMW phenomena in a larger regional and temporal context. Firstly, the relationship of the community to sturgeon (*Acipenser spp.*) is both ongoing and significant. While there are difficulties of comparability inherent in the analysis of fish remains that make it difficult to estimate the true proportion of sturgeon in the diet (see Colley 1990; Willis and Boehm 2014; Webb 2018), comparison with other assemblages and with other classes of zooarchaeological data indicate that sturgeon were overwhelmingly important to the community of Metepenagiag over a long period of time. A partial estimate based solely on number of identified specimens (NISP) has indicated that sturgeon represent 86% of all zooarchaeological remains from Metepenagiag sites (Webb et al. 2013), a much higher proportion than is found in sites along other rivers elsewhere in the Maine–Maritimes area (Spiess and Halliwell 2011). This focus is also reflected in contemporary interest in the community in sturgeon; people remember sturgeon as not only an important food fish but as an animal with a special, spiritual connection to the people and the places around the modern community. Many have recounted the story that each Mi'kmaq community in northeastern New Brunswick inscribed their canoes with particular and differentiating symbols, and that the symbol for Metepenagiag was the sturgeon. While the existence of this knowledge in the community does not need independent verification, it was also recorded by seventeenth-century French missionaries (Ganong 1910). The relationship between sturgeon, people, and place in the community of Metepenagiag represents a complex set of persistent and multifaceted entanglements.

Secondly, it is important to note how community memory flows through and crosscuts archaeological variability, and despite changes in how people engage with them, meanings and connections to places persist and are renewed and transformed through time. These recast archaeological understandings, enlivening the past with contemporary meaning. It may be possible to delimit archaeological activities using radiometric dates at places like Augustine Mound, but their active presence in community life transcends these frameworks, as indicated by the teachings passed down by Elder Joe Augustine of the Augustine Mound as a place of contemporary community importance. From this perspective, archaeological phenomena such as Adena and Meadowood can be recast as a set of interfaces of the community with the larger world around them.

Discussion and Conclusion

In the years since the excavation of many of the sites in the Metepenagiag Site Complex, we have continued to refine our understanding of EMW manifestations in the Maritime Peninsula (Blair 2004a, 2004b; Cudmore 2016; McEachen 1996; Pelletier-Michaud 2017; Taché 2008, 2011a, 2011b). At the same time, ongoing analysis of Early Woodland manifestations in their presumed cores (such as the Adena in the Ohio Valley) have revealed a significant lack of coherence (see Aument 1990). As Hays notes, "the potential for variability in the mortuary practices and material remains within a valley or watershed is so great that the [sic] any one valley may contain nearly the entire range of variability that exists throughout the Adena area" (Hays 1994:399). This lack of coherence is evident at Adena-affiliated sites outside of the Ohio Valley. For example, Heckenberger et al. (1990:130) observe a similar pattern in Vermont: "[A] similar pattern of variability is characteristic of coeval sites throughout the broader region. In some respects, the variability between grave lots at the Boucher site is as pronounced as the variation between cemeteries, not only within the Middlesex complex, but also between complexes." This view is expanded on significantly in the recent re-evaluation of that site undertaken by Robinson (2016).

Our analysis suggests that construction of temporal and spatial boundaries within the EMW need to be refined. Ritual activity that we have generally conceptualized as belonging to the EMW extend into the MMW, and, as a result, the use of culture-historical phenomenon such as Adena, Middlesex, and Meadowood to structure the archaeological sequence inevitably leads to contradiction and inconsistency. While elements of these phenomenon are widely distributed in the Northeast as internally coherent clusters of key traits, when observed at a landscape level that integrates multiple kinds of sites, EMW manifestations are only loosely related to the Early Woodland in areas to the south and west, while MMW manifestations equate even more poorly with Middle Woodland phenomena in those same areas. This is consistent with Heckenberger et al.'s (1990:137) observation that "conceptions of somewhat arbitrarily defined boundaries in time and space have hindered past understanding of Early Woodland cultural developments in the region."

In our approach to classifying sites, we have suggested differences between ceremonial and habitation-related places; this should not be a means of downplaying mortuary aspects of some of these habitation sites, as the presence of mortuary components in sites is a key concern for descendant Mi'kmaq communities and individuals. Furthermore, the categorization of sites as "ceremonial" and "mortuary" at once confounds the ceremonial aspects of everyday life and obscures a key archaeological difficulty in distinguishing mortuary ritual from non-mortuary ceremony; due to endemic soil acidity in the region, the presence or absence of human remains is not always a possible mechanism to distinguish between the two. While the general practice of segregating mortuary sites from non-mortuary contexts continues throughout the Maritime Woodland (see Leonard 1996) when attempting to understand the larger cultural context, we should contextualize particular site assemblages with larger landscape-level analysis to avoid overly emphasizing the economic behaviour that may be evident at particular classes of sites. Conversely, the careful management of items for mortuary contexts should not be read as a delineation of ceremonial life; as others have suggested elsewhere, non-mortuary ceremonial activities likely were deeply integrated into all facets of life, and served to express deep relationships between people, place, land, and animal and spirit beings (Betts et al. 2012; Ingraham et al. 2015; Robinson 2016). It would be a mistake to completely disarticulate ideology from economy (see Rowley-Conwy 2004). The examination of sites at a local landscape level, as we have attempted here, seeks integration of these various dimensions. A key example is the relationship between sturgeon and the community of Metepenagiag; while there can be no doubt that sturgeon was an economically important fish throughout the last 3,000 years, it is also clear that evidence of sturgeon fishing is deeply and continuously connected with both Metepenagiag's ceremonial life and spiritual identity.

However, equally salient is the disentangling of economic behaviour from social and ideological systems in the archaeological way of generating meaning, such that mortuary behaviour, ceremonial expressions, and the focus on key, highly productive resources should not lead us to inferences about change (such as increasing trends in intensification of resource extraction and social inequality) in a way that overshadows the importance of hunter-gatherer-fisher lifeways and perspectives, and the particular way communities interconnect with each other through a series of undirected webs of relationships. After all, EMW manifestations in the Far Northeast integrate local engagements in complex ways. Turnbull (1976) anticipated some of these conclusions when he observed that "the presence of quantities of the dominant local material in the site certainly points to a local orientation. In the broader Northeast, the spread of the material over 2 million square miles, the temporal range, and the lack of habitation sites speaks not of a single movement of one people, but of an extensive interconnection of local peoples." Further, these relationships remain hard to set into spatial or temporal hierarchies. As discussed above, if these relationships had involved transmission of ideas, objects, or people from a core in the Midwest or the Great Lakes to a periphery in the Far Northeast, we might have expected that EMW sites containing Early Woodland material have the following characteristics: (1) they would be later, (2) they would reflect the devolution of form and localization of materials over time, and (3) clusters of forms and objects in the hinterland would be partial, lacking elements or occurring in lower numbers relative to their occurrence in the core. None of these suppositions are supported by the evidence we have presented here. Although the radiocarbon plateau is a confounder, Adena/Middlesex artifacts occur at Metepenagiag as early or earlier than they occur in other parts of the broader Northeast. Indeed, the earliest dates from the Augustine Mound fall to the steeper portions of the calibration curve, slightly ahead of the plateau (see table 5.5 and figure 5.12). Further, the earliest expressions are forms mapped onto local materials—Adena bifaces occur as local quartz forms in the early period, while later they are made of exotic (nonlocal) materials and are supplemented by a much wider range of Adena-like objects. The same appears to be true of Meadowood forms. In a larger sense, a necessary characteristic for understanding the large-scale regional patterning in the Early Woodland is the integration of groups of heterogeneous complementarities. From this point of view, we need to resist imposing hierarchical systems on destratified, heterogeneous relationships, and resist the cooption of regional patterning into narratives that involve subordination and peripheralization. Archaeological notions of exchange and networks are influenced by basic understandings of social and economic life and particular conceptualization of interconnectivity—what Escobar has called hierarchical or "arborescent" networks. This conventional understanding of social networks has an inherent logic of order, structured around centralization and hierarchy building, and is centre-out and top-down.

It is the logic of core and periphery, and has been naturalized and universalized in terms of social order by "capitalism and its drive to accumulation, and by ruling structures in which the few privilege at the expense of the many" (Escobar 2008:275). In the context of the EMW of the Far Northeast, we must consider the fit of the evidence with decentralized systems that integrate heterogeneity, diversity, and overt lack of directionality.

While we might also expect external influences and interventions to create disjuncture in the archaeological record, when taken as a whole, the Metepenagiag Site Complex can best be characterized by deep patterns of continuity. The overwhelming focus on tool production using local white quartz, the regular occupation of landforms in and around the community over thousands of years, and the intense and persistent focus on sturgeon (Webb et al. 2013) indicate a broad pattern that extends back to at least 3,000 years and continues up to the disruption of the colonial period.

So how do manifestations like Adena and Meadowood map onto local practices? Loring has suggested these patterns may reflect social signalling in the deployment of different Early Woodland manifestations, as might result from affiliation of individuals within a group to different moieties (Loring 1985). More recently, others have suggested we consider the role of social networks as a mechanism enabling the movement of people between groups, a view that moves us past the narrow conceptualization of migration and replacement (Pluckhahn 2020:5). Sassaman and others point to the expressions of "group solidarity, territorial rights, and mythological heritage" (Railey 1996:84); Sassaman (2005:337) also suggests a continuity of Archaic practices into the Early Woodland, where key monumental sites and ritual centres "were duplicated in form across the landscapes of their respective cultural milieus, reflecting literally the histories of migration, diffusion, and colonization that linked communities of people across regions and generations."

As Bernardini (2004) notes, the view that monumental structures served as places for gathering and reproducing social ties (a view which emphasizes referential meaning) is increasingly being supplemented by models that explore experiential meaning—how monuments were experienced. These insights resonate with the archaeological and cultural history of Metepenagiag. We have adopted here a view of the Early Woodland landscape for the Northeast from the inside looking out—from the vantage of Metepenagiag, local places are experienced by Mi'kmaq people within the context of their social, ritual, and ceremonial lives, and as places where the community expresses their connection to others—both other humans woven together through relationships and experiences enacted over broad space and time, and other non-human beings, like sturgeon. Interactions with sturgeon (and other non-human and more-than-human entities) create a seasonal rhythm to these activities and experiences, both creating a link between people and the riverscapes in the community and providing a ceremonial framework through time.

On the other hand, our analysis suggests that mortuary activity is not simply correlated with annual seasonal aggregation and feasting, in that mortuary activity within the community proper that was undertaken using methods and ideas shared over the broader Northeast occurred in several temporally restricted episodes, while the connection between the community and these sacred places persisted over centuries through to the present. This record resists simple explanations that privilege one particular moment or sets of moments, as might occur if we were to encapsulate the relationship of sturgeon, mound building, and interregional relationships into a theoretical framework to understand social relationships through feasting. While such explanations may be narrowly true of particular moments and experiences, here we have sought to avoid the plucking of particular threads from the fabric of community life in favour of contemplating the whole cloth. The temporal rhythm of life, death, practice, and ceremony are woven together by memory, the performance of community acts, and pulses of gathering and dispersing. The importance of the ceremonial places in the Metepenagiag landscape, in other words, transcends the specific events of interment, suggesting memorialization and community connection to place in a way that weaves together widely disparate ritual acts.

However we proceed with our understanding of the EMW, our research suggests the importance of transcending the narrow classification of tools and sites. While the EMW portion of the Metepenagiag Site Complex is rife with tension between internal cohesion and continuity, and external stimuli, the evidence presented here encourages us to break down internal/external and consider a set of locally grounded ritual practices that touch on and connect people over broad regions, enabling a consideration of the ways in which people may have come together at Metepenagiag to express relationships with each other and with the world around them over thousands of years.

Acknowledgements

This research was funded by the Natural Sciences and Engineering Research Council of Canada (Strategic Grant program), and the Social Science and Humanities Research Council of Canada. We wish to particularly acknowledge the contribution through major foundational research undertaken by Christopher Turnbull; not only did he work with the community through the early days of the first government-to-government collaboration of its kind in Canada, but his thoughts on both community-driven collaboration and the Early Woodland have always been well ahead of their time. We also acknowledge the important contributions of (in alphabetical order) Patricia Allen, the late

Madeline Augustine, David Black, Drew Gilbert, Elizabeth Gorman, Gabriel Hrynick, the late Tricia Jarratt, Matthew Litvak, Ramona Nicholas, Karine Taché, Brent Suttie, Andrew Taylor, Pam Ward, W. Jesse Webb, and Melanie Wiber, as well as the support of Metepenagiag Heritage Park Inc. and Metepenagiag Mi'kmaq Nation.

References Cited

Allen, Patricia

1980 The Oxbow Site: Chronology and Prehistory in Northeastern New Brunswick. Master's thesis, Department of Anthropology, Memorial University of Newfoundland, St. John's.

1981 *The Oxbow Site: Chronology and Prehistory in Northeastern New Brunswick.* Manuscripts in New Brunswick Archaeology No. 1. Historical Resources Administration, Fredericton.

1988 *Southwest Miramichi Survey and Testing Project: 1987.* Manuscripts in New Brunswick Archaeology No. 23, Archaeological Services, Fredericton.

1994 *Metepenagiag: New Brunswick's Oldest Village.* Goose Lane Editions, Fredericton.

2005 *The Oxbow Site 1984: Metepenagiag Mi'kmaq First Nation, Miramichi, New Brunswick.* Manuscripts in New Brunswick Archaeology No. 39, New Brunswick Culture and Sport Secretariat, Fredericton.

Amsden, Charles

1932 The Loom and its Prototypes. *American Anthropologist* 32(2):216–235.

Augustine, Madeline, Christopher Turnbull, Patricia Allen, and Pamela Ward

2006 *To Hold it in my Hand.* Manuscripts in New Brunswick Archaeology No. 43. Heritage Branch, Wellness, Culture, and Sport, Fredericton.

Augustine, Noah, and John McLaughlin

2006 Memorandum of Understanding between UNB on Archaeological and Heritage Research, Metepenagiag Heritage Park Inc., and Metepenagiag Mi'kmaq Nation. Manuscript on file, Metepenagiag Heritage Park and University of New Brunswick, Fredericton.

Aument, Bruce W.

1990 Mortuary Variability in the Middle Big Darby Drainage of Central Ohio between 300 BC and 300 AD, Vol. 1. PhD dissertation, Department of Anthropology, Ohio State University, Columbus.

Belcher, William R.

1989 Prehistoric Fish Exploitation in East Penobscot Bay, Maine: The Knox Site and Sea-Level Rise. *Archaeology of Eastern North America* 17:175–191.

Bernardini, Wesley

2004 Hopewell Geometric Earthworks: A Case Study in the Referential and Experiential Meaning of Monuments. *Journal of Anthropological Archaeology* 23(3):331–356.

Betts, Matthew W., Susan E. Blair, and David W. Black

2012 Perspectivism, Mortuary Symbolism, and Human-Shark Relationships on the Maritime Peninsula. *American Antiquity* 77(4):621–645.

Black, David W.
1992   *Living Close to the Ledge: Prehistoric Human Ecology of the Bliss Islands, Quoddy Region, New Brunswick, Canada.* Occasional Papers in Northeastern Archaeology No. 6, Copetown Press, Dundas, Ontario.

Blair, Susan E.
2004a   Ancient Wolastoq'kew Landscapes: Settlement and Technology in the Lower Saint John River Valley, Canada. PhD dissertation, Department of Anthropology, University of Toronto, Toronto.

2004b   *Wolastoqiyik Ajemseg: The People of the Beautiful River at Jemseg,* vol. 2: *Archaeological Results.* Manuscripts in New Brunswick Archaeology 36E. Archaeological Services, Fredericton.

2007   Lukuwakn, Metepenagiag's "Place of Work." Paper presented at the 39th Canadian Archaeological Association Conference, St. John's, Newfoundland.

Blair, Susan E., Tricia L. Jarratt, and Pamela Ward
2014   Weaving Together Two Ways of Knowing: Archaeological Organic Artifact Analysis and Indigenous Textile Arts. *North American Archaeologist* 35(4): 295–302.

Blair, Susan E., and Pamela Ward
2013   The Metepenagiag Site Complex. In *Underground New Brunswick: Stories of Archaeology,* edited by P. Erickson and J. Fowler, pp. 7–16. Nimbus Press, Halifax.

Blair, Susan E., W. Jesse Webb, and Matthew K. Litvak
2013   Identifying the Presence of Sturgeon in Ancient Riverscapes: A Case Study from Northeastern New Brunswick, Canada. Paper presented at the 7th International Sturgeon Symposium, Nanaimo, British Columbia.

Bollwerk, Elizabeth A., and Shannon Tushingham, eds.
2016   *Perspectives on the Archaeology of Pipes, Tobacco and Other Smoke Plants in the Ancient Americas.* Springer, New York.

Bourque, Bruce J.
1971   Prehistory of the Central Maine Coast. PhD dissertation, Department of Anthropology, Harvard University, Cambridge, Massachusetts.

1994   Evidence for Prehistoric Exchange on the Maritime Peninsula. In *Prehistoric Exchange Systems in North America* edited by T. Baugh and J. Ericson, pp. 23–46. Springer, Boston, Massachusetts.

Bourgeois, Vincent, and Patricia Allen
2005   *The Mitchell Site: 1998 Heritage Impact Assessment Project at Metepenagiag Mi'kmaq First Nation.* Manuscripts in New Brunswick Archaeology No. 38. Archaeological Services, Fredericton.

Bowman, Sheridan
1990   *Radiocarbon Dating.* Vol. 1. University of California Press, Oakland.

Braun, David P.
1980   On the Appropriateness of the Woodland Concept in Northeastern Archaeology. In *Proceedings of the Conference on Northeastern Archaeology,* edited by J. A. Moore, pp. 93–108. Research Report 19, Department of Anthropology, University of Massachusetts, Amherst.

Claasen, Cheryl
2015   Beliefs and Rituals in Archaic Eastern North America: An Interpretive Guide. University of Alabama Press, Tuscaloosa.

Clay, R. Berle
1983   Pottery and Graveside Ritual in Kentucky Adena. *Midcontinental Journal of Archaeology* 8:109-126.
1986   Adena Ritual Spaces. In *Early Woodland Archeology*, edited by K. Farnsworth, pp. 581–595. Center for American Archaeology Press, Kampsville, Illinois.
1987   Circles and Ovals: Two Types of Adena Space. *Southeastern Archaeology* 6(1): 46–56.
1998   The Essential Features of Adena Ritual and Their Implications. *Southeastern Archaeology* 7(1):1–21.
2005   Adena: Rest in Peace? In *Woodland Period Systematics in the Middle Ohio Valley*, edited by Darlene Applegate and Robert Mainfort, pp. 94–110. University of Alabama Press, Tuscaloosa.
2014   What Does Mortuary Variability in the Ohio Valley Middle Woodland Mean? Agency, Its Projects, and Interpretive Ambiguity. *Southeastern Archaeology* 33(2):143–152.

Cochran, Donald R.
1996   The Adena/Hopewell Convergence in East Central Indiana. In *A View from the Core: A Synthesis of Ohio Hopewell Archaeology*, edited by Paul J. Pacheco, pp. 340–352. The Ohio Archaeological Council Conference Publication, Columbus.

Colley, Sarah M.
1990   The Analysis and Interpretation of Archaeological Fish Remains. *Archaeological Method and Theory* 2:207–253.

Conolly, James
2018   Hunter-Gatherer Mobility, Territoriality, and Placemaking in the Kawartha Lakes Region, Ontario. *Canadian Journal of Archaeology* 42(2):185–209.

Crawford, Gary W., Jessica L. Lytle, Ronald F. Williamson, and Robert Wojtowicz
2019   An Early Woodland Domesticated Chenopod (*Chenopodium berlandieri* subsp. *Jonesianum*) Cache from the Tutela Heights Site, Ontario, Canada. *American Antiquity* 84(1):143–157.

Cudmore, Lauren
2016   Macro-Regional Meadowood: A Comparative Approach to Early Woodland Lithic Tool Production in the Maritimes and Ontario. Master's thesis, Department of Anthropology, University of New Brunswick, Fredericton.

Curry, Dennis. C.
2018   A Chronicle of Prehistoric Archaeology in the Middle Atlantic Region. In *Middle Atlantic Prehistory: Foundations and Practice*, edited by H. Wholey and C. Nash. Rowman and Littlefield, New York.

Donahue, Nancy
1978   A Study of the Textiles from the Augustine Site in Relation to the Historic and Prehistoric Textile Technologies of Eastern North America. Honours thesis, Department of Anthropology, University of New Brunswick, Fredericton.

Dragoo, Don W.

1963   *Mounds for the Dead.* Annals of Carnegie Museum 37, Pittsburgh.

1976   Adena and the Eastern Burial Cult. *Archaeology Eastern North America* 4:1–9.

Emin, Adele

1978   An Archaeological Survey of the Augustine Mound Terrace and Red Bank Native Reserve No. 7, Red Bank, Northumberland Co., New Brunswick. Manuscript on file, Province of New Brunswick Archaeological Services, Heritage Branch, Culture and Sport Secretariat, Fredericton.

Escobar, Arturo

2008   *Territories of Difference: Place, Movements, Life, Redes.* Duke University Press, Durham, North Carolina.

Evans, Craig

2006   Provenancing Archaeological Copper. Honours thesis, Department of Anthropology, University of New Brunswick, Fredericton.

Fiedel, Stuart J.

2001   What Happened in the Early Woodland? *Archaeology of Eastern North America* 29:101–142.

Ganong, William F.

1910   The Identity of the Animals and Plants Mentioned by the Early Voyagers to Eastern Canada and Newfoundland. Transactions of the Royal Society of Canada, Third Series, Ottawa, Ontario.

Gordon, Jolene

1990   Mi'kmaq Textiles: Sewn-Cattail Matting BkCp-1 Site, Pictou Nova Scotia. Curatorial Report 80. Nova Scotia Museum, Halifax.

2002   Mi'kmaq Textiles. In *Collection-collectionneurs: Textiles d'Amérique et de France.*, edited by Jocelyne Mathieu and Christine Turgeon, Actes du colloque tenu à Québec, du 4 au 7 octobre 2000, Les Presses de l'université Laval.

Gorman, Elizabeth, and Susan E. Blair

2008   Continuity and Change at the Augustine Mound, New Brunswick, Canada. Paper presented at the 73rd Annual Meeting of the Society for American Archaeology, Atlanta.

Granger, Joseph E.

1978   *Meadowood Phase Settlement Pattern in the Niagara Frontier Region of Western New York State.* Anthropological Paper 65, Museum of Anthropology. University of Michigan, Ann Arbor.

1981   The Seward Site Cache and a Study of the Meadowood Phase Cache Blade in the Northeast. *Archaeology of Eastern North America* 9:63–103.

Grantz, Denise L.

1986   Archaeological Investigation of the Crawford-Grist Site #2 (36FA262): An Early Woodland Hamlet. *Pennsylvania Archaeologist* 56(3–4):1–21.

Greenman, Emerson F.

1932   The Excavation of the Coon Mound and an Analysis of the Adena Culture. *Ohio State Archaeological and Historical Quarterly* 41:336–523.

Griffin, James B.

1942   Adena Pottery. *American Antiquity* 7:344–358.

Hart, J. P., Hetty Jo Brumbach, and Robert Lusteck

2007   Extending the Phytolith Evidence for Early Maize (*Zea mays ssp. mays*) and Squash (*Cucurbita sp.*) in Central New York. *American Antiquity* 72(3): 563–583.

Hays, Christopher T.

1994   Adena Mortuary Patterns and Ritual Cycles in the Upper Scioto Valley, Ohio. PhD dissertation, Department of Anthropology, State University of New York at Birmingham.

2010   Adena Mortuary Patterns in Central Ohio. *Southeastern Archaeology* 29(1): 106–120.

Heckenberger, Michael J., James B. Petersen, Louise A. Basa, Ellen R. Cowie, Arthur E. Spiess, and Robert E. Stuckenrath

1990   Early Woodland Period Mortuary Ceremonialism in the Far Northeast: A View from the Boucher Cemetery. *Archaeology of Eastern North America* 18:109–144.

Henry, Edward R.

2017   Building Bundles, Building Memories: Processes of Remembering in Adena-Hopewell Societies of Eastern North America. *Journal of Archaeological Method and Theory* 24(1):188–228.

2018   Earthen Monuments and Social Movements in Eastern North America: Adena-Hopewell Enclosures on Kentucky's Bluegrass Landscape. PhD dissertation, Department of Anthropology, Washington University in St. Louis.

Henry, Edward R., and Casey R. Barrier

2016   The Organization of Dissonance in Adena-Hopewell Societies of Eastern North America. *World Archaeology* 48(1):87–109.

Ingraham, Robert C., Brian S. Robinson, Kirstin D. Sobolik, and A. Sky Heller

2015   "Left for the Tide to Take Back": Specialized Processing of Seals on Machias Bay, Maine. *The Journal of Island and Coastal Archaeology* 11(1):89–106.

Jarratt, Tricia L.

2015   The Augustine Mound Copper Sub-Assemblage: Beyond the Bead. Master's thesis, Department of Anthropology, University of New Brunswick, Fredericton.

Johanson, Jessie L., Kandace D. Hollenbach, and Howard J. Cyr

2020   Food Production in the Early Woodland: Macrobotanical Remains as Evidence for Farming along the Riverbank in Eastern Tennessee. *Southeastern Archaeology* 39(1):1–15.

Kidder, Tristam R., Lori Roe, and Timothy M. Schilling

2010   Early Woodland Settlement and Mound Building in the Upper Tensas Basin, Northeast Louisiana. *Southeastern Archaeology* 29(1):121–145.

Kroeber, Alfred L.

1948   *Anthropology: Race, Language, Culture, Psychology, Prehistory*. Harcourt Brace, New York.

Leonard, Kevin M.

1995   Woodland or Ceramic Period: A Theoretical Problem. *Northeast Anthropology* 50: 19–30.

1996 Mi'kmaq Culture during the Late Woodland and Early Historic Periods. PhD dissertation, Department of Anthropology, University of Toronto, Toronto, Ontario.

Lester, Joan
1987 "We didn't make fancy baskets until we were discovered": Fancy-Basket Making in Maine. In *A Key into the Language of Woodsplint Baskets*, edited by Ann McMullen and Russell G. Handsman pp. 38–59. American Indian Archaeological Institute, Washington, Connecticut.

Levine, Mary Ann, Michael Nassaney, and Kenneth E. Sassaman
1999 *The Archaeological Northeast*. Bergin and Garvey, Westport.

Lewis, R. Barry
1996 *Kentucky Archaeology*. University Press of Kentucky, Lexington.

Loring, Stephen
1985 Boundary Maintenance, Mortuary Ceremonialism and Resource Control in the Early Woodland: Three Cemetery Sites in Vermont. *Archaeology of Eastern North America* 13:93–127.

Lowery, Darrin L.
2012 The Delmarva Adena Complex: A Study of the Frederica Site, Kent County, Delaware. *Archaeology of Eastern North America* 40:27–58.

Mainfort, Robert C., Jr.
1989 Adena Chiefdoms? Evidence from the Wright Mound. *Midcontinental Journal of Archaeology* 14(2):164–178.

McCord, Beth K., and Donald R. Cochran
2008 The Adena Complex: Identity and Context in East-Central Indiana. In *Transitions: Archaic and Early Woodland Research in the Ohio Country*, edited by Martha P. Otto and Brian G. Redmond, pp. 334–360. Ohio University Press, Athens.

McEachen, Paul J.
1996 The Meadowood Early Woodland Manifestation in the Maritimes: A Preliminary Interpretation. Master's thesis, Archaeology Unit, Memorial University of Newfoundland, St. Johns.

McEachen, Paul, Patricia Allen, Patrick Julig, and Darrel G. Long
1999 The Tozer Site Revisited: Implications for the Early Woodland Period in New Brunswick. *Canadian Journal of Archaeology/Journal Canadien d'Archéologie* 22(2): 157–166.

McMullen, Ann
1992 Talking through Baskets: Meaning, Production, and Identity in the Northeast Woodlands. In *Basketmakers: Meaning and Form in Native American Baskets,* edited by Linda Mowat, Howard Morphy, and Penny Dransart, pp. 19–36. Pitt Rivers Museum Monograph No. 5, University of Oxford, Oxford.

McKern, William C.
1937 An Hypothesis for the Asiatic Origin of the Woodland Culture Pattern. *American Antiquity* 3:138–143.

Mills, William C.
1902 Excavations of the Adena Mound. *Ohio Archaeological and Historical Society Publications* 10:452–479. Columbus, Ohio.

Monaghan, G. William, and Edward W. Herrmann
2019   Serpent Mound: Still Built by the Adena, and Still Rebuilt during the Fort Ancient Period. *Midcontinental Journal of Archaeology* 44(1):84–93.

Mueller, Natalie G.
2018   The Earliest Occurrence of a Newly Described Domesticate in Eastern North America: Adena/Hopewell Communities and Agricultural Innovation. *Journal of Anthropological Archaeology* 49:39–50.

Otto, Martha P., and Brian G. Redmond, eds.
2008   Transitions: Archaic and Early Woodland Research in the Ohio Country. Ohio University Press, Athens.

Pauketat, Timothy R., and Kenneth E. Sassaman
2020   *The Archaeology of Ancient North America*. Cambridge University Press, Cambridge.

Pelletier-Michaud, Alexandre
2017   The Bristol-Shiktehawk Bifaces and Early Woodland Ceremonialism in the Middle St. John Valley, New Brunswick. Master's thesis, Department of Anthropology, University of New Brunswick, Fredericton.

Petersen, James B.
1995   Preceramic Archaeological Manifestations in the Far Northeast: A Review of Recent Research. *Archaeology of Eastern North America* 23:207–230.

Pluckhahn, Thomas J., Neill J. Wallis, and Victor D. Thompson
2020   The History and Future of Migrationist Explanations in the Archaeology of the Eastern Woodlands with a Synthetic Model of Woodland Period Migrations on the Gulf Coast. *Journal of Archaeological Research* 28(4):1–60.

Purtill, Matthew P., Jeremy A. Norr, and Jonathan B. Frodge
2014   Open-Air "Adena" Paired-Post Ritual Features in the Middle Ohio Valley: A New Interpretation. *Midcontinental Journal of Archaeology* 39(1):59–82.

Rafferty, Sean M.
2001   They Pass Their Lives in Smoke, and at Death, Fall into the Fire: Smoking Pipes and Mortuary Ritual during the Early Woodland Period. PhD dissertation, Binghamton University, Binghamton, New York.
2004   *Smoking and Culture: The Archaeology of Tobacco Pipes in Eastern North America.* University of Tennessee Press, Knoxville.
2006   Evidence of Early Tobacco in Northeastern North America? *Journal of Archaeological Science* 33(4):453–458.

Railey, Jimmy A.
1996   Woodland Cultivators. In *Kentucky Archaeology*, edited by R. Barry Lewis, pp. 79–125. University Press of Kentucky, Lexington.

Redmond, Brian G.
2016   Connecting Heaven and Earth: Interpreting Early Woodland Nonmortuary Ceremonialism in Northern Ohio. *Midcontinental Journal of Archaeology* 41(1): 41–66.
2017   Late Archaic Ritualism in Domestic Contexts: Clay-Floored Shrines at the Burrell Orchard Site, Ohio. *American Antiquity* 82(4):683–701.

Ritchie, William A.

1955   *Recent Discoveries Suggesting an Early Woodland Burial Cult in the Northeast*. New York State Museum and Science Service Bulletin 40. University of the State of New York, Albany.

Ritchie, William A., and Don W. Dragoo

1960   *The Eastern Dispersal of Adena*. New York State Museum and Science Service Bulletin 379. Albany.

Robinson, Brian S.

1992   Early and Middle Archaic Period Occupation in the Gulf of Maine Region: Mortuary and Technological Patterning. In *Early Holocene Occupation in Northern New England*, edited by Brian Robinson, James Petersen, and Ann Robinson, pp. 63–116. Occasional Publications in Maine Archaeology No. 9, Maine Historic Preservation Commission, Augusta.

1996   Archaic Period Burial Patterning in Northeastern North American. *The Review of Archaeology* 17(1):33–44.

Robinson, Francis J., IV

2016   The Initiation and Maintenance of the Early Woodland Interaction Sphere (ca. 3,000-2,000 BP): The View from Six Northeastern Mortuary Sites. PhD dissertation, Department of Anthropology, State University of New York at Albany.

Rowley-Conwy, Peter

2004   How the West Was Lost: A Reconsideration of Agricultural Origins in Britain, Ireland, and Southern Scandinavia. *Current Anthropology* 41: S83–S99.

Rutherford, Douglas E.

1989   The Archaic/Ceramic Period Transition in New Brunswick and Maine: An Analysis of Stemmed Biface Morphology. Master's thesis, Archaeology Unit, Memorial University of Newfoundland, St. Johns.

1991   The Ceramic Period in New Brunswick. In *Prehistoric Archaeology in the Maritime Provinces: Past and Present Research*, edited by Michael Deal and Susan Blair, pp. 109–119. Reports in Archaeology 8, Council of Maritime Premiers, Fredericton, New Brunswick.

Sanger, David

1974   Recent Meetings in Maine/Maritimes Archaeology. *Man in the Northeast* 7:128–129.

Sanger, Matthew C., Brian D. Padgett, Clark S. Larsen, Mark Hill, Gregory D. Lattanzi, Carol E. Colaninno, and R. J. Speakman

2019   Great Lakes Copper and Shared Mortuary Practices on the Atlantic Coast: Implications for Long-Distance Exchange during the Late Archaic. *American Antiquity* 84(4):591–609.

Sassaman, Kenneth E.

2005   Poverty Point as Structure, Event, Process. *Journal of Archaeological Method and Theory* 12:335–364.

2010   *The Eastern Archaic, historicized*. Altamira Press, Lanham, Maryland.

Spiess, Arthur E., and David B. Halliwell
2011 Fish Remains Found at Pre-Columbian Archaeological Sites in Maine: Freshwater, Diadromous and Estuarine Fish. *The Maine Archaeological Society Bulletin* 51(2):1–26.

Stewart, Francis L.
1981 Analysis of the Faunal Sample from the CfDl1 Oxbow Site, Appendix E. In *The Oxbow Site: Chronology and Prehistory in Northeastern New Brunswick*, New Brunswick Manuscripts in Archaeology No. 1, New Brunswick Department of Tourism, Recreation and Heritage, Fredericton.
1982 Faunal Remains from the Augustine Mound (CfDl2) of Northeastern New Brunswick. Manuscript on file, Province of New Brunswick Archaeological Services, Heritage Branch, Culture and Sport Secretariat, Fredericton.

Stothers, David M., and Timothy J. Abel
1993 Archaeological Reflections of the Late Archaic and Early Woodland Time Periods in the Western Lake Erie Region. *Archaeology of Eastern North America* 21:25–109.

Suess, Hans E.
1970 Bristlecone-Pine Calibration of the Radiocarbon Time-Scale 5200 B.C. to the Present. In *Radiocarbon Variations and Absolute Chronology*, edited by Ingrid Olsson, pp. 303–311. John Wiley and Sons, New York.

Suttie, Brent S.
2006 Mejipkei and Taboogul Mejipkei Pit Features on the Miramichi: Final Technical Report. Manuscript on file, Province of New Brunswick Archaeological Services Unit, Heritage Branch, Culture and Sport Secretariat, Fredericton.

Swartz, B. K., Jr. (editor)
1971 *Adena: The Seeking of an Identity.* Ball State University, Muncie, Indiana.

Taché, Karine
2005 Explaining Vinette I Pottery Variability: The View from the Batiscan Site, Québec. *Canadian Journal of Archaeology/Journal Canadien d'Archéologie* 29(2): 165–233.
2008 Structure and Regional Diversity of the Meadowood Interaction Sphere. PhD dissertation, Department of Archaeology, Simon Fraser University, Barnaby, British Columbia.
2011a *Structure and Regional Diversity of the Meadowood Interaction Sphere.* Memoires of the Museum of Anthropology, Vol. 48. University of Michigan, Ann Arbor.
2011b New Perspectives on Meadowood Trade Items. *American Antiquity* 76(1): 41–79.

Tuck, James
1984 *Maritimes Provinces Prehistory.* Canadian Prehistory Series, National Museum of Man, Ottawa.
1991 The Archaic Period in the Maritime Provinces. In *Prehistoric Archaeology in the Maritime Provinces: Past and Present Research*, edited by Micahel Deal and Susan Blair, pp. 29–57. Reports in Archaeology 8, Council of Maritime Premiers, Fredericton.

Turnbull, Christopher J.
1976 The Augustine Site: A Mound from the Maritimes. *Archaeology of Eastern North America* 4:50–63.
1980 The Augustine Mound. Manuscript on file, Province of New Brunswick Archaeological Services, Heritage Branch, Culture and Sport Secretariat, Fredericton.
1986 *The McKinley Collection: Another Middlesex Tradition Component from Red Back, Northumberland County, New Brunswick.* Manuscripts in New Brunswick Archaeology No. 17E. Archaeological Services, Fredericton.
Tushingham, Shannon, and Jelmer Eerkens
2016 Hunter-Gatherer Tobacco Smoking in Ancient North America: Current Chemical Evidence and a Framework for Future Studies. In *Perspectives on the Archaeology of Pipes, Tobacco and Other Smoke Plants in the Ancient Americas*, edited by Elizabeth Anne Bollwerk and Shannon Tushingham, pp. 211–230. Springer, Switzerland.
Waldron, John, and Elliot M. Abrams
1999 Adena Burial Mounds and Inter-Hamlet Visibility: A GIS Approach. *Midcontinental Journal of Archaeology* 24(1):97–111.
Wallis, Wilson D., and Ruth S. Wallis
1955 *The Micmac of Eastern Canada.* University of Minnesota Press, Minneapolis.
Webb, W. Jesse
2018 A Late Maritime Woodland Peskotomuhkati Fishery from the Mainland Quoddy Region, Southwestern New Brunswick, Canada. Master's thesis, Department of Anthropology, University of New Brunswick, Fredericton.
Webb, W. Jesse, Susan E. Blair, and Matthew K. Litvak
2013 Identifying the Presence of Sturgeon in Ancient Riverscapes: A Case Study from Northeastern New Brunswick, Canada. Paper presented at the 7th International Sturgeon Symposium, Nanaimo, British Columbia.
Webb, William S.
1962 The Adena People. *The Ohio State Archaeological and Historical Quarterly* 61:6–9.
Webb, William S., and Raymond S. Baby
1957 *The Adena People, No. 2.* The Ohio Historical Society. Columbus.
Webb, William S., and Charles E. Snow
1945 *The Adena People.* University of Kentucky Reports in Anthropology and Archaeology No. 6. Lexington, Kentucky.
Whitehead, Ruth H.
1980 *Elitekey: Micmac Material Culture from 1600 AD to Present.* Nova Scotia Museum Curatorial Report, Nova Scotia Museum, Halifax.
Whittaker, William E., and William Green
2010 Early and Middle Woodland earthwork enclosures in Iowa. *North American Archaeologist* 31(1):27–57.
Willis, Lauren M., and Andrew R. Boehm
2014 Fish Bones, Cut Marks, and Burial: Implications for Taphonomy and Faunal Analysis. *Journal of Archaeological Science* 45(1):20–25.

Wintemberg, William J.

1937   Artifacts from Presumed Ancient Graves in Eastern New Brunswick. *The Proceedings and Transactions of the Royal Society of Canada Transactions,* Section 11:205–209. Royal Society of Canada, Ottawa.

Wright, Alice P. and Edward R. Henry, eds.

2013   *Early and Middle Woodland Landscapes of the Southeast.* University Press of Florida, Gainesville.

Wright, James V.

1999   *A History of the Native People of Canada, Vol. II (1,000 BC–AD 500).* Mercury Series Paper 152, Archaeology Survey of Canada, Canadian Museum of Civilization, Hull, Quebec.

6

A CHRONOLOGICAL AND TYPOLOGICAL FRAMEWORK FOR BIFACIAL STONE TOOLS IN THE MARITIME PENINSULA DURING THE CERAMIC PERIOD

ADRIAN L. BURKE

Abstract

The Maritime Peninsula currently lacks a chronological and typological framework for the classification of bifacial stone tools for the Ceramic (Woodland) period. Since the publication of Petersen and Sanger's ceramic sequence in 1991, archaeologists from the region have been able to better situate their ceramic assemblages in time. Unfortunately, this is not the case for lithic assemblages. This is particularly problematic for the interior of the Maritime Peninsula, which has rich lithic assemblages but few ceramic remains. This chapter proposes a framework for the bifacial stone tools (primarily stemmed bifaces or projectile points) from sites across the Maritime Peninsula dating to the Ceramic period. These sites are securely dated to contexts postdating the Archaic period, and I include Contact-period sites up to and including the seventeenth century. Because the Maritime Peninsula contains several quarry and workshop complexes, I include aspects of the reduction sequences or *chaînes opératoires* as part of the framework. These technological aspects add detail and additional diagnostic criteria that go beyond simple typology and morphology, thus refining the framework. The intention of this chapter is to create a lithic sequence or framework that will be complementary to Petersen and Sanger's ceramic sequence, and that is specific or purpose-built for the archaeology of the Maritime Peninsula.

Résumé

La Péninsule Maritime ne possède pas de cadre chronologique ou typologique pour la classification des outils bifaciaux en pierre taillée pour la période céramique (sylvicole). Depuis la publication de la séquence céramique de Petersen et Sanger en 1991, les archéologues de la région peuvent mieux situer leurs collections céramiques dans le temps. Malheureusement ce n'est pas le cas pour les collections lithiques. C'est particulièrement problématique pour les sites de l'intérieur qui possèdent beaucoup de restes lithiques, mais peu ou pas de céramique. Dans ce chapitre je propose un cadre pour les outils en pierre bifaciaux, principalement les bifaces avec emmanchement et les pointes de projectile, provenant de sites de la Péninsule Maritime datant de la période céramique. J'utilise des sites qui sont datés d'après l'Archaïque et j'inclus les sites de la période de Contact jusqu'au 17ᵉ siècle. Étant donné que la Péninsule Maritime possède plusieurs sites de carrière et des ateliers de taille, j'inclus aussi les séquences de réduction ou chaînes opératoires dans ce cadre. Les aspects technologiques ajoutent des détails et des critères diagnostiques qui nous permettent d'aller au-delà des simples typologies et morphologies et nous permettent ainsi de raffiner le cadre proposé. Mon intention c'est de créer une séquence ou cadre lithique qui pourra compléter la séquence céramique de Petersen et Sanger, et qui est faite sur mesure pour l'archéologie de la Péninsule Maritime.

Affiliation

– Département d'anthropologie, Université de Montréal, Quebec, Canada

Since the publication of Petersen and Sanger's ceramic sequence in 1991, archaeologists working in the Maritime Peninsula (figure 6.1) have been able to better situate their ceramic assemblages in time and space. Unfortunately, no comparable chronological, stylistic, or typological framework exists for the lithic assemblages of the region. This is most problematic for the numerous sites and contexts that are suspected to date to the Woodland or Ceramic periods but which have not produced ceramics. Some local or regional projectile-point sequences have been proposed, such as those for Penobscot Bay (Bourque 1971), Passamaquoddy Bay (Davis 1978; Sanger 1979, 1986, 1987), and the Miramichi River (Allen 1981, 1989, 2005), and these have proven useful to archaeologists working in those regions (see also Blair 2004a:Figure 2.2, p. 25–27).

This chapter proposes a chronological lithic framework primarily focused on bifacial stone tools from sites across the Maritime Peninsula dating to the Ceramic and Contact periods (3050–250 BP). When possible, I only use sites that are securely dated to contexts postdating the Archaic period, and I include Contact period sites up to and including the seventeenth century (table 6.1). Some site contexts that include ceramics and which can be assigned to a sub-period of the Ceramic period based on the Petersen and Sanger sequence are included even if no radiocarbon dates are available. I have also included some older collections that provide useful comparative material but which are poorly dated (e.g., Erskine's collections from Nova Scotia). The sites included in this analysis are from an area corresponding to the traditional definition of the Maritime Peninsula (Bourque 1989; Burke 2000; Hoffman 1955a, 1955b, 1967), which is delimited on the west by the Kennebec River–Chaudière River drainages (figure 6.1). This area includes most of the state of Maine; the regions of Côte-Sud, Bas-Saint-Laurent and Gaspésie in Quebec; and the provinces of New Brunswick and Nova Scotia. I have included Prince Edward Island in my analysis but only in a limited way due to a lack of familiarity with the recent archaeological record in that province. I have not attempted to divide the Maritime Peninsula into an interior and a coastal zone for this analysis, as has been done in the past by other researchers, but, rather, I have created an artificial boundary between the southwest and northeast parts of the region (figure 6.1). This division emerged during my analysis of the data and will be explained below. This division is hinted at by Robinson in his 1996 article, but he focuses primarily on the coastal–interior division. Because the Maritime Peninsula contains several quarry and lithic workshop complexes, I include aspects of the reduction sequences, or *chaînes opératoires*, as part of the proposed framework. These technological aspects add detail and additional diagnostic criteria that go beyond simple typology and morphology, thus helping to refine the framework proposed here.

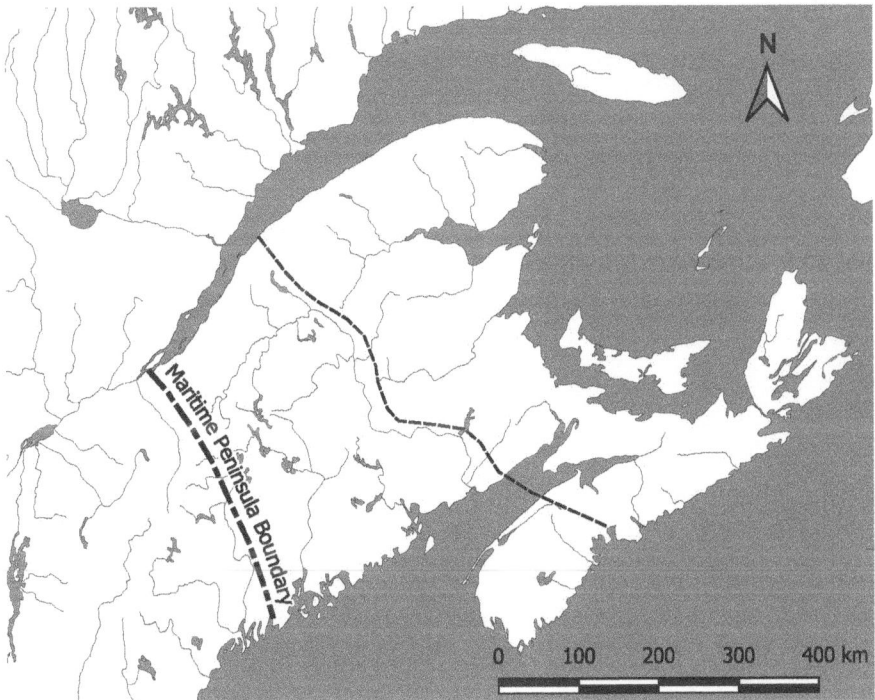

Figure 6.1. The Maritime Peninsula region as defined in this chapter. The narrow dashed line divides the study area into southwest and northeast sectors.

Table 6.1. Compilation of projectile points from sites in the Maritime Peninsula dated to the Ceramic period. Taxonomy referred to by original authors is retained in column "Ceramic period date".

Borden code / Site number	Site name	Province or State	Component or Area	Level	Radiocarbon date	Ceramic period date	Projectile points	References
CkEe-2	Davidson	QC	Area A	level 2 & 3	1560±150 & 1970±100	early Middle Woodland	stemmed	Chalifoux, Burke & Chapdelaine p. 66
CkEe-5	McInnes	QC	Structure I, hearth		1400±90 direct association	late Middle Woodland (PSS pottery)	Jack's Reef corner notched	Chalifoux, Burke & Chapdelaine p. 73, photo 5.3
DgDq-1	Cap Chat	QC	North and South zones		620±115 & 540±115	Late Woodland (CWS pottery)	side notched & stemmed	Barré 1978 figure 36 & 37
CkEe-9	Pelletier	QC	Area I and II	2	560±70 & 340±60	Late Ceramic and Contact	side and corner notched	Chalifoux, Burke & Chapdelaine p. 57-58, photo 5.5 & 6.4
31,17	Ruth Moore	Maine	1991–1993 excavations	basal shell layer	2815±85	Early Ceramic (Vinette I pottery)	straight stemmed (broad stem, short)	Cox & Lawless 1994 figure 12 M, no pagination
30,21	Knox	Maine	1986 excavations	Assemblage 1	2720±90 to 2020±70	Early Ceramic	wide and narrow side notched, one Adena-like stemmed	Belcher 1989 plate 6

Borden code / Site number	Site name	Province or State	Component or Area	Level	Radiocarbon date	Ceramic period date	Projectile points	References
74,148	Bob	Maine	1993 excavations	Area A, feature 19		CP1 pottery 3050–2150 BP	shallow side notched (eared or group 2)	Mack, Sanger & Kelley 2002 p. 45–47, plate 17
31,17	Ruth Moore	Maine	1991-1993 excavations	basal black soil layer		Early Ceramic (Vinette I pottery)	stemmed (straight, expanding & contracting)	Cox & Lawless 1994 figure 12 N-R, no pagination
80,15	Reversing Falls	Maine	2017 and 2018 excavations		2190±30 & 1759±30	early Middle Woodland	contracting and straight stemmed	Hrynick et al. 2019 and photo from author
29,9	Turner Farm	Maine	Occupation 4	2GF and 1GF	2105±75 to 875±70		lobate stemmed and narrow stemmed	Bourque 1995 p. 174–178
41,4	Kidder Point	Maine	1975 and 1982 excavations	Assemblage K		CP2 pottery 2150–1650 BP	stemmed and side notched	Spiess 1983 p. 68–71, plates 4–13 & 4–14
90.2D	Sharrow	Maine	1987 trench area	stratum IV & V	1510±80 (feature 22, N15 E25) direct association		side notched	Petersen 1991 p. 66–67, figure 48 (5 total, one from feature 22)
31,17	Ruth Moore	Maine	1991–1993 excavations	coarse crushed shell layer		Middle Ceramic (dentate & PSS pottery)	stemmed and wide side notched	Cox & Lawless 1994 figure 12 G-I, no pagination

Borden code / Site number	Site name	Province or State	Component or Area	Level	Radiocarbon date	Ceramic period date	Projectile points	References
various sites	Allagash waterway	Maine	surface collections			Middle and Late Woodland	side and corner notched	Butler & Hadlock 1962 p. 24, plate IX
118,188	Casey	Maine	1993 excavations	feature 1, N100 W100	1010±50 direct association?		corner notched	Will 1996 figure 4
43,24	Fernald Point	Maine	1976 and 1977 excavations	housepit 1	radiocarbon dates mentioned but not given	Ceramic period, pottery (CP 4 & 5)	corner notched	Sanger 1989 figure 5, p. 12–18
29,9	Turner Farm	Maine	Occupation 4	1 GF and above	875±70		side and corner notched	Bourque 1995 p. 178 plate 7.3
29,9	Turner Farm	Maine	Occupation 4	1 GF and above	875±70		triangular (Madison/Levanna)	Bourque 1995 p. 178, plate 7.4
30,42	Goddard	Maine	1979 excavations	Area 5 (pit)	770±70 direct association	Late Ceramic	side notched	Bourque & Cox 1981 p. 13–16, plate II
155,8	Birch Point	Maine	1953 excavations (Abbe Museum collection)			1250–750 BP Late Ceramic	corner notched	Seeber 1987 p. 35, plate 2–11
74,148	Bob	Maine	1993 excavations	Area A, feature 21		CP5-6 pottery 950–400 BP	side notched (group 3)	Mack, Sanger & Kelley 2002 p. 45–47, plate 16

Borden code / Site number	Site name	Province or State	Component or Area	Level	Radiocarbon date	Ceramic period date	Projectile points	References
146,1	Hodgdon	Maine	1974, 1975 and 1979 excavations			Late Ceramic CWS pottery (CP4-5)	side and corner notched, triangular	Lahti et al. 1981 p. 23, plate 1
73,9	Hirundo	Maine	1972 excavations	Area B		1000–400 BP (CWS pottery)	side and corner notched	Sanger 1973 plate IV
30,42	Goddard	Maine	1979 excavations			Late Ceramic	triangular	Bourque & Cox 1981 p. 13–16, plate II
96,02	Ntolonapemk	Maine	1999–2000 excavations			Late Ceramic to Contact period	triangular, corner and side notched, small stemmed «Contact period» point	Brigham et al. 2001 figure 8 p. 34
154,5	Venus of Munsungun	Maine	1953 excavations (Abbe Museum collection)			1250–350 BP Late Ceramic and Protohistoric	corner notched and small stemmed	Seeber 1987 p. 35, plate 2–3

Borden code / Site number	Site name	Province or State	Component or Area	Level	Radiocarbon date	Ceramic period date	Projectile points	References
31,17	Ruth Moore	Maine	1991–1993 excavations	fine crushed shell layer		Late Ceramic and Contact (CWS pottery, European brass & pipe stems)	side and corner notched	Cox & Lawless 1994 figure 12 A-F, no pagination
42,43	Flye Point-2	Maine	1980 and 1982 excavations	House feature with hearth	420±60 & 490±90 direct association	Late Ceramic	side and corner notched	Cox 1983 figure 4
26,34	Ann Hilton	Maine	1988 excavations			Early Contact (16th–17th century) European clay pipe fragments and European flint flakes	short and small stemmed	Will and Will 1989 p. 4–6, figure 5
BfDd-24	End of Dyke	NS	2012 excavations	Feature 44	2490±30, 1550±30 & 1520±30	early and middle Middle Ceramic	broad side notched (expanding stem) & contracting stem with flared shoulders (Tusket or bipoint)	CRM Group 2014 plate 223, p. 288 (BfDd-24.5135, 12882, 12883)
BfDa-1	St. Croix	NS				early Middle Woodland Period (ca. 2350–2150 BP)	contracting stemmed or 'Tusket'	Milner 2014 figure 7.1, p. 84–88

Borden code / Site number	Site name	Province or State	Component or Area	Level	Radiocarbon date	Ceramic period date	Projectile points	References
BfDd-24	End of Dyke	NS	2012 excavations	Feature 9 (hearth complex)		Middle Ceramic (pottery)	expanding stem	CRM Group 2014 plate 115, p. 137 (BfDd-24.14058+59)
various sites	Tusket Falls and Gaspereau Lake	NS				Tusket phase (AD 200–1000)	contracting stemmed (Tusket)	Erskine 1998 p. 64–70, plate 22 & figure 6
BjCo-7?	Merigomish Harbour; shell heaps A & D	NS				Middle Ceramic based on pottery	contracting stemmed (Tusket or Bipoint?), wide side notched	Smith & Wintemberg 1929 p. 21–22, plate IV
BjCj-9	Delorey Island	NS	Area 1 & 2	Level 2 & 3	1595±80 to 810±70 & 460 BP TL date	AD 350 to Contact	stemmed, side and corner notched	Nash 1986 p. 39–55, figure 11
BeCs-3	Brown	NS	1977,1978 and 1985 excavations, mostly central portion		1230±70 direct association		side notched	Sheldon 1988 p. 54, figure 13, specimen m, BeCs-3:633+768
BfDa-1	St. Croix	NS				late Middle to Late Woodland Period (2000–500 BP)	corner notched	Milner 2014 figure 7.1, p. 84–88

Borden code / Site number	Site name	Province or State	Component or Area	Level	Radiocarbon date	Ceramic period date	Projectile points	References
BfDd-24	End of Dyke	NS	2012 excavations	Feature 7 (hearth complex)		Middle and Late Ceramic (pottery)	corner notched	CRM Group 2014 plate 106, p. 126 (BfDd-24.11017)
various sites	Yarmouth Coast	NS	1987			Middle and Late Woodland	side and corner notched	Davis 1991, plate 6, p. 87
BfDd-24	End of Dyke	NS	2012 excavations	Feature 41 (pit)		late Middle and Late Ceramic (pottery)	side notched	CRM Group 2014 plate 216, p. 274 (BfDd-24.12182)
BeCs-3	Brown	NS	1977, 1978 and 1985 excavations, mostly central portion			1300 BP to Contact	Group 1 expanding stem (corner & side notched)	Sheldon 1988 p. 51–55
AlDf-24	Port Joli	NS	2008–2012 excavations	Area C, feature 4 (house floor)	660±40	later Late Maritime Woodland	side and corner notched	Betts & Holyoke 2019 figure 7.23, Betts 2019 for dates
BgDb-7	Melanson	NS	Northwestern sub-area 1986	level 3	560±60 direct association		side notched	Nash & Stewart 1990 figure 30, specimen k (BgDb-7-5-3)
BaGd-2	Indian Gardens	NS	Low Terrace, 1985 excavations			Late Ceramic (CWS pottery) and Protohistoric	corner notched and triangular	Deal et al. 1987 plate 3, p. 179–183
various sites	Indian Gardens, Gaspereau Lake and Bear River	NS				Indian Gardens phase (AD 1000–1500)	side notched	Erskine 1998 p. 64–70, plates 22, 23 & figure 6

Borden code / Site number	Site name	Province or State	Component or Area	Level	Radiocarbon date	Ceramic period date	Projectile points	References
BgDc-12	Toby	NS	2014 surface collection			Late Ceramic	side notched	Davis MacIntyre & Associates 2015
BcDc-4	Eisenhauer shell heap	NS				Late Ceramic based on pottery	corner notched	Smith & Wintemberg 1929 p. 114–115, plate XXIII
BjCj-1, BjCj-5, BjCj-6, BjCj-8, BjCj-12 & BjCj-13	Tracadie Harbour	NS				Ceramic period	side and corner notched	Rosenmeier 2010 figure 5
BgDb-7	Melanson	NS	Northwestern sub-area 1986	pits 1 to 13		Ceramic period	corner-removed/stemmed, side notched, & corner notched	Nash & Stewart 1990 p. 74–79
AlDf-24	Port Joli	NS	2008–2012 excavations	Area C, level 2	380±40	Protohistoric	corner notched	Betts & Holyoke 2019 figure 7.18, Betts 2019 for dates
CfDl-1	Oxbow	NB	1978, 1979 & 1984 excavations		2640±50 & 2600±60	Early Ceramic 2600-2200 BP	small expanding stem	Allen 1981, Allen 1989 p. 52–53, Allen 2005

Borden code / Site number	Site name	Province or State	Component or Area	Level	Radiocarbon date	Ceramic period date	Projectile points	References
BkDm-14	Jemseg Crossing	NB		component 5	2520±70 & 2460±60	2800–2400 BP (earlier Early Maritime Woodland)	side notched	Blair 2004b p. 256–258, plate 18.1
BkDw-5	Mud Lake Stream	NB	1983 excavations		2470±110 BP indirect association	Early Ceramic	side notched (box base)	Deal n.d., Rutherford 1991 p. 114–115
BlDn-12	Fulton Island	NB	1971, 1973 and 1974 excavations		>2075±45 point below this date	dentate and rocker dentate pottery (CP2-3, 2150-1350 BP)	contracting stemmed or bipoint (group 3)	Foulkes 1981 p. 81–97, figure 13
CfDl-1	Oxbow	NB	1978, 1979 & 1984 excavations	level 19	three later dates but rejected	Early Ceramic	large stemmed	Allen 1981, Allen 1989 p. 52–53, Allen 2005
CeDw-8	Bernard	NB		surface collection		Early Woodland or Little Gap	expanding stem (wide side notch or corner removed)	Turnbull 1990
CfDl-1	Oxbow	NB	1978, 1979 & 1984 excavations		2145±65 & 2120±65 direct association	early Middle Ceramic 2200-1800? BP	bipoint	Allen 1981, Allen 1989 p. 53–54, Allen 2005
BlDo-4	Bullfrog	NB			1855±70	Middle Maritime Woodland (CP2b)	contracting stemmed or bipoint	Blair 2004a p.10, table 1.1

Borden code / Site number	Site name	Province or State	Component or Area	Level	Radiocarbon date	Ceramic period date	Projectile points	References
CfDl-1	Oxbow	NB	1978, 1979 & 1984 excavations		1745±70 & 1675±50 direct association	late Middle Ceramic 1800-? BP	contracting & straight stemmed	Allen 1981, Allen 1989 p. 53–54, Allen 2005
BlDn-12	Fulton Island	NB	1971, 1973 and 1974 excavations		1680±70 level association	ceramics	straight stemmed (group 2)	Foulkes 1981 p. 81–97, figure 13
BkDw-5	Mud Lake Stream	NB	1983 excavations			Middle Ceramic based on pottery and horizontal distribution and morphology	expanding stem (wide corner notched)	Deal 1986 p. 82–85, figure 8 (see corrected figure 8 in Man in the Northeast No. 34, 1987)
BgDr-11	Teacher's Cove	NB	1970 and 1972 excavations			AD 1 to 1100 or Late Period	side and corner notched (expanding stem or Group 2)	Davis 1978 p. 20, 31, plate VI
ClDq-1	Old Mission Point	NB	1972 & 1973 excavations			2000 BP to contact, Middle and Late Ceramic Period	straight & contracting stemmed, and corner notched (oldest to youngest)	Turnbull 1973, Turnbull & Turnbull 1974, Allen n.d.
BjDh-3		NB	2018 excavations		(1180 and 930 BP)	Late Maritime Woodland	side and corner notched	Christian Thériault, personal communication March 2020

Borden code / Site number	Site name	Province or State	Component or Area	Level	Radiocarbon date	Ceramic period date	Projectile points	References
BgDr-5	Carson	NB	1969 excavations	Assemblage 2, Section A	1120±65 BP (feature 12) & 925±80 (feature 6a)	Ceramic Period ca. 1000 BP	side and corner notched (expanding stem or group 1)	Sanger 1987 p. 36–37, plate 10
CbDd-1	Skull Island	NB	1990 and 1991 excavations	Lot 3	680±70 direct association in burial	Late Ceramic	corner notched	Leonard 1996 p. 73–75, figure 38, and original photo print from author
CfDl-1	Oxbow	NB	1978, 1979 & 1984 excavations	level 6		Late Ceramic CWS pottery	stemmed (small)	Allen 1989 p. 55–56
CiDg-1	Barnaby's Nose	NB	1970, 1972, 1985	surface collection		AD 900–1000 based on nearby sites radiocarbon dates and CWS	corner notched	Keenlyside 1990
BkDl-5	Mill Brook	NB				Late Maritime Woodland	corner notched	Holyoke 2012 p. 131–132, figure 5.14
BlDn-27	Swan Creek Lake	NB				Late Maritime Woodland	corner notched	Holyoke 2012 p. 81–85, figure 4.4 & 4.5
CfDl-1	Oxbow	NB	1978, 1979 & 1984 excavations			Late Ceramic	side and corner notched	Allen 1981, 1989 & 2005
CbDd-4	Indian Point	NB	surface collections 2000–2001			Late Woodland	corner notched	Leonard 2002 figure 24

Borden code / Site number	Site name	Province or State	Component or Area	Level	Radiocarbon date	Ceramic period date	Projectile points	References
CfDk-48	Davidson	NB	1987 and surface collections			Ceramic Period	contracting stemmed, wide side notched, corner notched	Allen 1988 p. 6–7, figures 12 & 16
BlDn-12	Fulton Island	NB	1971, 1973 and 1974 excavations			Late Ceramic levels and Contact	side and corner notched (group 1)	Foulkes 1981 p. 81–97, figure 13 and Holyoke 2012
CcCm-9	Wakelin	PEI	1979–1981 excavations			2500–2000 BP (pottery)	contracting stemmed (some with flared shoulder), bipoints, straight stemmed	Keenlyside 1983 p. 5–6
CcCm-12	MacDonald	PEI	1979–1981 excavations			AD 800–1000 (CWS pottery)	corner notched and stemmed	Keenlyside 1983 p. 3–6

Biface Typologies and Chronological Frameworks

As Brian Robinson eloquently explained in 1996, the use of a single diagnostic artifact to define an archaeological culture is ill-advised, and it rarely works anyway (Robinson 1996). An entire assemblage is more useful, and probably more faithfully reflects some social or political entity in the past. My purpose here is not to create a new typology of diagnostic bifaces and projectile points, but rather to create a chronological framework that can help archaeologists place their bifacial tools in time. This chronological framework will not reference specific archaeological cultures or other taxa, just as Petersen and Sanger did not in their 1991 ceramic sequence.

In the Maritime Peninsula, the first point or biface typologies for the Late Archaic and Ceramic periods were proposed by Bourque and Sanger in the 1970s (e.g., Bourque 1971, 1976; Sanger 1979). Erskine had proposed an earlier point sequence for Nova Scotia in the 1960s but it was not widely available or applied (Erskine 1998:Figure 6). Bourque's typology referenced the Ritchie (1961) typology from New York for lack of any regional sequence that was closer, and was focused on his work on the central Maine coast. Sanger's typology was consolidated in the 1980s and was primarily focused on the Passamaquoddy Bay area of Maine and New Brunswick (Sanger 1979, 1986, 1987). In both cases, the most diagnostic forms of bifaces and points of the very end of the Late Archaic were the narrow-stemmed and stemmedbroadspear forms. Some were seen to possibly continue into the Early Ceramic in the form of narrow, elongated points, with straight or contracting stems, because these were common in occupations that were stratigraphically above the Late Archaic levels and therefore associated with the Early Ceramic period (Sanger 1986:Plate 2; see also Sanger 2008). There were also side-notched points that resembled Early Woodland Meadowood types (box base), but these were not securely dated at the time and were simply associated with the Early Woodland based on point sequences from further west, from Ontario and New York. Narrow-stemmed forms seem to continue into the Middle Ceramic period in the Sanger sequence based on his early syntheses (Sanger 1979, 1986). A small, expanding-stem form was also added as typical of the Middle Ceramic (Sanger 1979:Figure on p. 152, point G). The typical Late Ceramic point in this sequence was a side- or corner-notched (expanding stem) variety that seemed to be widely distributed in Maine and New Brunswick, including in the interior (Sanger 1979, 1986).

In northeastern New Brunswick, Allen's work during the 1970s and 1980s at deeply stratified sites along the Miramichi River, primarily at the Oxbow site, made it possible to securely date within a stratified sequence a series of projectile-point types or morphologies and thus create a point sequence for this part of New Brunswick (Allen 1981, 1988, 1989, 2005). Allen (2005:56) summarizes the projectile-point sequence as follows:

At the base of the site, medium to large stemmed points, reminiscent of Late Archaic or Transitional period forms, are found. These were followed by small, slightly expanding-stemmed points. This type of point, by about 2,100 years ago, was superseded by bipointed forms that, in turn, appear to develop into several varieties of late, small stemmed points that are common in the Miramichi River District [...]. Most recent in the sequence are side and/or corner notched points that were not well represented in the most recent Oxbow levels and are therefore considered to occur very late in the cultural sequence.

Allen's sequence was slightly different than the Sanger Passamaquoddy sequence but it still begins with a stemmed point in the Early Woodland (figure 6.2). This point is not as narrow as the Passamaquoddy stemmed points, but Allen also makes the connection with the very end of the Archaic, suggesting at least some continuity in these projectile-point types. This is followed by a small expanding-stem form from 2600 to 2200 BP (Allen 1980, 1981, 1988, 1989; Rutherford 1991). This was followed in turn by a bipointed form. The contracting stem is on occasion separated from the blade by a slight shoulder. This bipointed form is also dated to the earlier part of the Middle Ceramic, approximately 2200 to 1800 BP. The bipointed form is followed by a medium-sized point with a wide and straight or contracting stem that is placed stratigraphically in the latter part of the Middle Ceramic, after 1800 BP. Sometime after 1000 BP, during the Late Ceramic period, side- and corner-notched forms were introduced in the Miramichi region.

In her analysis of the Fulton Island site in the lower Saint John River, Foulkes (1981) was able to reproduce part of the point sequence proposed by Allen in terms of morphology and dated stratigraphic context. At Fulton Island, group 3 points or bifaces with contracting stems are equivalent to the bipointed forms from Oxbow and are dated to the same time period (Foulkes 1981:94–95). These are followed by bifaces with straight and wide stems of group 2, dated to after 1800 BP and probably no later than 1000 BP (Foulkes 1981:95–96). Finally, the group 1 bifaces are side- and corner-notched points which lack secure dating but are found in the upper stratigraphic levels, just as at Oxbow (Foulkes 1981:96–97).

Oxbow and Fulton Island are important sites because they provide dated stratigraphic contexts going back to the Archaic, which is rare in the Maritime Peninsula. At the Sharrow site, a comparable, deeply stratified site in Maine, projectile points are rare in the Ceramic-period levels. Those that are present are small and stemmed and not particularly diagnostic in their morphology (Petersen 1991). All of these sites are also notable because they lack a clear biface morphology or type for the Early Ceramic. Sanger (2008) and Allen (1981), for

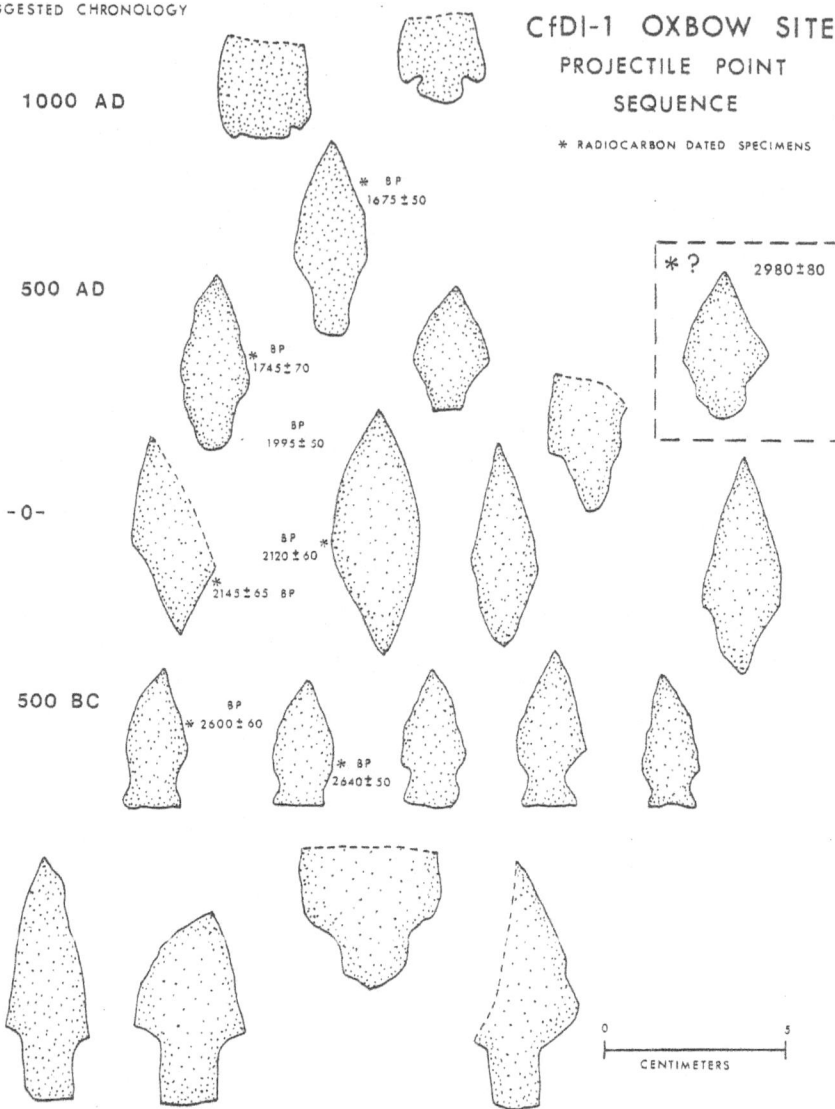

Figure 6.2. Projectile point sequence for the Oxbow site, Miramichi, New Brunswick.
Source: From Allen (1980:Figure 57) with permission of the author.

example, have suggested that the narrow- and wide-stemmed points are typical of the Early Ceramic, and that they may represent continuity from the very end of the Archaic. Unfortunately these points lack clear radiocarbon dates. On the other hand, archaeologists have in the past associated side-notched points with squared or box bases as being diagnostic of the Early Woodland. This can be problematic when we consider that the typical Early Woodland box-base point will typically be made on a biface that is highly consistent in shape and morphology (i.e., Meadowood Onondaga chert cache blades). Fortunately, some dated contexts do occur that contain side-notched points that resemble the box-base forms of the Early Ceramic found to the west of the Maritime Peninsula in the St. Lawrence Valley and New York. At the Jemseg Crossing site, Blair describes these forms and assigns them to 2800–2400 BP (earlier Early Maritime Woodland) based on two radiocarbon dates (Blair 2004b:256-258, Plate 18.1). At Mud Lake Stream, Deal (n.d., 1986) describes an Early Ceramic component that contains typical side-notched, box-base-style points. These can be safely dated to the Early Ceramic based on at least one radiocarbon date (Rutherford 1991:114–115). Occasionally, lobate-stemmed points similar to Adena-style points are found in the Maritime Peninsula. At the Knox site in Maine, one is dated to the time span 2700–2000 BP based on several radiocarbon dates (Belcher 1989:Plate 6). Foulkes's group 4 bifaces have contracting blunt stems and she associates them with Adena points (Foulkes 1981:90, 93–94). One complete specimen (BlDn-12:100) is directly associated with a radiocarbon date of 2655±85 at Fulton Island (Foulkes 1981:90).

The use of diagnostic point morphologies and typologies from other regions like New York or Ontario can be justified in cases where the contexts are well controlled stratigraphically and chronologically using absolute dates. Otherwise, it is best to remain prudent when assigning a side-notched point that has a square base to the Early Ceramic since look-alikes exist for the Middle and Late Ceramic (see site CkEe-22 in Témiscouata, Quebec, for example; Eid 2017a). It would be interesting in the future to apply a measurable index such as the dart-arrow index to distinguish two similar morphologies from different periods as Hildebrandt and King (2012) have proposed. The same can be said for a point with a short, contracting stem; is this an Adena-like point or a later Middle Ceramic point? Turnbull has already raised this issue in terms of archaeological assemblages where the dating is problematic, specifically with regard to the Late Archaic (Terminal or Transitional) and Early Woodland in the Maritime Peninsula (Turnbull 1990; see also Blair 2004a, Sanger 2008). Is it appropriate to use terms like "Meadowood" or "Middlesex" to talk about local populations on the middle Saint John River, for example? In the case of the Bernard-site assemblage, Turnbull (1990) suggests that perhaps the "local" Early Ceramic point is a point with wide side notches, creating a slightly flared base on the stem. These are reminiscent of the small, stemmed points with slightly flared or expanding bases that Allen describes for the earliest part of the Middle Woodland. These points are also not dissimilar from the points described by Chrétien (1995) as the "local" Early Ceramic points found alongside Meadowood Onondaga chert cache blades on Québec City—region sites. Elsewhere in the Maritime Peninsula, the local Early Ceramic point may be a narrow-stemmed variety if one relies on the Passamaquoddy Bay sequence. Finally, at the Ruth Moore site on Great Gott Island in mid-coast Maine, a small point with a wide and straight stem and weak shoulders was found in a basal shell layer in association with Vinette I pottery and a radiocarbon date of 2815±85 BP (Cox and Lawless 1994:Figure 12, point M).

On the other end of the Ceramic period sequence, the early Contact period has produced some securely dated contexts with projectile points. At least two point types seem to be used during the sixteenth and seventeenth centuries in the Maritime Peninsula. One is a side- or corner-notched variety (expanding stem) with very narrow notches that is in seamless continuity with the side- and corner-notched varieties typical of the Late Ceramic. These points are found in many late Ceramic contexts in Maine, Quebec, New Brunswick, and Nova Scotia (table 6.1). At the CkEe-9 site in Témiscouata, Quebec, one such point is directly associated to a hearth dated to 340±60 BP and to a glass bead dating to the early seventeenth century (Chalifoux et al. 1998). A rather different type of point has been assigned to the early Contact period (late sixteenth and early seventeenth century) by Will and Cole-Will (1989) for the central coast of Maine. At the Ann Hilton site, a series of small points (1.9 cm to 3.3 cm in length) with contracting stems and slight or weak shoulders were found in direct association with European clay-pipe fragments and European flint flakes (Will and Cole-Will 1989:4-6, Figure 5). Two other sites in Maine (N'tolonapemk and Venus of Munsungun) have produced similar small, stemmed points that the excavators have assigned to the Contact period (Brigham et al. 2001:Figure 8; Seeber 1987:Plate 2–3).

A simplified chronological sequence of the point morphologies presented above is compiled in table 6.2 (see also Blair 2004a:Figure 2.2). The carefully dated stratified sequences of the lower Miramichi and Saint John River valleys provide the most reliable sequences and dates at this time (Allen 1981, 1989, 2005; Blair 2004a, 2004b; Foulkes 1981); however, archaeologists should be prudent when extending these sequences to Maine, Nova Scotia, or Prince Edward Island. I have attempted to fill in the gaps with the sites in table 6.1 that have provided dated contexts either based on radiocarbon dates or ceramic decorative styles. There appear to be some differences between the northeast and the southwest sectors of the Maritime Peninsula, but the geographic coverage is patchy at best. These differences are indicated in table 6.2. To summarize, the Early Ceramic has no real diagnostic point form other than the small point with a slightly expanding stem from the Northeast area. The Middle Ceramic is also poorly defined other than the bipointed forms and the wide and straight or contracting stem forms that are found at Oxbow. In Nova Scotia, there is a similar form that often has pronounced shoulders (Tusket-style point) and seems to be associated with the early Middle Ceramic. The latter half of the Middle Ceramic is the least well represented in the sequence; however, some time before 1000 BP a new form appears. It is a side- or corner-notched point (sometimes referred to as an expanding stem) that is notable for its narrow (2 mm–3 mm wide) and deep notches that are placed close to the bottom of the blade (cf. Sanger 1987:36). The blade is triangular (isosceles) or slightly convex. This form becomes popular across the Maritime Peninsula during the Late Ceramic period and continues to be used into the early Contact period. It is found in dated contexts in Maine, Quebec, New Brunswick, and Nova Scotia (figures 6.3–6.7, table 6.1). I describe the technological aspects of this point type in the next section.

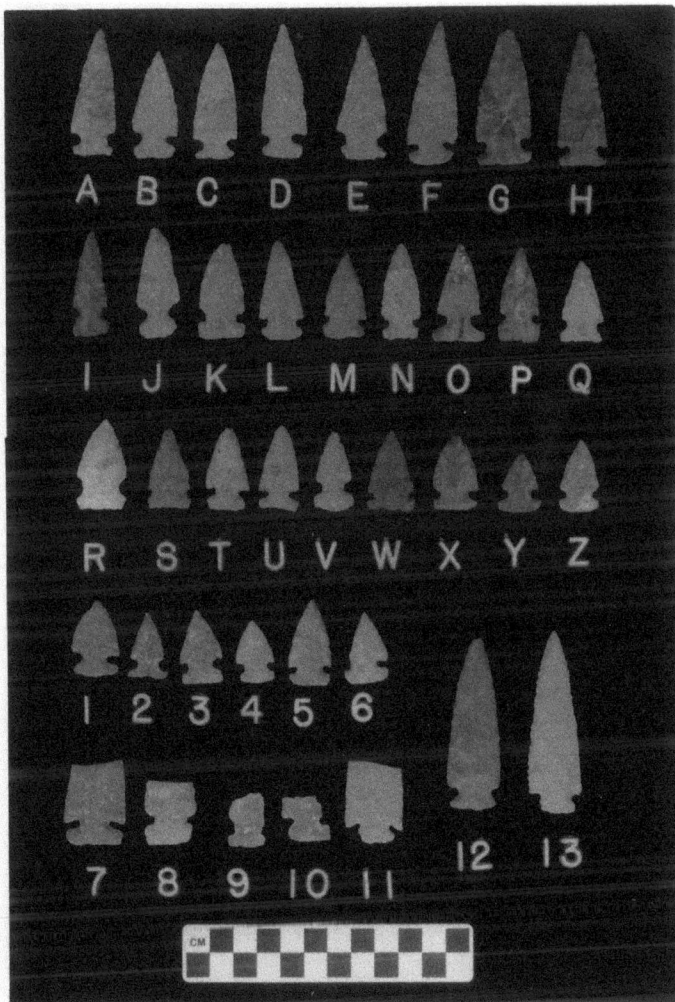

Figure 6.3. Ceramic-period notched points from the Goddard site, Penobscot Bay, Maine. *Source:* Photo courtesy of Steven Cox and the Maine State Museum.

Figure 6.4. Projectile points from Passamaquoddy Bay Late Ceramic sites (reproduced from Sanger 1987:Figure 8): (A)—(B) McAleen; (C) Teacher's Cove; (D–E) Minister's Island; and (F) Eidlitz. All sites are on the New Brunswick side of the bay.
Source: With permission of the Canadian Museum of History.

Figure 6.5. Projectile points from the Carson site, Passamaquoddy Bay, New Brunswick. Reproduced from Sanger (1987:Plate 10). Group I bifaces are the corner- and side-notched (expanding stemmed) points A–J and N–P.
Source: With permission of the Canadian Museum of History.

Figure 6.6. Ceramic-period projectile points from the Brown site, south-shore Nova Scotia. Reproduced from Sheldon (1988:Figure 13). These are group 1 expanding-stemmed points as defined by Sheldon. Point m, at the bottom right (BeCs-3:633+768), is radiocarbon dated by direct association to 1230±70 BP. *Source:* With permission of the Nova Scotia Museum.

Figure 6.7. Late Ceramic-period points from the Pelletier site (CkEe-9), Témiscouata, Quebec. *Source:* Photo by the author.

Technological Aspects of Biface Typologies

For this analysis, it is necessary not only to look at the shape of a tool but also to understand how it is made; that is, how can the technological choices and gestures that lead to a bifacial tool reflect a "technological style" (cf. Lechtman and Merrill 1977). The French technological approach (Inizan et al. 1995) based on the linked concepts of *schéma opératoire* and *chaîne opératoire* can be applied if there is enough information to reconstruct how bifaces were made and also to distinguish between one technological "style" and another. The *schéma opératoire* (operational scheme) can be seen as the mental abstraction that includes all of the steps, gestures, and choices necessary to produce a biface, a sort of strategy that is known to the knapper and which can be shared (Inizan et al. 1995; Soressi

Table 6.2. Summary of bifacial projectile point morphologies by Ceramic sub-period (chronology based on Petersen and Sanger 1991). The SW and NE sectors refer to the sectors defined in the map in figure 6.1. For site-specific dates and morphologies, refer to table 6.1.

			Regional Maritime Peninsula Point Morphology	Extra-Regional Point Morphology
Early Ceramic	CP1	3050-2150 BP	SW: narrow straight and contracting stemmed NE: straight stemmed, followed by small expanding stemmed (2600-2200 BP)	side notched (Meadowood box base), lobate stemmed (Adena)
early Middle Ceramic	CP2	2150-1650 BP	SW: stemmed and side notched (Nova Scotia - contracting stem with pronounced shoulders) NE: bipointed/contracting stem	
middle Middle Ceramic	CP3	1650-1350 BP	SW: side notched NE: wide straight or contracting stem	
late Middle Ceramic	CP4	1350-950 BP	side and corner notched?	[SW: corner notched triangular Jack's Reef?]
early Late Ceramic	CP5	950-650 BP	side and corner notched, blade is triangular to slightly convex, notches are narrow and placed low on the blade	
late Late Ceramic	CP6	650-400 BP	side and corner notched, blade is triangular to slightly convex, notches are narrow and placed low on the blade	SW: Triangular (Levanna)
early Contact	CP7	400-300 BP	A) side and corner notched, blade is triangular to slightly convex, notches are narrow and placed low on the blade B) small contracting stemmed	SW: Triangular (Levanna) including points made of copper alloy

and Geneste 2011). The *chaîne opératoire* is the concrete embodiment of the *schéma opératoire*. It must be seen as specific to a raw material and a technological tradition of a specific time, place, and community (e.g., the Touladi chert biface reduction sequence found at the Late Ceramic lithic workshops in Témiscouata, described below). Consequently, in this section, I look at projectile points but also bifacial preforms and bifaces dating to the Late Ceramic. While projectile points have more attributes that seem to be time sensitive or diagnostic, such as straight and narrow stems or corner and side notches, my intent is not to isolate these forms but to look at them, along with the bifaces that are found in the same contexts, as part of a continuum. My working hypothesis is that in some cases the techno-logical attributes of bifaces may be just as diagnostic as the proximal or hafting element of a projectile point. In addition, over the past 40 years, archaeologists working in the Maritime Peninsula have remarked on the increased number over time of small scrapers (endscrapers and thumbnail scrapers) in Ceramic contexts, and the same trend seems to be true for bipolar tools such as wedges and bipolar cores (cf. Black 1992). I suspect that all of these lithic technological choices are part of a generalized Late Ceramic toolkit that people in the Maritime Peninsula used up to and during the time of contact with Europeans (cf. Holyoke 2012:204). One major problem exists, however: it was impossible for me to analyze the bifaces and projectile points used for this study in person. As a result, what I propose here is a tentative framework that will have to be validated by the actual on-site analysis of the bifacial tools themselves.

Quarries and Lithic Workshops: An Ideal Place to Study Technology

In northeastern North America, projectile-point typologies have typically relied on morphology (e.g., Ritchie 1961). Only occasionally is a technological attri-bute used to distinguish a point type, such as serrated edges, bevelling along the blade, or basal grinding. Furthermore, most projectile points found on archae-ological sites are not pristine and have been reworked or are broken, which confounds the use of typologies. This is why quarries and nearby lithic work-shops are the best place to start when trying to figure out the idealized forms (morphologies or types) that people are trying to produce. More importantly, these places allow us to look at the entire reduction-production sequence of a projectile point. This includes the bifacial preforms and bifaces that are eventually converted into projectile points. On some lithic workshops close to quarry sources such as in Témiscouata, or at Munsungun and Mount Kineo, Maine, bifacial preforms and bifaces number in the hundreds, if not thousands (Burke 2000, 2007; Chalifoux et al. 1998; Eid 2017a, 2017b; McGuire 1908; Seeber 1987; Will 1996; Willoughby 1901; see also Spiess and Hedden 1983 for workshops using cobbles). It is precisely on these lithic workshops where we can reconstruct and understand the technological processes, the *chaînes opératoires*, specific to each time period and each raw material. The combination of this technological information on biface manufacture with more traditional mor-phological characteristics will be used here to better define the Late Ceramic projectile points and bifaces that are characteristic of the Maritime Peninsula. Sadly, I do not have the necessary data at this time to carry out the same kind of analyses for the Early and Middle Ceramic bifacial technologies (but see Blair 2004a for Early Ceramic bifacial technologies).

While quarries and lithic workshops are notoriously difficult to date, we are fortunate to have several lithic workshops that have been radiocarbon dated or which have produced ceramics that can be assigned to a Ceramic sub-period. Moreover, the lithic workshops in question are often single occupation sites or have a short lifespan (one or two generations). To compensate for the small number of dated contexts, table 6.1 provides several additional sites from the Maritime Peninsula that have produced projectile points dated to the Ceramic period. The following lithic workshops are useful in understanding the bifacial reduction-production technology of the inhabitants of the Maritime Peninsula during the Late Ceramic period: the Pelletier site (CkEe-9) on Lake Touladi in Témiscouata, Quebec; the Casey site (118-188) on Moosehead Lake near Mount Kineo, Maine; and the Venus of Munsungun (154-5) and Birch Point (155-8) sites on Munsungun Lake, also in Maine. Several other lithic workshops that date to the Ceramic period are known for these three quarry-source areas, but I will limit my analysis here to these workshops since they have been the object of the most detailed technological studies and they date to the same sub-period, the Late Ceramic. One other site, Kidder Point (41-4) on the central coast of Maine, is interesting because the occupants used the local beach cobbles of rhyolite to manufacture bifaces. The site's bifacial technology is described by Spiess and Hedden in their 1983 monograph. The workshop is not securely dated but is most likely Ceramic period.

The Pelletier site is a Late Ceramic and early Contact period site with at least two occupation areas (Burke 1993; Chalifoux et al. 1998). The technological analysis of the bifacial production was initially done by me (Burke 1993, 2000, 2007). Eid (2017a, 2017b) then reanalyzed most of the Témiscouata lithic workshops, including Pelletier, using the French technological approach (figure 6.8). Eid's analysis was much more detailed than mine, and included the refitting of flakes to cores and bifacial blanks/preforms. With this new, detailed understanding, it is possible to reconstruct the bifacial *chaîne opératoire* related to bifacial production in Touladi chert during the Late Ceramic (Eid 2017b:10-19). Knappers created most of the bifacial blanks out of tabular chunks that came from the quarry and not from large flake blanks. Reduction followed a predictable sequence leading to the production of bifaces that are symmetrical laterally and in plan (see figure 6.8 for examples of the phases described below; consult Eid 2107a, 2017b, for further details). The final thinning (phase 3B in Eid's terminology) of the biface is done late in the sequence and leads to the finished biface (phase 4; Eid 2017b). This biface is thin (<8 mm thickness) and has a biconvex (lenticular) cross-section. The most common outline of this biface is a leaf shape with slightly excurvate or convex blade sides and a base that is rounded, creating a continuous contour. The second option for this final phase of the biface is a form that is reminiscent of the cache blades of the Early Woodland and has a blade that starts with straight sides that then curve toward the base in an almost parallel fashion, and a straight to slightly convex base, creating a slight corner at the junction of the sides and the base. Finally, a third finished biface form is also produced. It has a triangular (isosceles) shape with straight sides and a straight base. It is not clear if some of these thinned bifaces were used as knives; however, in this case I am interested primarily in the projectile points that were made out of these bifaces.

There is no doubt that the phase 4 (*sensu* Eid 2017b) finished bifaces are indeed the "preforms" for the projectile points (figure 6.8). What is curious, however, is that in all three cases the final intent for the projectile point is similar, no matter what the morphology of the bifacial preform. Two narrow (2 mm–3 mm wide) notches are produced toward the base of the biface. The notches vary whether they are corner or side notches, and there is clearly a continuum from one to the other. This suggests to me that the intention of the knapper is simply to create the notches as near as possible to the base but not necessarily that the knapper would distinguish between side or corner notches (I suspect that many archaeologists might also have a hard time separating the two). The only apparent difference in the end product is that corner notches produce more pronounced barbs, which may be an intentional outcome for some of the points. Some of the notches can be relatively open or shallow, but many are quite deep, sometimes up to 5 mm, and are parallel and narrow, suggesting a specialized tool. Copper tools may have been used for pressure flaking the notches, and some of the small rods, "awls," and "spatulas" made of copper that are found on sites around the Gulf of Maine and near Shediac, New Brunswick, would be ideally suited for pressure flaking the notches (cf. Leonard 1996; see also Hadlock 1941 for examples). The base of the finished and notched point can be slightly curved and convex, or straight. This form is simply the relict base of the biface preform and is usually not reworked, suggesting that the notching is indeed the final step in the manufacture of the tool. This is supported by a biface from the Casey site that has the beginnings of a notch at one corner of the base but which must have snapped the biface tip during the notching process, according to Will (figure 6.9; Will 1996:234). The blade margins also remain either straight or slightly convex, true to the original biface preform. Occasionally the blade margins are slightly serrated, but it is not clear if this is a later and intentional retouch alteration. The thin, biconvex (lenticular) cross-sections of these points also suggest that there is little retouch along the blade margins after phase 3b. Bases are not ground but some notches show signs of grinding and/or wear.

At the Casey site on Moosehead Lake in Maine, Will (1996) has been able to reconstruct the bifacial reduction-production sequence (figure 6.9). Will's analysis is based on years of experience analyzing stone tools and debitage from the region, but also on his extensive experience as a knapper of local materials, which gives him considerable insight into the technological choices made by the knappers at the Casey site. The raw material used is Mount Kineo rhyolite, which comes from quarries about 12 km west of the site. Will has knapped this material many times and understands the challenges posed by the raw material, and there are several errors in manufacture that Will identifies at the Casey site, such as end shock. The reduction sequence that Will presents resembles the sequence described above for the Late Ceramic in Témiscouata (Will 1996:232-234, Figure 4). It is not clear if the bifacial blanks are started on quarry blocks or on large flake blanks because the more advanced preforms arrive at the Casey site already shaped, and therefore these steps appear to have taken place at the quarries themselves (Will 1996:234): "Thinning, shaping, edge straightening and notching were the final manufacturing steps that presumably took place at the campsite (Callahan's stages 4 and 5)." (Will cites Callahan's stages because these represent one of the few widely used bifacial reduction sequences in North America.) Nonetheless, the intention of at least part of the bifacial reduction sequence was to produce side- and corner-notched points that resemble closely those from Témiscouata and other parts of the Maritime Peninsula. The *schéma opératoire* and the *chaîne opératoire* that lead to this projectile point are very similar to those from Témiscouata despite the difference in the raw material (figure 6.9). The chert from Témiscouata can be said to be more easily worked and responds better, especially to pressure flaking. Kineo rhyolite is a tough (hard) material that is hard to pressure flake, and which often crushes along the edge of a thin biface if not prepared properly prior to percussion flaking.

Interestingly, at the Kidder Point site on the central coast of Maine, Spiess and Hedden (1983:88-94) have been able to reconstruct the bifacial reduction-production sequence using the same material, but in this case the rhyolite has been glacially transported from central interior Maine and is found in large cobbles on the beach. Assemblage K at the site probably dates to the early Middle Ceramic period, but the reduction sequence resembles that from Casey. The finished bifaces have similar dimensions (length, width, thickness), but the shape is more reminiscent of cache blades with a straight base and slightly convex sides (Spiess and Hedden 1983:68-71, Plates 4–14). What is interesting in this case is that these bifaces do not seem destined to be converted into points. They have a change in retouch that occupies the bottom 2 cm of the blade on both sides, which Spiess and Hedden interpret as necessary for hafting these bifaces for use as knives. The projectile points associated with this assemblage are quite diverse and include side-notched and stemmed varieties.

In her master's thesis, Seeber analyzed the lithic materials from two Ceramic period sites on Munsungun Lake: Venus of Munsungun and Birch Point (Seeber 1987). These sites are campsites and lithic workshops, much like Pelletier and Casey. Seeber's detailed analysis uses a methodology that is detailed and rigorous but not widely applied to sites in the Northeast. The reduction-production sequence is presented using descriptive terms like "face paring" or "platform isolating" (Seeber 1987:81–100). There are few photos and no drawings. Knappers at both sites seem to have spent a lot of time producing bifaces, only a few of which were converted into side- and corner-notched points. The reduction sequence seems to begin at these workshops on flake blanks and not on quarry blocks. There also seems to be more use of pressure flaking in the earlier steps of the bifacial reduction sequence than at Pelletier or Casey. Seeber also identifies some differences between the two Munsungun sites in terms of the bifacial reduction sequence, primarily in the order of the steps identified (face paring, edge dulling, rub buffeting, margin regularizing and contouring, pressure flaking, and notching, to use her terms). My personal analysis of the materials from the Munsungun Lake Ceramic-period sites suggests that the Munsungun chert behaves much in the same way as the Touladi chert from Témiscouata and, therefore, should not pose any different constraints on the bifacial reduction sequence or *chaîne opératoire*. It is hard, however, to propose any other parallels between the technological aspects visible at Pelletier and Casey and those described by Seeber for Venus of Munsungun and Birch Point without reanalyzing the bifacial tools. But, to be clear, the biface preforms from the Munsungun sites that are presented in Seeber's study are almost identical in morphology to those found on Late Ceramic sites in Témiscouata (e.g., Seeber 1987:Plates 5–2, 5–3, 5–6).

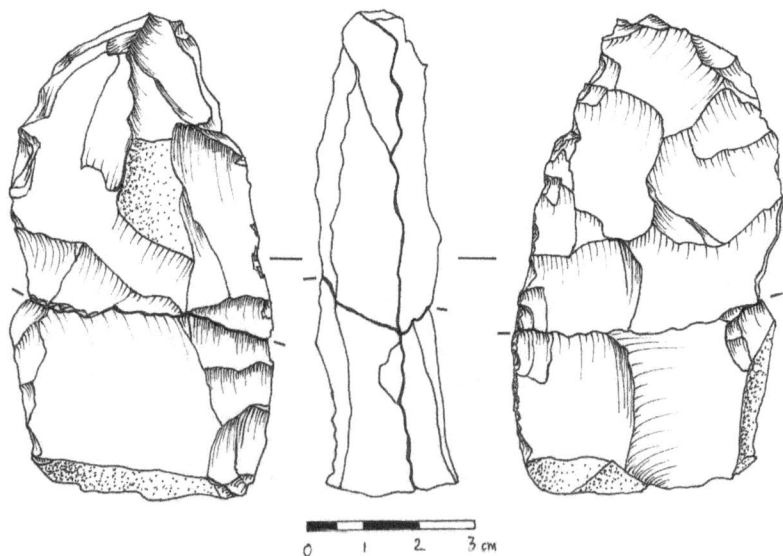

Figure 6.8a. Bifacial reduction sequence for the Late Ceramic occupations at the Pelletier site, Témiscouata, Quebec, as reconstructed by Patrick Eid (2017a, 2017b); bifacial blank on a quarry block (CkEe-9.881).

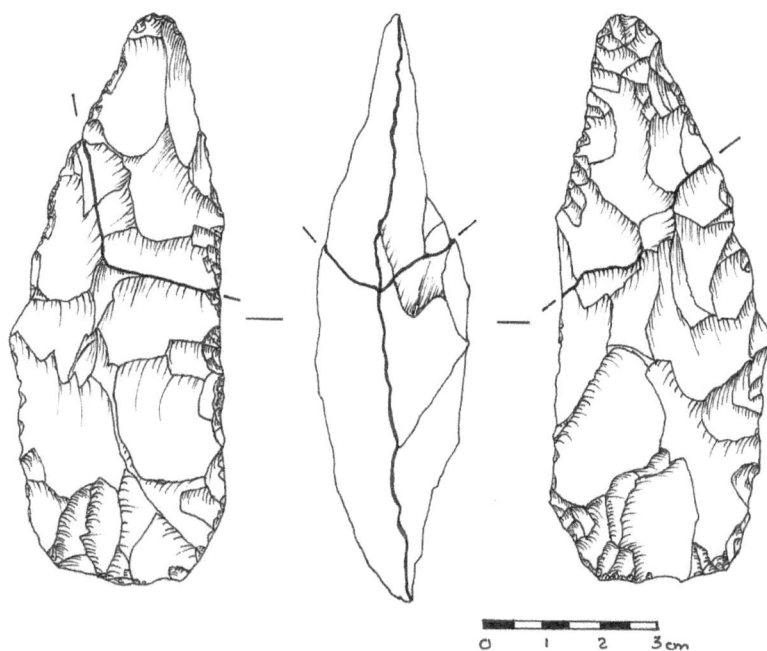

Figure 6.8b. Bifacial preform, phase 2 (CkEe-9.572-647).

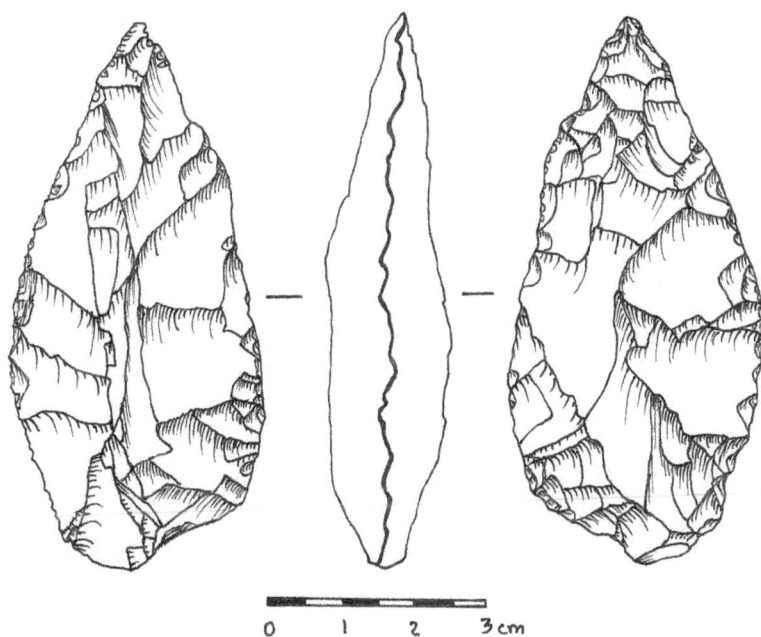

Figure 6.8c. Biface, phase 3 (CkEe-9.658).

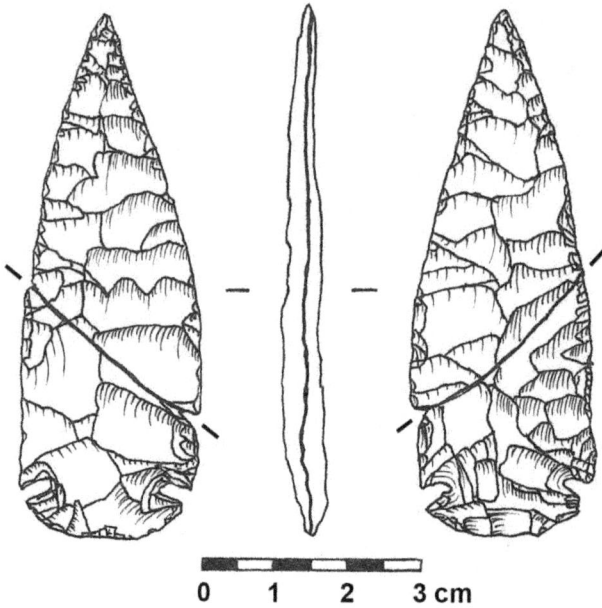

Figure 6.8d. Corner-notched biface, phase 4 (CkEe-9.670-671). Reproduced from Eid (2017b:Figures 6–9). *Source:* All drawings by Marianne-Marilou Leclerc. Reproduced with permission of the author and the artist.

Figure 6.9. Biface reduction sequence from the Casey site, Moosehead Lake, Maine. *Source:* From Will (1996:Figure 4) with permission from the journal *Archaeology of Eastern North America.*

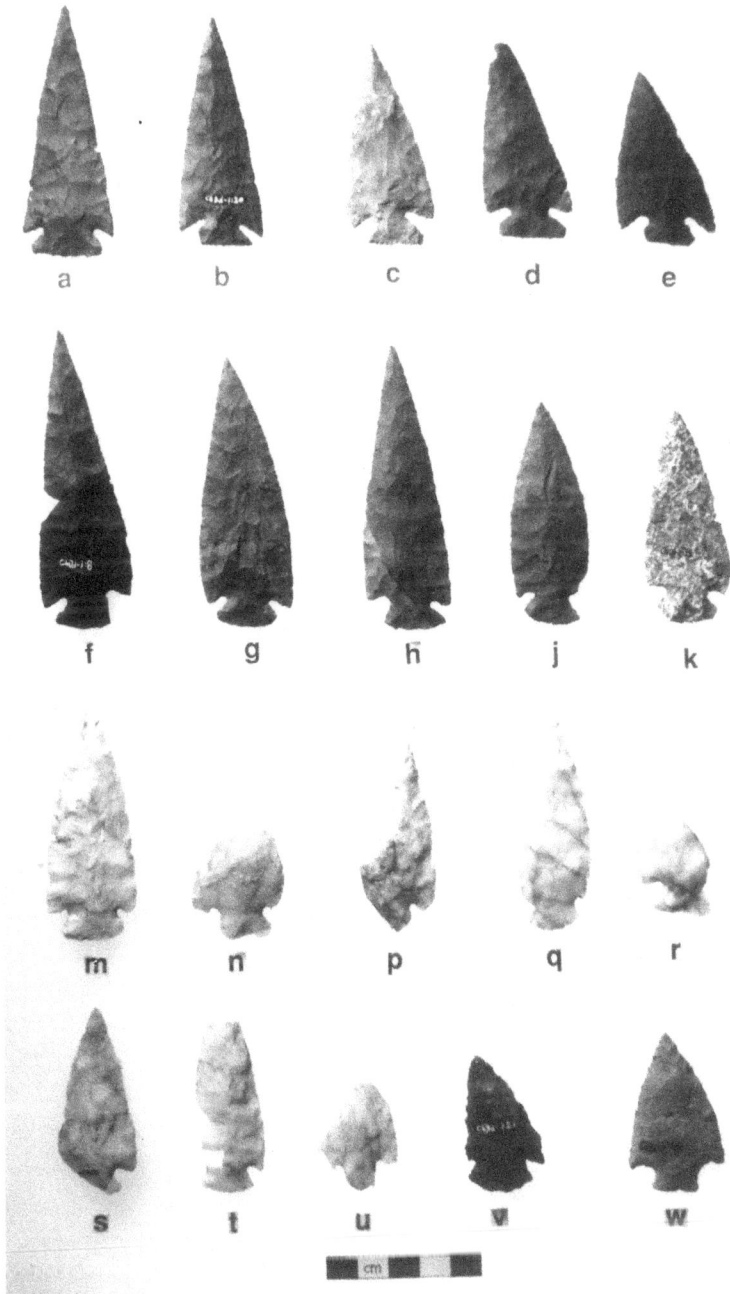

Figure 6.10. Corner-notched projectile points from a burial context from Skull Island (CbDd-1), Shediac, New Brunswick. The points were all found together and in direct association with a radiocarbon date of 680 ± 70 BP.

Source: Photo courtesy of Kevin Leonard; corresponds to Leonard (1996:Figure 38).

Discussion and Conclusion

In this chapter I have tried to assemble and summarize data on bifacial stone-tool technology from the Maritime Peninsula. The emphasis has been on stemmed bifaces or projectile points. No collections were physically analyzed or reanalyzed for this chapter, which is a serious limitation, particularly in terms of the technological analysis of bifaces and projectile points. Some detailed technological data was fortunately available for the well-known quarry sources areas of Maine and Quebec. During my analysis of the data available, it became clear that there is no apparent distinction between the interior and the coast of the Maritime Peninsula in terms of the projectile-point typologies, or even the general bifacial reduction sequences. On the other hand, there appears to be a difference between the southwest and the northeast portions of the study area (figure 6.1, table 6.2). This is somewhat contrary to what Robinson had proposed in 1996, since he had focused primarily on the coastal—interior differences, but in his case only for Maine. In rereading his article, however, it seems clear that he sees a distinction (boundary?) between the southwest and the northeast parts of Maine. The differences I have described in this chapter are primarily visible in the bifacial technology in terms of the influence of extra-regional styles or types that appear on occasion (e.g., box-base side-notched, triangular Levanna; table 6.2). These represent widespread projectile-point horizons that can be found as far as southern New England, New York, and the St. Lawrence River Valley, and they do not necessarily represent the local bifacial technology (cf. Boudreau 2008; Ritchie 1961).

The data in table 6.1 point to the fact that it is difficult to go beyond some general point morphologies or types for the Early and Middle Ceramic. This is in part due to a lack of dated features and/or well-controlled stratigraphic contexts producing bifaces and projectile points. In some sub-regions of the Maritime Peninsula, such as the lower Saint John River valley and the Miramichi River valley (Allen 1981, 1988, 1989, 2005; Blair 2004a, 2004b; Holyoke 2012), archaeologists have been able to get a better handle on the Early and Middle Ceramic biface technology, but it is hard to extend these sequences with confidence to the entire Maritime Peninsula. This stratigraphic "challenge" is further compounded given that there has not been enough detailed analysis of the complete bifacial technological sequence that leads to what we consider to be diagnostic projectile-point morphologies for these periods. A locally produced, Early Ceramic, side-notched box-base point that resembles the classic Meadowood box-base point will inevitably be more variable in morphology than the original made on an Onondaga chert cache blade. This is because the *schéma opératoire* leading to the production of the biface, and then the point, is not as rigid or standardized in the Maritime Peninsula, at the "margins" of the Meadowood interaction sphere (cf. Chrétien 1995 for a clear demonstration of this for Meadowood sites in the Québec City region). It is perhaps more productive to look at these points as local "copies" of an extra-regional style.

There is more interpretive potential if we work on reconstructing the local or regional bifacial technology that produced a wide variety of stemmed points that were used during the Early and Middle Ceramic. These points are numerous and are made in a variety of local materials, primarily quartz in eastern New Brunswick, quartzite in Nova Scotia and Prince Edward Island, and rhyolites on the southern coast of New Brunswick and Maine. Working to reconstruct the *chaînes opératoires* of points made of less fine-grained materials is admittedly a challenge, but this does not diminish the importance that these technologies had to the people of the Maritime Peninsula since the end of the Archaic and for at least 1,500 years during the Ceramic period. At the moment, I am hesitant to propose any obvious trends in the bifacial technology related to these stemmed points during the Early and Middle Ceramic, but there seems to be a clear technological change at some time in the late Middle Ceramic that leads to a new type of narrow, side- and corner-notched point.

The side- and corner-notched points that seem to have captured the imagination of the Late Ceramic-period inhabitants of the Maritime Peninsula did not appear out of nowhere, nor did the *schéma opératoire* that was put into action at several quarries and lithic workshops in the interior. The earliest date we have for a side-notched point with narrow, deep notches is from the Brown site in Nova Scotia (Sheldon 1988). Here, a date of 1230±70 is in direct association with the point BeCs-3:633+768 (Sheldon 1988:Figure 13, specimen m) (figure 6.6). At the Casey site, in Maine, the bifaces and corner-notched point described by Will (1996; figure 6.9 here) are dated to 1010±50. It seems likely then that this type of projectile point (corner- and side-notched, with narrow notches), the accompanying finished bifaces (triangular, leaf-shaped), and the bifacial reduction sequence that precedes these thin bifaces were put in place sometime in the late Middle Ceramic sub-period (CP4; see Petersen and Sanger 1991). The point of origin is hard to establish, based on the patchy coverage that we have (see table 6.1), but I am willing to propose that this is a regional, homegrown, Maritime Peninsula concept, by which I mean that the *schéma opératoire* was shared across the region. The "finished product" (the side- and corner-notched projectile point) is surely the easiest element of this biface reduction sequence to recognize for archaeologists. But it is clear, based on the analysis of quarry-related workshops at Moosehead Lake, Munsungun Lake, and Touladi Lake, that this reduction sequence is put into practice using different raw materials while following generally similar steps, choices, and gestures. When more detailed analyses of the knapping products (bifaces and debitage) are done, some variability does show up in this sequence, which is to be expected (Eid 2017a, 2017b; Seeber 1987; Will 1996, 2000).

The Late Ceramic bifacial reduction sequence that I describe here, with its side- and corner-notched projectile points, is widely distributed across the Maritime Peninsula, being found in Quebec, Maine, New Brunswick, and Nova Scotia (tables 6.1–6.2, figures 6.2–6.9). It is found on the coast, along the major river valleys, and in the interior uplands. It lasts into the Contact period, as evidenced by the Pelletier site in Témiscouata, Quebec. This implies that the Indigenous knappers of the Maritime Peninsula were using the quarries and secondary deposits of raw materials on the coast and in the interior into the early seventeenth century to manufacture stone tools (Chalifoux et al. 1998; Leonard 1996; Seeber 1987; Spiess 1995; Wellman 1973). This bifacial technology is accompanied by a high number of small scrapers (also referred to as endscrapers and thumbnail scrapers) that are most often manufactured out of fine-grained materials like chert or chalcedony. Also of interest from a lithic technology perspective is the increased use during the Late Ceramic of bipolar reduction technology. The presence of wedges (*pièces esquillées*) and bipolar cores on sites from the Maritime Peninsula is significant for the Late Ceramic, and suggests an important role for this complementary mode of reduction and production. The presence of these three elements—side- and corner-notched projectile points with narrow notches, numerous small scrapers made of fine-grained raw materials, and wedges and bipolar cores—together can be considered diagnostic of the Late Ceramic for the Maritime Peninsula (see also Holyoke 2012 for the lower Saint John River valley).

Finally, it is important to note that the bifacial technology that produced the fine, thin, side- and corner-notched projectile points was enacted within a social context, and probably had a symbolic dimension or was connected in some way to group identity. The Late Ceramic Maritime Peninsula point style is not known outside of the Maritime Peninsula based on published data and my personal experience working in archaeology in the St. Lawrence River Valley, New England, and New York. In addition, these projectile points were seen as "valuable" enough to be included as burial offerings on at least one occasion, at a burial excavated on Skull Island (CbDd-1), near Shediac, by Leonard (1996). This exceptional burial included the twenty corner-notched points pictured in figure 6.10, as well as paint stones, marcasite crystals, a ground-stone adze, a stone pipe bowl, scrapers, bifaces, ceramics, plants including food plants, and copper artifacts. The points are remarkably consistent in morphology despite the use of different raw materials. The burial, including the projectile points, is directly dated by a radiocarbon date of 680±70 BP. These symbolic or identity dimensions have not been explored in this chapter, but they certainly merit further exploration, in part by looking more carefully at the specific archaeological contexts in which these points are found.

The fact that the side- and corner-notched type of projectile point was used for over 700 years attests to its popularity and importance in the lives of the Indigenous people of the Maritime Peninsula. At earlier times during the Ceramic period, other point styles came into the region from further south and west (table 6.2) but the people of the Maritime Peninsula seem to have maintained their own regional "styles" throughout the Ceramic period, beginning even in the Late Archaic. This process of regionalization seems to have increased or accelerated during the Ceramic period, based on the bifacial technology presented here, and the ceramic technology of the Maritime Peninsula points to the same trend (Petersen and Sanger 1991; see also Bourgeois 1999). On the one hand, the Maritime Peninsula seems to have become its own distinct cultural and social entity, or region, sometime during the Late Archaic or Early Ceramic period. On the other hand, and in a continuation of this "regionalization" process during the ensuing 3,000 years, the Indigenous groups occupying the Maritime Peninsula seem to have gradually become separate political, social, and cultural entities (Burke 2000). These groups would become the First Nations that we know today: Penobscot, Passamaquoddy, Wolastoqiyik, and Mi'kmaq.

Acknowledgements

Thank you to Ken Holyoke and Gabe Hrynick for allowing me to contribute to this book even though I did not participate in the original Canadian Archaeological Association session in 2019. A special thanks to Ken Holyoke for all his help putting this chapter together, and for helping me find sites and reports I did not know about. Also, thank you to the many other people that helped me by pointing me in the right direction of reports and sending me files: Art Spiess, Katie Cottreau-Robbins, Gabe Hrynick, Arthur Anderson, Kevin Leonard, and Christian Thériault. Thanks to Steve Cox and Kevin Leonard for letting me use their excellent original photos of projectile points. Thank you to Cora Woolsey for her advice on the features and dates from the End of Dyke site in Nova Scotia; any misinterpretations are my responsibility, of course. Thank you to the Nova Scotia Museum and to the Canadian Museum of History for permission to reproduce images. Finally, thanks to Ken Holyoke, Gabe Hrynick, and an anonymous reviewer for their comments on a previous draft of this work.

References Cited

Allen, Patricia

n.d.   *Old Mission Point—Restigouche Culture History*. Report submitted to the Archaeology Branch, Province of New Brunswick. Fredericton.

1980   The Oxbow Site: Chronology and Prehistory in Northeastern New Brunswick. Master's thesis, Department of Anthropology, Memorial University of Newfoundland, St. John's.

1981   *The Oxbow Site: Chronology and Prehistory in Northeastern New Brunswick.* New Brunswick Manuscripts in Archaeology Series 2, No. 1. Department of Historical and Cultural Resources, Province of New Brunswick, Fredericton.

1988   *Southwest Miramichi Survey and Testing Project: 1987.* New Brunswick Manuscripts in Archaeology 23. Municipalities, Culture, and Housing, Fredericton, New Brunswick.

1989   The 1984 Oxbow Archaeology Project. Draft Manuscript on file at the Archaeology Branch, New Brunswick Department of Municipalities, Culture and Housing, Fredericton, New Brunswick.

2005   *The Oxbow Site 1984: Metepenagiag Mi'kmaq First Nation, Miramichi, New Brunswick.* New Brunswick Manuscripts in Archaeology 39. Archaeological Services, Heritage Branch, Culture and Sport Secretariat, Fredericton, New Brunswick.

Barré, Georges

1978   *Cap Chat (DgDq-1) : un site du Sylvicole Moyen en Gaspésie. Les cahiers du patrimoine 1.* Ministère des Affaires culturelles du Québec, Quebec.

Belcher, William R.

1989   The Archaeology of the Knox Site, East Penobscot Bay, Maine. *Maine Archaeological Society Bulletin* 29(1):33–46.

Betts, Matthew W.

2019   Chronology (Chapter 4). In *Place-Making in the Pretty Harbour: The Archaeology of Port Joli, Nova Scotia,* edited by Matthew W. Betts, pp. 115–127. Canadian Museum of History and University of Ottawa Press, Ottawa.

Betts, Matthew W., and Kenneth R. Holyoke

2019   Lithic Technology and Other Artifacts (Chapter 7). In Place-Making in the Pretty *Harbour: The Archaeology of Port Joli, Nova Scotia,* edited by Matthew W. Betts, pp. 217–324. Canadian Museum of History and University of Ottawa Press, Ottawa.

Black, David W.

1992   *Living Close to the Ledge: Prehistoric Human Ecology of the Bliss Islands, Quoddy Region, New Brunswick, Canada.* Occasional Papers in Northeastern Archaeology No. 6. Copetown Press, Dundas, Ontario.

Blair, Susan E.

2004a   Ancient Wolastoq'kew Landscapes: Settlement and Technology in the Lower Saint John River Valley, Canada. PhD dissertation, Department of Anthropology, University of Toronto, Toronto.

Blair, Susan E. (editor)

2004b   *Wolastoqiyik Ajemseg: The People of the Beautiful River at Jemseg. Volume 2: Archaeological Results (Jemseg Crossing Archaeology Project).* New Brunswick Manuscripts in Archaeology 36E. Archaeological Services, Heritage Branch, Culture and Sport Secretariat, New Brunswick, Fredericton.

Boudreau, Jeff

2008   *A New England Typology of Native American Projectile Points.* Alphagraphics, New Bedford, Massachusetts.

Bourgeois, Vincent G. J.
1999   A Regional Pre-Contact Ceramic Sequence for the Saint John River Valley. Master's thesis, Department of Anthropology, University of New Brunswick, Fredericton.

Bourque, Bruce J.
1971   Prehistory of the Central Maine Coast. PhD dissertation, Department of Anthropology, Harvard University, Cambridge, Massachusetts.
1976   The Turner Farm Site: A Preliminary Report. *Man in the Northeast* 11:21–30.
1989   Ethnicity on the Maritime Peninsula. *Ethnohistory* 36(3):257–284.
1995   *Diversity and Complexity in Prehistoric Maritime Societies: A Gulf of Maine Perspective.* Interdisciplinary Contributions to Archaeology. Plenum Press, New York.
2001   *Twelve Thousand Years: American Indians in Maine.* University of Nebraska Press, Lincoln.

Bourque, Bruce J., and Steven L. Cox
1981   Maine State Museum Investigation of the Goddard Site, 1979. *Man in the Northeast* 22:3–27.

Brigham, Michael, Robert N. Bartone, Jessica A. Reed, and Ellen R. Cowie
2001   Introduction to the Archaeological Phase III Excavations at NTOLONAPEMK, the Eastern Surplus Company Superfund Site, 96.02. *The Maine Archaeological Society Bulletin* 41(2):27–39.

Burke, Adrian L.
1993   The Pelletier Site (CkEe-9), Témiscouata: A Lithic Workshop and Habitation Site. Master's thesis, Department of Anthropology, Université de Montréal, Montréal.
2000   Lithic Procurement and the Ceramic Period Occupation of the Interior of the Maritime Peninsula. PhD dissertation, Department of Anthropology, University at Albany—SUNY, Albany, New York.
2007   Quarry Source Areas and the Organization of Stone Tool Technology: A View from Quebec. Archaeology of Eastern North America. *Archaeology of Eastern North America* 35:63–80.

Butler, Eva L., and Wendell S. Hadlock
1962   *A Preliminary Survey of the Munsungan-Allagash Waterway.* Bulletin VIII. Robert Abbe Museum, Bar Harbor, Maine.

Callahan, Errett
2000   *The Basics of Biface Knapping in the Eastern Fluted Point Tradition: A Manual for Flintknappers and Lithic Analysts.* 4th ed. (reprinted from *Archaeology of Eastern North America*, vol. 7, 1979, pp. 1–180). Piltdown Productions, Lynchburg, Virginia.

Chalifoux, Éric, Adrian L. Burke, and Claude Chapdelaine
1998   *La préhistoire du Témiscouata: Occupations amérindiennes dans la haute vallée de Wolastokuk. Paléo-Québec No. 26.* Paléo-Québec. Recherches amérindiennes au Québec, Montréal.

Chrétien, Yves
1995   Les lames de cache du site Lambert et l'influence de la culture Meadowood dans la région de Québec. In *Archéologies québécoises. Paléo-Québec No. 23*, edited

by Anne-Marie Balac, Claude Chapdelaine, Normand Clermont, and Françoise Duguay, pp. 185–201. Recherches amérindiennes au Québec, Montréal.

Cox, Steven L.
1983   The Blue Hill Bay Survey. *Maine Archaeological Society Bulletin* 23(2):21–30.

Cox, Steven, and Gary Lawless
1994   *The Indian Shell Heap:Archaeology of the Ruth Moore Site.* Robert Abbe Museum, Bar Harbor, Maine.

Cultural Resource Management Group Limited (CRM Group)
2014   *End of Dyke Mitigation 2012, Gaspereau Lake Reservoir, Kings County, Nova Scotia, Final Report.* Heritage Research Permit Number: A2012NS093. Report submitted to Nova Scotia Power Incorporated and the Special Places Program of the Nova Scotia Department of Communities, Culture and Heritage, Halifax.

Davis, Stephen A.
1978   *Teacher's Cove:A Prehistoric Site on Passamaquoddy Bay.* New Brunswick Archaeology Series 1, Number 1. Historical Resources Administration, Fredericton.
1991   Yarmouth Coastal Survey. Heritage Research Permit A1987NS07. In *Archaeology in Nova Scotia 1987 and 1988. Curatorial Report No. 69*, edited by Stephen A. Davis, Charles Lindsay, Robert Ogilvie, and Brian Preston, pp. 69–88. Nova Scotia Museum, Halifax.

Davis MacIntyre & Associates Limited
2015   *Starr's Point Crown Lands Transfer:Archaeological Resource Impact Assessment (Detail Report BgDc-12, Heritage Research Permit A2014NS017).* Report submitted to Coordinator, Special Places, Nova Scotia Communities, Culture and Heritage, Halifax.

Deal, Michael
1986   Late Archaic and Ceramic Period Utilizaton of the Mud Lake Stream Site, Southwestern New Brunswick. *Man in the Northeast* 32:67–94.
n.d.   *Susquehanna and Ceramic Period Utilization of the Mud Lake Stream (BkDw-5) Site, Southwestern New Brunswick.* Report on file at Archaeology Branch, Department of Historical and Cultural Resources, Province of New Brunswick, Fredericton.

Deal, Michael, Judith Corkum, Dora Kemp, Jeff McClair, Susan McIlquham, Alex Murchison, and Barbara Wells
1987   Archaeological Investigations at the Low Terrace Site (BaDg2), Indian Gardens, Queens County, Nova Scotia. In *Archaeology in Nova Scotia 1985 and 1986. Curatorial Report No. 63*, edited by Stephen A. Davis, Charles Lindsay, Robert Ogilvie, and Brian Preston, pp. 149–228. Nova Scotia Museum, Halifax.

Eid, Patrick
2017a   Analyse techno-économique des chaînes opératoires lithiques du Témiscouata (Québec), durant le Sylvicole et la période de Contact. PhD dissertation, Département d'anthropologie, Université de Montréal, Montréal.
2017b   Les artefacts importés dans un contexte de carrières: la techno-économie des industries lithiques du Témiscouata (Québec) durant le Sylvicole et la période de Contact. *Journal of Lithic Studies* 4(2). doi:10.2218/jls.v4i2.2543.

Erskine, John Steuart
1998   *Memoirs on the Prehistory of Nova Scotia, 1957-1967.* Nova Scotia Museum special report edited by Michael Deal. Nova Scotia Museum, Halifax.

Foulkes, Ellen V.
1981   Fulton Island: A Stratified Site in the Saint John River Valley of New Brunswick. Master's thesis, Department of Anthropology, Trent University, Peterborough, Ontario.

Hadlock, Wendell S.
1941   *Three Shell Heaps on Frenchman's Bay. Bulletin 6, Robert Abbe Museum.* Robert Abbe Museum, Bar Harbor, ME.

Hildebrandt, William R., and Jerome H. King
2012   Distinguishing between Darts and Arrows in the Archaeological Record: Implications for Technological Change in the American West. *American Antiquity* 77(4):789–799.

Hoffman, Bernard G.
1955a   Historical Ethnography of the Micmac of the Sixteenth and Seventeenth Centuries. PhD dissertation, Department of Anthropology, University of California, Berkeley.
1955b   Souriquois, Etechemin, and Kwedech—A Lost Chapter in American Ethnography. *Ethnohistory* 2(1):65–87.
1967   Ancient Tribes Revisited: A Summary of Indian Distribution and Movement in the Northeastern United States from 1534 to 1779, Parts I-III. *Ethnohistory* 14(1–2):1–46.

Holyoke, Kenneth R.
2012   Late Maritime Woodland Lithic Technology in the Lower Saint John River Valley. Master's thesis, Department of Anthropology, University of New Brunswick, Fredericton.

Hrynick, Gabriel, Arthur Anderson, Katherine Patton, W. Jesse Webb, Christopher Brouillette, Trevor Lamb, and Alex Pelletier-Michaud
2019   *Report on the 2017–2018 Universities of New Brunswick, Toronto, and New England Fieldwork in Washington County, Maine.* Report submitted to the Maine Historic Preservation Commission and the Passamaquoddy Tribal Historic Preservation Office, Augusta, Maine.

Inizan, Marie-Louise, Michèle Reduron-Ballinger, Hélène Roche, and Jacques Tixier
1995   *Technologie de la pierre taillée (Préhistoire de la Pierre Taillée, Tome 4).* Cercle de Recherches et d'Etudes Préhistoriques (C.R.E.P.), Meudon, France.

Keenlyside, David L.
1983   In Search of the Island's First People. *The Island Magazine* 13:3–7.
1990   *An Archaeological Survey of the Upper Reaches of the Tracadie Estuary, New Brunswick. New Brunswick Manuscripts in Archaeology 26.* Municipalities, Culture, and Housing, New Brunswick, Fredericton.

Lahti, Eric, Arthur Spiess, Mark Hedden, Robert Bradley, and Alaric Faulkner
1981   Test Excavations at the Hodgdon Site. *Man in the Northeast* 21:19–36.

Lechtman, Heather, and Robert S. Merrill
1977   *Material Culture: Styles, Organization, and Dynamics of Technology.* West Publishing Co., St. Paul, Minnesota.

Leonard, Kevin J. M.
1996   Mi'kmaq Culture during the Late Woodland and Early Historic Periods. PhD dissertation, Department of Anthropology, University of Toronto, Toronto.
2002   Jedaick (Shediac, NB): A Nexus Through Time. Report prepared for the Shediac Bay Watershed Association, Shediac Bridge, New Brunswick. Ms. in possession of the author.

Mack, Karen, David Sanger, and Alice R. Kelley
2002   *The Bob Site: A Multicomponent Archaic and Ceramic Period Site on Pushaw Stream, Maine.* Occasional Publications in Maine Archaeology No. 12. Maine Archaeological Society, Augusta.

McGuire, Joseph D.
1908   Ethnological and Archaeological Notes on Moosehead Lake, Maine. *American Anthropologist* 10:549–557.

Milner, Cameron A.
2014   The Precontact Village at St. Croix (BfDa-1), Nova Scotia: Explorations of Site Size and Stratigraphic Integrity. Master's thesis, Department of Archaeology, Memorial University of Newfoundland, St. John's.

Nash, Ronald J.
1986   *MI'KMAQ: Economics and Evolution.* Nova Scotia Museum Curatorial Report No. 57. Nova Scotia Museum, Halifax.

Nash, Ronald J., and Frances L. Stewart
1990   *Melanson: A Large Micmac Village in Kings County, Nova Scotia.* Nova Scotia Museum Curatorial Report No. 67. Nova Scotia Museum, Halifax.

Petersen, James B.
1991   *Archaeological Testing at the Sharrow Site: A Deeply Stratified Early to Late Holocene Cultural Sequence in Central Maine.* Occasional Publications in Maine Archaeology No. 8. Maine Archaeological Society and the Maine Historic Preservation Commission, Augusta.

Petersen, James B., and David Sanger
1991   An Aboriginal Ceramic Sequence for Maine and the Maritime Provinces. In *Prehistoric Archaeology in the Maritime Provinces: Past and Present Research*, edited by Michael Deal and Susan Blair, pp. 121–178. Reports in Archaeology No. 8. The Council of Maritime Premiers, Maritime Committee on Archaeological Cooperation, Fredericton.

Ritchie, William A.
1961   *A Typology and Nomenclature of New York Projectile Points.* New York State Museum and Science Service Bulletin Number 384 (revised 1971). The University of the State of New York and The State Education Department, Albany.

Robinson, Brian S.
1996   Projectile Points, Other Diagnostic Things, and Culture Boundaries in the Gulf of Maine Region. *Maine Archaeological Society Bulletin* 36(2):1–24.

Rosenmeier, Leah Morine

2010   Findings and Queries from Tracadie Harbour. *Archaeology in Nova Scotia: 2009 News* 1:9–16.

Rutherford, Douglas E.

1990   Reconsidering the Middlesex Burial Phase in the Maine–Maritimes Region. *Canadian Journal of Archaeology* 14:169–181.

1991   The Ceramic Period in New Brunswick. In *Prehistoric Archaeology in the Maritime Provinces: Past and Present Research*, edited by Michael Deal and Susan Blair, pp. 109–119. Reports in Archaeology No. 8. The Council of Maritime Premiers, Maritime Committee on Archaeological Cooperation, Fredericton.

Sanger, David

1979   The Ceramic Period in Maine. In *Discovering Maine's Archaeological Heritage*, edited by David Sanger, pp. 99–115, 152–153. Maine Historic Preservation Commission, Augusta.

1986   An Introduction to the Prehistory of the Passamaquoddy Bay Region. *American Review of Canadian Studies* 16(2):139–159.

1987   *The Carson Site and the Late Ceramic Period in Passamaquoddy Bay, New Brunswick*. Canadian Museum of Civilization Mercury Series, Archaeological Survey of Canada Paper No. 135. National Museums of Canada, Ottawa.

1989   Insights into Native American Life at Fernald Point. In *An Island in Time: Three Thousand Years of Cultural Exchange on Mount Desert Island*, edited by A. McMullen and D. Kopec, pp. 5–20. Bulletin XII. Robert Abbe Museum, Bar Harbor, Maine.

2008   Discerning Regional Variation: The Terminal Archaic Period in the Quoddy Region of the Maritime Peninsula. *Canadian Journal of Archaeology* 32(1):1–42.

Sanger, David, and Robert G. MacKay

1973   The Hirundo Archaeological Project—Preliminary Report. *Man in the Northeast* 6:21–29.

Seeber, Pauleena MacDougall

1987   A Comparison of Archaeological Remains from Two Ceramic Period Sites at Munsungun Lake, Maine. Master's thesis, Quaternary Studies, University of Maine, Orono.

Sheldon, Helen Louise

1988   *The Late Prehistory of Nova Scotia as viewed from the Brown Site*. Nova Scotia Museum Curatorial Report No. 61. Nova Scotia Museum, Halifax.

Smith, Harlan I., and W. J. Wintemberg

1929   *Some Shell-Heaps in Nova Scotia*. National Museum of Canada Bulletin 47, Anthropological Series 9. National Museum of Canada, Ottawa.

Soressi, Marie, and Jean-Michel Geneste

2011   The History and Efficacy of the *Chaîne Opératoire* Approach to Lithic Analysis: Studying Techniques to Reveal Past Societies in an Evolutionary Perspective. *PaleoAnthropology*:334–350.

Spiess, Arthur E.

1995   Early Contact Period Context. *Maine Archaeological Society Bulletin* 35(2):1–20.

Spiess, Arthur E., and Mark H. Hedden
1983   *Kidder Point and Sears Island in Prehistory.* Occasional Publications in Maine
        Archaeology No. 3. The Maine Historic Preservation Commission, Augusta.
Turnbull, Christopher J.
1973   *Old Mission Point Excavations 1972.* Report submitted to Archaeology Branch,
        Historical Resources Administration, Province of New Brunswick, Fredericton.
1990   *The Bernard Collection: A Tobique Complex site from the mid-St. John River Valley,
        New Brunswick.* New Brunswick Manuscripts in Archaeology 25. Municipalities,
        Culture, and Housing, Fredericton, New Brunswick.
Turnbull, Christopher J., and Susan W. Turnbull
1974   Preliminary Report of the 1973 Excavations at Old Mission Point (ClDq-1),
        Northern New Brunswick. In *Archaeological Salvage Projects 1973*, edited by
        William J. Byrne, pp. 151–162. Archaeological Survey of Canada Paper No. 26.
        Mercury Series. National Museum of Man, National Museums of Canada,
        Ottawa.
Wellman, Alice N.
1973   *The La Pomkeag Site (156-1)—A Preliminary Report.* Report on file at the
        Robert Abbe Museum and Department of Anthropology, University of Maine,
        Orono.
Will, Richard T.
1996   An Example of Late Middle Ceramic (Woodland) Period Biface Production
        Technology from Moosehead Lake, Maine. *Archaeology of Eastern North
        America* 24:227–238.
2000   A Tale of Two Flint-Knappers: Implications for Lithic Debitage Studies in
        Northeastern North America. *Lithic Technology* 25(2):101–119.
Will, Richard, and Rebecca Cole-Will
1989   A Preliminary Report on the Ann Hilton Site. *Maine Archaeological Society
        Bulletin* 29(2):1–11.
Willoughby, Charles C.
1901   Prehistoric Workshops at Mt. Kineo Maine. *American Naturalist* 35:213–219.

7

GEOCHEMICAL PROVENANCE OF COPPER IN PRE-CONTACT ARTIFACTS ON THE MARITIME PENINSULA, EASTERN CANADA

Determining Source Using Laser Ablation-Inductively Coupled Plasma-Mass Spectrometry

Jacob Hanley,[1] Anna Terekhova,[1] Paige Drake,[1] Katie Cottreau-Robins,[2] Roger Lewis,[2] Brent Suttie,[3] and Brandon Boucher[4]

Abstract

Owing to its versatility, and its cultural and spiritual significance, copper was procured over thousands of years by the Wabanaki peoples throughout the Far Northeast and used in the fabrication of tools and objects for personal adornment, ceremony, gift, and trade. From an archaeological perspective, little is known about the source of the copper used in daily life and how the copper moved across Indigenous cultural landscapes in the region. In this study, minimally destructive laser ablation–inductively coupled plasma–mass spectrometry (LA-ICP-MS) is used to characterize the trace element chemistry of pre-Contact artifacts from Late Archaic (5000–3500 BP) to Late Maritime Woodland (1500–500 BP) archaeological sites in Nova Scotia, New Brunswick, Prince Edward Island, and Maine (Black 2002; Lewis 2006, 2007, 2011; Sanger and Renouf 2006). The goal of employing LA-ICP-MS is to address a copper artifact knowledge gap and, ultimately, provide insights concerning the collection, movement, and trade of this significant natural metal. Through the development of a robust analytical protocol, and comparison of artifact chemistry to the chemistry of 86 copper source samples from the Lake Superior region and the Appalachians, the results of the study reported in this chapter show that, contrary to the historically emphasized Lake Superior model, no artifacts analyzed from the Maritime Peninsula have trace element compositions consistent with copper sources from the Lake Superior region. Furthermore, of those artifacts to which provenance can be assigned, all have compositions consistent with sources in the Bay of Fundy region.

Résumé

Matériau polyvalent, souvent porteur d'une valeur culturelle et spirituelle, le cuivre a été exploité durant des milliers d'années par les peuples Wabanaki de la Péninsule Maritime, qui en façonnaient aussi bien des outils que des parures et des objets destinés aux cérémonies, aux cadeaux et aux échanges. L'archéologie en sait peu sur l'origine du cuivre utilisé dans les activités quotidiennes, ou sur la manière dont le cuivre circulait à travers les paysages culturels Autochtones de la région. Cette étude présente les résultats de la caractérisation par spectrométrie de masse à plasma à couplage inductif par ablation laser (LA-ICP-MS/SM-PCI-AL), une méthode microscopiquement destructrice, du profil chimique d'éléments traces d'artéfacts pré-contact provenant de sites archéologiques datant de l'Archaïque supérieur (5000-3500 AA) au Sylvicole maritime tardif (1500-500 AA) de la Nouvelle-Écosse, du Nouveau-Brunswick, de l'Île-du-Prince-Édouard et du Maine (Black 2002; Lewis 2006, 2007, 2011; Sanger and Renouf 2006). L'utilisation de la SMPCI-AL vise à combler un vide de connaissances en ce qui concerne les objets de cuivre et obtenir des informations sur l'acquisition, la circulation et les échanges de ce métal. L'élaboration d'un protocole d'analyse rigoureux et la comparaison des profils chimiques des artéfacts à ceux de 86 sources de cuivre natif de la région du lac Supérieur et des Appalaches nous permettent d'infirmer le modèle classique centré sur les Grands Lacs en révélant qu'aucun des artéfacts du Péninsule Maritime analysé jusqu'ici ne présente un profil d'éléments traces compatible avec les sources de cuivre de la région du lac Supérieur. De plus, tous les artéfacts dont l'origine a pu être déterminée présentent une composition comparable aux sources de cuivre de la baie de Fundy.

Affiliations

1. Department of Geology, Saint Mary's University, Nova Scotia, Canada (corresponding author: jacob.hanley@smu.ca)
2. Nova Scotia Museum, Nova Scotia, Canada
3. Archaeology and Heritage Branch, New Brunswick Department of Tourism, Heritage and Culture, New Brunswick, Canada
4. Department of Earth Sciences, University of New Brunswick, New Brunswick, Canada

The chemical and isotopic analysis of archaeological materials at a microscopic scale involves sampling by largely non-destructive methods using "microbeam" techniques that remove tiny amounts of the artifact for chemical compositional analysis. Such methods can provide significant insight into the provenance (i.e., geographic or geological origin of artifact raw materials) of objects that are of cultural or archaeological significance. For metallic artifacts in particular, surface corrosion (i.e., oxidation and hydration of the metal to produce a patina) can change the original composition of the metal, requiring methods to sample the fresh material under this corrosion layer. Traditionally, chemical analysis of fresh metal in such artifacts has required invasive sampling methods and large sample volumes, which is quite destructive. This has been primarily due to limitations in the bulk analytical techniques available to archaeological sciences historically, and such techniques are still used today. While the preservation of the artifact is a priority during collection, conservation, storage, and study, this must be carefully reconciled with the need for researchers to reduce uncertainties in provenance studies, particularly when fresh metal cannot be readily analyzed in an artifact.

Laser ablation-inductively coupled plasma-mass spectrometry (LA-ICP-MS) is a microbeam method that has significantly refined archaeometric studies of material provenance, and has considerable advantages over other methods (e.g., INAA: instrumental neutron-activation analysis; XRF: X-ray fluorescence spectroscopy; μ-SR-XRF: micro-synchrotron radiation X-ray fluorescence; μ-PIXE: micro-particle-induced X-ray emission). As with other microbeam techniques, LA-ICP-MS is minimally invasive, offers high spatial resolution (i.e., ability to accurately target the analysis at specific locations on a single object with a microscopic beam) and requires little to no sample preparation. The method allows for the chemical and isotopic composition of artifacts to be determined in situ without cutting or powdering objects of significant cultural value.

In North America, there has been considerable work done to identify the geographic/geological origins of copper within copper artifacts, and to differentiate between natural and refined (European) copper and its alloys. The first suspected use of copper in what is now Canada dates back to between 6800 BP (Ehrhardt 2009) and 5560 BP (Beukens et al. 1992). Several studies have been undertaken to elucidate where Indigenous peoples in central and eastern North America procured their copper (e.g., Cooper et al. 2008; Dussubieux et al. 2008; Fenn 2001; Fitzgerald et al. 1993; Hancock et al. 1991; Hill 2012; Hill et al. 2016, 2018, 2019; Junk 2001; Lattanzi 2007, 2008; Levine 1999, 2007a, 2007b; McKnight 2007; Mulholland and Pulford 2007; Rapp and Allert 1984; Rapp 1985; Rapp et al. 1980, 2000; Whitehead 1993; Whitehead et al. 1998), but no studies of source provenance have been conducted on artifacts from

Canadian provinces within the Maritime Peninsula, with the exception of a single analytical study that used INAA to characterize copper artifacts from three burial localities. In that study, all artifacts were found to be composed of smelted/refined copper and copper alloys of European origin (Whitehead 1993; Whitehead et al. 1998) and are not pre-Contact.

The Lake Superior region (Keweenaw Peninsula, Michigan, and Mamainse Point, Ontario) is rich in large copper deposits classified as rift-related, volcanic, redbed-associated copper deposits (Brown 1992; Kirkham 1995). These were extensively exploited by Indigenous peoples locally and beyond, and were later mined commercially for over a hundred years (e.g., Halsey 2018, and references therein). While the importance of these large deposits to the Old Copper Culture is undisputed, an inherent bias in copper provenance studies in North America has arisen which focuses on the Lake Superior region (i.e., the Lake Superior model) as the assumed source of copper prior to European contact and trade (cf. Ehrhardt 2009; Fenn 2001; Hancock et al. 1991; Hill and Neuman 1966; Holmes 1901; Lattanzi 2007, 2008; Levine 1999, 2007a, 2007b; Rapp et al. 2000; Reeder 1961 [1903]). However, some studies have contradicted this hypothesis (see Bassett et al. 2019; Fenn 2001; Hill 2012; Hill et al. 2018, 2019; Lattanzi 2007, 2008; Levine 1999, 2007a, 2007b; Rapp et al. 2000; Seeman et al. 2019). Through chemical analysis by relatively destructive means (e.g., XRF, INAA) and, more recently, microbeam methods (e.g., LA-ICP-MS), combined with multivariate statistical methods of data analysis, the listed studies have argued that some artifacts found in the eastern United States and central Canada (Ontario, Quebec) were likely sourced from other copper mineralization throughout the Appalachian region in the northeastern United States and Canada (Anselmi 2004; Dussubieux and Walder 2015; Fenn 2001; Fields et al. 1971; Goad and Noakes 1978; Hancock et al. 1991, 1995; Hill et al. 2016; Levine 2007a, 2007b; Rapp, 1985; Rapp and Allert, 1984; Rapp et al. 1980, 2000). In particular, the INAA results of Levine (2007a, 2007b) suggest the presence of copper from the Bay of Fundy region at Late Archaic (5000–3500 BP) sites in central Canada (McCollum site, Allumette Island, Québec), and at multiple Early Woodland (1500–500 BP) sites in eastern Canada and the Atlantic northeastern United States.

The application of microbeam methods to archaeological metals found in North America has been relatively limited (Cooper et al. 2008; Dussubieux et al. 2008; Dussubieux et al. 2019; Hawkins et al. 2016; Hill 2012; Hill et al. 2016, 2018, 2019; Lattanzi 2007, 2008; McKnight 2007; Seeman et al. 2019) and only some of these studies (Lattanzi 2007; Seeman et al. 2019; Bassett et al. 2019; Hill et al. 2016, 2018, 2019; Lattanzi 2007; Seeman et al. 2019) were focused on copper provenance from natural copper sources (rather than discriminating European from natural copper; see Bassett et al. 2019; Dussubieux and Walder 2015; Hawkins et al. 2016; and authors therein). A review of this literature suggests that, until very recently (Dussubieux et al. 2019), there has been a lack of unified approach from study to study regarding best analytical practices. In particular, there has been considerable variability in, or a lack of information presented regarding, (i) data reduction approaches and reporting formats (e.g., details about how trace element concentrations were calculated, inconsistencies in the number and diversity of trace elements analyzed from study to study, reporting of uncertainties and sources of error); (ii) diversity and suitability of certified standard reference materials (SRM) used for quality control and data quantification (e.g., ensuring copper SRM are used when measuring trace elements in copper artifacts and sources—i.e., "matrix matching"; ablation characteristics of SRM); (iii) sampling density in individual source samples and artifacts (e.g., number of analyses of an object or a source sample needed to be representative and to identify outliers); and (iv) the diversity and number of potential copper source samples employed (e.g., number of samples from a single geographic/geological location needed for representativity; variations in the total number of potentially important different sources used for provenance studies). This makes it difficult to compare data sets from different studies, and to evaluate the robustness of commonly used multivariate statistical approaches for copper provenance determination. Nonetheless, these studies suggest that while Lake Superior copper sources are well represented in the Woodland and Archaic archaeological copper records, other sources (e.g., Appalachians) were likely also important.

In this study, we present composition (trace element) data obtained using the LA-ICP-MS method, collected from 197 pre-Contact artifacts (with 8 to 20 analyses per artifact) composed of naturally sourced, elemental copper from 22 Late Archaic (5000–3500 BP) to Late Maritime Woodland (1500–500 BP) archaeological sites in the Maritime Peninsula. These data are compared to a new reference database (developed in this study) generated for natural copper source localities in the Canadian Maritimes (Nova Scotia and New Brunswick), Newfoundland and Labrador, the Lake Superior region (Michigan and Ontario), and the Atlantic Northeast of the United States (New Jersey, Pennsylvania) with goals to (i) propose recommendations for analytical protocols for LA-ICP-MS copper provenance studies; (ii) define simple and robust graphical tools that can be used to establish the provenance of pre-Contact artifacts, specifically to differentiate Lake Superior- from Appalachian-sourced copper; and (iii) determine from which sources the copper in Maritime Peninsula artifacts was procured.

Background and Sample
(Artifact and Copper Source) Descriptions

Access to archaeological copper samples (artifacts) was facilitated by the Nova Scotia Museum (NSM), the provincial repository of archaeological collections. The copper artifacts are components of larger archaeological collections from a range of sites in the Maritime Peninsula study area (figure 7.1). They come from collections that were discovered, assembled, and characterized by provincial, academic, and/or professional archaeologists and Indigenous community members over a hundred-year period, beginning with the Harlan I. Smith and W. I. Wintemberg investigations in the Merigomish Harbour area of Pictou County, Nova Scotia (Smith and Wintemberg 1929). The copper artifacts from outside Nova Scotia come from museums, provincial archaeology offices, and university collections. Short-term loans were organized between the NSM and collections-holding institutions in New Brunswick, Prince Edward Island, and Maine to facilitate testing. Copper artifacts collected in the early twentieth century were loaned by the Canadian Museum of History, in Ottawa. The artifacts analyzed include copper beads of different shapes and sizes, awls, a gorge, a spear point, rings from the strands of a head dress, and modified and unmodified nodules or nuggets (figure 7.2). Table 7.1 summarizes rudimentary archaeological site details pertaining to the artifacts analyzed.

The goals of this research, and the advantages of the LA–ICP–MS method specifically, were discussed in detail with First Nation groups and representatives. Fundamental to the project has been engagement with Indigenous communities and sharing how and why artifacts may be studied. Meeting with community members to address questions and concerns, organizing opportunities for hands-on participation, and sharing outcomes have been critical to the collaborative framework design of this project as has been the guidance and direction provided by community. The Augustine Mound copper collection represents a significant component of the research presented. Working together with the Metepenagiag Mi'kmaq Nation and Nova Scotia Mainland Mi'kmaq Grand Council was critical to facilitating analysis of the artifacts and to addressing research questions important to the community. This approach builds on the framework of dialogue and collaboration set by previous Augustine Mound archaeological researchers (Turnbull 1976; Turnbull, 1978; Allen et al. 1994; Jarratt 2013; Blair et al. 2014) and stimulates shared learning and stewardship and a movement from past practices.

Copper specimens from potential source environments were analyzed from two regions (figure 7.1). From the Lake Superior region, 22 copper samples were analyzed from locations in Michigan (Keweenaw Peninsula, 20 samples) and Ontario (Mamainse Point, 2 samples). These comprised 15 samples from historic copper deposits (mined previously) and 7 "float" specimens (i.e., not in situ) obtained near former mining operations in areas where copper deposits have been eroded at surface. The float specimens were not obtained from tailings areas and represent naturally positioned, loose

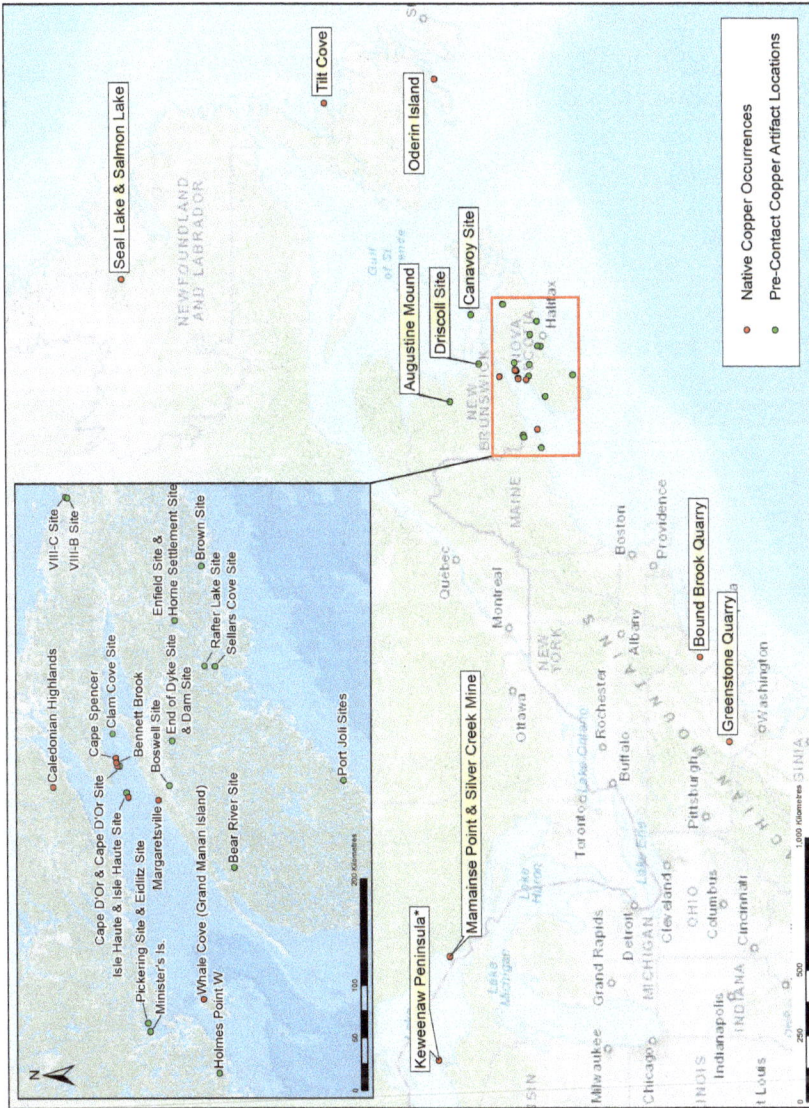

Figure 7.1. Natural geological copper occurrences (either as outcrop/mine or float samples) and pre-Contact copper artifact site locations included in the study to date. Note* that 20 natural copper sample locations on the Keweenaw Peninsula are not shown but are summarized in table 7.2.

Source: Map developed by M. Meuse-Dallien, NSM. Map GIS Service Layer Credits: Esri, HERE, Garmin, Intermap, Increment P Corp., GEBCO, USGS, FAO, NPS, NRCAN, GeoBase, IGN, Kadaster NL, Ordnance Survey, Esri Japan, METI, Esri China (Hong Kong), swisstopo, © OpenStreetMap contributors, the GIS User Community, Esri, Garmin, GEBCO, NOAA, and NGDC.

samples of copper. From the northeast Appalachians region, 64 copper samples were analyzed from locations in Nova Scotia (NS; 42 samples), New Brunswick (NB; 13 samples), Newfoundland and Labrador (NFLD; 6 samples), Pennsylvania (PA; 2 samples), and New Jersey (NJ; 1 sample). These comprised samples from both historic copper deposits and mineralized outcrops. Table 7.2 lists details pertaining to sample locations. All NS, NB, NJ, PA, NFLD samples, and nine samples from the Lake Superior region, were obtained from outcrop or underground workings directly by professional mineralogists/collectors who were engaged by the authors, whereas other samples were obtained from the private collections of the first author. Copper deposits in all of these study areas belong to deposit styles known as volcanic redbed and redbed copper deposits that occur in association, most commonly, with metamorphosed and hydrothermally mineralized subaerial flood basalts commonly interlayered with sedimentary rocks (shales, sandstones, conglomerates) (Kirkham 1995).

Figure 7.2. Examples of the diversity of pre-Contact copper artifacts analyzed in this provenance study: (A) nodules and nuggets (Port Joli, Horne Settlement, and Isle Haute Sites); (B) long, thin-walled tubular beads of different shapes and sizes (Sellars Cove site on left side) and awl (Rafter Lake site on right side); (C) thick-walled tubular rings (Augustine Mound site; top and side profile views); (D) tubular beads on strands of hide (Augustine Mound Site); and (E) Spear point (Augustine Mound site).
Source: Nova Scotia Museum.

Table 7.1. Pre–Contact copper artifacts and associated archaeological sites.

SITE NAME	BORDEN NO.	No. TESTED	CULTURAL PERIOD	SITE FEATURE
End of Dyke Site	BfDd-24	39	Late Archaic/ Woodland/ Historic	habitation
Dam Site	BfDd-10	7	Late Woodland	general activity
Sellars Cove Site	BdCx-1	8	Early/Mid/Late Woodland	shell midden
Ilse Haute Site	BhDf-1	2	Late Woodland	encampment
Horne Settlement	BfCv-3	5	Late Archaic/ Woodland	general activity
Rafter Lake Site	BeCx-3	1	Late Archaic/ Woodland gen. activity/ encampment	
Brown Site	BeCs-3	1	Late Woodland/ Historic	encampment
Clam Cove Site	BhDc-5	4	Mid Woodland to Contact shell midden/ encampment	
Enfield Site	BfCv-5	1	Late Woodland	general activity
Bear River Site	BdDk-1	1	Woodland	shell midden
Eidlitz Site	BgDs-4	1	Late Woodland	shell midden
Cape d'Or Site	BhDe-1	1	Woodland	shell midden
Cape d'Or Site	BhDe-2	1	Woodland	gen. activity/lithic workshop
Pickering Site	BgDr-2	1	Early Woodland	general activity
VIII-C Site	BjCo-3	1	Late Woodland	shell midden
VIII-B Site	BjCo-2	1	Woodland	shell midden
Ministers Is. Site*	BgDs-10	1	Early/Mid/Late Woodland	shell midden/ encampment
Canavoy Site	CcCq-1	2	Late Archaic/ Woodland	encampment
Port Joli Site	AlDf-24	1	Late Woodland	shell midden/ habitation
Port Joli Site	AlDf-30	2	Middle Woodland	shell midden/ sweathouse
Boswell Site*	BfDf-8	5	Transitional Archaic/Mid Woodland	encampment

SITE NAME	BORDEN NO.	No. TESTED	CULTURAL PERIOD	SITE FEATURE
Holmes Pt. West*	62.8 Maine	4	Late Woodland	habitation
Driscoll Site*	CbDd-4	17	Late Woodland to Historic	habitation
Augustine Mound	CfDl-2	90	Early Woodland	burial mound

Twenty-four precontact archaeological sites have provided copper artifacts for LA-ICPMS testing. The basic Cultural Period and Site Feature ascriptions, are taken from site records filed between 1913 and 2009 and illustrate a long period of archaeological recording varied in detail and level of field study and analysis. Cultural Period designations reflect generalized terminology used in archaeology; however, this study incorporates and recognizes the formalized Mi'kmaw terminology for cultural periods (See Lewis 2006, 2007, 2011). Artifacts from sites with * have been analyzed but the data has not been included. Evaluation of source provenance is in progress for these objects. Archaeological site records, such as MARI forms and field reports, are stewarded by the regional archaeology regulatory offices (See References section). Where site records were not robust, site details were confirmed by associated archaeologists via personal communication.

Analytical Methods

Sample Preparation and Analytical Method

All artifacts and natural copper source samples were analyzed by the LA-ICP-MS microbeam technique at the Department of Earth Sciences, University of New Brunswick (UNB). A comprehensive introduction to this analytical method is described for those unfamiliar with the approach by Hirata (2018) and authors therein, which describe key parts of the instrumentation, and the reasons for selecting specific instrument parameters for the measurement of trace elements in solid materials, including metals. Due to the size constraints of the laser ablation chamber, artifacts were analyzed in a sequence that maximized the number of artifacts that would fit within the sample holder dimensions (figure 7.3). Artifacts larger than 2.5 cm were mounted in small bricks of paraffin wax that were customized to allow the artifacts to rest within the bricks securely. Samples smaller than 2.5 cm were mounted in paraffin and/or conservators wax packing on top of, or within, the cores of drilled-out cylindrical epoxy pucks, allowing for stabilization and levelling of the artifacts. For some larger objects that exceeded the sample holder space, extremely small fragments (<0.2 cm) that had fallen off naturally over time were taken from each sample. Native copper source samples were mounted into acrylic pucks and then ground down and polished to expose fresh natural copper without patina (corroded/altered surface layers formed by oxidation and hydration of the metal).

The LA-ICP-MS system at UNB consists of a Resonetics RESOlution M-50 (193 nm ArF excimer) laser with S 155 Laurin Technic cell coupled to an

Table 7.2. Summary of natural sources of copper analyzed for provenance study.

COPPER SOURCE	LOCATION	#SAMPLES
Horseshoe Cove (Cape D'Or)	NS	16
Colonial Copper Mine (Cape D'Or)	NS	12
Isle Haute	NS	8
Margaretsville	NS	3
Bennett Brook (Cape D'Or)	NS	1
Cape Spencer	NS	2
Whale Cove (Grand Manan Island)	NB	12
Caledonian Highlands	NB	1
Seal Lake	NFLD	1
Tilt Cove	NFLD	3
Oderin Island	NFLD	1
Salmon Lake	NFLD	1
Mamainse Mine, Mamainse Pt.	ON	1
Silver Creek Mine, Mamainse Pt.	ON	1
Ahmeek Mine	MI	1
Centennial Mine	MI	2
Quincy Mine	MI	1
South Hecla Mine	MI	1
"Float" Samples	MI	7
Caledonia Mine	MI	1
Phoenix Mine	MI	1
Calumet Mine	MI	1
Central Mine	MI	1
Isle Royale Mine	MI	1
Osceola Mine	MI	1
White Pine Mine	MI	1
Copper Falls Mine	MI	1
Bound Brook Quarry	NJ	1
Greenstone Quarry	PA	2

Notes: Location abbreviations: NS=Nova Scotia, Canada; NB=New Brunswick, Canada; NFLD=Newfoundland and Labrador, Canada; ON=Ontario, Canada; MI=Michigan, USA; NJ=New Jersey, USA; PA=Pennsylvania, USA.

Agilent 7700x quadrupole ICP-MS. Ablation (the sampling process that removes sub-microgram amounts of sample) and ICP-MS (the measurement process) parameters were optimized for the measurement of trace elements in a copper matrix. Typically, 8–20 measurements were taken in each artifact and native copper source sample. Table 7.3 summarizes analytical instrumentation and parameters/settings for measurements and data reduction, and measured isotopes/dwell times. Figure 7.3 shows examples of typical LA-ICP-MS ablation "craters" or "pits" left behind after analysis.

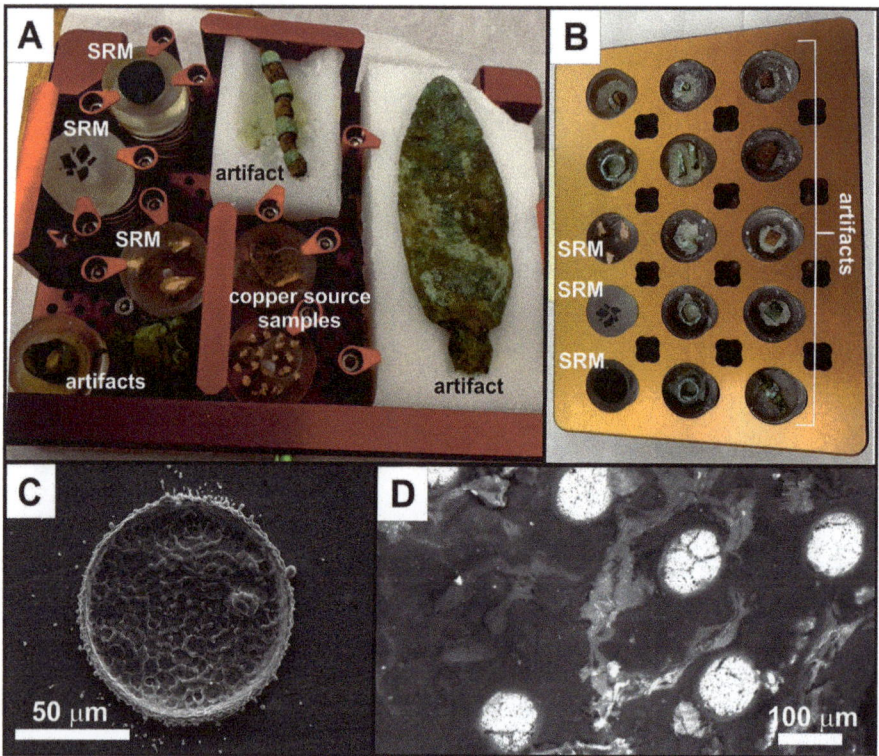

Figure 7.3. LA-ICP-MS sample holders showing artifacts, copper source samples, and standard reference material (SRM) arrangements and ablation pit characteristics: (A) "Universal"-type sample holder for the S-155 Laurin Technic Cell ablation chamber showing the 2.5-cm-diameter epoxy pucks containing the SRM, natural copper source samples, and artifacts stabilized in position with mounting pins and wax. (B) Sample holder for smaller artifacts with dimensions less than 2.5 cm. Artifacts shown are stabilized in 2.5 cm diameter epoxy pucks using conservation wax. (C) Scanning electron microscope (SEM) secondary electron image (an image type showing surface features) showing a circular ablation pit (90 um-diameter) in the polished surface of a copper source sample. (D) SEM image (backscattered electron image, an image type showing differences in density) showing artifact ablation pits. Darker areas are lower density regions composed of patina (altered/corroded surface layers). Brighter circular areas indicate where the laser has penetrated into metallic copper under the patina.
Source: Nova Scotia Museum.

Standard Reference Materials (SRM),
Ablation Signal Handling, and Data Quantification

SRM must be frequently analyzed during each LA-ICP-MS session to enable fundamental steps in robust data reduction (i.e., correction of instrument drift, external calibration of analyte sensitivities) and to allow for quality control monitoring (e.g., inter-standard determination of accuracy and precision; see, e.g., Dussubieux et al. 2019). In the early stages of development of the analytical protocol, the ablation characteristics and homogeneity of copper and brass SRM from the National Institute of Standards and Technology (NIST) were investigated as these standards have been used routinely by other researchers in studies of copper artifact provenance. The SRM investigated were SRM 400 (Unalloyed Copper – Cu VII) and SRM 1124 (Free Cutting Brass – UNC C36000). In general, the number of elements with certified concentrations is relatively small in the available and relevant NIST SRM for in situ metallic copper analysis. While this did not ultimately limit the usefulness of these standards for this study, which focuses on the use of only a small number of elements for provenance determination, it does reduce the flexibility to explore variations in some potentially important discriminating elements (e.g., Au, In, Mo). The main limitation with the NIST SRM, however, was their very poor ablation characteristics. This study used (and recommends) SRM from MBH Analytical Ltd. (United Kingdom; "residuals in refined copper" standard numbers 39X 27866, 39X 27869, and 39X 17872) that contain a wide range of certified trace elements that are likely to be dissolved constituents in copper, and therefore suitable for a study of metal artifact chemistry. The SRM from MBH Analytical Ltd. showed excellent ablation behaviour and homogeneity. Additionally, the concentrations of certified analytes in these SRM are relatively high (compared to some other SRM reported in the literature in provenance studies; e.g., Dussubieux et al. 2019) and the inter-SRM range in concentrations is wide ($>10^1$ to 10^3 parts per million; table 7.3), offering flexibility in data reduction and a means to robustly evaluate the accuracy of analyses by inter-SRM comparisons. A pressed sulfide powder pellet (MASS1) standard from the United States Geological Survey was also used to quantify mercury (Hg), molybdenum (Mo), manganese (Mn), and gallium (Ga), which are not certified in the MBH Analytical standards. As the matrices are substantially different (i.e., matrix mismatch), larger uncertainties in the calculated Hg and Mo concentrations in copper are likely; thus, reported values should be treated as semi-quantitative only.

Raw laser ablation data was reduced using the Iolite data-reduction software package (University of Melbourne) on the Igor Pro compiler (version 6). Reference standard files were prepared from certified element concentration data, and the reference materials were measured regularly during LA-ICP-MS sessions. With the exception of a few elements that could only be quantified using MASS1, all data reported were quantified using the MBH Analytical standards. Copper was used as the internal standard for data quantification (table 7.3).

Table 7.3. LA–ICP–MS operating conditions and data-acquisition parameters.

LA

Model	Resonetics RESOlution M-50 with S-155 Laurin Technic cell
Wavelength	193 nm
Pulse duration (FWHM)	20 ns
Repetition rate	2.5 Hz
Spot diameter	90 μm
Energy density	~4 J/cm^2

ICP-MS

Model	Agilent 7700x with dual external rotary pumps
Forward power	1500W
Sampling depth	4.0 to 5.0 mm
Gas flow rates:	
Carrier (He)	300 mL/min
Make up (Ar)	930 mL/min
ThO+/Th+	<0.1
U+/Th+ (NIST 610)	1,05

Data acquisition/reduction

Total sampling time	0.7162 s
Detector mode	Dual mode
Data reduction software	Iolite platform on Igor Pro 6
Internal standardization	Cu wt% (99.9 for native copper)
Primary (calibration) standards	MBH39X278-66, MBH39X278-69, MBH39x178-72, MASS-1
Secondary (QC) standard	MBH39X278-66, MBH39X278-69, MBH39x178-72, MASS-1
Isotopes determined (dwell time 10 ms) (in italics, monitors of contamination by patina/contamination on surfaces)	^{27}Al,^{31}P,^{34}S,^{56}Fe,^{59}Co,^{60}Ni,^{65}Cu,^{66}Zn,^{75}As,^{95}Mo,^{107}Ag,^{111}Cd, ^{115}In,^{118}Sn,^{121}Sb,^{125}Te,^{197}Au,^{202}Hg,^{208}Pb,^{209}Bi.
Quadrupole settling time	5 ms
Analysis time	background (20s), ablation (20s), washout (5s)

Importantly, the LA–ICP–MS method minimizes sample damage resulting in a series of microscopic pits in the sample surface that (ideally) penetrate through the patina surface layers and into fresh copper. A representative transient ICP-MS signal illustrating the different stages of ablating a copper artifact with a patina layer is shown in figure 7.4. To maximize the likelihood that fresh copper could be sampled, each artifact was visually inspected to locate the best areas for ablation (i.e., where the patina layer was thinnest). A qualitative assessment of this was done under binocular microscope. The optimal areas for analysis were those with reddish-brown (see artifact in centre of frame in figure 7.2A), submetallic, and moderately reflective appearance, as these represent areas where fresh copper was typically intersected within a few seconds of ablation, starting at the sample surface. This is in contrast to areas that have a greenish-blue (see artifact in right of frame in figure 7.2A), weakly reflective appearance or, most commonly, a porous green-white, non-reflective appearance, where patina was thickest. After measurements, ablation signals were examined to identify the point in time at which the transition from the patina to fresh copper occurred. This could be identified readily in transient signals at the time where specific elements preferentially depleted (e.g., Ag) and enriched (e.g., Pb, Zn, As, Fe) in the patina showed an increase or decrease, respectively, in measured isotope count rate to a relatively constant level (see portions of signal interval labelled "patina" and "fresh copper" in figure 7.4). Routinely, this patina layer comprised no more than ~10 seconds of the total ablation signal where areas with reddish-brown coloration were selected. For the determination of trace element concentrations in fresh copper, the last ~10 seconds of each ablation signal was selected and quantified (figure 7.4).

In some source samples and artifacts, examination of the transient signals showed the presence of occasional short-duration high count-rate events ("spikes") that represent contaminating mineral or rock particles included in fresh copper (e.g., silver inclusions in copper signal, shown in figure 7.4). Like the patina layer, these inclusions must be rejected when selecting signal intervals for quantification, otherwise, anomalously high concentrations for some trace elements will be reported in average artifact compositions, increasing sample heterogeneity and negatively impacting the provenance determination.

Results and Discussion

Trace element data for potential copper source locations from which the copper in artifacts was derived are tabulated in table 7.4 (Supplementary File A) and artifact trace element data is listed in table 7.5 (Supplementary File B). These data files can be obtained by visiting https://press.uottawa.ca/the-far-northeast .htm. The ultimate goal of this research is to provide chemical criteria that can be used to reconcile the trace element composition of artifacts with geological sources. Based on the entire analyte list quantified, only five elements (Ni, As,

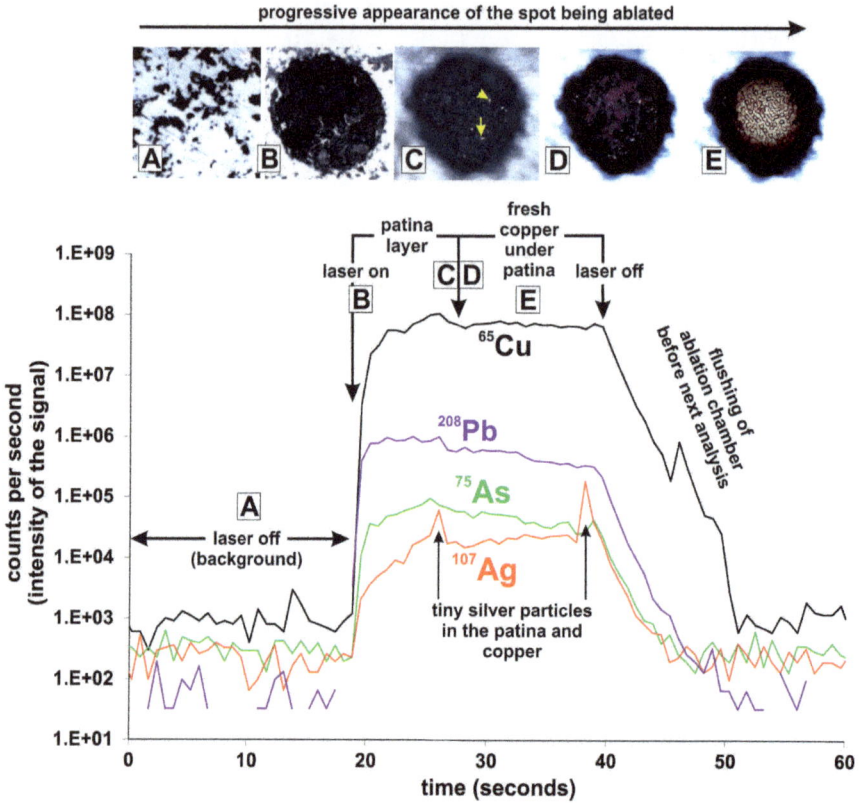

Figure 7.4. LA-ICP-MS transient signal showing the ablation of a single spot in a copper artifact with a thick patina layer. The x axis is time (s); y axis is the instrument signal intensity for isotopes of a small selection of major and trace elements being measured. Signals are labelled with the corresponding elements isotope mass being measured (65Cu, 208Pb, 75As, and 107Ag). Along the top are photomicrographs (taken with a reflected light microscope) showing the progressive appearance of the location on an artifact surface as the LA-ICP-MS analysis takes place. From 0 to ~20s (A), the laser is kept off, and a "background" signal is collected during which the signals for all isotopes measured are low. At ~20s (B) the laser is turned on and immediately the signals for the measured isotopes increase; in the spot image (B) a circular ablation pit appears as the patina is removed by the laser. Between ~20 and ~28s, an interval of patina is progressively ablated. At ~28s the laser beam passes through the boundary between the patina and the fresh copper underneath. In the spot images (C) and (D) this transition is seen as the ablation pit gets deeper; in (C) the first signs of fresh copper are visible (yellow arrows pointing to small bright areas); in (D) slightly tarnished (reddish colour) fresh copper is visible. The microscope is focused through (C) and (D) on the bottom of the pit and the surface of the sample appears blurry. From ~28 to ~41s an interval of fresh copper is progressively ablated, corresponding to section of the entire signal that will be quantified to yield the concentrations of Pb, As, and Ag in the copper. Image (D) shows the bottom of the ablation pit in the fresh copper interval showing bright metal. Note the lower Ag and higher Pb and As signal in the patina layer interval compared to the fresh copper interval. Note also two Ag inclusions contaminating the signal. The Ag inclusion in the fresh copper would result in a slightly higher Ag concentration for the quantified interval, requiring rejection or reassigning of the quantified interval to be shorter to exclude the inclusion. At ~41s the laser is turned off, followed by a gradual decrease of count rates for all measured isotopes down to background levels (flushing of ablation chamber) before the next analysis spot is selected.

Ag, Zn, and Pb) were routinely above detection limits and/or showed consistent differences in absolute concentration between samples from different localities. To make the data and interpretation as accessible to end users as possible, we chose to utilize simple graphical methods of data presentation rather than multivariate statistical approaches.

Homogeneity of Copper in Sources and Artifacts

Discussion of the complications to provenance studies created by heterogeneous copper source chemistry has been discussed previously (e.g., Mauk and Hancock 1998). Three considerations arise with respect to heterogeneity that are relevant to provenance assignment.

The first issue relates to the natural range in concentration in dissolved (solid solution) trace elements within a given copper sample, and population of copper samples from a source location. It is critical to the success of provenance results that the heterogeneity of each source and artifact be adequately evaluated through sufficient analyses of both source and artifact. With increasing number of analyses, the range in true (dissolved) concentration of each trace element will increase but outliers (if they exist, resulting from contamination by patina or mineral/rock inclusions—see below) will be recognizable. As a general guideline, it is recommended that at least eight spot analyses per artifact be obtained to ensure adequate representativity and allow recognition of outliers. However, transient signals during LA-ICP-MS measurements should be monitored in real time, as much as possible, to assess whether, due to the frequently encountered contaminating phases, additional analyses are needed to adequately evaluate true source composition.

More analyses are recommended for copper source samples in order to accurately evaluate the absolute range in concentrations in dissolved trace elements. Figure 7.5A–B show box-whisker plots for two sources, one based on 173 analyses from copper samples taken from 16 different outcrop locations over an area of several thousand square metres at Horseshoe Cove, Cape d'Or (Nova Scotia), and the other based on 40 analyses from copper samples taken from 5 different mines on the Keweenawan Peninsula over 10s of kilometres scale. The results of these measurements show that at a variety of scales, "source" copper compositions can be considerably narrow. With the exception of Fe, As, Co, and Ag at the Cape d'Or locality, the total variability is within an order of magnitude for each trace element, with the Q1–Q3 interquartile range much smaller for most elements. Total variability for the Keweenawan Peninsula sources is wider, but the Q1–Q3 interquartile range is still well within an order-of-magnitude variance for the majority of trace elements.

The second issue relates to the occurrence of mineral or alloy inclusions, or rock fragments, within the copper from natural occurrences (and, therefore, in the artifacts). While it is possible that some of these phases may be coeval with the copper (i.e., precipitated at the same time copper was deposited in the rock), it is more likely that these phases are not linked to copper deposition but are rather spatially coincident to the site of sampling. It is likely that this has impacted both the reported source composition variability and the outcome of artifact provenance studies reported in the literature by both bulk and in situ (microbeam) analytical methods, because such mineral and rock phases can introduce orders-of-magnitude variability in copper composition, and elevated average or centroid compositions in multivariate statistics (cf. silicate contamination in copper—Hurst and Larson 1958; Levine 2007a; elevated and highly variable Pb in copper from galena or other Pb-rich phases—Dussubieux et al. 2008 and Hill et al. 2016; elevated and highly variable Fe, As, Ni in copper from inclusions of sulfarsenide or arsenide mineral phases—Hill et al., 2018). The advantage of in situ methods is that chemical heterogeneity within single samples can be rapidly assessed, and any contaminating patina or inclusions of other minerals in copper (host-rock fragments, coeval or non-coeval mineral phases) can be screened and avoided in the transient signal during data processing (by precluding the parts of the signal containing the contaminating inclusion, or rejecting the analyses entirely). Figure 7.5C shows a box-whisker plot for an artifact (a spearhead from Augustine Mound; artifact 2507) analyzed 34 times, targeting the thinnest patina possible and excluding the patina layer, based on inspection, from the quantified signal (table 7.5). Trace element concentration variabilities in artifacts should be similar to that in natural sources that are analyzed on fresh surfaces (no patina) and are typically within an order of magnitude. However, in the case of the object analyses plotted in figure 7.5C, rejection of 10 ablation signals showing inclusions of Ag within the copper greatly reduces the interquartile range and shifts the mean value from ~37 to ~6 parts per million. When combined with a poor representation of the natural heterogeneity in copper sources, the likely consequence of contaminating phases on provenance determination is considerable uncertainty in the accuracy of provenance determination.

A third consideration is assessing the effect of oxidation and corrosion (patina formation) on the chemistry of underlying "fresh" copper. Previous studies of copper artifacts have noted the preferential enrichment and depletion in some elements associated with corrosion and the formation of a patina layer (e.g., Dussubieux et al. 2008; Moreau and Hancock 1999). As with the evaluation of contaminating inclusions, examination of transient LA-ICP-MS signals (figure 7.4) allows selection of unmodified copper beneath a patina layer. This assumes that the trace element composition of fresh metal (metallic Cu, free of oxides, hydroxides) has not been modified, an assumption that remains to be tested in future studies. Comparison of the trace element concentrations in patina and underlying "fresh" copper on a box-whisker plot for 20 objects (figure 7.5D)

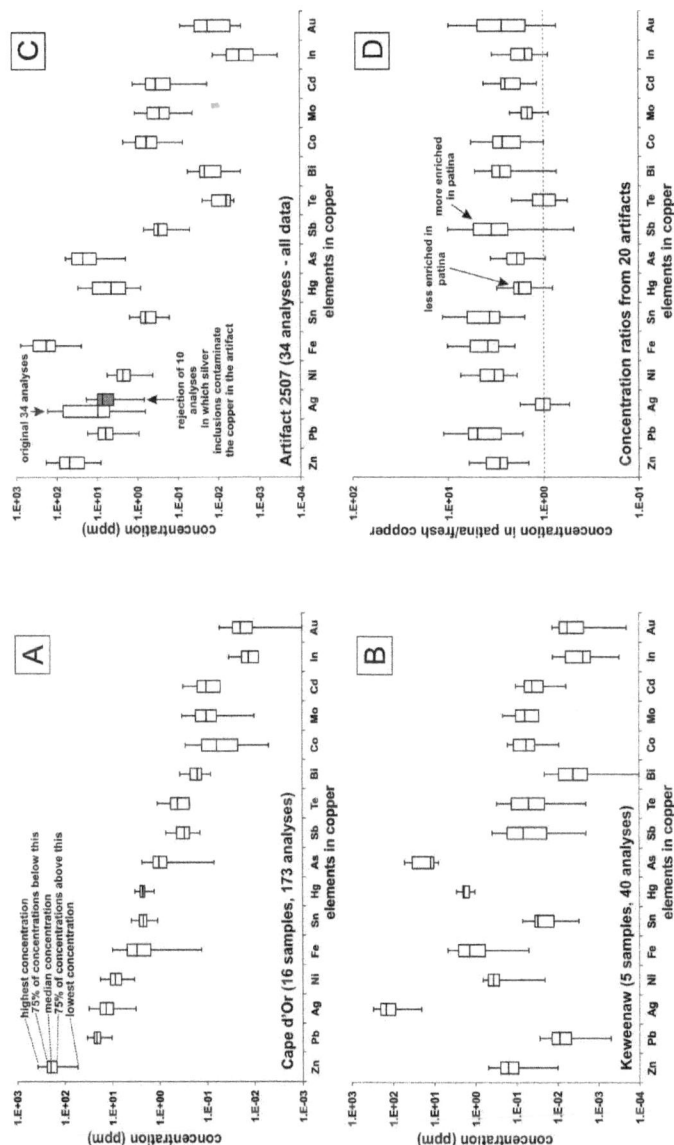

Figure 7.5. Box plots summarizing trace element concentrations and ratios in selected source copper samples and artifacts following data processing. Box-whisker symbols for each trace element show the median value of all concentrations measured for that element in a sample, the upper and lower quartile, and maximum and minimum values (the "whiskers" highest and lowest concentrations, respectively). Elements with larger ranges in concentration (i.e., large range between upper and lower quartile) and large overall data range (between max. and min. values) are more heterogenous in the source sample or artifact, or contain contaminating metal particles. (A) Box plot for 173 analyses of native copper from 16 different outcrop samples taken from Horseshoe Bay, Cape d'Or, Nova Scotia. (B) Box plot for 40 native copper analyses from five separate outcrop samples from the Keweenaw Peninsula, Lake Superior region. (C) Box plot of 34 analyses from an artifact (2507; spear head from Augustine Mound site). The box-whisker symbol filled in grey represents 24 analyses of silver, and sits next to the white box-whisker symbol for 34 analyses of silver from the same sample. The removal of 10 analyses (outliers) containing contaminating native silver inclusions results in a lower mean and median values, narrower interquartile range, and reduction in the maximum-minimum range for silver in the sample. (D) Box plot of average concentration ratios between patina and underlying fresh copper (= concentration in patina ÷ concentration in fresh copper) obtained from many analyses of 20 artifacts. Dashed line is 1:1 line (patina concentration=fresh copper concentration). Elements with ratios farther from the 1:1 line are more enriched in the patina relative to elements that are closer to the 1:1 line.

shows that while most elements increase in concentration in patina relative to the underlying copper, others (Ag and Sb) do not. Furthermore, the degree of relative enrichment is variable from element to element for those that are patina-enriched. While systematic differences in patina and fresh copper composition (i.e., consistently higher concentrations in the patina for all elements) are the result of overestimation of the Cu content of the patina (i.e., above ~100% Cu), non-systematic differences reinforce that analyses that do not resolve fresh metal from patina may negatively impact provenance determination.

Chemical Differentiation of Copper Sources

Copper Sources Differentiated Using Ternary Diagrams

Ternary diagrams are barycentric plots for discrimination of source chemistry involving three variables that sum to a constant. They are a widely utilized graphical tool in earth science and metallurgical fields that are straightforward for the non-specialist to use, but their effective application to provenance studies relies on demonstrating that sufficiently distinct compositional fields can be defined using only three chemical parameters. Investigation of many different combinations of the trace elements Ni-As-Ag-Pb-Zn (table 7.4, Supplementary File A) led to the development of five ternary diagram variants that provide the best possible separation of copper source compositions. Figures 7.6 and 7.7 show these ternary diagrams with compositional fields for different sources of copper. It should be noted that good separation of sources is not possible using a single ternary diagram, but when used in conjunction with one another it is possible to separate the majority of copper sources into distinct fields with little or no overlap. Thus, the successful application of these diagrams also relies on obtaining a reasonably large database for source chemistry to ensure that the heterogeneity of the natural sources are represented:

(i) As-Pb(x50)-Ag ternary: Nova Scotia Bay of Fundy sources (figure 7.6A) define tight fields at the Pb and Ag apices (corners), and more diffuse fields between the Pb and Ag apices, but extending only halfway through the ternary toward the As apex. No source compositions lie near the As apex. New Brunswick Bay of Fundy sources (figure 7.6B) plot very close to (and mainly on) the As (Caledonian Highlands) and Ag (Grand Manan) apices, respectively, whereas sources from NFLD (figure 7.6C) plot close to (and on) the Pb and Ag apices. Other sources (NJ, PA, and the Lake Superior region; figure 7.6D–E) are very Pb-poor and occur along the As-Ag join. The NJ, PA, and Lake Superior (Keweenawan Peninsula and Mamainse Point) sources can be clearly differentiated from one another along the As-Ag join. Likewise, most sources at or near Cape d'Or (Cape Spencer, Horseshoe Bay, Colonial Copper Mine) and Tilt Cove and Oderin Island (Newfoundland) can be differentiated

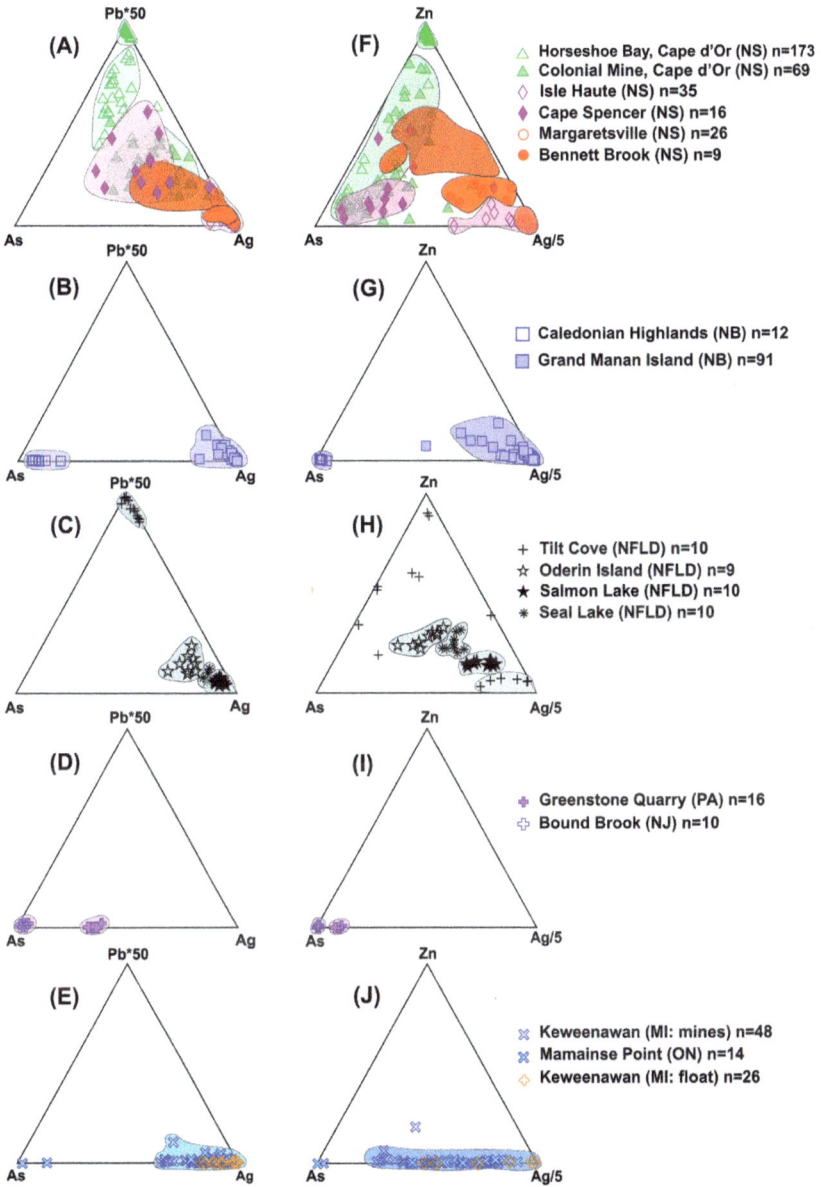

Figure 7.6. Ternary diagrams showing the relative concentration of three trace elements per diagram, utilizing different combinations from the Ni-As-Ag-Pb-Zn data for copper source samples analyzed. The relative position of source data fields in these diagrams is distinct for many sources analyzed. The closer to one of the vertices (the corners of the triangular plot), the more relatively enriched in that element the sample is. Diagrams (A)–(E) show relative As-Pb-Ag concentrations with Pb multiplied by 50. Diagrams (F)–(J) show relative As-Zn-Ag concentrations with Ag divided by 5. Scaling factors (Pbx50, Ag/5) at vertices are arbitrary and used only to distribute the data more evenly across the ternary diagram for clearer visual separation of the different sample groups. Compositional fields are shaded to show the overall range in compositions for different source locations.

easily from Lake Superior, NJ, and PA sources. Additionally, some Cape d'Or sources (Horseshoe Bay and Colonial Copper Mine) can be differentiated from Salmon Lake and Seal Lake (Labrador) sources. However, there is significant overlap between Lake Superior, Salmon and Seal Lakes, Grand Manan Island, Margaretsville, Bennett Brook, and Isle Haute sources that all lie at or near the Ag apex.

(ii) As–Zn–Ag/5 ternary: Compositional fields are distributed very similarly to those in the As–Pb(x50)–Ag ternary, with a few significant differences. Nova Scotia Bay of Fundy sources (figure 7.6F) once again define tight fields at the Zn and Ag apices but also show a spread along the As–Zn join on the left side, and spreading into the centre, of the diagram. Compositions near the Ag apex show some scatter into the diagram, but the Zn–Ag join is free of data points. New Brunswick Bay of Fundy sources (figure 7.6G) again plot very close to (and mainly on) the As (Caledonian Highlands) and Ag (Grand Manan) apices, and show slightly more spread away from these apices than in the As–Pb(x50)–Ag ternary, in particular, for the Caledonian Highland source that spreads farther along the As–Ag join. Sources from NFLD (figure 7.6G) show much more scatter than in the previous diagram, in particular the Tilt Cove source, which shows two diffuse fields, one near the Ag apex and one spread out over most of the top part of the diagram. Fields from the other NFLD sources are still distinct from one another, focused near the Ag apex, but extend farther into the centre of the diagram from the Ag apex. Other sources (NJ, PA, and the Lake Superior region; figure 7.6I–J) are very Zn-poor and occur along the As–Ag join. As in the previous ternary, the NJ, PA and Lake Superior sources can be clearly differentiated from one another along the As–Ag join. Likewise, some sources at or near Cape d'Or (Cape Spencer, Horseshoe Bay, Colonia Copper Mine) and Oderin Island can be differentiated easily from the Lake Superior, NJ, and PA sources. Additionally, this diagram allows the Labrador sources to be differentiated from LS, NJ, and PA sources, and allows some Cape d'Or sources (Horseshoe Bay and Colonial Copper Mine) to be differentiated from Oderin Island, Salmon Lake, and Seal Lake sources. However, there is significant overlap between Lake Superior, Tilt Cove, Grand Manan Island, Margaretsville, Bennett Brook, and Isle Haute sources that all lie at or near the Ag apex, and some overlap between Cape d'Or sources and the PA source is seen. On the other hand, individual Cape d'Or sources are better resolved from one another at the Ag apex.

(iii) Ni–Ag/50–Pb ternary: Bay of Fundy source fields (figure 7.7A) occupy the area along the Ni–Pb join and the Ni–Ag join with some spread

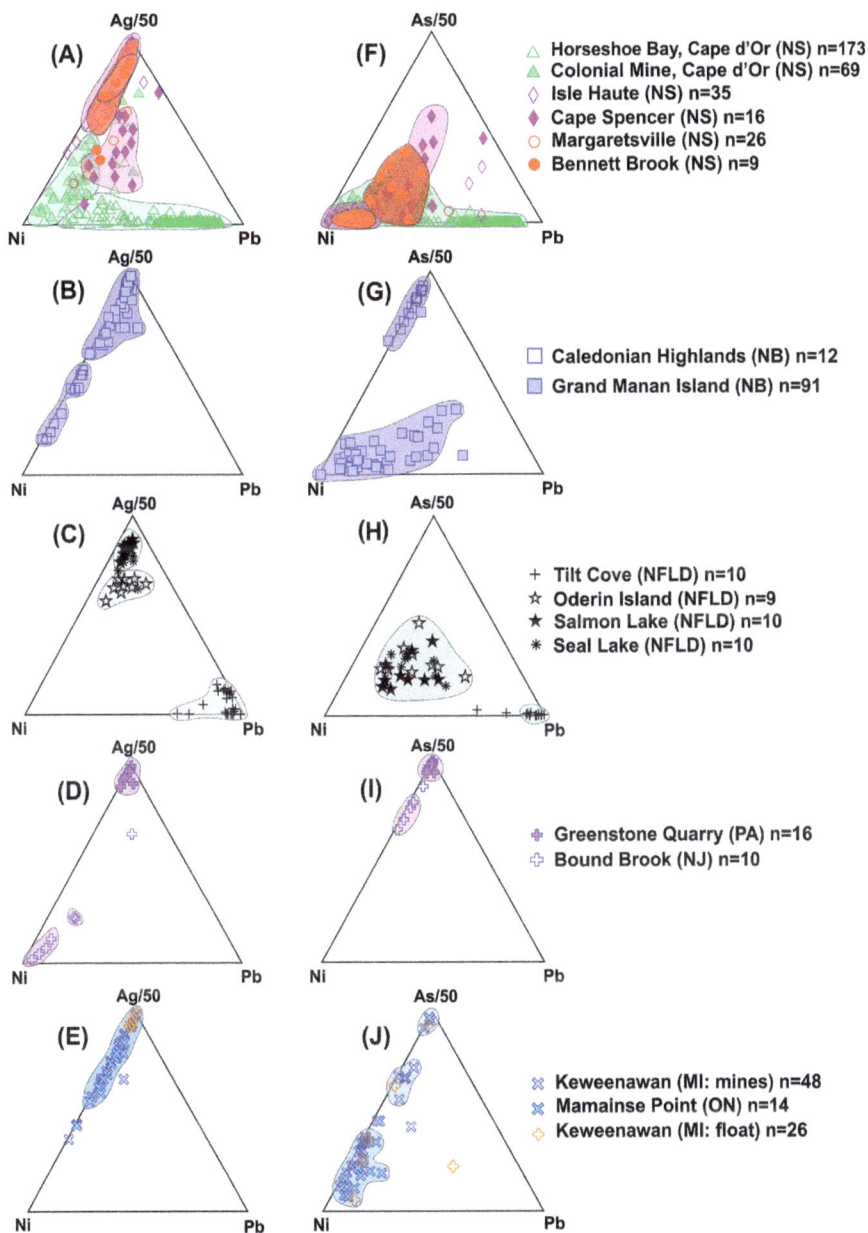

Figure 7.7. Ternary diagrams showing the relative concentration of three trace elements per diagram, utilizing different combinations from the Ni-As-Ag-Pb-Zn data for copper source samples analyzed. Diagrams (A)–(E) show relative Ni-Ag-Pb concentrations with Ag divided by 50. Diagrams (F)–(J) show relative Ni-As-Pb concentrations with As divided by 50.

into the centre of the diagram from the Ni apex. The area along the Ag-Pb join, and toward the centre from this join, is empty. Specific Cape d'Or sources (Horseshoe Bay and Colonial Copper Mine) are well resolved from one another and from Isle Haute, Bennett Brook, Margaretsville, and Cape Spencer fields. New Brunswick Bay of Fundy sources (figure 7.7B) lie in different areas along the Ni-Ag join. This allows differentiation of the Caledonian Highlands source from Grand Manan samples, which lie closer to the Ag apex. However, there is major overlap between NS and NB sources along the Ni-Ag join, preventing discrimination. Similar to the As-Pb (x50)-Ag ternary, NFLD sources (figure 7.7C) lie near two of the apices, with Tilt Cove near the Pb apex, and the other sources (Oderin Island, Salmon and Seal Lakes) near the Ag apex, showing some spread toward the centre of the diagram. Sources from Lake Superior, NJ, and PA (figure 7.7D–E) lie along the Ni-Ag join or at the Ni and Ag apices, allowing differentiation between NJ copper that lies at the Ni apex. However, fields for Lake Superior, NFLD (except Tilt Cove), PA, and the Ag-rich sources from the Bay of Fundy show considerable overlap with one another along the Ni-Ag join. On the other hand, two Cape d'Or sources (Colonial Copper Mine and Horseshoe Bay) are well resolved and only show overlap with the NJ (Bound Brook) and Caledonian Highlands sources, an overlap that can be resolved using one of the other two ternaries already described.

(iv) Ni-As/50-Pb ternary: All Bay of Fundy sources in NS and NB, except the Caledonian Highlands (figure 7.7F–G), lie along the Ni-Pb join with most groups showing some spread into the centre of the diagram away from the centre of the Ni-Pb join. The degree of spread differentiates some of these sources from one another. Caledonian Highlands copper is well resolved, lying near the As apex along the Ni-As join. Newfoundland and Labrador sources (figure 7.7H) show overlap in the central area of the diagram, except for Tilt Cove, which lies at the Pb apex. Both the NJ and PA sources lie along Ni-As join, near the As apex, and are well resolved from all Bay of Fundy sources. Lake Superior sources lie along the Ni-As join with most analyses nearer the Ni apex. However, the degree of spreading away from the Ni-As join into the centre of the diagram is minimal, allowing reasonable differentiation of Lake Superior sources from all Bay of Fundy sources, which are less As-rich and more Pb-rich.

Overall, the ternary diagrams, when used in conjunction with one another, may provide a tool for discrimination provided artifacts have a similar or smaller compositional spread than in individual source compositions. On the other hand, some sources show sufficient overlap in all diagrams (e.g., Grand Manan compared to Salmon Lake, Seal Lake, and Oderin Island, and to other Bay of Fundy sources) such that other discriminators must be used to differentiate these. An important result from this exercise is the lack of overlap and/or the differences in field positions between Lake Superior and Bay of Fundy sources.

Copper Sources Differentiated using Abundance vs. Category Plots ("Spider" Diagrams)

Figures 7.8 and 7.9 show the results of all source sample analyses (table 7.4, Supplementary File A), by location or region, in plots with logarithmic concentration (in parts per million) on the y axis and the five diagnostic trace elements along the x axis. Lines connect concentration data points for single copper analyses. The resulting patterns illustrate relative enrichments and depletions in the trace elements between each source location or region. The characteristics of each copper source are summarized below.

Copper sources from the Bay of Fundy region in NS and NB (figure 7.8A–H, figure 7.9A) have seven distinct patterns:

(i) Horseshoe Bay (Cape d'Or)—elevated Ni-Ag-Pb, low As, and highly elevated Zn.

(ii) Cape Spencer (10 km northeast of Cape d'Or) and one variant from the Colonial Copper Mine (Cape d'Or) with a relatively "flat" pattern—low Ni, elevated Ag-As-Zn with an As peak, and elevated or low Pb.

(iii) A second variant from the Colonial Copper Mine—with a similarly "flat" pattern as in (ii)—low Ni, peaks of elevated Ag and Zn separated by slightly lower As, and low Pb.

(iv) Margaretsville—two variants—both with variable but generally low Ni, highly elevated Ag, and either low As-Zn and low Pb or elevated As-Zn and low Pb. Bennett Brook (Cape d'Or) copper shares similar characteristics as the second variant from Margaretsville, having low Ni, highly elevated Ag, elevated As-Zn, and low Pb.

(v) Copper sources from Grand Manan Island and Isle Haute—are very similar to one another, but distinct from other sources in the Bay of Fundy region described here, showing highly elevated Ag, low Ni-As-Zn, and very low Pb. The Ag content of Grand Manan copper is higher than Isle Haute.

(vi) Caledonian Highlands (north shore Bay of Fundy)—elevated Ni, very high Ag, and extremely high As (As >> Ag), low Zn, and very low Pb.

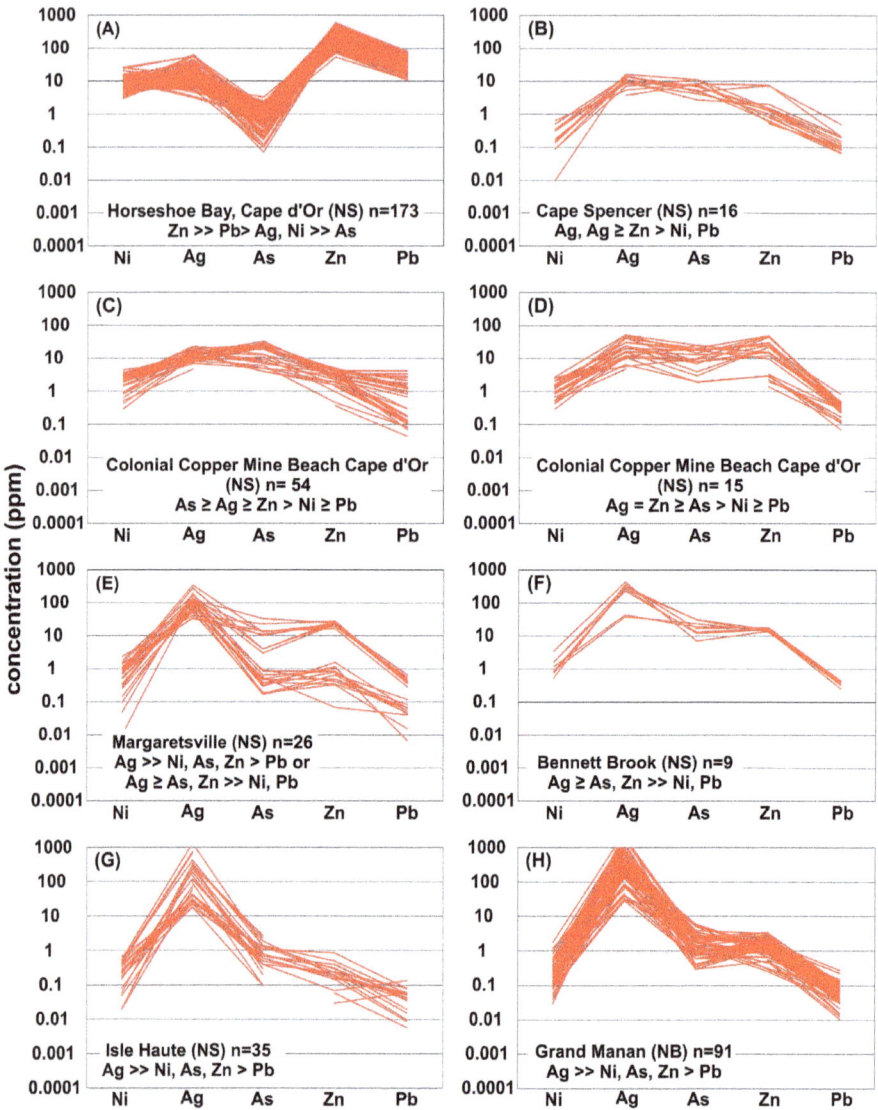

Figure 7.8. Abundance patterns ("spider" diagrams) involving Ni, Ag, As, Zn, and Pb for copper source sample analyses (Nova Scotia—and New Brunswick—source localities; table 7.2). Trace element concentrations for the five diagnostic metals are shown on logarithmic scale on y axes, and metals are shown as categories on x axes. Individual red lines connect the concentrations of metals from a single analysis. For example, in (A) a total of 173 analyses of copper from Horseshoe Bay at Cape d'Or are shown, corresponding to 173 red lines all with the same overall shape or "abundance pattern." For example, the abundance pattern for (A) can be described by Zn being the highest concentration metal of the five diagnostic elements, with Pb being the second highest in concentration, followed by Ag and Ni showing similar concentration levels, and finally As with the lowest concentration. The relative abundance patterns for each source are diagnostic and for the majority of sources are unique to each source.

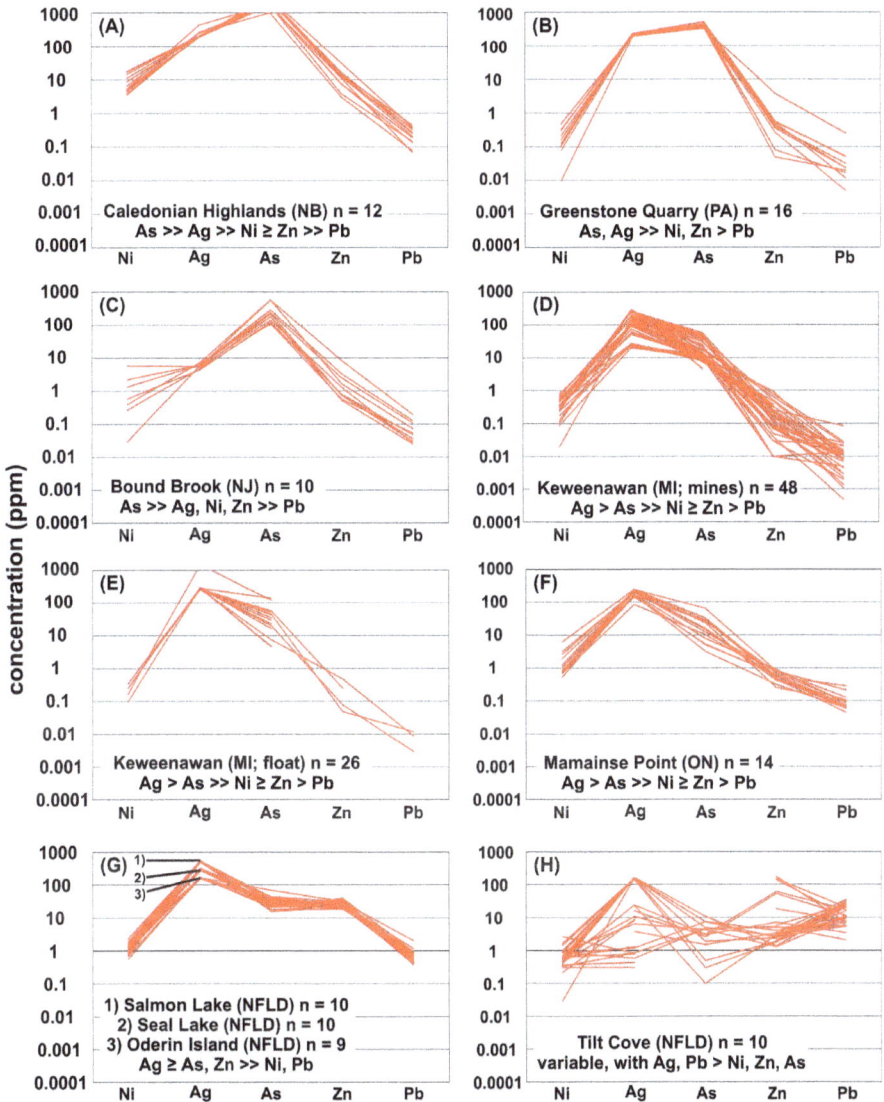

Figure 7.9. Abundance patterns for New Brunswick, Lake Superior, Pennsylvania, New Jersey, and Newfoundland and Labrador sources. See diagram general description in figure 7.8 caption.

Copper sources from the Greenstone Quarry (PA) and Bound Brook (NJ) (figure 7.9B–C) are distinct from the Bay of Fundy sources, with the exception of the Caledonian Highlands (NB), which is similar. The PA and NJ sources have much higher As, and lower Zn and/or Pb than the Bay of Fundy sources. The PA source has low Ni-Zn and very low Pb, but very high Ag and As, with As comparable to Ag (or slightly higher than Ag). The NJ source has very high As, elevated Ag, low but variable Ni-Zn, and very low Pb. Caledonian Highlands copper can be differentiated from the PA and NJ sources by its much higher As and Ni contents, its higher Zn (compared to PA), and its higher Ag (compared to NJ).

Copper sources from the Lake Superior occurrences (Keweenawan Peninsula and Mamainse Point) (figure 7.9D–F) are all similar to one another, with a characteristic highly elevated Ag and As, elevated Ag:As ratio, and very low Ni, Zn, and Pb. Copper from float and mine settings are indistinguishable from one another, whereas copper from Mamainse Point has lower overall concentrations of Ag and As compared to Keweenawan copper. The Lake Superior sources are differentiated from the NB, NJ, and PA sources mainly by their much lower As content, and from other Bay of Fundy sources by their much lower Ag and higher As content (compared to Isle Haute and Grand Manan), or by their much lower Pb contents and much higher Ag:Pb and As:Pb ratios (compared to Cape d'Or, Margaretsville, Cape Spencer, and Bennett Brook sources).

Lastly, copper sources from NFLD (figure 7.9G–H) are characterized by low Ni, highly elevated Ag, elevated As-Zn, and low Pb (Salmon and Seal Lakes, Oderin Island), or by generally highly variable Ag-As-Zn, low Ni, and elevated Pb (Tilt Cove). Salmon Lake, Seal Lake, and Oderin Island are very similar but have distinctly different Ag contents. Their patterns are distinct from other sources, with the exception of Margaretsville and Bennet Brook sources whose patterns are very similar. To differentiate these two Bay of Fundy sources from the NFLD sources, some additional parameters must be considered (see below). The reason for the poor heterogeneity of the Tilt Cove sample is unknown and is being investigated further. Importantly, however, its high variability in composition and largely mismatched patterns from one analysis to another are inconsistent with other copper sources, providing a means of differentiating it from other sources in provenance assignments.

Undifferentiated Sources: "Difficult" Cases

Copper sources from Margaretsville (high Zn variant), Bennett Brook (at Cape d'Or), and three of the NFLD localities (Salmon Lake, Seal Lake, and Oderin Island) cannot be easily discerned using the graphical tools presented here. There is a distinct difference in the Ag content of Salmon Lake copper (higher than the two NS sources), whereas the patterns are nearly identical. Thus, provided that patina is penetrated and fresh copper is accessed by LA-ICP-MS, it should be possible to differentiate the Salmon Lake from Margaretsville (high Zn variant) and Bennett Brook, but this is the only possible approach. No other elements analyzed (table 7.4, Supplementary File A) show any differences in concentration between the two. With respect to Seal Lake and Oderin Island, the Ag contents are too similar to the two NS sources to be a reliable discriminator, and, once again, the patterns are identical. In this case, examination of the indium (In) content of the copper is helpful, and this is the only case where the element provides a means for additional discrimination between any of the sources discussed. The In content (table 7.4, Supplementary File A) of Seal Lake and Oderin Island copper is consistently higher (by an order of magnitude) than the two NS sources. The In content of Salmon Lake copper, however, is undifferentiated from the NS sources (thus the need to use Ag alone).

A second example is between Grand Manan and Isle Haute copper, and copper from the Lake Superior region. While the criteria presented for differentiating the Bay of Fundy sources from the Lake Superior sources are robust for artifacts showing relatively narrow ranges in composition (i.e., good heterogeneity), there may be cases where the patterns or plot positions of artifacts lend some ambiguity to the provenance decision. This can be readily resolved by examining the bismuth (Bi) content of the artifact, which for Lake Superior sources is always an order of magnitude lower in concentration than any of the Bay of Fundy sources (table 7.4, Supplementary File A).

Provenance of Maritime Peninsula Pre-Contact Copper Artifacts

Ternary Diagrams

As a first test of the discrimination diagrams in assigning a source to the artifact copper, the artifact trace element data (table 7.5, Supplementary File B) was plotted in the described ternary diagrams (figure 7.10) for comparison to the compositional fields defined for Bay of Fundy copper sources and Lake Superior copper sources in figures 7.6 and 7.7. Figure 7.10 shows all individual artifact analyses (128 objects, ~1,200 individual LA-ICP-MS analyses) for all objects as black circles. While there is considerable scatter in artifact plot positions on the ternary diagrams, more than was expected given the ranges in source compositions, there are some important first-order observations that can be made with respect to provenance. First, the scatter in the artifact data indicates that the compositional variability in the artifacts is larger than the known source compositions, and that there likely are other sources relevant to the artifact provenance that have not been evaluated in this study. Second, much of the data are clustering in areas (or are absent from areas) consistent with the fields from source ternary diagrams. For example, in the Ni-Ag/50-Pb ternary (figure 7.10A–B), there is some clustering of artifact data near the Ag apex, and along the Ni-Pb join nearest the Ni and Pb apices, and slightly less data overall plotting along the Ag-Pb join. In the As-Zn-Ag/5 ternary (figure 7.10C–D), the artifact data closer along the As-Zn and Zn-Ag joins and near the As apex, along the As-Ag join. In the As-Pb(x50)-Ag and Ni-As/50-Pb diagrams (figure 7.10E–F and G–H, respectively), this clustering is much more pronounced, with the bulk of artifact data concentrated along the Pb-Ag, and Ni-Pb joins, respectively. Importantly, areas where artifact data density is the highest do not correspond to the areas where the fields for Lake Superior copper sources reside, and, in general, the overall distribution of the data in the diagrams is not consistent with Lake Superior sources. This is best shown in the Ni–As/50-Pb diagram, which appears to be most appropriate to differentiate Lake Superior from Bay of Fundy sources. Comparison of the artifact data distribution with other source compositional fields in figures 7.6 and 7.7 indicate that other sources (e.g., Caledonian Highlands, NJ, PA) are also unlikely to explain the spread in artifact data within the diagrams.

Comparison of an individual artifact's compositional position in figure 7.10 reinforces the value of these diagrams for provenance classification. Analyses of artifact 2507 (spearhead), shown previously in figure 7.5C, plot in all four ternary diagrams in figure 7.10 within the broad fields for Bay of Fundy sources, clearly dissimilar to Lake Superior sources. Notably, the spread in data points for the artifact illustrates the impact of contaminating Ag inclusions (previously mentioned) on the provenance assignment, spreading the data range away from the Ag apex. Rather, the filtered data (devoid of Ag inclusions) clusters tightly closer to the Apex, consistent with sources at Cape d'Or (Colonial Copper Mine or Horseshoe Cove; figures 7.6–7.7).

Abundance ("Spider") Diagrams

Graphical comparisons of the relative abundance patterns (figures 7.8 and 7.9) of copper sources to the trace element data for a wide range of artifacts (table 7.5, Supplementary File B) allows for details classification, considering the relative and absolute abundances of all five diagnostic trace elements. Both the trace element patterns (relative abundances of diagnostic trace elements within a single artifact, compared to candidate sources) and the absolute abundances of these trace elements (compared to candidate sources) were compared. Figure 7.11 shows examples of six artifacts plotted on the same format of abundance-category diagrams, as were the copper sources in figures 7.8 and 7.9. There were five major outcomes of this exercise:

> (i) Approximately 85% of the artifacts analyzed have abundance patterns consistent with sources characterized here. The remaining 15% of artifacts could not be unambiguously assigned a provenance or had abundance patterns that were distinctly uncharacteristic of the sources characterized (e.g., figure 7.11A). Identification of the provenance of these artifacts are limited by the diversity of source copper in the data set, consistent with the observations earlier in ternary diagrams that a large number of artifacts do not have data that clusters in areas consistent with characterized sources.

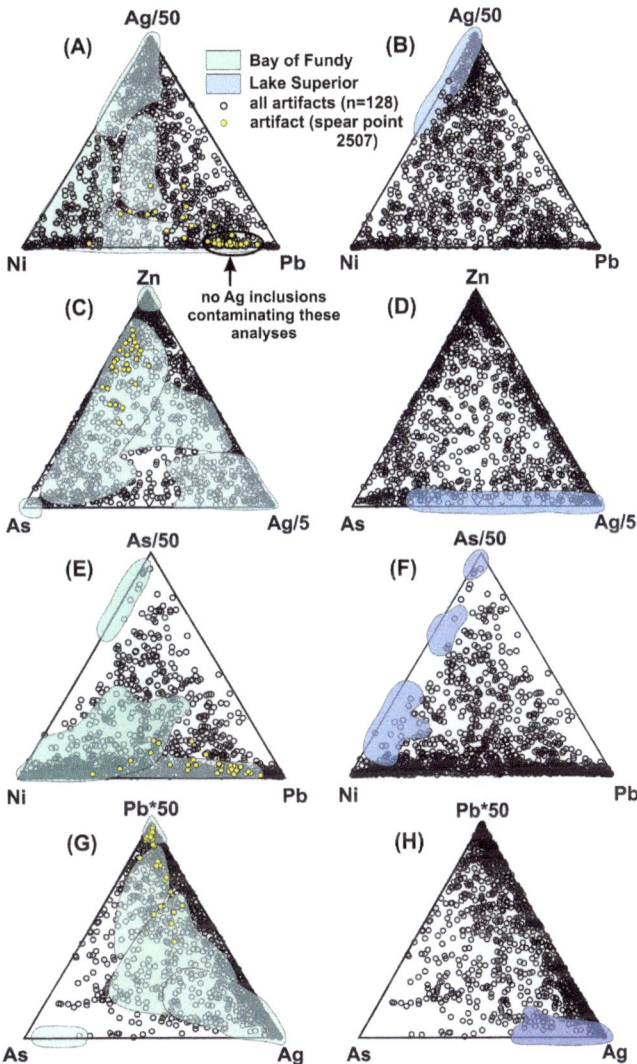

Figure 7.10. Ternary diagrams showing all copper artifact data (~1200 individual LA-ICP-MS analyses; black circles) and fields of composition for all Bay of Fundy copper sources (diagrams A, C, E, and G) and Lake Superior copper sources (diagrams B, D, F, and H) based on all source-sample analyses (from figures 7.6, 7.7). Lake Superior—source compositions generally plot close to the Ag, As, and Ni vertices and along the Ag-Ni, As-Ni, and As-Ag sides of the diagrams and show characteristically very low Pb-Zn concentrations, whereas Bay of Fundy—source compositions are more diverse in compositional scatter but show typically higher concentrations of Pb and Zn relative to Ag-As-Ni. Note that artifact compositions do not cluster within fields consistent with Lake Superior sources. In particular, diagrams (E)–(F) showing As/50-Ni-Pb and (G)–(H) showing As-Pbx50-Ag illustrate that artifacts generally (but not all) adhere to the Bay of Fundy–source composition distributions. Also shown are the LA-ICP-MS analyses for a single artifact, a spear point (artifact 2507) from the Augustine Mound site (yellow circles) to illustrate the distribution of analyses from a single artifact within the artifact analysis population. The LA-ICP-MS analyses of clean copper, free of Ag-rich inclusions, are circled in (A). Note the compositional spread in the other analyses of copper from the artifact containing contaminating Ag-rich mineral inclusions, obscuring its provenance fingerprint.

(ii) Importantly, none of these artifacts show the characteristic patterns of Lake Superior copper, with its hallmark highly elevated Ag and As, elevated Ag/As ratio, and very low Ni, Zn, and Pb (Ag > As >> Ni ≥ Zn > Pb).

(iii) Of the artifacts that could be assigned sources based on comparisons of abundance patterns and absolute concentrations for each of the diagnostic trace elements, almost all show compositions consistent with Bay of Fundy sources (e.g., figure 7.11B–F; ~29% Margaretsville or Bennett Brook, ~25% Colonial Copper Mine, ~10% Margaretsville, ~11% Cape Spencer or Colonial Copper Mine, ~8% Cape Spencer, ~5% Margaretsville or Colonial Copper Mine; one artifact matching Grand Manan and Isle Haute sources).

(iv) In agreement with earlier statements made in this study, artifacts containing contaminating inclusions (e.g., figure 7.11D) yield ambiguous patterns that are inconsistent from analysis to analysis, reinforcing the need to carefully review each analysis and its impact on the overall pattern, mean concentration, and concentration ranges associated with an artifact.

(v) In some cases, artifact heterogeneity may challenge the success of assigning (graphically) a provenance, despite exclusion of inclusions, and with best attempts at isolating fresh copper from patina in the LA-ICP-MS transient signals. Figures 7.11C–D show such artifacts. However, even in these cases, the relative magnitude in concentration of diagnostic elements, and their corresponding abundance pattern, allows some sources and most certainly preclude other sources. Still, there are likely to be cases where some artifacts are so heterogeneous that the graphical methods fail and provenance cannot be assigned.

As mentioned earlier, as part of this exercise, differentiation/clarification of (i) Margaretsville and Bennett Brook copper from sources in Newfoundland and Labrador and (ii) Grand Manan and Isle Haute copper from copper in the Lake Superior region required the examination of the absolute abundances of two additional trace elements (In and Bi; table 7.5, Supplementary File B).

Conclusions and Future Implications

The proposed graphical tools highlight a preliminary but innovative approach to resolving copper provenance for artifacts analyzed by LA-ICP-MS that is accessible to a wide range of end users of the data. Using a series of ternary discrimination diagrams and abundance-category-type ("spider") diagrams

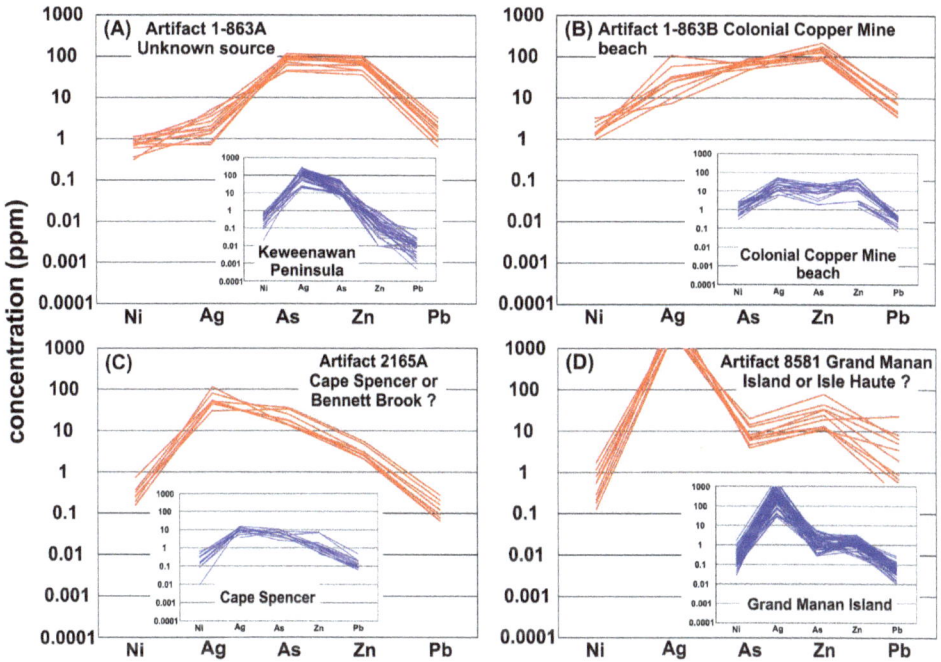

Figure 7.11. Trace-element abundance patterns (Ni-Ag-As-Zn-Pb; in red) for representative copper artifacts listing artifact number and interpreted source based on comparison of patterns to copper-source data (figures 7.8, 7.9; table 7.5 – Supplementary File B). Insets show copper source patterns in blue. (A) Artifact 1-863A (unknown provenance) does not have relative abundances of the diagnostic trace elements matching any analyzed natural copper. For comparison, Lake Superior copper (inset) has a characteristically enrichment pattern of Ag > As >> Ni ≥ Zn > Pb with the hallmark of very low Ni, Zn, and Pb relative to Ag and As. This indicates that the source for this artifact cannot be copper from the Keewenaw Peninsula. (B)–(D) Artifacts 1–863 B, 2165A, and 8581 patterns showing different, distinct abundance patterns. Insets show the relevant source compositions for comparison. Note that while relative enrichment patterns are conservative, the absolute abundance of the diagnostic trace elements are sometimes slightly higher in artifacts compared to their sources. This reflects the ablation of patina (containing less than ~100% Cu) in some artifacts, and overestimate of the Cu content of this patina during data reduction. While this impacts the absolute concentrations of trace elements in the quantified analysis of the artifact, it has a negligible impact on the relative abundance patterns for the purposes of provenance assignment.

involving the trace elements Ni-As-Ag-Pb-Zn, Lake Superior copper can be readily differentiated from various sources of copper in the northern Appalachians based on graphical comparisons of source patterns and fields, as well as comparisons of the order-of-magnitude absolute range in concentrations for the diagnostic elements between sources and artifacts. Individual Appalachian sources can also be differentiated from one another with a high degree of certainty. The success of this approach relies on careful scrutiny of contaminating alloy or mineral inclusions in time-intensity signals, avoidance of artifacts with thick patina layers (and detailed examination of each object to select the best areas for ablation), and creation of a reasonably large data set (recommend at least eight analyses of each object or source) to ensure that sample homogeneity (or lack thereof, owing to contaminating inclusions) can be properly assessed.

The results of this study suggest that the artifacts from Archaic and Woodland sites in Nova Scotia, New Brunswick, and Prince Edward Island, including the Augustine Mound, originated from non–Lake Superior sources of copper. Whereas the majority of objects have compositions consistent with geological sources of copper in, and surrounding, the Bay of Fundy, a significant number of artifacts (15%) have compositions that could not be matched to any existing source compositions in the present database but likewise have compositions inconsistent with a Lake Superior origin.

As with any active research project where new data is regularly introduced, complex questions linked to cultural history, human interactions, and regional movements have emerged. Beyond this method-focused chapter, such questions are being explored and discussed through the continued interdisciplinary interplay (Repko 2008) of the geochemical provenance data, archaeological site record, and Indigenous traditional knowledge. Central questions include:

(i) Why is Lake Superior copper absent from the Maritime Peninsula archaeological record? Is this simply a practice of procuring close at hand what was needed or desired, or does this reflect a preference for a copper that was easier to work (i.e., small crystals and nuggets vs. large float fragments)? Also important to consider in terms of preference for a local source is the local cultural significance of copper. Cape d'Or, or L'mu'juiktuk in Mi'kmaq, is "one of the most storied places in Mi'kma'ki," and plays large in Mi'kmaw traditional knowledge and as a recorded resource location "that had great value" (Sable et al. 2012; Gloade 2020).

(ii) What are the unknown sources? Were these local sources and, if so, are they documented currently or historically? If they were sourced from other parts of what is now the Maritime region or northeastern United States, how does this better inform relationships of trade and exchange between Indigenous groups? Continued expansion of the copper source data set to include, in particular, other sources in the central and southern Appalachians (cf. Hill et al. 2019) is a priority.

(iii) Can the diversity in sources for artifacts recovered at a single archaeological site reflect reuse of copper sourced from different areas over generations? What are the compositional relationships between artifacts from different sites, at individual sites, and closely associated objects (e.g., copper beads from a single strand)? Was copper being procured from a variety of sources at one time for various end uses?

(iv) Was Bay of Fundy copper more prevalent than previously thought? Given the limitations in bulk analytical methods discussed here and potential improvements on existing analytical protocols, will reanalysis of samples from other sites in North America by LA-ICP-MS tighten constraints on copper provenance, revealing a greater role for copper from the Bay of Fundy region in North American Indigenous cultures prior to European contact?

In general, given its significance as a source of copper, and the complexity of source compositions revealed in this study, the inclusion of copper-source material from a diversity of source locations in the Far Northeast into studies of North American copper-artifact provenance is strongly encouraged. The results present a successful application of the LA-ICP-MS analytical approach that utilizes appropriate SRM and resolves concerns with bulk analytical approaches and sample heterogeneity that commonly introduce uncertainties into copper provenance studies. Evidently, the Bay of Fundy region was a significant source of copper regionally for the Maritime Peninsula and beyond, reinforcing the INAA results of Levine (2007a, 2007b) that first suggested Bay of Fundy copper at Late Archaic and Early Woodland sites well outside of the Maritime Peninsula. Specifically, for the Woodland period in the Maritime Peninsula, the study to date supports the pre-Contact procurement of copper as an activity largely defined by Bay of Fundy copper source locations, and Cape d'Or in particular. The Bay of Fundy, and Cape d'Or in particular, were consistent and persistent places used over thousands of years to collect and gather a material of practical and cultural meaning and value.

Acknowledgements

The Geology Department at Saint Mary's University and the Archaeology Section of the Nova Scotia Museum began the Copper Project as part of the NSM Research Associate Program six years ago. The advancement of the project is directly connected to the keen interest and participation of several organizations, institutions, First Nations, and community members. The chapter authors would like to thank everyone who has helped and contributed to the Copper Project. In particular, we acknowledge the following supporters: the Nova Scotia Museum board of governors; NS Department of Communities, Culture and Heritage; Department of Earth Sciences, University of New Brunswick; the Nova Scotia Mi'kmaq Mainland Grand Council; Archaeological Services Branch of the New Brunswick Department of Tourism, Heritage and Culture; Passamaquoddy First

Nation; Metepenagiag Mi'kmaq Nation; Prince Edward Island Indigenous Affairs Secretariat and Archaeology Office; Northeastern Prehistory Laboratory, University of Maine; Canadian Museum of History; Royal Ontario Museum; CRM Group Ltd.; Department of Earth Sciences, Memorial University of Newfoundland; Department of Anthropology, University of Maine; the Saint Mary's University Community and Student Engagement committee; and the Natural Sciences and Engineering Research Council. The authors also thank Jessica Whattam and Matt Meuse Dallien for their hours of data crunching, research, and map-making.

References Cited
Allen, Patricia M., and Red Bank First Nation
1994   *Metepenagiag: New Brunswick's Oldest Village.* Goose Lane Editions, Fredericton.
Anselmi, Lisa M.
2004   A Brief Historical Retrospective of Investigation of Archaic to Contact Period Copper-Based Metal Artifacts in Northeastern North America. *Ontario Archaeology* 78:81–93.
Beukens, Roelf P., Laurence A. Pavlish, Ronald G. V. Hancock, Ronald M. Farquhar, Graham C. C. Wilson, Patrick J. Julig, and William Ross
1992   Radiocarbon Dating of Copper-Preserved Organics. *Radiocarbon* 34:890–897.
Black, David W.
2002   Out of the Blue and Into the Black: The Middle-Late Maritime Woodland Transition in the Quoddy Region, New Brunswick, Canada. In *Northeast Subsistence-Settlement Change A.D. 700–1300,* edited by John P. Hart and Christina B. Rieth, pp. 301–320. New York State Museum Bulletin 496, New York.
Blair, Susan E., Tricia L. Jarratt, and P. Ward
2014   Weaving Together Two Ways of Knowing: Archaeological Organic Artifact Analysis and Indigenous Textile Arts. *North American Archaeologist* 35(4): 295–302.
Brown, Alexander C.
1992   Sediment-Hosted Stratiform Copper Deposits. *Geoscience Canada* 19: 121–141.
Cooper, Harold K., M. J. M. Duke, Antonio Simonetti, and Guang C. Chen
2008   Trace Element and Pb Isotope Provenance Analyses of Native Copper in Northwestern North America: Results of a Recent Pilot Study Using INAA, ICMP-MS, and LA-MC-ICP-MS. *Journal of Archaeological Science* 35: 1732–1747.
Dussubieux, Laure, Aurélie Deraisme, Gérard Frot, Cristopher Stevenson, Amy Creech, and Yves Bienvenu
2008   LA-ICP-MS, SEM-EDS and EPMA Analysis of Eastern North American Copper-Based Artefacts: Impact of the Corrosion and Heterogeneity on the Reliability of the LA-ICP-MS Compositional Results. *Archaeometry* 50: 643–657.

Dussubieux, Laure, and Heather Walder
2015   Identifying American Native and European Smelted Coppers with pXRF: A Case Study of Artifacts from the Upper Great Lakes Region. *Journal of Archaeological Science* 59:169–178.

Dussubieux, Laure, Mark A. Hill, and Gregory D. Lattanzi
2019   Comparison of Different Sets of External Standards for the LA-ICPM-MS Analysis of North American Copper Artifacts. *Journal of Archaeological Science Reports* 24:1076–1082.

Ehrhardt, Kathleen L.
2009   Copper Working Technologies Contexts of Use and Social Complexity in the Eastern Woodlands of Native North America. *Journal of World Prehistory* 22: 213–235.

Fenn, Thomas R.
2001   Geochemical Investigation of Prehistoric Native Copper Artifacts, Northern Wisconsin. Master's thesis, Department of Geology and Geophysics, University of New Orleans.

Fields, P. R., John Milsted, Eiler Henrickson, and R. Ramette
1971   Trace Impurity Patterns in Copper Ores and Artifacts. In *Science and Archaeology*, edited by Robert. H. Brill, pp. 131–143. MIT Press, Cambridge, Massachusetts.

Fitzgerald, William R., Laurier Turgeon, Ruth Holmes Whitehead, and James W. Bradley
1993   Late Sixteenth-Century Basque Banded Copper Kettles. *Historical Archaeology* 27:44–57.

Gloade, Gerald
2020   L'mu'juiktuk Cape d'Or. Electronic document, http://www.mikmaweydebert .ca/home/ancestors-live-here/cape-dor/.

Goad, Sharon I., and John Noakes
1978   Prehistoric Copper Artifacts in the Eastern United States. In *Archaeological Chemistry: A Sourcebook on the Applications of Chemistry to Archaeology,* edited by Zvi Goffer, pp. 335–346. Wiley, New York.

Halsey, John R.
2018   *Prehistoric Copper Mining in Michigan.* Anthropological Papers No. 99, University of Michigan Press, Ann Arbor.

Hancock, Ronald G. V., Laurence A. Pavlish, Ronald R. Farquhar, R. Salloum, William A. Fox, and Graham C. Wilson
1991   Distinguishing European Trade Copper and North-Eastern North American Native Copper. *Archaeometry* 33:69–86.

Hawkins, Alicia L., Joseph A. Petrus, Lisa M. Anselmi, and Gary Crawford
2016   Laser Ablation-Inductively Coupled Plasma-Mass Spectrometry Analysis of Copper-Based Artifacts from Southern Ontario and the Chronology of the Indirect Contact Period. *Journal of Archaeological Science* 6:332–341.

Hill, Mark A.
2012   *The Benefit of The Gift: Social Organization and Expanding Networks of Interaction in the Western Great Lakes Archaic.* International Monographs in Prehistory, Berghahn Series, New York.

Hill, Mark A., Diana M. Greenlee, and Hector Neff
2016   Assessing the Provenance of Poverty Point Copper through LA-ICP-MS Compositional Analysis. *Journal of Archaeological Science Reports* 6:351–360.

Hill, Mark A., Gregory D. Lattanzi, Matthew C. Sanger, and Laure Dussubieux
2019   Elemental Analysis of Late Archaic Copper from the McQueen Shell Ring, St. Catherine's Island, Georgia. *Journal of Archeological Science Reports* 24: 1083–1094.

Hill, Mark A., Mark F. Seeman, Kevin C. Nolan, and Laure Dussubieux
2018   An Empirical Evaluation of Copper Procurement and Distribution: Elemental Analysis of Scioto Valley Hopewell Copper. *Archaeological and Anthropological Sciences* 10:1193–1205.

Hill, Walter E. Jr., and Robert W. Neuman
1966   Copper Artifacts from Prehistoric Archaeological Sites in the Dakotas. *Science* 154 (3753):1171–1173.

Hirata, Takafumi
2018   Laser Ablation – Inductively Coupled Plasma Mass Spectrometry. In *Encyclopedia of Geochemistry*, edited by William M. White, pp. 801–810. Springer International Publishing, Cham, Switzerland.

Holmes, William H.
1901   Aboriginal Copper Mines of Isle Royale, Lake Superior. *American Anthropologist* 3:684–696.

Hurst, Vernon J., and Lewis H. Larson
1958   On the Source of Copper at the Etowah Site, Georgia. *American Antiquity* 24(2):177–181.

Jarratt, Tricia L.
2013   The Augustine Mound Copper Sub-assemblage: Beyond the Bead. Master's thesis, Department of Anthropology, University of New Brunswick, Fredericton.

Kirkham, Rodney V.
1995   Volcanic Redbed Copper. In *Geology of Canadian Mineral Deposit Types*, edited by O. R. Eckstrand, W. D. Sinclair, and R. I. Thorpe, pp. 241–252. Canada Communication Group Publishing, Ottawa, Canada.

Lattanzi, Gregory D.
2007   The Provenance of Pre-contact Copper Artifacts: Social Complexity and Trade in the Delaware Valley. *Archaeology of Eastern North America* 35:125–137.

2008   Elucidating the Origin of Middle Atlantic Pre-contact Copper Artifacts Using Laser Ablation. *North American Archaeologist* 29:297–326.

Levine, Mary A.
1999   Native Copper in the Northeast: An Overview of Potential Sources Available to Indigenous Peoples. In *The Archaeological Northeast*, edited by Mary A. Levine, Kenneth E. Sassaman, and Michael S. Nassaney, pp. 183–199. Bergin & Garvey, Westport, Connecticut.

2007a   Determining the Provenance of Native Copper Artifacts from Northeastern North America: Evidence from Instrumental Neutron Activation Analysis. *Journal of Archaeological Science* 34:572–587.

2007b   Overcoming Disciplinary Solitude: The Archaeology and Geology of Native Copper in Eastern North America. *Geoarcheaology* 22:49–66.

Lewis, Roger J.

2006   Mi'kmaq Rights and Title Claim: A Review of the Pre-Contact Archaeological Factor. *Mi'kmaq Maliseet Nations News*, June 16–17. Truro, Nova Scotia.

2007   Pre-Contact Fish Weirs: A Case Study from Southwest Nova Scotia. Master's thesis, Department of Anthropology, Memorial University of Newfoundland, St. John's.

2011   Mi'kmaik Teloltipnik L'nuk: "How Lnu Lived in Mi'kmakik". In *T'an Wetapeksi'k: Understanding from Where We Come: Proceedings of the 2005 Debert Research Workshop, Debert, Nova Scotia, Canada*, edited by Tim Bernard, Leah M. Rosenmeier, and Sharon L. Farrell, p. 22. Confederacy of Mainland Mi'kmaq, Truro, Nova Scotia.

McKnight, Matthew D.

2007   The Copper Cache in Early and Middle Woodland North America. PhD dissertation, Department of Anthropology, Pennsylvania State University, State College.

Mauk, Jeffrey L., and Ronald G. V. Hancock

1998   Trace Element Geochemistry of Native Copper from the White Pine Mine, Michigan (USA): Implications for Sourcing Artifacts. *Archaeometry* 40:97–107.

Moreau, Jean-Francois, and Ronald G. V. Hancock

1999   The Effects of Corrosion on INAA Characterizations of Brass Kettles of the Early European Contact Period in Northeastern North America. *Journal of Archaeological Science* 20:1119–1125.

Mulholland, Susan C., and Mary H. Pulford

2007   Trace Element Analysis of Native Copper: The View from Northern Minnesota, USA. *Geoarchaeology* 22:67–84.

Rapp, George, Jr.

1985   The Provenance of Artifactual Raw Materials. In *Archaeological Geology*, edited by George Rapp Jr. and John A. Gifford, pp. 353–375. Yale University Press, New Haven, Connecticut.

Rapp, George, Jr., and James Allert

1984   Trace Element Discrimination of Discrete Sources of Native Copper. In *Archaeological Chemistry III*, edited by Joseph B. Lambert, pp. 273–293. American Chemical Society, Washington DC.

Rapp, George, James Allert, Vanda Vitali, Zhichun Jing, and Eiler Henrickson

2000   *Determining Geologic Sources of Artifact Copper: Source Characterization Using Trace Element Patterns*. University Press of America, Lanham, Maryland.

Rapp, George, Jr., Eiler Henrickson, Michael Miller, and Stanley Aschenbrenner

1980   Trace Element Fingerprinting as a Guide to the Geographic Sources of Native Copper. *Journal of Metals* 32:35–45.

Reeder, John T.

1961 [1903]   Evidences of Prehistoric Man on Lake Superior. *Prehistoric Copper Mining in the Lake Superior Region, A Collection of Reference Articles,* edited by Roy W. Drier and Octave J. Du Temple, pp. 135–144. Calumet, Michigan.

Repko, Allen F.
2008   Interdisciplinary Research: Process and Theory. Sage Publications, Los Angeles.

Sable, Trudy, and Bernie Francis
2012   *The Language of this Land, Mi'kma'ki*. Cape Breton University Press, Sydney, Nova Scotia.

Sanger, David, and Priscilla Renouf (editors)
2006   *The Archaic in the Far Northeast*. University of Maine Press, Orono.

Seeman, Mark F., Kevin C. Nolan, and Mark A. Hill
2019   Copper as an Essential and Exotic Hopewell Metal. *Journal of Archaeological Science Reports* 24:1095–1101.

Smith, Harlan I., and William J. Wintemberg
1929   *Some Shell-Heaps in Nova Scotia*. Bulletin No. 47, National Museum of Man, Ottawa.

Turnbull, Christopher J.
1976   The Augustine Site: A Mound for the Maritimes. *Archaeology of Eastern North America* 4:50–62.
1978   Introductory Report of Investigations at the Augustine Mound National Historic Site (CfDl-2), New Brunswick. Manuscript on file, Archaeological Services Branch, Fredericton.

Whitehead, Ruth Holmes
1993   *Nova Scotia: The Protohistoric Period 1500–1630*. Curatorial Report 75. Nova Scotia Museum, Halifax.

Whitehead, Ruth Holmes, Laurence A. Pavlish, Ronald M. Farquhar, and Ronald G. V. Hancock
1998   Analysis of Copper Based Metals from Three Mi'kmaq Sites in Nova Scotia. *North American Archaeologist* 19:279–292.

8

"AND WE SHOWERED WITH A THOUSAND PRAISES THE WOMAN WHO HAD BEEN THE FIRE'S GUARDIAN"

Ancestral Wabanaki Gender and Place-making in the Woodland Period

M. Gabriel Hrynick[1] and Matthew W. Betts[2]

Abstract

In many hunter-gatherer societies, gender is an essential way in which the social and spiritual world is structured. Wabanaki language, ethnohistory, oral tradition, and archaeology all attest to gender as a crucial yet malleable way that Ancestral Wabanaki made their place within and interacted with the world around them. Close scrutiny of gender in the Woodland period, we argue, helps to illuminate how relationships were made among people, nature, and the cosmos. Changing and reifying these relationships offered ways for people to adapt to social and environmental change. In this chapter, we consider Woodland-period gender at scales ranging from single artifacts to local landscapes to track the ways that Ancestral Wabanaki made their homes and histories in the Atlantic Northeast.

Résumé

Le genre est l'un des éléments centraux de l'organisation de l'univers social et spirituel de nombreuses sociétés de chasseurs-cueilleurs. Le fait que le genre ait été un élément central mais flexible de la manière dont les anciens Wabanaki organisaient leur place dans le monde et leurs interactions avec leur environnement est confirmé par la linguistique, l'ethnohistoire, les traditions orales et l'archéologie. Une étude rapprochée de la place du genre durant la période Sylvicole apporte, selon nous, un éclairage nouveau sur la manière dont les relations entre les humains, la nature et le cosmos étaient construites. La possibilité de réifier et transformer ces relations permettait aux humains de s'adapter aux changements sociaux et environnementaux. Dans cet article, nous examinons le rôle du genre à la période Sylvicole, à une échelle allant de l'artéfact au paysage local, afin de comprendre comment les anciens Wabanaki habitaient leur monde et créaient leurs histoires dans le nord-est de la région atlantique.

Affiliations

1. Department of Anthropology, University of New Brunswick, New Brunswick, Canada
2. First Peoples and Early Canada, Canadian Museum of History, Quebec, Canada

In the Atlantic Northeast, archaeologists have started to consider gender and ritual as overlapping aspects of hunter-gatherer life (e.g., Betts 2019; Hrynick and Betts 2017, 2019; Robinson and Ort 2011). Spanning the Palaeoindian to the Late Maritime Woodland period, some of this work has drawn on classic ethnographic studies that, presaging recent interest in ontologies (e.g., Descola 2013; Viveiros de Castro 1998, 2004a, 2004b), recognized that economic and ritual actions are not mutually exclusive for many hunter-gatherer groups (e.g., Brightman 1973; Hoffman 1955; Tanner 1979). In the Atlantic Northeast—as elsewhere—archaeologists remain largely reliant on historical analogy to identify gender actions in the archaeological record, along with analogies to action and materiality that draw on general trends among foraging peoples. However, careful attention to historical and ontological context can offer further assistance.

In this chapter, we consider gender at a series of overlapping spatial and temporal scales as ways ancestral Wabanaki people negotiated social and cosmological relations during the Middle and Late Maritime Woodland periods at Port Joli Harbour, within the Wabanaki homeland of the Maritime Peninsula (see introduction, this volume). In Wabanaki sacred ecology (following Hornborg 2013), gendered action is fundamental to proper relational or spiritual action. That is, the actions of men and women are critical to maintaining relationships with the often-powerful subjects of the natural world. Therefore, focusing on gendered action situates Ancestral Wabanaki as agents who could change or reify their cosmological relationships in response to environmental and cultural change. Here, then, we focus narrowly on gender as an act of *place-making*; that is, as a way people could define spiritual and domestic places on the landscape, or make landscapes into privileged spaces and homelands (Betts 2019; Creese 2018). Questions of home, homeland, and ethnicity therein span the history of the Atlantic Northeast, and are reliant on local histories in which people relate to one another and the cosmos to constitute themselves and their worlds (e.g., Betts 2019; Betts et al. 2012; Lelièvre 2017; Pawling 2016). Such relationships are maintained or changed through cultural tools for managing them. Hunter-gatherers often integrate these tools into everyday action, so that even mundane domestic activities are relational, or world renewing (an extended review of hunter-gatherer relational ontologies in general are beyond the scope of this chapter; for discussion and approaches, see, e.g., Betts et al. 2012, 2015; Cipolla 2019; Descola 2013; Harris and Cipolla 2017; Hill 2011; Hornborg 2013; Hrynick and Betts 2017; Tanner 1979; Viveiros de Castro 1998, 2004a, 2004b; Watts 2013).

Sacred Ecology and Gender in the Far Northeast

Hoffman (1955:504) observed that Wabanaki cosmology existed within a broad Northeastern Algonquian framework, which anthropologists would now term a relational ontology. In this ontology animals are conceived as "other-than-human persons" (Hallowell 1960) with the same capability of a spirit, or soul, which may be as potent, and often more potent, than humans (see Feit 1973; Martin 1978; Tanner 1979; Viveiros de Castro 1998, 2004a, 2004b). In such a cosmology, common in North and South American Indigenous societies, maintaining proper relationships with these powerful subjects is of primary importance. Across the Far Northeast, these relationships are maintained by a mix of broad prescriptions and proscriptions of behaviour to attend to relations with entities in the natural world. For example, among the Cree, Hallowell (1960) observed that maintaining relationships with powerful entities called gamekeepers was critical. Gamekeepers were often powerful animal-persons, who ensured successful hunts, safety, and general band success. Some of these gamekeepers, such as bears, appear to have been defined as broadly important across the Far Northeast, while other relationships with particular animals and their keepers may have been at the group, family, or even individual level.

Human action was critical to the maintenance of these relations. These included quotidian actions that all members of society participated in, as well as more specialized and overtly ritual or shamanistic activities, the latter often to address specific situations, such as locating game or treating illness (see Hoffman 1955:344-504; Hornborg 2006; Lockerby 2004; Wallis and Wallis 1955:142-170). Gendered action was an important aspect of daily Algonquian and Wabanaki life (and indeed Indigenous life throughout the continent), and critical to the maintenance of relationships between humans and non-human persons. As we describe below, the ethnohistoric literature is replete with evidence of difference in gendered practice and action; some overtly proscribed, and some simply deeply embedded in routine, everyday practices. It is important to point out that while proscriptions on certain actions were part of this quotidian maintenance of relations, taboo is not an adequate nor appropriate term to describe the scope of this practice. Tanner (1979) has noted elegantly the failure of a dualistic nature-culture framework to account for these ontological systems. He observed that "motivated religious thought" and "common sense" are inseparable in Algonquian cosmology—essentially, the material and spiritual worlds are inexorably entangled. "Right" action in such a cosmology is just a way of being, of interacting and living in a world full of human and other-than-human persons. In short, gendered actions are overtly social, and may therefore be fundamentally entwined with all aspects of culture. Disentangling them, piecemeal, may not be appropriate or even possible. Thus, understanding the intricate ways Algonquian hunter-gatherers responded to their environment or made their world and their place in it requires attention to relational processes that are local and historical, and acknowledgement of the agentive participation of all members of society, including the non-human ones.

Wabanaki Gender and Material Culture, and Making Gendered Spaces

We should acknowledge at the outset that we recognize the risks of essential-izing gender in both the archaeological record and the historic record from which we draw analogies; each of these is reported from a series of Western gender biases which, to some degree, likely imposed Western gender categories onto Indigenous peoples (Axtell 1981). However, we reiterate here that we are interested in actions performed by different genders, such that the emphasis is on difference in action and how that is embedded in relational ontologies. Secondly, within the limited analytical frameworks we have for describing past gender, we are interested in gender within its specific Wabanaki and historical context. The relational emphasis of our approach here is not an attempt to begin from defined Western-styled genders to describe the past but to explore the ways in which gendered relationships were constitutive of the ancient Wabanaki world. In other words, we do not purport to fully account for maleness, female-ness, or third-gender categories in themselves but, rather, to illustrate that, insomuch as these categories can be ascertained through the ethnohistoric and archaeological record, the interplay among them was culturally significant and historically generative.

Gender pervaded both daily activities and specific shamanistic practices of the Indigenous peoples of the Far Northeast. Gonzalez (1981:1-2) has suggested that the early ethnohistoric literature about Wabanaki gender is most abundant and robust in matters of economy and material culture because Europeans were interested in learning how Indigenous people made a living in what was to Europeans an unfamiliar place. Thus, ironically, although gender has often been conceived of as either opaque or essentialized in the archaeological record (see Hays-Gilpin 2008), it should be among the most visible social constructs archaeologically, given the ethnohistoric record's emphasis on the ways gender intersects economic production, material culture, ritual, and myriad social and political actions. As Sassaman (1992) noted, gender variation or difference should in many instances be reflected in archaeologically visible ways. Indeed, in Flannery's (1939:166-176) remarkably useful tabulations of comparable Algonquian and Iroquoian culture traits from early Historic-period accounts, she lists about 10% of the traits as being explicitly concerned with sex or gender. This percentage is conservative about the visibility of gender in ethnohistoric accounts and the importance of gender as an ordering principle in that it deals only with explicitly sexed and/or gendered traits or activities that are also comparable over an enormous geographic area. It also does not account for some activities that, at least for the Wabanaki record with which we are familiar, are gendered but may not be easily compared. Crucially, many of these are associated with specific items or spaces, meaning that from a practical standpoint many of them can be tracked using direct historic analogy into the past and situated within rich historical context.

Beyond the importance of gendered action provided by a tabular summary, ethnographic accounts suggest that gender—like other relational principles—pervaded Algonquian life in ways that were sometimes locally defined and sometimes broadly held, a point summarized in Flannery's (1939) review. For instance, menstrual seclusion, gendered divisions of hunted game, whether men or women build dwellings, and gendered leadership potentially vary across her survey area. This is unsurprising, in the context of hunter-gatherer relational ontologies broadly and, more narrowly, eastern Algonquian hunter-gatherers. In the broad sense, the mechanisms of relational ontology are crucial ways to define and assert identity, and to create it. This is socially, historically, and environmentally contingent and malleable. Relational ontology is a not a way to assert gendered difference; rather, asserting gendered difference is a way to maintain a relational ontology. The phenomenon of an "animal friendship" in Algonquian hunter-gatherer ontology is one example of a commonly held ontological mechanism (the animal friendship) manifesting in diverse ways (variation in the species of the animal friend). In this ontology, hunters with special relationships to specific prey had to maintain those relationships over the hunter's life. These friendships could sometimes be passed on to a hunter's family or band if they exhibited appropriate concern for the specific animal (Martin 1978:121-122; Tanner 1979:139) The mechanism of gender could also exhibit variability in the way people related to animals—including, incidentally, as a way of showing deference to specific animals (e.g., Le Clerq 1910:227).

In table 8.1, we have collated some rules about gendered activities, both mundane and explicitly ritual, from ethnographic accounts of the Wabanaki. This table is far from exhaustive, but codes information from some major primary or secondary accounts. The assumed ethnic or regional scope of the inferences are provided in works listed in the references column. Much of the data are derived from Hoffman's (1955:211) summary of Mi'kmaq ethnohistoric material. We emphasized that material because our focus here is on Nova Scotia archaeological contexts. This chart highlights that many tasks had clear material correlates and settings and were associated with specific genders. That many of these tasks could be expected to produce material correlates and so permeate the archaeological record suggests that gender also may account for some repeated patterns evident in the region's archaeological record—a case we have made elsewhere specifically with regards to architectural spaces (Hrynick and Betts 2014, 2017; Hrynick et al. 2012). As with Flannery's data, there is an economic emphasis in many of these gendered activities. Leonard's (2017) recent study of gender and Wabanaki dice games provides an example of the overlap of economic activity, gender, and relational principles. He ascribes the origins of *waltes*—a Wabanaki dice game in which the players quickly use a wooden bowl to flip the dice held within—to pre-Contact games using the pits of plums, likely harvested by women. Leonard uses this specific gendered action as a point of departure for a more detailed study of *waltes*, gender relations, and mobility.

Beyond direct historical connections of gendered activities, some artifacts recovered on the Maritime Peninsula are explicitly gendered. For instance, some petroglyphs on the Maritime Peninsula display phallic imagery, likely associated with shamanism (Hedden 1985; see Vastokas and Vastokas 1973:86–89). Women and men, evident from their unique clothing, figure prominently in the corpus of Mi'kmaw petroglyphs at Kejimkujik. Our own research has identified a series of unreported overtly phallic groundstone artifacts in contexts that range from the Archaic through the Woodland (also Lacroix 2015:85).

Contrasting with the overt male imagery of these artifacts, we have also identified a series of clay-lined *Mya arenaria* (softshell clam) shells with associated charcoal that corresponds to spark holders reported in the ethnohistoric literature, as we discuss below (also Betts 2019). Finally, there is evidence for gendered divisions of dwellings and sites, as we have reported in detail elsewhere (Hrynick et al. 2012; Hrynick and Betts 2014, 2017).

Table 8.1. Table collating a selection of accounts of gendered tasks in terms of gender, where the task was carried out, and what materials the task involved. Task location has been simplified to be domestic, meaning inside the dwelling or related to the construction of the dwelling; camp, meaning outside but within a residential area; riverine, meaning in or around a river; lacustrine, meaning around a freshwater body; ocean, referring to activities at or around estuaries, oceans, or the littoral; field/forest, to refer to non-residential terrestrial spaces not by bodies of water; ritual, to refer to activities associated with specific ritual places or structures; and generalized, referring to activities that occurred in a range of different spaces. Question marks indicate inferences made where the text was not explicit but was still detailed enough to permit a degree of confidence in interpretation. This table is non-exhaustive but emphasizes the degree to which ancient Wabanaki activities were gendered, and encourages consideration of how those activities may be reflected in the archaeological record spatially or artifactually.

Manufacturing				
Task	Gender(s)	Task Setting	Task Materials	References
Arrow manufacture	Men	domestic, camp? generalized?	wood, stone, feather	Denys 1908; Hoffman 1955:211; Lescarbot
Bow manufacture	Men	domestic?	wood, sinew, cordage, ax, knife, shell	Denys 1908; Hoffman 1955:211
Warclub manufacture	Men	domestic?	stone? wood?	Hoffman 1955:211
Fishtrap/weir manufacture	Men	riverine	wood, stone	Denys 1908; Hoffman 1955:211
Snowshoe frame manufacture	Men	domestic?	wood	Denys 1908; Hoffman 1955:211
Canoe frame manufacture	Men	?	wood	Denys 1908; Hoffman 1955:211
All other wood manufacture	Men	?	wood	Deny 1908; Hoffman 1955:211
Tobacco pipe manufacture	Men	?	wood, lobster claw, stone, bone	Denys 1898:215; Hoffman 1955:211
Manufacture of birch bark containers	Women	domestic? camp?	birchbark, bone needles	Denys 1908; Hoffman 1955:211
Snowshoe cording	Women	?	sinew, cordage	Denys 1908; Hoffman 1955:211
Goose feather robe manufacture	Women	?	feather	Denys 1908; Hoffman 1955:211

Hide clothing manufacture	Women	?	hides, needles (bone?)	Denys 1908; Hoffman 1955:211
Rush matting manufacture	Women	domestic?	rushes	Denys 1908; Hoffman 1955:211; Lescarbot 1914
Jewelry manufacture	Women	domestic?	stone? clay?	Lescarbot 1914:201
Gathering firewood	Women	field/forest	stone tools?	Speck 1935:79
Washing clothing	Women	?	?	Speck 1935:105
Moving wigwam	Women	generalized	packs? toboggans? sledges?	Denys 1908; Hoffman 1955:211
Setting-up wigwam	Women	domestic	posts, birch bark, bone needles	Denys 1908; Hoffman 1955:211; Thwaites 1898:40–41
Transport of camp gear	Women	generalized	packs? toboggans; sledges?	Denys 1908; Hoffman 1955:211; Lescarbot 1914:210
Hunting and Food Preparation				
Hunting	Men	field/forest	projectiles/snares	Denys 1908; Hoffman 1955:211
Fishing	Men	riverine, lacustrine, ocean	bone hooks, leisters, nets	Wallis and Wallis 1955:185a
Transport of game to camp	Women	generalized	cordage? toboggans? sledges?	Denys 1908:404-405; Hoffman 1955:211
Cooking food	Women	domestic, camp	ceramic vessels	Denys 1908; Hoffman 1955:211
Dressing game	Women	domestic, camp?	hide scrapers	Rand 1894:57
Food preservation	Women	domestic, camp?	?	Denys 1908; Hoffman 1955:211; Rand 1894:91
Hide preparation	Women	camp?	hide scrapers	Denys 1908; Hoffman 1955:211
Collection of maple sap	Women	field/forest	birchbark containers	Rasle 1724
Boiling of maple sap	Women			Rasle 1724
Shamanistic and Specific Religious Practices				
Menstrual seclusion	Women			Mailard 1758:51
Scapulimancy	Men	ritual	bone	Speck 1997
Sweathouses - healing	Men (adult)	ritual	medicinal plants, sweathouse	cf. Prins and McBride 2007:35–36

Sweathouses-divination	Men (adult)	ritual	medicinal plants, sweathouse	cf. Prins and McBride 2007:35–36
Setting-up sweathouses	Men	ritual	birchbark, wood, posts, stone	Hoffman 1955:306
Pecking petroglyphs	Men?	ritual (bedrock outcrops)	hammerstone	inferred from shamanistic association (Hedden 2004)
Preservation of fire in winter	Women	generalized	shell, woodchuck skin, rotted wood or yellow birch	Lockerby 2004:408–409 [Maillard ca. 1740]; Nicolar 2007:196-198
Wearing a string of red beads	Women	generalized	beads (stone?), cord?	Speck 1935:29
Wearing gorget	Men	generalized	stone	Speck 1935:29
Wearing bone amulet	Men	generalized	moose bone, bear, racoon penis bone	Speck 1935:29
Miscellaneous				
Dancing at special events	Men and Women	camp?	Men: moose antler rattle; Women: wooden club	Wallis and Wallis 1955:186
Drumming at special events	Men and Women	camp?	drum or roll of birchbark	Maillard 1758
Playing ball	Men and Women			Brown 1889:45
Playing shinny?	Women	riverine/lacustrine (frozen)	stick, block of wood	Flannery 1939:89; Dubious according to Favour 1974
Playing waltes	Men and Women	camp?	wood or bone dice	Wallis and Wallis 1955:195–200
Stone slinging	Men and Women	camp, generalized	stones, rawhide line	Speck 1940:47, 86, 170, 180
Bark biting	Children of either gender and Women	camp	birchbark	Butler and Hadlock 1957:48

Source: This table is derived from primary and secondary sources indicated in the references column and draws heavily on Hoffman's (1955) summary of Mi'kmaq historic accounts. This table glosses, we expect, variation within the Wabanaki homeland.

Port Joli Harbour: A Case Study in Gendered Actions, Objects, Spaces, and Places

Port Joli Harbour is located on Nova Scotia's South Shore and is home to a series of coastal sites primarily dating ca. 1500–400 cal BP, spanning the Middle Maritime Woodland to Protohistoric periods. Intensive occupation of Port Joli began with the development of the harbour itself (Betts 2019; Neil et al. 2014). Extensive archaeological work has tracked the dynamic culture history of this harbour and has been published in detail elsewhere (see Betts et al. 2017; Betts 2019), but we review the salient settlement and subsistence points here: (1) by 1450 cal BP occupation of the harbour was intensive, marked by the rapid accumulation of soft-shell clam in large middens, some over 1 m thick, with indistinguishable radiocarbon dates from upper and lower strata (Betts 2019; (2) potentially contemporaneous occupations occur throughout the occupational sequence at Port Joli Harbour; (3) Late Maritime Woodland economic shifts largely follow those described elsewhere in the region (Black 2002, and this volume): structurally there are fewer deep, clam-rich shell middens, increased terrestrial mammal (especially cervid) hunting, and decreased reliance on birds; and (4) during the Late Maritime Woodland, sites became larger and more numerous, many overlying Middle Maritime Woodland deposits, and others as new task-specific sites.

Apparently regionally unique to Port Joli are large, relatively sterile, soft-shell clam middens, which we interpret as communal summer clam-processing middens (Betts 2019; Betts et al. 2017). Year-round occupation of the harbour in smaller campsites appears to span the entire occupational sequence, augmented by sizable warm-season aggregations at some large sites, such as AlDf-24, first emphasizing clam processing and perhaps storage, and then fishing and cervid hunting/processing.

History of Spatial Organization at Port Joli Harbour

Concurrent with a focus on studies of ancient Wabanaki economies at Port Joli Harbour, which focused primarily on shell middens, we undertook an intensive study of architecture that emphasized the identification of architectural features and, when possible, sought to excavate them in full horizontal extent with high-resolution spatial control (Hrynick and Betts 2019; Hrynick et al. 2012). The result was a detailed understanding of divisions of space at the intra-feature and site level, as well as of the settlement pattern of the Woodland-period occupation of the harbour. More detailed information about methods, seasonality inferences, and chronostratigraphy may be found in Betts (2019). In the sections that follow, we outline the organization of space at Port Joli sites with specific reference to gender. We posit that the changing historical context of shifting gendered places, at multiple scales, is a way to track gender at Port Joli Harbour. Our understanding of gender at these places relies on direct historical analogy, which is simultaneously historical context for gendered action proxied by the spatial organization we outline.

Middle Maritime Woodland

As described in the ethnographic record, Wabanaki houses were constructed by women (see table 8.1). Given that, cross-culturally, hunter-gatherers usually erect a shelter anywhere they spend the night (Binford 1990), a woman assembling a house was likely among the first actions at Port Joli Harbour, sometime around 1500 cal BP (1540±40 BP). However, the oldest structure identified in Port Joli is actually a sweat house (figure 8.1), found stratigraphically below two Middle Maritime Woodland house floors. These structures are located ca. 300 m inland from the shore on a knoll in the midst of a fen, at a site designated AlDf-30 (figure 8.2). Fauna in the adjacent "kitchen midden" suggests these houses were cold-season structures (Betts et al. 2017), but the sweathouse, we surmise, was used in the warm season (Hrynick and Betts 2017), which was probably the first season the harbour was ever occupied.

About 500 m to the northeast from AlDf-30, but 250 m closer to the coast, is the largest known extant shell midden from Nova Scotia, AlDf-24 Area A (figure 8.3). This large, almost featureless midden developed rapidly, ca. 1500 cal BP. We expect that houses were either erected on the beach or in Area B, a black-soil midden directly behind the Area A midden, on the forest side. The available fauna from the Area A midden indicates a warm-season occupation

Figure 8.1. Photograph, facing approximately northwest, of the AlDf-30 sweathouse feature.

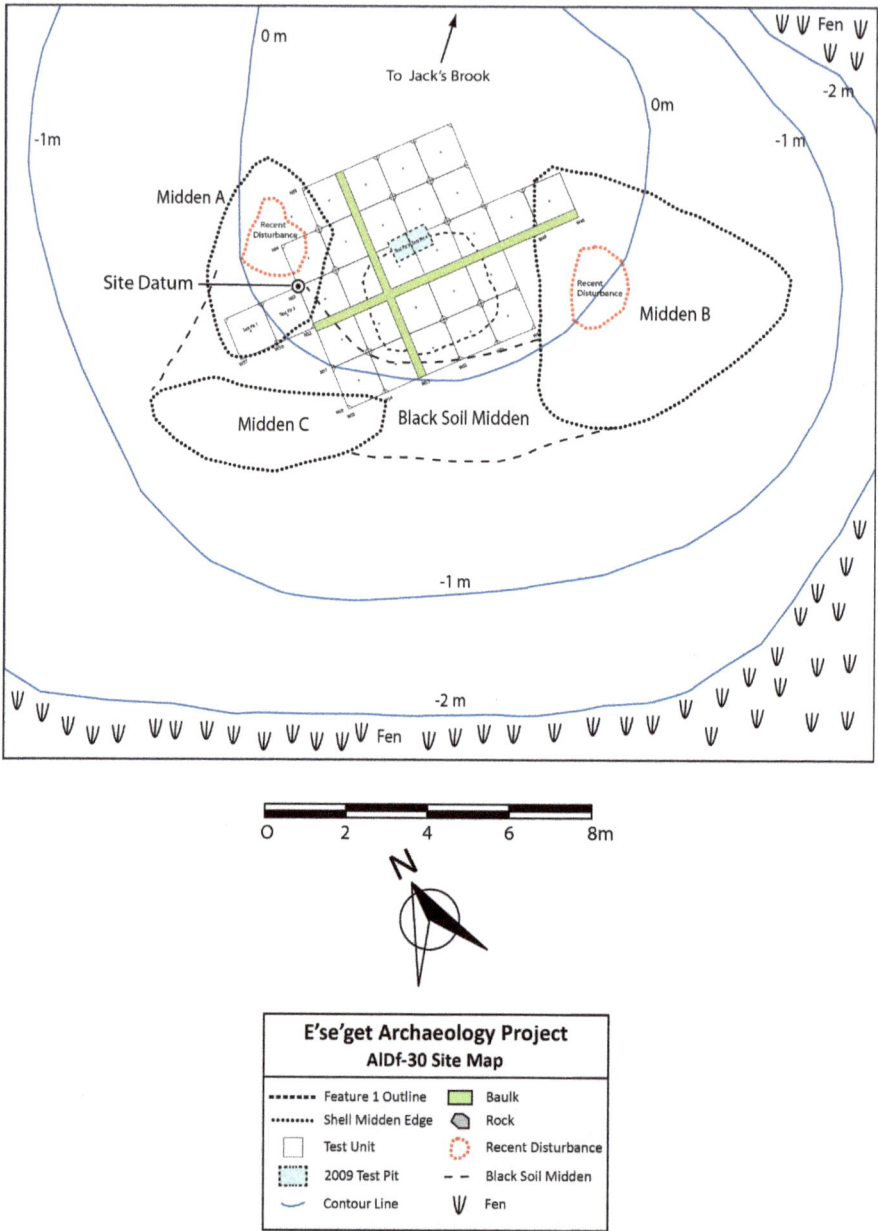

Figure 8.2. Map of AlDf-30 (reproduced from Betts 2019).

(Betts 2019), and the radiocarbon dates, which are essentially contemporary from the top of the midden to the bottom, suggest rapid accumulation, likely the result of summer aggregations for communal processing and storage (Betts et al. 2017). The midden also dates to approximately 1500 cal BP.

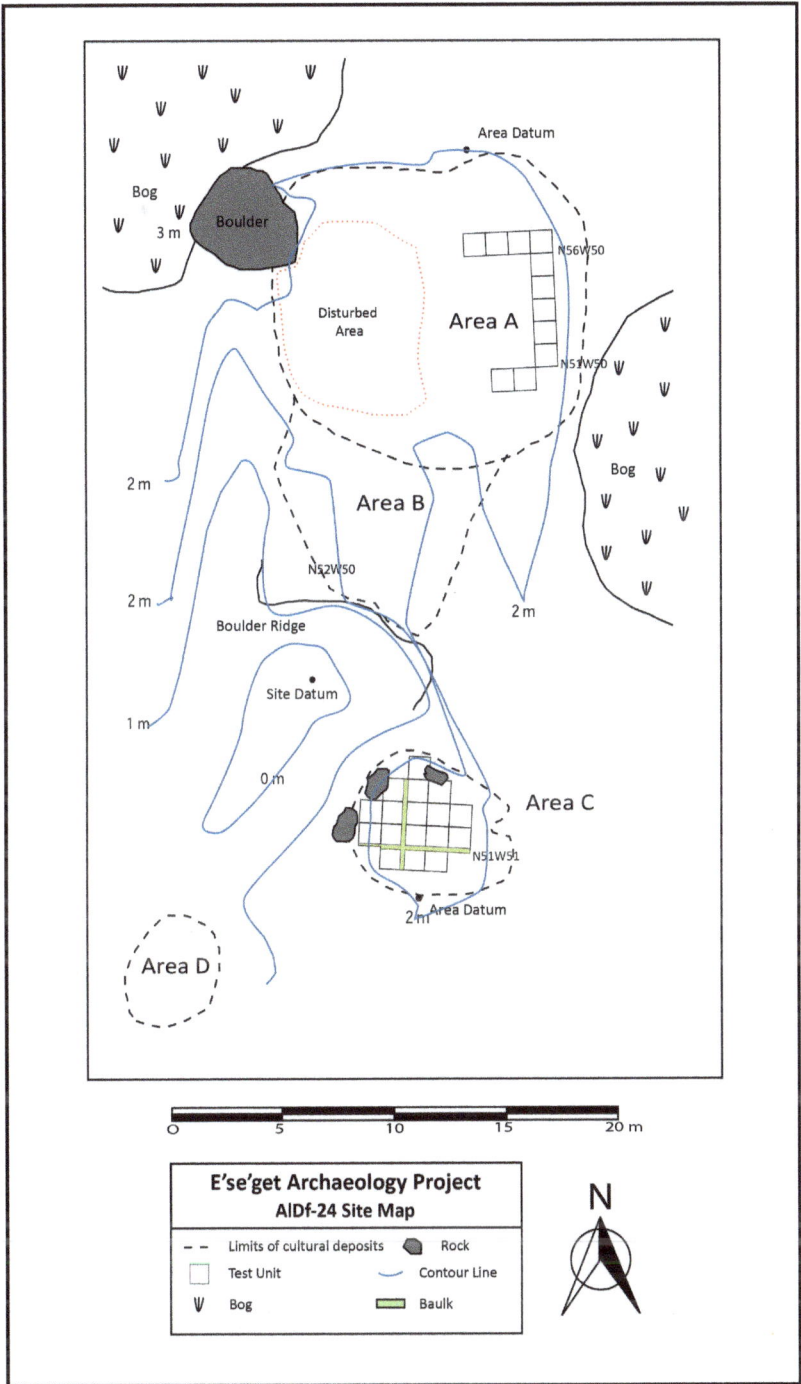

Figure 8.3. Map of AlDf-24 (reproduced from Betts 2019).

We believe the AlDf-24 Area A midden, and the unidentified houses associated with it, were accompanied by the construction of the sweathouse excavated at AlDf-30. While the midden and its associated wigwams were a public location (Betts 2019), the sweathouse likely was not. Sweathouses are, after dwellings, among the most mentioned structures in the region's ethnographic record (e.g., Denys 1908; Le Clerq 1910; Wallis and Wallis 1955:123). Unlike dwellings, which were constructed by women but occupied by whole families, sweathouses were male spaces, associated with shamanism and healing in many cases, and host to explicitly secluded male activity (Denys 1908:416; Wallis and Wallis 1955:308; see Hrynick and Betts 2014, 2017). The shamanistic association with some sweats further emphasizes the likely male context of the sweathouses. Mechling (1959:175) and Wherry (2003:56), for instance, note that, while extant, early ethnographic references to women as semi-specialized religious practitioners are exceedingly rare.

The secluded nature of AlDf-30 and its location within a fen, close to a freshwater stream, would have made it an ideal location for sacred male activities—indeed, even today the locale feels isolated and private from other sites at Port Joli. The sweathouse itself was a semi-subterranean basin approximately 2.5 m to 3 m in diameter. A cairn of large stones was constructed in the centre of the structure, with one large boulder dominating the pile. The sweathouse lacked artifactual material and charcoal, but did contain one piece of ceramic and a fire-cracked stone. Its stratigraphic position and association with the sherd indicate it was used in the Middle Maritime Woodland. We believe that fire-heated rocks were brought into the sweathouse and placed around the cairn. Ethnographic accounts (see Hrynick and Betts 2017) indicate that similar sweathouse features sometimes had medicines poured over or smeared on them, which would vaporize to become an inhalant. Pollen analysis from the nearby fen indicates that it contained plants suited to this use (Neil et al. 2014). In summary, the initial use of AlDf-30 was likely by men, who used it to heal and to spiritually prepare themselves for their interactions with the objects and subjects of the natural world (Hrynick and Betts 2017, 2019).

Is there evidence of similar female spaces and female ritual at Port Joli? The notion of secluded male space certainly suggests that women's ritual may have also been separated, but work at Port Joli suggests it may have been highly visible. Cross-culturally, shellfish harvesting and processing is often the domain of women (Waselkov 1987:96-99). It therefore may be possible to view the intensive activity that resulted in the construction of the most visible human feature in Port Joli, the AlDf-24 Area A midden, as a woman's space. This is supported by the artifact assemblage from the midden, which is nearly devoid of lithics and dominated by ceramics, which are mostly made and used by women in the global ethnographic record (the literature is clear that men mostly made stone tools). In terms of ritual, however, a new class of artifacts was discovered at Port Joli, which directly evokes female ritual and transforms the midden into a place of female-centred ceremony as well as domestic production.

Five unmodified clamshell valves filled with raw clay mixed with charcoal (figure 8.4) were recovered from the AlDf-24 Area A midden (Betts 2019).

Figure 8.4. Clay-lined softshell-clam spark holders from AlDf-24 Area A.

These artifacts correspond to a type described in the ethnographic literature and associated exclusively with women (Betts 2019). Clam shells were lined with clay, and fungi or rotting wood were placed in them as a fuel source. A spark was placed in this tinder and, when the clam valves were closed over it, the punk would smoulder in a low-oxygen environment for a long duration. Maillard (1758, in Lockerby 2004:408–409) reported:

> To preserve fire [...] we would entrust it to the care of our war-chief's women, who took turns to preserve the spark, using half-rotten pine wood covered with ash. Sometimes this fire lasted up to three moons. When it lasted the span of three moons, the fire became sacred and magical to us. [...] We would all gather together and [...] when our numbers were complete, we would gather round and, without regard to rank or age, light our pipes at the fire. We would suck in the smoke and keep it in our mouths, and one by one would puff it out into the face of the woman who had last preserved the spark, telling her that she was worthy above all to share in the benign influence of the Father of Light, the Sun, because she had so skillfully preserved His emanations.

Similar artifacts have not been reported elsewhere, which is notable given that such processing middens are otherwise unreported in the archaeological record on the Maritime Peninsula. The presence of spark holders in this unique midden context suggests such female activities may have taken place in locations that were largely created and maintained by women, and which were associated with substantial gatherings of people.

While female-dominated spaces were open, accessible, and public, at Port Joli the sweathouse was a secluded, formal, task-specific structure (and contrasting with a variety of more expedient sweat houses described in the ethnohistoric record). However, we do not think this formality is surprising: the landscape was new, it was being intensively exploited, and relationships with this new environment and the animals in it needed to be maintained. Furthermore, a dramatic feature (the shell midden) was being constructed a short distance away, and this new constructed female space may have needed a formal male counterpart. Additionally, in such a new locale, everything balanced on the successful procurement of natural species (clams and other fauna, such as deer). In the ethnographic record, Wabanaki sacred ecology calls for addressing such resource precarity with pronounced ritual. Finally, and perhaps most importantly, if the initial occupation of the harbour involved aggregations of many families for the purposes of shellfish gathering and processing, an activity that appears to have been involved with group ceremony focused on women, then ritual male activity may have been an obligation, as well as a mechanism to reinforce group activities and assuage any social tensions which may have developed. While there is good ethnographic evidence to support these interpretations, what is fundamentally clear is that as soon as the landscape was inhabited by ancient Mi'kmaq, it was segregated into gendered and sacred spaces at multiple settlement scales and arranged as a sacred and social landscape whose organization ensured a proper interaction with the subjects of the natural and spiritual worlds.

Within habitation sites, however, spatial segregation was also important, but perhaps less rigid than it would be later in the historical sequence at Port Joli Harbour. Shortly after the use of AlDf-30 as a sweathouse, it was converted to a dwelling feature. Inhabitants repurposed the interior stone architecture of the sweathouse as an axial feature, dividing the subsequent dwelling features into two halves. At this time, a sweathouse may have been shifted to nearby AlDf-31 (Betts 2019). Relying largely on historic analogy, the axial division of dwelling space is suggestive of gendered divisions of domestic space, although the small number of artifacts in the feature precludes identifying robust spatial patterning (Hrynick and Betts 2014).

Late Maritime Woodland

The Late Maritime Woodland at Port Joli was marked by less intensive communal processing of shells toward an emphasis on terrestrial mammal and fish runs by ca. 1300 BP (Betts et al. 2017). Plausibly, such intensification—especially surrounding herring runs—would be expected to be associated with aggregation, which likely occurred closer to rivers at the head of the harbour (Betts 2019). At Port Joli, in the Late Maritime Woodland AlDf-24 Area C, well-defined spatial seclusion at the site scale appears to be less pronounced, as the large summer processing midden in Area A stopped accumulating just prior to the Late Woodland transition at the site. Rather, shell middens accumulated next to dwellings, which were likely occupied in the cold season. During this period, we have not identified any purpose-specific sweathouses, nor any large processing middens or clay-lined clam shells in Port Joli. Given the lack of sweathouses generally identified in the archaeological record, this may reflect archaeological visibility and current models for archaeological testing, or it may reflect a switch to more expedient sweating practices on a landscape more familiar to its inhabitants.

At AlDf-24 Area C, a Late Maritime Woodland dwelling feature was characterized by repeated reuse over a short period of time. These intensive occupations produced a remarkably persistent division of space in the dwelling, with a robust (ca. 7,000 pieces) of lithic debitage clustered on the northwest of the dwelling, contrasting with ceramics confined mostly to the southeast of the dwelling feature, along with scrapers (especially near the hearth) and bifaces.

This pronounced patterning is consistent with near-universal agreement in the ethnographic literature that Wabanaki dwelling features were spatially segregated by gender (Hrynick et al. 2012). In Port Joli, this intense separation of activities within the domestic space occurred at a time when distinct middens were diminished from their Middle Maritime Woodland predecessors. As sites became more complex and less spatially segregated, there appears to have been an increased emphasis on this codified, gendered practice within the house, at least at winter sites. We have yet to excavate the one of the large summer aggregations sites located at the head of the harbour, but we expect considerable spatial patterning to have occurred there as well.

Discussion: Gender and Place-Making at Port Joli Harbour

While we share in concerns raised by other archaeologists about the risks of superficially equating artifacts and actions with particular genders (e.g., Ginge 1996) and of simplifying gendered categories in prehistory, undue caution can also serve to mask consideration of what the ethnohistoric record suggests was a central way Wabanaki people related to one another, their worlds, and the cosmos (see table 8.1 and discussion, above). Robust culture-historical research empowered by theoretical focus on historical process has led to a recognition that hyper-emphasis on equifinality risks accepting ecologically derived general models that obscure culture and agency.

A crucial result of recent theoretical work about hunter-gatherer relational ontologies has been to broaden anthropological focus on the immediate inter-action between hunter and prey and overt shamanism as the primary cosmo-logical actions of hunter-gatherers to maintain relationships among people, people and things, and people and cosmological beings (e.g., Betts et al. 2012, 2015; Hill 2011; Zedeño 2009). For archaeologists, such relationships are chal-lenging to interpret because while economic activities are often quite visible archaeologically, the quotidian actions used to maintain human-animal relation-ships are often commonplace, and thus are masked as routine domestic activity. That episodic shamanistic behaviours were primarily associated with males also led them to be foregrounded in ethnohistoric accounts, obscuring the important role of women in maintaining spiritual relationships. One way to address this is to foreground the agencies and actions of both men and women in how ancient Wabanaki made their places in the world. In relational societies, domestic activity—that is, the everyday actions of men and women, their routines—was evidence of a spiritual act. If so, the archaeological record is replete with evidence of relationality. This offers a relational and culturist window onto persistent questions of Wabanaki place and domestic action. It also opens notions of pro-curement and use of the landscape as overt spiritual acts. The relationships with animals notwithstanding, the question of family hunting territories leaps to mind, in which the relation between male hunter, and place and game has been the primary concern (Snow 1968).

Studies of hunter-gatherers tend to envision evidence of territories as embedded in implicitly male activity, proxied, for instance, by the acquisition of toolstone from distant places (e.g., Loring 2018), or in migrations in the pursuit of prey. Port Joli and the apparent role of women as ritual actors in aggregation emphasizes a socially integrative role they apparently played in such aspects of hunter-gatherer lifeways. For example, they moved fire around the landscape, and when they arrived at summer aggregation centres like AlDf-24, they used fire as an apparent means to unify groups in shared ritual. Furthermore, the large aggregations and the group movements they entailed appear to have centred on the collection of clams, which was also the domain of women. At Port Joli, aggregations may have required gendered ritual due to the explicit requirements of reducing tensions inherent in large groups, the tendency to require clear and appropriate signalling when others are present, and for maintaining the proper human-animal relationships in the presence of large groups of people. Whatever the rational between the ritual and the large midden associated with it, both the routine economic activity and the formal ritual created Port Joli as a special place. The large midden at AlDf-24 A was, quite literally, a monument to place-making in this special harbour.

The seclusion of males in a special location at AlDf-30 to engage in sweats is also place-making. While gendered seclusion to create homosocial spaces is common cross-culturally among hunter-gatherers (see Endicott 1999:413), the relational, heterosocial underpinning of this deserves further attention. Seclusion and notions of seclusion are relative. For instance, Berndt (1965) has argued that gendered seclusion and secrecy in Australian Aboriginal religious practice may in actuality be viewed as a socially constrained form of interaction between genders, including shared ritual knowledge.

The actions we have outlined here do not form a unified theory of ancient Wabanaki gender. Rather, they offer a series of examples that implies two things: gender is visible in quotidian actions that are abundant in the archaeological record, and, theoretically, gendered actions were important history—and place-making practices. The former realization may encourage archaeologists in the region to further explore gender, and, in doing so, form more holistic connections among specific actions and gender. From there, diachronic and regional diversity against general trends can help to illuminate gendered agency.

While limited, the archaeological data outlined here along with the ethno-historic data (table 8.1) suggest some patterns to explore, and some patterns that appear particularly historically robust with regard to gender. The first of these may be the overwhelming tendency toward specialized ritual action (often secluded) associated with men, while women's ritual action was more public, and indeed quite probably the most visible of all activities in the archaeological record.

Conclusions

Among hunter-gatherers, gender is often considered in narrow economic terms, couched as the division of labour, while architecture is considered primarily as simply shelter. Yet, as we argue here, gender was not epiphenomenal to how people made their places at Port Joli Harbour, a realization that lends itself to a multi-scalar consideration of the implications of gendered action and agency in the Far Northeast. Emboldened by increasing theoretical interest in historical process and the relational ontology, we anticipate opportunity for theoretically robust and historically contextualized examinations that move beyond descriptive approaches to the gendered divisions of labour to situate gendered action in the archaeological record of the Far Northeast in much the way it appears in the ethnographic record for Algonquian hunter-gatherers, in that myriad gendered behaviours, seclusions, and inclusions were crucial to the maintenance of the world. Taken together, the artifacts and spaces we have described here suggest that the gendered relationships so crucial to Historic-period Algonquian hunter-gatherers were present before and at Contact. Gender was a crucial historical process pervading quotidian and ritual life, and as such was a locus for people to respond to and create their world at Port Joli Harbour, and throughout the Far Northeast.

Acknowledgements

Both authors contributed equally to this chapter. We thank Ken Holyoke for inviting us to participate in this volume, and the various participants for helpful comments received at the 2019 Québec City Canadian Archaeological Association session from which it developed. Funding for this research was provided by the Canadian Museum of History. Various forms of institutional support for this research were provided by the Universities of Connecticut and New Brunswick. David Black and Lauren Cudmore each contributed to this research and provided comments on portions of it, for which we thank them. Acadia First Nation has been a supporter of and collaborator on this project since its inception, for which we are profoundly grateful. Finally, we would like to thank Ken Holyoke, again, and an anonymous peer reviewer for their insightful comments on this work.

References Cited

Axtell, James
1981   *The Indian Peoples of Eastern America: A Documentary History of the Sexes.* Oxford University Press, New York.

Berndt, Catherine H.
1965   Woman and the "Secret Life." In *Aboriginal Man in Australia*, edited by Ronald M. Berndt and Catherine H. Berndt, pp. 238–282. Angus and Robertson, Sydney.

Betts, Matthew W. (editor)
2019   *Place-Making in the Pretty Harbour*. Canadian Museum of History Mercury Series. University of Ottawa Press, Ottawa.

Betts, Matthew W., David W. Black, and Susan E. Blair
2012   Perspectivism, Mortuary Symbolism, and Human-Shark Relationships on the Maritime Peninsula. *American Antiquity* 77(4):621–645.

Betts, Matthew W., Meghan Burchell, and Bernd R. Schöne
2017   An Economic History of the Maritime Woodland Period in Port Joli Harbour, Nova Scotia. *Journal of the North Atlantic* Special Volume 10:18–41.

Betts, Matthew W., Mari Hardenber, and Ian Stirling
2015   How Animals Create Human History: Relational Ecology and the Dorset-Polar Bear Connection. *American Antiquity* 80(1):89–112.

Binford, Lewis R.
1990   Mobility, Housing, and Environment: A Comparative Study. *Journal of Anthropological Research* 46(2):119–152.

Black, David W.
2002   Out of the Blue and Into the Black: The Middle-Late Maritime Woodland Transition in the Quoddy Region, New Brunswick, Canada. In *Northeast Subsistence-Settlement Change: A.D. 700–1300*, edited by John P. Hart, and Christina B. Rieth, pp. 301–320. New York State Museum Bulletin #496. University of the State of New York/State Education Department, Albany.

Brightman, Robert A.
1973   *Grateful Prey: Rock Cree Human-Animal Relationships*. Canadian Plains Research Center, Regina.

Brown, Mrs. W. W.
1889   *Some Indoor and Outdoor Games of the Wabanaki Indians*. Transactions of the Royal Society of Canada Vol. 6, Montréal.

Butler, Eva L., and Wendell S. Hadlock
1957   *Uses of Birch-bark in the Northeast*. Robert Abbe Museum Bulletin VII. Robert Abbe Museum, Bar Harbor, Maine.

Cipolla, Craig N.
2019   Taming the Ontological Wolves: Learning from Iroquoian Effigy Objects. *American Anthropologist* 121(3):613–627.

Creese, John L.
2018   Place-Making in Canadian Archaeology. *Canadian Journal of Archaeology* 42:46–56.

2013   Rethinking Early Village Development in Southern Ontario: Toward a History of Place-Making. *Canadian Journal of Archaeology* 37(2):185-218.

Denys, Nicolas
1908   *Description and Natural History of the Coasts of North America (Acadia)*. The Champlain Society, Toronto.

Descola, Philippe
2013   *The Ecology of Others: Anthropology and the Question of Nature.* Prickly Paradigm
        Press, Chicago.
Endicott, Karen L.
1999   Gender Relations in Hunter-Gatherer Societies. In *The Cambridge Encyclopedia
        of Hunters and Gatherers*, edited by Richard B. Lee, and Richard Daly, pp. 411–
        418. Cambridge University Press, Cambridge.
Favour, Edith
1974   *Indian Games, Toys, and Pastimes of Maine and the Maritimes.* Bulletin X. Robert
        Abbe Museum, Bar Harbor, Maine.
Feit, Harvey A.
1973   The Ethno-Ecology of the Waswanipi Cree, or How Hunters Can Manage
        Their Resources. In *Cultural Ecology: Readings on the Canadian Indians and
        Eskimos*, edited by Bruce Cox, pp. 115–125. McLelland and Stewart,
        Toronto.
Flannery, Regina
1939   *An Analysis of Coastal Algonquian Culture.* Anthropological Series No. 7. Catholic
        University of America Press, Washington.
Ginge, Birgitte
1996   Identifying Gender in the Archaeological Record: Revising Our Stereotypes.
        Etruscan Studies 3(1):65–74.
Gonzalez, Ellice B.
1981   *Changing Economic Roles for Micmac Men and Women: An Ethnohistorical Analysis.*
        Mercury Series No. 72, National Museums of Canada, Ottawa.
Hallowell, A. Irving
1960   Ojibwa Ontology, Behavior, and World View. In *Culture in History: Essays in
        Honor of Paul Radin*, edited by Stanley Diamond, pp. 19–52. Columbia
        University Press, New York.
Harris, Oliver J. T., and Craig N. Cipolla
2017   *Archaeological Theory in the New Millennium: Introducing Current Perspectives.*
        Routledge, Oxford.
Hays-Gilpin, Kelley Ann
2008   Gender. In *Handbook of Archaeological Theories*, edited by R. Alexander Bentley,
        Herbert D. G. Maschner, and Christopher Chippindale, pp. 335–349. AltaMira
        Press, Lanham, Maryland.
Hedden, Mark
1985   Sexuality in Maine Petroglyphs (Comments on Cover for Spring 1985 MAS
        Bulletin). *Maine Archaeological Society Bulletin* 25(1):3–9.
2004   Passamaquoddy Shamanism and Rock Art in Machias Bay, Maine. In *Rock Art
        of Eastern North America*, edited by Carol Diaz-Granados, and James R. Duncan,
        pp. 319–343. University of Alabama Press, Tuscaloosa.
Hill, Erica
2011   Animals as Agents: Hunting Ritual and Relational Ontologies in Prehistoric
        Alaska and Chukotka. *Cambridge Archaeological Journal* 21(3):407–426.

Hoffman, Bernard G.

1955   The Historical Ethnography of the Micmac of the Sixteenth and Seventeenth Centuries. PhD dissertation, Department of Anthropology, University of California, Berkeley.

Hornborg, Anne-Christine

2006   Visiting the Six Worlds: Shamanistic Journeys in Canadian Mi'kmaq Cosmology. *Journal of American Folklore* 119(473):312–336.

2013   Mi'kmaq Landscapes: From Animism to Sacred Ecology. Ashgate Publishing, Burlington, Vermont.

Hrynick, M. Gabriel, and Matthew W. Betts

2014   Identifying Ritual Structures in the Archaeological Record: A Maritime Woodland Period Sweathouse from Nova Scotia, Canada. *Journal of Anthropological Archaeology* 35:92–105.

2017   A Relational Approach to Hunter-Gatherer Architecture and Gendered Use of Space at Port Joli Harbour, Nova Scotia. *Journal of the North Atlantic* (Special Volume) 10:1–17.

2019   Features. In *Place-Making in the Pretty Harbour*. Canadian Museum of History Mercury Series. University of Ottawa Press, Ottawa.

Hrynick, M. Gabriel, Matthew W. Betts, and David W. Black

2012   A Late Maritime Woodland Period Dwelling Feature from Nova Scotia's South Shore: Evidence for Patterned Use of Domestic Space. *Archaeology of Eastern North America* 40:1–25.

Lacroix, Dominic

2015   Mobility, Ceremonialism, and Group Identity in Archaic Newfoundland. PhD dissertation, Memorial University of Newfoundland, St. John's.

Le Clerq, Chrestien

1910   *New Relations of Gaspesia with the Customs and Religions of the Gaspesian Indians.* Edited by William F. Gonong. Champlain Society, Toronto.

Lelièvre, Michelle

2017   *Unsettling Mobility: Mediating Mi'kmaw Sovereignty in Post-contact Nova Scotia.* University of Arizona Press, Tucson.

Leonard, Kevin

2017   Why Waltes was a Woman's Game. In *Prehistoric Games of North American Indians: Subarctic to Mesoamerica*, edited by Barbara Voorhies, pp. 19–33. University of Utah Press, Salt Lake City.

Lescarbot, Marc

1914   *History of New France*, Volume III. Champlain Society, Toronto.

Lockerby, Earle

2004   Ancient Mi'kmaw Customs: A Shaman's Revelations. *The Canadian Journal of Native Studies* 24(2):403–423.

Loring, Stephen

2018   To the Uttermost Ends of the Easrt… Ramah Chert in Time and Space. In *Ramah Chert: A Lithic Odyssey*, edited by Jenneth E. Curtis, and Pierre M. Desrosiers, pp. 169–219. Parks Canada and Avataq Cultural Institute, Inukjuak, Quebec.

Maillard, Antoine Simon

1758   *An Account of the Customs and Manners of the Micmakis and Maricheets Savage Nations, Now Dependent on the Government of Cape Breton.* Hooper and Morley, London.

Martin, Calvin

1978   *Keepers of the Game: Indian-animal Relationships and the Fur Trade.* University of California Press, Berkeley.

Mechling, William H.

1959   The Malecite Indians with Notes on the Micmacs (Concluded). *Anthropologica* 8:1–160.

Neil, Karen, Konrad Gajewski, and Matthew Betts

2014   Human-Ecosystem Interactions in Relation to Holocene Environmental Change in Port Joli Harbour, Southwestern Nova Scotia, Canada. *Quaternary Research* 81(2):203–212.

Nicolar, Joseph

2007   *The Life and Traditions of the Red Man.* Edited by Annette Kolodny. Duke University Press, Durham, North Carolina.

Pawling, Micah

2016   Wabanaki Homeland and Mobility: Concepts of Home in Nineteenth-Century Maine. *Ethnohistory* 63(4):621–643.

Prins, Harald E. L., and Bunny McBride

2007   Asticou's Island Domain: Wabanaki Peoples at Mount Desert Island 1500-2000. 2 vols. Abbe Museum and National Park Service, Boston.

Rand, Silas T.

1894   *Legends of the Micmacs.* Wellesley Philological Publications, New York.

Rasles, Sebastien

1896 [1724]   *Lettres édifiantes et curieuses escrites des missions étrangères par quelques missionaires de la Compagnie de Jésus.* In Jesuit Relations 67. Burrows Brothers, Cleveland.

Robinson, Brian S., and Jennifer C. Ort

2011   Palaeoindian and Archaic Period Traditions: Particular Explanations from New England. In *Hunter-Gatherer Archaeology as Historical Process*, edited by Kenneth E. Sassaman, and Donald H. Holly Jr., pp. 209–226. University of Arizona Press, Tucson.

Sassaman, Kenneth E.

1992   Lithic Technology and the Hunter-Gatherer Sexual Division of Labor. *North American Archaeologist* 13(3):249–262.

Snow, Dean

1968   Wabanaki "Family Hunting Territories." *American Anthropologist* 70(6): 1143–1151.

Speck, Frank G.

1935   Penobscot Tales and Religious Beliefs. *Journal of American Folklore* 48:1–107.

1997   *Penobscot Man: Life History of a Forest Tribe in Maine.* University of Maine Press, Orono.

Tanner, Adrian

1979   *Bringing Home Animals: Religious Ideology and Mode of Production of the Mistassini Cree Hunters.* St. Martin's Press, New York.

Thwaites, Rueben Gold (editor)

1898   *Jesuit Relations and Allied Documents: Travels and Explorations of the Jesuit Missionaries in New France 1610 – 1791 (Vol III, Acadia).* Burrows Brothers, Cleveland.

Vastokas, Joan M., and Romas Vastokas

1973   *Sacred Art of the Algonkians: A Study of the Peterborough Petroglyphs.* Mansard Press, Peterborough, Ontario.

Viveiros de Castro, Eduardo

1998   Cosmological Deixis and Amerindian Perspectivism. *Journal of the Royal Anthropological Institute* 4:469–488.

2004a   Exchanging Perspectives: The Transformation of Objects into Subjects in Amerindian Ontologies. *Common Knowledge* 10:463–484.

2004b   Perspectival Anthropology and the Method of Controlled Equivocation. *Tipití* 2(1):3–22.

Wallis, Wilson D., and Ruth Sawtell Wallis

1955   *The Micmac Indians of Eastern Canada.* University of Minnesota Press, Minneapolis.

Waselkov, Gregory A.

1987   Shellfish Gathering and Shell Midden Archaeology. *Advances in Archaeological Method and Theory* 10:93–210.

Watts, Christopher (editor)

2013   *Relational Archaeologies: Humans, Animals, Things.* Routledge, London.

Wherry, Leah

2003   Wabanaki Women Religious Practitioners. Master's thesis, Department of Anthropology, University of New Brunswick, Fredericton.

Zedeño, María Nieves

2009   Animating by Association: Index Objects and Relational Taxonomies. *Cambridge Archaeological Journal* 19(3):407–417.

ALL OUR RELATIONS

Re-Animating the Mi'kmaw Landscape on Nova Scotia's Chignecto Peninsula

9

Michelle A. Lelièvre [1], Alyssa Abram,[2]
Cynthia Martin,[3] and Mallory Moran[4]

Abstract

We report the preliminary results of our archaeological fieldwork at Qospemk (at the lake), or Newville Lake, and Spruce Island, both located at the eastern edge of Nova Scotia's Chignecto Peninsula. Bordered by the Minas Basin to the south and Chignecto Bay to the west, the Chignecto Peninsula is unique among the regions of the Far Northeast; its shores experience the highest and most powerful tides in the world, and its onshore landscape—carved by the retreat of glaciers from 13,000 to 11,000 BP—is dominated by a series of low hills that rise rapidly from the southern coast. We focus particularly on the period after 3400 BP, when Shaw et alia (2010) argue the Minas Basin experienced a rapid tidal expansion. Preliminary radiocarbon dates from Qospemk suggest possible human dwelling here as early as ca. 3300 BP, a time period that archaeologists refer to as the Late or Terminal Archaic, and that some Mi'kmaw researchers and Elders describe as Mu Awsami Saqiwe'k, or Not So Recent People. Guided by the research principles articulated by members of the Mi'kmawey Debert Elders' Advisory Council, and framed through the diverse expertise of our research team (which includes Indigenous and non-Indigenous members, formally trained archaeologists, and artists), we offer an interpretation of our preliminary archaeological findings that emphasizes the relatedness of today's L'nuk with L'nuk of the past.

Résumé

Nous rapportons ici les résultats préliminaires de nos fouilles à Qospemk («au lac», Newville Lake,) et Spruce Island, deux sites situés sur la côte est de la péninsule de Chignectou, en Nouvelle-Écosse. Bordée au sud par le bassin des Mines et à l'ouest par la Baie de Chignectou, la péninsule de Chignectou est un endroit unique dans l'extrême Nord-Est (*Far*

Northeast). Ses rives sont battues par les plus grandes et plus puissantes marées du monde, et son paysage, sculpté par le retrait des glaciers de 13 000 à 11 000 ans AA, est marqué par une série de basses collines s'élevant rapidement vers le nord à partir de la côte sud. Nous nous concentrons tout spécialement sur la période postérieure à 3 400 AA, date à laquelle le bassin des Mines aurait selon Shaw et alia (2010) subi une expansion rapide de l'amplitude des marées. Les datations radio-carbone préliminaires du site Qospemk suggèrent la possibilité d'une occupation humaine dès ca. 3 300 ans avant aujourd'hui, une période nommée « Archaïque supérieur » ou « Archaïque final » par les archéolo-gues et que certains chercheurs et aînés Mi'kmaw décrivent en tant que Mu Awsami Saqiwe'k, « Ceux d'il y a plutôt longtemps ». L'interprétation de nos résultats archéologiques préliminaires, basée sur les principes de recherche élaborés par le *Mi'kmawey Debert Elders' Advisory Council* (Julien et al. 2016) et construite autour des expertises diverses de notre équipe de recherche (qui inclut des membres autochtones et non-autochtones, des archéologues professionnels et des artistes), met l'accent sur la parenté entre les L'nuk d'aujourd'hui et les L'nuk du passé.

Affiliations
1. Department of Anthropology and American Studies Program, William & Mary, Virginia, United States
2. Millbrook First Nation, Nova Scotia, Canada
3. BFA, Millbrook First Nation, Nova Scotia, Canada
4. Department of Anthropology, William & Mary, Virginia, United States

The current volume challenges its contributors to reconsider human dwelling in the Far Northeast from 3000 BP until the arrival of Europeans. We welcome this opportunity, in part, because we are among a growing group of researchers who are exploring the deep pasts of Indigenous peoples by combining local Indigenous and Eurocentric ways of observing and interpreting the world (see Bartlett 2011; Julien et al. 2016; Laluk 2017; Lepofsky et al. 2017). The broad objective of our research has been to understand Teloltipnik L'nuk, or how L'nuk (the People) lived on the Chignecto Peninsula—a 1,500 km² triangle of land on what is now mainland Nova Scotia, jutting into the Bay of Fundy and situated in the Sipekne'katik and Siknikt districts of Mi'kma'ki (see figure 9.1).[1]

---

1. Chignecto, or Sikniktuk in Mi'kmaw, is translated as "at the draining place" (see "Ta'n Weji-sqalia'tiek," Mi'kmaw Place Names, https://placenames.mapdev.ca/, accessed November 15, 2021). Sipekne'katik (also Sikipne'katik) is spelled

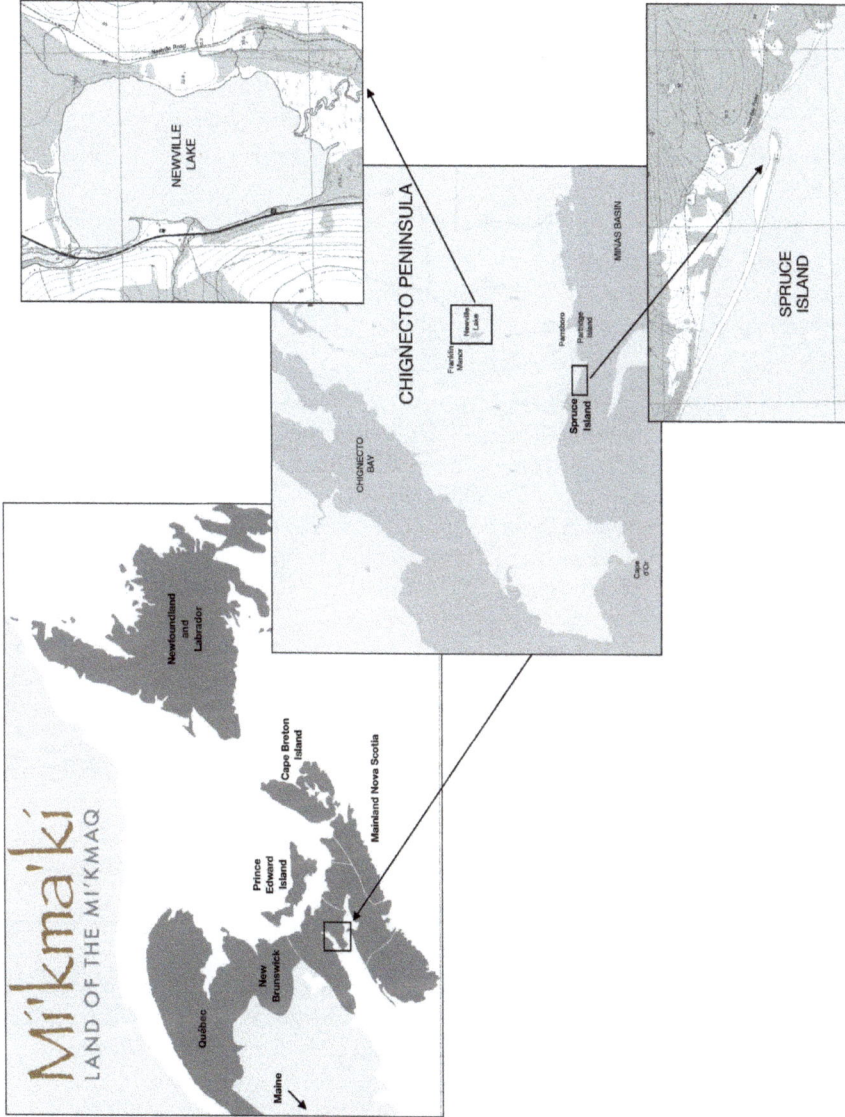

Figure 9.1. *Top left:* Map of Mi'kma'ki showing boundaries of the traditional Mi'kmaw territories and contemporary province names. *Centre:* Inset map of Chignecto Peninsula. *Top right:* Inset map of Qospemk (Newville Lake). *Lower right:* Inset map of Spruce Island. *Source:* Map of Mi'kma'ki used with permission of the Mi'kmawey Debert Cultural Centre.

Our team includes Mi'kmaw (Cynthia Martin and Alyssa Abram) and non-Mi'kmaw (Michelle Lelièvre and Mallory Moran) researchers working in partnership with the Confederacy of Mainland Mi'kmaq in Millbrook, Nova Scotia, and with William & Mary, in Williamsburg, Virginia.[2] Our work has thus far combined Mi'kmaw stories, oral histories, and oral testimonies with archaeological, archival, geological, cartographic, and remote sensing data to investigate what Julien et alia (2016:37) describe as the Mi'kmaq's "complex and deep attachments to land and place." Through these explorations we hope to reconnect Mi'kmaq from various regions of Mi'kma'ki to ancestral places from which they have been dislocated.

Boasting the world's highest and most powerful tides, and an onshore landscape dominated by a series of low hills that rise rapidly from the coast, the Chignecto Peninsula seems to defy human scale. Standing atop the cliffs of L'mu'juiktuk (Place of the Dogs, or Cape d'Or), looking northeast along the

---

"Shubenacadie" in English and translates as "area of wild potato/turnip." (See Roger Lewis and Trudy Sable, "Cultural Landscapes," http://mikmawplacenames .ca/cultural-landscapes/, accessed November 15, 2021. The Chignecto Peninsula has been variably attributed to two different traditional Mi'kmaw territories. Wicken (1994:452) includes the western third of the Chignecto Peninsula with the eastern half of New Brunswick, forming the Sikniktewaq political district. Wicken attributes the eastern portion of Chignecto Peninsula to the Sipekne'katik district. Bernard et alia (2015:16) maintain this division, abbreviating the spelling of Sikniktewaq to "Siknikt."

Roger Lewis, Trudy Sable, and William Jones suggest that the historically documented districts are more representative of post-Contact interactions with Europeans than pre-Contact cultural landscapes. They propose boundaries to traditional districts based on "natural physiographic features such as watersheds, river systems, climatic conditions, and geological formations" (see http://mikmawplacenames.ca /cultural-landscapes/, accessed November 15, 2021). They also note that these districts should not be imagined as fixed; they were adjustable according to fluctuations in the population and climatic changes.

The notes that local Mi'kmaw researcher Don (Byrd) Awalt compiled from conversations with his grandmother provide oral testimony to the connection between the Chignecto Peninsula and the eastern area of New Brunswick. The notes report that, even though several generations of the Bonis family lived at Qospemk, they always considered Memramcook, New Brunswick, their home (Awalt, n.d.).

Mi'kma'ki translates as the "Land of the Mi'kmaq" and includes eight traditional Mi'kmaw districts in the Canadian provinces of Nova Scotia, New Brunswick, Prince Edward Island, Newfoundland and Labrador, and Québec, and in the state of Maine.

2. In 2016, our team also included Mi'kmaw researcher Jodi Howe. In 2019, we were joined by non-Mi'kmaw researcher Allison Loveridge.

shore of Advocate Bay, what appears to be a small beach cobble is, in fact, an adult-sized boulder. At its eastern edge is the Minas Passage, where each high tide is estimated to bring a volume of water "greater than the combined flow of all the World's rivers" (Shaw et al. 2010:1081). This setting is appropriate for the oral traditions that L'nuk have told for generations (see Battiste 1997; Leland 1884; Rand 1971 [1894]; Sable and Francis 2012).[3] Many of these stories are of the hero Kluskap—himself a giant—for whom the hills, islands, and waterways of the Chignecto Peninsula are the setting for several of his feats of cunning and benevolence for the Mi'kmaq and other Eastern Algonquian peoples. The Kluskap stories provide remarkably accurate details about the topography and geology of the Chignecto Peninsula and other regions of Mi'kma'ki (see Gloade 2008; Sable 2011; Sable and Francis 2012; Shaw et al. 2010). For example, Kluskap is said to have raised from the earth a causeway (wo'qn or spine) to facilitate Mi'kmaw travels to and from Chignecto Bay in the north and Partridge Island in the south (see figure 9.1). This story describes the glacial esker or boar's back that winds along River Hebert from Qospemk (at the lake, or Newville Lake) to Chignecto Bay (see Rand 1971[1894]:292; Sable 2011:164). Additionally, the many different versions of Kluskap's confrontation with Giant Beaver share several details that explain local geographic phenomena: Giant Beaver builds a dam across a large body of water, the dam wreaks havoc as it floods land on which L'nuk rely, the dam is eventually broken, and the consequences of this rush of water are embedded in the land- and waterscapes of Mi'kma'ki, including Cape Split on the south shore of the Minas Basin, and the accumulated driftwood at Atuomjek (a sandy place, or Advocate Harbour).[4] Kluskap also punishes Giant Beaver by throwing stones that become places, such as Five Islands and Spencer's Island in the Minas Basin (see Beck 1972; Pacifique 1934; Parsons 1925; Rand 1919, 1971 [1894]; Sable 2011; Sable and Francis 2012; Speck 1915).

Archaeologists and other researchers have long used such stories to help identify and interpret places of human dwelling in the Far Northeast. Marine geoscientist John Shaw and his colleagues used the Kluskap–Giant Beaver story as evidence to support their hypothesis that a catastrophic event in the Minas Basin around 3400 BP led to the destruction of a gravel barrier that stretched across the Minas Passage from around Parrsboro to Cape Blomidon (Shaw et al. 2010:1088). The researchers examined 148 radiocarbon dates taken from areas

---

3. Mi'kmaq is a plural noun that refers to the Mi'kmaq as a people. Mi'kmaw is a singular noun and an adjective that modifies both singular and plural nouns (see Pacifique 1990).

4. The Mi'kmawey Debert Cultural Centre (MDCC) translates Atuomjek as "Driftwood Haven." http://www.mikmaweydebert.ca/home/ancestors-live-here/advocate-harbour/, accessed November 15, 2021.

around the Minas Basin and Chignecto Bay to determine the chronology of high- and low-water thresholds over the past 5,000 years (Shaw et al. 2010:1081). The results indicate that the tidal expansion experienced in the Bay of Fundy and Gulf of Maine during the early Holocene was delayed in the Minas Basin until after 3400 BP, and then increased rapidly (Shaw et al. 2010:1080). The researchers suggest that the rapid destruction of a gravel barrier (not unlike the sudden breaking of a beaver dam) may explain the dramatic rise of tides in the Minas Basin during this period (Shaw et al. 2010:1088-1089). Shaw and his colleagues consider the Giant Beaver story to be how L'nuk, who dwelled in this region, interpreted the gravel barrier's destruction and the subsequent dramatic changes to their land- and waterscapes.

We are interested in the hypothesis that Shaw and his colleagues offer because the fieldwork we have been conducting is taking place at sites north and west of the town of Parrsboro, which is the northern terminus of the gravel barrier they postulate. The sediments that would have composed this barrier are the same outwash deposits laid down by retreating glaciers that formed a delta extending south of Parrsboro into the Minas Basin and north into a steep valley known as the Parrsboro Gap (see Davis and Browne 1996:27; Shaw et al. 2010:1089; Stea and Wightman 1987; Swift and Borns 1967). If the catastrophic event that Shaw et alia (2010) hypothesize is accurate, what might that mean for the L'nuk who dwelled on the Chignecto Peninsula and in other regions of Mi'kma'ki after 3400 BP?

As we discuss below, Kluskap stories, oral testimonies, archival data, and preliminary archaeological evidence suggest L'nuk were dwelling in this eastern region of the Chignecto Peninsula well before and after the arrival of Europeans, during time periods that archaeologists working in northeastern North America have termed the Late Archaic (5000–3000 BP) and the Transitional Archaic (4100–2700 BP. See Campbell 2016:59), Woodland (3000–500 BP), and Protohistoric or Contact periods (1500–1700 AD). Archaeologists define these periods by similarities in technology, foodways, and/or burial practices. But there is a long-standing tradition in archaeology of conflating the technologies that researchers deem typical of these temporal categories with the peoples who lived during these times; hence, archaeological terms such as "Red Paint People." When our team met to discuss a first draft of this chapter, Cynthia expressed concern that some of these terms—the lingua franca of archaeology—may alienate some members of our Mi'kmaw audience. Recognizing the disconnect that some community members experience with archaeological conventions for describing and interpreting their past, Mi'kmaw archaeologist and curator of ethnology at the Nova Scotia Museum, Roger Lewis, developed with Mi'kmaw Elders a chronological framework for categorizing changing eras of human dwelling in this region "through the lens of relatedness and kin group" (Rosenmeier 2010:70; see also Lewis 2006).[5] This framework, which the Elders named Mi'kmakik Teloltipnik L'nuk (How the People Lived in Mi'kma'ki), is the result of deliberative discussions of how today's people (Kiskukewe'k L'nuk) relate to L'nuk of the past. As Rosenmeier (2010:71) notes, the language that the Elders use to describe these phases reflects "an underlying assumption of relatedness through time." In this framework, the arbitrary Late Archaic becomes Mu Awsami Saqiwe'k (Not So Recent People) and Woodland becomes Kejikawek L'nuk (Recent People) (see Davis 2011:22; Lewis 2006; Julien et al. 2016:43).

We explore these ideas of relatedness through time and the "recentness" of people who lived from approximately 3400 BP to the time of European contact. The preliminary results of our investigations on the Chignecto Peninsula do not allow us to formulate traditional archaeological hypotheses to investigate possible archaeological correlates for the catastrophic event that Shaw et alia (2010) hypothesize (e.g., a shift in subsistence strategy, redistributions of settlements, exploitation of new resources, etc.). Nor are we able to contribute to important conversations regarding changes during this period, such as the adoption of horticulture or village formation. Such contributions may be possible in the future as more (and more detailed) archaeological investigations are completed. However, as we met to discuss how we would present the work we've completed thus far, Cynthia encouraged us to consider the preliminary nature of our evidence not as a disadvantage but as an invitation for further exploration, and as an opportunity to ask questions—particularly questions that might expand our audience to include not only archaeologists working in the Far Northeast but also this region's Indigenous peoples. For example, could we consider the significance of our research to lie not (or not only) in the quantity, morphology, and patterning of the artifacts we collected? Could we use the evidence we've gathered thus far to tell a story of how L'nuk lived in Mi'kma'ki? Could we tell that story in a way that connects (and in some cases reconnects) Mi'kmaq to this region? And by telling this story, could we help archaeologists trained in the Eurocentric conventions of the discipline to understand a Mi'kmaw interpretation of the past in which today's people consider people from 3,000 years ago to be "recent?"

The preliminary nature of our archaeological findings means that our attempts to answer these questions are somewhat speculative. The story we offer

---

5. The MDCC is administered through the Confederacy of Mainland Mi'kmaq, a First Nations tribal council. While still in the planning stages, the MDCC will interpret the Debert Palaeoindian archaeological site and the surrounding landscape. It will also share, protect, and explore "the stories of the Mi'kmaq's earliest ancestors and those who came after them" (https://www.mikmaweydebert.ca/welcome/about-mdcc/, accessed November 15, 2021).

depends on two premises: First, how Kejikawek L'nuk lived includes not only the material aspects of life, such as obtaining and processing food, but also sharing with kin and other relations experiences of being on the land, crossing the water, adapting to the climate, and being disconnected from the land, water, and resources on which they relied. Second, to understand how today's L'nuk conceive their relatedness to Kejikawek L'nuk we must consider an archaeological past that extends beyond the period of contact with Europeans. One of the hallmarks of Mi'kmaw relatedness is the shared experience of connection *and* disconnection from their ancestral lands and waters. We focus on two characteristics of the artifacts that we've collected thus far to explore this relatedness: (a) the varieties of materials that L'nuk used to craft the tools and debitage we've recovered from Qospemk (Newville Lake, site numbers BjDc-06 and BjDc-07) and Spruce Island (BiDc-01), and (b) the tool-making techniques that L'nuk applied to these lithic materials and, possibly, to green bottle glass. We suggest that the varieties of materials provide evidence for how the L'nuk lived in Mi'kma'ki by maintaining connections to the places where they could obtain them—either by travelling to outcrops, quarrying, and transporting materials elsewhere (see Blair 2010), congregating in a place of prominence to trade them, and/or participating in networks that brought materials to them (see Deal 1989, 1998; Sable 2011). Additionally, the observation of similar lithic toolmaking techniques being applied to bottle glass may provide evidence that L'nuk maintained knowledge over time even as they were disconnected from ancestral places and networks. No longer able to access (or access as easily) the places where lithic materials were quarried or traded—and recognizing the physical qualities of glass—the worked bottle glass may indicate that Mi'kmaq adapted their techniques.[6] The appearance of worked bottle glass at Qospemk and Spruce Island may, therefore, be evidence of connection not only through time but also across space.

Background

On our very first morning working together in July 2017, Michelle (the project director) welcomed the crew and began diving into the details of the field season with a PowerPoint presentation. After the presentation, Cynthia asked a simple question: Why were we doing this work? Cynthia wanted to gauge the sincerity of the project's objectives and establish a mutual understanding of those objectives among the members of our research team. L'nuk know that they have been

---

6. Our thanks to Michael Deal for noting the European tradition of using bottle glass to make basic scraping and cutting tools. Deal suggests that the glass tools found at Qospemk and Spruce Island "may be a case of lithic technology being re-introduced to the Mi'kmaq" (Deal, pers. comm. 2020; see also Deal and Hayden 1987; and Kostro and Martin 2019).

in Mi'kma'ki since time immemorial. So, if the project's objective was to demonstrate the presence of Mi'kmaq on the Chignecto Peninsula, then what type of proof did we need to find and why was such proof necessary? Michelle has been contemplating the importance of these questions ever since Cynthia asked them. In the moment, Michelle suggested that the project's objective was more about demonstrating and proving Mi'kmaw presence to non-Mi'kmaw audiences; that is, to a general public that more often acknowledges the presence of the superhuman Kluskap than the more mundane human presence of Mi'kmaq who have dwelled on the lands and waters of the Chignecto Peninsula; to academic archaeologists skeptical that Mi'kmaw connections stretch back to "time immemorial"; and to the museum curators and public historians whose interpretations of the region have favoured the history of the French and British settlers over that of the Indigenous population. Demonstrating long-term Mi'kmaw presence and persistence in the face of European colonization, erasure, and encroachment seemed like a worthy goal that would contribute to "decolonizing" the academic, touristic, and public-history landscapes.

But as our work on the Chignecto Peninsula has progressed, our objectives have broadened to consider not only non-Indigenous audiences but also Mi'kmaw community members who have been disconnected from the ancestral places we have been studying. This shift has been in direct response to our engagements with past and present Mi'kmaw residents of the Chignecto Peninsula, Mi'kmaw researchers, and Mi'kmaw Elders, particularly members of the Mi'kmawey Debert Elders' Advisory Council (MDEAC). The MDEAC has provided guidance for the establishment of a cultural centre that will interpret the Debert Palaeoindian archaeological site and surrounding landscape on mainland Nova Scotia. The MDEAC, in conversation with Mi'kmawey Debert Cultural Centre (MDCC) staff, developed three principles to guide this work (see Julien et al. 2016). The first principle is that Mi'kmaq understand themselves to be descended from the people who came before them in Mi'kma'ki (Julien et al. 2016:39). This understanding of relatedness between the present and the deep past does not mean that Mi'kmaq believe that "there has been no linguistic, cultural, or biological change among the people who have lived in Mi'kma'ki since the last glaciation" (Julien et al. 2016:40). However, Mi'kmaq understand that they share a long-term history of experience with L'nuk who lived in this region before the arrival of Europeans. The second principle is that Mi'kmaw Elders look to the past for healing and spirituality, not only for knowledge and information (Julien et al. 2016:44). This principle underscores the importance of ancestral places to contemporary Mi'kmaq because of their potential to heal the wounds of intergenerational trauma that Mi'kmaq have suffered as European encroachment on these places—and genocidal policies such as residential schooling—severed their cultural, spiritual, and practical ties to them. The final guiding principle that the MDEAC has offered is that Mi'kmaq respect know-ledge of the past and are dedicated to learning more about their people, L'nuk (Julien et al. 2016:49). This dedication to knowing more about how L'nuk lived in Mi'kma'ki over the long-term has created new knowledge, including the identification of additional ancestral places around Debert, the integration of interdisciplinary sciences and Mi'kmaw knowledge to understand the surround-ing landscape (see Bernard et al. 2015), and the investigation of places where multiple forms of evidence converge; for example, in places such as Spruce Island and Qospemk, where Kluskap stories are coincident with the presence of archaeological remains, tool stone outcrops, oral histories and testimonies, and archival records.

These principles provide the foundation for researching the Mi'kmaw past according to Mi'kmaw values. They also complement the Two-Eyed Seeing framework for learning we have been using to conduct our research on the Chignecto Peninsula. Mi'kmaw Elder Albert Marshall describes Two-Eyed Seeing as "learning to see from one eye with the strengths of Indigenous knowledges and ways of knowing, and from the other eye with the strengths of Western knowledges and ways of knowing, and using both these eyes together, for the benefit of all" (Bartlett et al. 2012:335; Bartlett et al. 2015:215).[7] Two-Eyed Seeing aims for co-learning between researchers whose expertise is grounded in different ways of knowing. Such co-learning requires building ongoing relationships between researchers who develop their expertise either through training in disciplinary conventions, through first-hand, intergenera-tional experience, or both. Two-Eyed Seeing has framed how we have con-ducted our primary research, how we have interpreted our preliminary results, and how we have presented these results to broader audiences (see Lelièvre et al. 2020). For example, while we have adhered to most of the archaeological conventions of subsurface testing, at the same time, we have attempted to be more mindful of the disturbance and disrespect our excavations cause to the vegetation, animals, human, and more-than-human presences in the places where we work. Cynthia has led our efforts to protect plant life from irreparable damage by minimizing root cutting, designating paths to reduce trampling, and, in some cases, temporarily transplanting vegetation for the duration of our excavations. These efforts have become integral for approaching our research with sincerity and a mutual respect for the various expertise our team members

---

7. The developers of Two-Eyed Seeing have anticipated some criticisms. Does the dualistic emphasis on "two" foreclose more nuanced perspectives? Is the emphasis on "seeing" inherently ablest? They emphasize "that Mi'kmaw understandings are but one view in a multitude of aboriginal and indigenous views. ... Thus, one might wish to talk about Four-Eyed Seeing, or Ten-Eyed Seeing, etc." (Bartlett et al. 2012:336).

offer. As such, we believe our work contributes to ongoing conversations within archaeology, Indigenous studies, and other disciplines about the potential that collaborative research holds for creating epistemic change; that is, for new kinds of knowledge and new ways of learning and sharing that knowledge (see Bartlett et al. 2015; Gonzalez 2016; Kovach 2015; McNiven 2016:28; Wylie 2015:203).

In many ways, the three principles articulated by the MDEAC and the Two-Eyed Seeing framework challenge some traditional archaeological approaches to understanding the deep past. Although some archaeologists have questioned the sharp line the discipline has created between the pre- and post-Contact periods (see Crellin 2020; Nieves 2021; Oland et al. 2012; Panich 2013; Silliman 2009), skepticism remains regarding Mi'kmaw and other Indigenous Peoples' claims of relatedness to peoples of the past. Archaeology has long equated discontinuities in artifact style, manufacturing technique, and/or the absence of certain artifact types as evidence for the discontinuity of particular groups of people (see Piers 1912; Rosenmeier 2010; Trigger 1980). Rather than interpreting such discontinuities as a common part of how people lived in the past, archaeologists have frequently explained them as signs of migration of peoples and/or ideas from another region. And these explanations have helped settler institutions dispossess Indigenous Peoples of their pasts and, in some cases, appropriate those pasts to legitimize settler encroachment and Indigenous assimilation (see Lelièvre 2017b; McNiven and Russell 2005).

Connecting L'nuk and Places

We felt the weight of this disciplinary legacy in 2019 when, on two occasions, we spoke directly to members of the MDEAC about our research. The first opportunity was at a monthly MDEAC meeting in the boardroom of the Confederacy of Mainland Mi'kmaq, during which Michelle deployed another PowerPoint presentation dense with photographs, archival documents, toponyms, Mi'kmaw family names, radiocarbon dates, and GIS (geographic information system)-generated maps that tried to condense into two dimensions multiple layers of bedrock and surficial geology, archaeological sites, old-growth forests, and places mentioned in Kluskap stories.[8] We quickly discovered that our presentation was an ineffective way of sharing what, for many of us, has been a very profound experience of being on the land in an unfamiliar region of Mi'kma'ki and being able, as Cynthia and Alyssa described it, to smell, touch, and see the materials and environment in which their ancestors lived. Such an experience

---

8. Our thanks to Nick Belluzzo, a PhD candidate in the Department of Anthropology at William & Mary, for preparing the base maps used in this presentation. See Sable 2011 for comparable maps.

could not be conveyed adequately in the artificial light and air-conditioned environment of a boardroom.

For us, the principles of relatedness through time, healing, and interdisciplinarity came to life when, a few months later, we welcomed members of the MDEAC and Mi'kmawey Debert Cultural Centre (MDCC) staff to Qospemk, where we were beginning our third season of fieldwork. We were first drawn to Qospemk through the work of respected Mi'kmaw Elder Doug Knockwood, who was a member of the MDEAC until his death in 2018. In his memoir, Doug describes in vivid detail his early life spent in and around Qospemk, a place he called "paradise" (Knockwood 2018:4). This memoir and archival records describe a thriving Mi'kmaw community at Qospemk and at the Franklin Manor Reserve a short distance to the northwest. Some parcels of land in this area were reserved for the use of the Mi'kmaq by the provincial and, later, federal governments. Other parcels were owned outright by Mi'kmaw families (Awalt, n.d.; Knockwood 2018:2). Oral histories collected by Don (Byrd) Awalt, a Mi'kmaw researcher and writer currently living in the coastal village of Port Greville, Nova Scotia, describe Qospemk in the early twentieth century as a place where several families lived year-round. Other families from communities around Mi'kma'ki resided there in the late summer to participate in the region's blueberry harvest (see Awalt, n.d.).

Many of the Elders we welcomed to Qospemk had travelled to the Chignecto Peninsula for the first time. Our plan was to bring them as close as possible to the southwest corner of the lake where we had concentrated our excavations and recovered the bulk of our archaeological artifacts. Instead, we lingered at the northwestern shore of Qospemk, steps away from where the houses of Mi'kmaw families who lived here in the nineteenth and twentieth centuries once stood. Rather than describing to the Elders the artifacts and their contexts, or even our efforts to care for the area's plant life, we mostly listened. We listened as the Elders described their feelings of experiencing firsthand a place they had previously only heard about from family members. Consequently, the Elders were most interested to learn about the families who had lived at Qospemk in the recent past. We had gathered names stretching back to the late seventeenth century from baptismal records, census returns, letters from federal Indian agents, oral histories and testimonies, photographs, and from families living in other regions of Mi'kma'ki. Among these names was Joseph (Joe) Cope, Cynthia's great-grandfather, whose service record from the First World War noted that he was born in Parrsboro in 1869. A guidebook that MDCC staff prepared for the Elders' visit included the names we had gathered and a map indicating the former locations of Mi'kmaw homes around the lake. Knockwood, Paul, Bonis (Bonas), Toney, Logan, Brooks, Hood, and Gloade were familiar names to the members of the MDEAC. One Elder commented that she had been told of family members who came from this region but she never knew their names. The MDCC staff also shared stories of the two trips they had made with Doug Knockwood to record stories of how he and his extended family lived at Qospemk and nearby places.[9] These stories were told with a combination of fondness for an Elder who advocated for the preservation and protection of Qospemk and sadness for the loss of a man so dedicated to his ancestral home.[10]

We consider the opportunity to introduce and, in some cases, reintroduce Elders to Qospemk to be one of the most significant contributions of our research because it works toward fulfilling the first of the three guiding principles established by the MDEAC. As Julien et alia (2016:44) argue: "When the Elders visit the sites, they speak of spiritual connections to the sites that are centered (*sic*) in knowing that people—mothers, fathers, grandparents, brothers, sisters, aunts, uncles, children—have lived there." By drawing on the knowledge of Doug Knockwood, Don (Byrd) Awalt, and Elder Charlie Paul, we were able to name the families who once lived there, identify the locations where their houses stood, and describe the activities in which they engaged to support themselves. In turn, the Elders' experiences of being at this place may have allowed them to ground (literally and metaphorically) their own memories of Qospemk—or the passing remarks about Qospemk made by a relative decades earlier—in the present moment of being at the place itself. This grounding, we argue, can be healing because, as Mi'kmaw Elder Murdena Marshall described it, healing is apprehending one's relationship to the entity that caused the illness (Julien et al. 2016:44-45).[11] By sharing the knowledge we had gathered with these Elders, we were providing them with a means to apprehend the trauma of dispossession and the vibrancy of the Mi'kmaw community that once thrived at Qospemk.

---

9. The MDCC website includes one of these stories, told outside of the St. Brigid's Catholic Church in Parrsboro: https://www.mikmaweydebert.ca/sharing -our-stories/exploring-our-histories/elders-stories/#prettyPhoto, accessed November 15, 2021.

10. Doug Knockwood also advocated for the protection of Mi'kmaw burials that several local residents have reported being located in the hills just to the west of Qospemk. Sara Beanlands, Steve Garcin, and staff from Boreas Heritage Consulting generously donated their equipment, time, and expertise to conduct ground-penetrating radar analyses of this area in June 2019. Garcin noted that some of the anomalies in the hills at the northwest corner of Newville Lake suggest buried artifacts and/or features, although the anomalies did not form a distinct pattern that would allow for an accurate interpretation (Garcin, pers. commun. 2020).

11. Elder Murdena Marshall was a member of the MDEAC until her death in 2019.

Interpreting 3,000 Years of Relatedness

It may be easier for non-Mi'kmaq to understand the feeling of relatedness Mi'kmaq have for L'nuk of the past when those L'nuk have Anglicized names and appear in settler documents such as census returns and church records. It may be more difficult to understand how that relatedness extends to L'nuk as far back as 3400 BP. In this section, we use the preliminary results of our archaeological fieldwork at Qospemk (BjDc-06 and BjDc-07) and Spruce Island (BiDc-01) to offer a possible interpretation of that connection.

Archaeological Fieldwork Conducted at Qospemk
(Newville Lake, Sites BjDc-06 and BjDc-07)

Like most of the lakes in this region, Qospemk was formed through the retreat and advance of glaciers. Wightman (1980:294) notes that the local surficial deposits indicate Newville Lake, as it is otherwise known, and Gilbert Lake (located 4 km south) formed one large body of water immediately following the last deglaciation. Sedimentation and vegetation growth gradually separated this body of water into two lakes (Wightman 1980:291). Qospemk's surficial deposits overlie two bedrock formations within the geological Cumberland Group. Underlying the northern portion of the lake is the Polly Brook Formation, which belongs to the Permian period. The southern quarter of Qospemk, where BjDc-06 and BjDc-07 are located, overlies the older Carboniferous-period Ragged Reef Formation, consisting of "fluvial sandstone, conglomerate, mudstone, rare coal, and lacustrine limestone" (see Keppie 2000).

As of the summer of 2019, our team had conducted three short seasons of archaeological fieldwork at Qospemk.[12] BjDc-06 was identified in 2016 after a brief shovel-test survey. Our team excavated a total of five shovel-test pits, the southern most of which yielded a possible reduction flake of quartzite or an unidentified felsitic material at 26 cm below surface. This artifact was found in association with charcoal that has been AMS (accelerator mass spectrometry) radiocarbon dated 3,406–3,206 calendar years before present (see figure 9.2; Lelièvre 2017a, 2018).[13]

---

12. Fieldwork at these sites was conducted under Nova Scotia Heritage Research Permits A2016NS053, A2018NS058, and A2019NS050. Permit reports are on file with the Culture and Heritage Division of the Department of Communities, Culture and Heritage in Halifax, Nova Scotia (see Lelièvre 2017a, 2019, and 2021).

13. The identity of neither the flake type nor the material has been confirmed. Comparable material was recovered during follow-up test excavations in 2018 (see Lelièvre 2019). Michael Deal and John Campbell viewed the images included in figure 9.2 in April 2020. Both cautioned against making macroscopic identifications from photos. Based on the location of the site and the texture visible in the photo, Campbell suggested the material may be a "reddish form of White Rock quartzite,"

Lab ID	Submitter ID	Material	Mat. Code	Depth (cm)	^{14}C YR BP	+/-	F ^{14}C	+/-	cal BP	Mi'kma'ki Teloltipnik L'nuk
UOC-4586	A2016NS053-02	Charcoal	AAA	23	163	47	0.9799	0.0057	290-0 (95.4%)	Kiskukewe'k L'nuk (Today's People)
UOC-4587	A2016NS053-03	Charcoal	AAA	26	3103	47	0.6796	0.0040	3406-3206 (91.5%)	Mu Awsami Saqiwe'k (Not So Recent People)
UOC-4588	A2016NS053-04	Charcoal	AAA	50	3045	47	0.6845	0.0040	3369-3140 (92.6%)	Mu Awsami Saqiwe'k (Not So Recent People)

Level	Depth below surface	Matrix description
1	0-28 cm	Reddish brown silty loam
2	28-32 cm	Charcoal staining
3	32-72 cm	Compacted light gray sand and gravel with a band of red silt/rust stained gravel at ~38-48 cm and ~66-69 cm
4	72-77 cm	Light gray sand, fine and uniform
5	77-97 cm	Mix of small pebbles and light grey sand

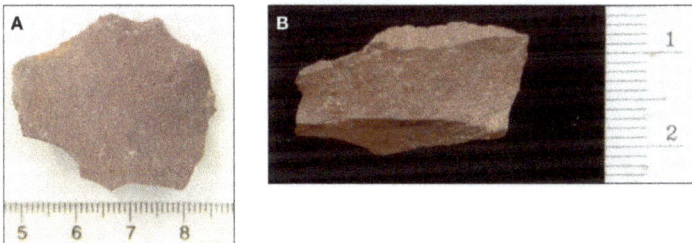

Figure 9.2. *Top:* AMS (accelerator mass spectrometry) radiocarbon analysis conducted by André Lalonde, AMS Laboratory, University of Ottawa, July 2017. All charcoal samples were collected from test pit 23, excavated at Qospemk (Newville Lake, BjDc-06) in July 2016. Raw dates calibrated using OxCal (see Lelièvre 2017a and 2018). *Middle:* Table summarizing matrix descriptions for test pit 23, excavated in July 2016. *Bottom:* Photos illustrating possible quartzite (or felsite) reduction flakes recovered from BjDc-06. (A) Artifact recovered in situ in 2016 from TP23 at 26 cm below surface. (B) Artifact recovered in 2018 in situ from test unit -2 N, -2 E at 14.5 cm below surface (see also figure 9.4).

Wanting to confirm that the dates were associated with cultural activity, we returned to Qospemk in 2018 and expanded this shovel-test pit by opening two 1-m-x-1-m test units. From one of these units (-2 N, -2 E), we recovered 15 samples of debitage, including flakes, chips, and indeterminate samples of a variety of crypto- and microcrystalline materials (see Ballin 2000). Two of the flakes exhibited

a source of which is located near the Gaspereau River in the Annapolis Valley (Campell, pers. comm. 2020).

retouch (see figure 9.4; Lelièvre 2019).[14] We also collected from the lakeshore south of our excavation units a sherd of green bottle glass that had been worked into a scraper (see figure 9.3A). While there are signs of retouch on three sides of this scraper, it is most distinct on the longest axis, which also bears a distinct linear groove along its edge.

Unable to return to BjDc-06 during the summer of 2019 due to flooding at the site, we shifted our test excavations to a terrace about 200 m south. There, we excavated 12 shovel-test pits. Two of these shovel tests yielded debitage, including 82 chips, flakes, and indeterminate samples from -15N, -5E. Our use of nested 3.18 mm and 6.35 mm screens allowed us to recover 30 chips of various materials that were less than or equal to 5 mm (see figures 9.5 and 9.6).[15]

Figure 9.3. Worked green bottle glass collected from Qospemk (Newville Lake, BjDc-06) and Spruce Island (BiDc-01). *Top:* 5 mm × 20 mm × 22 mm scraper collected from the lakeshore at Qospemk in 2018. Two edges are worked. A shallow groove appears on the worked side of the longest axis. *Bottom:* 4 mm × 14 mm × 24 mm sherd of modified bottle glass excavated at Spruce Island (BiDc-01) in July 2016 from test pit 6 at approximately 69 cm below surface.

---

14. These units were not complete by the end of the 2018 field season and were reburied to continue excavation in 2019. In July 2019, the area of these units was flooded due to excessive rain during the winter and spring. Fieldwork planned for the summers of 2020 and 2021 was cancelled due to the COVID-19 pandemic. We hope to complete the excavation of these units in 2022.

15. These materials have preliminarily been identified using an 8 x magnification hand lens as chert, chalcedony, quartzite (or felsite), and unidentified. These artifacts have not yet been examined using more powerful magnification or chemical analysis.

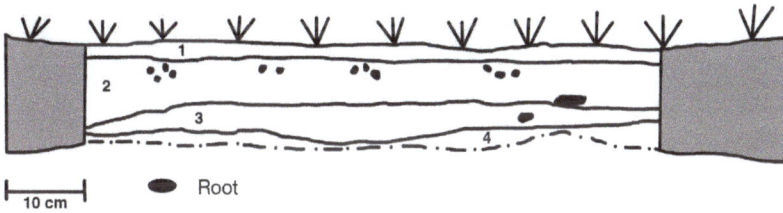

Figure 9.4. *Top:* Select artifacts collected from test unit -2N, -2E at BjDc-06 in 2018. (A) Flake collected from the north side of unit, level 2, at 8 cm below the southwest corner. (B) Flake collected from the north side of unit, level 2. Found in the screen. (C) Flake collected in the screen from level 4 back dirt and wall scrapings. (D) Flake recovered from level 3 at 6.5 cm from north wall, 14 cm from east wall, and 10 cm below southwest corner. *Middle:* Profile drawing of the west wall of unit -2N, -2E. *Bottom:* Level descriptions for unit -2N, -2E.

LEVEL	DEPTH (cm)	CHALCEDONY				CHERT				QUARTZITE (OR FELSITE)				UNIDENTIFIED				TOTAL by DEPTH
		Chip <= 5mm	Chip 5-9mm	Flake	Indeter.	Chip <= 5mm	Chip 5-9mm	Flake	Indeter.	Chip <= 5mm	Chip 5-9mm	Flake	Indeter.	Chip <= 5mm	Chip 5-9mm	Flake	Indeter.	
1	15	-	-	-	2	1	-	1	-	1	1	-	-	2	-	-	-	8
1	22	3	1	1	-	3	5	2	2	6	5	3	-	-	2	-	-	33
4/5/6	40	1	-	-	-	3	4	3	2	6	10	-	1	2	2	-	-	34
Wall scrapings	N/A	-	-	-	-	1	2	-	-	-	-	1	-	1	2	-	-	7
TOTAL ARTIFACTS BY MATERIAL		8				29				34				11				

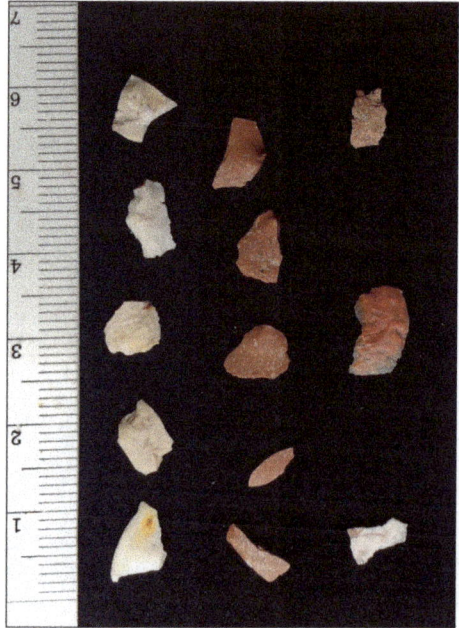

Figure 9.5. *Top:* Table summarizing debitage recovered from test pit -15N, -5E in July 2019 at Qospemk (Newville Lake, BjDc-07). Debitage types based on Ballin 2000. Material types tentatively identified in the field using an 8 × magnification hand lens. *Bottom:* Photos illustrating material types of select debitage samples: (Left) chips >5mm collected from 22 cm below surface organized by material type; and (Right) chips >5mm collected from 40 cm below surface organized by material type (see also figure 9.6).

LEVEL	DEPTH (cm)	COLOUR	TEXTURE
1	0-24	10YR/2/2 - Very Dark Brown	Granular sandy loam
2	24-26	10YR/2/1 - Black	Massive silt
3	24-34	10YR/4/2 - Greyish brown	Massive silty very fine sand
4	28-42	10YR/3/2 - Very dark greyish brown	Silty sand (coarser than 3)
5	36-42	10YR/4/2 - Dark greyish brown	Coarse sand
6	40-46	10YR/2/1 - Black	Platy silty clay
7	46-50	10YR/4/2 - Dark greyish brown	Massive silty coarse sand

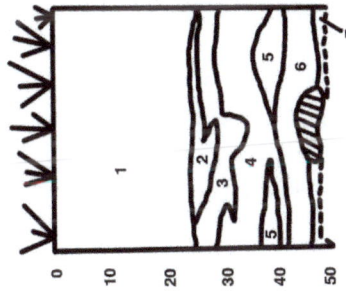

Figure 9.6. *Left:* Profile drawing of west wall of shovel test -15E, -5N excavated at Qospemk (Newville Lake, BjDc-07) in July 2019. *Middle:* Photo of the west wall of shovel test -15E, -5N. Debitage collected from approximately 15 cm, 22 cm, and 40 cm below surface (see figure 9.5). *Right:* Level descriptions for shovel test -15E, -5N.

Archaeological Fieldwork Conducted at Spruce Island (BiDc-01)

Seventeen kilometres southwest of Qospemk, and toward the western edge of Shaw et alia's (2010) proposed gravel barrier, is Spruce Island; so named for the narrow strip of spruce trees towering over most of its 1.5 km length. Spruce Island is south of the hamlet of Black Rock and north of the landmark also known as Black Rock, most of which is only visible at low tide (see figure 9.1). On the south side of the spit is a cobble beach. On the north side is a gravel shore that slopes steeply toward a narrow cove. At low tide this cove is almost passable on foot, but the rapidly rising tide makes exploring the area dangerous. The entire spit of Spruce Island has surficial marine deposits. The bedrock geology is likely the same as the mainland in this area, which is part of the Carboniferous Parrsboro Formation, consisting of "fluvial sandstone, calcrete limestone, conglomerate, mudstone" (Keppie 2000).[16]

In 2016, our team excavated nine test pits at Spruce Island. We selected this spit as a testing location because an archaeological site had been tentatively identified here in 1934, when a Boy Scout troop collected several trade beads and donated them to the Nova Scotia Museum. Then curator, Harry Piers, noted in the accession ledger that Mi'kmaq had been reported camping in the area until around 1864 (see Nova Scotia Museum 1933–1937). Oral testimony we collected in 2017 included recollections from the twentieth century of a Mi'kmaw man who walked 3.5 km west along the shore from Spruce Island to purchase groceries in Diligent River (Lelièvre 2017a:23).

Our shovel tests at Spruce Island yielded artifacts from the post-Contact period, including a shell embroidery bead and a sherd of worked bottle glass (figure 9.3B). Though waterworn, this bottle glass shows some possible signs of being modified for use as a tool; for example, its sides are tapered and one edge has signs of retouch. The glass sherd was recovered at approximately 69 cm below surface in the bottom level a shovel-test pit (TP6) that was placed just north of the wooded portion of Spruce Island at the spit's far eastern end (see Lelièvre 2017a). The matrix was highly compacted pinkish orangey-brown clayey silt with pebbles (see Lelièvre 2017a:Appendix B). Yet the churn of the rapid tidal changes and the extensive erosion along the Minas Basin mean that the context for the glass sherd may be unreliable.

So Near and Yet So Far?

When we met to discuss how to present our preliminary results for this chapter, Cynthia remarked how fascinated she was by the spatial proximity of our chronologically distant finds. The glass scraper that had been recovered in 2018 was only a few centimetres above where we had excavated our best examples

---

16. The scale of the 2000 bedrock geology map (see Keppie 2000) is not fine enough to distinguish the spit from the mainland.

of modified flakes (see figure 9.4). To date, we have not determined the sedimentation rate at Qospemk, nor have we recovered flakes and debitage in association with a feature that would allow us to determine their provenience with greater confidence. However, Cynthia's comment that these artifacts are so near in space, yet so distant in time resonates with approaches in landscape and Indigenous archaeologies that interpret archaeological sites as places where multiple temporalities are present (see Ingold 1993; Million 2005). Indeed, on the day the glass scraper was recovered, we also recovered a flake of Minas Basin chert (see figure 9.4D).

Our evidence is insufficient to connect the glass scrapers collected at Qospemk and Spruce Island with a particular person (or even with an Indigenous person), but there are several Indigenous individuals whose names appear repeatedly in oral testimonies, archival records, and ethnographic accounts from the region. These individuals include Peter Toney, Thomas Bonis, John Logan, among others.[17] It is possible that one of these individuals, or someone related to him, made and used this tool. The glass scraper also connects that individual to others through the knowledge he would have learned in order to manipulate the raw material into a useable tool.[18] Such knowledge would include the crystalline

---

17. These names include Peter Toney, John Logan, Lemey Paul, William Paul, Newell (Noel) Paul, John Lewis, Newell (Noel) Bonis (Bonus/Barrio), Joseph Brooks, Sam Knockwood, and John Knockwood. We recognize that such records must be approached cautiously and critically. Few census returns accurately enumerated Indigenous peoples, not every Mi'kmaw would have been baptized (or had a baptism recorded), records kept by Europeans reflect European biases against Mi'kmaw kinship and gender relations, and names are often recorded incorrectly. Thus, the names that frequent the nineteenth- and early-twentieth-century records of Qospemk may misrepresent the Mi'kmaq who dwelled there and/or underrepresent the Mi'kmaq who had connections to the region.

   One name that can be traced through several records is Thomas Bonis, who likely lived from the late eighteenth/early nineteenth century until the late nineteenth century. A Thomas Bonus appears in the 1852 baptismal record of his son, is mentioned in a story about several Mi'kmaq who brought apple trees to the Mi'kmaw reserve of Franklin Manor several decades before the Second World War, and is described by Silas Rand as Rand's "aged friend" in "A Wizard Carries Off Glooscap's (*sic*) Housekeeper," a story Bonis told Rand in Cumberland County on June 10, 1870 (Rand 1971 [1894]:293; see also Awalt, n.d.). Genealogical research on Mi'kmaw families at Qospemk conducted by Don (Byrd) Awalt traces four generations of a Bonis family. Thomas Bonis and his brother Noel were believed to be the last Bonis families to live at Qospemk permanently. Their great-grandfather, Francis, is said to be the first Mi'kmaw to have a permanent residence at Qospemk in the early eighteenth century (Awalt, n.d.).

18. This is a point that Mary Ellen Googoo made in her response to David Black's presentation on lithic materials at the 2005 Debert Research Workshop. Googoo noted, "when I was thinking about the tools they (Palaeoindians) would have made,

properties of bottle glass and the flaking techniques that create a sharpened edge (on bottle-glass tools, see Clark 1981; Deal and Hayden 1987; Harrison 2003; Kostro and Martin 2019; Porter 2015). And the knowledge applied to green bottle glass in the post-Contact period would have been learned first on comparably cryptocrystalline lithic materials, both before and after the arrival of Europeans. The development of the expertise necessary to create these tools and the sharing of that expertise with others over time is one way to understand the "recentness" of Kejikawek L'nuk. They are Recent People, in part because they passed on their knowledge to Today's People, and that knowledge is manifest in objects such as green bottle-glass scrapers.

While the techniques applied to create lithic and glass tools tell a story about how knowledge may have been passed across generations, the materials themselves may suggest changes in how L'nuk accessed places in Mi'kma'ki. The varieties of lithic materials that we have recovered from the two sites at Qospemk indicate that the L'nuk who dwelled there had access to several different sources of toolstone (see figures 9.2, 9.4, and 9.5). Acquiring these materials either by directly quarrying them, collecting them as cobbles, or trading for them would have required access to places beyond the shores of Qospemk. Some of these material types appear, at low magnification, to be of varieties similar to those found along the shore of Scot's Bay and within the fissures of basalt formations at L'mu'juiktuk.

Indeed, Qospemk's description in the story of Kluskap raising up a wo'qn to aid the Mi'kmaq in their travels situates this place within a long-term land- and waterscape through which L'nuk and, later, Europeans travelled to and from other parts of the Maritime Peninsula and the region's islands (see Campbell 2016; Clermont 1989; Deal 1989; Sable 2011; Smith 1934:123). Qospemk is connected to the north shore of the Minas Basin, including places such as Spruce Island, by the Hebert and Farrells (formerly Parrsboro) Rivers and a portage between Gilbert and Jeffers Lake. To the north, River Hebert continues out of Qospemk and empties into the Cumberland Basin. Stories from the eighteenth and nineteenth centuries report heroic feats of navigation as Mi'kmaq paddled approximately 185 km from Halifax to New Brunswick in one day, following the Shubenacadie River to the Minas Basin, timing the crossing of the Minas Basin with the tides, taking the rivers and portages north from Parrsboro (approximately 7 km east of Spruce Island) to River Hebert, and eventually crossing the Cumberland Basin to New Brunswick (see Awalt n.d.; MGC 2009:17; Whitehead 1991:213).[19]

---

well, one thing I've learned is that, through oral tradition, things can really be passed on" (see Black 2011:123).

19. To date, seven archaeological sites have been identified along this corridor: BjDc-01 to BjDc-07. Two of those (BjDc-06 and BjDc-07) have been identified through

In the centuries following contact with Europeans, access to these places and the varieties of toolstone would have diminished as Europeans drained, cleared, and bounded the land, and as L'nuk's social and trade networks were disrupted. Thus, the adaptation of green bottle glass for use as a raw material for tool manufacture may suggest that L'nuk lived by preserving knowledge and surviving dispossession through time.

Conclusion

On the Chignecto Peninsula, the period between 3400 and 500 BP was book-ended by catastrophe. If Shaw et alia's (2010) hypothesis is correct, a catastrophic storm around 3400 BP destroyed a gravel barrier connecting the north and south shores of the Minas Basin, causing tides to the east of the Minas Passage to rise rapidly. Such an event may have disrupted the travel routes of the Mu Awsami Saqiwe'k, the Not So Recent People, and/or may have provided new opportunities for access to resources.[20] Around 500 BP, L'nuk began to encounter new peoples whose ideologies and technologies eventually threatened their very existence. In this chapter, we have tentatively explored the intervening years through the archaeological and oral-historical evidence we have begun to collect on the Chignecto Peninsula. We have used our preliminary results, our experience of working within the Two-Eyed Seeing framework, and our inspiration from the Mi'kmawey Debert Elders' Advisory Council's research principles to explore what it means for Mi'kmaq to consider L'nuk from three millennia ago to be Recent People.

Julien et alia (2016) emphasize that a Mi'kmaw understanding of being descendent from the first peoples to inhabit Mi'kma'ki following the last deglaciation is grounded in shared experience. We have attempted to use the (thus far) modest collection of debitage and glass tools from Qospemk and Spruce Island to offer possible stories for what that shared experience entailed. How L'nuk lived in Mi'kma'ki during this period included sharing experiences of continuity (e.g., transferring knowledge related to tool manufacture) and discontinuity, dislocation, dispossession, and disconnection from places such as Qospemk.

---

our sub-surface testing. The others were identified through isolated finds, some of which were reported to John Erskine in the mid-twentieth century. Two of these sites (BjDc-01 and BjDc-02) are located along River Hebert. The remaining sites are located at Qospemk. Our thanks to Stephen Powell and Sara Beanlands for drawing our attention to these sites.

20. Lewis (2006) and Rosenmeier (2010) translate Mu Awsami Saqiwe'k as "Not So Recent People," although saqiwe'k translates as "old," which may mean this period translates as "Not as Old People," gesturing more to the Ancient People than the Recent People.

In our conversations about the research we've been conducting on the Chignecto Peninsula, Cynthia has reminded us that, while the experience of being on the land and learning more about her ancestors has been rewarding, it has also been incredibly painful. As her knowledge grows so does her awareness of the traumatic losses her ancestors experienced. We hope that sharing the knowledge we have been collecting and generating inspires each of us—Mi'kmaq and non-Mi'kmaq—to work towards healing by examining our own relationships to that pain.

Acknowledgements

We would like to thank the staff of the Mi'kmawey Debert Cultural Centre in Millbrook, Nova Scotia. Tim Bernard, Sharon Farrell, Gerald Gloade, and Leah Rosenmeier have supported our project in every way from the beginning. The members of the Mi'kmawey Debert Elders' Advisory Council honoured us with their presence at Qospemk in July 2019. Since 2017, Don (Byrd) Awalt has generously shared his time and research with us. Cameron and Ann Fullerton and Rod Harrington granted permission to access their properties at Qospemk. Sara Beanlands, Steve Garcin, and the staff of Boreas Heritage Consulting have shared their data related to the Chignecto Peninsula, conducted ground-penetrating radar surveys at two sites along Qospemk, and constructed digital elevation models of these sites using drone data. The archaeological, oral-historical, and archival research has been supported by two fellowships from the Reves Center for International Studies at William & Mary, the Dean of Arts and Sciences Faculty Research Fund at William & Mary, a Nova Scotia Museum Research Grant, and a Franklin Research Grant from the American Philosophical Society. We also thank the anonymous reviewers of this chapter.

References Cited

Awalt, Don (Byrd)

ca. 2020   Mna'q Wisuiknemt… T'an Teliaqsɨpnek Wejkwa'taqnek Micmac/Mi'kmaw Kji-matnakewinu/Undefeated… A History of Micmac/Mi'kmaw Warrior and Other Resources. Manuscript on file, Department of Anthropology, William & Mary, Williamsburg, Virginia.

Ballin, Torben Bjarke

2000   Classification and Description of Lithic Artifacts: A Discussion of Basic Lithic Terminology. *Lithics* 21:9–15.

Bartlett, Cheryl M.

2011   Integrative Science/Toqwa'tu'kl Kijitaqnn: The Story of Our Journey in Bringing Together Indigenous and Western Scientific Knowledges. In *T'an Wetapeksi'k: Understanding From Where We Come. Proceedings of the 2005 Debert Research Workshop. Debert, Nova Scotia, Canada*, edited by Tim Bernard, Leah

Morine Rosenmeier, and Sharon Farrell, pp. 179–186. Eastern Woodland Print Communications, Truro, Nova Scotia.

Bartlett, Cheryl M., Murdena Marshall, and Albert Marshall

2012 Two-Eyed Seeing and Other Lessons Learned within a Co-learning Journey of Bringing Together Indigenous and Mainstream Knowledges and Ways of Knowing. *Journal of Environmental Studies and Sciences* 2:331–340.

Bartlett, Cheryl M., Murdena Marshall, Albert Marshall, and Marilyn Iwama

2015 Integrative Science and Two-Eyed Seeing: Enriching the Discussion Framework for Healthy Communities. In *Ecosystems, Society, and Health: Pathways Through Diversity, Convergence, and Integration*, edited by Lars K. Hallström, Nicholas P. Guehlstorf, and Margot W. Parkes, pp 280–326. McGill-Queen's University Press, Montréal, Quebec, and Kingston, Ontario.

Battiste, Marie

1997 Introduction. In *The Mi'kmaw Concordat*, edited by J. (Sákéj) Youngblood Henderson, pp. 13–20. Fernwood, Halifax.

Beck, Jane C.

1972 The Giant Beaver: A Prehistoric Memory? *Ethnohistory* 19(2):109–122.

Bernard, Tim, Leah Rosenmeier, and Sharon Farrell

2015 Mi'kmawe'l Tan Teli-kina'muemk: Teaching about the Mi'kmaq. Electronic document, https://www.mikmaweydebert.ca/home/wp-content/uploads/2015/06/Mikmawel_Tan_Telikinamuemk_Final_Online.pdf, accessed November 15, 2021.

Black, David

2011 Background, Discussion and Recommendations for Extending the Analysis of Lithic Materials Used by Palaeoindians at the Debert and Belmont Sites. In *T'an Wetapeksi'k: Understanding From Where We Come. Proceedings of the 2005 Debert Research Workshop. Debert, Nova Scotia, Canada*, edited by Tim Bernard, Leah Morine Rosenmeier, and Sharon Farrell, pp. 111–131. Eastern Woodland Print Communications, Truro, Nova Scotia.

Blair, Susan

2010 Missing the Boat in Lithic Procurement: Watercraft and the Bulk Procurement of Tool-Stone on the Maritime Peninsula. *Journal of Anthropological Archaeology* 29:33–46.

Campbell, John Andrew

2016 Mu Awsami Keji'kewe'k L'nuk Mi'kma'ki: New Perspectives on the Transitional Archaic Period in Southwestern Nova Scotia. Master's thesis, Department of Archaeology, Memorial University of Newfoundland, St. John's.

Clark, Jeffrey T.

1981 Glass Scrapers from Historic North America. *Lithic Technology* 10(2/3):31–34.

Clermont, Norman

1986 L'adaptation maritime au pays des Micmacs. In *Les Micmacs et la mer*, edited by Charles Martijn, pp. 11–27. Recherches amérindiennes au Québec, Montréal.

Crellin, Rachel J.

2020 *Change and Archaeology*. Routledge, London.

Davis, Stephen A.
2011 Mi'kmakik Teloltipnik L'nuk – Saqiwe'k L'nuk: How Ancient People Lived in Mi'kma'ki. In *T'an Wetapeksi'k: Understanding From Where We Come. Proceedings of the 2005 Debert Research Workshop. Debert, Nova Scotia, Canada*, edited by Tim Bernard, Leah Morine Rosenmeier, and Sharon Farrell, pp. 11–22. Eastern Woodland Print Communications, Truro.

Davis, Derek S., and Sue Browne
1996 *The Natural History of Nova Scotia*. 2 Volumes. Nimbus Publishing and the Nova Scotia Museum, Halifax.

Deal, Michael
1989 The Distribution and Prehistoric Exploration of Scots Bay Chalcedonies. Paper presented at the 22nd Annual Meeting of the Canadian Archaeological Association, Fredericton.

Deal, Michael (editor)
1998 *Memoirs on the Prehistory of Nova Scotia, 1957-1967. By John Steuart Erskine.* Nova Scotia Museum Special Report. Nova Scotia Museum, Halifax.

Deal, Michael, and Brian Hayden
1987 The Persistence of Pre-Columbian Lithic Technology. In *Lithic Studies among the Contemporary Maya*, edited by Brian Hayden, pp. 235–331. University of Arizona Press, Tucson.

Gloade, Gerald
2008 Mi'kmawey Debert Cultural Centre: Cultural Memory Timeline Embedded in the Mi'kmaq [*sic*] Legends of Kluskap. In *Preserving Aboriginal Heritage: Technical and Traditional Approaches*, edited by Carole Dignard, Kate Helwig, Janet Mason, Kathy Nanowin and Thomas Stone, pp. 245–251. Canadian Conservation Institute, Ottawa.

Gonzalez, Sara L.
2016 Indigenous Values and Methods in Archaeological Practice: Low-Impact Archaeology through the Kashaya Pomo Interpretive Trail Project. *American Antiquity* 81(3):533–549.

Harrison, Rodney
2003 "The Magical Virtue of these Sharp Things": Colonialism, Mimesis and Knapped Bottle Glass Artefacts in Australia. *Journal of Material Culture* 8(3): 311–336.

Ingold, Tim
1993 The Temporality of the Landscape. *World Archaeology* 25(2):152–174.

Julien, Donald M., Tim Bernard, and Leah M. Rosenmeier (with review by the Mi'kmawey Debert Elders' Advisory Council)
2016 Paleo is Not Our Word: Protecting and Growing a Mi'kmaw Place. In *Archaeologies of Placemaking: Monuments, Memories, and Engagement in Native North America*, edited by Patricia E. Rubertone, pp. 35–57. Routledge, New York.

Keppie J. D. (compiler)
2000 *Geological Map of the Province of Nova Scotia*. Nova Scotia Department of Natural Resources, Minerals and Energy Branch, Map ME 2000-1, scale 1:500 000.

Knockwood, Doug
2018   Doug Knockwood, Mi'kmaw Elder: Stories, Memories, Reflections. Roseway, Halifax.
Kostro, Mark and Alexandra G. Martin
2019   Knapped Glass Tools at the Eighteenth-Century Brafferton Indian School. In *Building the Brafferton: The Founding, Funding and Legacy of America's Indian School*, edited by Danielle Moretti-Langholtz and Buck Woodard, pp. 206–216. Muscarelle Museum of Art, Williamsburg.
Kovach, Margaret
2015   Emerging from the Margins: Indigenous Methodologies. In *Research as Resistance: Revisiting Critical, Indigenous, and Anti-Oppressive Approaches,* edited by Susan Strega and Leslie Brown, pp. 43–64. Canadian Scholars' Press and Women's Press, Toronto.
Laluk, Nicholas C.
2017   The Indivisibility of Land and Mind: Indigenous Knowledge and Collaborative Archaeology within Apache Contexts. *Journal of Social Archaeology* 17(1): 92–112.
Leland, Charles G.
1884   *The Algonquin Legends of New England.* Houton, Mifflin, Boston.
Lelièvre, Michelle A.
2017a   Report on the Sub-surface Testing of Three Sites (BjDc-06, BiDc-01, and BiDc-02) near Parrsboro, Cumberland County, Nova Scotia, July 2016. Permit A2016NS053. Manuscript on file with the Department of Communities, Culture, and Heritage. Halifax.
2017b   Constructing a Sacred Chronology: How the Nova Scotian Institute of Science Made the Mi'kmaq a People Without Prehistory. *Ethnohistory* 64(3):401–426.
2018   Report on the Sub-surface Testing and Site Visits around Advocate Harbour, Parrsboro, and Gerrish Valley, Cumberland County, Nova Scotia, July 2017. Permit A2017NS034. Manuscript on file with the Department of Communities, Culture, and Heritage. Halifax.
2019   Report on Sub-surface Testing at BjDc-06 and Site Visits at Newville Lake, Cumberland County, Nova Scotia. July 2018. Permit A2018NS058. Manuscript on file with the Department of Communities, Culture, and Heritage. Halifax.
2021   Report on Ground Penetrating Radar Surveys at BjDc-06 and the Northwest Area of Newville Lake and Sub-surface Testing at BjDc-07 in Cumberland County, Nova Scotia. July 2019. Permit A2019NS050. Manuscript on file with the Department of Communities, Culture, and Heritage. Halifax.
Lelièvre, Michelle A., Cynthia Martin, Alyssa Abram, and Mallory Moran
2020   Bridging Indigenous Studies and Archaeology Through Relationality? Collaborative Research on the Chignecto Peninsula, Mi'kma'ki. *American Indian Quarterly* 44(2):171–195.
Lepofsky, Dana, Chelsey Geralda Armstrong, Spencer Greening, Julia Jackley, Jennifer Carpenter, Brenda Guernsey, Darcy Mathews, and Nancy J. Turner

2017   Historical Ecology of Cultural Keystone Places of the Northwest Coast. *American Anthropologist* 119(3):448–463.

Lewis, Roger

2006   Mi'kmaq [*sic*] Rights & Title Claim: A Review of the Precontact Archaeological Factor. *Mi'kmaq Maliseet Nations News*, 16–17 June. Truro.

McNiven, Ian J.

2016   Theoretical Challenges of Indigenous Archaeology: Setting an Agenda. *American Antiquity* 81:27–41.

McNiven, Ian J., and Lynette Russell

2005   *Appropriated Pasts: Indigenous Peoples and the Colonial Culture of Archaeology.* AltaMira Press, Lanham, Maryland.

Membertou Geomatics Consultants (MGC)

2009   Phase 1 - Bay of Fundy, Nova Scotia Including the Fundy Tidal Energy Demonstration Project Site Mi'kmaq [*sic*] Ecological Knowledge Study. Electronic document, https://fundyforce.ca/resources/f1c21770b59114114866 df4d49139581/2009-Phase-I-MEKS-FORCE-MembertouGeomatics-Consultants.pdf, accessed November 15, 2021.

Million, Tara

2005   Developing an Aboriginal Archaeology: Receiving Gifts from White Buffalo Calf Woman. In *Indigenous Archaeologies: Decolonising Theory and Practice*, edited by Claire Smith and Hans Martin Wobst, pp. 39–51. Routledge, New York and London.

Nieves, Josué R.

2021   "These Their Women Bear after Them, with Corne, Acorns, Morters, and All Bag and Baggage They Use": An Archaeological History of Indigenous Households along the Rappahannock River, Virginia. PhD dissertation, Department of Anthropology, William & Mary, Williamsburg, Virginia.

Nova Scotia Museum

1933–1937   Provincial Museum Accession Book. September 1933–November 1937. Manuscript on file at the Heritage Division of the Nova Scotia Department of Communities, Culture and Heritage, Halifax.

Oland, Maxine, Siobhan M. Hart, and Liam Frink (editors)

2012   *Decolonizing Indigenous Histories: Exploring Prehistoric/Colonial Transitions in Archaeology.* University of Arizona Press, Tucson.

Pacifique, Père

1934   *Le Pays des Micmacs.* Chez Ducharme, Montréal.

1990   *The Micmac Grammar of Father Pacifique.* Translated and retranscribed by John Hewson and Bernard Francis. Memoir 7. Algonquian and Iroquoian Linguistics, Winnipeg.

Panich, Lee M.

2013   Archaeologies of Persistence: Reconsidering the Legacies of Colonialism in Native North America. *American Antiquity* 78(1):105–122.

Parsons, Elsie Clews

1925   Micmac Folklore. *Journal of American Folklore* 38(147):55–133.

Piers, Harry

1912 Brief Account of the Micmac Indians of Nova Scotia and Their Remains. *Proceedings of the Nova Scotian Institute of Science* 13, Part 2:99–125.

Porter, Colin A.

2015 Identification and Analysis of Utilized Glass in Early Colonial Contexts: A Case Study from 17th-century Rhode Island. *Technical Briefs in Historical Archaeology* 9:1–15.

Rand, Silas T.

1919 *Micmac Place-Names in the Maritime Provinces and Gaspé Peninsula Recorded between 1852 and 1890.* Surveyor General's Office, Ottawa.

1971 [1894] *Legends of the Micmacs.* Longmans, Green, New York.

Rosenmeier, Leah

2010 Towards an Archaeology of Descent: Spatial Practice and Communities of Shared Experience in Mi'kma'ki. PhD dissertation, Department of Anthropology, Brown University, Providence, Rhode Island.

Sable, Trudy

2011 Legends as Maps. In *T'an Wetapeksi'k: Understanding From Where We Come. Proceedings of the 2005 Debert Research Workshop. Debert, Nova Scotia, Canada*, edited by Tim Bernard, Leah Morine Rosenmeier, and Sharon Farrell, pp. 151–171. Eastern Woodland Print Communications, Truro.

Sable, Trudy, and Bernie Francis

2012 *The Language of this Land: Mi'kma'ki.* Cape Breton University Press, Sydney.

Shaw, John, Carl L. Amos, David A. Greenberg, Charles T. O'Reilly, D. Russell Parrott, and Eric Patton

2010 Catastrophic Tidal Expansion in the Bay of Fundy, Canada. *Canadian Journal of Earth Sciences* 47:1079–1091.

Silliman, Stephen W.

2009 Change and Continuity, Practice and Memory: Native American Persistence in Colonial New England. *American Antiquity* 74(2):211–230.

Smith, A. Tanner

1936 Transportation and Communication in Nova Scotia, 1749 to 1815. Master's thesis, Department of History, Dalhousie University, Halifax.

Speck, Frank

1915 Penobscot Tales. Some Micmac Tales from Cape Breton Island. Some Naskapi Myths from Little Whale River. *Journal of American Folklore* 28:52–77.

Stea, Ralph R., and Daryl M. Wightman

1987 Age of the Five Islands Formation, Nova Scotia, and the Deglaciation of the Bay of Fundy. *Quaternary Research* 27:211–219.

Swift, Donald J. P., and Harold W. Burns, Jr.

1967 A Raised Fluviomarine Outwash Terrace, North Shore of the Minas Basin, Nova Scotia. *The Journal of Geology* 75(6):693–710.

Trigger, Bruce

1980 Archaeology and the Image of the American Indian. *American Antiquity* 45(4): 662–676.

Whitehead, Ruth Holmes
1991   *The Old Man Told Us: Excerpts from Mi'kmaw History 1500-1950*. Nimbus Publishing Ltd., Halifax.
Wicken, William
1994   Encounters with Tall Sails and Tall Tales: Mi'kmaq [*sic*] Society 1500–1760. PhD dissertation, Department of History, McGill University, Montréal.
Wightman, Darryl M.
1980   Late Pleistocene Glaciofluvial and Glaciomarine Sediments on the North Side of the Minas Basin, Nova Scotia. PhD dissertation, Department of Geology, Dalhousie University, Halifax.
Wylie, Alison
2015   A Plurality of Pluralisms: Collaborative Practice in Archaeology. In *Objectivity in Science: New Perspectives from Science and Technology Studies*, edited by Flavia Padovani, Alan Richardson, and Jonathan Y. Tsou, pp. 189–210. Springer, Dondrecht, Netherlands.

VARIATION AMID HOMOGENEITY

An Examination of Early Ceramic Period Technologies from the Penobscot River Valley in Maine

Bonnie D. Newsom

Abstract

The introduction of Aboriginal pottery in Maine and the Canadian Maritimes marks an important technological and cultural shift among peoples living in the region. These early pots, commonly referred to as Vinette 1 pottery, often serve as a relative dating tool in reconstructions of archaeological sites and cultural landscapes based on their defining technological and morphological characteristics, such as fabric-impressed interior and exterior surfaces, coarse grit temper, conoidal bases, and thick vessel walls. Early ceramic vessels with these particular characteristics are widespread across the region. Such homogeneity in traits has been interpreted as an indicator of widespread social interaction, and studies to discern technological variation within this horizon style have been rare. To begin to fully understand the socio-cultural dynamics associated with the initial manufacture and use of pottery in the region, localized studies to identify heterogeneity within the horizon style are necessary. To that end, this paper presents the results of a study designed to discern distinctive technological characteristics of Early Ceramic period ceramics in the Penobscot River Valley, Maine.

Résumé

L'adoption de la poterie par les peuples autochtones du Maine et des provinces maritimes canadiennes marqua pour eux un changement culturel et technologique important. Ces premiers vases, du style communément appelé Vinette 1, servent souvent de repère de datation relative dans l'analyse des sites archéologiques et des paysages culturels. Leurs principaux attributs morphologiques et technologiques incluent les impressions textiles sur leurs surfaces intérieures et extérieures, l'utilisation de dégraissants minéraux grossiers, une base conoïdale et des parois épaisses. Les récipients céramiques datant de cette période et présentant ces caractéristiques sont communs à la grandeur de la région. L'homogénéité de ces attributs a été interprétée comme indicatrice d'interactions sociales dynamiques au début du Sylvicole. Bien peu d'études se sont cependant appliquées à discerner des variations technologiques à l'intérieur de cet horizon. Il est pourtant crucial de pouvoir identifier ces traits hétérogènes à l'échelle locale si l'on souhaite parvenir à une plus grande compréhension des dynamiques socioculturelles associées aux débuts de la fabrication et de l'utilisation de la céramique. Dans cette optique, cet article présente les résultats préliminaires d'une étude visant à définir les attributs technologiques caractérisant les récipients du début de la période Céramique dans la vallée de la rivière Penobscot, au Maine.

Affiliation
– Department of Anthropology, Climate Change Institute, University of Maine, Maine, United States (bonnie.newsom@maine.edu)

Early Ceramics and Archaeological Interpretations

Indigenous peoples in Maine and the Canadian Maritimes integrated clay pots into their lifeways roughly 3,000 years ago, marking one of the most visible and important material culture shifts in regional archaeology. Early Wabanaki potters approached their craft in ways similar to their neighbours across New England and into New York and Canada, creating clay pots with similar surface treatments, temper types, and morphology. The first ceramics in the Maine–Maritimes region resemble the New York Vinette 1 type, as defined by Ritchie and MacNeish (1949), and exhibit characteristics such as fabric-impressed interior and exterior surfaces, coarse grit temper, straight walls, conoidal bases, and rounded or sometimes pointed rims.

In a 1973 meeting of archaeologists working in the Maine–Maritimes region, participants agreed to a "moratorium on named types" based on interpretive implications of typological nomenclature that may not apply to the region (Sanger 1974:128; Leonard 1995). Despite this, the Vinette 1 construct and its defining suite of attributes have influenced Maine–Maritimes ceramic analyses and interpretations. For example, Petersen and Sanger (1991:126) acknowledge similarities between the first Aboriginal ceramics in the Maine–Maritimes region and the Vinette 1 type, and they interpret the shared ceramic traits as a "horizon style" indicative of widespread social interaction. Given the endless options people have in manipulating clay to meet their needs, understanding the social and cultural meaning behind such apparent homogeneity in pottery across a broad region is important. Yet, the influence of the Vinette 1 construct across the Northeast has skewed our interpretations away from the vantage point of the potter, resulting in few efforts to differentiate how potters approached their craft technologically and identify what those differences might mean culturally. This, in turn, has inhibited our understanding of the socio-cultural dynamics associated with the initial manufacture and use of ceramics in the Maine–Maritimes region.

The goal of this chapter is to look beyond the "normative" (Claassen 1991; Lyman and O'Brien 2004) concept of the Vinette 1 horizon style in order to highlight ceramic variability, acknowledge Indigenous agency in the ceramic production process, and advance our understanding of the socio-cultural dimensions of the first pottery. I do this through a comparative analysis of Early Ceramic period (ca. 3050–2150 BP) pottery from 10 archaeological sites in the Penobscot River Valley in central Maine. I approach the study using agency and technological style as theoretical scaffolding. In the following sections, I provide background information on archaeological studies of the first pottery in the Northeast, followed by a discussion of the theoretical and methodological approach taken here; then, I present the results of my analysis and offer an interpretive discussion and some preliminary conclusions.

Given the diversity in archaeological labels applied to the time period and associated ceramics explored here, a note on terminology is warranted (see Leonard 1995). Labels such as Early Woodland, Early Ceramic, or Ceramic period 1 (Petersen and Sanger 1991) are used regionally to represent the period between ca. 3050 and 2150 BP, and pottery associated with, and diagnostic of, this time period may be referred to in the literature as Ceramic period 1 pottery, Early Woodland pottery, or Vinette 1 pottery. In what follows, I use "early" when referencing the first ceramic(s) or pottery in the region and "Early Ceramic" to refer to the associated time period. When referencing studies outside of the Maine–Maritimes region, I use nomenclature published by regional scholars when quoting them directly.

Research on Early Ceramics in the Northeast

Research focused specifically on the first ceramics in the Maine–Maritimes region has been sparse, hampered by limited data sets and few ceramics specialists. Studies of early ceramics exist for the region, but they are often generated as part of a larger research focus such as archaeological site reports or regional ceramic chronologies (Borstel 1982; Bourgeois 1999; Deal 1986; Kristmanson 1992; Mack et al. 2002; Petersen and Sanger 1991). In the 1980s, several key studies on early ceramics demonstrated the utility of exploring variability to address anthropological questions (Doyle et al. 1982; Hamilton 1985; Petersen and Hamilton 1984). For example, Doyle and colleagues (1982)

conducted a comparative analysis of early ceramics recovered from five archaeological sites in diverse ecological settings in southwestern Maine. Based on a
comparison of ceramic attributes, the authors report that the ceramics in the
samples are "relatively uniform throughout their range of distribution" (Doyle
et al. 1982:15), except with regard to fibre perishables used in ceramic surface
treatments, which they note varied in terms of coastal and interior cordage twist
patterns. Cordage is produced by spinning fibres together to create strands that
can then be twisted together to make a thicker, stronger strand. When producing
cordage, there are two options with respect to spin and twist—either S-spin,
Z-twist or Z-spin, S-twist (Hurley 1979; figure 10.1 below). These classifications
reflect whether the cordage maker uses a right-over-left or left-over-right technique when twisting strands of fibres together. The two techniques are distinguished by the angle of the cordage, which may be visible on the surface of
fabric- or cordage-impressed clay pots. Doyle and colleagues (1982:15) revealed
that S-twist cordage was evident at both coastal and interior sites, whereas
Z-twist cordage was only present in samples from coastal sites, leading them to
speculate that different coastal and interior populations may have occupied
Maine during the Early Ceramic period.

Subsequent studies on early ceramics in Maine continued this line of inquiry,
and based on a review of fibre perishable data across the Northeast, Petersen and
Hamilton (1984:435) observed the coastal and interior twist distinction in their
analysis of 26 sites in Maine. They suggested that differences in cordage twist preference is "indicative of different social groups" (Petersen and Hamilton 1984:438).
I return to this topic later in this chapter, but it is important to note here that not
only did these studies showcase variability in early ceramics, they helped reinforce
the value of a non-typological analytical approach to regional ceramics.

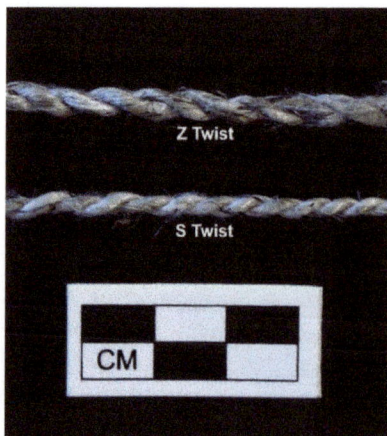

Figure 10.1. Examples of Z- and S-twist cordage made by the author from milkweed fibres.

Regionally, studies of the first pottery have been much broader in focus and research on early ceramics has gained momentum in recent years (Bunker 2002; Mitchell 2017; Taché 2005; Taché et al. 2008; Taché and Craig 2015; Taché and Hart 2013). These researchers take various approaches to their studies focusing on ceramic technology and variability in more detail, thereby moving us beyond strictly typological analyses or general descriptions. In this vein, Bunker (2002) conducted a technological analysis of two early ceramic vessels (ca. 3000–2150 BP) recovered from the Beaver Meadow Brook and Eddy sites in the Merrimack River Valley in New Hampshire. She acknowledges that early potters in the area "participated in a single cultural tradition, geographically linked to the interior watersheds of [...] central and northern New England" (Bunker 2002:220). She also points out that these potters were technologically savvy and made manufacturing decisions informed by their needs and social contexts—a theme that is emerging more frequently through ceramics studies in the Northeast (Chilton 1996, 1998, 1999; Kristmanson and Deal 1993; Mitchell 2017; Newsom 2017; Pretola 2000, 2002; Stapelfeldt 2009; Taché 2005). A case in point is Bunker's (2002:222) interpretation that potters' selection of thick walls made these pots "suitable for slow simmering next to a fire, in coals, or on the edge of a hearth." She challenged Fowler (1966:53), who interpreted thick walls and coarse temper as evidence of Indigenous peoples' lack of knowledge of pottery production. Bunker (2002:221) argues that this view is unwarranted because, based on her study, potters were aware of the characteristics of a successful cooking pot.

Similar to Bunker (2002), other ceramics researchers have focused on the technical aspects of early pottery, and Taché's (2005) study of ceramics at the Batiscan site in Quebec is a good example of this. In that study, she examined pottery variability as part of her exploration of the Meadowood Interaction Sphere—an archaeological construct denoting regional social interaction during the Early Woodland period (ca. 3000–2400 BP). Taché (2005:173) analyzed technological, techno-stylistic, morphological, and use-related characteristics of early pottery at the Batiscan site and compared them to ceramic data regionwide. She observed several characteristics in the Batiscan-site sample that varied from the Vinette 1 type as defined by Ritchie and MacNeish (1949). For example, Taché noted that some pots lacked cordage impressions and that pots at Batiscan generally had thinner vessel walls and rims than at other sites. She also observed variability in pot size, and that lip shapes varied based on cordage twist direction (Taché 2005:193-199). Her proposed explanations for this variability include location-based environmental constraints, potters' experimentation with new technology, acquiring a "mastery" of the craft, functional differences in pots, and differences between imported and locally made pots.

Mitchell (2017) took a slightly different approach to identifying variation within Ritchie and MacNeish's (1949) Vinette 1 type, whereby she conducted a study blending petrography with geoarchaeology to examine the technological choices of early potters in New York. She focused specifically on temper, coiling techniques, and firing conditions, and used agency and technological-style approaches to examine these characteristics (Mitchell 2017:100). Based on her analysis of potters' manufacturing choices, she showed that these early ceramics varied in terms of clay sources, the type and amount of crushed rock added to the clay matrix, firing atmosphere, and firing conditions. Through a detailed examination of ceramic fabrics (clays and inclusions), Mitchell (2017) divided vessel lots into three primary groups based on ceramic "recipes." These included a quartz-rich group, a feldspar-rich group, and a mafic-rich group, and, according to Mitchell (2017:232), dark mafic-rich rocks were "more commonly sought after than either feldspar or quartz-rich rock combined." Like other studies discussed here, Mitchell's research exemplifies how variation within early ceramics are revealed when analyses move beyond typological classifications.

Theoretical Framework

A recurring theme among the studies discussed above is the interplay between technology, choice, variability, and homogeneity in early ceramics. The present study builds on these technology studies and is guided by human-centred approaches of agency (Dobres 1999, 2000; Dobres and Robb 2000, 2005; Gardner 2007; Sassaman 2000) and technological-style (Childs 1991; Costin 1999; Hegmon 1998; Lechtman 1977) theories—two complementary frameworks that move archaeological inquiry beyond normative interpretations of material culture toward more humanistic representations of the past. Agency, defined by Brumfiel (2000:250) as "the intentional choices made by men and women as they take action to realize their goals," is a useful paradigm for humanizing archaeological research because it acknowledges people's influence on their material and social spheres by way of their actions, beliefs, and decisions, and that those spheres are intimately connected. However, in order to validate agency theory as effective in understanding past peoples, archaeologists need methodological tactics designed to "get at" agency (Dobres and Robb 2005). This is where technological style becomes useful as a complementary theoretical tool.

The concept of technological style has been around archaeology for some time and was pioneered by Lechtman (1977:5), who recognized that "the activities themselves which produce the artifacts are stylistic." Technological style is the product of technological choices made along an operational sequence or behavioural chain within the context of natural and social constraints and opportunities (Lemonnier 1992, 1993; Schiffer and Skibo 1997). Archaeologists and ethnoarchaeologists have increasingly designed material culture studies with a technological-style focus (Braun 2010; Childs 1991; Costin 1999; Gosselain 1992; Hegmon et al. 2000; Mahias 1993; Stark et al. 1998; van der Leeuw 1991, 1993).

In the Northeast, Chilton (1996, 1998, 1999) applied a technological-style approach to her analysis of Aboriginal ceramics from three Late Woodland (ca. 950–350 BP) sites in New England and New York. Her analysis identified distinct differences in the technological choices made by Algonquian and Iroquoian potters, showing that choices identified within the ceramic manufacturing process could be used to interpret social organization. Specifically, she focused on potters' choices regarding paste characteristics, shaping techniques, and temper type, and this approach enabled her to identify a greater degree of diversity among Algonquian pots than among Iroquoian ones. Chilton (1996, 1998, 1999) concluded that differences in Algonquian and Iroquoian pots reflected differences in the scale and context of ceramic production, the intended use of pots, and the social basis for choices made during the ceramic manufacturing process. What is important to note here is that Chilton would not have seen these differences had she approached the study using predetermined types based on a priori attribute patterns defined by archaeologists through normative approaches.

The present study emulates Chilton's approach, and, as a conceptual framework for this study, I attempt to capture the interdependent nature of people and their material culture by emphasizing the role and power of human decision-making on their material world. The intent here is to acknowledge potters' agency and view material culture from the vantage point of the people acting on it as a way to move beyond interpretations linked to the Vinette 1 type and other normative approaches to ceramic studies in the Maine–Maritimes region. Theoretically and methodologically, it is aligned with a recent comparative analysis of Middle Ceramic period (ca. 2150–950 BP) pottery from coastal and interior sites in the Penobscot River Valley (see Newsom 2017), showing technological variation in ceramic attributes based on site location, which in some cases was maintained across multiple temporal units. With a few exceptions, the sites in both studies are the same.

Sites and Data Sets

This chapter focuses on potters living in the Penobscot River valley of Maine, where past archaeological research provides a robust ceramics data set to explore potters' choices and ceramic technologies (Belcher 1988; Borstel 1982; Bourque 1995; Mack et al. 2002; Newsom 1999, 2017; Petersen and Sanger 1987; Sanger et al. 1977). The ceramic samples selected for this study were recovered from 10 sites located in three distinct areas within the Penobscot River Valley—a northern area, a central area, and a coastal area (figure 10.2). The locations selected fall within three distinct physiographic divisions—the eastern lowlands region, the central interior region and the Penobscot Bay region, as defined by McMahon (1990). These are distinguished from one another based on differences in environmental characteristics such as climate, vegetation, soils, and topography.

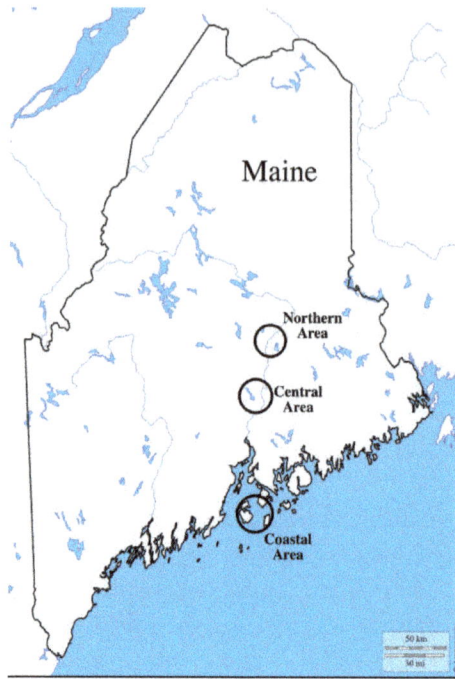

Figure 10.2. Map depicting study areas, Penobscot River Valley, Maine.

Examining ceramic data from three distinct settings within one river system allows scrutiny of potters' choices in a localized way. I opted to focus on samples from one river system because previous ceramics and seasonality data from coastal and interior sites in Maine have pointed to two distinct populations occupying these settings prior to European contact—one coastally adapted group, and another group adapted to interior settings (Petersen and Hamilton 1984; Petersen 1996; Sanger 1996a), therefore, some level of variability in early ceramics might be expected. Here, I discuss each of these areas briefly and provide the reader with some archaeological context for the samples included in this study. Henceforth, sites and their associated samples will be referred to as "Northern," "Central," or "Coastal" based on their locations within the river system. See table 10.1 for additional details on individual sites included in this study.

The Northern ceramics sample was recovered from three sites located on the Piscataquis River near Howland, Maine (figure 10.3). The Piscataquis River is a western branch of the Penobscot River, and archaeological sites in this area have produced evidence of Indigenous families[1] using these locations during

---

1. One reviewer cautioned against use of the term "families" as it implies a particular type of social structure. My rationale for using the term is twofold: first, references

Table 10.1. Site summaries.

Site Name/Number	# of CPI Vessel lots/sherds	Site Setting	Ceramic Periods Represented	References
Northern Sites				
Seboeis Site/108-38	3/28	River/Stream Confluence	Early to Late	Newsom and Sanger (1998) Newsom (1999)
Bo Island Site/108-36	1/1	Island at River Confluence	Early to Middle	
108-27	1/6	Riverbank (high terrace)	Early to Middle	
Central Sites				
Hirundo Site/73-9	6/63	Streambank	Early to Late	Sanger et al. (1977)
Young Site/73-10	4/91	Streambank	Early to Middle	Borstel (1982)
Eddington Bend Site/74-8	3/5	Riverbank (high terrace)	Early to Late	Newsom (2017)
74-136	2/60	Streambank	Early to Late	Mack et al. (1998)
Bob Site/74-148	9/91	Streambank	Early to Late	Mack et al. (2002)
Coastal Sites				
Knox Site/30-21	5/630	Coastal Island Shell Midden	Early to Late	Belcher (1988)
Turner Farm Site/29.9	24/323	Coastal Island Shell Midden	Early to Late	Bourque (1995)

the Archaic and Ceramic periods (ca. 9000–450 BP) (Cook and Spiess 1981; Newsom and Sanger 1998; Newsom 1999; Sanger and Newsom 2000). Much of the archaeological research conducted in this area has occurred through cultural resources management projects, and the sites selected for this study are a case in point. University of Maine archaeologists excavated sites in the Howland area between 1995 and 1997 in connection with the federal relicensing process for the Howland Dam (Newsom and Sanger 1998; Newsom 1999).

The early ceramic sample from this area consists of 35 sherds recovered from the Seboeis site and site 108-27—two deeply stratified riverbank sites located at the confluences of two small tributaries and the Piscataquis River. The Bo Island site (108-36) is also included in this sample. It is a small island site at the

---

to families are not absent from the anthropological and archaeological literature for the region (Hrynick and Betts 2017; Sanger 1996a, 2005; Snow 1968; Speck 1915, 1927, 1940), and I see my use of the term here appropriate given these previous uses; and second, the term is an alternative to labels such as "occupants" or "inhabitants," which tend to objectify past peoples, thereby dehumanizing them. This counters what I seek to do as an archaeologist; therefore, I retained the term here, meaning no disrespect to the reviewer.

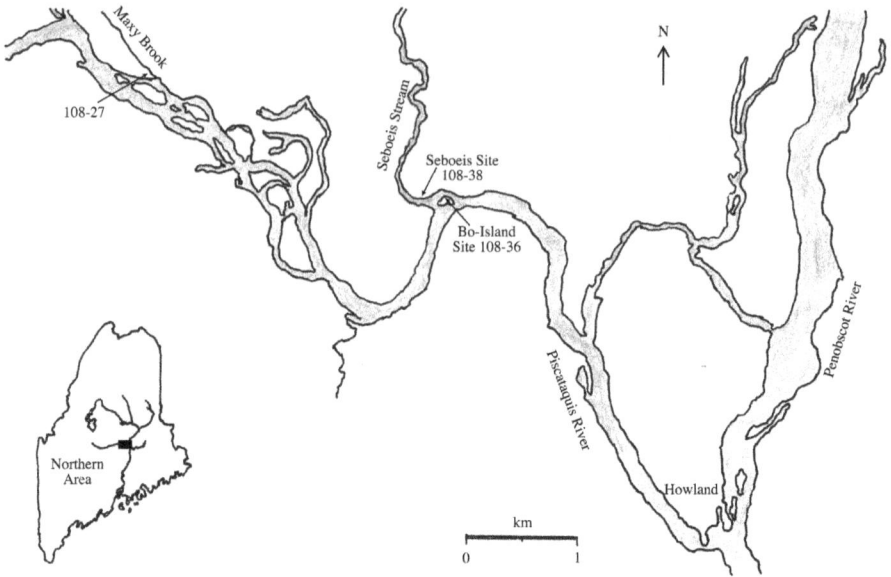

Figure 10.3. Map depicting sites in the Northern area.
Source: Adapted from Newsom (1999).

confluence of the Piscataquis and Penobscot Rivers. These sites produced evidence of Indigenous peoples using this area throughout the Ceramic period (ca. 3050–450 BP) indicating repeated use of these locations over time; however, early ceramics are sparse in comparison to ceramics assigned to the Middle Ceramic period and evidence of Indigenous occupation during the Late Ceramic period (ca. 950–450 BP) is also poorly represented (Newsom 1999).

The ceramic sample from the Central Penobscot River drainage area consists of 310 sherds recovered from four sites—the Hirundo site (73-9); Young site (73-10); Bob site (74-148), and site 73-136, all of which are in the vicinity of Pushaw Stream, a small tributary stream of the Stillwater (Penobscot) River (figure 10.4). Early ceramics from the Eddington Bend site (74-8) on the main stem of the Penobscot River are included in this sample as well. Evidence of Native American families living in the central Penobscot River Valley suggests repeated use of the area from the Late Palaeoindian (ca. 9500 BP) through the Historic period (ca. 400–200 BP) (Mack et al. 2002; Sanger et al. 1992; Sanger 1996b). Significant archaeological research has occurred in this area, either through cultural resources management studies or academic research, and multiple ceramics studies exist from this region (Borstel 1982; Mack et al. 1998; Mack et al. 2002; Mack 2016; Newsom 1999; Newsom 2017). Similar to sites in the Northern area, Early Ceramic sites are fewer than Middle Ceramic ones. However, Kelley (2006) reports that half of the sites near Pushaw Stream have an Early Ceramic component,

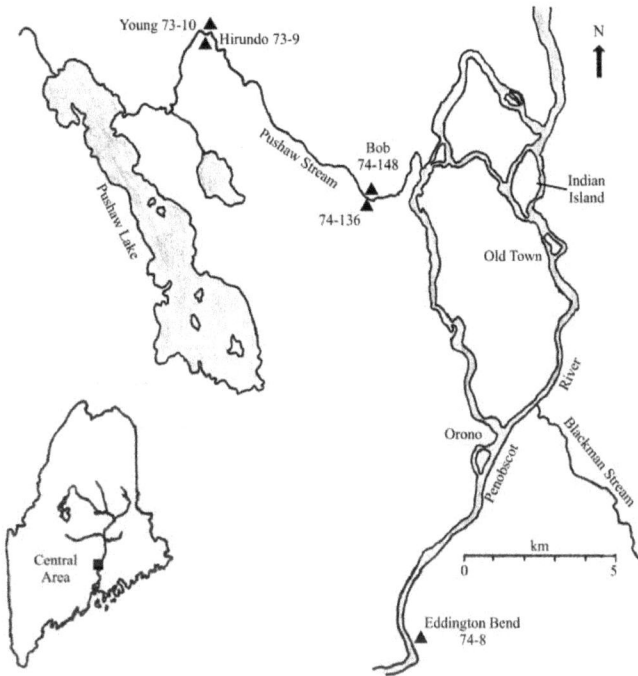

Figure 10.4. Map depicting sites in the Central area.
Source: Adapted from Newsom (1999).

and she points out that this counters Fiedel's (2001) contention that the Early Ceramic period is not well represented in New England due to climatic factors.

The Coastal ceramic sample consists of 953 sherds, which were recovered from two offshore island sites in Penobscot Bay (figure 10.5). One is the Knox site (30-21) located on Pell Island in East Penobscot Bay. Pell Island is situated on a pluton of course-grained granite with outcrops present adjacent to the site and Aboriginal potters may have accessed these outcrops for tempering materials (Belcher 1989). The site was excavated by the University of Maine in 1976 and 1986. Belcher's (1988) study of the Knox site indicates that Native families occupied this location throughout much of the Ceramic period, with the period between ca. 1600 and 1200 BP representing the "most intense occupation of the site" (Belcher 1988:3). Ceramics from the Knox site were analyzed previously by Belcher (1988) and also included in ceramic comparative studies by Mack (1994) and Newsom (2017).

The Turner Farm site (29.9) on North Haven Island in Penobscot Bay is the second Coastal site included in this study. It is a multi-component site with evidence of Native families occupying this location from the Late Archaic (ca. 5300–3000 BP) through the Late Ceramic periods (Bourque 1995; Spiess

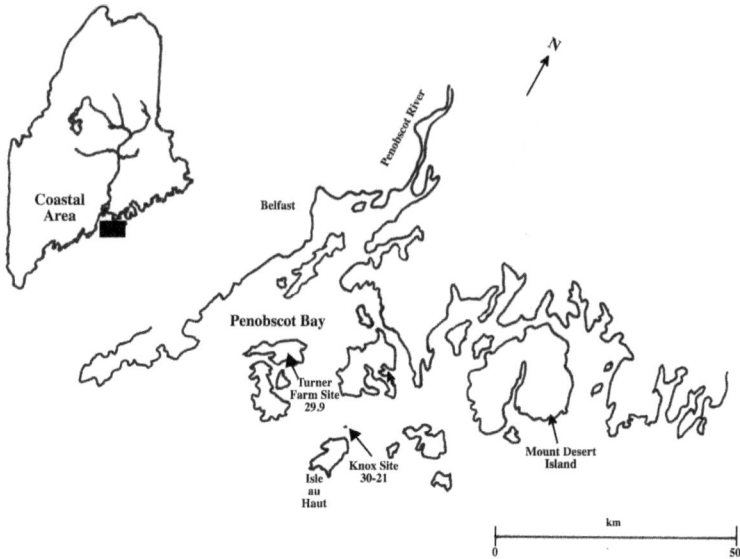

Figure 10.5. Map depicting sites in the Coastal area.
Source: Adapted with permission from Belcher (1988).

and Lewis 2001). The site is situated on a high terrace near a gravel beach, with eroding bluffs, fresh and brackish marshes, and tidal flats located nearby. Archaeological research at this site has focused heavily on the Late Archaic components and lithic and faunal materials (Bourque 1995; Spiess and Lewis 2001). Ceramics from the site span the Ceramic period but published data on this assemblage are limited (Bourque 1995).

Eleven radiocarbon dates associated with early ceramics at the sites included in this study range from 2920 ± 60 (Beta-142045) at the Bob site in the Central area (Mack et al. 2002) to 2020 ± 90 (Beta-20614) at the Knox site in the Coastal area. Except for one recent radiocarbon date of 2510 ± 30 (Beta-558632) on ceramic residues at the Turner Farm site, all dates are from published reports and were obtained prior to 2005. Beta Analytic provided updated calibrations on dates that they produced originally (details on radiocarbon dates from sites in this study are presented in table 10.2; for a detailed discussion of radiocarbon dates associated with early ceramics in the region, see Taché and Hart 2013).

Methods

This analysis compares potters' manufacturing choices in the Penobscot River Valley, and the unit of analysis here is the vessel lot. Defined as "the reconstructed remains of discrete ceramic vessels" (Petersen 1980:11), a vessel-lot analysis reduces statistical misrepresentation of the collection and aids in intra- and

Table 10.2. Radiocarbon dates associated with early ceramics.

Site # and Name	Radiocarbon Lab #	Conventional ^{14}C Age (BP)[a]	cal BP[b] range 95% CI	cal BC range 95% CI	Material Dated	Variables[c]	Citation
108-36 Bo Island Site	Beta-98089	2180 ± 90	2351-1951	402-2	hemlock; feature fill charcoal	d13C=-27.6 o/oo	Newsom (1999)
108-38 Seboeis Site	Beta-98091	2590 ± 100	2867-2361	887-542	birch; feature fill charcoal	d13C=-26.4 o/oo	Newsom (1999)
74-148 Bob Site	Beta-66766	2280 ± 70	2489-2069	540-120	feature fill charcoal	d13C=-26.1 o/oo	Mack et al. (2002)
	Beta-142045	2920 ± 60	3230-2880	1281-931	feature fill charcoal	d13C=-26.1 o/oo	
29.9 Turner Farm Site	SI-2398	2575 ± 75	indetermined	indetermined	Mya	unavailable	Bourque (1995)
	SI-2407	2530 ± 65	indetermined	indetermined	Sea Urchin	unavailable	
	GX-2463	2275±130	indetermined	indetermined	Charcoal	unavailable	
	Beta-558632	2510 ± 30	2740-2489	791-540	Residues on interior surface of CP1 vessel	d13C=-18.7 o/oo	current study
30-21 Knox Site	Beta-20614	2020 ± 90	2302-1738	516-117	Charcoal	est. d13C=-25.0 o/oo	Belcher (1988)
	Beta-20261	2270 ± 70	2465-2066	689-55	Charcoal	est. d13C=-25.0 o/oo	
	Beta-17374	2720 ± 90	3137-2543	1188-594	Charcoal	est. d13C=-25.0 o/oo	

a: All conventional ^{14}C dates are reported as published previously except for Beta 558632 (Turner Farm 29.9 residue sample); b: Calibrations conducted by Beta Analytic in 2020 using OxCal version 4.3 (Ramsey 2009) and IntCal13 database (Reimer et al. 2013); c: d13C values published previously; estimated values of 25.0 o/oo were used for the Knox Site (30-21) where actual values were not available.

inter-site analytical comparisons. Additionally, as Carr (1993:97) points out, "it is the whole vessel, not the sherd, that is the technological, functioning system that interfaces the material world, people, and culture and that is subject to physical and cultural selection." Therefore, a vessel-lot approach supports my aim to explore pottery from the vantage point of the maker, who focuses on the pot holistically.

In total, 58 vessel lots comprised of 1,298 ceramic sherds are included in this study. I analyzed each vessel lot using an attribute analysis of technological choice (Chilton 1996, 1998, 1999). This type of approach differs from typological analyses in that it places equal emphasis on all attributes and does not diminish the importance of variability in a data set (Petersen 1985; Wright 1967). Attribute analyses are applied routinely to ceramic studies in the Maine–Maritimes region but may be limited in terms of which attributes are selected for analysis. For example, Petersen and Sanger (1991:122) identify temper type, surface treatment, and decorative application as being "most sensitive for ceramic differentiation," and, as a result, other choices along the ceramic production sequence, such as temper size and density or wall thickness, may get overlooked during the analytical and interpretive processes. In the present analysis, I examine a broad suite of attributes to highlight potters' manufacturing choices and to minimize a priori assumptions about their interpretive value. The attributes selected for analysis include body and rim thickness, rim eversion, lip shape, primary and secondary surface treatments, cordage twist, inclusion type, and density (for a detailed discussion of attribute definitions and methods, see Newsom 2017:220-222).

Prior to this study, ceramics within each collection underwent varying levels of analysis by other researchers, and I used previously established sherd counts and vessel lots when available. Unpublished ceramic analyses conducted by James Petersen and Kathleen Ferguson were curated with the Hirundo site (73-9) ceramics collection. These were reviewed prior to this analysis, and although their analytical methods were similar, I elected to reanalyze the early ceramic sample for this study. Additionally, I conducted a new attribute analysis on early ceramics from all sites, and recorded both quantitative and qualitative data. Quantitative data such as maximum rim thickness were measured to the nearest .01 mm using digital calipers, and attributes were analyzed either macroscopically or with a 20 x binocular microscope. All attribute data were entered into a Microsoft Access database, and records associated with this analysis are on file in the University of Maine's Anthropology Department. The results of this analysis are presented below.

Results

This analysis revealed both similarity and variation in potters' choices among the Penobscot River Valley early ceramic samples. Here, I discuss these results in the context of three categories—vessel morphology, fabric (paste) character-istics, and surface treatment.

Vessel Morphology

Vessel lots from the three areas show remarkable similarity in morphological characteristics, including average body thickness, rim thickness, and lip shape. For example, average body thicknesses for the Northern (n=5), Central (n=20), and Coastal (n=26) samples measure 9.81 mm, 10.02 mm, and 10.08 mm, respectively. Likewise, rim-thickness measurements taken 1 cm below the lip show little variation based on site location, measuring an average of 7.97 mm in the Central sample (n=13) and 8.03 mm in the Coastal sample (n=10). The Northern sample had only one rim which measured slightly smaller (6.51 mm) than the averages at the other two locations.

Lip shape was also similar across the three locations, classified here as flat, round, pointed, or a combination of more than one shape. Vessel lots with flat lips and round lips occur in similar percentages in the Coastal and Central samples, whereas pointed lips, a common trait of the Vinette 1 type (Ritchie and MacNeish 1949), are rare overall, occurring on two vessels in the Central sample, one of which is in combination with a flat lip shape.

While certain rim attributes show similarities across the three locations, this is not the case for rim eversion, where the Central (n=16) and Coastal (n=8) samples differ. Specifically, vessel lots with direct (straight) rims dominate the Central sample (62.5%; n=10) and excurvate (curving outward) rims dominate the Coastal sample (87.5%; n=7). This variation may reflect a functional differ-ence between the two samples as excurvate rims are typically designed for pouring and they allow easier access to the pot's contents than a rim that is direct or curves in.

Ceramic Fabrics

Rice (2015:456) defines ceramic fabrics as "the composition of a fired ceramic, including clay, inclusions, and pores and excluding surface treatment." Choices related to ceramic fabrics centre on clay and inclusion selection, which are among the first decisions potters make in the manufacturing sequence. Here, I present data on inclusion type and density, both of which are linked to potters' decisions about pot performance, strength, firing, and workability.

Inclusion type refers to the kind of aplastics (organics, grit [crushed rock or minerals], shell, grog, etc.) present within the clay matrix and these are often referred to as temper. The term "temper" implies an intentional addition by the potter (Rice 2015:83-84). Discerning between aplastics occurring naturally in the clay and those added by the potter was not attempted here, so I have opted to use "inclusion" when referring to aplastics within the clay matrix.

Grit inclusions are most common in the vessel lots analyzed here and 91.3% (n=53) of the vessel lots display this type exclusively; the remaining vessel lots (n=5) have a mix of grit and shell/organic inclusions. Grit inclusions within the overall sample are comprised of combinations of feldspars, quartz, and micas, suggesting that crushed granite served as a common inclusion source. However, primary inclusion type (i.e., the most abundant inclusion within the clay matrix) varies based on location. In the Coastal sample, vessel lots with feldspars (62.0%; n=18) outnumber those with quartz (31.9%; n=11); this is also the case for the Northern sample (feldspar 80%, n=4; quartz 20%, n=1). Conversely, the Central sample shows an opposite trend, in which quartz (83.3%; n=20) is more prevalent than feldspar (16.6%; n=4) as the primary inclusion type (figure 10.6). A two-tailed Fisher's exact test (p=0.000579) indicates that a statistically significant association exists between the variables of primary inclusion type and location based on the samples in this study.

Inclusion density represents the percentage of aplastics present in the clay matrix (figure 10.7). Analysis of inclusion densities for all sites from the Penobscot River valley samples indicates that vessel lots with inclusion densities ranging between 3% and 5% are most common, representing 50% (n=29) of the total sample. However, vessel lots with higher and lower-density percentages also occur. Vessel lots with low inclusion densities (1%–2% of the ceramic matrix) represent 20.6% (n=12) of the sample, whereas those with high inclusions densities (10%–20% of the ceramic matrix) represent 29.3% (n=17) of the sample. When the data are compared spatially, the Northern sample has a higher percentage of vessel lots (60%; n=3) with higher density inclusions than the other two locations (figure 10.8).

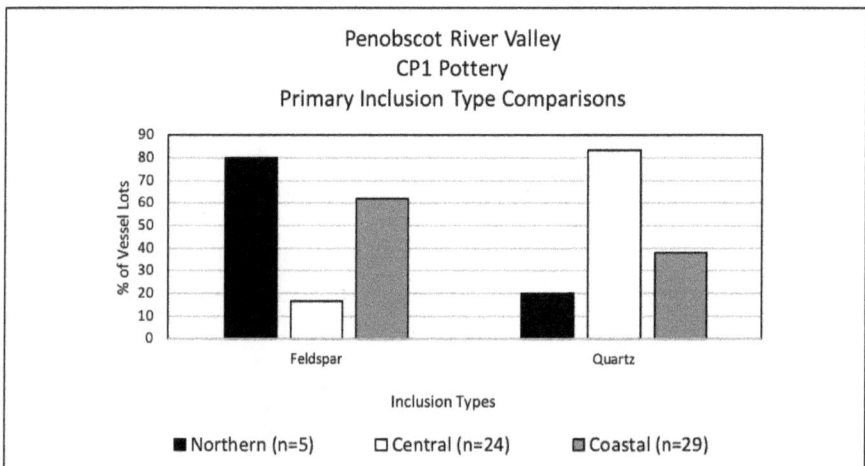

Figure 10.6. Primary inclusion type by location within the Penobscot River Valley.

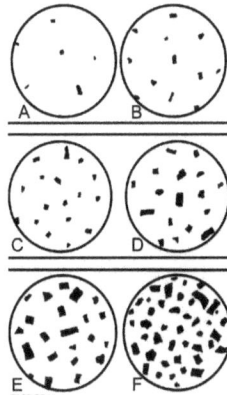

Figure 10.7. Inclusion density chart. (A) 1%; (B) 2%; (C) 3%; (D) 5%; (E) 10%; and (F) 20%. *Source:* Adapted from Philpotts 1989.

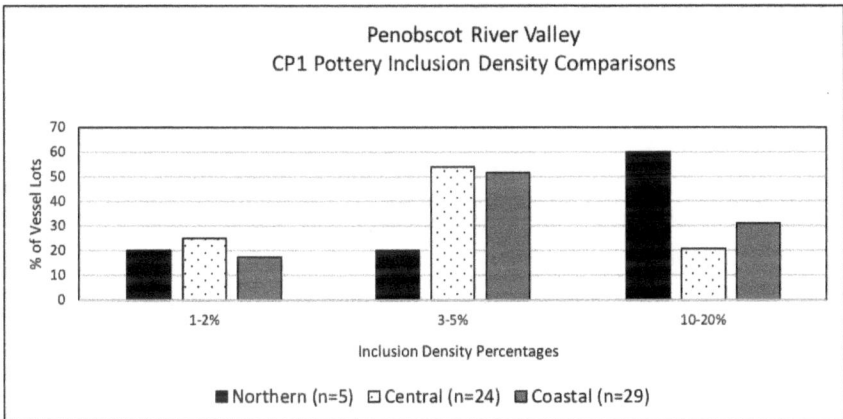

Figure 10.8. Inclusion density by location within the Penobscot River Valley.

Surface Treatments

Surface treatment is one of the last manufacturing choices a potter makes prior to firing a pot and often represents techniques used by the potter before the clay dries completely. All vessel lots in this study exhibit cordage-based impressions on the interior and exterior surfaces of the pot. Cordage imprints on a vessel indicate the use of fibre perishables as part of the surface-treatment stage of manufacture. During the Early Ceramic period, potters in the Maine–Maritimes region impressed vessel surfaces with fibre perishables, such as cordage and netting. These impressions typically exist on both the interior and exterior surfaces of early ceramics. This is a hallmark characteristic of the Vinette 1 type. Some sherds lack cordage impressions, indicating that in some cases, cordage-based surface treatment did not cover the vessel's surface entirely. Most vessel lots exhibit secondary smoothing, with 82.7% (n=48) of the entire sample exhibiting this trait. Interestingly, all of the coastal vessels from both the Turner Farm and Knox sites display secondary smoothing over cordage impressions. This is not the case for the Central and Northern samples, where subsequent smoothing is not evident on 33.3% (n=8) and 40% (n=2) of the vessel lots, respectively.

Figure 10.9. Turner Farm rim sherd showing S-twist cordage impression on the vessel interior.

Both Z- and S-twist cordage patterns occur on vessel lots in this study, and overall, Z- spin, S-twist cordage is most common (82.6%; n=43) (figure 10.9) and dominates all three samples. S-spin, Z-twist cordage is present in small percentages within the Coastal (17.3%; n=7) and Central (10%; n=2) samples and is non-existent in the Northern sample. These distributions would appear to be inconsistent with interior and coastal twist patterns identified for the Maine–Maritimes region (Petersen 1996; Petersen and Hamilton 1984; Petersen and Sanger 1991). However, the results of a two-tailed Fisher's exact test (p=0.294) suggest that there is not a statistically significant association between cordage twist and location based on the samples in this study.

Discussion

The results of this analysis show important technological variation among early ceramics in the Penobscot River Valley, and each location is distinguished from the others in different ways. Morphologically, the Coastal and Central samples differ in terms of rim eversion (figure 10.10). Excurvate rims are more prevalent in the Coastal sample than in the Central sample, and this variation may be based on pot function. According to Rice (2015:422), characteristics of cooking pots generally include an orifice that is accessible for adding or removing food and a slight constriction at the neck to inhibit boil overs (see also Skibo 2013). Additionally, excurvate rims help facilitate transfer of a pot's contents and may aid in accessing the pot contents for stirring or serving. Of note, food residues were observed on 15 vessel lots from the Coastal sample, as opposed to only three vessel lots with residues in the Central sample.

Residue studies on early ceramics led Taché and Craig (2015:79) to propose that the first pots in the region were used to prepare aquatic species for feast events or oil exchange. This interpretation has been subject to some debate (Skibo et al. 2016; Taché et al. 2019). All sites in this study are locations where

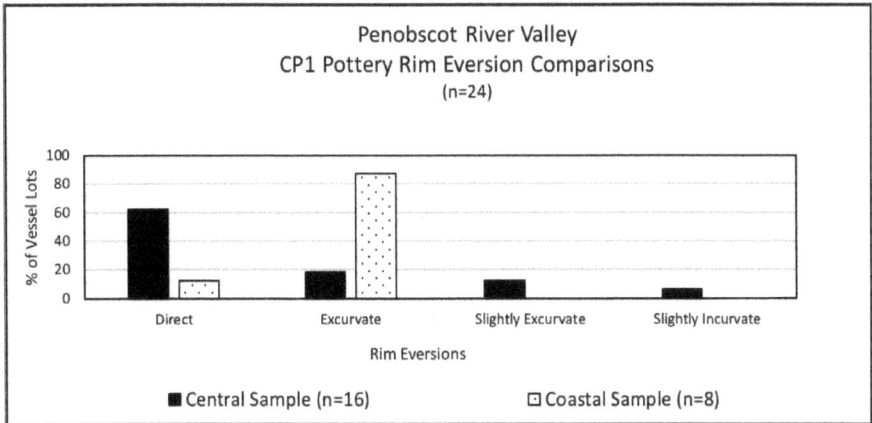

Figure 10.10. Rim eversion types by location within the Penobscot River Valley. SlExc=slightly excurvate; SlInc=slightly incurvate.

Native families would have access to diverse fish species. Although faunal remains from the inland sites are not well preserved, the faunal record at the Turner Farm site in the Coastal sample is well documented (Spiess and Lewis 2001). These data may offer some insight on food shifts accompanying the introduction of ceramics. For example, Spiess and Lewis (2001) report changes in faunal remains between the Late Archaic Susquehanna (ca. 4000–3500 BP) occupation at the site and the subsequent Ceramic period occupation; specifically, faunal data show increasing evidence of seal hunting beginning in the Early Ceramic period. They also note an increased reliance on moose, beaver, flounder, sturgeon, and bird.

The morphology of early pottery at this site would support practices such as simmering meat or processing seal fat for oil, which may or may not require heat (Bogoraz-Tan 1904; Harry and Frink 2009). Additionally, early ceramic-vessel lots in this location show a preference for feldspar-rich inclusions, which are optimal for cooking pots because feldspar has a similar thermal coefficient to clay (Rye 1976). The combination of excurvate rims and feldspar inclusions in vessel lots at the Turner Farm site support the interpretation that early ceramics served as cooking pots. However, determining whether or not they were used to cook seal, process blubber or fish for oil, or to cook something else altogether, remains to be tested.

It is unclear why direct (straight) rims dominate the Central sample. Mack (2002:92) reports a hazelnut fragment from an Early Ceramic period feature at the Bob site in this location. It is possible that early pottery in the Pushaw Stream area was used to roast and/or perhaps collect nuts. These activities would not require excurvate rims, nor would they leave encrusted residues on the vessel surface, but they would require an orifice that makes the contents accessible.

Ceramic fabrics at the three locations also differ. The use of quartz as primary inclusion in the Central sample is notable and could point to quartz's utility in increasing a vessel's mechanical strength (Vekinis and Kilikoglou 1998), which might be an attractive characteristic for pots that are moved from place to place. The high thermal expansion rate of quartz makes a pot less resistant to thermal shock; therefore, its use in pots that are repeatedly heated and cooled is not ideal. That does not preclude a person from using quartz in a cooking pot. Finer grades of quartz can be effective tempers for cooking vessels, particularly if accompanied by thin vessel walls (Rice 2015; Rye 1976). The reliance of quartz-rich inclusions in the Central area could also reflect what is available locally for temper, and sourcing ceramic inclusions would be a valuable research effort in this regard.

Access to resources plays an important role in influencing ceramic recipes. A case in point is potters' temper choices, which may be constrained by what is available environmentally; however, people globally use a wide range of tempers (sand, fur, shell, plant materials, etc.) and as such, temper choices within any given setting have the potential to be highly variable. That being said, the choice to use feldspar-rich inclusions in the Northern area may have been a by-product of what was available locally. Dale (1907:148) refers to historic quarries with granites rich in feldspar roughly 40 miles west of the Howland area. These sources may have been accessed by potters directly; conversely, transport of feldspar-rich granites by ice or fluvial activity may have influenced what was available as cobbles downstream. Cobbles closer to the source may retain more feldspar than cobbles farther away because it is more susceptible to weathering than quartz (Alice Kelley, pers. comm. 2017) and may have influenced potters' temper choices.

However, findings in a study on Middle Ceramic period pottery from the Northern area show a similar preference for feldspar-rich granites, suggesting long-term reliance on this material for temper (Newsom 2017). A preference for high-density inclusions in vessel lots from the Northern area during the Middle Ceramic period is also evident, which is similar to the present study (Newsom 2017). When taken collectively, these inclusion data hint at a manufacturing practice that includes dense, feldspar-rich tempers, which remains consistent through time.

The final suite of attributes discussed here relates to surface treatment. Secondary smoothing over cordage impressions occurred at all locations and is a common trait among early ceramics. We cannot be certain as to why potters smoothed over cordage impressions; however, Velde and Druc (1999:119) note that "the smoothed surface of a ceramic, made by wiping the surface when the clay is plastic or the polishing on semidry surface orients the particles. This gives a resistance to heat transfer to the surface," and aids in slow cooking by helping to keep heat in. Based on this, smoothing would be an appropriate follow-up technique for a cooking pot with a textured surface that was initially cord-wrapped paddled to consolidate coils. Additional research on correlations between cooking-pot characteristics and secondary smoothing on early pottery surfaces may help explain the practice of secondary smoothing on pots in the region.

Cordage twist patterns on ceramic surfaces in this study are the final attribute discussed here and have been identified as temporally and spatially sensitive in Maine and other parts of the Northeast. Petersen (1996) identified "discontinuities" in coastal and interior cordage twist patterns during the Early Ceramic period and again between ca. 1350 and 950 BP (or "Ceramic Period 4") suggesting a coastal preference for Z-twist cordage and an interior preference for S-twist cordage. The results of the Penobscot River Valley early ceramic analysis do not align with coastal and interior twist patterns identified previously. S-twist cordage is most common on early ceramics in all three samples, including the Coastal sample. However, this study did not show these distributions to be statistically significant and additional research on this topic is needed.

It has been proposed that distinctions in Z- and S-twist cordage in the Maine–Maritime region reflect different learning networks and may be indicative of distinct social groups (Petersen and Hamilton 1984; Petersen 1996; Petersen and Sanger 1991). Petersen (1996:113) speculates that left- and right-handedness may account for deviations from the majority pattern, but as Minar (2001:389) points out, proportions of left-and right-handed people appear to be fairly consistent across human populations, and as such would result in consistent proportions of Z- and S-twist cordage, which she states is not the case. The issue is also complicated by debates on whether handedness is influenced by biological or cultural factors (for a review of debates on handedness, see Sassaman and Rudolphi 2001).

Minar (2001:390) tested the hypothesis that cordage twist is influenced by handedness using survey data from contemporary fibre crafters and found that all left-handed crafters in her study group spun fibres in the same direction as most right-handed crafters, and that it was a minority of the right-handed crafters that spun fibres in the opposite direction. Minar concluded that handedness does not determine spin direction.

Additionally, the distinction between coastal and interior cordage twist patterns in Maine shifts in the Late Ceramic period, and Z-twist appears to dominate cordage twist techniques in both coastal and interior settings (Petersen 1996). This apparent pattern shift suggests that cultural factors account for cordage twist patterns in Maine. While learning networks may be the influencing factor in cordage twist patterns observed in Maine, cultural influences (e.g., gender protocols, craft specialization, cultural taboos, identity markers) may also account for regional cordage twist patterns. Of note, the Coastal sample studied here is inconsistent with early ceramic coastal and interior twist patterns previously identified for Maine, and although not statistically significant in the present study, this points to the need for additional research into models of coastal and interior populations distinctions.

Conclusions

In the introduction to this chapter, I proposed that normative approaches to the first ceramics in the region have skewed our interpretations away from the vantage point of the potter, resulting in a neglect of potters' agency and few efforts to differentiate how potters approached their craft technologically. As a result, our perspective on the socio-cultural dynamics associated with the introduction of ceramics into Indigenous lifeways is narrow. This chapter broadens archaeological perspectives by highlighting variability in potters' choices with regard to how they approach their craft. It is clear from this study that potters within the Penobscot River Valley shared a common ceramic heritage, and that Petersen and Sanger's (1991) early ceramic "horizon style" seems appropriate. Ceramic vessels from the three areas were not so distinct that one would recognize them as being made by culturally disassociated potters. In fact, the potters living during the Early Ceramic period made nearly identical choices with respect to rim thickness, body thickness, and surface treatment at the three locations. However, variability in potters' choices is evident when examined through a technological-choice lens, and whether those choices are linked to pottery function, availability of resources, or other cultural factors remains unresolved. I have offered some possible explanations for the variability identified here, and these certainly warrant further exploration. By centering our archaeological inquiries on the agency and technological choice of potters, we can begin to tease out variability in our data sets and, more importantly, place Indigenous potters where they belong, at the forefront of our ceramics inquiry.

Acknowledgments

Thanks go to Alexis Allard, Morgan McGraw, Abby Mann, and Serena Webster, who assisted me with various aspects of the data analysis. Chris Patrick at Beta Analytic was helpful in responding to my requests for updated calibrations of radiocarbon dates. I also extend thanks to Paula Work at the Maine State Museum for her assistance with access to the Turner Farm ceramics collection. Dr. Arthur Spiess of the Maine Historic Preservation Office responded generously to my requests for information on sites and collections. The editors of this volume and the anonymous reviewers improved this manuscript significantly with their thoughtful comments and gracious assistance. Finally, I am extremely grateful to my Wabanaki ancestors for sharing their skills and knowledge with me in this indirect way. This research was funded in part by a University of Maine Academic Prominence Initiative grant. Any errors or omissions in this chapter are my own.

Data Availability Statement

Ceramics from all sites except for the Turner Farm sample are curated at the University of Maine's Anthropology Department, South Stevens Hall, University of Maine. Turner Farm ceramics are curated at the Maine State Museum, Augusta. Ceramic attribute data sheets are on file at the University of Maine Anthropology Department, South Stevens Hall, University of Maine.

References Cited

Belcher, William R.

1988   Archaeological Investigations at the Knox Site (30–21), East Penobscot Bay, Maine. Master's thesis, Quaternary Studies, University of Maine, Orono.

1989   Prehistoric Fish Exploitation in East Penobscot Bay, Maine: the Knox Site and Sea-Level Rise. *Archaeology of Eastern North America* 17:175–191.

Bogoraz-Tan, Vladimir G.

1904   *The Chuckchee, vol. 1: Material Culture.* E. J. Brill, New York.

Borstel, Christopher

1982   *Archaeological Investigations at the Young Site, Alton, Maine.* Occasional Publications in Maine Archaeology 1. Maine Historic Preservation Commission, Augusta.

Bourgeois, Vincent G. J.

1999   A Regional Pre-Contact Ceramic Sequence for the Saint John River Valley. Master's thesis, Department of Anthropology, University of New Brunswick, Fredericton.

Bourque, Bruce

1995   *Diversity and Complexity in Prehistoric Maritime Societies: A Gulf of Maine Perspective.* Plenum Press, New York.

Braun, Gregory

2010   Technological choices: Ceramic Manufacture and Use at the Antrex Site (AjGv-38). *Ontario Archaeology* 89(90):69–96.

Brumfiel, Elizabeth M.

2000   On the Archaeology of Choice: Agency Studies as a Research Stratagem. In *Agency in Archaeology*, edited by Marcia Anne Dobres and John Robb, pp. 249–255. Routledge, London and New York.

Bunker, Victoria

2002   An Analysis and Interpretation of Early Ceramics from Sewalls and Amoskeag Falls, Merrimack River Valley, New Hampshire. In *A Lasting Impression: Coastal, Lithic and Organic Research in New England Archaeology*, edited by J. Kerber, pp. 207–222. Praeger, Westport, Connecticut.

Carr, Christopher

1993   Identifying Individual Vessels with X-Radiography. *American Antiquity* 58(1): 96–117.

Childs, S. Terry

1991   Style, Technology, and Iron Smelting Furnaces in Bantu-Speaking Africa. *Journal of Anthropological Archaeology* 10(4):332–359.

Chilton, Elizabeth S.

1996   Embodiments of Choice: Native American Ceramic Diversity in the New England Interior. PhD dissertation, Department of Anthropology, University of Massachusetts, Amherst.

1998   The Cultural Origins of Technical Choice: Unraveling Algonquian and Iroquoian Ceramic Traditions in the Northeast. In *The Archaeology of Social Boundaries*, edited by Miriam Stark, pp. 132–160. Smithsonian Institution Press, Washington DC.

1999   Ceramic Research in New England: Breaking the Typological Mold. In *The Archaeological Northeast*, edited by Mary Ann Levine, Kenneth E. Sassaman, and Michael S. Nassaney, pp. 97–111. Bergin and Garvey, Westport, Connecticut.

Claassen, Cheryl

1991   Normative Thinking and Shell-Bearing Sites. *Archaeological Method and Theory* 3:249–298.

Cook, David S., and Arthur E. Spiess

1981   Archaeology of the Piscataquis Ahwagan: Preliminary Results. *Maine Archaeological Society Bulletin* 21(1):29–38.

Costin, Cathy L.

1999   Formal and Technological Variability and the Social Relations of Production: Crisoles from San Jose de Moro, Peru. In *Material Meanings: Critical Approaches to the Interpretation of Material Culture*, edited by Elizabeth S. Chilton, pp. 85–102. University of Utah Press, Salt Lake City.

Dale, T. Nelson

1907   *The Granites of Maine* U.S. Geological Survey Bulletin 313. Department of the Interior, Washington, DC.

Deal, Michael

1986   Late Archaic and Ceramic Period Utilization of the Mud Lake Stream Site, Southwestern New Brunswick. *Man in the Northeast* 32:67–94.

Dobres, Marcia-Anne

1999   Of Paradigms and Ways of Seeing: Artifact Variability as if People Mattered. In *Material Meanings: Critical Approaches to the Interpretation of Material Culture*, edited by Elizabeth S. Chilton, pp. 7–23. University of Utah Press, Salt Lake City.

2000   *Technology and Social Agency: Outlining a Practice Framework for Archaeology.* Blackwell, Malden, Massachusetts.

Dobres, Marcia-Anne, and John E. Robb

2000   Agency in Archaeology Paradigm or Platitude? In *Agency in Archaeology*, edited by Marcia-Anne Dobres and John E. Robb, pp. 1–17, Routledge, New York.

2005   "Doing" Agency: Introductory Remarks on Methodology. *Journal of Archaeological Method and Theory* 12(3):159–166.

Doyle, Richard A., Nathan D. Hamilton, and James B. Petersen
1982 Early Woodland Ceramics and Associated Perishable Industries from Southwestern Maine. *Maine Archaeological Society Bulletin* 22(2):4–21.

Fiedel, Stuart J.
2001 What Happened in the Early Woodland? *Archaeology of Eastern North America* 29:101–142.

Fowler, William S.
1966 Ceremonial and Domestic Products of Aboriginal New England. *Bulletin of the Massachusetts Archaeological Society* 27:3–4.

Gardner, Andrew
2007 *Agency Uncovered: Archaeological Perspectives on Social Agency, Power, and Being Human.* Left Coast Press, Walnut Creek, California.

Gosselain, Olivier P.
1992 Technology and Style: Potters and Pottery among Bafia of Cameroon. *Man* 27(3):559–586.

Hamilton, Nathan D.
1985 Maritime Adaptation in Western Maine: The Great Diamond Island Site. PhD dissertation, Department of Anthropology, University of Pittsburgh, Pittsburgh.

Harry, Karen, and Liam Frink
2009 The Arctic Cooking Pot: Why Was It Adopted? *American Anthropologist* 111: 330–343.

Hegmon, Michelle
1998 Technology, Style and Social Practices: Archaeological Approaches. In *The Archaeology of Social Boundaries*, edited by Miriam T. Stark, pp. 264–279. Smithsonian Institution Press, Washington, DC.

Hegmon, Michelle, Margaret C. Nelson, and Mark J. Ennes
2000 Corrugated Pottery, Technological Style, and Population Movement in the Mimbres Region of the American Southwest. *Journal of Anthropological Research* 56(2):217–240.

Hrynick, M. Gabriel, and Matthew W. Betts
2017 A Relational Approach to Hunter-Gatherer Architecture and Gendered Use of Space at Port Joli Harbour, Nova Scotia. *Journal of the North Atlantic* 1001:1–17.

Hurley, William M.
1979 *Prehistoric Cordage Identifications of Impressions on Pottery.* Taraxacum, Washington, DC.

Kelley, Alice R.
2006 Archaeological Geology and Postglacial Development of the Central Penobscot River Valley, Maine, USA. PhD dissertation, Interdisciplinary Program, University of Maine, Orono.

Kristmanson, Helen
1992 The Ceramic Sequence for Southwestern Nova Scotia: A Refinement of the Petersen-Sanger Model. Master's thesis, Department of Anthropology, Memorial University of Newfoundland, St. John's.

Kristmanson, Helen, and Michael Deal
1993   The Identification and Interpretation of Finishing Marks on Prehistoric Nova Scotian Ceramics. *Canadian Journal of Archaeology / Journal Canadien d'Archéologie* 17:74–84.

Lechtman, Heather
1977   Style in Technology—Some Early Thoughts. In *Material Culture: Styles, Organization, and Dynamics,* edited by Heather Lechtman and Robert Merrill, pp. 3–20. West Publishing, St. Paul, Minnesota.

Lemonnier, Pierre
1992   *Elements for an Anthropology of Technology.* Museum of Anthropology, University of Michigan, Ann Arbor.
1993   *Technological Choices: Transformation in Material Cultures since the Neolithic.* Routledge, New York.

Leonard, Kevin
1995   Woodland or Ceramic Period: A Theoretical Problem. *Northeast Anthropology* 50:19–30.

Lyman, R. Lee, and Michael J. O'Brien
2004   A History of Normative Theory in Americanist Archaeology. *Journal of Archaeological Method and Theory* 11(4):369–396.

Mack, Karen E.
1994   Archaeological Investigations at the Todd Site (17-11), Muscongus Bay, Maine. Master's thesis, Quaternary Studies, University of Maine, Orono.
2016   *Final Mitigation Report on Phase III Archaeological Investigations at the Eddington Bend Site (Site 74.8) in Eddington Bend, Penobscot County, Maine.* Report on file Maine Historic Preservation Commission, Augusta.

Mack, Karen E., David Sanger, and Alice R. Kelley
2002   *The Bob Site: A Multicomponent Archaic and Ceramic Period Site on Pushaw Stream, Maine.* Occasional Publications in Maine Archaeology, Maine Historic Preservation Commission, Augusta.

Mack, Karen E., David Sanger, Catherine Quinn, and Alice R. Kelley
1998   *Phase III Archaeological Investigations of the Bob Site, Pushaw Stream, Maine.* Report on file Maine Historic Preservation Commission, Augusta.

Mahias, Marie-Claude
1993   Pottery Techniques in India: Technical Variants and Social Choice. In *Technological Choices,* edited by Pierre Lemonnier, pp. 157–180. Routledge, London.

McMahon, Janet S.
1990   The Biophysical Regions of Maine: Patterns in the Landscape and Vegetation. Master's thesis, Department of Botany and Plant Pathology, University of Maine, Orono.

Minar, C. Jill
2001   Motor Skills and the Learning Process: The Conservation of Cordage Final Twist Direction in Communities of Practice. In *Journal of Anthropological Research* 57(4):381–405.

Mitchell, Ammie M.

2017   The Symbolism of Coarse Crystalline Temper: A Fabric Analysis of Early Pottery in New York State. PhD dissertation, State University of New York, Buffalo.

Newsom, Bonnie D.

1999   Ceramic Period Archaeology along the Lower Piscataquis River, Maine. Master's thesis, Quaternary Studies, University of Maine, Orono.

2017   Potters on the Penobscot: An Archaeological Case Study Exploring Human Agency, Identity, and Technological Choice. PhD dissertation, University of Massachusetts, Amherst.

Newsom, Bonnie D., and David Sanger

1998   *Phase II Archaeological Investigations of the Howland Reservoir, Central Maine.* Report on file Maine Historic Preservation Commission, Augusta.

Petersen, James B.

1980   *The Middle Woodland Ceramics of the Winooski Site A.D. 1–1000.* New Series, Monograph 1. Vermont Historical Society, Burlington, Vermont.

1985   Ceramic Analysis in the Northeast: Resume and Prospect. In *Ceramic Analysis in the Northeast: Contributions to Methodology and Culture History.* Occasional Publications in Northeastern Anthropology no. 9, edited by James B. Petersen, pp. 5–25. Franklin Pierce College, Ringe, New Hampshire.

1996   Fiber Industries from Norther New England: Ethnicity and Technological Traditions During the Woodland Period. In *A Most Indispensable Art: Native Fiber Industries from Eastern North America,* edited by James B. Petersen, pp. 101–119. University of Tennessee Press, Knoxville.

Petersen, James B., and Nathan D. Hamilton

1984   Early Woodland Ceramic and Perishable Fiber Industries from the Northeast: A Summary and Interpretation. *Annals of Carnegie Museum* 53:413–445.

Petersen, James B., and David Sanger

1987   *Phase II Testing at the Eddington Bend Site (74–78) Penobscot County, Maine.* Report on file at the Maine Historic Preservation Commission, Augusta, Maine.

1991   An Aboriginal Ceramic Sequence for Maine and the Maritime Provinces. In *Prehistoric Archaeology in the Maritimes: Past and Present Research,* edited by Michael Deal, pp. 121–178. The Council of Maritime Premiers, Reports in Archaeology, Fredericton, New Brunswick.

Philpotts, Anthony R.

1989   *Petrography of Igneous and Metamorphic Rocks.* Prentice Hall, Englewood Cliffs, New Jersey.

Pretola, John

2000   Northeastern Ceramic Diversity: An Optical Mineralogy Approach. PhD dissertation, University of Massachusetts, Amherst.

2002   An Optical Mineralogy Approach in Northeastern Ceramic Diversity. In *A Lasting Impression: Coastal, Lithic and Organic Research in New England Archaeology,* edited by J. Kerber. Praeger, Westport, Connecticut.

Ramsey, Christopher B.

2009   Bayesian Analysis of Radiocarbon Dates. *Radiocarbon* 51(1):337–360.

Reimer, Paula J., Edouard Bard, Alex Bayliss, J. Warren Beck, Paul G. Blackwell, Christopher Bronk Ramsey, Caitlin E. Buck, Hai Cheng, R. Lawrence Edwards, Michael Friedrich, Pieter M. Grootes, Thomas P. Guilderson, Haflidi Haflidason, Irka Hajdas, Christine Hatté, Timothy J. Heaton, Dirk L. Hoffmann, Alan G. Hogg, Konrad A. Hughen, K. Felix Kaiser, Bernd Kromer, Sturt W. Manning, Mu Niu, Ron W. Reimer, David A. Richards, E. Marian Scott, John R. Southon, Richard A. Staff, Christian S. M. Turney, and Johannes van der Plicht
2013   IntCal 13 and Marine 13 Radiocarbon Age Calibration Curves 0–50,000 Years cal BP. *Radiocarbon* 55:1869–1887.

Rice, Prudence M.
2015   *Pottery Analysis: A Sourcebook.* 2nd ed. University of Chicago Press, Chicago, Illinois.

Ritchie, William A., and Richard S. MacNeish
1949   The Pre-Iroquoian Pottery of New York State. *American Antiquity* 15(2): 97–124.

Rye, Owen S.
1976   Keeping Your Temper Under Control. *Archaeology and Physical Anthropology in Oceania* 11:205–211.

Sassaman, Kenneth
2000   Agents of Change in Hunter Gatherer Technology. In *Agency in Archaeology,* edited by Marcia-Anne Dobres and John Robb, pp. 148–168. Routledge, New York.

Sassaman, Kenneth E., and Wictoria Rudolphi
2001   Communities of Practice in the Early Pottery Traditions of the American Southeast, *Journal of Anthropological Research* 57(4):407–425.

Sanger, David
1974   Recent Meetings on Maine–Maritimes Archeology: A Synthesis, *Man in the Northeast* 7:128.

1996a   Testing the Models: Hunter-Gatherer Use of Space in the Gulf of Maine, USA. *World Archaeology* 27(3):512–526.

1996b   Gilman Falls Site: Implications for the Early and Middle Archaic of the Maritime Peninsula. *Canadian Journal of Archaeology / Journal Canadien d'Archéologie* 20:7–28.

2005   Pre-European Dawnland: Archaeology of the Maritime Peninsula. In *New England and the Maritime Provinces: Connections and Comparisons,* edited by Stephen J. Hornsby and John G. Reid, pp. 15–31. McGill-Queen's University Press, Kingston and Montréal.

Sanger, David, William R. Belcher, and Douglas Kellog
1992   Early Holocene Occupation at the Blackman Stream Site, Central Maine. In *Early Holocene Occupations in Northern New England,* edited by B. S. Robinson, J. B. Petersen and A. K. Robinson, pp. 149–161. Vol. 9. Maine Historic Preservation Commission, Augusta.

Sanger, David, Ronald B. Davis, Robert G. MacKay, and Harold W. Borns Jr.
1977   The Hirundo Archaeological Project—An Interdisciplinary Approach to Central Maine Prehistory. In *Amerinds and their Paleoenvironments in Northeastern*

North America, edited by W. B. Newman and B. Salwen, pp. 457–471. Annals of the New York Academy of Sciences, Vol. 288. New York Academy of Sciences, New York.

Sanger, David, and Bonnie D. Newsom

2000   Middle Archaic in the Lower Piscataquis River, and its Relationship to the Laurentian Tradition in Central Maine. *Maine Archaeological Society Bulletin* 40(1):1–22.

Schiffer, Michael.B., and James Skibo

1997   The Explanation of Artifact Variability. *American Antiquity* 62(1):27–50.

Skibo, James M.

2013   *Understanding Pottery Function: Manuals in Archaeological Method, Theory, and Technique.* Springer New York.

Snow, Dean

1968   Wabanaki "Family Hunting Territories." *American Anthropologist* 70(6): 1143–1151.

Speck, Frank G.

1915   The Family Hunting Band as the Basis of Algonkian Social Organization. *American Anthropologist* 17(2):289–305.

1927   Family Hunting Territories of the Lake St. John Montagnais and Neighboring Bands. *Anthropos* 22(3/4):387–403.

1940   *Penobscot Man.* University of Pennsylvania Press, Philadelphia.

Spiess, Arthur E., and Robert A. Lewis

2001   *The Turner Farm Fauna.* Occasional Publications in Maine Archaeology No. 11. Maine Historic Preservation Commmission and Maine Archaeological Society, Augusta, Maine.

Stapelfeldt, Kora

2009   A Form and Function Study of Precontact Pottery from Atlantic Canada. Master's thesis, Department of Archaeology, Memorial University of Newfoundland, St. John's.

Stark, Miriam T., Mark D. Elson, and Jeffery J. Clark

1998   Social Boundaries and Technical Choices in Tonto Basin Prehistory. In *The Archaeology of Social Boundaries*, edited by Miriam Stark, pp. 208–231. Smithsonian Institution, Washington, DC.

Taché, Karine

2005   Explaining Vinette I Pottery Variability: The View from the Batiscan Site, Québec. *Canadian Journal of Archaeology / Journal Canadien d'Archéologie* 29:165–233 .

Taché, Karine, and Oliver E. Craig

2015   Cooperative Harvesting of Aquatic Resources and the Beginning of Pottery Production in North-Eastern North America. *Antiquity* 89(343):177–190.

Taché, Karine, and John P. Hart

2013   Chronometric Hygiene of Radiocarbon Databases for Early Durable Cooking Vessel, Technologies in Notheastern North America. *American Antiquity* 78(2):359.

Taché, Karine, Manon Bondetti, Alexandre Lucquin, Marjolein Admiraal, and Oliver E. Craig

2019   Something Fishy in the Great Lakes? A Reappraisal of Early Pottery use in North-Eastern North America. *Antiquity* 93(371):1339–1349.

Taché, Karine, Daniel White, and Sarah Seelen

2008   Potential Functions Of Vinette I Pottery: Complementary Use of Archaeological and Pyrolysis Gc/Mc Data. *Archaeology of Eastern North America* 36:63–90.

van der Leeuw, Sander E.

1991   Variation, Variability and Explanation in Pottery Studies. In *Ceramic Ethnoarchaeology,* edited by W. A. Longacre, pp. 11–39. The University of Arizona Press, Tucson.

1993   Giving the Potter a Choice: Conceptual Aspects of Pottery Techniques. In *Technological Choices: Transformations in Material Cultures since the Neolithic*, edited by Pierre Lemonnier, pp. 238–288. Routledge, London.

Vekinis, G., and Vassilis Kilikoglou

1998   Mechanical Performance of Quartz-Tempered Ceramics: Part II, Hertzian Strength, Wear Resistance and Applications to Ancient Ceramics. *Archaeometry* 40(2):281–292.

Velde, Bruce, and Isabelle C. Druc

1999   Archaeological Ceramic Materials: Origin and Utilization. Springer, New York and Berlin.

Wright, James V.

1967   *The Laurel Tradition and the Middle Woodland Period*. National Museum of Canada Bulletin No. 217(79), Ottawa.

11

LATER LATE MARITIME WOODLAND SETTLEMENT IN PESKOTOMUHKATIHKUK

Re-Envisioning Chronology, Shellfishing, and Site Formation at the Cusp of Contact

A. Katherine Patton,[1] Susan E. Blair,[2] and W. Jesse Webb[3]

Abstract

This chapter examines the later Late Maritime Woodland (ca. 900–450 cal. BP) in the Quoddy Region of New Brunswick, Canada, and Maine, United States. Shell-bearing deposits from this period are structurally complex and exhibit variable assemblages of faunal remains. The complexity of the archaeological record is compounded by the difficulty in identifying components from this period in the region. As a result, patterning in shellfish harvesting, fishing, and mobility is ambiguous. We incorporate the existing data set with results from recent excavations to examine inter-site variability in shellfish assemblages, site-formation processes, and radiocarbon chronology to re-evaluate the timing and duration of settlement in particular locations on the landscape. Rather than clearly showing increasing nucleated and sedentary settlements, our results open the possibility that households were dispersed, or fragmented, along coastlines. Peskotomuhkati ideas of community at this time, therefore, may confound conventional archaeological thinking about village life.

Résumé

Cet article se penche sur la période du Sylvicole maritime supérieur tardif (ca. 900-450 cal. BP) dans la région Quoddy du Nouveau-Brunswick (Canada) et du Maine (USA). Les sites à coquillages de cette période sont structurellement complexes et présentent des restes fauniques très variables. Cette complexité des sites archéologiques s'ajoute au fait que les composantes attribuables à cette période sont difficiles à identifier dans la région. Il est donc ardu de tirer de ces données ambiguës des schèmes de mobilité, de pêche et d'exploitation des mollusques. Nous ajoutons aux données actuelles les résultats de fouilles récentes et examinons la variabilité intersite des assemblages de mollusques, des processus de formation des sites et des datations radiocarbones pour finalement réévaluer la chronologie et la durée des occupations dans certains endroits du paysage. Là où l'on aurait pu s'attendre à une tendance claire vers une centralisation et une sédentarisation des établissements, nos résultats suggèrent plutôt une distribution éclatée, ou fragmentée, des foyers le long des côtes. Il semble donc que le concept de communauté qui existait chez les Peskotomuhkatiyik à cette époque s'accorde mal avec le concept archéologique conventionnel de "vie de village".

Affiliations

1. Department of Anthropology, University of Toronto, Ontario, Canada
2. Department of Anthropology, University of New Brunswick, New Brunswick, Canada
3. Independent Researcher, New Brunswick, Canada

While recent research has exposed the breadth and diversity of late pre-Contact settlement and economic practices on the Maritime Peninsula and the far Northeast, our ability to integrate them into a single system that is coherent at multiple scales remains elusive (Hart and Reith 2002). This is particularly true of later Late Maritime Woodland (LMW; see table 11.1) settlement in the Quoddy Region (QR) of southwestern New Brunswick, Canada, and the northern coast of Maine, United States (figure 11.1). The QR forms a significant part of Peskotomuhkatihkuk, the ancestral homeland of the Peskotomuhkatiyik (Passamaquoddy), a nation of the Wabanaki Confederacy. Multi-component, thickly deposited shell-bearing sites that date to between approximately 2200 and 900 cal. BP (the Middle Maritime Woodland [MMW] and the earlier LMW periods) are the most visible type of archaeological site in this region, and, as a result, many research programs have framed broader Maritime Woodland models of settlement around them (Black 1992; Blair 1997; Davis 1978; Hrynick et al. 2019; Matthew 1884). These shell-bearing sites also produce well-preserved assemblages of vertebrate faunal remains, allowing for the integration of important economic dimensions in these model-building exercises.

This approach to model construction is consistent with larger theoretical approaches, where the most visible element in a diverse system becomes the central mode, with less frequent variations allowing for elaboration around it. Our understanding of diversity here is a fairly simple one—a spatiotemporal unit that contains within it a number of different types at any given time (see Black 1992, 1993). It is this diversity with respect to what archaeologists call "sites" and how they are distributed across landscapes that is our focus here, and as a part of this, we consider the issue of visibility (what archaeologists look for and choose as a focus of study) and how we allocate meaning to various types within the larger system.

There is, however, another type of shell-bearing site in the QR that has a dramatically different character than the MMW/earlier LMW sites described above; these sites are small, ephemeral, and usually composed of multiple loci or distinct and non-contiguous deposits of shell. These are much less impressive than the large, deep, stratigraphically complex shell-bearing sites, and as such have often been overlooked as a focus of research. As a corollary, they are less "visible" in the archaeological imagination. Building on the work of Black (1988, 1992, 1993, 2002) and Sanger (1987), we propose that some of these smaller, patchy shell-bearing sites could be key to understanding the changing character of settlement in the QR beginning around 1000 cal. BP, shortly before the later LMW period (ca. 900–450 cal. BP). To date, later LMW settlement and economy have remained somewhat resistant to integration into overarching Maritime Woodland models (Hrynick and Black 2016). There are likely a number of reasons for this, but perhaps the most significant is the rarity of large, visible, multi-component shell-bearing sites in the later LMW. This has complicated model construction in this period by removing the central mode around which we have organized settlement models in both earlier periods, and for the Maritime Woodland as a whole.

In this chapter, we bring together the results of recent archaeological research in the QR and draw on previously published data to explore what these small, ephemeral sites represent in terms of human activities and social relations, as well as where they "fit" in terms of chronology. Previously, we (Blair et al. 2016) problematized diversity in QR shell-bearing sites as a shift in settlement that breaks a previous trajectory toward increasing centralization and complexity; in this chapter, we also consider whether the process of sorting sites into types and arranging them into meaningful systems obscures a key characteristic— settlement diversity itself. As a part of this examination, we explore how the physical structure of sites and their distribution, as well as the shellfish taxa that comprise them, might be linked in complex ways, and how an examination of this landscape might help us to address questions pertaining to transitions in settlement and economy that took place between the earlier and later LMW.

Peskotomuhkatiyik and Peskotomuhkatihkuk

The few historical and ethnographic records that exist on the Peskotomuhkatiyik describe them as a largely egalitarian people, with political leaders known as *sagamores*. The leadership was "precarious" as allegiance, largely pertaining to decisions around warfare, was voluntary (Biard in Thwaites 1896b:75). Early historical accounts suggest that Wabanaki *sagamores* made formal agreements with one another concerning how tribes were distributed across the region (Prins 1994). For the Peskotomuhkatiyik, this resulted in a traditional territory, or homeland, known as Peskotomuhkatihkuk, that includes the region between the Union River in Maine and Point Lepreau in New Brunswick (Sanger et al. 2006). Central to this homeland are the geographical features now referred to as Passamaquoddy and Cobscook Bays[1] on the coast (Prins 1994:100), as well as key lakes and rivers in the interior (Pawling 2016; Soctomah 2005).

Historically, Peskotomuhkatiyik were mobile hunter-gatherer-fishers (Champlain 1922 in Biggar 1922; Lescarbot 1610 in Thwaites 1896a:83; Soctomah 2005). Early historical accounts describe lightly inhabited coastlines, with people "scattered over wide spaces" (Biard in Thwaites 1896b:73). At times, these early French chroniclers appear contradictory; Lescarbot (in Thwaites 1896a:83), for example, wrote that Peskotomuhkatiyik lived in "bands" along the coast until the winter, when they moved to interior lakes to hunt terrestrial fauna, while Champlain (in Biggar 1922), describes contact year-round on the coast. Differing accounts of the character and timing of coastal settlements such as these may reflect the flexible character of Peskotomuhkati households and autonomy in individual decision-making. According to Prins (1994:98; Prins and McBride 2007:16–18), household membership in all Wabanaki bands during the seventeenth century was voluntary, and while bands might move seasonally within territories under the leadership of *sagamores*, membership was malleable and fluctuated in size over time. Peskotomuhkati daily, routinized activities were organized around the family, or household, which was a small, flexible social unit with ties to particular stretches of coastline or hunting grounds (Pawling 2016; Prins and McBride 2007:16–18). According to Sanger and colleagues (2006), individual households could travel freely among related kin groups, which gave people access to multiple fishing, hunting, and gathering locations. On the coast, some of these locations included clam ovens, which could be used by several households (Matthew 1884:22).

According to Soctomah (2005:175), however, families gathered in larger groups at ancient ancestral villages in the spring in order to harvest diadromous fish. In some places, like Meddybemps, Maine, archaeological evidence from the

---

1. For the sake of clarity, and to enable a modern reader to identify particular geographical features, we refer to these places by their the modern, state-recognized form. However, we feel it is important to acknowledge that these toponyms are modifications of the original (anglicized or poorly translated) while many other original toponyms have been entirely excised from official state records, and replaced (see, later, St. Croix and St. Stephen, for example).

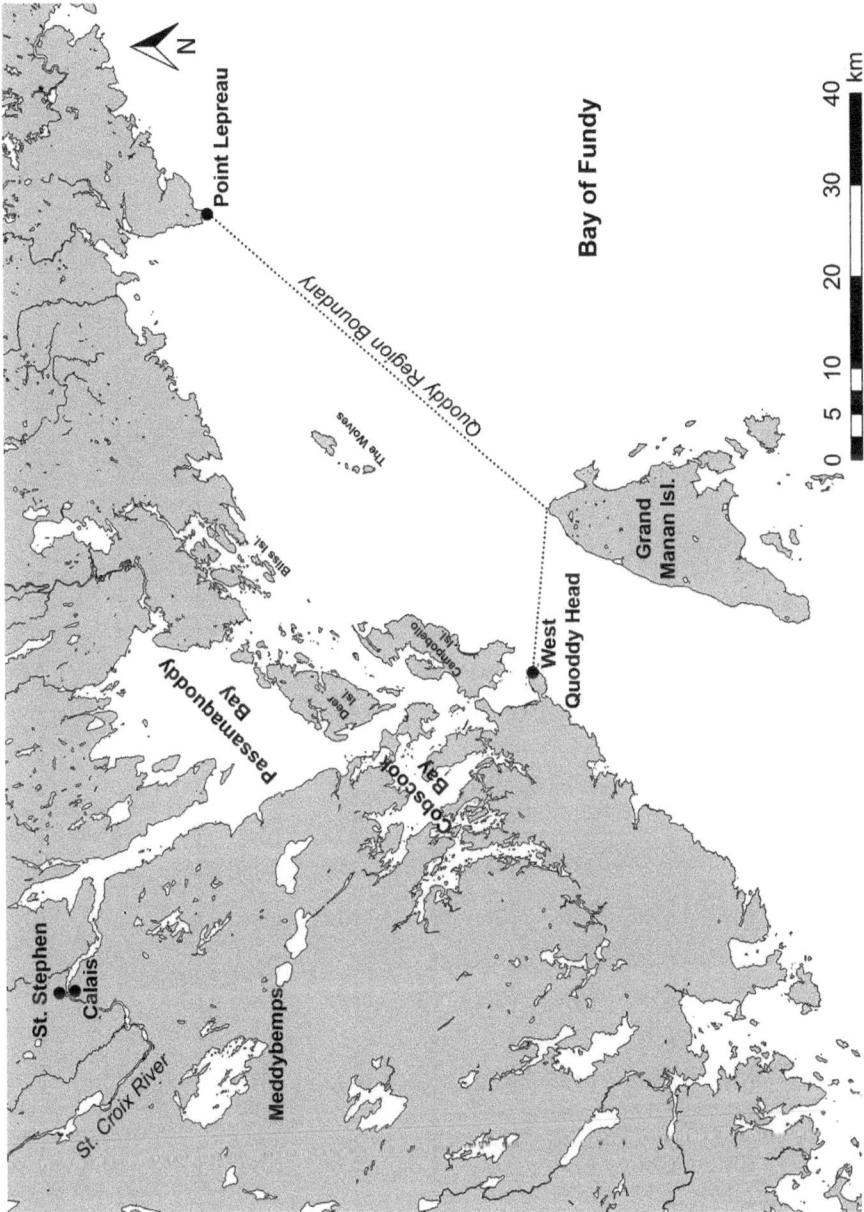

Figure 11.1. The Quoddy Region.
Source: C. Shaw.

N'tolonapemk site reinforces this historical recognition of place, extending back several thousand years. Soctomah (2005:1) also describes gatherings to harvest fish at the first waterfalls on the St. Croix River at St. Stephen, New Brunswick, and the movement of families from the interior to this location at the end of the winter into the nineteenth century (see also Bassett 2015:14). Families came to this place each spring "since time immemorial," and a fire, symbolic of the gathering, burned until "the last family left [...] and moved closer to the bounds of the ocean" (Soctomah 2005:1). This description conveys a sense that even larger gatherings of people were composed of individual households that made their own decisions about when to arrive and how long to stay. Settlement at all scales—households, communities, and regions—and the social relations that shaped them, were enormously flexible (Sanger et al. 2006). As Prins and McBride (2007:17) write, for example, "everyone retained the right to determine their own affairs and was free to leave the area and, if so accepted, join a neighboring community."

Table 11.1. Cultural-Historical Periods for the QR.

Cultural-Historical Periods	Approx. date range (cal. BP)
Early Maritime Woodland	3400–2200
Middle Maritime Woodland	2200–1300
Earlier Late Maritime Woodland	1300–900
Later Late Maritime Woodland	900–450
Proto-contact	450–350
Contact/post-contact	350–present

Modified from Hrynick and Black (2016). Our chronology differs slightly in that we mark the beginning of the proto-contact period as AD 1500 (or 450 cal. BP), three years after Cabot's voyage to the eastern shore of North America. This is the first documented European presence in the Northeast other than the Norse 500 years before this date. Contact/post-contact period date approximates early French and English settlements along the eastern seaboard (i.e. approximately AD 1600 or 350 cal. BP).

Archaeological Perspectives on Maritime Woodland Settlement

As initial archaeological research in the region focused on MMW and earlier LMW settlement, several scholars addressed the disjuncture between the archaeological and historical accounts of settlement and landscape. Archaeological approaches to seasonality based on vertebrate and invertebrate faunal remains consistently revealed that pre-Contact Peskotomuhkatiyik were either on the coast year-round or were preferentially on the coast in the winter (Black 1993:99; Bourque 2004:84; Sanger 1996). The insight that long-standing pre-Contact patterns of seasonality might have been overturned and economies reorganized around trade with Europeans led many to conclude that historical information in general might not be appropriately extended before Contact (Bourque 1973; Sanger 1982, 1987:124).

Building on this research into seasonality, Sanger (1987, 1988, 1996) proposed that Maritime Woodland settlement and mobility as a whole was a form of cold-weather foraging involving a high degree of residential mobility (*sensu* Binford 1980). Black, however, challenged the idea that a single economic and settlement tradition characterized the Maritime Woodland and instead proposed long-term transformations in resource focus and subsistence—trends that he suggested culminated in a gradual transition from residential to logistical mobility (Black 2002:314; *sensu* Binford 1980). Drawing on Snow (1980), Black (1992:153, 2002:314; see also Hrynick and Black 2016) proposed that, through time, Maritime Woodland settlement might have become increasingly concentrated such that, by the LMW, it was organized around nucleated permanent base camps. In the QR, only the Bocabec site (figure 11.2) might meet this description. Excavated by George Matthew in 1883, it was one of the first archaeological sites explored in the region and is also a large, stratigraphically complex shell-bearing site. Matthew recorded 30 surface depressions, many of which he and subsequent researchers have identified as house depressions (Hrynick and Black 2016; Matthew 1884). Black ventured that other comparable sites could have been located at river mouths, and, as such, would have been susceptible to destruction by marine erosion and historic-period settlement (Black 1992:153, 2002). On the other hand, oral and written accounts of the St. Croix fishing village (Bassett 2015:14; Soctomah 2005) record seasonal gatherings of a large number of people within a settlement model that could be characterized as either fairly mobile or relatively sedentary, as does work further afield, such as at the Goddard site in Maine (Bourque and Cox 1981; Petersen et al. 2004).

While archaeological research in the greater Northeast has tended to focus on the divide between horticultural (to the south of the Kennebec River), and foraging societies (to its north) (Snow 1980), recent perspectives that focus on the larger Wabanaki and Algonquian context for the region shed additional light on landscape, settlement, and household. For example, in southern New England, Leveillee et al. (2006) and Chilton (2002) proposed alternate models for village life that invite us to reimagine preconceived notions of what constitutes community, and what villages might have looked like on the ground. Chilton (2002, 2010) proposed that, while there is some evidence for Late Woodland permanent or semi-permanent villages on the southern New England coast, the evidence has been perplexingly absent from the interior. Instead, she proposed that interior horticulturalists maintained a relatively high degree of mobility and settlement flexibility during the Late Woodland, as they had well into the Contact period. In a similar vein, Leveillee et al. (2006) addressed specifically the arrangement of archaeological features at two coastal Rhode Island sites. These features

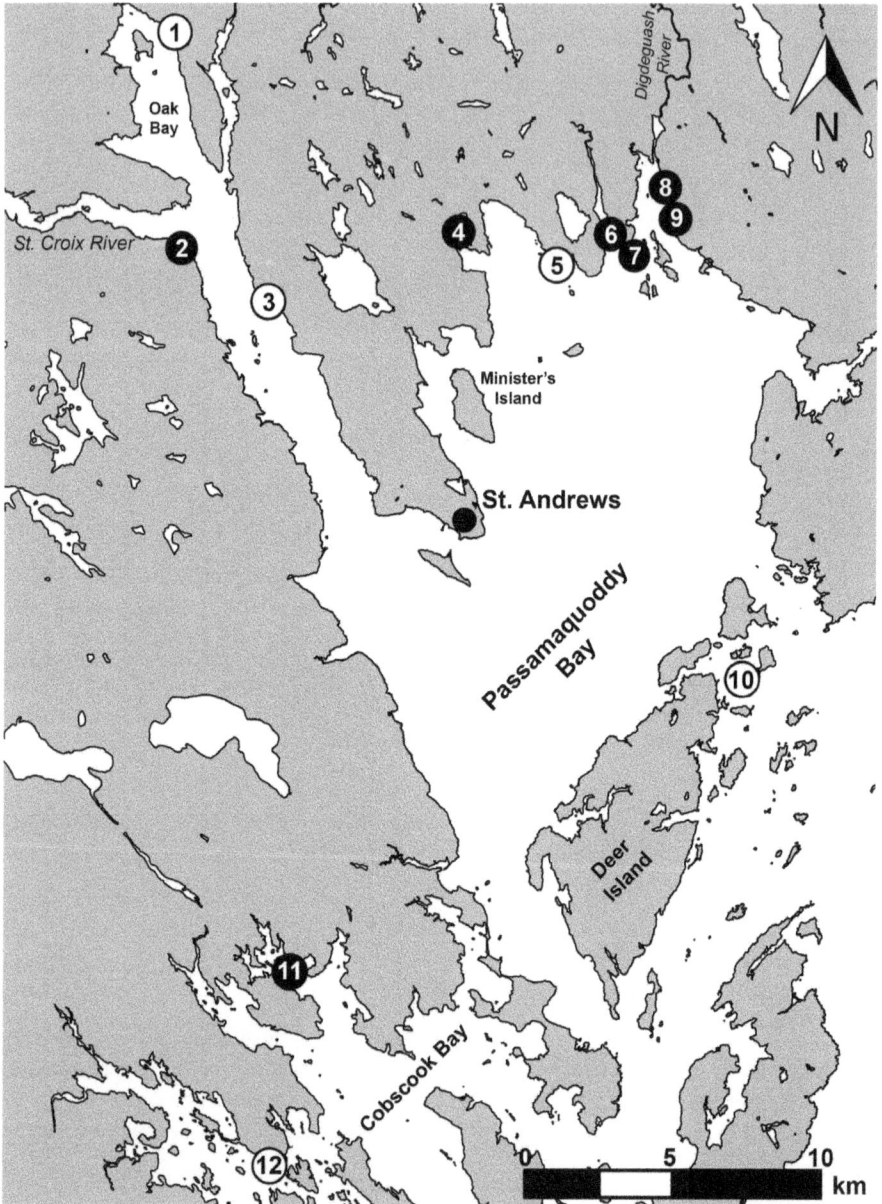

Figure 11.2. Quoddy Region archaeological sites. Open circles denote MMW/earlier LMW shell-bearing sites and closed circles later LMW sites: 1. Oak Bay (BhDt-4), 2. Devil's Head (ME 97.10), 3. Sand Point (BgDs-6), 4. Birch Cove sites (see Figure 5), 5. Teacher's Cove (BgDr-11), 6. Bocabec (BgDr-1), 7. Orr's Point (BgDr-7), 8. McAleenan (BhDr-1), 9. Carson (BgDr-5), 10. Weir (BgDq-6) and other Bliss Island sites (see figure 11.4), 11. Sipp Bay sites (See figure 11.6), and 12. Reversing Falls (ME 80.15).

are spread over a large area (in one case, along the shoreline of a body of water); individually, these features might represent dispersed, autonomous households, but taken together they represent a larger settlement. Drawing on these ideas, Blair and colleagues (2016) proposed that, while related households might have lived for part of the year in direct proximity to each other at the large shell-bearing sites during the MMW/earlier LMW, around 1000 cal. BP households started to disperse themselves along continuous stretches of shoreline. Boats would have facilitated settlement, mobility, resource procurement, and transport for generations on the coast, but in a dispersed or scattered household model, boats specifically allowed people to move freely among dispersed networks of relations in order to acquire access to different resource locations. In this model, settlement could be harder to recognize archaeologically because of our practice of equating it with discrete contiguous deposits ("sites" and "components"), particularly in small-scale societies (Dunnell 1992).

Insights from southern New England encourage us to re-examine the broader regional ethnohistoric record and, in particular, the intersection between the Peskotomuhkati homeland, a landscape rich in history and meaning, and household. Like other Wabanaki peoples that inhabit the Maine–Maritimes region, the concept of homeland encompasses Peskotomuhkati cultural values about the integration of human social relationships and the land (Pawling 2016). It includes specific locations on the landscape (places to build weirs and dwellings, harvest and process shellfish, or gather berries, among other things), the pathways people use to travel between them by boat or on foot, and the social networks that people rely on to enable these continued practices through time (J. Patton 2014; Pawling 2016; Sanger et al. 2006:317). Many of the original place names within Wabanaki territory reveal an intimate knowledge of the landscape, a knowledge that reflects the potential of productive environments and the challenges of travelling through the region (Prins 1994). Though a modern term, "homeland" references historical access to lands that particular Indigenous groups were connected to prior to dispossession in the colonial world (Pawling 2016, 2017). Wabanaki sense of place, then, exists at multiple scales. Specific locations on the landscape recorded as meaningful in language and cosmology (Sanger et al. 2006), for example, or what we might call "place-worlds" (*sensu* Basso 1996), are often difficult to locate archaeologically as cultural knowledge is often privileged to community members or has been lost over the course of time (Sanger et al. 2006). The idea of homeland, however, incorporates meaning beyond the particular locations that we, as archaeologists, tend to examine toward a larger, integrated landscape, and as such is a reasonable lens through which to explore the history of Peskotomuhkati settlement in—and movement through—the region.

At the same time, as noted above, the primary social unit among all Wabanaki peoples was the household. Peskotomuhkati households were autonomous with flexible membership and settlement (Pawling 2016; Prins 1994; Sanger et al. 2006). The individual deposits of shell that we work with at these shell-bearing sites represent short-term and highly localized activities that we propose, as others have done (Hunter et al. 2014), likely represent the actions of households. While "household archaeology" is not unified body of theory, archaeologists working with this framework focus on the household as the central unit of analysis (Hayden and Cannon 1982; Hendon 1996; Madella et al. 2013; Sobel et al. 2006; Wilk and Rathje 1980). Typically, these studies focus on domestic structures as the primary link to household activities in the archaeological record (e.g., Coupland and Banning 1996). Yet, we know that the form, structure, and meaning of households are historically contingent. Several households might live within a single dwelling, making it difficult to find individual household units; a single household might live in multiple dwellings, and, importantly, household activities extend well beyond the confines of architecturally defined spaces (Beaudry 2015; Hunter et al. 2014; Briz i Godino and Madella 2013; Robin 2002). Thus, households operate at a variety of scales that are often difficult to disentangle from one another and from other kinds of human interaction. However, small-scale depositional episodes, as can be discerned in some shell-bearing sites, may reveal traces of highly localized practices that occurred on a small scale, like a household (Beaudry 2015:3; Briz i Godino et al. 2013:27). The shell-bearing sites that we examine here typically consist of superimposed, stratigraphically observable depositional episodes, or discrete, shallow loci spread across an area horizontally, each of which could represent household shellfish harvesting and processing episodes.

Wabanaki shellfishing is particularly poorly documented in historical accounts, although the archaeological record of the QR indicates that shellfishing must have been a significant factor in decision-making around settlement and seasonality. According to French historical accounts, shellfishing took place from May to mid-September, but clams were also essential for survival in the winter months (Biard in Thwaites 1896b:80-81; Champlain in Biggar 1922:308; Soctomah 2009:3, 11). Matthew (1884:22), for example, notes that in the nineteenth century Peskotomuhkatiyik harvested clams in the fall specifically for processing and storage for winter consumption. Biard (Thwaites 1896b:77) writes that women generally collected shellfish (see also Soctomah 2009:4), reflecting perhaps a cosmological association among women, littoral zones, and shellfish, a socio-spatial structuring principle in the broader Northeast. J. Patton (2014), for example, notes that, in southern New England, littoral zones were female spaces for collecting shellfish, whereas deep waters were male. Taking an explicitly structuralist approach, Nash (1997) contends that, among the Mi'kmaq, also a Wabanaki nation, intertidal zones were "feminine in nature." Several scholars note, however, that cosmological associations with a particular place or activity do not necessarily translate into rigid gender divisions of space or tasks (Hunter et al. 2014; J. Patton 2014). Thus, while Wabanaki shellfishing in the past was largely considered women's work, as seems to be the case in most parts of the world (Claassen 1991; Moss 1993), there may have been instances where people of all ages and genders participated.

Large, Stratigraphically Complex Shell-Bearing Sites in the QR

While there are a number of shell-bearing site types in the QR, most research has focused on large, stratigraphically complex sites that are typically 50 cm–100 cm in depth. These sites are often considered to be the key type in much of the Maritime Woodland. While they may have non-shell-bearing deposits that date to the Early Maritime Woodland (ca. 3400–2200 cal. BP), these sites typically date between about 2200 and 1000 cal. BP, spanning the MMW to earlier LMW periods. Coastal erosion and submergence, in conjunction with periodic storm tides, have been taking place over the course of several thousand years in the QR (Bush and Lemmen 2019:382-383; Desplanque and Mossman 1999; Shaw et al. 1994). As a result, many of these large sites are chronologically "shingled" (Sanger 1988), with older settlement being closer to the beach and more recent inhabitancy generally further from the shore. These sites have been documented, and in some cases sampled, on both mainland and insular locations (Black 1992, 1993; Davis 1978; Matthew 1884; Sanger 1987). They have been interpreted as places where groups of single-family units or households settled for relatively long stretches while practising a larger cycle of residential mobility, favouring outer coasts in warmer seasons and inner coasts during cold seasons (Hrynick and Black 2016). Stratification at some sites, like the Weir (BgDq-6) site on Bliss Island, consists of over a hundred identifiable strata that alternate between shell-fish-dense deposits, gravel dwelling floors, and soil development (Black 1992, 2002; figure 11.3 here). Because most of these sites have been sampled only, it is difficult to understand the precise nature of overall settlement structure. Black (1992:36-37), however, contends that while individual households might repeatedly visit these places on a seasonal basis, these were not organized villages, as the location of specific dwellings within the settlement appears to shift over time.

The shellfish taxa that comprise the shell-bearing deposits in these sites are diverse. For example, the shellfish assemblage at Teacher's Cove (Davis 1978), located in the northern mainland of the QR, consists almost entirely of soft-shell clam (*Mya arenaria*). At Teacher's Cove and several other sites sampled in the mid- to late twentieth century, these observations operate at a general, qualitative level as shellfish were uncollected and unquantified. Similar descriptions of other northern QR sites such as Sand Point and Oak Bay suggest that soft-shell clams are most abundant, but that several other shellfish taxa, including green sea urchin (*Strongylocentrotus droebachiensis*), northern whelk (*Buccinum undatum*), common mussel (*Mytilus edulis*), and horse mussel (*Modiolus modiolus*), are also present (Matthew 1884; Pearson 1970). On the other hand, Black provided a high level of controlled quantification of shellfish assemblages for two insular MMW/earlier LMW sites, at Weir and Partridge Island (Black 1992, 1993). At both of these sites, soft-shell clams occurred in significant frequencies, often comprising more than half of the shellfish assemblages by mass (table 11.2). New data from the Reversing Falls site (ME 80.15) on Cobscook Bay in the western QR show that soft-shell clams make up approximately 55% of the shellfish assemblage by mass (Anderson et al., 2021; see also Hrynick et al. 2019:24–26). These three sites, however, also show that other shellfish taxa are well represented. Green sea urchin, for example, ranges in site-wide totals from 9% to 33%, horse mussels from approximately 9% to 34%, and lesser amounts of northern whelks, striped dogwinkles (*Nucella ostrina*), and common mussels. Relative quantities of shellfish taxa vary enormously between each deposit (Hrynick et al. 2019:24), which appears to reflect distinct depositional episodes relating to the timing of specific shellfish-harvesting episodes (see also Black 1993:60–66). For example, at Reversing Falls, green sea urchin comprises over 56% of a single stratigraphic deposit, while common mussels and horse mussels combined make up 45% of a second bulk sample collected in a different excavation unit (Anderson et al., 2021). Although analysis of bulk samples has only begun at Reversing Falls, results from these preliminary samples illustrate the stratigraphic complexity of this site as well as the horizontal and vertical diversity in shellfish assemblages at these MMW/earlier LMW sites.

Figure 11.3. Photograph of an exposed profile at the Weir site (BgDq-6) illustrating the stratigraphic complexity of Middle Maritime Woodland/early Late Maritime Woodland sites.
Source: Courtesy of David W. Black.

Table 11.2. Relative percentages of shellfish taxa identified to species by mass from three Middle Maritime Woodland/early Late Middle Woodland shell-bearing sites.

	# of samples	Sample Dimensions	Soft-shell clam	Horse mussel	Common mussel	Mussel spp.	Green sea urchin	Northern whelk	Striped Dogwinkle	Other taxa present	source
Reversing Falls (ME 80.15)	6	1-2.15 litres each	54.7% (1896.3 gr.)	9.4% (79.4 gr.)	0.9% (31.9 gr.)	2.3% (79.4 gr.)	32.7% (1134.2 gr.)	0.2% (7.4 gr.)	—	Periwinkles, Rough barnacle, Chiton sp., Limpet sp., Mya trucata, Arctic saxicave	Anderson et al. in press
Weir (BgDq-6)	30	Variable volumes (20x20 cm from each stratigraphic deposit)	51%	14%	1%	—	29%	5%	<1%	Ten-ridged whelk, Stimpson's whelk, Periwinkles, Limpet sp.,Barnacle sp.,Arctic saxicave, Deep-sea scallop, Bean mussel	Black 2002:311 (see also Black 1992:99-100)
Partridge Island (BgDr-48)	44	Variable volumes (20x20 cm from each stratigraphic deposit)	41.7%	33.7%	8.8%	—	9%	<1%	5.9%	Periwinkles, Ten-ridged whelk, Bean mussel, Heart shell, Astarte, Limpet sp., Barnacle sp., Deep-sea scallop, Arctic saxicave, Surf clam	Black 1993:56-63

The Earlier LMW to Later LMW Transition

While large, stratigraphically complex shell-bearing sites are a visible expression of Maritime Woodland settlement and economy prior to approximately 1000 cal. BP, archaeological data suggests that these locations stopped being used for shellfishing and settlement (figure 11.4). Why, after over a thousand years of relatively constant seasonal inhabitancy, did people cease these activities at these locations, and how did Ancestral Peskotomuhkatiyik reconfigure settlement across the landscape? A precise answer to that question remains elusive with the current evidence; Sanger (1987) proposed that soft-shell clam beds might have been overharvested during the earlier LMW as a result of human population increase in the region. Many of these large shell-bearing sites show evidence for expansion during the earlier LMW, which might have occurred in response to increasing community size. Black (2002:314) notes that the later LMW seems to coincide with the onset of the Medieval Climatic Anomaly (MCA), providing additional context for environmental and resource factors, though it is not clear how climate or warming might have intersected with settlement realignment.

We propose that part of the answer lies with a more complete understanding of the nature of the settlement pattern with which people replaced the older system. To do so, we closely examine the other kind of QR shell-bearing site: the shallow, ephemeral, and patchy sites that became the dominant form after approximately 1000 cal. BP. Some scholars have hypothesized that at least some of these sites are nineteenth-century "baiter's mounds" (Black and Turnbull 1986:400; see also Black 1992, 1993:56). Indeed, between 1850 and 1875, a clam-harvesting industry in Maine focussed on providing soft-shell clams as bait in the inshore fishery (Hanks 1963:1). BgDr-49, on Partridge Island, for example, was composed exclusively of soft-shell clams and lacked vertebrate faunal remains. It also produced exclusively post-Contact artifacts, which led Black (1993:56) to see the site as representing a single episode of soft-shell clam harvesting and processing, perhaps associated with the nineteenth-century bait fishery.

Notwithstanding this evidence, there are several shallow, ephemeral shell-bearing sites in the QR that have produced pre-Contact dates that can be assigned to the later LMW and/or artifacts diagnostic of this period. By and large, these later LMW sites consist of horizontally differentiated shallow patches of shell (<40 cm). Three sites located on in the Northern QR on Digdeguash Harbour (see figure 11.2), for example, have produced radiocarbon dates or artifact types common to the later LMW. A single radiocarbon assay from McAleenan site (BhDr-1) produced a date of 680 ± 160 BP, or a 2-sigma range of 955 to 325 cal. BP (Sanger 1987:89-90; see table 11.3 here) and the Carson site (BgDr-5) produced radiocarbon assays indicating inhabitancy spanning the earlier and later LMW. Orr's Point is undated, but ceramic fragments collected during Sanger's (1987:98) excavations are diagnostic of Petersen and Sanger's (1993) Ceramic period 4 and Ceramic period 5 (including shell-tempering), suggesting an earlier-to-later LMW occupation.

On Bliss Island (figure 11.5), the Lighthouse Cove (BgDr-60) and Pintlowes Cove (BgDr-61) sites vary in terms of structure and area but also consist of patchy, shallow deposits of soft-shell clam. While they have yet to be radiometrically dated, based on other evidence Black suggested that these sites represented single-component pre-Contact occupations, likely during the later LMW (Black 1988, 1992; see table 11.3 here). The Lighthouse Cove site, for example, produced two sherds of shell-tempered pottery, which is generally considered diagnostic of the later LMW (Black 1988:102). Drawing on the site's structure and lithic assemblage, Black proposed that the site was likely the result of activity over a relatively short period of time approximately 1,000 to 1,200 years ago. He provided a similar interpretation for another small, shallow deposit on Bliss Island, the Ledge site (BgDq-5). This site is also composed of patchy shell deposits, though these differ in important ways from the Lighthouse and Pintlowes Cove sites. Representing more diverse and more recent activities than the first two, the Ledge site produced a layer of soft-shell clam and horse mussel, and another layer comprised entirely of green sea urchin.

The Devil's Head site (97.10 ME) includes two proto-Contact period loci and a single later LMW locus, Area A (Hrynick et al. 2017). Area A includes an oval-shaped, gravel-lined dwelling feature that articulates with a shallow shell deposit dominated by soft-shell clam. A radiocarbon assay from moose bone in Area A yielded a date of 801 ± 29 BP or 767–676 cal. BP (2-sigma), placing it within the later LMW. Ceramic densities were relatively low in Area A, consisting of three sherds of grit-tempered pottery, decorated with cord-wrapped stick, in common with other LMW sites.

While these small, patchy sites have also been subjected to long-term erosional processes which could have obscured or perhaps obliterated archaeological deposits, there are several indications that these deposits do indeed form a distinct group of shell-bearing site in the QR. First, while the large, deep sites are chronologically shingled, very few have produced any deposit dated after 1000 cal. BP; where later LMW deposits do occur, they are stratigraphically above earlier deposits rather than to the landward edge of the site (Black 2002:331). This suggests that what we identify as small, ephemeral sites are not simply the back ends of badly eroded larger sites. Second, as we discuss below, these small sites are generally characterized by a low density of vertebrate faunal remains and appear to reflect an economic strategy focussed on a few specific vertebrate and invertebrate species, whereas large, deep shell-bearing sites are often taxonomically rich and diverse, even within particular units and stratigraphic deposits.

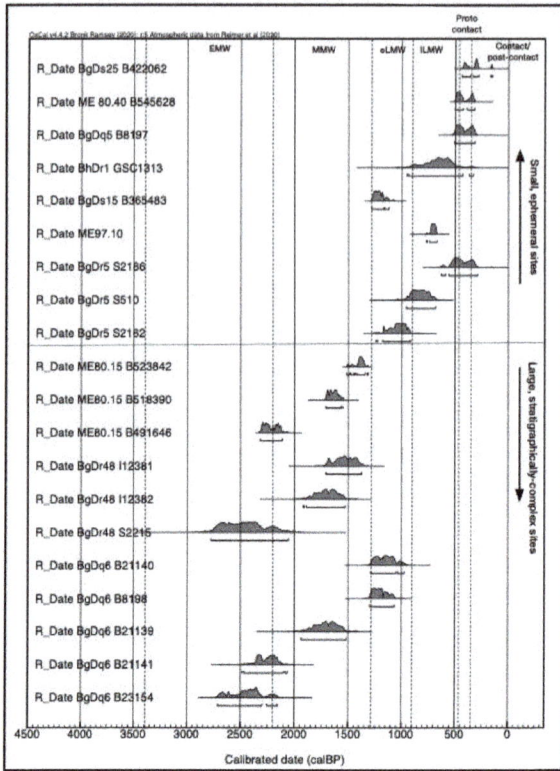

Figure 11.4. Probability distributions for dates from the three large, deeply stratified shell-bearing sites (Weir, Partridge Island, and Reversing Falls) and for dated, small, ephemeral sites. These were calibrated using OxCal version 4.3.2. (Bronk Ramsey 2017) and the IntCal atmospheric curve (Reimer et al. 2013). Some lab abbreviations are shortened: B=Beta; S=SI. The remaining follow standard lab abbreviations.

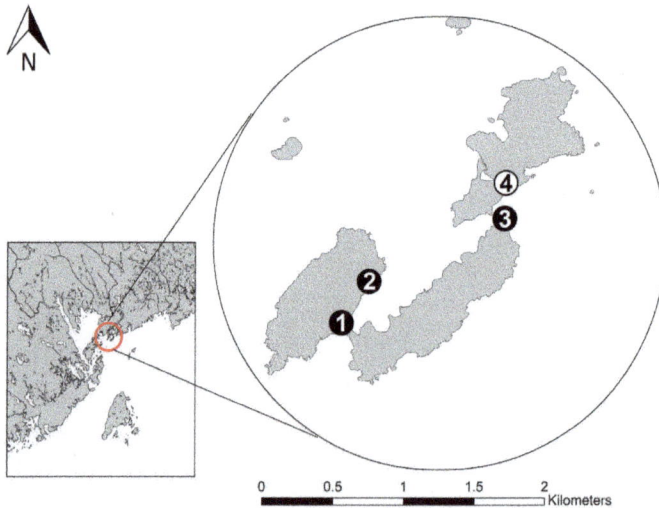

Figure 11.5. Bliss Island archaeological sites. Open circles denote Middle Maritime Woodland/earlier Late Maritime Woodland (LMW) shell-bearing sites, and closed circles denote later LMW sites: 1. Lighthouse Cove (BgDr-60), 2. Pintlowes Cove (BgDr-61), 3. Ledge (BgDq-5), 4. Weir (BgDq-6).

Table 11.3. Conventional and Calibrated radiocarbon dates for all later LMW sites discussed.

Site name	Borden/ Site number	Material	$^{14}C \pm 1$-sigma Yrs. BP. Delta ^{13}C corrected	Delta ^{13}C	Cal BP Yrs. ± 2-sigma	Lab number	Reference
Carson	BgDr-5	charcoal	1120±65	-25.0	1226-1211 (1.3%) 1183-926 (94.1%)	SI-2187	Sanger 1987
Carson	BgDr-5	charcoal	925±80	-25.0	965-689 (95.4%)	S-510	Sanger 1987
Carson	BgDr-5	charcoal	420 ±90	-25.0	635-595 (3.9%) 562-291 (91.5%)	SI-2186	Sanger 1987
McAleenan	BhDr-1	charcoal	680±160	-25.0	953-945 (0.2%) 939-429 (93.7%) 374-367 (0.2%) 360-328 (1.2%)	GSC-1313	Sanger 1987
Ledge site	BgDq-5	charcoal	380±50		510-314 (95.4%)	Beta-8197	Black 1992:210
Devil's Head	ME97.10	terrestrial mammal bone	801±29	-24.0	767-676 (95.4%)	AA-106617	Hrynick et al. 2017
Birch Cove	BgDs-25	terrestrial mammal bone	270+/30	-24.2	436-352 (42.8%) 334-281 (46.4%) 169-152 (6.2%)	Beta-422062	Blair et al. 2017
BgDs-15	BgDs-15	terrestrial mammal bone	1270±30	-21.7	1288-1172 (92.3%) 1159-1147 (1.3%) 1132-1129 (0.2%) 1108-1091 (1.6%)	Beta-365483	Webb 2018
Sipp Bay II	ME80.40	terrestrial mammal bone	380±30	-23	505-426 (61.5%) 392-319 (33.9%)	Beta-545628	Hrynick et al. 2019

New Evidence from Birch Cove and Sipp Bay

With the goal of understanding the later LMW, we have participated in several recent projects that afford new insight into these diffuse and ephemeral deposits of shell. We report here analysis from projects focused on two different mainland areas, including sites in and around Birch Cove (Blair et al. 2017), located in the northern QR, and sites at Sipp Bay, in Cobscook Bay in the western QR (Hrynick et al. 2019). In each case, bulk samples were collected from each excavated deposit, and the quality and quantity of samples is good compared to a number of sites that were excavated to a greater extent. Samples differed in mass and volume, with 1 L samples collected at Birch Cove and 1 L to 2.5 L samples collected from the Sipp Bay sites. All samples were sorted using nested screens (8 mm, 4 mm, and 2 mm). Materials passed through 8 mm and 4 mm screens were sorted in full, while those from 2 mm screens were usually subsampled. At BgDs-25, 50% or 100% of the 2 mm screens were analyzed. For the Sipp Bay sites, a riffle splitter was used to subsample the 2 mm fraction such that 25% was of the total sample was analyzed. While differences in small-screen subsampling might underestimate quantities of highly friable taxa such as green sea urchins and common mussels, we are only able to report coarse trends in shellfish assemblages with this methodology.

Birch Cove

In 2015, Blair, K. Patton, and Horne (Blair et al. 2017) sampled BgDs-25, a mainland site in the Caughey-Taylor Nature Preserve at the mouth of Birch Cove, a small embayment off of Bocabec Bay in the northern QR (figure 11.6). BgDs-25 is one of a series of mostly small, ephemeral shell-bearing sites that are located along the Birch Cove shoreline. BgDs-25 is composed of at least two distinct loci, and was first identified through its erosional face and patches of shell at the base of trees in a low-lying swale. Blair and colleagues selected this site for excavation because earlier testing had suggested that it matched the profile for later LMW sites described by Black (1993, 2004). Excavation produced a single fragment of French earthenware, suggesting an early Contact-era date. The likely seventeenth-century inhabitancy was later supported by a single radiocarbon assay that produced a date of 270 ± 30 BP (2-sigma calibration of 440–150 cal. BP).

Locus 1 is a shallow shell deposit (<20 cm in depth) consisting almost exclusively of soft-shell clam located on a rock ledge; however, Locus 2 is structurally more complex. Several factors, including high densities of gravel and concentrations of lithic artifacts, suggest that a dwelling had been constructed here. Locus 2 also contained evidence of multiple shell dumps, with the deepest part consisting of relatively unfragmented shell. Soft-shell clam made up approximately 96% of the shellfish taxa by mass at this site (table 11.4). Northern whelks were the next most frequently occurring taxa, at 3.5%. Northern whelks were particularly abundant in lower deposits (layers 3, 3a, and 4) in unit 4, comprising between approximately 9% and 12% of the identified shell by mass in those parts of the site (table 11.5).

In addition to BgDs-25, several other sites have been sampled around Birch Cove, including BgDs-15. While BgDs-25 is on the outer arm of Birch Cove, BgDs-15 is at its inner margin, where a brackish water pond captures freshwater flowing in from the surface and from a small stream, and is regularly charged with tidal salt water. In 2004, the University of New Brunswick conducted a field school that included the partial excavation of BgDs-15, which features shallow (≤30 cm depth) cultural deposits consisting of an admixture of marine shell and black soil (Dickinson et al. 2005; Webb 2018). A shell-free complex hearth feature was partially excavated and is presumed to be stratigraphically associated with the shell-bearing deposit. A radio-carbon assay of 1270 ± 30 BP was obtained from mammal bone from the site, placing it at 1091–1288 cal. BP at the 2-sigma range (within the earlier LMW). A second date of 160 ± 30 BP was obtained on wood charcoal from Feature 1; however, this date was rejected due to the obvious pre-Contact character of the feature. While the shell from BgDs-15 has not been quan-titatively analyzed, it appears to be predominantly soft-shell clam with trace amounts of mussel and whelk. The material culture from the site was relatively scant, with only a single amorphous biface and 14 friable, undecorated grit-tempered pre-Contact pottery sherds recovered from the excavation units.

In addition to terrestrial faunal remains, the field-collected zooarchaeo-logical sample also included 977 fishbone specimens, most of which were attributed to Atlantic tomcod (80% NISP [number of identified specimens]) and indeterminate small gadids (probable tomcod; 19%), with trace amounts of clupeids (<1%). Laboratory processing of column and bulk samples from Feature 1 yielded an additional 3,217 fishbone specimens, of which 1,723 could be identified. Again, the sample is dominated by Atlantic tomcod (79% NISP) and small gadids (20%), with a small number of clupeids (1%). These data, in conjunction with a nearby potential fish trap (figure 11.6), suggest a relatively specialized subsistence strategy targeting winter-spawning tomcod in Birch Cove. Fish-skeletal-part frequencies are indicative of in situ provi-sioning, which is consistent with a residential mobility pattern (Webb 2018; *sensu* Binford 1980).

Sipp Bay

In 2018, K. Patton and colleagues (Hrynick et al. 2019) tested two thin, patchy mainland shell-bearing sites on Sipp Bay, Maine, on lands owned by the Maine Coast Heritage Trust (figure 11.7). A third site (ME 80.41) has been docu-mented but is untested. Mapping and preliminary testing at ME 80.25 and ME 80.40 (Sipp Bay I and II, respectively) show that they match descriptions of later LMW sites identified by Black (1992, 1993), but parts of these sites would appear not dissimilar in form from the slightly earlier-dated BgDs-15 (Webb 2018) and Locus 1 at the later-dated BgDs-25 (Blair et al. 2017). ME 80.25 and ME 80.40 each cover a long stretch of a rocky ledge (35 m–60 m) but are relatively shallow (<25 cm in depth; figure 11.8A). Shell-bearing deposits at both sites were typically 10 cm–15 cm in thickness and differen-tiated horizontally by non-shell-bearing deposits (Hrynick et al. 2019:29–36). At ME 80.40, for example, shell-free test units were observed within a metre of the shell-rich erosional face (figure 11.8B). There are no radiocarbon dates for ME 80.25, but artifacts found during subsurface testing here suggest both pre-Contact and late-nineteenth/early-twentieth-century use. Of note are three fragments of grit-tempered ceramics, which could indicate site use from the MMW through to the later LMW (Hrynick et al. 2019:30). ME 80.40 produced a single radiocarbon date on terrestrial mammal bone of 380 ± 30 BP, which, when calibrated (2-sigma range), provides date ranges of 505–315 cal. BP. A closer look at the probability distribution for this date shows that it is most likely later LMW or proto-Contact period. Preliminary analysis of bulk samples shows that soft-shell clam comprises over 99% of shellfish by mass at both sites (table 11.4). While a few vertebrate faunal remains were identified in samples at these sites, both sites show an almost exclusive focus on soft-shell clam harvesting.

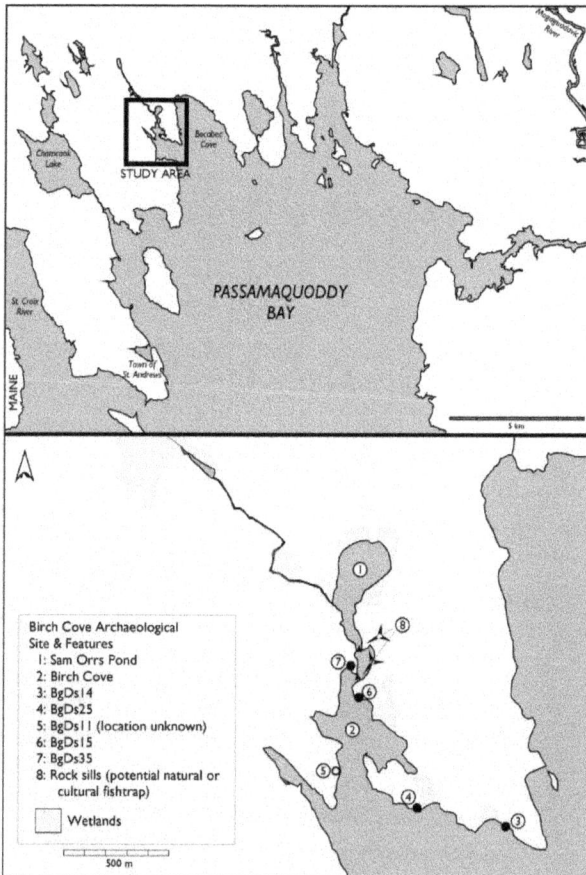

Figure 11.6. Birch Cove archaeological sites and landscape features.

Figure 11.7. Sipp Bay archaeological sites.

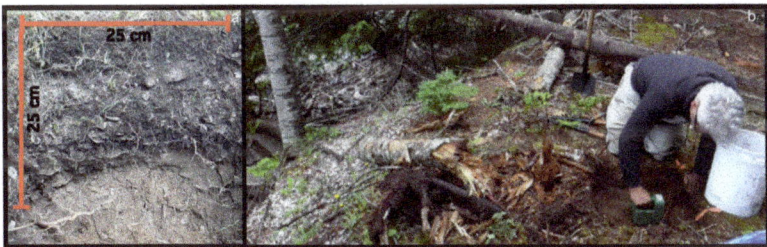

Figure 11.8. Photographs of tested Sipp Bay I and II sites, illustrating their depth and patchy character. (A) south profile of test unit 3 at ME 80.25; (B) excavation of test unit 2 at ME 80.40. Tim Spahr is shown in the picture.

Table 11.4. Mass and relative percentages of identified shellfish taxa at BgDs–25, Sipp Bay I, and Sipp Bay II.

	# of litre samples	Soft-shell clam	Horse mussel	Blue mussel	Mussel spp.	Green sea urchin	Northern whelk	Periwinkle sp.	Acorn barnacle	Total mass of identified taxa
BgDs-25	23	95.6% (7609 gr.)	–	–	0.9% (71.6 gr.)	–	3.5% (281.1 gr.)	<0.1% (0.4 gr.)	–	796.2 gr.
Sipp Bay I (ME 80.25)	3	99.9% (3657.8)	<0.1% (0.01 gr.)	–	<0.1% (0.13 gr.)	–	<0.1% (0.15 gr.)	–	<0.1% (0.02 gr.)	3658.1 gr.
Sipp Bay II (ME 80.40)	2	99.3% (1174.8 gr.)	–	–	0.6% (7.3 gr.)	0.1% (1.5 gr.)	–	–	<0.1% (0.1gr.)	1183.7 gr.

Table 11.5. Mass and relative percentages of identified shellfish taxa from four bulk samples collected from BgDs-25.

Sample # and provenience	Soft-shell clam	Mussel spp.	Northern whelk	Periwinkle sp.	Total
Sample 6: Unit 4, layer 4	88.4% 337.7 gr.	2.2% 8.4 gr.	8.5% 35.6 gr.	<0.1% 0.4 gr.	382.1 gr.
Sample 13: Unit 4, layer 4	89.3% 434.7 gr.	2.2% 10.7 gr.	8.5% 41.1 gr.	-	486.5 gr.
Sample 15: Unit 4 layer 3 (pocket A)	81.3% 302 gr.	6.4% 23.6 gr.	12.4% 45.96 gr.	-	371.6 gr.
Sample 23: Unit 4 layer 3	86.8% 624.6 gr.	0.8% 5.7 gr.	12.4% 89.4 gr.	-	719.77 gr.

Discussion

At the beginning of this chapter, we proposed to examine whether the process of creating site types has obscured our ability to recognize the character of settlement change in the pre-Contact archaeological record of the QR. From the shell-bearing sites presented here, we can see that diversity exists at two scales that likely reflect the activities of individuals or small groups of people such as households. The large, stratigraphically complex MMW/earlier LMW shell-bearing sites show considerable taxonomic diversity, which likely reflects household flexibility and intimate knowledge of complex environments on land and sea. The kinds of plants and animals, including shellfish, that live within microlocal habitats can be enormously diverse, even within a small region (Thomas et al. 1983). This means that the shellfish taxa that show up in archaeological sites derive from shoreline habitats that exhibit varying salinity levels, wave exposure, substrate character, and other highly localized ecological factors (Moss 2012). Some shellfish would have been harvested immediately in front of the sites themselves, and in these cases, people likely harvested shellfish in the same locations they processed and consumed them. Shellfish harvesting and processing would have been scheduled around other activities, or red tides,[2] but also around daily and fortnightly tidal regimes (Black 1993:62-63; Sanger 1987:118). The three MMW/earlier LMW sites presented here contain many layers of shells from epifaunal shellfish taxa, such as horse and common mussels, green sea urchins, and northern whelks. All except common mussels favour lower intertidal-to-subtidal zones and, thus, would have been most easily

---

2. The term red tide describes a harmful marine algal bloom (red dinoflagellate *Protogonyaulax tamarensis*) that typically occurs in later summer/early fall and is linked to potent neurotoxic saxitoxin and analogues, which when consumed as a result of eating shellfish can cause paralytic poisoning (Medcof et al. 1947; Sherman-Caswell and Hurst 1988).

harvested during spring tides, occurring twice within each lunar month (Berrill and Berrill 1981; Black 1993:62-63; Brady and Scheibling 2006; Speller et al. 2016; Zagata 2008). Green sea urchins, which were likely harvested for their gonads (Black 1992:123), might provide the most precise indicators for seasonality of all shellfish species identified within the study sites. Green sea urchin move along substrates in response to food availability and water temperature, and are susceptible to mass die-offs if temperatures in shallow waters are above 12° C for sustained periods (Brady and Scheibling 2006), perhaps making it unlikely that they would occur in shallow waters in large numbers in warmer months. Significantly, their gonads are largest in the late fall through to the early spring (Black 1993:89; Brady and Scheibling 2006), suggesting that the urchin lenses we find in these sites likely pertain specifically to cold-season harvesting.

Soft-shell clam, however, make up significant proportions of these same shell-bearing sites, and at Reversing Falls they are the most frequently occurring shellfish species by mass. While several northern mainland QR MMW/earlier LMW shell-bearing sites are located adjacent to large clam flats, the three presented here are located adjacent to large bedrock outcrops and along rocky foreshores. Both Sanger (1987:118) and Ames (2002) have demonstrated how boats allow hunter-gather-fishers to traverse large areas on a more regular basis than terrestrial hunter-gatherers to collect and transport resources in bulk. Using boats, Ancestral Peskotomuhkatiyik could harvest soft-shell clams from any number of tidal flats in the QR. Clams and other shellfish could have been harvested year-round, but late fall through spring harvesting would have mitigated some of the risks associated with red tides. Such toxic algae blooms are inconsistent in timing and intensity but generally occur from the spring through to autumn and are most common in the warmest months. Red tides may be more common in the post-industrial age due to pollution (Black 1993:87) but could have occurred prior as well. Several Indigenous populations around the world rely on a number of indicators, such as changes in water colour, changes in air quality, and animal behaviour, to determine when red tides are coming or are present (Sahadevan 2016; Williams and Perez-Corral 2001). Burns and Sanger (1971:12) note that Peskotomuhkatiyik in the QR recognized the connection between toxic shellfish and red tides and relied on their knowledge and experience to mitigate the likelihood of getting ill.

The evidence to date suggests that shellfish harvesting took on a different character after 1000 cal. BP. This shift seems to have taken place several decades to as much as a century after the onset of the MCA (Jones et al. 1999; Masson-Delmotte et al. 2013:386). Climate change could have influenced the kinds of plants and animals that were available in the QR, which, by extension, would have constrained the kinds of choices made by Ancestral Peskotomuhkatiyik living there. Climate research shows, however, that environmental changes associated with the MCA were often regional in character, timing, and degree (Masson-Delmotte et al. 2013:409). Preliminary research in the Gulf of Maine, for example, indicates a reduction in seawater temperature amplitude during the MCA; summers were cooler and winters warmer (Betts et al. 2021:39; Wanamaker et al. 2011). While many shellfish taxa are sensitive to changes in temperature and other aspects of their habitat, others, including several of the taxa we have identified in MMW/early LMW sites, can tolerate fluctuations in sea temperature (e.g., see Dinesen and Morton 2014; Reedy-Meyer and Rick 2019). This means that the relationship between warming or cooling temperatures and available shellfish taxa in a given region is complex (see, e.g., Cerrato et al. 2013). As several scholars have noted (Betts et al. 2019; Wolff and Holly 2019), we cannot at present assess the ways in which Indigenous lifeways, including settlement and shellfishing, in any location in the far Northeast were propelled by regional climate change associated with the MCA.

What the current evidence suggests, however, is that people shifted focus to a smaller number of vertebrate and invertebrate species. In several cases, the shellfish assemblages indicate that Ancestral Peskotomuhkatiyik focussed almost exclusively of soft-shell clam. While later LMW peoples would have continued to use boats for travel and transport, these sites are smaller and patchier and may represent the activities of smaller populations. At ME 80.40, clam deposits are interspersed with non-shell-bearing lithic scatters (Hrynick et al. 2019:33-35). The very structure of such sites conveys a sense of intermittent inhabitancy focussed on a few key tasks and resources.

Each one of these small sites, however, is also unique in some way and suggests that diverse harvesting and consumption practises were dispersed along coastlines rather than concentrated in central locations; there are remarkably few vertebrate faunal remains at either Sipp Bay site, while animal bone is more abundant at BgDs-15 and BgDs-25. In addition to soft-shell clam, BgDs-25 also produced evidence for periodic, and likely tide-dependent, northern whelk harvests. The Ledge site differs again; the green sea urchin lens may reflect seasonal and targeted harvesting at fortnightly (spring) low tides. Tomcod occur in astonishingly high frequencies at BgDs-15, though this impression may be an artifact of sampling bias. While this kind of mass capture of tomcod could reflect specialized-task group harvest for a stored economy, several lines of evidence indicate that these fish were consumed fresh and on-site (Webb 2018). Each of these sites is different from one another in terms of economy, and to some degree structure, and it is this diversity that we consider here.

These sites also reaffirm the view that there was a major shift away from the pattern of the MMW/earlier LMW, when settlement was centred on key sites. While small, ephemeral sites like these may be outlying extraction sites representing some kind of extension of a centralized, nucleated settlement, the evidence at present does not necessarily support it. Insights gleaned from ethnohistorical perspectives on settlement, coupled with emerging perspectives from southern New England, encourage us to consider other possibilities. These views suggest that the "fragmentation" of settlement into smaller family units might obscure it from an archaeological perspective by rendering the linkages between tasks, place, and household difficult to see. Small, ephemeral sites equally could fit with a model of dispersed settlement that lacks a centralized hub (*sensu* Chilton 2010; Leveillee et al. 2006). Such a model does not require us to account for absent sites and allows us to envisage either a stable or growing population base for the period after 1000 cal. BP. For example, if one were able to amass all the archaeological material and deposits from the various later LMW components around Birch Cove into a single deposit, it would likely be as or more substantial than the thick MMW deposits of the preceding period. This proposed model has parallels with McFayden's (2014:122) understanding of the "spatial and temporal conditions of Mesolithic life" in Britain. While ephemeral flint scatters in Wiltshire have been interpreted as evidence for marginality during the Mesolithic, McFayden argues instead that these hunter-gatherers created space differently than the later Neolithic peoples in the same area. Thus flint scatters are more than locations or the remnants of isolated and unconnected activities; they reveal important information about how people lived their lives and are integrated and connected to other activities embedded in regional landscapes. Gathering flint scatters together, as McFayden (2014:126) does, they no longer convey a sense of marginality, but rather show us a uniquely Mesolithic way of creating space and "living spatially" in small, interconnected settlements.

Similarly, we suggest that the small, ephemeral, shell-bearing sites presented in this study may in fact represent "fragmented settlements" that are not unlike the "dispersed villages" model proposed for the later LMW in southern New England. Just as Leveillee et al. (2006:86) suggest the Narragansett may have structured their social landscape around family autonomy within larger collectivities, we propose that personal and household autonomy might also have been a structuring principle influencing settlement in the QR. Individuals could rely on vast social networks fostered by flexibility in household and band membership to acquire access to any number of microlocal resource locations within the QR, and perhaps beyond the traditional homeland (Pawling 2016; Sanger et al. 2006). This vast, flexible social network might explain the diversity of both sites and assemblages after approximately 1000 cal. BP, and counter notions of sparse inhabitancy embedded within European historical accounts.

Though our proposed settlement model for the later LMW diverts our view away from trajectories of increasing sedentism on the coast and complexity, it does not negate or contradict oral-historical and archaeological evidence for seasonal fishing villages at places like the first waterfall on the St. Croix (Bassett 2015; Soctomah 2005) or beyond the Peskotomuhkati homeland (Bourque and Cox 1981; Nash and Stewart 1990). Central to our argument is social and residential flexibility, flexibility that would allow and enable individuals and households to gather at important resource and/or social/ceremonial locations at specific times in the year. Households, and the people that comprised them, however, might come and go on their own terms, thus exhibiting the kind of autonomy described by ethnohistorical accounts. The broader, shared patterns of dispersal in the Northeast might indeed lead to commonalities in the later LMW and, in this sense, may reflect shared but subtly distinctive understandings of social space that transcend the economic realities (horticulture in southern New England, food foraging in the Maritime Peninsula) that underpin them.

Finally, we propose that our inability to see this kind of fragmented settlement stems from the very structure of archaeological research, in particular the imposition of concepts such as "site" onto what would have been a continuous human presence across landscapes (Dunnell 1992; Dunnell and Dancey 1983; Lacy 1999; Lucas 2001:167-170). The site concept leads to a conflation of a locale containing a concentration of material (the archaeological context) with the circumscription of past activities (the systemic context, *sensu* Schiffer 1972). This conflation is most evident in the concept of archaeological component, which, in its original formulation, corresponded to the notion of community (Phillips and Willey 1953:628; Rouse 1955:713). Several scholars have raised concerns about the constructed nature of these concepts and their influence on archaeological interpretation (see Lucas 2001:167-170; Lyman et al. 1997; O'Brien and Lyman 2000). Nonetheless, "component"—a set of archaeological remains clustered into a "site" reflecting a set of temporally limited past activities—remains a key way to conceptualize meaningful human activity in the past. Continuity of material culture is inherent in the component concept, which relies on contiguous, localized stratigraphic deposits (O'Brien and Lyman 2000:126). While this definition of components has allowed us to make interpretative correlations between temporally and spatially associated artifacts, it has at the same time impeded our ability to make correlations between noncontiguous deposits of archaeological materials. In effect, we only regard groups of components as settlements when materials are concentrated sufficiently to create identifiably continuous layering in a local area. Should components ever reach a particular state of dispersal, our narrow approach to component, activity, and site could easily render the settlement itself—a place where a group of closely connected people built structures, carried out tasks, and interacted with one another—archaeologically "invisible." This renders each deposit of archaeological material as a "site" in and around Birch Cove or Sipp Bay, for example, conveying the idea that the activities within each locale are distinct from the activities at other locales, and that each is socially circumscribed. Reflective consideration of the construct of site, however, reminds us of the spaces in between, as well as the mobility possible between them.

Conclusion

Almost 20 years ago, Black (2002:313) noted that there was "greater uncertainty" about the ancestral Peskotomuhkati settlement and subsistence practices of the later LMW than earlier in the Maritime Woodland. Despite recent work at a number of these sites, patterning in later LMW-dated archaeological sites is still remarkably difficult to discern. We propose, however, that small, ephemeral sites, such as the ones we present here, could represent a shift from a kind of nucleated settlement toward dispersal. In these "fragmented settlements," networks of closely related households could stretch themselves along contiguous coastlines and focus on micro-local resources. This model would help to explain the diversity in vertebrate and invertebrate remains and site structure that seems to characterize these sites. We cannot be entirely sure of the impetus for this transition, but we propose that flexible kin and social networks permitted it to take place, and that the result is a distribution of ephemeral and distinct shell-bearing sites. Our proposed settlement model also requires us to reflect on the constraints that can be imposed on our interpretations by fundamental archaeological constructs such as "site" and "component." While central to how we do archaeology, many human activities extend well beyond archaeologically defined sites and point toward a larger landscape of integrated human action.

Acknowledgments

We are grateful to Donald Soctomah, Passamaquoddy Tribal Historic Preservation Officer in Maine, and Hugh Akagi, chief of the Peskotomuhkati Nation in New Brunswick for their support for research within Passamaquoddy/Peskotomukati territory. Thanks also to the Town of Pembroke, Maine, the Cobscook Community Learning Centre, the Nature Trust of New Brunswick, the Hunstman Marine Science Centre, and Sheila Washburn for facilitating and permitting several aspects of this research. The Maine Coast Heritage Trust granted permission for us to undertake field work at the Sipp Bay Preserve and we are especially grateful to Deirdre Whitehead for her assistance with this work. Many thanks also to Gabe Hrynick and Arthur Anderson for collaborating on the Maine-centred research in this chapter, and to students from the University of Toronto, the University of New Brunswick, and the University of Maine, and to Tim Spahr for help during field and lab work. This research has been generously funded by the Insight Program of the Social Sciences and Humanities Research Council of Canada, the National Geographic Society, and the Archaeology Centre and the Faculty of Arts and Science at the University of Toronto. We offer our appreciation to Gabe Hrynick and Ken Holyoke for their invitation to contribute to this volume, to David Black for feedback on an earlier version of this chapter, and to anonymous reviewers whose feedback improved this work.

References Cited

Ames, Kenneth

2002   Going by Boat: The Forager-Collector Continuum at Sea. In *Beyond Foraging and Collecting: Evolutionary Change in Hunter-Gatherer Settlement Systems,* edited by William Fizthugh and Junko Habu, pp. 17–50. Kluwer/Plenum Press, New York.

Anderson, Arthur, A. Katherine Patton, and M. Gabriel Hrynick

2021   Wabanaki Subtidal Shellfish Harvesting: An Ecological and Archaeological Study of Horse Mussels and Barnacles at the Reversing Falls Site, Maine, USA. *Archaeology of Eastern North America* 48.

Bassett, Edward

2015   *Cultural Importance of River Herring to the Passamaquoddy People.* Sipayik Environmental Department, Pleasant Point Reservation, Passamaquoddy Tribe, Perry, Maine.

Basso, Kevin

1996   *Wisdom Sits in Places: Landscapes and Language among the Western Apache.* University of New Mexico Press, Albuquerque.

Beaudry, Mary C.

2015   Households Beyond the House: On the Archaeology and Materiality of Historical Households. In *Beyond the Walls: New Perspectives on the Archaeology of Historical Households,* edited by Kevin R. Fogle, James A. Nyman, and Mary C. Beaudry, pp. 1–22. University Press of Florida, Gainesville.

Berrill, Michael, and Deborah Berrill

1981   *A Sierra Club Naturalist's Guide: The North Atlantic Coast, Cape Cod to Newfoundland.* Sierra Club Books, San Francisco.

Betts, Matthew W. and M. Gabriel Hrynick

2021   *The Archaeology of the Atlantic Northeast.* University of Toronto Press, Toronto.

Betts, Matthew W., David W. Black, Brian Robinson, and Arthur Spiess

2019   Coastal Adaptations to the Northern Gulf of Maine and Southern Scotia Shelf. In *The Archaeology of Human-Environmental Dynamics on the North American Atlantic Coast,* edited by Leslie Reeder-Myers, John A. Turck, and Torben C. Rick, pp. 44–80. University Press of Florida, Gainesville.

Binford, Lewis R.

1980   Willow Smoke and Dogs' Tails: Hunter-Gatherer Settlement Systems and Archaeological Site Formation. *American Antiquity* 45:4–20.

Biggar, Henry P. (editor)

1922   *The Publications of the Champlain Society: The Works of Samuel de Champlain,* Vol. 1. Champlain Society, Toronto.

Black, David W.

1988   *Bliss Revisited: Preliminary Accounts of the Bliss Islands Archaeology Project Phase II.* Archaeological Services, New Brunswick Department of Tourism, Recreation and Heritage, Fredericton.

1992   *Living Close to the Ledge: Prehistoric Human Ecology of the Bliss Islands, Quoddy Region, New Brunswick, Canada.* Occasional Publications in Northeastern Archaeology, No. 6. Copetown Press, Dundas.

1993   *What Images Return: A Study of the Stratigraphy and Seasonality of a Shell Midden in the Insular Quoddy Region, New Brunswick.* New Brunswick Archaeology 27, the Partridge Island Archaeology Project, Vol. 1. Municipalities, Culture and Housing, Fredericton, New Brunswick, Canada.

2002   Out of the Blue and into the Black: The Middle-Late Maritime Woodland Transition in the Quoddy Region, New Brunswick, Canada. In *Northeast Subsistence-Settlement Change: A.D. 700–1300,* edited by Hart, John P. and Cristina R. Rieth, pp. 301–320. New York State Museum Bulletin 496, New York State Education Department, Albany.

Black, David W., and Chris Turnbull

1986   Recent Archaeological Research in the Insular Quoddy Region, New Brunswick, Canada. *Current Anthropology* 27(4):400–402.

Blair, Susan E.

1997   The Prehistoric Archaeology of the Grand Manan Archipelago: Cultural History and Regional Integration. Master's thesis, Department of Anthropology. University of New Brunswick, Fredericton.

Blair, Susan E., Margaret Horne, A. Katherine Patton, and W. Jesse Webb

2017   Birch Cove and the Protohistoric Period of the Northern Quoddy Region, New Brunswick, Canada. *Journal of the North Atlantic* 31:59–69.

Blair, Susan E., A. Katherine Patton, and W. Jesse Webb

2016   Movement and Landscape in the Late Maritime Woodland and Protohistoric Quoddy Region of the Gulf of Maine. Paper presented at the 83rd Meeting of the Eastern States Archeology Federation, Langhorne, Pennsylvania.

Bourque, Bruce J.

1973   Aboriginal Settlement and Subsistence on the Maine Coast. *Man in the Northeast* 6:3–20.

2004   *Twelve Thousand Years: American Indians in Maine.* University of Nebraska Press, Lincoln.

Bourque, Bruce J., and Steven L. Cox

1981   Excavations at the Goddard Site, Brooklin, Maine: A Preliminary Report. *Man in the Northeast* 22:3–28.

Brady, Sheanna M., and Robert E. Scheibling

2006   Changes in Growth and Reproduction of Green Sea Urchins, *Strongylocentrotus droebachiensis* (Muller), during Reproduction of the Shallow Subtidal Zone after Mass Mortality. *Journal of Experimental Marine Biology* 335: 277–291.

Briz i Godino, Ivan, and Marco Madella
2013   The Archaeology of Household—an Introduction. In *The Archaeology of Household,* edited by Marco Madella, Gabriella Kovacs, Brigitta Kulcsarne-Berzsenyi, and Ivan Briz i Godino, pp. 1–5. Oxbow Books, Oxford.

Bronk Ramsey, C.
2017   Methods for Summarizing Radiocarbon Datasets. *Radiocarbon* 59(2): 1809–1833.

Burns, Jim, and David Sanger
1971   Accounts of Faunal Material from Three Shell Midden Sites Near St. Andrew's New Brunswick. Manuscript 978, on file at the Canadian Museum of History Archives, Ottawa.

Bush, Elizabeth, and Donald S. Lemmen (editors)
2019   *Canada's Changing Climate Report.* Government of Canada, Ottawa.

Cerrato, Robert, Phillip V. Locicero, and Steven L. Goodbred
2013   Response of Mollusc Assemblages to Climate Variability and Anthropogenic Activities: A 4000-year Record from a Shallow Bar-Built Lagoon System. *Global Change Biology* 19:3024–3036.

Chilton, Elizabeth
2002   "Towns They Have None": Diverse Subsistence and Settlement Strategies in Native New England. In *Northeast Subsistence-Settlement Change: A.D. 700–1300,* edited by Hart, John P. and Cristina R. Rieth, pp. 289–300. New York State Museum Bulletin 496, New York State Education Department, Albany.
2010   Mobile Farmers and Sedentary Models: Horticulture and Cultural Transitions in Late Woodland and Contact Period New England. In *Ancient Complexities: New Perspectives in Pre-Columbian North America,* edited by Susan Alt, pp. 96–103. University of Utah Press, Salt Lake City.

Claassen, Cheryl
1991   Gender, Shellfishing, and the Shell Mound Archaic. In *Engendering Archaeology: Women and Prehistory,* edited by Joan M. Gero and Margaret W. Conkey, pp. 276–300. Basil Blackwell. Cambridge, Massachusetts.

Coupland, Gary, and Edward B. Banning (editors)
1996   *People Who Lived in Big Houses: Archaeological Perspectives on Large Houses.* Monographs in World Archaeology, No. 27. Prehistory Press, Madison, Wisconsin.

Davis, Stephen A.
1978   *Teacher's Cove: A Prehistoric Site on Passamaquoddy Bay.* New Brunswick Archaeology No. 1. New Brunswick Department of Historical and Cultural Resources, Fredericton.

Desplanque, Con, and David J. Mossman
1999   Tides of the Fundy. *Geographical Review* 89(1):23–33.

Dickinson, Pamela J., Susan E. Blair, and D. W. Black
2005   Technical Report on the 2004 University of New Brunswick Archaeological Field School (License Number 2004 NB7). Manuscript on file, Archaeological Services Branch, Fredericton.

Dinesen, Grete E., and Brian Morton
2014 Review of the Functional Morphology, Biology, and Perturbation Impacts on the Boreal, Habitat-Forming Horse Mussel *Modiolus Modulus* (Bivalvia: Mytilidae: Modiolinae). *Marine Biology Research* 10(9):845–870.

Dunnell, Robert C.
1992 The Notion Site. In *Space, Time, and Archaeological Landscapes*, edited by Jacqueline Rossignol and LeAnn Wandsnider, pp. 21–41. Springer, Boston.

Dunnell, Robert C., and William S. Dancey
1983 The Siteless Survey: A Regional Scale Data Collection Strategy. *Advances in Archaeological Method and Theory* 6:267–287. Academic Press, New York.

Hanks, Robert W.
1963 *The Soft-shell Clam*. United States Department of the Interior, Fish and Wildlife Service, Bureau of Commercial Fisheries, Washington, DC.

Hart, John P., and Cristina R. Rieth
2002 *Northeast Subsistence-Settlement Change: A.D. 700–1300*. New York State Museum Bulletin 496, New York State Education Department, Albany.

Hayden, Brian, and Aubrey Cannon
1982 The Corporate Group as an Archaeological Unit. *Journal of Anthropological Archaeology* 1:132–158.

Hendon, Julia A.
1996 Archaeological Approaches to the Organization of Domestic Labour: Household Practice and Domestic Relations. *Annual Review of Anthropology* 25: 45–61.

Hrynick, M. Gabriel, and David W. Black
2016 Cultural Continuity in Maritime Woodland Period Domestic Architecture in the Quoddy Region. *Canadian Journal of Archaeology* 40(1):23–76.

Hrynick, M. Gabriel, W. Jesse Webb, Christopher E. Shaw, and Taylor C. Testa
2017 Late Maritime Woodland to Protohistoric Culture Change and Continuity at the Devil's Head Site, Calais, Maine. *Archaeology of Eastern North America* 45:85–108.

Hrynick, M. Gabriel, Arthur Anderson, A. Katherine Patton, W. Jesse Webb, Christopher Brouillette, Trevor Lamb, and Alexandre Pelletier-Michaud
2019 *Report on the 2017–2019 Universities of New Brunswick, Toronto, and New England Fieldwork in Washington County, Maine*. Submitted to the Maine Historic Preservation Commission, Augusta, and the Passamaquoddy Tribal Historic Preservation Office, Sipayik, Maine.

Hunter, Ryan, Stephen W. Silliman, and David B. Landon
2014 Shellfish Collection and Community Connections in Eighteenth-Century Native New England. *American Antiquity* 79(4):712–729.

Jones, Terry J., Gary M. Brown, L. Mark Raab, Janet L. McVickar, W. Geoffrey Spaulding, Douglas J. Kennett, Andrew York, and Phillip L. Walker
1999 Environmental Imperatives Reconsidered: Demographic Crises in Western North America during the Medieval Climatic Anomaly. *Current Anthropology* 40(2):137–170.

Lacy, David M.

1999   Myth Busting and Prehistoric Land Use in the Green Mountains of Vermont. In *The Archaeological Northeast,* edited by Mary Ann Levine, Kenneth E. Sassaman, and Michael S. Nassaney. Bergin and Garvey, Westport, Connecticut.

Leveillee, Allan, Joseph Waller, and Donna Ingham

2006   Dispersed Villages in Late Woodland Period South-Coastal Rhode Island. *Archaeology of Eastern North America* 34:71–89.

Lucas, Gavin

2001   Critical Approaches to Fieldwork: *Contemporary and Historical Archaeological Practice.* Routledge, London.

Lyman, R. L., Michael J. O'Brien, and Robert C. Dunnell

1997   *The Rise and Fall of Culture History.* Springer, Boston.

McFayden, Lesley

2014   Making Space in the Late Mesolithic of Britain. In *Structured Worlds: The Archaeology of Hunter-Gatherer Thought and Action,* edited by Aubrey Cannon, pp. 116–127. Routledge, London.

Madella, Marco, Gabriella Kovacs, Brigitta Kulcsarne-Berzsenyi, and Ivan Briz i Godino

2013   *The Archaeology of Household.* Oxbow Books, Oxford.

Masson-Delmotte, Valérie, Michael Schultz, Ayako Abe-Ouchi, Juerg Beer, Andry Ganopolski, Jesus Fidel González-Rouco, Eystein Jansen, Kurt Lambeck, Jürg Luterbacher, Timothy Naish, Timothy Osborn, Bette Otto-Bliesner, Terrence Quinn, Rengaswamy Ramesh, Maisa Rojas, XueMei Shao, and Axel Timmerman.

2013   Information from the Paleoclimate Archives. In *Climate Change 2013: The Physical Science Basis, Contribution of Working Group 1 to the Fifth Assessment Report of the Intergovernmental Panel on Climate Change,* edited by T. F. Stocker, D. Qin, G.-K. Plattner, M. Tignor, S. K. Allen, J. Boschung, A. Nauels, Y. Xia, V. Bex, and P. M. Midgley, pp. 383–464. Cambridge University Press, Cambridge.

Matthew, George F.

1884   Discoveries of a Village of the Stone Age at Bocabec. *Bulletin of Natural History of New Brunswick* 3(2):6–29.

Medcof, John Carl, A. H. Leim, A. B. Needler, A. W. H. Needler, J. Gibbard, and J. Naubert

1947   Paralytic Shellfish Poisoning on the Canadian Atlantic Coast. *Bulletin of the Fisheries Research Board of Canada* 75:1–32.

Moss, Madonna L.

1993   Shellfish, Gender, and Status on the Northwest Coast: Archaeological, Ethnographic, and Ethnohistorical Records of the Tlingit. *American Anthropologist* 95(3):631–652.

2012   Understanding Variability in Northwest Coast Faunal Assemblages: Beyond Economic Intensification and Cultural Complexity. *The Journal of Island and Coastal Archaeology* 7(1):1–22.

Nash, Ronald J.

1997   Archetypal Landscapes and the Interpretation of Meaning. *Cambridge Archaeological Journal* 7(1):57–69.

Nash, Ronald J., and Frances Stewart
1990   *Melanson: A Large Micmac Village in Kings County, Nova Scotia.* Nova Scotia Museum Curatorial Report No. 67. Nova Scotia Museum, Halifax.

O'Brien, Michael J., and R. Lee Lyman
2000   *Applying Evolutionary Archaeology: A Systematic Approach.* Springer, Boston.

Patton, Jonathan K.
2014   Considering the Wet Homelands of Indigenous Massachusetts. *Journal of Social Archaeology* 14(1):87–111.

Pawling, Micah
2016   Wabanaki Homeland and Mobility: Concepts of Home in Nineteenth-Century Maine. *Ethnohistory* 63(4):621–643.
2017   *Welastekwey* (Maliseet) Homeland: Waterscapes and Continuity with the Lower St. John River Valley, 1794–1900. *Acadiensis* 46(2):5–34.

Pearson, Richard
1970   Archaeological Investigations in the St. Andrew's Area, New Brunswick. *Anthropologica* 12(2):181–190.

Petersen, James B., Malinda Blustain, and James W. Bradley
2004   "Mawooshen" Revisited: Two Native American Contact Period Sites on the Central Maine Coast. *Archaeology of Eastern North America* 32:1–71.

Petersen, James B., and David Sanger
1993   An Aboriginal Ceramic Sequence for Maine and the Maritime Provinces. In *Prehistoric Archaeology in the Maritime Provinces: Past and Present Research*, edited by Michael Deal and Susan Blair, pp. 113–170. Reports in Archaeology No. 8. Council of Maritime Premiers, Fredericton, New Brunswick.

Phillips, Phillip, and Gordon Willey
1953   Method and Theory in American Archeology: An Operational Basis for Culture-Historical Integration. *American Anthropologist* 55(1):615–633.

Prins, Harold E. L.
1994   Children of Gluskap: Wabanaki Indians on the Eve of the European Invasion. In *American Beginnings: Exploration, Culture, and Cartography in the Land of Norumbega*, edited by Emerson W. Baker, Edwin A. Churchill, Richard D'Abate, Kristine L. Jones, Victor A. Konrad, and Harold E. L. Prins, pp. 95–118. University of Nebraska Press, Lincoln.

Prins, Harold E. L., and Bunny McBride
2007   *Asticou's Island Domain: Wabanaki Peoples at Mount Desert Island—1500–2000.* Acadia National Park Ethnographic Overview and Assessment Vol. 1. Abbe Museum, Bar Harbor, Maine, and National Park Service Ethnography Program, Northeast Region, Boston.

Reedy-Meyers, Leslie, and Torben C. Rick
2019   Sea Level Rise and Sustainability in Chesapeake Bay Coastal Archaeology. In *The Archaeology of Human-Environmental Dynamics on the North American Atlantic Coast*, edited by Leslie Reeder-Myers, John A. Turck, and Torben C. Rick, pp. 107–136. University Press of Florida, Gainsville.

Reimer, Paula J., Edouard Bard, Alex Bayliss, J. Warren Beck, Paul G. Blackwell, Christopher Bronk Ramsey, Caitlin E. Buck, Hai Cheng, R. Lawrence Edwards,

Michael Friedrich, Pieter M. Grootes, Thomas P. Guilderson, Haflidi Haflidason, Irka Hajdas, Christine Hatté, Timothy J. Heaton, Dirk L. Hoffman, Alan G. Hogg, Konrad A. Hughen, K. Felix Kaiser, Bernd Kromer, Sturt W. Manning, Mu Niu, Ron W. Reimer, David A. Richards, E. Marian Scott, John R. Southon, Richard A. Staff, Christian S. M. Turney, and Johannes van der Plicht

2013   Intcal13 and Marine13 Radiocarbon Age Calibration Curves 0–50,000 Years cal BP. *Radiocarbon* 55(4):1869–1887.

Robin, Cynthia

2002   Outside of Houses. *Journal of Social Archaeology* 2(2):245–268.

Rouse, Irving

1955   On the Correlation of Phases of Culture. *American Anthropologist* 57(4):713–722.

Sahadevan, P.

2016   Indigenous Technical Knowledge of the Fisher Folk of Kerala (South India). *International Journal of Fisheries and Aquatic Studies* 4(6):334–338.

Sanger, David

1982   Changing Views of Aboriginal Settlement and Seasonality on the Gulf of Maine. *Canadian Journal of Archaeology* 2(2):195–203.

1987   *The Carson Site and the Late Ceramic Period in Passamaquoddy Bay, New Brunswick.* Archaeological Survey of Canada Paper No. 135. National Museum of Canada, Ottawa.

1988   Maritime Adaptations in the Gulf of Maine. *Archaeology of Eastern North America* 16:81–99.

1996   Testing the Models: Hunter-Gatherer Use of Space in the Gulf of Maine, USA. *World Archaeology* 27(3):512–526.

Sanger, David, Micah Pawling, and Donald Soctomah

2006   Passamaquoddy Homeland and Language: The Importance of Place. In *Cross-Cultural Collaboration: Native Peoples and Archaeology in the Northeastern United States*, edited by J. Kerber, pp. 314–328. University of Nebraska Press, Lincoln.

Schiffer, Michael B.

1972   Archaeological Context and Systemic Context. *American Antiquity* 37(2): 156–165.

Shaw, J., R. B. Taylor, D. L. Forbes, M.-H. Ruz, and S. Solomon

1994   Sensitivity of the Canadian Coast to Sea-Level Rise. Open File Report 2825, Geological Survey of Canada, Ottawa.

Shumway, Sandra E., Sally Sherman-Caswell, and John W. Hurst

1988   Paralytic Shellfish Poisoning in Maine: Monitoring a Monster. *Journal of Shellfish Research* 7(4):643–652.

Sobel, Elizabeth, D. Ann Trieu Gahr, and Kenneth Ames (editors)

2006   *Household Archaeology on the Northwest Coast.* Archaeological Series 16. International Monographs in Archaeology, Ann Arbor.

Soctomah, Donald

2005   *Let Me Live as My Ancestors had 1850–1890: Tribal Life and Times in Maine and New Brunswick.* Tribal Historic Preservation Office, Sipayik.

2009   *Save the Land for the Children 1800–1850: Passamaquoddy Tribal Life and Times in Maine and New Brunswick.* Tribal Historic Preservation Office, Sipayik.

Snow, Dean R.
1980   *The Archaeology of New England.* Academic Press, New York.

Speller, Jeffrey, A. Katherine Patton, and Susan E. Blair
2016   Proto-historic and Early Historic Period Shellfishing in the Quoddy Region. Paper presented at the Eastern States Archaeology Federation meeting in Langhorne, Pennsylvania.

Thomas, Martin Lewis Hall, David C. Arnold, and A. Ronald, A. Taylor
1983   The Rocky Intertidal Communities. In *Marine and Coastal Systems of the Quoddy Region, New Brunswick,* edited by Martin Lewis Hall Thomas, pp. 35–73. Canadian Special Publication of Fisheries and Aquatic Sciences 64. Department of Fisheries and Ocean, Ottawa.

Thwaites, Ruben G.
1896a   *The Jesuit Relations and Allied Documents: Travels and Explorations of the Jesuit Missionaries in New France, 1610–1791, Vol I. Acadia 1610–1613.* The Burrows Brothers, Cleveland.

1896b   *The Jesuit Relations and Allied Documents: Travels and Explorations of the Jesuit Missionaries in New France, 1610–1791, Vol III. Acadia 1611–1616.* The Burrows Brothers, Cleveland.

Wanamaker, Alan D., Karl J. Kreutz, Bernd R. Schone, and Douglas S. Introne
2011   Gulf of Maine Shells Reveal Changes in Seawater Temperature Seasonality During the Medieval Climate Anomaly and the Little Ice Age. *Palaeogeography, Palaeoclimatology, and Palaeoecology* 302(1–2):43–51.

Webb, W. Jesse
2018   A Late Maritime Woodland Peskotomuhkati Fishery from the Mainland Quoddy Region, Southwestern New Brunswick, Canada. Master's thesis, Department of Anthropology, University of New Brunswick, Fredericton.

Wilk, Richard, and William Rathje
1980   Household Archaeology. *American Behavioral Scientist* 25(6):617–639.

Williams, M. J., and V. Q. Perez-Corral
2001   Management Strategies for Harmful Algae Blooms. In *Harmful Algae Blooms 2000,* edited by G. M. Hallengraeff, S. I. Blackburn, C. J. Bolch, and R. J. Lewis. Intergovernmental Oceanographic Commission of UNESCO, Paris.

Wolff, Christopher B., and Donald H. Holly, Jr.
2019   Sea Ice, Seals, and Settlement: On Climate and Culture in Newfoundland and Labrador. In *The Archaeology of Human-Environmental Dynamics on the North American Atlantic Coast,* edited by Leslie Reeder-Myers, John A. Turck, and Torben C. Rick, pp. 16–43. University of Florida Press, Gainesville.

Zagata, Craig, Christy Young; Joanne Sountis, and Melanie Kuehl
2008   Mytilus edulis. Animal Diversity Web. Electronic document, https://animaldiversity.org/accounts/Mytilus_edulis/, accessed January 28, 2020.

12

THE CHANGING ROLE OF CERAMICS DURING THE WOODLAND PERIOD IN THE FAR NORTHEAST

Evidence from Some Large Ceramic Assemblages in New Brunswick and Nova Scotia

CORA A. WOOLSEY

Abstract

Ceramics changed throughout the Woodland period as the priorities and allegiances of potters changed. Region-wide pottery styles—stretching from as far north and east as Labrador and Nova Scotia to as far west and south as the American Bottom flood plain—affirm that ideas, and potentially people, travelled vast distances and maintained connections cross-culturally. These styles have been the subject of much research and sequence building, but the reasons for changes through time have remained relatively unexplored. Because ceramics are closely tied with the domestic sphere, and with subsistence activities, they are sensitive to changes in the broader social realm, making them an excellent source of information about group dynamics and women in particular. The aim of this chapter is to synthesize ceramic data from several large sites in New Brunswick and Nova Scotia to characterize the changes that occurred over time and to explain these changes as part of larger social dynamics. One important source of information about social dynamics comes from the distribution of ceramics through time, with very few ceramics surviving from the Early Woodland, then large numbers from the Middle Woodland, and an apparent decline in numbers during the Late Woodland. Another important source of information comes from changing manufacturing processes, indicating changing priorities through time. Looked at from this perspective, ceramics only became important to subsistence during the Middle Woodland period, and probably shifted to a sacred role during the Late Woodland.

Résumé

Les variations observées dans la poterie de la période Sylvicole reflètent les changements de priorités et d'allégeances des artisans qui les fabriquaient. La cohérence des styles céramiques à l'intérieur d'une région allant du Labrador à la vallée du Mississippi, en passant par la Nouvelle-Écosse, suggère que les idées – et possiblement les personnes – traversaient de grandes distances dans un contexte de connexions interculturelles. Si de nombreuses études se sont penchées sur ces styles dans le but d'en extraire des séquences typologiques, les raisons expliquant leurs transformations demeurent relativement inexplorées. De par leur appartenance à la sphère domestique et leur rôle dans les activités de subsistance, les récipients de céramique sont directement affectés par les transformations sociales. Cela en fait d'excellents témoins des dynamiques culturelles à l'échelle des groupes, notamment en ce qui a trait au monde des femmes. Cet article présente une synthèse des données céramiques provenant de plusieurs sites d'importance au Nouveau-Brunswick et en Nouvelle-Écosse, et vise à 1) décrire les changements observés sur le plan temporel, et 2) expliquer ces changements à l'intérieur de dynamiques sociales plus larges. La répartition temporelle de la poterie peut nous en dire beaucoup sur ces dynamiques sociales. Très peu de récipients du Sylvicole inférieur sont parvenus jusqu'à nous, alors qu'on les retrouve en abondance au Sylvicole moyen, avant qu'ils deviennent en apparence plus rares au Sylvicole supérieur. Les transformations des techniques de fabrication nous fournissent également des renseignements sur les priorités changeantes des artisans durant ces périodes. Vue sous cet angle, la poterie semble n'avoir occupé un rôle de subsistance important qu'à partir du Sylvicole moyen, avant de probablement passer dans la sphère du sacré au Sylvicole supérieur.

Affiliation

– Department of Computer Science, University of New Brunswick/The Learning Lab, The Ville Cooperative, New Brunswick, Canada

Across the Northeast of North America, ceramics changed in similar ways at particular points in time. The pseudo-scallop shell decoration, accompanied by new ways of building and firing pots, appeared between 2,200 and 2,000 years ago (Petersen and Sanger 1991), later disappearing around 1,600 years ago. Cord marks as a dominant decoration or texturing tool appeared more gradually in different places between ca. 1,500 and 1,100 years ago, supplemented or replaced in many places between 1,100 and 1,000 years ago. Although many researchers have concluded that these widespread changes indicate connections across the Northeast, regional and local variation suggests significant in situ development of ceramic manufacturing traditions. These changes, visible in the Maine–Maritimes region as well, have frequently been noted and pointed to as evidence for interaction occurring throughout the Woodland period. Yet little has been said concerning why the peoples of the Maine–Maritimes region participated in such far-flung horizons, or what social factors influenced pottery manufacture (Petersen 1997:87).

This is not for a lack of study or interest in the subject. Petersen and Sanger (1991) published one of the most concise ceramic chronologies in North America, built by looking at ceramics and ceramic dates from 78 sites in the Maine–Maritimes region and surrounding areas. Their model, dividing ceramic change into seven ceramic-era periods (or CPs), has become the main tool by which ceramics in this region are researched. Petersen (1988) made an important observation that one decoration tool, the pseudo-scallop shell (PSS) tool, was remarkably widespread and constrained between ca. 2200 BP and 1600 BP, leading him to propose a "pseudo scallop shell horizon" that offered compelling evidence for contact between vastly disparate peoples. Similarly, Mason (1970) noted that PSS decorations seem to have originated and spread outward from a proto-Iroquoian source, while dentates are more closely associated with the American Bottom flood plain and the Hopewell culture.

Another important ceramic analyst for the Maine–Maritimes region, Wright (1972) considered the ways that the Laurel and Saugeen traditions from the Great Lakes region articulated with traditions distant in all directions, and offered one of the most compelling explanations for the differences in patterning during the Middle and Late Woodland: patrilocal versus matrilocal residence. He observed that, though decoration types such as dentates and cord-wrapped-stick impressions occurred ubiquitously across eastern and central North America, a more heterogeneous mixture of ceramic styles and manufacturing practices existed in regions inhabited by groups of the Algonquian-language group, such as northern Ontario and Quebec, the Maritime provinces, and the eastern coast of the United States. He posited that this was because, in these regions, women—who made pottery—tended to marry into new groups, bringing their pottery knowledge with them, in turn being influenced and influencing other women's practices, creating a mixture of traditions and knowledge. In contrast, regions inhabited by Iroquoian groups tended to be matrilocal, where women learned and practised pottery manufacture within the same community throughout their lives without significant outside influences on their pottery-making practices. This mechanism—women moving to other places and influencing the local traditions—was taken up sporadically by other researchers (e.g., Engelbrecht 1972; Martelle 2002) and was also proposed as the responsible mechanism for the movement of maize across the Northeast by Martin (2008).

More recently, researchers have investigated how to better understand ceramic change by refining existing evidence. Studies relevant to the Maine–Maritimes region include studies on collections from here and from the related regions of New England, the St. Lawrence drainage, and the Great Lakes region. Stapelfeldt (2009) developed a chronology of ceramic morphology in the Maine–Maritimes region showing that, later in time, ceramic shapes changed from conoidal (pointed bottom) to globular (rounded bottom). This was the first research in the region that focused primarily on morphology rather than on decorations to build a chronology. Taché and Hart (2013) significantly tightened the radiocarbon sequence from the Early Woodland for the Maine–Maritimes region by omitting dates with a 1-sigma range greater than 30 years. From this more robust evidence, they found that ceramics had probably been around from as early as 3500 BP, at least in the St. Lawrence drainage. Curtis (2004) showed that ceramics in the Great Lakes region changed significantly between 1400 and 1200 BP and proposed a Middle–Late Woodland transition. She further found that ceramics provided evidence supporting the in situ model of Iroquoian development rather than the migration model of Iroquoian origins. Woolsey (2018) showed a similar phenomenon in Nova Scotia, demonstrating that ceramics at the Gaspereau Lake Reservoir Site Complex changed gradually over time. This showed that, even though new techniques and decorative tools were adopted, the ceramic manufacturing tradition had evolved in situ, likely as a result of pressures arising from the larger group and beyond. Despite these advances, work on the complex history that ceramics reveal throughout the Woodland period has only just begun, and we do not yet have even the beginnings of an explanatory model for ceramic change.

In this chapter, I review evidence about ceramic change through time in the Maine–Maritimes region from the invention or adoption of ceramics around 3000 BP until their near-disappearance, around 500 BP, at the end of the Woodland period in New Brunswick, Nova Scotia, and Prince Edward Island, and their dramatic decrease in parts of Maine (figure 12.1). Since the push to establish regional chronologies and better understandings of interactions in the Northeast some three decades ago (e.g., Lenius and Olinyk 1990; Petersen and Sanger 1991), a synthesis of ceramic evidence in the Far Northeast has not been undertaken. The purpose of this review is to propose a model of ceramic change through time and to propose explanations for change based on evidence from the Maine–Maritimes region. The following discussion focusses on changes in ceramic distribution (numbers of ceramics appearing at different locations through time) and manufacturing attributes (specifically, lamellar character, temper percentages and mineral type, wall thickness, and coil breaks) to unravel which changes were technological in nature and why these changes occurred. Although significantly more can be learned about ceramics, research to date reveals broad ceramic trends that suggest several cultural changes at the regional scale. Broadly, these changes are (1) the introduction of ceramics from other regions sometime around 2800 BP with concomitant ceramic knowledge but insignificant impact on the technological system; (2) an influx of "fineware" around 2200 BP that accompanied the movement of women with connections to other regions; (3) a gradual shift toward more expedient ceramic vessel manufacture sometime after 1500 BP that likely resulted from increasingly large and frequent gatherings; (4) a shift away from domestic ceramics toward more ceremonial ceramics sometime after 1000 BP, although ceramics were still used in varying amounts and, in some places, for domestic purposes; and (5) the near-disappearance of ceramics sometime after European contact, possibly resulting from culture contact and access to new goods.

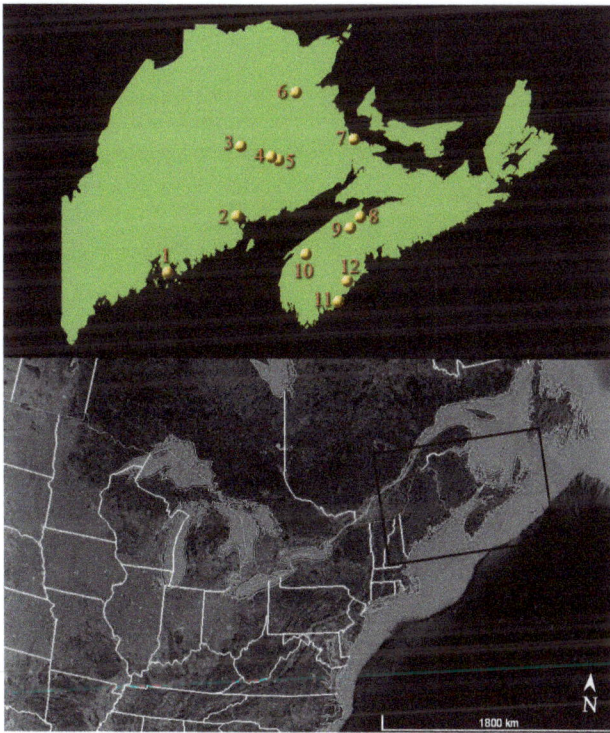

Figure 12.1. Ceramic-bearing sites in the Maine–Maritimes region: (1) Goddard; (2) Mud Lake Stream; (3) George Frederick Clark (actually a number of sites within a ca. 100 km radius of Woodstock, New Brunswick); (4) Fulton Island; (5) Jemseg; (6) Oxbow; (7) Skull Island; (8) Melanson; (9) Gaspereau Lake Reservoir; (10) L'sitkuk Bear River; (11) Port Joi; and (12) Eel Weir.

Methods for Evaluating Ceramic Change

The following is a discussion about the choice of attributes that formed the basis of this research. Some attributes have received significantly more attention in the Maine–Maritimes region than others, especially decorations, yet it has not always been clear why these attributes receive so much attention or what these attributes indicate about culture. Here, I discuss my analytical strategy for a more in-depth understanding of ceramic change, suggesting attributes that have the most value for understanding pottery change and the cultural factors these changes indicate.

Ceramic analysis in the Maine–Maritimes region is challenging because of the high heterogeneity of ceramic styles and decorative strategies compared with relatively small assemblage sizes. This heterogeneity characterizes all extant ceramic collections, with no instances of strong standardization or what could be considered types.[1] Because types do not emerge intuitively, as they do in other regions (such as the southwestern United States), researchers have usually based their analysis on attribute variability rather than on typologies (e.g., Allen 1981; Bourgeois 2004:118; Kenyon 1986:19; Kristmanson 1992; Laybolt 1999:12-14; Nash and Stewart 1990:107; Petersen and Sanger 1991; Sanger 1974; for attribute analysis in other parts of the Northeast, see Chilton 1998:146; Engelbrecht 1978; Wright 1967:3, 1980).

The difficulty of building a chronology or explaining change through time using attribute-based analysis lies in sorting out which attributes are significant in terms of culture change or stability and which are relatively inconsequential (Read 2007; van der Leeuw 1991). Inconsequential attributes are those that do not indicate anything particularly important about the circumstances in which the pottery was made, at least with the information archaeologists have at their disposal. For instance, lip shape has relatively few constraints (i.e., there is not much technological or aesthetic reason to prefer one shape over another) and lip shapes on ceramics from the Maine–Maritimes region have not so far been shown to have chronological, ethnic, or technological significance, either as a stand-alone attribute or as part of a cluster of attributes. Therefore, this attribute appears to be inconsequential to Far Northeast ceramic analysis at the time of

---

1. Researchers have sometimes proposed that some ceramic horizon styles (e.g., Laurel, Point Peninsula, or Vinette 1) might be considered types. However, due to the proliferation of varieties and caveats that necessarily accompany these types due to high variation in the Far Northeast, Sanger (1974) proposed that researchers use an attribute-based approach rather than a typological analysis, a convention that has since been followed widely, if not ubiquitously, in the Maine–Maritimes region. The possible exception to this rule is the use of the ware concept (e.g., Bourque 1995), proposed as a middle ground between the type system and the attribute-based system by Rice (1976).

this writing.[2] On the other hand, tempering materials are highly constrained technologically and geographically (Bebber 2017; Feathers 2006; O'Brien et al. 1994; Tite et al. 2001), so changes in tempering materials through time have been shown to be chronologically significant (Feathers 2008) as well as indicative of location and raw-material sources (Druc 2013). The same has been shown to be true here in the Maine–Maritimes region (Petersen and Sanger 1991; Woolsey 2018). Temper is therefore a significant attribute that has become important in ceramic analysis across North America (e.g., Bronitsky and Hamer 1986; Hoard et al. 1995; Michelaki and Hancock 2011), although, other than cursory examinations, it has not been studied to the same degree in the Maine–Maritimes region (but see MacIntyre 1988; Newsom 2017, this volume; Taché 2005; Woolsey 2018).

The choice of which attributes are significant rests on understanding what information each attribute can yield. Increasingly, ceramic researchers advocate for using manufacturing attributes as the basis of analysis because they tend to remain stable through time, indicating which skills were passed on through a learning lineage (*sensu* Crown 2001).[3] Manufacturing practices, such as processing temper, forming the walls, and paddling, promote motor habits, which are hard to change, particularly if learned in childhood (Roddick 2009:85). When one or more manufacturing attribute changes in a pottery assemblage, a new learning lineage is in evidence (Crown 2007). New learning lineages come about because of a population change or replacement that introduced new skills (Gosselain 2016:44) or a new need[4] arising from the larger group that would make the original skills obsolete or would require development of new skills (Arnold 2008; White 2017; but see Smith 2005 for possible sources of accidental change). As many researchers have shown (e.g., Arnold 2008;

---

2. Here, inconsequential should not be confused with meaningless, random, or having no effect on performance.

3. See Crown (2007, 2014), Lave (1991), Lave and Wenger (1991), Minar and Crown (2001), Sassaman and Rudolphi (2001), Mills (2018) and Wenger (1999) for more on learning lineages and the larger theoretical framework of communities of practice.

4. I follow Wilk (2001:113) in defining needs as "the entire field socially defined as luxuries and necessities, the full range of conceivable standards of living in a particular time and social setting." In other words, needs are not utilitarian and different from desires, nor do they necessarily arise from changing circumstances, but they can be manufactured separate from circumstances and can even be the cause of change. Importantly, needs are not met in order of their proximity to survival or utilitarian goals but according to other forces that are specific to the context in which they arise. Wilk notes that "need is part of the technological design process, because anyone manufacturing anything is working with an idea of the needs of the user." It is for this reason that archaeologists can use formal and technological attributes of pottery to understand what needs potters were trying to meet.

Chilton 2000; Fowles et al. 2007; Gosselain 1992; Sassaman 2010; White 2017), new needs could arise from anything ranging from shifts in economic factors, resource base, kinship organization, settlement patterns, shifting contact with other groups, warfare, starvation, and beyond. Furthermore, the ways potters responded to these needs could manifest in any or all of the realms of decorative function, technological function, materials sourcing and processing behaviours, landscape use, and more.[5] Therefore, manufacturing attributes—those attributes that indicate manufacturing processes such as forming, firing, procuring, and processing—seem to be most salient to social production and organization (Mills 2018; Roux 2003).[6] The choice of attributes to analyze therefore entails careful consideration of what each attribute indicates alone as well as in relation to other attributes.

Decorative attributes have received the bulk of attention in the Maine–Maritimes region (e.g., Curtis et al. 2019; Kristmanson and Deal 1993), but their relationship to cultural factors remains elusive. The main value archaeologists traditionally have placed on decorations has been as a chronologically sensitive attribute cluster, but their significance to the lives of the people who made pottery is harder to uncover. Surface decorations have been shown in other regions to be important ideological markers that can be compared with manufacturing attributes to reveal cultural trends such as "circulation of people, things, and ideas" (Gosselain 2016:37). Because of their visibility to both pottery users and non-users alike, they are efficient conveyers of messages. Yet they are also more fluid than manufacturing attributes, easily adopted by others, making them poor indicators of ethnicity (Dorland 2018) or boundaries (Gosselain 2017; Mills 2018). However, they can contribute significantly to understanding (sometimes changing) identities (Gosselain 2008). Decorations

---

5. Research on motor habits has shown that potters prefer to maintain their practice unchanged unless pushed by outside factors (e.g., market demand or changing nutritional requirements) to adopt new skills, materials, or methods (e.g., Costin 1991; Gosselain 2008:75; Roddick 2009:85; Sillar and Tite 2000). Because of this inherent stability of pottery manufacturing practice through time, ceramics can be reverse-engineered to understand what needs potters were trying to meet, which aspects of ceramics were passed down through generations, what was left up to individual preferences or circumstances, and why otherwise stable attributes may have changed when they did (Peirce 2005).

6. This is particularly true of those attributes that would indicate learning lineages by how stable they remain through time. Learning lineages, the lines through which knowledge is transferred and which often follow other lines such as kinship, has been shown to be an important part of analyzing archaeological ceramics because the forms ceramics take are directly relatable to the ways knowledge about ceramics are passed on (e.g., Chatfield 2010; Crown 2001; Gosselain 2016; Mills 2018; Sassaman and Rudolphi 2001; Wallaert 2001).

in the Maine–Maritimes region can therefore be profitably reframed to better understand what potters were "saying" with their pots and how this changed over time.

In this research, decoration horizons are considered in terms of what people may have been signifying in their use of decorative tools, and are compared with measures and attributes more suggestive of the learning lineages out of which pots in the Far Northeast emerged. These include the measurement of *distributions of ceramics through time* (actual numbers within temporal and spatial bounds), the forming attributes of *coil breaks and lamellar character*, and the ingredient attributes of *tempering materials and processing practices* (e.g., temper minerals, temper particle size, and sieving and cleaning practices).

Distributions

Distributions are important because they result from scale of production, indicating needs and pressures arising from the larger group (Costin 1991). While poor artifact preservation makes the numbers of surviving ceramics semiquantitative at best, comparison of ceramic numbers at different points in time and proximal in space yields relative information, particularly in regard to increase and decline of production scale. Production scale can change because of many factors, including subsistence strategy or settlement patterns, shifts in economic activities, new ceremonial or ideological practices, or changes in population, among others.

Forming Attributes

Coil breaks and lamellar character result from coil building and paddling after the initial shape is formed (figures 12.2 and 12.3). Changes in these attributes result from changes in how vessel walls are built. The greater the paddling, the more smoothed together become the coil breaks, and the more compacted and vertically oriented become the lamellae in the cross-section of the wall, allowing for an estimate of the amount of paddling a pot underwent. Because paddling is both a risky (*sensu* Hoard et al. 1995:831; Lancy 2012:118) practice and a time-consuming step in the manufacturing sequence,[7] the degree of paddling (indicated by lamellar direction and number of coil breaks, or lack of them) suggests the degree of expediency desired by the potter (Arnold 1985). This, in turn, suggests what value and significance the pot has (e.g., whether an expedient vessel for single-use or a unique and elaborately decorated gift) (Costin 1991; Woolsey 2018).

---

7. Neupert (2007) reported one case of pottery manufacture that included four separate paddling stages. Not all sequences have so many paddling stages, but Neupert's example shows that paddling can significantly increase the time ceramic manufacture takes.

Figure 12.2. Sherds exhibiting (A) coil breaks, both concave and convex faces; and (B) a lack of coil break. The former tend to be smoother, with well-developed coils very smooth and less-well-developed coils appearing rough and/or jagged. Sherds lacking coil breaks exhibit breakage patterns that do not follow horizontal orientations, as coil breaks tend to do.
Source: Photos by Cora Woolsey.

Ingredients

Finally, tempering material changes result from changing subsistence practices, changing geographical sources, changing expediency requirements, or changing learning lineages (Costin 1991; Druc 2013; Vitelli 1995). There can be many reasons why tempering materials become important (or become less important), including aesthetics, efficiency, ideology, factionality, sacredness/ceremonialism, and techno-function (Braun 2015; Feathers 2003, 2006; Kilikoglou et al. 2007; Myers 2006; Schiffer and Skibo 1997; Sillar and Tite 2000). Regardless of reasons for spatial or temporal differences in pottery-ingredient attributes, these

Figure 12.3. Lamellar direction from vertical lamellae (*left*) moving to oblique (*centre three*) and ending in U-shaped lamellae (*right*). Vertical lamellae are discernible in sherds that have been intensely paddled and are correlated with PSS and dentate decorations, thin walls (often as low as 0.5 cm), compact pastes, a lack of coil breaks, exfoliation of the surfaces, and vertical cracking around the rim. Oblique lamellae indicate less intensive paddling and are correlated with cord marks, thicker walls (averaging 0.8 cm), less compact pastes, and smooth or jagged horizontal coil breaks. U-shaped lamellae indicate very little or no paddling, and are correlated with cord marks, coarser pastes, thick walls (1 cm or larger), and smooth horizontal coil breaks. *Source:* Photos by Cora Woolsey.

differences can be powerful indicators of boundaries (Bowser 2000; Druc 2013) or, conversely, of a lack of boundaries where boundaries are expected to exist (Feathers 2008; Herbert 2008; Mortimer 2011).

Noting changes is not enough; a mechanism must be identified to explain change. In this discussion, I make several assumptions about mechanisms of ceramic stability and change based on ethnoarchaeological studies of pottery and knowledge transmission, and on research previously conducted on this region. First is that women and girls made pottery (as they did elsewhere in North America and as they do in most small-scale societies) and that women moved from other locations to marry men in exogamous bands (Fiedel 1994). This research is also built on the assumption that potters passed their knowledge on to their students who went on to pass these skills on to other students, creating learning lineages (cf. Minar and Crown 2001) that can be traced through motor habits that remain stable (Mills 2018:1055) and knowledge that would have been difficult to acquire without a teacher (Herbert 2008; Kamp 2001:430). It is also an assumption underlying this research that potters changed their practices if attractive options or pressure were presented from outside of pottery manufacture (Arnold 2008; Gosselain 2016) that pushed potters toward new and more expedient methods, greater elaboration or labour loading[8] to make

---

8. "Labour loading" is a phenomenon noted in cases where artifacts are more elaborate, made of more expensive material, or treated with more elaborate care than necessary to achieve the utilitarian purpose of the artifact. See Hayden's (1995) prestige technology, Pfaffenberger's (2001) pre-energized template, and Neff's (2014) costly signalling for concepts involving labour loading.

higher-value products, the need for faster production, or the need for better-quality products (a culturally determined concept that is context-specific). Distributions of ceramics, forming techniques, and raw materials are examined from this framework to identify possible mechanisms for change in the Far Northeast.

Maine and the Maritimes

Ceramic studies to date reveal a difference in ceramic trajectories between the Maritime provinces as a whole and Maine; in this, several differences can be singled out. First is the lower numbers of Early Woodland pottery in the Maritimes compared to Maine, while Maine has somewhat fewer Early Woodland ceramics than elsewhere. Another difference is that, after European contact, ceramic traditions continued in Maine for at least another two centuries, while in the Maritimes ceramics largely disappeared from view (discussed more fully below). A third difference is that in Maine, shell-tempered ceramics appear to have been more prominent than in the Maritimes, although again, shell tempering did not predominate as it did in neighbouring regions. Given these differences, I refer to the Maritime provinces throughout this chapter unless the evidence can be generalized to the Far Northeast or to the Northeast of North America.

Sites Studied in This Research

The research presented here is the result of studying several large ceramic collections and some smaller ones from New Brunswick and Nova Scotia (figure 12.1, tables 12.1 and 12.2). The aim in studying large collections is to gain a finer-grained understanding of how ceramics changed through time. In smaller collections, the assumption must be made that many specimens are chronologically separate unless sites were single component and constrained in time. Indeed, within smaller collections, ceramics tend to exhibit little relationship to each other, either in time period or manufacturing materials and processes, which I have come to interpret as showing that different people from different places deposited their pots in the archaeological record. In contrast, larger sites tend to have many more links visible among the ceramics, and technological progressions can sometimes be seen, such as at Gaspereau Lake.

I am aware that basing a model mostly on larger sites—which may be exceptional rather than representative—can introduce bias. While this needs to be kept in mind, there are also reasons to avoid considering all the ceramic collections from a region together, such as has been frequently done in this region as researchers attempted to refine the Far Northeast ceramic sequence. The first is that including all ceramic collections together masks the variability from site to site. In other words, looking at a ceramic collection from a camp site on a major portage route between Quebec, New Brunswick, and Maine may cause us to consider Iroquoian influences more heavily, which may not be borne out from the evidence from the New Brunswick coast. The second reason is that considering more ceramic assemblages together requires exponentially more time and effort, and could easily constitute a life's work. Considering the difficulty of tracking down collections, travelling to where they are housed, and fully understanding the context in which they occur, it seems better to deeply understand some important collections rather than to poorly understand many collections. The third is that there is good reason to believe that the larger the ceramic collection, the more representative it is. If ceramics represent potters, and potters represent groups who need pottery, then the larger the collection, the more likely it consists of more people with the same pottery needs. Large collections make those needs easier to study. While it may be true that the people represented in smaller ceramic collections may be categorically different than those in larger settlements or base camps, both the ceramic evidence and other kinds of evidence suggest that people across the Far Northeast were crossing paths, and may even have been the same people in both small and large sites.

In this research, I looked at sites that could reveal changes at a fine resolution. The largest sites were considered first, but some collections are not available for study, such as the Oxbow ceramic collection, so the existing literature is the only source of evidence. Additionally, I chose sites that could reveal something important about a particular period, such as the Skull Island site and the Jemseg site. Finally, I incorporated evidence from publications and my own observations of smaller sites for illustrative purposes. I emphasize that the collections selected are not meant to be a representative sample in a quantitative sense but rather were selected to answer questions I and others have had about why ceramics changed. This study is informed by over 10 years analyzing ceramics in New Brunswick and the observations I have made during that time. For my work using more quantitative and systematic samples of ceramics and fuller discussions of ceramic sampling, I direct the reader to my work on the Gaspereau Lake Reservoir ceramic assemblage (Woolsey 2017, 2018, 2020) and George Frederick Clarke collection (Woolsey 2010).

Table 12.1. Sites studied in depth for this research.

Site Name	Province	Number of Sherds
Gaspereau Lake Reservoir	Nova Scotia	18,609
Jemseg	New Brunswick	331
Skull Island	New Brunswick	1260

Table 12.2. Sites mentioned in this research that were not studied in depth or are not large enough to be included as a standalone discussion.

Site Name	Province	Number of Sherds
George Frederick Clarke Collection	New Brunswick	183
Eel Weir	Nova Scotia	~2500
Mud Lake Stream	New Brunswick	68
Port Joli	Nova Scotia	3,934
Oxbow	New Brunswick	3,980
Fulton Island	New Brunswick	1,508
Melanson	Nova Scotia	1,018
L'sitkuk Bear River	Nova Scotia	~2,800
Goddard	Maine	13,000–18,000*

* This number comes from Steven Cox (pers. comm. August 3rd, 2017), who conservatively estimates the number of all sherds collected by private collectors, excavated by field schools, and analyzed by James B. Petersen from the original excavation to be somewhere between 8,000 and 10,000 sherds in total, but acknowledges that the number could be as high as 18,000. Uncertainty exists because the assemblage is unevenly catalogued.

The following sections present evidence and interpretations for how and why ceramics changed during the Early (3000–2150 BP), Middle (2150–1050 BP), and Late (1050–500 BP) Woodland periods in the Maritime provinces of the Far Northeast, and a transition between 1450 and 1050 BP.

Early Woodland (3000–2150 BP)

Early Woodland pottery in the Northeast, commonly referred to as Vinette 1 pottery, tends to be undecorated and fabric-impressed, both inside and outside (figure 12.4). Attributes usually considered together to indicate Vinette 1 pottery include coarse grit temper, relatively thick walls, coil breaks, and conical or beaker-shaped morphology with a lack of a neck region (Ritchie and MacNeish 1949; Taché 2005). They contrast with later ceramics in their tendency to lack decoration (although this is not a hard-and-fast rule; see Allen 1981; Taché 2005) and their asymmetrical circumference (Newsom, this volume; Taché et al. 2008).

Many researchers consider one of the hallmarks of the Early Woodland period to be the invention or adoption of ceramics (e.g., Bourgeois 2004:117; Keenlyside 1999:70-71; Leonard 1995; Sanger 1986, 1988); however, this argument has proven problematic, particularly for the Maine–Maritimes region. First, ceramics did not appear in large numbers in this region until the Middle Woodland, and are distributed sporadically (Taché et al. 2008) before this time, suggesting that ceramics were not a significant or consistent part of the

Figure 12.4. Sherds with fabric or cord impression. These may have been made during the Early Woodland; however, they have not been directly dated and their date remains uncertain.
Source: Photo by Cora Woolsey.

subsistence strategy of the peoples living in the Maine–Maritimes region. Colder climate and acidic soil have been suggested to explain overall lower numbers of sherds and vessel lots when compared to adjacent areas such as New York (Brumbach 1979:25), but these explanations cannot account for the fact that total number of Early Woodland sherds is an order of magnitude lower than elsewhere. The difference cannot be attributable to freeze/thaw action or other destructive factors alone. Second, the significantly larger number of Middle Woodland compared to Early Woodland ceramics theoretically should resemble a gradual incline in numbers through time if distributions are a function of temporal degradation; instead, the numbers climb steeply around the Early–Middle Woodland transition, at ca. 2100 BP, in both Maine and the Maritimes. Ceramics therefore appear to have been made in smaller numbers than elsewhere during the Early Woodland, a relatively minor addition to the toolkit rather than a paradigm-shifting hallmark of the period.

A third problem with ceramics marking the beginning of the Woodland period is that ceramics were already being made prior to 3000 BP in other parts of eastern North America, possibly as early as 4,500 years ago (Beck et al. 2002; Sassaman 2010). Taché and Hart (2013:366) proposed that, in the Northeast, Early Woodland pottery may have been made as early as 3450 BP, as evidenced from early dates at the Batiscan site in Quebec, among others. Finally, ceramics in the Maritime provinces appear to have largely left the domestic toolkit, declining in numbers from 1000 BP in domestic contexts to almost nothing after 500 years ago. In Maine, ceramic manufacture continued into the Historic period, but that area also shows a decline in numbers after 1000 BP. These factors make ceramics potentially a poor representation of a Woodland cultural complex.

Theoretically, sporadic deposits of ceramics could result from a particular economic situation in which women travelling to a region with their pots or their pottery-making knowledge may leave pots in the archaeological record but not in significant amounts. Their knowledge is not passed on to others because pottery is not part of the economic or subsistence strategy of the group. Sassaman (1992, 2010) argued that, in eastern North America, the adoption of pottery by different Archaic cultures depended on whether they were matrilocal or patrilocal, the latter giving men—who controlled the soapstone trade—more decision-making power about container and cooking technologies. Soapstone is rare in the Maine–Maritimes region, so clearly the same situation does not apply here, but Sassaman's work illustrates that ceramics were not necessarily adopted on utilitarian or technological grounds alone. In the Northeast broadly, other container technologies, such as birchbark jars and baskets (Speck 1931), may have been more prestigious than ceramics, leaving little room or appetite for ceramics.

Another possible factor in the apparent low ceramic numbers is the small number of Early Woodland sites and artifacts overall. Early Woodland sites are often difficult to identify based on artifact assemblages because forms have not been as well delineated as for other periods, such as for the Late Archaic (Fiedel 2001:107-110). Additionally, Early Woodland components are often more ephemeral or impacted than subsequent layers (e.g., Allen 2005:52-54; Black 2002:310-311; Laybolt 1999:144). This might be explained by a lower population during the Early Woodland in the Far Northeast, as proposed by Fiedel (2001), or by the possible destruction of large Early Woodland sites along waterways and coastal areas. If the former case is true, lower numbers of ceramics need to be taken in this context and compared with other artifact classes to determine whether they do indeed reflect significantly lower numbers. Investigating this problem is beyond the scope of this chapter except to mention that, even in the context of Early Woodland sites, which frequently exhibit an increase in the number of scrapers compared with the earlier Terminal Archaic (Rutherford 1990:332-333), ceramic numbers may still appear in less frequency than would be expected if they are important to the subsistence strategy. Additionally, the Jemseg site, with a substantial Early Woodland component, needs to be considered in how we evaluate site distributions from the Early Woodland, since in this case the Early Woodland component is extensive. If low numbers result from destroyed or poorly identified sites, the view of Early Woodland ceramics as unimportant to the subsistence strategy may need to be re-evaluated.

Despite the small collection sizes and possibly low impact of ceramic technology on the subsistence strategy of the Maritime provinces, the fact that ceramics were extant in the Maine–Maritimes region from at least 2,800 years ago (Taché and Hart 2013) signifies a change from earlier periods. Many sites that have a substantial ceramic assemblage contained a very small number of possible Early Woodland ceramic sherds (usually one to ten), with two exceptional sites in New Brunswick that contain larger numbers of Early Woodland ceramics: the Oxbow site on the Miramichi River (Allen 1981, 2005) and the Jemseg site on the Saint John River (Bourgeois 2004). The Oxbow site yielded an enigmatic assemblage, about which many questions remain concerning the date of some potentially early decorations, and may not ultimately aid in understanding the history of ceramic manufacture in this region.[9] However, the Jemseg site is of great importance in understanding the Early Woodland period.

The Jemseg Site

The Jemseg site yielded the only typical Early Woodland ceramic collection in the Maine–Maritimes region of a substantial number of sherds (Bourgeois 2004). Although no complete vessels come from the site, the ceramics are similar to Early Woodland pottery elsewhere in their fabric-impressed exteriors, relatively coarse grit temper, and somewhat uneven wall thickness. Three dates were acquired on ceramics exhibiting attributes characteristic of Vinette 1 spanning the entire Early Woodland period (table 12.3, figure 12.5) and show that ceramics were manufactured over approximately 800 years ago, and, furthermore, that the tradition remained relatively stable. These ceramics show pronounced coil breaks, indicating coil-building and thin walls. However, unlike later thin-walled ceramics, no paddling is evident: lamellar character is completely lacking, indicating that the walls were thinned through a different method.

Table 12.3. Radiocarbon dates acquired from Jemseg site vessel lots. All dates are listed as direct-dated, although Bourgeois (2004:121) mentions charcoal as the dated material.

Vessel Lot	Date	I-Sigma Range	ID
Vessel 2	2870	80	Beta-156019
Vessel 9	2460	60	O-9618
Vessel 1	2140	60	(Beta-105892)
Vessel 7*	2230	50	Not listed

*Not considered Vinette 1 by Bourgeois (2004:121) because it is undecorated.

9. I refer readers to Allen (1981, 2005) for more information about the Early Woodland component of the Oxbow site and to Petersen and Sanger (1991:121-25) for a discussion of possible early PSS and dentate decorations at this site.

Calibrated Age Ranges

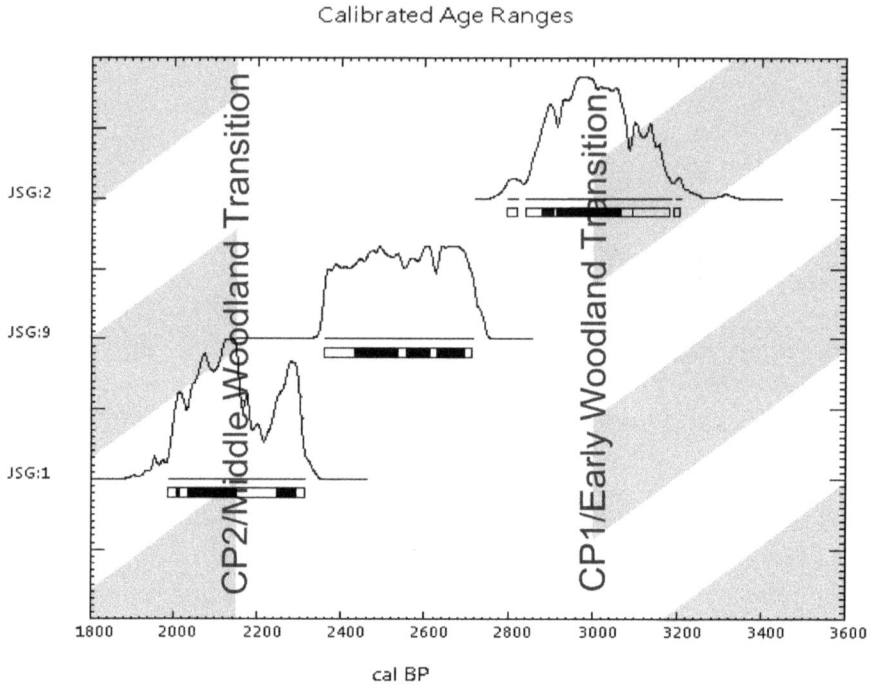

Figure 12.5. Calibrated radiocarbon dates acquired on ceramics from the Jemseg site. Black blocks show 1-sigma ranges, white blocks show 2-sigma ranges. Dates calibrated with Calib (Reimer et al. 2013) using the Intcal13 curve.

The ceramics from the Jemseg site suggest that manufacturing practices were quite different between the Early and Middle Woodland periods. The thin walls of the Jemseg Early Woodland ceramic vessels would have been difficult to achieve without paddling, if they were made the same way as later ceramics using the coiling technique. Yet the coil breaks clearly show that coils were used to build up the walls. Even more difficult to explain is the difference between the Jemseg ceramics and other assemblages, some of which exhibit no coil breaks at all, such as the Gaspereau Lake Reservoir assemblage.

One manufacturing practice that might explain the attributes of the Jemseg ceramics was proposed by Kutruff and Kutruff (1996:164), writing about ceramics from the Mound Bottom site in Tennessee ca. 1,000 years ago. This method consists of digging a hole in the ground that was roughly conical, lining it with fabric, and pressing coils of clay along the wall. The vessel would have been left to dry in place, which would result in crisp fabric impressions, as they usually are on Early Woodland ceramics, whereas they tend to be "partially smoothed" and partly obscured on later ceramics that have been fabric-paddled. This method would also explain how the Jemseg Vinette 1 ceramics were remarkably thin-walled (0.5 cm–0.7 cm rim thickness) without using paddling, since free-standing vessels would likely have collapsed at that thinness without paddling. It would also explain why the shapes tend to be more asymmetrical and lacking necks (Woolsey 2018; see also Taché 2005). Finally, this method would explain how some fabric-impressed ceramics from the Early Woodland lack coil breaks, as clay can just as easily be patted into the mould as it can be coiled. Patted-in clay would result in a complete lack of coil breaks but an identical morphology to using coils with a mould. It is even plausible that both techniques could exist at the same site.

The near-ubiquitous fabric impression in Early Woodland ceramics may be meant to evoke basketry, an idea that convinced some researchers that textiles may have been the preferred container technology of the Early Woodland period (Beck et al. 2002:3; Blitz 2015; Speck 1931). These early pots would not have required significant skill to build, even though the firing regime would most likely have involved knowledge passed on from a teacher (Crown 2001:455), so attributes showing motor habits would not be as evident as in later pots. This would lead to a situation of high heterogeneity of forming attributes and sizes among Vinette 1 ceramics as well as variable pastes and hardness, a situation observable among Early Woodland collections (Taché 2005). The low demand for pottery could have incentivized potters not to give much time to developing stable firing regimes and processes for procuring and processing ingredients, explaining this high heterogeneity in Early Woodland ceramics.

Middle Woodland (2150–1450 BP)

Around 2200 BP, a new kind of pottery flooded the Northeast, including the Maine–Maritimes region. Usually decorated with PSS or dentate stamps, this pottery is almost always more plentiful than earlier pottery. It departs from the earlier pottery in many respects. The conical or oval shape of the Early Woodland changed to a conoidal shape with neck constriction and rounded shoulders (figure 12.6). It is symmetrical, or near-symmetrical, and wall thickness is more even. It is thoroughly paddled, evidenced by the thin walls (sometimes as thin as 0.5 cm), highly lamellar character that runs vertical to the wall axis, compact paste, and a lack of coil breaks. This pottery is also harder-bodied and redder as a result of oxidizing firing

Figure 12.6. Reconstructed pottery vessel from Maquapit Lake in central New Brunswick. Note the decoration all the way down to the base.
Source: Courtesy of the New Brunswick Museum.

regimes, with finer pastes and smaller temper particles, and with smoothing on the interiors. During the earlier Middle Woodland (2150–1650 BP), pottery reached a peak in thinness and hardness, prompting many researchers to call this period the height of ceramic manufacturing skill (e.g., Bourque 2001; Petersen and Sanger 1991).

Another difference between the Early and Middle Woodland periods is the introduction of decoration to a majority of pots. Decoration strategies were elaborate and usually covered the whole exterior surface, often in carefully placed zones or bands of discrete decorations (figures 12.7–12.9). Zoning takes the form of rows of horizontal and oblique tool impressions, chevrons, and horizontal rows of punctates. The two main decorative tools, PSS and dentate, were never used together, except for on a very small number of exceptions,[10] which may mean that the tools were emblemic and signify different affiliations. What these affiliations may have been is unknown. However, considering the rise of the so-called Hopewell Interaction Sphere around the same time, and the prominence of the Laurel and Point Peninsula cultures in the related regions of the Great Lakes and St. Lawrence drainage, the entire Northeast may have circulated pottery knowledge even as far as the Maine–Maritimes region.

---

10. It is possible that both PSS and dentate tools appear on different zones of some ceramics that are fragmented and not recognized as belonging to the same vessel, masking the incidence of these tools combined on a single vessel. Because this would be a significant find, in my own work, I have looked for this in the George Frederick Clarke collection (roughly 200 sherds), the Bliss Island ceramics (roughly 180 sherds), the Gaspereau Lake Reservoir ceramics (roughly 3,000 were analyzed), the Bear River ceramics (roughly 3,000 sherds, but I was not able to examine them exhaustively), the Fulton Island and Jemseg sherds (not examined exhaustively), and various private collections. When time permitted (for instance, when examining the GFC collection for my master's and the Gaspereau ceramics for my PhD), I put significant effort into assigning each sherd to a vessel lot on the basis of fabric, surface treatment, and colouration, in addition to decorations. I therefore felt a high degree of confidence that I was not missing extant tool combinations, at least in these collections. Bourque (2001:80) also notes that "only a very few sherds bearing both kinds of decoration have been reported" from Maine, and it is probable that at least some of these rare instances result from a PSS tool appearing to be dentate because of variations in pressure while impressing with the tool. It is also noteworthy that no mentions of both PSS and dentate tools occurring on the same sherd or in the same vessel lot appear in the literature from the Maine–Maritimes region, to my knowledge, although this last might admittedly result at least some of the time from the practice of grouping sherds into vessel lots mostly on the basis of deco- ration. Nevertheless, given the absence of references to both PSS and dentate tools together, and given my own experience looking for just this sort of phenomenon and not finding it, I am of the opinion at the time of this writing that this separation was an important ideological division.

Emblemic and assertive style are concepts proposed by Wiessner (1983) to explain different kinds of information transmission through material culture. In contrast to assertive style, which she suggests mainly communicates something about the personal identity of the user or maker, emblemic style "has a distinct referent and transmits a clear message to a defined target population [...] about conscious group affiliation or identity, such as an emblem or a flag" (Wiessner 1983:257). Although Wiessner notes Wobst's (1977) prediction that emblemic style would likely be poorly developed in hunter-gatherer groups because of a lack of an overarching nationality and limited networks of information transmission, she observes that the simpler an emblem is, the easier it is to adopt as an identity marker and to be spread through prolific artifact types such as projectile points. Pottery would also seem to be a good candidate for this given its visibility to others during use (Neff 2014). It is this quality that has encouraged other researchers (e.g., Carr, 1995; Saunders 2001) to adopt emblemic style in analyzing pottery. In particular, Saunders (2001:79) noted that pottery can be used to signify allegiance in what she called a "negotiated tradition," such as the case of Altamaha pottery, which signified an alliance of the Indigenous population of what would become Georgia with the Spanish missionaries from roughly 1600 to 1700 CE.

Mason (1970) and others (Finlayson 1977; Gates St-Pierre and Chapdelaine 2013; Petersen 1997; Spittal 2017) pointed out that dentate is associated more closely with the Ohio and Illinois Hopewell cultures, whereas PSS is associated with the Laurel and Saugeen cultures of the Great Lakes region. Affinities to these distant regions might well have been signalled through pottery. However, though conformity with decorative conventions is evident in the near-ubiquitous use of one or the other of these two tools, variability in how pots were made and decorated is high and no standardization is evident. Variability of temper, wall thickness, and morphology indicate that rules (*sensu* Michelaki 2008:337), if they existed, were only loosely followed. Middle Woodland potters worked within a tradition but felt comfortable deviating from conventions while still making pots recognizable as belonging to those conventions.

Middle Woodland pottery is categorically different from Early Woodland pottery with no real transitional forms (see also Petersen 1997:87; Ritchie and MacNeish 1949:103). Although Petersen and Sanger (1991:123) found that ceramics made before and after 2150 BP shared characteristics that show they are related through time (an assessment also supported by the Jemseg collection), there are no vessels currently in the literature or common knowledge that show a gradual shift or transitional stage, as there are at the transition to the Late Woodland. Middle Woodland pottery relates to earlier pottery in "vessel lip, rim and even overall vessel body morphology similarities and generally similar temper types, sizes and proportions between these different ceramics," as noted by

Figure 12.7. Sherds belonging to a PSS-decorated vessel from the Fulton Island site, New Brunswick. *Source:* Photo by Cora Woolsey.

Figure 12.8. A PSS-decorated sherd from the George Frederick Clarke collection. *Source:* Photo by Cora Woolsey.

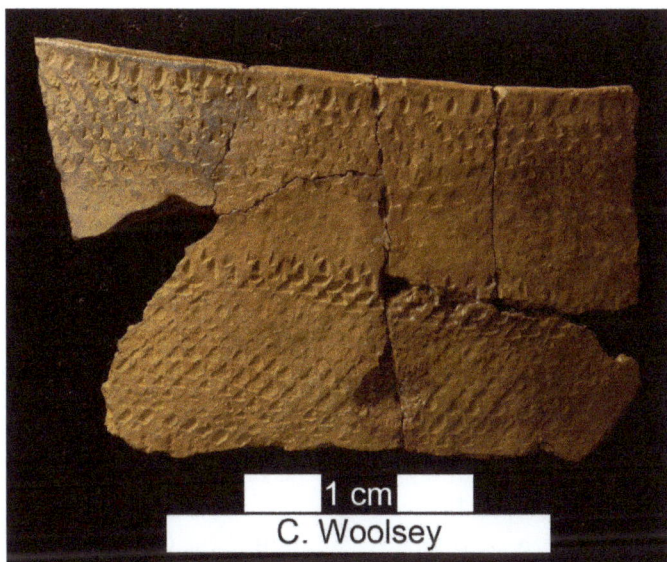

Figure 12.9. Sherds belonging to a triangular dentate-decorated vessel from the Gaspereau Lake Reservoir Site Complex. Average thickness (measurements n=9) is 0.41 cm (S.D.=0.01571, variance=0.000025). *Source:* Photo by Cora Woolsey.

Petersen and Sanger (1991:123). Yet while this continuity between the two periods suggests a long-lived ceramic tradition, it does not suggest a gradual evolution over time but, instead, an abrupt change that caused ceramics also to change.

Presumably, a transitional form would incorporate attributes from two periods and would gradually move from one form to another. Attributes that could be expected would be oblique or U-shaped lamellae with the introduction of paddling, moving gradually to vertical lamellae. We might also expect to see colours gradually brighten from dull grey or brown to medium brown to brick red. These transitional forms are not reported in the literature, nor have I observed them at the Jemseg site or other sites with Early or Middle Woodland ceramics. Some ceramics from the Oxbow site dated to the Early Woodland period bear PSS and dentate decorations, and may ultimately prove to be these missing links, but Allen (1981, 2005) has not described them as such; further investigation will be needed to decide how they fit into the history of ceramic change.

My own investigations of the forming attributes of the Jemseg pottery assemblage, the only assemblage in this region containing a substantial CP1 (3000–2150 BP) as well as a CP2 (2150–1650 BP) ceramic sample, suggests that a new method was introduced rather suddenly into the existing ceramic man-ufacturing tradition around 2,100 years ago (Woolsey 2019). The practice of coiling and smoothing a free-standing jar as opposed to coiling a jar inside a mould would have required a new set of skills that would have taken some time to learn, and even more so the ability to further shape the pot and thin and compact the walls through paddling (Arnold 1985:202-205). Paddling—the act of "spanking" the pot wall with a flat paddle while bracing it from the other side using an anvil stone or the potter's own hand—is a particularly risky practice because the clay must not be allowed to dry out, the paste must not be too coarse, and the potter must have significant motor control over the process of repeatedly turning the pot and striking the wall with the paddle without thinning the walls too much or too quickly (Crown 2007).[11] While this was apparently not as much of a concern in earlier or later pottery, early Middle Woodland ceramic (2150–1650 BP) assemblages show that this was not acceptable to potters and that pots tend to conform to conventions of very thin and even walls and very symmetrical shapes (figure 12.10). Developing the skills and knowledge to competently paddle a coil-built pot requires much more practice than coil-building alone (Arnold 1985:202-205), as I have discovered in my own pottery-making practices (also see Gates St-Pierre 2001 for an example from the Great Lakes region); these skills seem doubly important given the remarkably thin and even walls of many Middle Woodland pots, often as thin as 0.5 cm around the rim. Paddling also adds significantly more time to the pottery *chaîne opératoire* (e.g., Neupert 2007).

Why would potters put so much effort into paddling and shaping their pots given the risk and the amount of practice and time needed to make these pots? The first evidence to consider is the effect this process has on the pot. Paddling compresses the wall and aligns the clay particles to create a stronger molecular bond; air holes are also driven out during paddling and coil breaks are smoothed together, eliminating these sources of weakness in the wall (Rice 2005 [1987]; Rye 1981). Potters can also achieve more and larger shapes using paddling, and symmetry becomes possible (although moulds can achieve symmetry if they are made using a symmetrical preform, such as a paddled pot; see, e.g., Charlton et al. 1991). These advantages translate into utility: constricted necks help with keeping heat in while simmering food (Hally 1983; Skibo 2013), and harder walls break down from use slower over time (Hally 1983; Skibo et al. 1997). Yet it is unlikely that potters during the Early Woodland—some 800 years—had no understanding of which pottery properties could be improved on, making utility an unsatisfactory explanation.

---

11. The significance of paddling to the manufacturing process has been explored by Arnold (1985), Crown (2007), Kamp (2001:430), and Rye (1981) in varying degrees. Additionally, ethnographic literature has frequently documented the importance of variability of paddling stages in different cultures (e.g., Neupert 2007). Skills required for paddling have been remarked upon by Arnold (1985), Gosselain (1992), and Herbert (2008). For an overview and further discussion on paddling, see Woolsey (2018).

Figure 12.10. Attributes of Middle Woodland pottery, including (A) PSS and (B) dentate decorations, (C) smoothed or anvil-pressed interiors (E), finely tempered pastes, even carbon cores (F), and vertically oriented lamellar character.
Source: Photos by Cora Woolsey.

The best clue to why manufacturing practices changed lies in the combination of coiling and paddling with elaborate and painstaking decorations, which would have required significant time to execute and which would contribute little to the utility of the pot compared with earlier fabric impression. The new decorative practices therefore can be considered a loading up of labour (*sensu* Hayden 1995; e.g., Longacre et al. 2000) onto pots in addition to the risky and time-consuming practice of paddling (Woolsey 2018) in what Quinn (2009; see also Hart et al. 2016, 2017; Neff 2014) calls "costly signaling." A term borrowed from biology but profitably applied using social-network analysis (e.g., Hart et al. 2016), costly signalling refers to when significant labour and/or resources have been allocated to transmitting a message (e.g., through very valuable materials) (Panter-Brick 2002; Quinn 2009).

This approach has been applied to pottery analysis in the Northeast. Hart et al. (2016) demonstrate that pottery made by groups in southern Ontario were signalling ties to each other between 1,450 and 1,650 years ago through elaborate collar decorations. Because the labour involved in creating collars on pottery "added unnecessary time and material costs" to the utilitarian function of the pottery (Hart et al. 2016:6), they would have been what Quinn (2009) considers costly.

The same concept can be applied to earlier Middle Woodland ceramics of the Maine–Maritimes region. These thin, symmetrical pots with their elaborate decorations and brick-red colour would have been aesthetically pleasing, both to look at and to hold, and the skill required to make them would have been obvious to potters and non-potters alike, a phenomenon Gell (1992) dubbed "the technology of enchantment." The pottery would have been an ideal vehicle to carry emblemic (Wiessner 1983) decorations that are easy to differentiate and to adapt, a good candidate for signalling affiliation to other groups or ideologies. Thus, Middle Woodland pots may have been made as objects of value on display for all to see (Dobres 2001:54), perhaps acting as a showcase of the potter's ability and allegiance. Potters might wish to signal affiliations with other regions as a means of promoting their own status within the group, as I will discuss.

The changing role of ceramics may have come about because of new cultural influences on the Maine–Maritimes region. Although new pottery-manufacturing practices may have evolved independently, the abrupt transition to a new skill set and knowledge base argues against this possibility, as does the emergence of emblemic decorations across several regions at roughly 2200 BP (e.g., Gates St-Pierre and Chapdelaine 2013; Mason 1970; Pauketat 2012:257-258; Penney 1981; Petersen 1988, 1997; Petersen and Sanger 1991:125; Syms et al. 2014; Wiersum 1973), including the Far Northeast. The pots, decorated with a set of tools common to all these different complexes, regions, and cultural manifestations, exhibit local and areal distinctiveness and are made using local materials. This means that it was the potters and their knowledge, not the pots, that were being imported, indicating a large-scale movement of women and, possibly, their families. A replacement of the population does not fit well with the evidence in most places (no signs of wide-scale conflict or evidence of a hiatus; e.g., Cantú Trunzo 2006; Charles and Buikstra 2006; Gates St-Pierre 2001; Gates St-Pierre and Chapdelaine 2013; Lepper 2006; Mason 1970) so it appears that these people became new members in the native groups.

The Hopewell Interaction Sphere, far-flung and influential, saw goods, ideas, and—probably—people moving across great distances (Lepper 2006; Spence 1982), evident in the wide dispersal of cultural materials associated with the Hopewell, Laurel, and Point Peninsula cultures and with the movement of raw materials and finished goods (Charles and Buikstra 2006). At the same time, people were bringing their ideas and goods to the largest Hopewell centres from faraway regions (Spense 1982:187): pilgrimage appears to have been an important activity during the earlier Middle Woodland period (Lepper 2006). Women from the emerging Hopewellian and Laurel cultural centres may have been travelling around the Northeast as trading partners, colonists, wives, and mothers of wives, and bringing their pottery-making knowledge with them. At the same time, women from the Far Northeast may have been sending their own knowledge throughout eastern and central North America through marriage, trade, and pilgrimage. These women might have travelled significant distances (as Wright 1972 proposes) and may have used pottery as a way of maintaining ties with their homelands (as Zuni and Puebloan women did in times of major restructuring and migration; Mills 2018:1060-1061). In this way, they may have signified to others their cultural backgrounds and reminded others of the value of those ties—namely, access to exotic goods such as platform pipes, gorgets, cache blades, and sharks' teeth—and their presence may have been welcomed by the native populations. The lack of evidence for a combination of Early and Middle Woodland pottery styles in the Far Northeast suggests that a new learning lineage—in other words, new teachers passing on new skills to a receptive generation of neophytes—was in place after 2200 BP.

Despite the evidence for connections to the south and west, the Far Northeast does not seem to have participated in Middle Woodland interaction spheres to the same degree as other regions. Long-distance exchange networks are less apparent than in earlier and later periods (Bourque 1994; Wright 1994), and Hopewell "hallmarks" such as complex earthworks and lavish burials are not in evidence. However, evidence for other large-scale changes were taking place after about 2,500 years ago in changing lithic technologies, language, and subsistence strategies (Blair 2004:275-276; Fiedel 1994:212). It seems likely that the whole of the Northeast was connected through interdigitation of regions and areas, such that people interacted most actively with nearby communities who were interacting with other nearby communities, and so on, while longer-distance travel would also have been undertaken, though less frequently. It is in this fashion that women may have received pottery-making knowledge from multiple geographic and cultural sources before moving to a new community and passing on their knowledge in turn. At the shift to the Middle Woodland period, this interdigitation may have begun to bring new pottery skills into the Far Northeast without necessarily also bringing the suite of material culture associated with Hopewell and Laurel contexts.

Middle–Late Woodland Transition (1450–1050 BP)

Researchers have found that ceramics after ca. 1350 BP tend to exhibit a different set of attributes from the previous period (Allen 2005; Bourgeois 1999;

Foulkes 1981; Kimball 2011; Petersen and Sanger 1991; Will 2014). The PSS decoration disappeared between about 1650 and 1350 BP, eventually to be replaced with cord marks or cord-wrapped-stick decorations, and dentate decorations decreased while evident fabric impression or fabric paddling reappeared (figure 12.11). Walls became thicker overall (Stapelfeldt 2009; e.g., Nash and Stewart 1990:114), pastes were more coarsely tempered (figure 12.12; Davis 1991:97), and the ceramics tended to be fired in more reduced atmospheres, which resulted in more greyish colouration with less distinct carbon cores (figure 12.13; Woolsey 2010, 2017). After ca. 1450 BP, ceramics exhibit a significant increase in coil breaks (e.g., Hamilton and Yesner 1985) and noticeable decrease in careful application of decorations, which sometimes appear haphazard or poorly executed (e.g., Foulkes 1981:205; Nash and Stewart 1990:108; figure 12.14 here). Shell temper became more common in some places, although it never replaced grit temper as it did in other regions, especially further south (Petersen and Sanger 1991:136). Because of coarser pastes, more expediently applied decorations, and thicker walls, many researchers (Davis 1991:97; Keenlyside 1999:66) feel that skill levels decreased.

Figure 12.11. Sherds belonging to a cord-marked vessel from between 1300 and 1000 BP recovered from the Commeau Hill site in Nova Scotia. Note the lack of decoration below the rim.
Source: Courtesy of the Province of New Brunswick and Kora Stapelfeldt.

Figure 12.12. Sherds belonging to a cord-marked vessel from the Gaspereau Lake Reservoir Site Complex. Note the coarse paste, coil-break pattern and thicker walls.
Source: Photo by Cora Woolsey.

Figure 12.13. Sherds belonging to a cord-marked vessel in the George Frederick Clarke collection.

Figure 12.14. Attributes of pottery during the Middle to Late Woodland transition, including (A) cord-mark decorations, (B) more homogeneous temper minerals (in this case, bluish-grey quartz), (C) scraped interior surfaces, (D) uneven carbon cores, (E) well-developed coil breaks, and (F) oblique lamellar direction. *Source:* Photos by Cora Woolsey.

From the perspective of ceramic manufacture and use in the Maritime provinces, the period usually thought of as the Late Woodland in fact appears to be two distinct times, a Middle–Late Woodland transition between 1450 and 1050 BP and a later Late Woodland period from 1050 to 500 BP (Woolsey 2020; see also Black 2002; Curtis 2004; Hart and Reith 2002; Hart and Brumbach 2009) (or possibly somewhat later—see below). The largest ceramic assemblage so far yielded in the Maine–Maritimes region, the Gaspereau Lake Reservoir ceramic assemblage from central Nova Scotia, shows a gradual increase in ceramic production at the transition to the Late Woodland, around 1,450 years ago, but a drop-off of ceramic production after ca. 1050 BP (Woolsey 2020). During the transition, a gradual change in ceramic manufacture is evident, moving from finely tempered, elaborately and carefully decorated thin-walled ceramics (figures 12.15 and 12.16) to thicker-walled, less intensively paddled, coarser pottery (figures 12.17–12.19; Woolsey 2018), similar to what others have observed elsewhere (e.g., Kristmanson 1992; Petersen and Sanger 1991; Stapelfeldt 2009). Less is known about pottery production at the site after 1000 BP because only one ceramic was dated to after this time, suggesting pottery production was not as intensive or was used differently during the Late Woodland (Woolsey 2018). This drop-off of ceramic numbers also seems to have happened at other sites around 1,000 years ago (e.g., Allen 2005; Hrynick et al. 2012:16; Bourgeois 1999; Deal 1986; Sanger 1987; Stapelfeldt 2009), leading Foulkes (1981) to propose a "post-ceramic period."

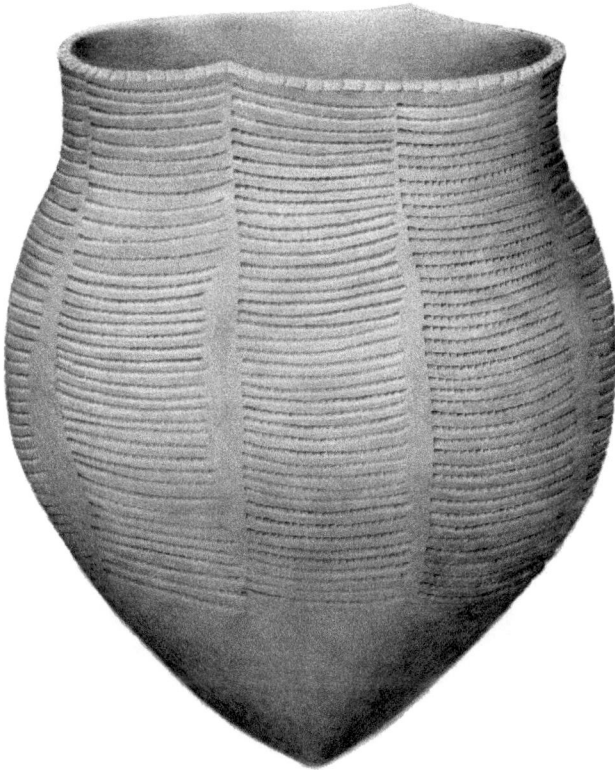

Figure 12.15. Artist's conception of what a dentate-decorated vessel lot from ca. 1500 BP from Gaspereau Lake, Nova Scotia, would have looked like.
Source: Cora Woolsey (illustration).

Figure 12.16. Sherds belonging to a dentate-decorated vessel from ca. 1500 BP recovered from the Gaspereau Lake Reservoir Site Complex in Nova Scotia. Note the carefully spaced and applied tool impressions, the exfoliation and spalling at the surface due to intense paddling, and the lack of obvious coil breaks.
Source: Photo by Cora Woolsey.

Figure 12.17. Artist's conception of a rocked-on cord-decorated vessel lot from ca. 1400 BP from Gaspereau Lake.
Source: Cora Woolsey (illustration).

Figure 12.18. Sherds belonging to a rocked-on cord-decorated vessel from ca. 1400 BP recovered from Gaspereau Lake. Note the larger tool impressions than the earlier dentate-decorated pottery. *Source:* From Woolsey (2017).

Black (2002) presented evidence for a transition that began somewhere around 1300 BP in the Quoddy Region on the coast of New Brunswick and Maine, which he called the Middle–Late Maritime Woodland Transition. In his view, a change in subsistence strategies around this time resulted in a different pattern of site formation that is marked by black-soil middens containing pit features, an increase in long-distance exchange of lithic materials, and an apparent pattern of cold-season occupation on mainland sites and warm-season occupation of insular sites such as the Bliss Islands. After this transitional period, sites became more ephemeral, lacking faunal remains and substantial middens, and were often in different locations from earlier sites. The change in site formation after 1000 BP suggests that "Late Maritime Woodland peoples in the Quoddy Region may have been shifting from a subsistence-settlement pattern emphasizing residential mobility to a pattern in which logistical mobility played a greater role" (Black 2002:306). At the same time, increased aggregation and/or longer-term residence are in evidence at larger sites such as the Goddard site in Maine and the Gaspereau Lake Reservoir site complex in Nova Scotia during the Late Woodland period. Black suggested that large aggregation sites at heads of tide on major rivers in the Maritime provinces probably exist but have yet to be discovered and may have been destroyed by development.

The Gaspereau Lake Reservoir Site Complex

A shift in subsistence strategies is certainly in line with evidence from the Gaspereau Lake Reservoir ceramic collection, which was only fully recovered in 2012 (Sanders et al. 2014). With ties to other Nova Scotia sites and sites beyond this region through long-distance exchange of lithics, sharks' teeth, and other trade items (Sanders et al. 2014:348-349), the Gaspereau Lake Reservoir Site Complex (made up of 21 closely spaced pre-European sites) is a good candidate for being one of the sites suggested by Black (2002) as a Late Woodland aggregation site. The ceramic assemblage consists of more than ca. 18,000 sherds, much larger than any known assemblage in the Maine–Maritimes region. The large numbers alone, most having been made after 1550 BP and before 1000 BP according to AMS (accelerator mass spectrometry) dating and evidence from attributes typical of the Late Woodland (Woolsey 2020), suggest a sizeable population that grew larger after the Middle Woodland period.

Because this assemblage is so large, it allows fine-grained analysis of manufacturing attributes that is not possible on smaller assemblages. In some ways, the assemblage conforms to expectations: the Early Woodland is represented by a vanishingly small number of sherds, while the Middle Woodland is represented by a much larger sample, evidenced by PSS and dentate decorations and characteristic red-bodied, thin-walled, finely tempered vessels. In other ways, however, the assemblage is anomalous: the Late Woodland is represented by many more vessels than the Middle Woodland, a distribution not usually seen in other assemblages (but see Sheldon 1988). Additionally, there are only a few shell-tempered ceramics. The ten AMS dates from carbonized foodstuffs on ceramic interiors show a continuous sequence from ca. 1600 BP to ca. 850 BP, with the largest number of dated vessel lots (n=9) falling between 1600 and 1050 BP (Woolsey 2020). The dated ceramics show a gradual change from highly paddled and carefully decorated to less well paddled and less carefully decorated, from variable temper to more homogeneous temper, from finer to coarser pastes, and from less iron oxide to more iron oxide in the paste (figure 12.14). The ceramics also show a remarkable lack of use wear, in contrast to other sites, where ceramics have microchipping on edges, build-ups of carbonized foodstuffs on interior surfaces, horizontal abrasion rings around neck interiors, and abrasion around the base on both interior and exterior surfaces. These are all missing or rare at

Gaspereau Lake, indicating that ceramics were used only once or a few times. Finally, vessels vary significantly in size, some potentially larger than 40 L, another remarkable feature of the assemblage and one of the features that Hayden (2001:40-41) lists as accompanying feasting and aggregation events.

Evident in these ceramic changes is the desire for more expedient manufacture. Paddling, a risky practice in terms of time wasted if a pot is ruined, decreased gradually from 1500 BP to 1050 BP. Temper amounts (including iron oxide) increased and organic temper began to be added; additionally, temper minerals became more homogeneous, suggesting that only one source was being accessed after 1500 BP. Temper protects clay from thermal shock during cooking as well as during the initial firing (Skibo 2013), and while increasing temper would not necessarily increase thermal-shock resistance during cooking, it would significantly reduce the chance of explosion during the initial firing, particularly if the pot were not yet fully dry (Woolsey 2018:281). Organic temper allows clay to dry faster (O'Brien et al. 1994:276-277; Skibo and Schiffer 1995), a trick taught to ceramic-arts students to allow them to build extra-large sculptures or rush work when deadlines are approaching (Karen Burk, pers. comm. 2009). The increase in temper percent and the addition of organic temper likely shows that potters were trying to hasten their production schedule, firing pots not fully dry and increasing the survival rate of pots during firing (Woolsey 2018:281). A drawback to increased temper, however, is reduced plasticity and, therefore, a reduction in the amount of paddling that a pot can withstand (Skibo 2013:52), as I have discovered with my own paddling experiments (Woolsey 2018:279). The resulting weakened walls with poorly smoothed coil joins may have been compensated for by increasing the amount of iron oxide, a mineral that fluxes ceramic material and causes it to chemically bond at lower temperatures. These changes would have allowed potters to cut corners in the production chain to turn out large numbers of pots within shorter timeframes. The question, then, is why potters would have wanted to turn out pots faster and produce larger quantities overall; to answer this, I turn to larger-scale changes taking place in the Far Northeast.

Evidence from the Gaspereau Lake Reservoir ceramics corroborates evidence from other sites, such as the Goddard and Bear River sites, pointing to an increase in size and/or frequency of large-scale gatherings after the Middle Woodland period. The minimal wear apparent on ceramics suggests that these pots were used but were not expected to have long use-lives (Woolsey 2017:114-124). This suggests that most pots were being made for specific events rather than for everyday use. This is in contrast to many Middle Woodland pots that show significant use wear in the form of carbonized encrustations, repair holes, extensive abrasion, polish on exteriors, and microchipping on lips. Considering the large numbers of pots, the expedient decorations, and the cutting down on manufacturing time by reducing or omitting steps such as paddling, potters appear to have been trying to increase output under tighter deadlines. Although deadlines are a part of any ceramic manufacture (e.g., seasons in which pottery can be made; Arnold 1985), potters at Gaspereau Lake after 1500 BP seem to have had to deal with increased pressure judging by the trade-offs of expediency for long use-lives. I suggest that the increased pressure arose from hosting large numbers of people during aggregation events, during which trade, feasting, and important political acts were carried out.

The large number of pots further suggests that these events were repeated frequently. Numerous exotic toolstones were found at Gaspereau Lake, including Ramah chert (Sanders et al. 2014:82, 106, 217, 348). Further, the majority of flakes and many projectile points were made of material that came from the Minas Basin, some 24 km from the site (Sanders et al. 2014:185); these are toolstones that have been found in other, distant sites such as the Goddard site in Maine (Sanger 1991) and the Jemseg site in New Brunswick (Black 2004). It is possible that Minas Basin chert was being accessed by people from all these distant sites to bring back home with them, especially the residents of Gaspereau Lake. However, given the large collection of flakes (n=376,546 from the End of Dyke site, the largest in the Gaspereau Lake Reservoir site complex) made primarily of Minas Basin chert and North Mountain quartzite, it is also possible that the aggregation activities included distributing these materials. Further evidence for this comes from the specialized lithic industry proposed by Nash and Stewart (1990) on the nearby and related Melanson site on the Gaspereau River. Evidently, people were aggregating at Gaspereau Lake in large numbers for large-scale gatherings and bringing toolstone with them; when they later dispersed, perhaps to gather at another location or to split off into nuclear-family residences along the coast or one of the river systems, they brought toolstone from Gaspereau Lake to these other locations. Such a pattern of moving around the region to attend large-scale gatherings at different locations is known from ethnohistoric records (Lelièvre 2017) and is supported by archaeological evidence that indicates most habitation sites are dispersed, single-family sites that were not occupied year-round (Black 2002). Pottery may also have been moving in a similar way.

Late Woodland Period (1050–500 BP)

At ca. 1050 BP, pottery became harder to find. Sites from after 1000 BP tend to be single component or disturbed and are really small, lacking pottery and often poorly preserved (Davis 1991:97; e.g., Foulkes 1981; Nash and Stewart 1990). One notable exception is the Skull Island site, where pottery, dated to ca. 650 BP in a single-component burial site, numbers 1,163 sherds, and 93 sherds in the adjacent shell midden (Leonard 1996). This context gives several clues about ceramic manufacture and use during the Late Woodland period in the Maritime provinces, and why ceramics became less visible at this time.

As mentioned earlier, some researchers have considered the possibility that ceramics declined in numbers or went out of use altogether owing to a lack of ceramic finds from the Late Woodland period. Although Foulkes (1981:234-235) acknowledged that the lack of evidence at the Fulton Island site in New Brunswick may have been the result of modern agricultural activity and disturbance, she cautioned that ceramics seemed to drop off gradually in other places around the Maritimes as well. Her observations have since been echoed by other researchers (e.g., Bourque 2001; MacIntyre 1988:326; Nash and Stewart 1990:114).

The drop-off in ceramic numbers could have occurred for several reasons. First, researchers have acknowledged the difficulty of telling ceramics apart during the latter part of the Late Woodland (e.g., Bourgeois 1999; Petersen and Sanger 1991; Kristmanson 1992:22-23). This may cause some ceramics to be labelled as earlier than they were actually made. Another possibility is that sites are increasingly disturbed in layers dating after 1000 BP, with later Late Woodland and Protohistoric sites often ephemeral, single component, or badly mixed. A third possibility is that ceramics simply stopped being made. Here, I propose a fourth possibility: that ceramics moved from domestic to ceremonial use and, therefore, are rarely discovered by archaeologists.

The Skull Island Site

The Skull Island site, which yielded the largest ceramic assemblage in the Maritime provinces from the Late Woodland, shows that ceramics were still being made but may be invisible to archaeologists because of a shift from domestic to mortuary and ceremonial contexts. The Skull Island site is a burial of several individuals in a single depositional event along with grave goods, including ceramic vessels. The ceramics are unusually well preserved due to their interment, which allowed Leonard (1996) to physically reconstruct several vessels (figure 12.20). The vessels bear certain signatures in manufacture, morphology, and decoration that make the probability of a single potter higher than in most sites. While the decorations are not all identical, the same tool, a cluster of porcupine quills that make a star shape in the clay, is discernible on most of the vessels. The cord marks are also similar among vessels. The method of construction left many coil breaks that are similar in character and roughness across the vessels, indicating similar or the same motor habits. The pots were clearly paddled, although not to the same extent as Middle Woodland pots. The morphology is also similar, and the same lip shape occurs on all the pots—an angled-outward, squared-off lip that is uncommon in this region. Leonard (1996:120) himself mentioned the likelihood of two pots having been made by the same potter, and other researchers (Stapelfeldt 2014) have also noted the likelihood of a single potter.

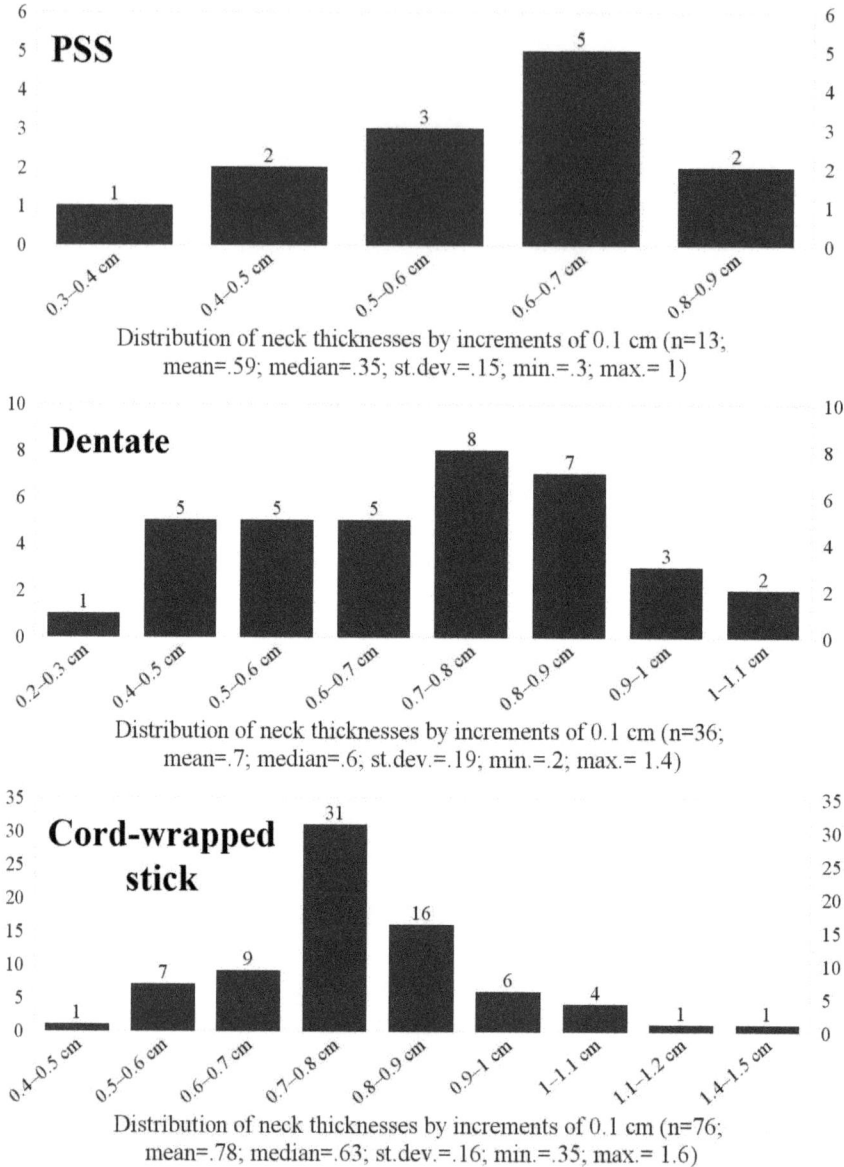

PSS

Distribution of neck thicknesses by increments of 0.1 cm (n=13; mean=.59; median=.35; st.dev.=.15; min.=.3; max.= 1)

Dentate

Distribution of neck thicknesses by increments of 0.1 cm (n=36; mean=.7; median=.6; st.dev.=.19; min.=.2; max.= 1.4)

Cord-wrapped stick

Distribution of neck thicknesses by increments of 0.1 cm (n=76; mean=.78; median=.63; st.dev.=.16; min.=.35; max.= 1.6)

Figure 12.19. Distributions of neck thicknesses for vessel lots decorated with PSS, dentate, and cord-wrapped stick in the Gaspereau Lake Reservoir ceramic collection for which this data has been collected. Student's t-test found that differences in thickness between PSS and dentate are significant (t-score=-1.87953, p=0.03319), and that thickness between PSS and cord-wrapped stick are even more clearly different (t-score=3.95921, p=0.000077). Differences between dentate and cord-marked are similar to those between PSS and cord-marked. Considering the three decorative-tool categories to represent roughly consecutive chronological periods (even though there is considerable overlap), then a gradual thickening of neck walls through time is in evidence.

Figure 12.20. Sherds belonging to a shell-tempered vessel from the Skull Island site.
Source: Photo by Cora Woolsey.

Jumping ahead in time for a moment, one of the first technological changes to occur during the Protohistoric period was the acquisition and use of copper kettles by the Mi'kmaq and other groups from the French (Whitehead 1993). These kettles showed up in burials almost immediately and were so ubiquitous that they earned the name "copper kettle burials" (Whitehead 1991). The importance of copper to Indigenous peoples during the pre-European and Contact eras is well documented (Leonard 1996; Whitehead 1991, 1993). Less well documented are the practices that occurred prior to this shift in burial practices, owing to the avoidance of excavating Indigenous graves in this region. In Skull Island, the one exception, human bones were placed inside or near ceramic vessels similar to the way they were placed in copper kettles in the following period, and copper nuggets were among the grave inclusions. This suggests that ceramics were important ceremonially, even though they were still tied to their utilitarian function as cooking pots, evidenced by conoidal bases and tempered pastes. It further suggests that copper kettles took over the mortuary function from ceramics after they became available through trade, even though they were also valued as cooking pots. Given this evidence, what has seemed like a discontinuation or decline of ceramic manufacture during the Late Woodland period may in fact have been a shifting of roles for ceramics from the domestic to the mortuary realm, making them mostly invisible to archaeologists.

The Decline in Ceramics from Domestic Contexts

If ceramics were moving toward a more ceremonial role, it seems possible that potters would also enjoy a more ceremonial status. There may no longer have been a need for every girl to learn pottery manufacture from her kin group as an essential skill, since pottery would not have been the only cooking tool, and other technologies, such as skin and birchbark containers and wooden vats, would have been used for the range of food-production needs of the group (Nash 1977; Rutherford 1991; Whitehead 1991, 1993). Ethnographic accounts of cooking mention that copper kettles were used in food preparation, but by no means did they replace all traditional Indigenous cooking technology, since wooden tubs were reportedly used in rendering fat (Champlain and Biggar 1971:153, 155; Denys et al. 1908:402, 406, 419; Nash 1977) and baskets and birchbark containers continued to be made and used up to the present (Petersen 1996; Whitehead 1987). In contrast, only one case of pottery making was ethnographically reported in this region (Champlain and Biggar 1971). It seems possible, in light of the evidence from Skull Island, that only one or two potters in each group would have made pottery, perhaps "on commission" or at the request of others for special occasions, and that pottery would not have been produced on as regular a basis as during the period prior to 1000 BP.

There are indications that the Late Woodland period was a time of increasing social complexity in the Far Northeast, of incipient chiefdoms in some areas (Leonard 1996), and of increasing territoriality. Trade increased significantly, evident in toolstone (Bourque 1994; Wright 1994), shark teeth (Betts et al. 2012), and probably a large range of both perishable and non-perishable goods as well as raw materials and crafted goods. This trend culminated in the Great Lakes region in the emergence of the Iroquoians (Curtis 2004; Gates St-Pierre and Chapdelaine 2013; Hart and Brumbach 2009; Martin 2008; Schillaci et al. 2017) and in the Mississippian groups further to the south (Brown et al. 1990; Emerson and Pauketat 2008; Feathers 2008; Kelly 1991; Little 1987; Perttula et al. 2001; Steponaitis 2009), but in the Maine–Maritimes region, some of these trends are also apparent. Although these different regions manifested very different cultural complexes, they probably influenced each other in a similar way as during the Middle Woodland. The Skull Island assemblage seems to show evidence of an emerging differential status in the amassing of wealth items that were ritually killed and placed in burials. The ethnographically reported town of Ouigoudi at the mouth of the Saint John River (Ganong 1899:262) may also have been one of the important "central places" (Nash et al. 1991) at which Black (2002) suggests people would have aggregated. Bear River was both an important archaeological site (Erskine 1986) and a gathering place for large groups during the Historic period (Ricker 1998), where people brought items to trade and to give.

Increasing complexity and more established long-distance exchange networks appear to have characterized the period after 1000 BP. Within this context, ceramics may have changed roles, moving from a food-preparation role supporting large gatherings to a ceremonial and mortuary role. Concomitantly, pottery knowledge may have become the purview of part-time specialists or brokers of sacred objects.

Evidence for Ceramic Manufacture During the Protohistoric Period

Although researchers have noted the decline of ceramic numbers, evidence for continued ceramic manufacture after European contact comes from both Maine and the Maritime provinces. This time frame, what Petersen and Sanger dubbed CP7, is represented by three dates from Nova Scotia and New Brunswick, and rather more from Maine, as several contexts that generally date ceramics to this time. Because evidence for ceramic manufacture is so small after European contact, it is important to consider what this evidence means for interpreting the role of ceramics. The radiocarbon dates acquired (listed in table 12.4) are statistically most likely to indicate pre-1600 CE, placing them more securely in the preceding CP6 (650–400 BP), but in the case of the Mud Lake Stream date, the 1-sigma range comfortably overlaps with CP7 (figure 12.21). All three dates are problematic, the latest date in particular, because of their large 1-sigma ranges. This lowers their value as evidence for ceramic manufacture after European contact.

The general dearth of Protohistoric ceramics suggests that, if ceramics continued to be made in the Maritime provinces, they were rare or are largely invisible to archaeologists owing to site destruction or mixing or a different depositional mechanism. The possible exception appears to be the southernmost tip of Nova Scotia, where Protohistoric ceramics were reported from the Port Joli site (Curtis et al. 2019). Unfortunately, they cannot yet add conclusive evidence for ceramic manufacture during this time because neither the date nor the number of ceramics from this context were provided. Given the proximity to the nearby Eel Weir site on the Mersey River that empties into the bay further up the coast, which also yielded a very late ceramic date (albeit a problematic one), this area of the Maritime provinces may ultimately prove similar to Maine in its late ceramic manufacturing tradition.

Table 12.4. List of dates directly associated with Protohistoric ceramics.
Dates come from Petersen and Sanger (1991) and Kristmanson (1992).

Site	Name	Date	δ	1-Sigma		2-Sigma	
				Range Cal BP	Probability	Range Cal BP	Probability
Mud Lake Stream	Beta-8163	300	80	289–466	1.0	1–25	0.027182
						140–221	0.110862
						260–513	0.861956
Eel Weir	Vessel 60	430	50	335–348	0.100236	318–393	0.21429
				456–527	0.899764	425–539	0.78571
Eel Weir	Vessel 66?*	AD 1520 (430)	50	335–348	0.100236	318–393	0.21429
				456–527	0.899764	425–539	0.78571

*It is possible that these are the same date. They are listed for two different vessels but are from the same site. Dates come from Kristamnson (1992), summarizing Ferguson (1982). Given this, the context listed as "direct" is uncertain.

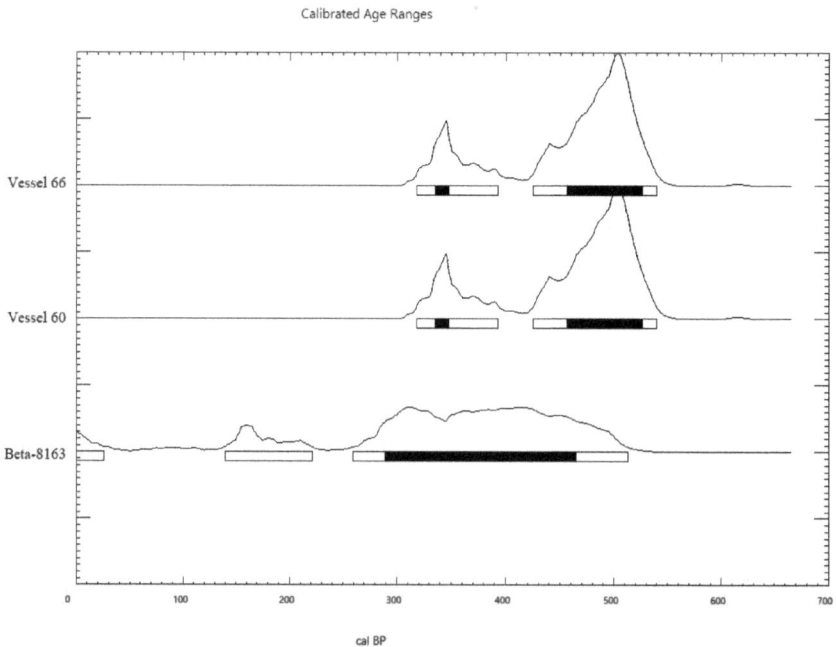

Figure 12.21. Protohistoric radiocarbon dates for ceramics from New Brunswick and Nova Scotia. The top two dates (Vessel 60 and Vessel 66) are from the Eel Weir site (Ferguson 1986) and reported by Kristmanson (1991). The bottom date (Beta-8163) is from Mud Lake Stream (Deal 1986) and reported by Petersen and Sanger (1991). Dates were calibrated using the Calib software program (Reimer et al. 2013) using the Intcal13 curve.

Conclusion: The Story(ies) of Pottery in the Far Northeast

Ceramics of the Maritime provinces have often been conceived of as belonging to a single, monolithic tradition that changed only in superficial ways through time. Yet evidence from ceramics as well as from glottochronology (e.g., Fiedel 1990), exchange networks (e.g., Bourque 1994; Wright 1994), and ethnohistoric accounts show that people were moving throughout the Northeast in ways that make an unchanging technological tradition unlikely. Ceramic analysis has sometimes suffered from seeing pottery as one long story with inexplicable and "chaotic" (Brose, quoted in Clark 1992:265) variation when it is in fact many, many stories of many women (and possibly men) in many places, each a node in a vast network of visible practices, fluid ideas, cumulative information, and independent innovation moving around the Northeast of North America.

Lelièvre (2017) showed how the Mi'kmaq during the Historic period moved through a vast, related, and sacred landscape, imbuing nodes and connections with spirituality and tradition continuously renewing investments in certain places. The mobility of peoples in the Far Northeast is a well-known cultural "trait," remarked upon throughout the Contact period by ethno-historians and scholars (Clarke 1968; Fiedel 1994; Ganong 1899, 1909; Hutton 1961; Le Clerq 1910; Lelièvre 2017; Whitehead 1991). This landscape of settlements "joining and splitting like quicksilver in a fluid pattern within its bounds" (Bragdon, quoted in Mann 2006:45) would have looked tremendously dynamic and culturally varied, during some times more than others. Different languages existed side by side; speakers of one language likely encountered speakers of other languages and dialects regularly, and migration and trans-humance was as much a part of life as food-getting. Clearly, no one potter would have represented the tradition of pottery manufacture better than another within this context of movement and knowledge sharing. Yet commonalities and shared understandings were also clearly carried over long distances, contrasting with the mix of local traditions to manifest as highly heterogeneous but relational pottery assemblages.

Pauketat (2001) elucidated the way material culture is best thought of as traces left behind by people negotiating many traditions at once. Pottery shows these traces exceptionally well compared with other artifact classes (Mills 2018) because the *chaîne opératoire* is rather complicated and requires skill building, knowledge acquisition, and creativity at all stages, leaving many crannies and opportunities to understand the constraints, identities, and allegiances of the potter. Because of its complex manufacture and subsequent use life, pottery performs many functions in the lives of people: as a connector with the landscape (Ingold 2011), as a display of skill and contestation of power during the act of making pottery (Dobres 2001), as a field for self-expression (Wiessner 1983), as a technological enhancement for food security (Claassen 1995), as objects of value (Neff 2014), as a conduit for the sacred (Emerson and Pauketat 2008), as heritage and memories of lived experience (Pauketat 2001), and many more. These perspectives on pottery could profitably be applied more fully to ceramic analysis of the Maine–Maritimes region.

Far Northeast pottery tells a very different story about what an Early Woodland potter would have thought and done from a potter of the Late Woodland. Almost everything about these two potters would have looked different: where and how they got their clay, which tools they would have used, how many people would have worked with them, and the ways in which their work would have been accepted or rejected. These outward signs would have suggested workings in their internal worlds, such as how developed was their sense of otherness, whom they would have considered their closest kin, how they went about acquiring the resources they needed, and what they would have hoped for the ones they loved.

We are a long way from understanding the complicated history of ceramic change through time in the Maritime provinces, as in other regions of the Northeast. The next step to understanding ceramics is developing a model of change. Here, I have looked at how ceramics may have moved from a fairly marginal addition to the domestic toolkit to an integral part of the subsistence strategy and, later, to an expedient technology used to support increasing aggregations at key points on the landscape, and, finally, to a mainly ceremonial and mortuary context. I offer women moving around the Northeast as a possible mechanism for the variability of ceramic assemblages in the Maritime provinces and elsewhere. Although insufficient evidence currently exists to conclude that this mechanism is the best fit, I hope it will serve as a starting point to advance ceramic studies in this region.

Acknowledgements

The research in this chapter was greatly aided by the guidance and support of many individuals, including Dr. Aubrey Cannon, Dr. David Black, Dr. Katie Cottreau-Robins, Dr. Chris McFarlane, Brent Suttie, and Dr. Matte Robinson. Thanks also to Kora Stapelfeldt for graciously providing images. I am indebted to the editors of this volume, Dr. Gabe Hrynick and Ken Holyoke, for inviting me to participate in the Canadian Archaeological Association session out of which this book came, since this chapter would probably not otherwise have been written. This chapter would also not have been possible without the funding and support of the Vanier Canada Research Scholarship, the Nova Scotia Museum, the University of New Brunswick, the Metepenagiag Heritage Park, and the Archaeology and Heritage Branch of the Province of New Brunswick.

References Cited

Allen, Patricia

1981   *The Oxbow Site: Chronology and Prehistory in Northeastern New Brunswick.* New Brunswick Manuscripts in Archaeology 1. Archaeological Branch Historical Resources Administration, Fredericton, New Brunswick.

2005   *The Oxbow Site 1984: Metepenagiag Mi'kmaq First Nation, Miramichi, New Brunswick.* New Brunswick Manuscripts in Archaeology 39. Archaeological Services, Heritage Branch, Province of New Brunswick, Fredericton.

Arnold, Dean E.

1985   *Ceramic Ecology and Cultural Process.* Cambridge University Press, Cambridge.

2008   *Social Change and the Evolution of Ceramic Production and Distribution in a Maya Community.* University Press of Colorado, Denver.

Bebber, Michelle Rae

2017   Tempered Strength: A Controlled Experiment Assessing Opportunity Costs of Adding Temper to Clay. *Journal of Archaeological Science* 86:1–13.

Beck, Margaret E., James M. Skibo, David J. Hally, and Peter Yang

2002   Sample Selection for Ceramic Use-Alteration Analysis: The Effects of Abrasion on Soot. *Journal of Archaeological Science* 29:1–15.

Betts, Matthew W., Susan E. Blair, and David W. Black

2012   Perspectivism, Mortuary Symbolism, and Human-Shark Relationships on the Maritime Peninsula. *American Antiquity* 77(4):621–625.

Black, David W.

2002   Out of the Blue and Into the Black: The Middle-Late Maritime Woodland Transition in the Quoddy Region, New Brunswick, Canada. In *Northeast Subsistence-Settlement Change A.D. 700–1300*, edited by John P. Hart and Christina B. Reith, pp. 301–320. New York State Museum Bulletin 496. New York State Museum, Albany.

2004   Ponapsqey. Stone Materials. In *Wolastoqiyik Ajemseg: The People of the Beautiful River at Jemseg, Volume 2: Archaeological Results, Jemseg Crossing Archaeology Project*, edited by Susan Blair, pp. 91–116. New Brunswick Manuscripts in Archaeology 36E. Archaeological Services, Heritage Branch, Province of New Brunswick Fredericton.

Blair, Susan

2004   *Wolastoqiyik Ajemseg: The People of the Beautiful River at Jemseg, Volume 2: Archaeological Results, Jemseg Crossing Archaeology Project.* New Brunswick Manuscripts in Archaeology 36E. Archaeological Services, Heritage Branch, Province of New Brunswick, Fredericton.

2009   Missing the Boat in Lithic Procurement: Watercraft and the Bulk Procurement of Tool Stone on the Maritime Peninsula. *Journal of Anthropological Archaeology* 29:33–46.

Blitz, John H.

2015   Skeuomorphs, Pottery, and Technological Change. *American Anthropologist* 117(4):665–678.

Bourque, Bruce

1994   Evidence for Prehistoric Exchange on the Maritime Peninsula. In *Prehistoric Exchange Systems in North America*, edited by Timothy G. Baugh and Jonathon E. Ericson, pp. 23–46. Springer, New York.

1995   *Diversity and Complexity in Prehistoric Maritime Societies: A Gulf of Maine Perspective*. Plenum, New York.

2001   *Twelve Thousand Years: American Indians in Maine*. University of Nebraska, Lincoln.

Bowser, Brenda J.

2000   From Pottery to Politics: An Ethnoarchaeological Study of Political Factionalism, Ethnicity, and Domestic Pottery Style in the Ecuadorian Amazon. *Journal of Archaeological Method and Theory* 7(3):219–248.

Bourgeois, Vincent G. J.

1999   A Regional Pre-Contact Sequence for the Saint John River Valley. Master's thesis, Department of Anthropology, University of New Brunswick, Fredericton.

2004   'Tahtuwalotewa Naka'Katkuhkewa: Ceramic Artifacts. In *Wolastoqiyik Ajemseg: The People of the Beautiful River at Jemseg, Volume 2: Archaeological Results, Jemseg Crossing Archaeology Project*, edited by Susan Blair, pp. 117–122. New Brunswick Manuscripts in Archaeology 36E. Archaeological Services, Heritage Branch, Province of New Brunswick, Fredericton.

Braun, Gregory Vincent

2015   Ritual, Materiality, and Memory in an Iroquoian Village. PhD dissertation, Department of Anthropology, University of Toronto, Toronto.

Bronitsky, Gordon, and Robert Hamer

1986   Experimental Ceramic Technology: The Effects of Various Tempering Materials on Impact and Thermal-Shock Resistance. *American Antiquity* 51(1):89–101.

Brown, James A., Richard A. Kerber, and Howard D. Winters

1990   Trade and the Evolution of Exchange Relations at the Beginning of the Mississippian Period. In *The Mississippian Emergence*, edited by Bruce D. Smith, pp. 251–80. University of Alabama, Tuscaloosa.

Brumbach, Hetty Jo

1979   Early Ceramics and Ceramic Technology in the Upper Hudson Valley. *The Journal and Bulletin of the Archaeology of New York State* 76:21–25.

Cantú Trunzo, Jennefer M.

2006   Political Economies and Peer Polities, Trade Networks, and Social Landscapes: Theorizing Hopewell in Middle Woodland Period New York State and Southern Ontario. *Northeast Anthropology* 72:55–76.

Carr, Christopher, and Jean-Christophe Komorowski

1995   Identifying the Mineralogy of Rock Temper in Ceramics Using X-Radiography. *American Antiquity* 60(4):723–749.

Champlain, Samuel, and Henry Percival Biggar

1971   *Voyages of Samuel de Champlain*. University of Toronto Press, Toronto.

Charles, Douglas K., and Jane E. Buikstra (editors)

2006   *Recreating Hopewell*. University Press of Florida, Gainesville.

Charlton, Thomas H., Deborah L. Nichols, and Cynthia Otis Charlton
1991   Aztec Craft Production and Specialization: Archaeological Evidence from the City-State of Otumba, Mexico. *World Archaeology* 23(1):98–114.

Chatfield, Melissa
2010   Tracing Firing Technology through Clay Properties in Cuzco, Peru. *Journal of Archaeological Science* 37:727–736.

Chilton, Elizabeth S.
1998   The Cultural Origins of Technical Choice: Unraveling Iroquoian and Algonkian Ceramic Traditions in the Northeast. In *The Archaeologies of Social Boundaries*, edited by Miriam T. Stark, pp. 132–160. Smithsonian, Washington, DC.

2000   Ceramic Research in New England: Breaking the Typological Mold. In *The Archaeological Northeast*, edited by Mary Ann Levine, Kenneth E. Sassaman, and Michael S. Nassaney, pp. 97–114. Bergin and Garvey, Westport, Connecticut.

Claassen, Cheryl P.
1995   A Consideration of the Social Organization of the Shell Mound Archaic. In *Archaeology of the Mid-Holocene Southeast*, edited by David G. Anderson and Kenneth Sassaman, pp. 235–258. University of Alabama, Tuscaloosa.

Clark, Caven P., Hector Neff, and Michael D. Glascock
1992   Neutron Activation Analysis of Late Woodland Ceramics from the Lake Superior Basin. In *Chemical Characterization of Ceramic Pastes in Archaeology*, edited by Hector Neff, pp. 255–267. Prehistory Press, Madison, Wisconsin.

Clarke, George Frederick
1968   *Someone Before Us: Our Maritime Indians*. Brunswick Press, Fredericton, New Brunswick.

Costin, Cathy Lynne
1991   Craft Specialization: Issues in Defining, Documenting, and Explaining the Organization of Production. *Archaeological Method and Theory* 3:1–56.

Crown, Patricia L.
2001   Learning to Make Pottery in the Prehispanic Southwest. *Journal of Anthropological Research* 57(4):451–469.

2007   Learning About Learning. In *Archaeological Anthropology: Perspectives on Method and Theory*, edited by James M. Skibo, Michael W. Graves, and Miriam T. Stark, pp. 198–217. University of Arizona Press, Tucson.

2014   The Archaeology of Crafts Learning: Becoming a Potter in the Puebloan Southwest. *Annual Review in Anthropology* 73:71–88.

Curtis, Jenneth Elizabeth
2004   Processes of Cultural Change: Ceramics and Interaction Across the Middle to Late Woodland Transition in South-Central Ontario. PhD dissertation, Department of Anthropology, University of Toronto Press, Toronto.

Curtis, Jenneth, Erin Ingram, and Matthew Betts
2019   The Ceramic Assemblage. In *Place-Making in the Pretty Harbour: The Archaeology of Port Joli, Nova Scotia*, edited by Matthew Betts, pp. 161–216. Mercury Series Archaeological Paper 182. Canadian Museum of History, Ottawa.

Davis, Stephen A.
1991   The Ceramic Period of Nova Scotia. In *Prehistoric Archaeology in the Maritime Provinces: Past and Present Research*, edited by Michael Deal and Susan Blair, pp. 85–100. Reports in Archaeology No. 8. Council of Maritime Premiers, Fredericton, New Brunswick.

Deal, Michael
1986   Late Archaic and Ceramic Period Utilization of the Mud Lake Stream Site, Southwestern New Brunswick. *Man in the Northeast* 32:67–94.

Denys, Nicholas, William Francis Ganong, and Victor Hugo Paltsits
1908   *The Description and Natural History of the Coasts of North America*. The Champlain Society, Toronto.

Dobres, Marcia-Anne
2001   Meaning in the Making: Agency and the Social Embodiment of Technology and Art. In *Anthropological Perspectives on Technology*, edited by Michael Brian Schiffer, pp. 47–76. University of New Mexico Press, Albuquerque.

Dorland, Steven G. H.
2018   Maintaining Traditions: A Study of Southern Ontario Late Woodland Ceramics Through a Communities-of-Practice Approach. *Journal of Archaeological Method and Theory* 25:892–910.

Druc, Isabelle
2013   What is Local? Looking at Ceramic Production in the Peruvian Highlands and Beyond. *Journal of Anthropological Research* 69:485–513.

Emerson, Thomas E., and Timothy R. Pauketat
2008   Historical-Processual Archaeology and Culture-Making: Unpacking the Southern Cult and Mississippian Religion. In *Belief in the Past: Theoretical Approaches to the Archaeology of Religion*, edited by David S. Whitley and Kelley Hays-Gilpin, pp. 167–188. Left Coast, Walnut Creek, California.

Engelbrecht, William
1972   The Reflection of Patterned Behavior in Iroquois Pottery Decoration. *Pennsylvania Archaeology* 42:1–15.

1978   Ceramic Patterning Between New York Iroquois Sites. In *Spatial Organization of Culture*, edited by Ian Hodder, pp. 141–152. University of Pittsburgh Press, Pittsburgh.

Erskine, John S.
1986   Unpublished Papers on the Archaeology of the Maritime Provinces. Edited by Michael Deal. St. Mary's University, Halifax.

Feathers, James K.
2003   Comments I: Accounting for Ceramic Change. *Archaeometry* 45(1):163–183.

2006   Explaining Shell-Tempered Pottery in Prehistoric Eastern North America. *Journal of Archaeological Method and Theory* 13(2):90–133.

2008   Origins and Spread of Shell-Tempered Ceramics in the Eastern Woodlands: Conceptual and Methodological Frameworks for Analysis. *Southeastern Archaeology* 27(2):286–293.

Ferguson, Robert S. O.
1986   Archaeological Site in Kejimkujik National Park. Nova Scotia. Manuscript on file at the Department of the Environment, Canada Parks.

Fiedel, Stuart J.

1990   Middle Woodland Algonkian Expansion: A Refined Model. *North American Archaeology* 11(3):209–230.

1994   Some Inferences Concerning Proto-Algonquian Economy and Society. *Northeast Anthropology* 48:1–11.

2001   What Happened in the Early Woodland? *Archaeology of Eastern North America* 29:101–142.

Finlayson, William David

1977   *The Saugeen Culture: A Middle Woodland Manifestation in Southeastern Ontario.* Mercury Series Archaeological Survey of Canada Paper No. 61. National Museum of Canada, Ottawa.

Foulkes, Ellen V.

1981   Fulton Island: A Stratified Site in the Saint John River Valley of New Brunswick. Master's thesis, Department of Anthropology, Trent University, Peterborough, Ontario.

Fowles, Severin M., Leah Minc, Samuel Duwe, and David V. Hill

2007   Clay, Conflict, and Village Aggregation: Compositional Analyses of Pre-Classic Pottery From Taos, New Mexico. *American Antiquity* 72(1):125–152.

Ganong, William F.

1899   *A Monograph of Historic Sites in the Province of New Brunswick. Contributions to the History of New Brunswick, Vol. 4.* Royal Society of Canada, Ottawa.

1909   *An Organization of the Scientific Investigation of the Indian Place-Nomenclature of the Maritime Provinces of Canada, Vol. 1.* Transactions of the Royal Society of Canada. J. Durie and Son, Ottawa.

Gates St-Pierre, Christian

2001   Two Sites, But Two Phases? Revisiting Kipp Island and Hunter Home. *Northeast Anthropology* 62:31–53.

Gates St-Pierre, Christian, and Claude Chapdelaine

2013   After Hopewell in Southern Québec. *Archaeology of Eastern North America* 41: 69–89.

Gell, Alfred

1992   The Technology of Enchantment and the Enchantment of Technology. In *Anthropology, Art, and Aesthetics*, edited by Jeremy Coote and Anthony Shelton, pp. 40–66. Oxford University Press, Oxford.

Gosselain, Olivier P.

1992   Technology and Style: Potters and Pottery Among Bafia of Cameroon. *Man* 27(3):559–586.

2000   Materializing Identities: An African Study. *Journal of Archaeological Method and Theory* 7(3):187–217.

2008   Thoughts and Adjustments in the Potter's Backyard. In *Breaking the Mould: Challenging the Past through Pottery*, edited by Ina Berg, pp. 67–79. Prehistoric Ceramics Research Group: Occasional Paper 6. BAR International Series 1861. Archaeopress, Oxford.

2011   Pourquoi le décorer? Quelques observations sur le décor céramique en Afrique. *Azania: Archaeological Research in Africa* 46(1):3–19.

2015   Roads, Markets, Migrants: The Historical Trajectory of a Male Hausa Pottery Tradition in Southern Niger. In *The Distribution of Technological Knowledge in the Production of Ancient Mediterranean Pottery*, edited by Walter Gauß, Gudrun Klebinder-Gauß, and Constance von Rüden, pp. 277–296. Proceedings of the International Conference at the Austrian Archaeological Institute at Athens 23rd–25th November 2012. Sonderschriften Österreichisches Archäologisches Institut, Vienna.

2016   The World is Like a Beanstalk: Historicizing Potting Practice and Social Relations in the Niger River Area. In *Knowledge in Motion: Constellations of Learning Across Time and Place*, edited by Andrew Roddick and Ann B. Stahl, pp. 36–66. University of Arizona Press, Tuscon.

2017   A Tradition in Nine Maps: Un-Layering Niger River Polychrome Water Jars. In *Balkan Dialogues: Negotiating Identity Between Prehistory and the Present*, edited by M. Gori and M. Ivanova, pp. 85–108. Routledge, London.

Hally, David J.

1983   Use Alteration of Pottery Vessel Surfaces: An Important Source of Evidence for the Identification of Vessel Function. *North American Archaeologist* 4:3–26.

Hamilton, Nathan D., and David R. Yessner

1985   Early, Middle, and Late Woodland Ceramic Assemblages from Great Diamond Island, Casco Bay, Maine. In *Ceramic Analysis in the Northeast: Contributions to Methodology and Culture History*, edited by James B. Petersen, pp. 5–25. Franklin Pierce College, Rindge, New Hampshire.

Hart, John P., Jennifer Birch, and Christian Gates St-Pierre

2017   Effects of Population Dispersal on Regional Signaling Networks: An Example from Northern Iroquoia. *Science Advances* 3(8):e1700497.

Hart, John P., and Hetty Jo Brumbach

2009   On Pottery Change and Northern Iroquoian Origins: An Assessment from the Finger Lakes Region of Central New York. *Journal of Anthropological Archaeology* 28:367–381.

Hart, John P., and Christina B. Reith (editors)

2002   *Northeast Subsistence-Settlement Change A.D. 700–1300*. New York State Museum Bulletin 496. New York State Museum, Albany.

Hart, John P., Termeh Shafie, Jennifer Birch, Susan Dermarkar, and Ronald F. Williamson

2016   Nation Building and Social Signaling in Southern Ontario: A.D. 1350–1650. *PLOS ONE* 11(5):e0156178.

Hayden, Brian

1995   The Emergence of Prestige Technologies and Pottery. In *The Emergence of Pottery*, edited by William K. Barnett and John W. Hoopes, pp. 257–266. Smithsonian, Washington, DC.

2001   Fabulous Feasts: A Prolegomenon to the Importance of Feasting. In *Feasts: Archaeological and Ethnographic Perspectives on Food, Politics, and Power*, edited by Brian Hayden and Michael Dietler, pp. 23–64. Smithsonian Institution, Washington, DC.

Herbert, Joseph M.
2008   The History and Practice of Shell Tempering in the Middle Atlantic: A Useful Balance. *Southeastern Archaeology* 27(2):265–285.

Hoard, Robert J., Michael J. O'Brien, Mohammad Ghazavy Khorasgany, and Vellore S. Gopalaratnam
1995   A Materials Science Approach to Understanding Limestone-Tempered Pottery from the Midwestern United States. *Journal of Archaeological Science* 22:823–832.

Hoopes, John W., and William K. Barnett
1995   The Shape of Early Pottery Studies. In *The Emergence of Pottery*, edited by William K. Barnett and John W. Hoopes, pp. 1–7. Smithsonian, Washington, DC.

Hrynick, Gabriel, Matthew W. Betts, and David W. Black
2012   A Late Maritime Woodland Period Dwelling Feature from Nova Scotia's South Shore: Evidence for Patterned Use of Domestic Space. *Archaeology of Eastern North America* 40:1–25.

Hutton, Elizabeth Ann
1961   The Micmac Indians of Nova Scotia to 1834. Master's thesis, Dalhousie University, Halifax.

Ingold, Tim
2011   *Being Alive: Essays on Movement, Knowledge, and Description*. Routledge, London.

Kamp, Kathryn A.
2001   Prehistoric Children Working and Playing: A Southwestern Case Study in Learning Ceramics. *Journal of Anthropological Research* 57(4):427–450.

Keenlyside, David L.
1999   Glimpses of Atlantic Canada's Past. *Revista Archaeología Americana* 16:49–76.

Kelly, John E.
1991   Cahokia and Its Role as a Gateway Center in Interregional Exchange. In *Cahokia and the Hinterlands: Middle Mississippian Cultures of the Midwest*, edited by Thomas E. Emerson and R. Barry Lewis, pp. 61–80. University of Illinois, Urbana.

Kenyon, Victoria Bunker
1986   Middle Woodland Ceramic Patterning in the Merrimack River Valley. *Archaeology of Eastern North America* 14:19–34.

Kilikoglou, Vassilis, George Vekinis, Y. Maniatis, and Peter M. Day
1998   Mechanical Performance of Quartz-Tempered Ceramics: Part I, Strength and Toughness. *Archaeometry* 40(2):261–279.

Kimball, Kessi Waters
2011   From Earth to Hearth: A Ceramic Analysis of the Ewing-Bragdon Site Collection. *The Maine Archaeological Society Bulletin* 51(2):29–51.

Kristmanson, Helen
1992   The Ceramic Sequence for Southwestern Nova Scotia: A Refinement of the Petersen/Sanger Model. Master's thesis, Department of Anthropology, Memorial University of Newfoundland, St. John's.

Kristmanson, Helen, and Michael Deal

1993   The Identification and Interpretation of Finishing Marks on Prehistoric Nova Scotian Ceramics. *Canadian Journal of Archaeology* 17:74–84.

Kutruff, Jenna Tedrick, and Carl Kutruff

1996   Mississippian Textile Evidence on Fabric-Impressed Ceramics from Mound Bottom, Tennessee. In *Ceramic Analysis in the Northeast: Resumé and Prospects*, edited by James Petersen, pp. 160–174. Franklin Pierce College, Rindge, New Hampshire.

Lave, Jean

1991   Situating Learning in Communities of Practice. In *Perspectives on Socially Shared Cognition*, edited by L. Resnick, J. Levine, and S. Teasley, pp. 63–82. APA, Washington, DC.

Lave, Jean, and Etienne Wenger

1991   *Situated Learning: Legitimate Peripheral Participation*. Cambridge University Press, Cambridge.

Lancy, David

2012   "First You Must Master Pain": The Nature and Purpose of Apprenticeship. *Anthropology of Work Review* 33(2):113–126.

Laybolt, Dawn A.

1999   Prehistoric Settlement and Subsistence Patterns at Gaspereau Lake, Kings County, Nova Scotia. Master's thesis, Department of Anthropology, Memorial University of Newfoundland, St. John's.

Le Clercq, Chrestien

1910   *New Relations of Gaspesia: With the Customs and Religion of the Gaspesian Indians*. Edited and translated by William F. Ganong. The Champlain Society, Toronto.

Lelièvre, Michelle A.

2017   *Unsettling Mobility: Mediating Mi'kmaw Sovereignty in Post-Contact Nova Scotia*. University of Arizona Press, Tuscon.

Lenius, Brian J., and Dave M. Olinyk

1990   The Rainy River Composite: Revisions to Late Woodland Taxonomy. In *The Woodland Tradition in the Western Great Lakes: Papers Presented to Elden Johnson*, edited by Guy Gibbon, pp. 77–112. Publications in Anthropology No. 4. University of Minnesota, Minneapolis.

Leonard, Kevin

1995   Woodland or Ceramic Period: A Theoretical Problem. *Northeast Anthropology* 50:19–30.

1996   Mi'kmaq Culture During the Late Woodland and Early Historic Periods. PhD dissertation, Department of Anthropology, University of Toronto, Toronto.

Lepper, Brad T.

2006   The Great Hopewell Road and the Role of the Pilgrimage in the Hopewell Interaction Sphere. In *Recreating Hopewell*, edited by Douglas K. Charles, and Jane E. Buikstra, pp. 122–133. University Press of Florida, Gainesville.

Little, Elizabeth A.

1987   Inland Waterways in the Northeast. *Midcontinental Journal of Archaeology* 12(1): 55–76.

Longacre, William A., Jingfeng Xia, and Tao Yang
2000   I Want to Buy a Black Pot. *Journal of Archaeological Method and Theory* 7(4):273–293.

Loring, Stephen
2013   Pottery from the North: Addendum to Stapelfeldt. *Arctic Studies Centre Newsletter* 20:31–32.

MacIntyre, Judith
1988   Appendix H: Results of Petrographic Analysis. In *The Late Prehistory as Viewed from the Brown Site*, edited by Helen Sheldon, pp. 307–329. Nova Scotia Museum Curatorial Report 61. Nova Scotia Museum, Halifax.

Mann, Charles C.
2015   *1491: New Revelations of the Americas Before Columbus*. Alfred A. Knopf, New York.

Martelle, Holly Anne
2002   Huron Potters and Archaeological Constructs: Researching Ceramic Micro-Stylistics. PhD dissertation, Department of Anthropology, University of Toronto, Toronto.

Martin, Scott W. J.
2008   Languages Past and Present: Archaeological Approaches to the Appearance of Northern Iroquoian Speakers in the Lower Great Lakes Region of North America. *American Antiquity* 73(3):441–463.

Mason, Ronald J.
1970   Hopewell, Middle Woodland, and the Laurel Culture: A Problem in Archaeological Classification. *American Anthropologist* 72(4):802–815.

Michelaki, Kostalena
2008   Making Pots and Potters in the Bronze Age Maros Villages of Kiszombor-Új-Élet and Klárafalva-Hajdova. *Cambridge Archaeological Journal* 18(3):355–380.

Michelaki, Konstantina-Eleni, and R. G.V. Hancock
2011   Chemistry Versus Data Dispersion: Is There a Better Way to Assess and Interpret Archaeometric Data? *Archaeometery* 53(6):1259–1279.

Mills, Barbara
2018   Intermarriage, Technological Diffusion, and Boundary Objects in the U.S. Southwest. *Journal of Archaeological Method and Theory* 25:1051–1086.

Minar, C. Jill, and Patricia L. Crown
2001   Learning and Craft Production: An Introduction. *Journal of Anthropological Research* 57(4):369–380.

Mortimer, Benjamin James
2011   Whose Pot is This? Analysis of Middle to Late Woodland Ceramics from the Kitchikewana Site, Georgian Bay Islands National Park of Canada. Master's thesis, Department of Archaeology, Trent University, Peterborough, Ontario.

Myers, Thomas P.
2006   Hominy Technology and the Emergence of Mississippian Societies. In *Histories of Maize: Multidisciplinary Approaches to the Prehistory, Linguistics, Biogeography, Domestication and Evolution of Maize*, edited by John E. Staller, Robert H. Tykot, and Bruce F. Benz, pp. 511–520. Academic Press, New York.

Nash, Ronald
1977   *Prehistoric and Cultural Ecology: Cape Breton Island, Nova Scotia.* Papers from the Fourth Annual Congress, edited by Richard J. Preston, pp. 131–156. Mercury Series Paper No. 40. National Museum of Man, Ottawa.

Nash, Ronald J., and Frances L. Stewart
1990   *Melanson: A Large Micmac Village in Kings County, Nova Scotia.* Curatorial Report Number 67. Nova Scotia Museum, Halifax.

Nash, Ronald J., Frances L. Stewart, and Michael Deal
1991   Melanson: A Central Place in Southwestern Nova Scotia. In *Prehistoric Archaeology in the Maritime Provinces: Past and Present Research,* edited by Michael Deal and Susan Blair, pp. 213–220. Reports in Archaeology No. 8. Council of Maritime Premiers, Fredericton, New Brunswick.

Neff, Hector
2014   Pots as Signals: Explaining the Enigma of Long-Distance Ceramic Exchange. In *Craft and Science: International Perspectives on Archaeological Ceramics,* edited by M. Martinón-Torres, pp. 1–11. Bloomsbury Qatar Foundation, Doha.

Neupert, Mark A.
2007   Contingency Theory and the Organizational Behavior of Traditional Pottery Production. In *Archaeological Anthropology: Perspectives on Method and Theory,* edited by James M. Skibo, Michael W. Graves, and Miriam T. Stark, pp. 139–162. University of Arizona Press, Tucson.

Newsom, Bonnie
2017   *Potters on the Penobscot: An Archaeological Case Study Exploring Human Agency, Identity, and Technological Choice.* PhD dissertation, Department of Anthropology, University of Massachusetts, Amherst.

O'Brien, Michael J., Thomas D. Holland, Robert J. Hoard, and Gregory L. Fox
1994   Evolutionary Implications of Design and Performance Characteristics of Prehistoric Pottery. *Journal of Archaeological Method and Theory* 1(3):259–304.

Panter-Brick, Catherine
2002   Sexual Division of Labour: Energetic and Evolutionary Scenarios. *American Journal of Human Biology* 14:627–640.

Pauketat, Timothy R.
2012   *The Oxford Handbook of North American Archaeology.* Oxford University Press, Oxford.

Pauketat, Timothy R. (editor)
2001   *The Archaeology of Traditions: Agency and History Before and After Columbus.* University Press of Florida, Gainesville.

Peirce, Christopher
2005   Reverse Engineering the Ceramic Cooking Pot. *Journal of Archaeological Method and Theory* 12(2):117–157.

Penney, Gerald
1981   A Point Peninsula Rim Sherd from L'Anse à Flamme, Newfoundland. *Canadian Journal of Archaeology* 5:171–173.

Perttula, Timothy K., Marlin F. Hawley, and Fred W. Scott
2001   Caddo Trade Ceramics. *Southeastern Archaeology* 20(2):154–196.

Petersen, James B.

1988   The Pseudo Scallop Shell Horizon Style in North American Prehistory. Paper presented at the 20th Annual Meeting of the Canadian Archaeological Association, Whistler, British Columbia.

1996   Fiber Industries from Northern New England: Ethnicity and Technological Traditions during the Woodland Period. In *A Most Indispensable Art: Native Fiber Industries from Eastern North America*, edited by James B. Petersen, pp. 100–119. University of Tennessee, Knoxville.

1997   A Prehistoric Native American Ceramic vessel from Lake Champlain. *Journal of Vermont Archaeology* 2:85–90.

Petersen, James B., and David Sanger

1991   An Aboriginal Ceramic Sequence for Maine and the Maritime Provinces. In *Prehistoric Archaeology in the Maritime Provinces: Past and Present Research*, edited by Michael and Susan Blair, pp. 113–170. Reports in Archaeology No. 8. Council of Maritime Premiers, Fredericton, New Brunswick.

Pfaffenberger, Brian

2001   Symbols Do Not Create Meaning—Actions Do: Or, Why Symbolic Anthropology Needs the Anthropology of Technology. In *Anthropological Perspectives on Technology*, edited by Michael Brian Schiffer, pp. 77–86. University of New Mexico Press, Albuquerque.

Quinn, Patrick Sean

2009   *Interpreting Silent Artefacts: Petrographic Approaches to Archaeological Ceramics.* Archaeopress, Ann Arbor, Michigan.

Read, Dwight W.

2007   *Artifact Classification: A Conceptual and Methodological Approach.* Left Coast Press, Walnut Creek, California.

Reimer, Paula J., Edouard Bard, Alex Bayliss, J. Warren Beck, Paul G. Blackwell, Christopher Bronk Ramsey, Caitlin E. Buck, Hai Cheng, R. Lawrence Edwards, Michael Friedrich, Pieter M. Grootes, Thomas P. Guilderson, Haflidi Haflidason, Irka Hajdas, Christine Hatté, Timothy J. Heaton, Dirk L. Hoffmann, Alan G. Hogg, Konrad A. Hughen, K. Felix Kaiser, Bernd Kromer, Sturt W. Manning, Mu Niu, Ron W Reimer, David A. Richards, E. Marian Scott, John R. Southon, Richard A. Staff, Christian S. M. Turney, and Johannes van der Plicht

2013   Intcal13 and Marine13 radiocarbon age calibration curves 0–50,000 Years Cal BP. *Radiocarbon* 55(4):1869–1887.

Rice, Prudence M.

1976   Rethinking the Ware Concept. *American Antiquity* 41(4):538–543.

2005 [1987]   *Pottery Analysis: A Sourcebook.* University of Chicago Press, Chicago.

Ricker, D. A.

1998   *L'sitkuk: The Story of the Bear River Mi'kmaw Community.* 2nd ed. Lockport, Roseway, Nova Scotia.

Ritchie, William A., and Richard S. MacNeish

1949   The Pre-Iroquoian Pottery of New York State. *American Antiquity* 15(2):97–124.

Roddick, Andrew Paul
2009   Communities of Pottery Production and Consumption on the Taraco Peninsula, Bolivia, 200 BC–300 AD. PhD dissertation, Department of Anthropology, University of California, Berkeley.

Roux, Valentine
2003   Ceramic Standardization and Intensity of Production: Quantifying Degrees of Specialization. *American Antiquity* 68(4):768–782.

Rutherford, Douglas E.
1990   Continuity of the Moorehead Phase Populations in New Brunswick and Maine. *Papers of the 21st Algonquian Conference* 21:329–336.
1991   The Ceramic Period in New Brunswick. In *Prehistoric Archaeology in the Maritime Provinces: Past and Present Research*, edited by Michael Deal and Susan Blair, pp. 101–112. Reports in Archaeology No. 8. Council of Maritime Premiers, Fredericton, New Brunswick.

Rye, Owen
1981   *Ceramic Technology: Principles and Reconstruction.* Taraxacum, Washington, DC.

Sanders, Mike, Angela Finnie, Kiersten Green, Robert Shears, and Kathryn Stewart
2014   *End of Dyke Site Mitigation 2012, Gaspereau Lake Reservoir, Kings County, Nova Scotia: Final Report.* Cultural Resource Management Group Limited, Halifax, Nova Scotia.

Sanger, David
1974   Recent Meetings on Maine–Maritimes Archaeology: A Synthesis. *Man in the Northeast* 13:128–129.
1986   An Introduction to the Prehistory of the Passamaquoddy Bay Region. *American Review of Canadian Studies* 16(2):139–159.
1987   *The Carson Site and the Late Ceramic Period in Passamaquoddy Bay, New Brunswick.* Archaeological Survey of Canada, Mercury Series Paper 135. Ottawa: National Museum of Civilization.
1988   Maritime Adaptations in the Gulf of Maine. *Archaeology of Eastern North America* 16:81–99.
1991   Five Thousand Years of Contact Between Maine and Nova Scotia. *The Maine Archaeological Society Bulletin* 31(2):55–61.

Sassaman, Kenneth E.
1992   Gender and Technology at the Archaic-Woodland Transition. In *Exploring Gender Through Archaeology: Selected Papers from the 1991 Boone Conference*, edited by Cheryl Claassen, pp. 71–80. Monographs in World Archaeology, No. 11. Prehistory, Madison, Wisconsin.
2010   *The Eastern Archaic, Historicized.* Altamira, New York.

Sassaman, Kenneth E., and Wictoria Rudolphi
2001   Communities of Practice in the Early Pottery Traditions of the American Southeast. *Journal of Anthropological Research* 57(4):407–425.

Saunders, Rebecca
2001   Negotiated Tradition? Native American Pottery in the Mission Period in La Florida. In *The Archaeology of Traditions: Agency and History Before and After*

Columbus, edited by Timothy R. Pauketat, pp. 77–93. University Press of Florida, Gainesville.

Schiffer, Michael Brian, and James M. Skibo

1997   The Explanation of Artifact Variability. *American Antiquity* 62:27–50.

Schillaci, Michael A., Craig Kopris, Søren Wichmann, and Genevieve Dewar

2017   Linguistic Clues to Iroquoian Prehistory. *Journal of Anthropological Research* 73(3):448–485.

Sheldon, Helen

1988   *The Late Prehistory as Viewed from the Brown Site.* Nova Scotia Museum Curatorial Report 61. Nova Scotia Museum, Halifax.

Sillar, Bill, and M. S. Tite

2000   The Challenge of "Technological Choices" for Materials Science Approaches in Archaeology. *Archaeometry* 42(1):2–20.

Skibo, James M.

2013   *Understanding Pottery Function.* Manuals in Archaeological Method, Theory and Technique. Springer, New York.

Skibo, James M., and Michael Brian Schiffer

1995   The Clay Cooking Pot: An Exploration of Women's Technology. In *Expanding Archaeology*, edited by James M. Skibo, William H. Walker, and Alex E. Nielsen, pp. 80–91. University of Utah Press, Salt Lake City.

Skibo, James M., Tamara C. Butts, and Michael Brian Schiffer

1997   Ceramic Surface Treatment and Abrasion Resistance: An Experimental Study. *Journal of Archaeological Science* 24:311–317.

Smith, Patricia E.

2005   Children and Ceramic Innovation: A Study in the Archaeology of Children. *Archaeological Papers of the American Anthropological Association* 15(1):65–76.

Speck, Frank G.

1931   Birch Bark in the Ancestry of Pottery Forms. *Anthropos* 26:407–411.

Spense, Michael W.

1982   The Social Context of Production and Exchange. In *Contexts for Prehistoric Exchange*, edited by Jonathon E. Ericson and Timothy K. Earle, pp. 173–198. Academic, New York.

Spittal, David A.

2017   The Blueberry Field Site (BcHa-23): A Middle Woodland Campsite in Wasaga Beach Provincial Park, Ontario. *Ontario Archaeology* 97:91–120.

Stapelfeldt, Kora

2009   A Form and Function Study of Precontact Pottery from Atlantic Canada. Master's thesis, Department of Archaeology, Memorial University, St. John's.

2014   A Form and Function Study of Pottery from Atlantic Canada: Variations on a Thesis. Paper presented at the Hamilton Chapter Meeting of the Ontario Archaeological Society, Ancaster, Ontario.

Steponaitis, Vincas P.

2009   *Ceramics, Chronology, and Community Patterns: An Archaeological Study at Moundville.* University of Alabama Press, Tuscaloosa.

Syms, E. Leigh, Teija Dedi, Gary Wowchuk, Kayleigh Speirs, and Susan Broadhurst
2014   Identifying New Late Woodland Ceramic Traditions in the Swan Valley, Western Manitoba. *Manitoba Archaeological Journal* 24(1–2):1–92.

Taché, Karine
2005   Explaining Vinette 1 Pottery Variability: A View from the Batiscan Site, Québec. *Canadian Journal of Archaeology* 29(2):165–233.

Taché, Karine, Daniel White, and Sarah Seelen
2008   Potential Functions of Vinette I Pottery: Complementary Use of Archaeological and Pyrolysis GC/MC Data. *Archaeology of Eastern North America* 36:63–90.

Taché, Karine, and John P. Hart
2013   Chronometric Hygiene of Radiocarbon Databases for Early Durable Cooking Vessel Technologies in Northeastern North America. *American Antiquity* 78(2):359–372.

Tite, M. S., Vassilis Kilikoglou, and G. Vekinis
2001   Review Article: Strength, Toughness and Thermal Shock Resistance of Ancient Ceramics, and Their Influence on Technological Choice. *Archaeometery* 43(3):301–324.

van der Leeuw, Sander
1991   Variation, Variability and Explanation in Pottery Studies. In *Ceramic Ethnoarchaeology*, edited by William Longacre, pp. 11–39. University of Arizona Press, Tucson.

Vitelli, Karen D.
1995   Pots, Potters, and the Shaping of Greek Neolithic Society. In *The Emergence of Pottery*, edited by William K. Barnett and John W. Hoopes, pp. 55–64. Smithsonian, Washington, DC.

Wallaert-Pêtre, Hélène
2001   Learning How to Make the Right Pots: Apprenticeship Strategies and Material Culture, a Case Study in Handmade Pottery from Cameroon. *Journal of Anthropological Research* 57(4):471–493.

Wenger, Etienne
1999   *Communities of Practice: Learning, Meaning, and Identity*. Cambridge University Press, Cambridge.

White, Joyce C.
2017   Changing Paradigms in Southeast Asian Archaeology. *Journal of Indo-Pacific Archaeology* 41:66–77.

Whitehead, Ruth Holmes
1987   Plant Fibre Textiles from the Hopps Site: BkCp-1. Nova Scotia Museum, Halifax.
1991   The Protohistoric Period in the Maritime Provinces. In *Prehistoric Archaeology in the Maritime Provinces: Past and Present Research*, edited by Michael Deal and Susan Blair, pp. 227–258. Reports in Archaeology No. 8. Council of Maritime Premiers, Fredericton, New Brunswick.
1993   *Nova Scotia: The Protohistoric Period 1500–1630*. Nova Scotia Museum, Halifax.

Wiersum, Wayne E.

1973   Salvage Archaeology Boreal Manitoba. *Bulletin of the Canadian Archaeological Association* 5:163–166.

Wiessner, Polly

1983   Style and Social Information in Kalahari San Projectile Points. *American Antiquity* 48(2):253–276.

Will, Richard

2014   Precontact Pottery from Moosehead Lake, Maine: Some Insights on Manufacture and Use. *The Maine Archaeological Society Bulletin* 54(1):1–46.

Wilk, Richard R.

2001   Toward an Archaeology of Needs. In *Anthropological Perspectives on Technology*, edited by Michael Brian Schiffer, pp. 107–122. University of New Mexico Press, Albuquerque.

Wobst, H. Martin

1977   Stylistic Behavior and Information Exchange. In *Papers for the Director: Research Essays in Honor of James B. Griffin*, edited by Charles E. Cleland, pp. 317–342. Museum of Anthropology Papers 61. University of Michigan, Ann Arbor.

Woolsey, Cora A.

2010   Ceramic Sherds in the George Frederick Clarke Collection: A Technological Approach. Master's thesis, Department of Anthropology, University of New Brunswick, Fredericton.

2017   A Historical Approach to Shifting Technologies of Ceramic Manufacture at Gaspereau Lake, Kings County, Nova Scotia. PhD dissertation, McMaster University, Hamilton, Ontario.

2018   Shifting priorities apparent in Middle and Late Woodland ceramics from Nova Scotia. *North American Archaeologist* 39(4):260–291.

2019   The Changing Role of Ceramics During the Woodland Period in the Far Northeast: Evidence from Some Large Ceramic Assemblages in New Brunswick and Nova Scotia. Paper presented at the Canadian Archaeological Association 50th Annual Meeting, Québec.

2020   A Direct-Dated Ceramic AMS Sequence from the Gaspereau Lake Reservoir Site Complex, Maine–Maritimes Region, Northeastern North America. *Radiocarbon* 62(2):419–437.

Wright, J. V.

1967   *The Laurel Tradition and the Middle Woodland Period.* National Museum of Canada Bulletin No. 217. Department of the Secretary of State, Ottawa.

1972   *Ontario Prehistory: An Eleven-Thousand-Year Archaeological Outline.* National Museum of Man, Ottawa.

1994   The Prehistoric Transportation of Goods in the St. Lawrence River Basin. In *Prehistoric Exchange Systems in North America*, edited by Timothy G. Baugh and Jonathon E. Ericson, pp. 47–72. Springer, New York.

13

THE WOODLAND PERIOD IN THE EASTERN TOWNSHIPS, QUEBEC
Adaptation and Continuity

Claude Chapdelaine

Abstract

The Eastern Townships constitute a region characterized by the Appalachian Plateau connected to the St. Lawrence River through the Saint-François and Chaudière Rivers. This chapter will summarize data related to the Early, Middle, and Late Woodland, providing the first synthesis of the archaeology of the area occupied by hunter-gatherers with a nomadic way of life. The connections with the Early Woodland Meadowood Interaction Sphere, the early Middle Woodland pseudo-scallop-shell horizon, the late Middle Woodland Melocheville ceramic tradition, the early Late Woodland Owasco style, and the St. Lawrence Iroquoians of the late Late Woodland are examined within the perspective of an evolving adaptive system with changing networks. The material culture, mostly ceramics and lithic tools and debitage, will be discussed, as well as the major lithic sources, to provide a better picture of the Woodland period from 3000 BP to Contact and to discuss cultural continuity and change within the study area.

Résumé

Les données archéologiques appuient la participation des groupes de l'Estrie au réseau d'interaction Meadowood du Sylvicole inférieur, un accès facilité par la connexion entre la vallée du Saint-Laurent et la rivière Saint-François. Cependant, c'est durant le Sylvicole moyen avec l'intégration de la poterie décorée d'empreintes ondulantes que la région semble être plus occupée. Au cours du Sylvicole supérieur, il n'y a aucun indice de changements majeurs dans le schème d'établissement, le réseau lithique et surtout pas dans l'utilisation des vases en terre cuite. Le contact avec les Iroquoiens du Saint-Laurent apparait sporadique. Un mode de vie axé sur le nomadisme se maintient tout au long du Sylvicole et la question de la continuité culturelle sera abordée. La culture matérielle, en particulier la poterie, les outils en pierre et le débitage, sera abordée ainsi que les principales sources de matières premières lithiques dans le but de présenter une image plus complète du Sylvicole de 3000 AA au Contact dans notre aire d'étude.

Affiliation

– Département d'anthropologie, Université de Montréal, Quebec, Canada

The Eastern Townships of Quebec have received little archaeological attention beyond the pioneer efforts of archaeologist René Lévesque in the early 1960s, under the influence of J.V. Wright (Lévesque 1962), and sporadic research by Bertrand Morin in the early 1980s (Morin 1981), followed by intensive research at the Bishop (BiEx-2) and île du Collège (BiEx-3) sites at Lennoxville (Transit Analyse 1990, 1991, 1992, 1995) and at BkEu-2 (Transit Analyse 1993) within a Cultural Resource Management context. Continuous fieldwork started in the second half of the 1990s with the efforts of Éric Graillon to uncover data from various new sites and on old sites like Vieux-Pont (Graillon 2001a; Dumont 2010). Within the Saint-François River Basin, fieldwork in the East Angus area was productive (Graillon 1999), with the discovery of several sites, including a Middle Archaic site identified as being part of the Gulf of Maine Archaic tradition (Chapdelaine et al. 2015). Pottery was found in limited number on a single site and few lithic tools could be attributed to the Woodland period. Graillon's excavations at the Gaudreau site near Weedon (Graillon 2013; Graillon et al. 2012) provided a large sample of pottery and lithic tools, indicating a strong Woodland presence at the confluence of the Saumon and Saint-François Rivers. Downstream from Sherbrooke, the recent discovery of the Kruger 3 site at Brompton also contributes to our understanding of the period (Graillon 2014; Graillon and Chapdelaine 2018, 2019). The Magog River was likely an important route to link Lake Memphrémagog to the Saint-François River. Site BhFa-3, excavated by the consulting firm Arkéos (1999), provides a useful addition to our database for the region (Joyal 1999). This site contains a large pottery assemblage pertaining mostly to the late Middle Woodland.

Within the second major hydrographic basin of the Eastern Townships, the Chaudière River, most of the known sites were surface collected over a long period by avocational archaeologists Jean Cliche and Catherine Rancourt. Their collections of about 35 sites were registered and made available for study (Graillon 1996, 1997a, 1997b, 1997c, 1998a, 1998b, 1998c, 2001b, 2012). The resulting database proved so attractive that I decided to move the Université de Montréal summer field school from Pointe-du-Buisson near Montréal to this sector of the Eastern Townships. Between 2001 and 2009, we worked on several sites, most of them multi-component, and we recovered new data on the Woodland occupation of the area dominated by Lake Mégantic (Chapdelaine 2007, 2009).

From this short review of the archaeological efforts to uncover data for the Eastern Townships, a few comments are in order. The region is not well covered, and several tributaries of the two major hydrographic basins still await basic surveys. Nevertheless, the total number of registered sites for the region is 105. A total of 23 sites are considered to have at least one Woodland component, and 19 sites contain pottery (table 13.1). Some radiocarbon dates are available, on which one can build a solid regional sequence (table 13.2). The Woodland components represent 22% of the known sites (23/105). Considering the scarcity of pottery at several of the Woodland sites, it is highly probable that the number of Woodland sites is underrepresented in this region based on the likelihood that several sites without pottery probably date to between 3000 BP and the Contact period.

Assuming that the connection between the region under study and the St. Lawrence Lowlands was the prevailing interaction force, the systematics for the Eastern Townships are strongly influenced by the chronology and cultural framework used along the St. Lawrence River. In return, the chronological and cultural framework of the St. Lawrence Lowlands, in its Quebec portion, is basically aligned to the framework developed in New York state by Ritchie (1980 [1969]). The terminology used in this chapter to present the prehistory of the Eastern Townships is thus the one currently used in Quebec and New York state, and differs slightly from the New England—Maritimes region, especially regarding the division of Ceramic-era phases (cf. Petersen and Sanger 1991).

It is thus no surprise that we divide the Woodland period into three subperiods: Early, Middle, and Late, with phases for the latter two. The first objective is to present a survey of the key sites and of the cultural markers for each subperiod. The adaptive system will be addressed from an empirical point of view. Settlement patterns, subsistence, and the identification of pottery styles, types of projectile points, and other cultural markers will be looked at in order to identify the driving forces behind the adaptation to local resources. Another topic will consider the major lithic sources and reconstructing the evolving interaction networks over time. The last matter will be to address whether the region was a theatre of major population movements or, rather, of continuity. The question of the cultural origin(s) of the Eastern Townships Indigenous settlers will be addressed by comparing data related to an interior adaptation to local sources against the external forces or influences visible within the assemblages.

The Eastern Townships: An Administrative Region with Ecological Features

The Appalachian Mountains are probably the most important feature of what is known as the Eastern Townships (ET) of Quebec. A few mountain peaks can be seen across the landscape and a number of lakes occupy the low altitudes, such as Lake Memphrémagog, Magog, Massawippi, Brompton, Saint-François, Mégantic, and Lac aux Araignées. The region is drained by a few rivers, mostly flowing from south to north, the main of which are the Saint-François and Chaudière, both leading to the St. Lawrence River. Several rivers feed into the Saint-François, the most important ones from west to east: Magog, Massawippi (including the Tomifobia, Niger, Coaticook, Moes, and Ascot Rivers), Eaton, and Saumon (figure 13.1).

The Saint-François River basin is one of the largest in the province of Quebec, covering 10,230 km², of which 75% is forested, 20% is under cultivation, and 4% consists of lakes and rivers (Graillon and Chapdelaine 2018:34). During the Woodland period, it is assumed that rivers and lakes within this hydrographic system were traversed using canoes. In this perspective, it is fundamental to consider our study area as an open and connected region, and not as an isolated region within the Appalachian Plateau.

The ET unfolds to the north via the Saint-François and Chaudière Rivers, with easy connection to the St. Lawrence River. They are also connected to the south by several rivers, such as the Magog River, leading to Memphrémagog Lake, and with portage access to the source of the Missisquoi River, flowing west to Lake Champlain, and the Coaticook River, with its source in Vermont.

Within the ET, how can one reach the Chaudière River from the Saint-François? Is it an easy route? The most logical access is to travel up the Saumon River to the base of Mount Mégantic. From there, a portage route described by Abenaki informants to David Thompson during an exploration of the Saint-François River in 1834, for the British American Land Company, led to a brook that empties into the lower part of Lake Mégantic (Verity and Péloquin 2011:46). From Lake Mégantic, it is possible to reach northern Maine through a mountain pass at Coburn Gore via the Dead River, which leads to the Kennebec River.

The ET is thus a region that is quite traversable, with various cultural influences identified in the archaeological record. It is also crucial to state that the climatic conditions during the time from 3000 BP to Contact were comparable to those prevailing today (Richard 1995). ET climatic conditions did not favour a sedentary life based on agriculture. During the entire prehistoric period, its inhabitants had a mobile way of life based on hunting, fishing, and gathering. Through their mobility, canoeing along rivers, they were aware of what was going on elsewhere in neighbouring regions, whether the St. Lawrence Lowlands to the north, the Lake Champlain area to the west, the Connecticut Valley to the south, or the Kennebec Valley to the east. Were the ET settlers influenced by these regions? The archaeological record will be examined in order to look for answers to this question, following a threefold division of the Woodland period, below.

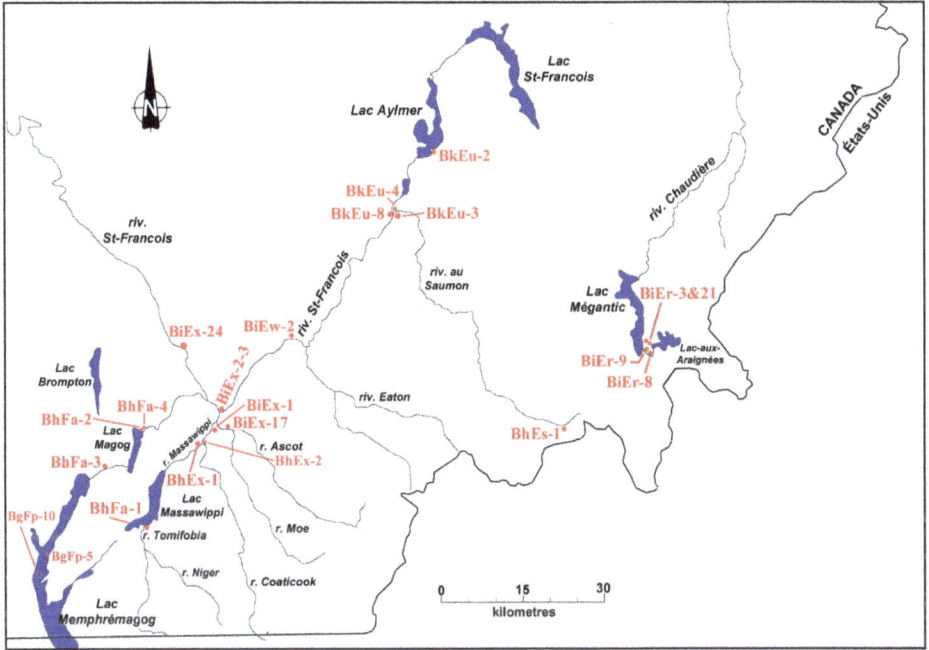

Figure 13.1. Distribution of Woodland sites in the Eastern Townships mentioned in this chapter.

Early Woodland

This time division of the Woodland Period is marked by the appearance of pottery and the development of the Meadowood Interaction Sphere (Taché 2011; Granger 1979). The identification of Early Woodland components relies mostly on the presence of pottery and lithic markers such as projectile points, end scrapers, and cache blades made of Onondaga chert (table 13.1). The presence of pottery known as Vinette 1 in the ET is identified at only two sites (Gaudreau and Bishop); the eight remaining sites attributed to the Early Woodland possess lithic evidence: Nepress, Nebessis, Gros Bouleau, and Chalet in the Lake Mégantic area, and Point Merry, Butler, Kruger 3, and BhEx-1 in the Saint-François basin (figure 13.1).

The Point Merry site is assigned to the Early Woodland because of a bird stone recovered from a probable burial mound destroyed in the early 1900s (Lévesque 1962). The bird stone is considered as a diagnostic type associated with the Meadowood Interaction Sphere (Clermont 1990). There are only six such specimens found in southern Quebec (Tremblay 2005). The complete bird stone from Point Merry in Magog does not have pop-eyes, and the polish of the raw material, probably a laminated siltstone (Graillon 1995:6), is excellent (figure 13.2). The length of the specimen is 17 cm, its body thickness 2 cm. It has four perforations, whereby it may be attached to a throwing stick. This type of artifact is also present at the Butler site, along the Ascot River (figure 13.3). The incomplete bird stone was collected at the Butler site by an avocational archaeologist, James Hosking, in a cultivated field along the Ascot River before its junction with the Massawippi River (Graillon 1994). This artifact is associated with a projectile point, a cache blade, and three triangular bifacial endscrapers made of Onondaga chert (Graillon 1994:80). Two small fragments of undecorated pottery may belong to this Early Woodland component, but they are too small to be assigned to the Vinette 1 pottery type.

In the Lake Mégantic area, four multi-component sites have produced several tools made of Onondaga chert. At BiEr-8, nine triangular bifacial endscrapers were identified, but only seven are made of Onondaga chert. It was sufficient to propose an Early Woodland occupation (Corbeil 2007:152, 172). The other site, BiEr-9, is different, with four triangular, bifacial endscrapers, none made of Onondaga chert (Chapdelaine and Beaulieu 2007:203). There is one in Mount Kineo rhyolite, two of red Munsungun chert, and one of green chert that may come from the Québec City region. These four triangular bifacial endscrapers are considered imitations of the highly distinctive type of endscraper made of Onondaga chert and circulating through the Meadowood Interaction Sphere (Taché 2011).

Two sites attributed to the Early Woodland time without pottery in the Lake Mégantic area are considered to be places where rituals took place but are not necessarily habitation sites. At Nebessis (BiEr-3) and Nepress (BiEr-21), a ritual occurred with the use of fire. At Nebessis, a concentration of endscrapers and utilized flakes made of chert were burned, along with red ochre and a quartz crystal, found near a hearth. Several tools exhibit potlids, and one fragmented triangular endscraper is a typical Meadowood tool made of Onondaga chert (Vidal 2007:238-239). At Nepress, a cache of bifaces made of Munsungun chert is accompanied by one Meadowood point and is associated to a triangular, bifacial endscraper of Onondaga chert and a fireplace dated to the Early Woodland period (table 13.2; Provençal et al. 2010).

The last site assigned to the Early Woodland without pottery is located at the junction of the Coaticook and Massawippi Rivers. BhEx-1 was first considered an Archaic site by Lévesque, in 1962. New ceramic data indicate that the site was occupied during the Late Woodland. A narrow and well-made biface from Lévesque's collection, possibly a cache blade, knapped from a red and yellow jasper, is tentatively assigned to the Early Woodland (figure 13.4). The retouch on the dorsal side has produced a ridge along the centre, and the knapping quality is high on both sides. The base is incomplete but seems to be straight or square, giving this biface a form similar to the bifaces from the Tozer site, in New Brunswick (Wintemberg 1937).

Two sites have produced Vinette 1 pottery, the oldest pottery in the Northeast: Gaudreau and Bishop. At both sites, a rim sherd with cord marks on the exterior and interior surfaces was identified. At Bishop, it is associated with a typical triangular, bifacial endscraper made of Onondaga chert (Clermont and Chapdelaine 1981:231, 234). These two cultural markers indicate a small occupation dating to the Early Woodland, and they could be imports or exotic artifacts that circulated within a larger network.

The same conclusion applies to the Gaudreau site, given the presence of more artifacts related to the Early Woodland. During the three-year project (2011–2013), a large quantity of artifacts was collected, encompassing 9,000 years of occupation, from the Late Palaeoindian (Graillon et al. 2012) to the Archaic (Gauvin 2015; Potter 2017) and all the Woodland periods to the Contact period. The Gaudreau site is thus multi-component and illustrates the problem of mixed assemblages deposited in a soil lacking distinct stratigraphic layers. The single Vinette 1 rim sherd identified at Gaudreau is associated with a small collection of lithic tools made of Onondaga chert (figure 13.5A), including nine triangular bifacial endscrapers (seven are clearly Onondaga chert, the other two grey chert), four cache blades (two are clearly Onondaga chert, one is red Munsungun chert, and one a black chert). A large biface made of Onondaga chert may be added to this collection (figure 13.5B), as well as a side-notched projectile point made of Onondaga chert recycled into an endscraper (figure 13.5A). A unique pendant with two perforations was found on the lower terrace of the Gaudreau site, where no artifact was identified to the Archaic period. The pendant may well date to the Early Woodland period (figure 13.6). The raw material might be a grey schist (Burke, pers. comm. 2019) and there has been a chemical reaction on one face, which may be related to the soil's acidity or the result of a ritual that left no trace otherwise.

Very small body fragments with cord marks on both sides have been tentatively identified as Early Woodland at the BiEx-24 site in Brompton (Graillon and Chapdelaine 2019). More compelling is the finding of a typical triangular, bifacial endscraper made of Onondaga chert. A pit feature of black soil within a sand matrix at 41 cm below the surface was associated in the field to a Woodland occupation. This shallow-pit feature was rich in charcoal, and an AMS (accelerator mass spectrometry) date of 2490 ± 20 BP supports the presence of a small Early Woodland component (table 13.2). It should be noted that a triangular bifacial endscraper made of black chert was also found (Graillon 2014).

A total of 10 components have been attributed to the Early Woodland in the ET, four from the Lake Mégantic region and six from within the Saint-François River Basin. The presence of tools made of Onondaga chert and, in particular, triangular bifacial endscrapers constitutes the basis of an affiliation to the Early Woodland, and the deep influence of the Meadowood culture is clearly visible in four sites, containing evidence of ritual practices similar to the ones discovered by archaeologists in the heartland of the Meadowood Interaction Sphere (Taché 2011).

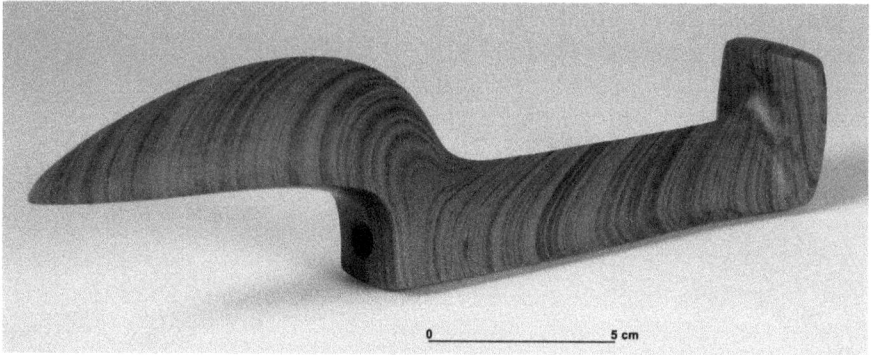

Figure 13.2. Bird stone from Point Merry, Magog.
Source: Musée de la nature et des sciences de Sherbrooke.

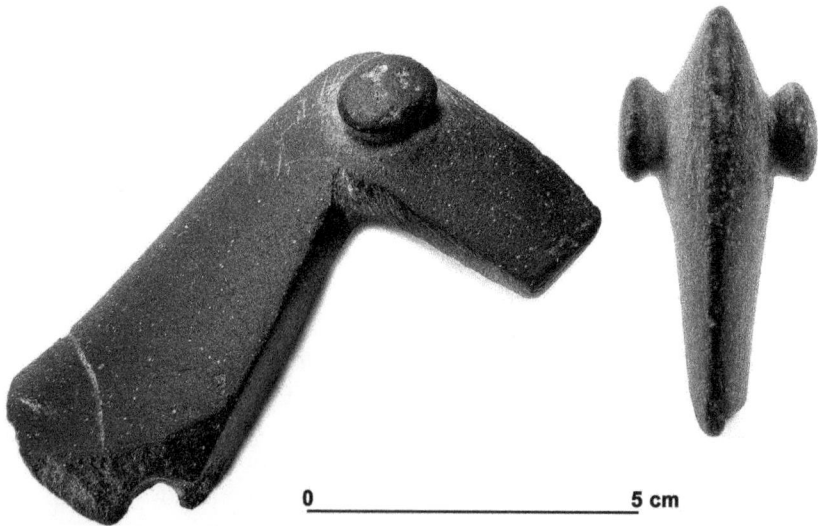

Figure 13.3. Bird stone from the Butler Site, Ascot River.
Source: Photo by Michael McCoy.

Figure 13.4. Biface made of red and yellow jasper from BhEx-1, junction of Saint-François and Coaticook Rivers.
Source: Photo by Claude Chapdelaine.

Figure 13.5A. Various Early Woodland tools from Gaudreau Site: upper row—small triangular, bifacial endscrapers made of Onondaga chert; middle row—long triangular, bifacial endscrapers made of Onondaga chert except BkEu-8.2070 made of Kineo rhyolite; lower row—cache blades made of Onondadag chert (BkEu-8.1481 & 2440), burnt red Munsungun chert (BkEu-8.1836) and BkEu-8.3040 made of black chert. *Source:* Photo by Claude Chapdelaine.

Figure 13.5B. Large biface made of Onondaga chert (BkEu-8.416) from Gaudreau Site.
Source: Photo by Claude Chapdelaine.

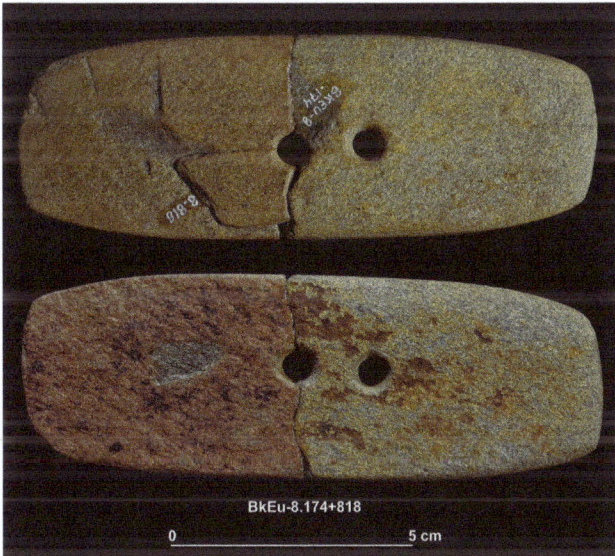

Figure 13.6. Pendant with two perforations from Gaudreau site.
Source: Photo by Claude Chapdelaine.

Table 13.1. List of Woodland sites in the Eastern Townships and selected attributes

Borden Code	Site*	Sector	Early Woodland	E. M. W.**	L. M. W.	E. L. W.	L. L. W.	Pottery	Lithic Objects	Remarks
BiEr-3	Nebessis	Mégantic	YES					NO	YES	Ritual with hearth
BiEr-8	Gros Bouleau	Mégantic	YES		YES		YES	YES	YES	Multicomponent
BiEr-9	Chalet	Mégantic	YES	YES	YES		YES	YES	YES	Multicomponent
BiEr-21	Nepress	Mégantic	YES					NO	YES	Cache and hearth
BkEu-2	Lac Aylmer	Lac Aylmer		YES	YES		YES	YES	YES	Multicomponent
BkEu-3	Fortier	Weedon		YES				YES	Platform pipe	Multicomponent
BkEu-8	Gaudreau	Weedon	YES	YES	YES	YES	YES	YES	YES	Base camp
BiEw-2	Cascades	East Angus		YES				YES		Small camp
BiEx-1	Vieux-Pont	Massawippi River		YES	YES			YES		Base camp
BiEx-2	Bishop	Lennoxville	YES	YES	YES	YES	YES	YES	YES	Multicomponent
BiEx-3	Ile du Collège	Lennoxville		YES	YES	YES	YES	YES	YES	Multicomponent
BiEx-17	Butler	Ascot River	YES					YES	Bird stone	Large site
BiEx-24	Kruger 3	Brompton	YES	YES	YES	YES		YES	YES	Portage site
BhEx-1		Coaticook R.	YES			YES	YES	YES	Cache blade	Multicomponent
BhEx-2		Coaticook R.			YES			YES		Small camp
BhFa-1	Tomifobia	Tomifobia		YES	YES	YES	YES	YES	YES	Base camp
BhFa-2	Pointe Merry	Magog	YES					NO	Bird stone	Ritual site?
BhFa-3	Magog	Magog		YES	YES			YES	YES	Base camp
BhFa-4	Maison Merry	Magog		YES	YES			YES		Single decorated fragment
BgFb-5		Memphrémagog		YES				YES		Underwater vessel
BgFb-10		Memphrémagog				YES		YES		Underwater vessel
BhEs-1	Laflamme	Montagne de Marbre			YES			NO	Bifaces	Near mountain pass and quarry

*Name used in the text in place of the Borden Code

** E. M. W.: Early Middle Woodland; L. M. W.: Late Middle Woodland; E. L. W.: Early Late Woodland;

Table 13.2. List of radiocarbon dates for Eastern Townships Woodland sites

Site	Region	Period	Tradition	Date	Remark	Source
BiEr-21	Mégantic	Early Woodland (3000–2400 BP)	Meadowood	3030±40 rcy BP	Charcoal (hearth)	Provençal et al. 2010
BiEx-24	Brompton	Early Woodland (3000–2400 BP)	Meadowood	2490±20 rcy BP	Charcoal (pit)	Graillon and Chapdelaine 2019
BiEr-9	Mégantic	Middle Woodland (2400–1500 BP)	Early	1980±70 rcy BP	Charcoal	Chapdelaine and Beaulieu 2007
BiEr-9	Mégantic	Middle Woodland	Early	101±60 rcy BP	Burnt bone (too young)	Chapdelaine and Beaulieu 2007
BhFa-3	Magog	Late Middle Woodland (1500–1000 BP)	Melocheville	1100±100 rcy BP	Charcoal	Joyal 2000
BhFa-3	Magog	Late Middle Woodland	Melocheville	280±90 rcy BP	Charcoal (too young)	Joyal 2000
BhFa-4	Magog	Late Middle Woodland	Melocheville?	1230±20 rcy BP	Charcoal	Artefactuel 2015
BhEs-1	Montagne de Marbre	Woodland (3000–500 BP)	?	850±40 rcy BP	Charcoal	Graillon 1997a
BiEx-2	Lennoxville	Middle Woodland (2400–1500 BP)	Early	1550±90 rcy BP	Charcoal	Transit Analyse 1995
BiEx-3	Lennoxville	Late Woodland	Owasco-like & Iroquoian	670±50 rcy BP	Charcoal	Transit Analyse 1995
BiEx-3	Lennoxville	(1000–400 BP)	Owasco-like & Iroquoian	730±60 rcy BP	Charcoal	Transit Analyse 1995
BiEx-3	Lennoxville	Late Woodland	Owasco-like & Iroquoian	690±50 rcy BP	Charcoal	Transit Analyse 1995
BiEx-3	Lennoxville	(1000–400 BP)	Owasco-like & Iroquoian	660±60 rcy BP	Charcoal	Transit Analyse 1995

Middle Woodland

The Middle Woodland time interval is long, at 1,400 years, between 2400 and 1000 BP. It is prudent to divide it into early (2400 to 1500 BP) and late (1500 to 1000 BP) Middle Woodland. Stylistic changes of pottery and new lithic tool types support this division.

Early Middle Woodland

The dominant pottery style of this period is the pseudo-scallop-shell impression. Collarless vessels are decorated with a tool producing wavy lines applied to the surface in various techniques, including direct stamping, stab, and drag, or push-pull and rocker-stamping. A total of 10 sites have produced this type of pottery (table 13.2). In the Saint-François River Basin, Vieux-Pont and Gaudreau are the key sites, and BiEr-9 in the Chaudière River Basin is the only site with pottery decorated with pseudo-scallop shell.

The Vieux-Pont site on the Massawippi River, not far from its junction with the Saint-François River, was recorded early in the 1950s (Lévesque 1962) and most of the collection comes from surface collecting by many avocational archaeologists over several decades. Limited fieldwork was carried out to verify the site's integrity (Graillon 2001a). The results led to the conclusion that the site is mostly disturbed and excavation was not recommended. Most of the decorated pottery belongs to the early Middle Woodland style (Dumont 2010), and an almost complete vessel (figure 13.7A) that was recovered is an excellent illustration of this style.

The Gaudreau site at Weedon generated a large sample of pottery fragments (Graillon 2013) that has not yet received the attention it deserves. Several large rim sherds are decorated with typical pseudo-scallop-shell impressions (figure 13.7B).

BiEr-9, or the Chalet site, is a large riverine site covering 150 m along the Araignée River (Chapdelaine and Beaulieu 2007). A minimum of four vessels and 11 body sherds is identified to the pseudo-scallop-shell tradition.

The other seven sites identified to this time period are characterized by a small amount of pottery, often less than five fragments, indicating a short occupation or the lack of importance of earthenware tools in the daily life of ET people. The general impression is that a mobile subsistence pattern was still the dominant adaptive strategy, and possibly the integration of pottery was less important than the advantages it might procure. At sites like Vieux-Pont, Gaudreau, and Chalet, the presence of a substantial amount of pottery could be the result of an extended stay at a base camp or the accumulation of several short-term occupations.

A monitor pipe or platform pipe made of steatite or soap stone was reported from BkEu-3 at Weedon (Lévesque 1962). This unique lithic implement is now lost, but, based on the photographs (figure 13.8), the base was heavily incised or grooved for an unknown purpose. This type of smoking pipe related to the Hopewell Interaction Sphere is unique in the ET and its chronological position remains unclear, like the specimens from Pointe-du-Buisson that were associated to the late Middle Woodland (Chapdelaine 1982; Gates St-Pierre and Chapdelaine 2013) but could also be of the early Middle Woodland period.

Late Middle Woodland

The dominant pottery style of this period uses cord-wrapped-stick impressions. Pottery decorated with dentate impressions is also known. One stylistic trait developed along the St. Lawrence Lowlands at that time is the use of an implement to make exterior circular punctates producing interior bosses. This decorative pattern is characteristic of the Melocheville tradition (Gates St-Pierre 2006). Projectile points such as Jack's Reef Corner Notched and Levanna types are also useful to identify components dating to this time period. A total of 10 sites have produced pottery decorated with cord-wrapped-stick impressions (table 13.1), but only one has a sizeable collection: BhFa-3 (Joyal 1999). Most of the rim sherds at this site are decorated following the style of the Melocheville tradition, which indicates a strong relationship with the St. Lawrence Lowlands (figure 13.9). At the Gaudreau site, the second in importance for this period, Jack's Reef Corner Notched points made of high-quality chert co-occur with rim sherds of the Melocheville tradition to indicate that the site was occupied with some intensity during the entire Middle Woodland. Two points that resemble Greene and Port Maitland types can be added to this component (figure 13.10).

The remaining eight sites are poor in pottery, with few fragments, suggesting short occupation (Artefactuel 2015; Graillon 2018). The general impression is that a mobile subsistence pattern was the dominant adaptive strategy, and the use of pottery was of secondary importance in daily life. It should be noted that seven sites contained pottery of the early and late Middle Woodland—providing a good argument to support continuity based on a stable adaptive system.

The chronological position of the Jack's Reef Corner Notched points between 1500 and 1000 BP is based on good evidence for southern Quebec (Gates St-Pierre and Chapdelaine 2013) and is a cultural marker of the late Middle Woodland. The Levanna point, however, is not restricted to that period. This triangular point has been found at several sites in association with pottery decorated with cord-wrapped stick (Clermont and Chapdelaine 1982; Joyal 1999; Petersen and Power 1985). However, on several sites of the ET where there is no pottery of this type, the presence of Levanna points is not automatically associated with the late Middle Woodland, especially when Late Woodland pottery is also recorded at the site. This is the case at the BiEr-8 site (Corbeil 2007). The Levanna-point type has been identified on several sites with Late Woodland pottery, and is assigned to this time period.

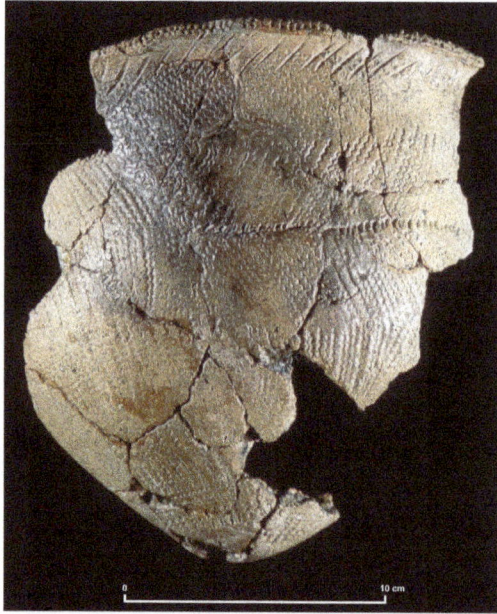

Figure 13.7A. An early Middle Woodland decorated vessel from Vieux-Pont Site.
Source: Photo by Claude Chapdelaine.

BkEu-8.651

BkEu-8.2072

BkEu-8.1864+1894

Figure 13.7B. Early Middle Woodland decorated rim sherds from Gaudreau Site.
Source: Photo by Claude Chapdelaine.

Figure 13.8. Middle Woodland monitor (platform) pipe from BkEu-3 at Weedon. *Source:* Photo modified from Lévesque 1962.

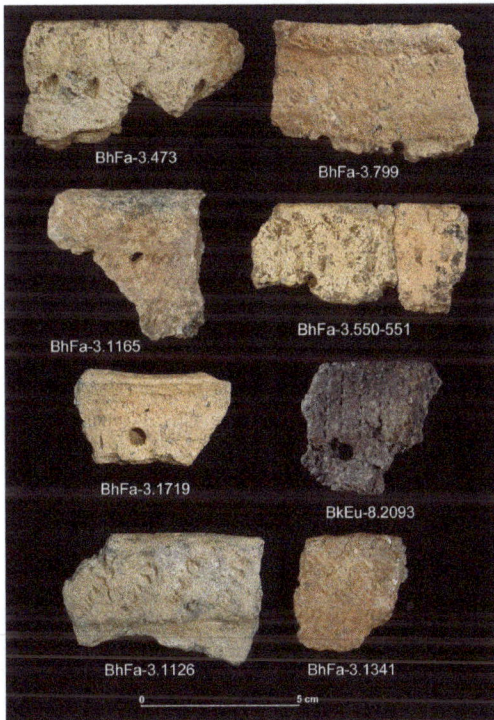

Figure 13.9. Late Middle Woodland cord wrap stick decorated rim sherds from BhFa-3 at Magog and one dentate decorated rim sherd from BkEu-8, Gaudreau site at Weedon. *Source:* Photo by Claude Chapdelaine.

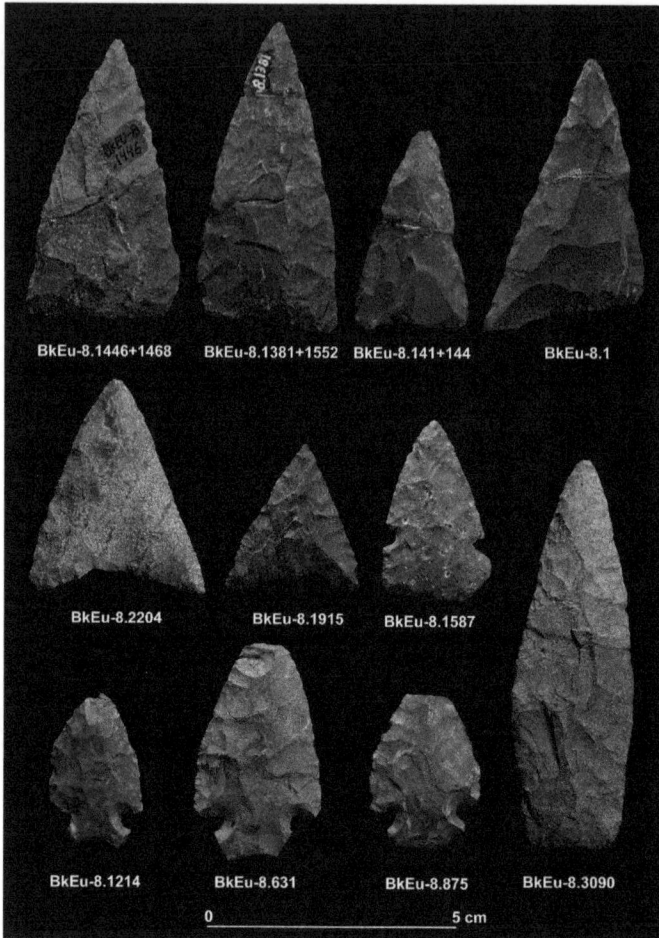

Figure 13.10. Projectile points associated to the late Middle Woodland component at Gaudreau site: upper row—large Levanna points made of local red slate; middle row—two Levanna points made of New Hampshire rhyolite (BkEu-8.2204) and grey chert (BkEu-8.1915) and one Port Maitland in mount Kineo rhyolite (BkEu-8.1587); lower row—three Jack's Reef Corner Notched made of Onondaga chert and a Greene point made of hornfels (BkEu-8.3090).
Source: Photo by Claude Chapdelaine.

Late Woodland

Major changes in the process of sedentarization happened at a relatively fast pace between 1200 and 800 BP in the St. Lawrence Lowlands. Those changes are visible to the west and north of the ET in settlement size, faunal remains, and material culture. The development of distinctive pottery styles allows for the identification of Late Woodland pottery with collared vessels and new, complex geometric motifs. It is possible to divide the 600 years of this time period (1000 to 400 BP) in three subperiods (early, middle, late). If the three subperiods are the accepted framework in the St. Lawrence Lowlands, two subperiods, an early Late Woodland (1000–700 BP) and a late Late Woodland (700–400 BP), are sufficient for the ET.

The sites identified to the early Late Woodland in the ET are defined mostly by a general similarity with Owasco pottery from New York state (Ritchie 1980 [1969]; Ritchie and Funk 1973; Ritchie and MacNeish 1949). The presence of Levanna points is attested on four of these sites containing Owasco-like pottery. The distinctive motifs with cord-wrapped-stick stamping are recognized at six sites (table 13.1) and large vessels were found at Gaudreau and île du Collège at Lennoxville (figure 13.11). An almost complete Owasco-like vessel found at the underwater site BgFp-10 in Lake Memphrémagog is curated at the Musée de la nature et des sciences de Sherbrooke (Graillon 2000).

The late Late Woodland time period is identified at seven sites in the ET, but the distinctive pottery is limited in number. The presence of a well-made collar decorated with a complex geometric design is typical of the earthenware produced after 700 BP, along with notching at the base of the collar and the use of incision and circular punctates under castellated rims. Considering the influences visible in the ET from the St. Lawrence Lowlands during the Melocheville tradition, and the intrusion of Owasco pottery by the same route, it is curious to see few St. Lawrence Iroquoian rim sherds of the late Late Woodland style. At Gaudreau, it is interesting to note the use of large circular punctates below a collar that is decorated with an unusual motif (figure 13.12). This vessel is not a conventional Iroquoian pot; an Algonquian potter is probably behind its production. A second vessel is more typical of the Iroquoian style, with notching at the base of collar, the complex motif, and two vertical incised lines below an incipient castellation (figure 13.12). A single smoking pipe of the trumpet type was found at Gaudreau and it may be the best indication of trade with Iroquoians (figure 13.12). The smoking pipe was left undecorated, and it is thus difficult to propose that a St. Lawrence Iroquoian made it. The surface does not have the usual finish of an Iroquoian smoking pipe, but the shape, paste, temper, and firing indicate a well-made specimen.

In the Lake Mégantic area, few vessels are identified to the late Late Woodland, and none are typical of the St. Lawrence Iroquoian tradition (Chapdelaine and Kennedy 2007). This came as a surprise to the author because, in the early 1990s, while working on St. Lawrence Iroquoian sites in the Cap Tourmente lowlands, northeast of Québec City (Chapdelaine 1993), an interaction between this region and Maine was established based on a strong correlation between the presence of Mount Kineo rhyolite on St. Lawrence Iroquoian sites (Tremblay 1997). It was assumed that some St. Lawrence Iroquoian vessels moving up the Chaudière River were used and broken on Mégantic sites since this type of pottery was found at several sites in Maine (Petersen 1990).

The late Late Woodland in the ET is identified on eight sites and not one site is a single component (table 13.1). On these multicomponent sites, the number of vessels identified to the late Late Woodland is few compared to pottery from other periods. This situation seems to suggest the interior population was less affected by what was going on in the St. Lawrence Lowlands after 700 BP. It is possible that new tensions or conflicts occurred, leading the interior population to avoid Iroquoians and be more self-sufficient.

Discussion

Our study area comprises two major river basins. The Chaudière Basin, in particular the Lake Mégantic region, was the centre of a long-term archaeological project, between 2002 and 2012 (Burke et al. 2014; Chapdelaine 2011, 2014, 2017; Chapdelaine and Corbeil 2017). The cultural sequence of this area is already published (Chapdelaine 2009), and the conclusions from the project are summarized below in conjunction with a discussion of the available data, mostly unpublished, from the Saint-François River Basin.

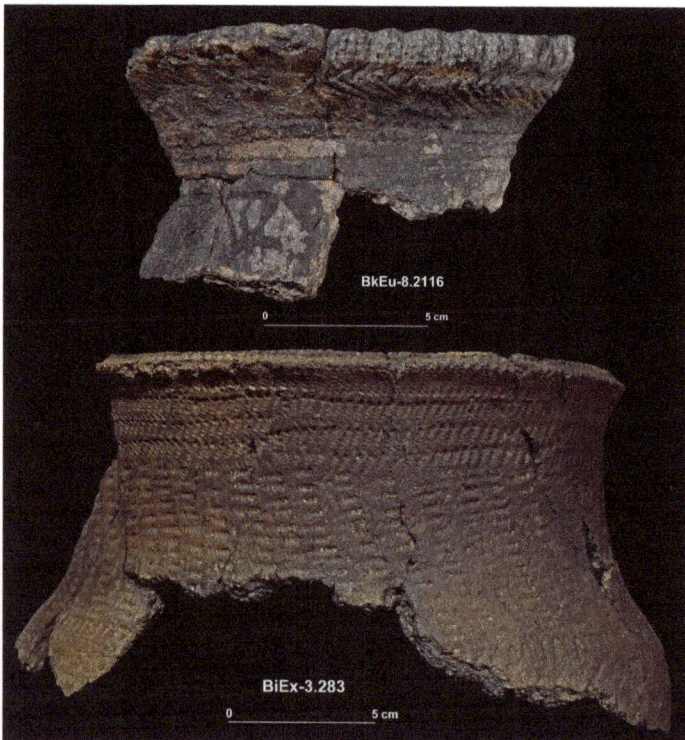

Figure 13.11. Two early Late Woodland rim sherds: BkEu-8.2116 from Gaudreau and BiEx-3.283 from Ile du Collège.
Source: Photos by Claude Chapdelaine (*above*) and Jolyane Saule with Claude Chapdelaine (*below*).

Figure 13.12. Late Late Woodland rim sherds and a smoking pipe from Gaudreau Site.
Source: Photo by Claude Chapdelaine.

Trends in the Settlement Pattern and Subsistence

The Lake Mégantic area is considered a more remote area, ensconced in the Appalachian Plateau, than the Saint-François River Valley. The groups inhabiting the Lake Mégantic area on a seasonal basis, around the upper Chaudière River and the terraces along the shores of the three major lakes (Mégantic, des Araignées, and des Joncs), were mobile. Sites are thus very small and located along the shorelines, which is unprotected. These sites were occupied during the summer and early fall, and it is no surprise that the most common tool is the scraping tool, used to prepare fur clothing toward the cold season. Soil acidity resulted in few faunal remains, except for small burnt bones on several sites in the two basins. Fish are underrepresented, and beaver is the dominant identified species. Cervids, bear, small rodents such as muskrat and porcupine, and turtles have been identified.

The most basic trend visible in the Woodland sites of the ET is continuity, especially in the location of sites and the presumed subsistence pattern based on hunting, fishing, and gathering. All the sites are located near a river or lake, and they are occupied during the warmer months. Only the Laflamme site (BhEs-1) found near Montagne de Marbre, a rhyolite source, close to a mountain pass is radiocarbon dated to the late Middle Woodland (table 13.2; Graillon 1997a). The fragmented bifaces found at this site cannot be conclusively assigned to the Woodland occupation. A bevelled axe found was considered by the excavators as a cultural marker of the Archaic period (Graillon 1997a:72). No other inland site that can be considered a habitation site has yet been located in our study area, and with the absence of pottery, it is difficult to connect these small settlements to a specific time interval.

Several sites are multi-component and their importance is often associated to a particular landscape (Tilley 1994; Ingold 2000). These sites may be part of a regional itinerary transmitted orally, which would explain a long occupation sequence through time (see Tessier 2017 regarding a site used over a long period as a carrying place near rapids). The accumulation of high artifact diversity helps provide clues to the cultural sequence, and the Gaudreau site is a good example with components ranging from the late Palaeoindian to the late Late Woodland, although it renders difficult the assignation of the assemblages to specific occupations. From our small database of 22 sites, we can divide them into two types of settlement. The first is the rich site, with an accumulation of pottery and lithics that can be either a single component like BhFa-3 (Magog) and BiEx-1 (Vieux-Pont) or a multi-component like BkEu-8 (Gaudreau) and BhFa-1 (Tomifobia). The second type of site with pottery and distinctive lithic tools are considered poor in artifact density and mostly multi-component. As a general conclusion, most of the Woodland sites in the ET are short term, and the number of occupations is the key factor to explain the quantity and diversity of artifacts on each site.

Trends in the Use of Pottery and External Influences

In 2009, we concluded that, for the Lake Mégantic area, the "nomadic way of life, the rolling hills and other environmental conditions of the Méganticois seem to have prevented the use of fragile earthenware vessels on a regular basis" (Chapdelaine 2009:161). This is true for the whole Woodland period of the Mégantic region but not for the Saint-François. Based on the number of estimated vessels, the site of Vieux-Pont was certainly a base camp or a site of repeated stops during the early Middle Woodland, and that BhFa-3, a site on the Magog River, was of the same importance during the late Middle Woodland.

The sites with the largest number of Late Woodland pottery are Bishop, île du Collège, and Gaudreau. Distinctive styles could be identified, in particular the Owasco and Iroquoian traditions, and there are few vessels exhibiting a St. Lawrence Iroquoian influence. The Gaudreau site, located at the strategic junction of the Saumon and Saint-François Rivers, was a popular location during the whole of the Woodland period, and certainly is a site that is key to understanding the major cultural and social trends that occurred during the last 3,000 years.

The use of earthenware vessels as a tool within the adaptive system of a human group is considered here a valuable approach (Arnold 1985; Braun 1983; Skibo 2013). For the people living in the ET, pottery was accessory and its adoption or production was limited, especially within a mobile hunter-gatherer adaptive system. This impression must not be a reason to believe that these groups, adapted to the interior region, did not achieve pottery production. A ceramic study based on neutron-activation analysis seems to indicate that some late Middle Woodland rim sherds from the ET could have been made locally (Chapdelaine and Kennedy 2007). This study needs more data, especially of natural clay samples close to key sites, to make a stronger case (see Tremblay et al., this volume). Although the pottery may have been made locally or obtained in an exchange network, the vessels can always be compared to that produced in neighbouring regions. Starting with the Early Woodland, it is no surprise that Vinette 1 pottery is scarce in the area and was probably a good obtained in exchange for local resources. Only three sites have produced this type of pottery with cord marks on both the exterior and interior surfaces. The rim sherd from the Bishop site (BiEx-2) is the most convincing, followed by the rim sherd from Gaudreau and the small body fragments from Kruger 3 (BiEx-24). In southern Quebec, at the Pointe-du-Buisson site, a rich, multi-component site, Vinette 1 pottery has been identified on several stations (Clermont and Chapdelaine 1982). Since the site is located on a massive clay bed, it was assumed that the Early Woodland pottery was made locally. A neutron-activation analysis was carried out to confirm this hypothesis (Clermont et al. 1999:68). The results were clear for the 24 Vinette 1 pottery samples: they could not have been made with the local, Pointe-du-Buisson clay. They are thus an imported good, as well as the cache blades and triangular, bifacial endscrapers made of Onondaga chert. With these results in mind, it is highly plausible to consider the Vinette 1 pottery in the ET as an exchange good coming from the Meadowood Interaction Sphere, operating on a very large geographic scale, with the St. Lawrence Valley as a major axis.

The first real adoption of pottery occurred in the early Middle Woodland. This type of pottery decorated with pseudo-scallop-shell impression is present on several sites but never in large numbers, except at sites such as Gaudreau and

Vieux-Pont. This decorated pottery is highly visible when present, but its incorporation could be regarded as superficial when considering the length of this time interval, about 900 years (2400–1500 BP). The late Middle Woodland, with a much shorter time interval of about 500 years (1500–1000 BP), presents higher pottery density in the ET. The largest rim sherd collection is located along the Magog River (Joyal 1999) and is linked to the Melocheville tradition, with cord-wrapped-stick impressions and the secondary use of circular punctates producing interior bosses. The presence of late Middle Woodland pottery in the Mégantic region is probably linked to an interior exchange network, while the Saint-François group were exchanging directly with the St. Lawrence Lowlands.

The number of sites exhibiting Late Woodland pottery is smaller than the preceding periods, and not a single site contains a component of that time period that could be a base camp. Since the Late Woodland could be divided into two subperiods, the shorter time interval must be considered. Few vessels identified to the Owasco style support the idea of a continuous link between the St. Lawrence Lowlands and the Saint-François interior group. It should be mentioned that St. Lawrence Lowlands pottery was influenced between 1000 and 700 BP by the Owasco tradition (Chapdelaine 1995). The local tradition imitates motifs common in New York state, but enough distinctions allow for a new concept, the Saint-Maurice interaction network, to account for the differences visible between the Quebec pottery and the Pickering and Owasco traditions (Morin 2001). From this perspective, groups of the Saint-François River Valley were participating in that social network, and we can imagine continuity between this Saint-Maurice network and the Melocheville tradition.

The late Late Woodland, especially between 600 and 400 BP, is normally highly visible in the archaeological record due to collared vessels with complex geometric motifs and well-made vessels with a castellated rim. The Iroquoian style seems to be dominant because of a new settlement pattern in the St. Lawrence Valley based on the construction of longhouses, occupied yearlong, and the integration of agriculture into the subsistence pattern. Large communities occupied these semi-permanent sedentary villages. These sites were occupied for a long period, probably 10 to 20 years, and the result is the production and discard in middens of a large number of broken pots. This feature contrasts with pottery assemblages from mobile hunter-gatherer groups and sedentary Iroquoians (see Moreau et al. 1991 for an assessment of the pottery density in the Lac Saint-Jean area occupied during the Woodland Period by hunter-gatherers). It is thus more likely that pottery innovation came from the Iroquoian world and that Algonquians were obtaining or copying Iroquoian vessels. However, the connection between the interior inhabitants of the Saint-François River and groups from the St. Lawrence Lowlands between 600 and 400 BP is not visible, with very few typical St. Lawrence Iroquoian vessels.

Contacts occurred between these groups, but it is not well supported by the actual ceramic data or by data from the Chaudière River trading route. It should be considered a break in the exchange pattern of pottery, not necessarily the entire network system, as we will see soon with the lithic network. The question that remains to be answered is why late Late Woodland pottery is less visible than pottery from earlier time intervals. The answer will not be a simple one, but what seems to me to be very clear is that the absence or scarcity of St. Lawrence Iroquoian pottery was not replaced by a local tradition. If I am right, it means that the production of pottery by interior groups was never an important adaptive tool, and that there was no increase over time in the use of pottery at summer camps as with Iroquoians at their villages. It seems that the ET inhabitants were less interested in exchanging goods to obtain pottery made by St. Lawrence Iroquoians. Local production probably occurred, and a few pots show an imitation of styles produced elsewhere (Chapdelaine and Kennedy 2007). Our study area lacks a large base camp of the Late Woodland period with a large collection of rim sherds. Based on the available data, the interior groups seem to be less attracted to domestic pottery, and the same could be said about smoking pipes, with a single specimen found at the Gaudreau site. The smoking pipe is of the trumpet form, with no decoration, and the exterior surface is not polished. The shape and craftsmanship quality are good, but it is impossible to determine if this ceramic artifact was made locally or obtained through an exchange network.

As a final comment on pottery, it is worth comparing the ET sequence to the Ceramic periods (CP) defined by Petersen and Sanger (1991) for the Maine and Maritime provinces. There are minimal adjustments to be made between those and our chronological framework. At a general level, based on shape and several technical and stylistic attributes, the Early Woodland and the entire Middle Woodland correspond to CP1-CP4 , while CP5-CP6 are coeval with the Late Woodland. The sequence from the undecorated Vinette 1 vessel to the transition from pseudo-scallop-shell impressions followed by dentate stamp and cord-wrapped-stick impressions is quite similar for the two regions. The distinction of an early Middle Woodland and a middle Middle Woodland, which was innovative in the early 1990s, is now a strong working hypothesis for the St. Lawrence River Valley sequence (Méhault 2017a, 2017b).

The main difference between the ET and Maine–Maritimes occurred during CP4, or late Middle Woodland, with the introduction of shell-tempered pottery along the coast, while the Melocheville tradition influences the inhabitants of the upper Saint-François and Chaudière River valleys. The increase of shell-tempered pottery during CP5 is considered here for the ET as a striking difference with pottery showing stylistic attributes similar to the Owasco tradition and a continuous rejection of shell temper in the process of making pottery.

The distinctions between the two regions are not evident during CP6 or late Late Woodland. A distinctive Algonquian pottery tradition is not yet well defined since influences from the Iroquoian world seem to be shared by both regions (Petersen 1990; Petersen et al. 2004).

Trends in Lithic Tools and External Influences

The most remarkable feature of the lithic industry in the ET is the general use of two local tool stones : quartz and red, silicified mudstone. These local stones are complemented by a general use of Kineo rhyolite from Maine. This external source was easily accessible through a mountain pass connecting the Chaudière River to the Dead and Kennebec Rivers toward Moosehead Lake.

The Appalachian Plateau was easily accessible from the St. Lawrence Valley, and it is no surprise that the Meadowood Interaction Sphere spread into our study area, with its diagnostic artifacts such as Vinette 1 pottery, bird stones, pendants, and numerous lithic tools made of Onondaga chert (mostly endscrapers, and a few points and cache blades). The extension of the Meadowood Interaction Sphere along the St. Lawrence Valley is a well-documented phenomenon (Taché 2011), especially at Pointe-du-Buisson in the Montréal area (Clermont 1978, 1990; Clermont and Chapdelaine 1982) and south of Québec City at Saint-Nicolas near the mouth of the Chaudière River (Chrétien 1995). The Meadowood Interaction Sphere entered the Appalachian Plateau from the Chaudière and Saint-François Rivers. Two ritual sites were documented in the Mégantic region, and exotic goods such as bird stones were recovered from the Saint-François basin, as well as several typical tools made of Onondaga chert. In a few sites, imitations of the typical Meadowood tool types were made out of local stone or from non-local sources from Maine (cache of red Munsungun chert bifaces at Nepress and a large, triangular, bifacial endscraper of Mount Kineo rhyolite at Gaudreau; see figure 13.5A).

Lithic tools as cultural markers for the Middle Woodland are few and the limited number of Jack's Reef Corner Notched points indicate a low exchange intensity for this type of good. It is worth mentioning that several points of this type, popular during the late Middle Woodland, are made of Onondaga chert (see the points from Gaudreau in figure 13.10). The Levanna type has been recorded on several sites and it is often made out of a local stone, like red, silicified mudstone, or from nonlocal material like Mount Jasper rhyolite, from New Hampshire, found at Gaudreau (see figure 13.10). Unfortunately, the Levanna point is not exclusive to the Late Woodland and its presence has been documented at several sites in association with typical late Middle Woodland pottery (Joyal 1999). The value of the Levanna point as a strong chronological marker is thus less useful in our study area while dealing with small sites and limited artifacts.

Two sources from outside our study area show a different density between our two major river basins. To the east, the presence of green Mount Kineo rhyolite is much more popular in the Mégantic region (Burke 2007), although it is consistently present in smaller number on sites in the Saint-François River basin, with the exception of the Gaudreau site. To the west, the Cheshire quartzite from Vermont is found regularly on sites in the Saint-François River Basin and is very rare in the Mégantic region.

Finally, several sites in the Lake Mégantic area have produced a good quantity of radiolarian green chert originating from the Québec City region (Letendre 2007). This green chert seems to be associated with Late Woodland occupations and it may have been exchanged for green Kineo rhyolite. This material occurs on many St. Lawrence Iroquoian sites along the St. Lawrence from the Québec City area to the Saguenay River in the St. Lawrence estuary (Chapdelaine 1993; Plourde 2012; Tremblay 1995). There is green chert in the assemblages of the Saint-François River Basin but it more closely resembles Hathaway chert from Lake Champlain in Vermont or Normanskill from the Hudson River Valley in New York.

Conclusion

The ET is an open region that is part of the Appalachian Plateau. Climate and soils did not readily facilitate or encourage agriculture. During the entire Woodland period, the inhabitants maintained a way of life based on mobility and a diversified exploitation strategy that used all available natural resources. Transport by canoe was fundamental during the warmer months.

This stable adaptive system based on mobility characterizes the whole Woodland period for the ET. The interior groups of the ET were in contact with neighbouring groups and participated in various exchange networks over the 3,000 years studied here. The Meadowood Interaction Sphere of the Early Woodland period is highly visible and the ET was an active participant, albeit on the periphery of this exchange network. Pseudo-scallop-shell decoration characterizes the early Middle Woodland pottery and is the first integration at a moderate scale of this type of domestic tool. The interior inhabitants thus adopted several pottery styles and this seems clear during the late Middle Woodland period with the production of collared or collarless vessels decorated with cord-wrapped stick, occasionally with dentate stamp. This type of decorative technique, with the use of exterior punctates producing interior bosses, is reminiscent of the Melocheville tradition of the St. Lawrence River. The Late Woodland period is still problematic. The number of sites producing pottery typical of this time period is limited. A few vessels are similar to Owasco pottery of New York state. Vessels similar to the transition style occurring between 800 and 600 BP in the St. Lawrence Valley were also registered in the ET. Typical

St. Lawrence Iroquoian pottery is not evident and few vessels can be attributed to the 600 to 400 BP interval.

Finally, the ET is an area connected to the St. Lawrence Valley with indirect access to regions to the south and east, allowing its inhabitants to be open to innovations coming from many directions. Adapted to a dissected plateau above the St. Lawrence Lowlands to the west and within the Appalachian Mountains, the interior settlers of the ET elected to live in a colder climate than their neighbours, exploiting the natural resources and thriving there for 12,000 years.

Acknowledgements

This chapter and recent fieldwork in Brompton and East Angus benefited from the financial support of the Fonds de recherche du Québec—Société et culture via the As^2 research group (Archéoscience/Archéosociale), Department of Anthropology, Université de Montréal. I would like to thank Adrian Burke for his thorough revision of this manuscript and for his generous and judicious comments. Jolyane Saule from Trent University made several constructive comments and she deserves our gratitude. I also acknowledge the input of Éric Graillon and its institution, the Musée de la nature et des sciences de Sherbrooke, for their dedication to fieldwork over the past 10 years, and for allowing me to use data from the Gaudreau site.

References Cited

Arkéos Inc.
1999   Prolongement du réseau de Gazoduc TQM vers le réseau de PNGTS, Travaux archéologiques. Volume 3a: Fouille au site BhFa-3, rivière Magog, Magog. Urgel Delisle & associés. For Gazoduc TQM. Manuscript on file, Ministère de la Culture et des Communications, Québec.

Arnold, Dean E.
1985   *Ceramic Theory and Cultural Process.* Cambridge University Press, Cambridge.

Artefactuel
2015   Fouilles archéologiques historiques et préhistoriques sur le site de la Maison Merry (BhFa-4), Magog. Manuscript on file, ministère de la Culture et des Communications, Quebec.

Braun, David P.
1983   Pots as Tools. In *Archaeological Hammers and Theories*, edited by Arthur S. Keene and James A. Moore, pp. 107–134. Academic Press, New York.

Burke, Adrian
2007   L'économie des matières premières lithiques en Estrie : la perspective géoarchéologique. In *Entre lacs et montagnes au Méganticois, 12 000 ans d'histoire amérindienne*, edited by Claude Chapdelaine, pp. 249–269. Paléo-Québec 32. Recherches amérindiennes au Québec, Montréal.

Burke, Adrian L., Gilles Gauthier, and Claude Chapdelaine
2014   Refining the Palaeoindian Lithic Source Network at Cliche-Rancourt Using XRF. *Archaeology of Eastern North America* 41:101–128.

Chapdelaine, Claude

1982 Les pipes à plateforme de la Pointe-du-Buisson: un système d'échanges à définir. *Recherches amérindiennes au Québec* 12(3):207–215.

1993 Eastern Saint Lawrence Iroquoians In The Cap Tourmente Area. In *Essays In St. Lawrence Iroquoian Archaeology*, edited by James F. Pendergast and Claude Chapdelaine, pp. 87–100. Copetown Press, Dundas, Ontario.

1995 An Early Late Woodland Pottery Sequence East of Lac Saint-Pierre: Definition, Chronology, and Cultural Affiliations. *Northeast Anthropology* 49:77–95.

2009 A Twelve Thousand Years Archaeological Sequence for the Mégantic Lake Area. In *Painting the Past with a Broad Brush: Papers in Honour of James Vallière Wright*, edited by David L. Keenlyside and Jean-Luc Pilon, pp. 143–174. Mercury Series, Archaeology Paper no. 170. Canadian Museum of Civilization, Gatineau, Quebec.

2011 Le site Cliche-Rancourt et le peuplement du sud-est du Québec au Paléoindien Ancien. In *Peuplements et préhistoire en Amériques*, edited by Denis Vialou, pp. 121–138. Collection : Documents Préhistoriques n° 28. Éditions du comité des travaux historiques et scientifiques, Paris.

2014 Douze mille ans d'histoire amérindienne au Québec, le plus vieux chapitre. *Archéologiques* 27:28–47.

2017 L'Archaïque moyen au Méganticois et le site BiEr-6, Lac des Joncs. In *L'Archaïque au Québec, six millénaires d'histoire amérindienne*, edited by Adrian L. Burke and Claude Chapdelaine, pp. 77–114. Paléo-Québec 36. Recherches amérindiennes au Québec, Montréal.

Chapdelaine, Claude (editor)

2007 Entre lacs et montagnes au Méganticois, 12 000 ans d'histoire amérindienne. Paléo-Québec 32. Recherches amérindiennes au Québec, Montréal.

Chapdelaine, Claude, and Simon Beaulieu

2007 Le site du Chalet, un espace de vie complexe. In *Entre lacs et montagnes au Méganticois, 12 000 ans d'histoire amérindienne*, edited by Claude Chapdelaine, pp. 181–218. Paléo-Québec 32. Recherches amérindiennes au Québec, Montréal.

Chapdelaine, Claude, and Pierre Corbeil

2017 Les occupations de l'Archaïque au site Cliche-Rancourt (BiEr-14) au Méganticois. In *L'Archaïque au Québec, six millénaires d'histoire amérindienne*, edited by Adrian L. Burke and Claude Chapdelaine, pp. 271–291. Paléo-Québec 36. Recherches amérindiennes au Québec, Montréal.

Chapdelaine, Claude, Éric Graillon, François Courchesne, Marie-Claude Turmel, Laurence Forget Brisson, François Hardy, Michel Lamothe, and Adrian Burke

2015 Cascades 5, une composante de la tradition de l'Archaïque du Golfe du Maine à East Angus, Estrie, Québec. *Recherches amérindiennes au Québec* XLV(2-3):93–126.

Chapdelaine, Claude, and Greg Kennedy

2007 L'origine de la céramique du Méganticois à l'aide de l'activation neutronique. In *Entre lacs et montagnes au Méganticois, 12 000 ans d'histoire amérindienne*, edited by Claude Chapdelaine, pp. 309–334. Paléo-Québec 32. Recherches amérindiennes au Québec, Montréal.

Chrétien, Yves

1995   Les lames de cache du site Lambert et l'influence de la culture Meadowood dans la région de Québec. In *Archéologies québécoises*, edited by Anne-Marie Balac, Claude Chapdelaine, Norman Clermont, and Françoise Duguay, pp. 185–201. Paléo-Québec 23. Recherches amérindiennes au Québec, Montréal.

Clermont, Norman

1978   Les crémations de Pointe-du-Buisson. *Recherches amérindiennes au Québec* 8(1):3–20.

1990   Le Sylvicole inférieur au Québec. *Recherches amérindiennes au Québec* 20(1):5–17.

Clermont, Norman, and Claude Chapdelaine

1981   Le site préhistorique de Bishop. *Recherches amérindiennes au Québec* 11(3):231–238.

1982   *Pointe-du-Buisson 4 : quarante siècles d'archives oubliées.* Recherches amérindiennes au Québec, Montréal.

Clermont, Norman, Claude Chapdelaine, and Greg Kennedy

1999   D'où vient la poterie Vinette 1 trouvée au Québec méridional? In *L'archéologie sous la loupe. Contributions à l'archéométrie*, edited by Jean-François Moreau, pp. 67–72. Paléo-Québec 29. Recherches amérindiennes au Québec, Montréal.

Corbeil, Pierre

2007   Sur une belle terrasse face au marais: le site du Gros Bouleau. In *Entre lacs et montagnes au Méganticois, 12 000 ans d'histoire amérindienne*, edited by Claude Chapdelaine, pp. 129–180. Paléo-Québec 32. Recherches amérindiennes au Québec, Montréal.

Dumont, Jessica

2010   Le Sylvicole moyen ancien au site Vieux-Pont (BiEx-1) à Lennoxville, analyse descriptive et comparative de la poterie. In *De l'archéologie analytique à l'archéologie sociale*, edited by Brad Loewen, Claude Chapdelaine, and Adrian L. Burke, pp. 219–241. Paléo-Québec 34. Recherches amérindiennes au Québec, Montréal.

Gates St-Pierre, Christian

2006   *Potières du Buisson, la céramique de tradition Melocheville sur le site Hector Trudel.* Mercury Series Archaeology Paper 168. Canadian Museum of Civilization, Gatineau, Quebec.

Gates St-Pierre, Christian, and Claude Chapdelaine

2013   After Hopewell in Southern Québec. *Archaeology of Eastern North America* 4:69–89.

Gauvin, Gaétan

2015   Exchange, Know-hows, and Interpersonal Segmentation: An Assessment of the Archaic Component of the Gaudreau (BkEu-8) Site, Weedon, Quebec. Mémoire de maîtrise, Département d'anthropologie, Université de Montréal, Montréal.

Graillon, Éric

1994   Inventaire de la collection archéologique James Hosking. Centre de recherche et d'animation en archéologie de l'Estrie (CRAAE), East Angus, Quebec.

1995 Dossier sur la pierre aviforme de la Pointe Merry (site BhFa-2). Manuscript on file, ministère de la Culture et des Communications, Quebec.

1996 Inventaire de la collection archéologique Cliche-Rancourt, volume 1 : le lac Aylmer. CRAAE, East Angus, Quebec.

1997a Intervention archéologique sur le site Laflamme (BhEs-1), Municipalité de Notre-Dame-des-Bois. Manuscript on file, ministère de la Culture et des Communications, Quebec.

1997b Inventaire de la collection archéologique Cliche-Rancourt, volume 2 : Le lac Mégantic. CRAAE, East Angus, Quebec.

1997c Inventaire de la collection archéologique Cliche-Rancourt, volume 3 : Le lac aux Araignées. CRAAE, East Angus, Quebec.

1998a Inventaire de la collection Lévesque : secteur du lac Mégantic (Sites BiEr-9 et BiEr-11). CRAAE, East Angus, Quebec.

1998b Inventaire de la collection archéologique Cliche-Rancourt, volume 4 : Décharge du lac des Joncs. CRAAE, East Angus, Quebec.

1998c Inventaire de la collection archéologique Cliche-Rancourt, volume 5 : Lac des Joncs. CRAAE, East Angus, Quebec.

1999 Deux saisons d'inventaire archéologique dans les limites de la Vile d'East Angus, étés 1997 et 1998. CRAAE, East Angus, Quebec.

2000 Découverte d'un vase amérindien dans les eaux du lac Memphrémagog, Canon de Potton (site BgFb-10). Manuscript on file, ministère de la Culture et des Communications, Quebec.

2001a Animation et évaluation archéologique sur le site du Vieux-Pont (BiEx-1), secteur Lennoxville/Ascot, été 2000. Manuscript on file, ministère de la Culture et des Communications, Quebec.

2001b Inventaire de la collection archéologique Cliche-Rancourt, volume 7 : Nouvelles découvertes sur les sites du secteur des lacs Mégantic, des Joncs et aux Araignées. CRAAE, East Angus, Quebec.

2012 Inventaire de la collection archéologique Cliche-Rancourt, volume 9 : Collection inédite du lac Aylmer. Musée de la nature et des sciences de Sherbrooke. Manuscript on file, ministère de la Culture, des Communications et de la Condition féminine, Quebec.

2013 Camp d'archéologie du Musée de la nature et des sciences de Sherbrooke: Évaluation du site Gaudreau (BkEu-8) de Weedon, été 2012. Manuscript on file, ministère de la Culture, des Communications et de la Condition féminine, Quebec.

2014 Inventaire archéologique dans l'arrondissement de Brompton, Ville de Sherbrooke, été 2013. Manuscript on file, ministère de la Culture et des Communications du Québec, Direction de l'archéologie et des institutions muséales, Musée de la nature et des sciences de Sherbrooke, Quebec.

2018 Mise à jour des collections archéologiques des sites Fortier (BkEu-3) et Weedon 2 (BkEu-4) du confluent des rivières au Saumon et Saint-François à Weedon en Estrie. Manuscript on file, ministère de la Culture et des Communications du Québec, Direction de l'archéologie et des institutions muséales, Musée de la nature et des sciences de Sherbrooke, Quebec.

Graillon, Éric, and Claude Chapdelaine

2018   Intervention archéologique sur les sites Kruger 2 (BiEx-23) et Kruger 3 (BiEx-24) de Brompton, été 2017. Manuscript on file, ministère de la Culture et des Communications, Quebec.

2019   Intervention archéologique sur les sites Kruger 2 (BiEx-23) et Kruger 3 (BiEx-24) de Brompton, été 2018. Manuscript on file, ministère de la Culture et des Communications, Quebec.

Graillon, Éric, Claude Chapdelaine, and Éric Chalifoux

2012   Le site Gaudreau de Weedon : un premier site Plano dans le bassin de la rivière Saint-François en Estrie. *Recherches amérindiennes au Québec* 42(1):67–83.

Granger, Joseph E.

1978   Cache Blades, Chert and Communication: A Reappraisal of Certain Aspects of Meadowood Phase and the Concept of a Burial Cult in the Northeast. In *Essays in Northeastern Anthropology in Memory of Marian E. White*, edited by William E. Engelbrecht and Donald K. Grayson, pp. 96–122. Occasional Publications in Northeastern Anthropology, no. 5. Department of Anthropology. Franklin Pierce College, Range, New Hampshire.

Ingold, Tim

2000   *The Perception of the Environment: Essays on Livelihood, Dwelling and Skill.* London, Routledge.

Joyal, Claude

1999   Occupations préhistoriques sylvicoles au site BhFa-3, rivière Magog en Estrie. *Archéologiques* 13:12–19.

Letendre, Myriam

2007   Le réseau des cherts au Méganticois. In *Entre lacs et montagnes au Méganticois, 12 000 ans d'histoire amérindienne*, edited by Claude Chapdelaine, pp. 271–308. Paléo-Québec 32. Recherches amérindiennes au Québec, Montréal.

Lévesque, René

1962   *Les richesses archéologiques du Québec*. La Société d'archéologie de Sherbrooke, Sherbrooke, Quebec.

Méhault, Ronan

2017a   Existe-t-il un « Sylvicole moyen médian » au Québec? *Archéologiques* 30:1–33.

2017b   Applying a Bayesian Approach in the Northeastern North America Context: Reassessment of the Temporal Boundaries of the "Pseudo-Scallop Shell Interaction Sphere." *Canadian Journal of Archaeology* 41(2):139–172.

Moreau, Jean-François, Érik Langevin, and Louise Verreault

1991   Assessment of the Ceramic Evidence for Woodland Period Culture in the Lac Saint-Jean Area. *Man in the Northeast* 41:33–64.

Morin, Bertrand

1981   *Évaluation archéologique dans les Cantons de l'Est*. Rapport présenté au Service d'archéologie et d'ethnologie, ministère des Affaires culturelles du Québec, Quebec.

Morin, Eugène

2001   Early Late Woodland Social Interaction in the St. Lawrence River Valley. *Archaeology of Eastern North America* 29:66–100.

Petersen, James B.
1990   Evidence of the Saint Lawrence Iroquoians in Northern New England: Population Movement, Trade, or Stylistic Borrowing. *Man in the Northeast* 40:31–39.

Petersen, James B., and Marjory W. Power
1985   Three Middle Woodland Ceramic Assemblages from the Winooski Site. In *Ceramic Analysis in the Northeast: Contributions to Methodology and Culture History*, edited by James B. Petersen, pp. 109–159. Occasional Publications in Northeastern Anthropology no. 9. Department of Anthropology. Franklin Pierce College, Rindge, New Hampshire.

Petersen, James B., John G. Crock, Ellen R. Cowie, Richard A. Boisvert, Joshua R. Toney, and Geoffrey Mandel
2004   St. Lawrence Iroquoians in Northern New England: Pendergast was "Right" and More. In *A Passion for the Past: Papers in Honour of James F. Pendergast*, edited by James V. Wright and Jean-Luc Pilon, pp. 87–123. Mercury Series Archaeology Paper 164. Canadian Museum of Civilization, Gatineau, Quebec.

Petersen, James B., and David Sanger
1991   An Aboriginal Ceramic Sequence for Maine and the Maritime Provinces. In *Prehistoric Archaeology in the Maritime Provinces: Past and Present Research*, edited by Michael Deal and Selma Blair, pp. 121–178. Reports in Archaeology 8. Council of Maritime Premiers, Maritime Committee on Archaeological Cooperation Fredericton, New Brunswick.

Plourde, Michel
2012   *L'exploitation du phoque à l'embouchure du Saguenay par les Iroquoiens de 1000 à 1534*. Mercury Series Archaeology Paper 171. Canadian Museum of Civilization, Gatineau, Quebec.

Potter, Bethany
2017   Lithic Raw Material Usage in the Archaic Northeast: Debitage Analysis of the Gaudreau Site, Weedon, Quebec. Master's thesis, Department of Anthropology, Université de Montréal, Montréal.

Provençal, Julie, Mariane Gaudreau, and Claude Chapdelaine
2010   La cache qui brûle, concentration inusitée d'outils lithiques du site Nepress (BiEr-21) au Méganticois. In *De l'archéologie analytique à l'archéologie sociale*, edited by Brad Loewen, Claude Chapdelaine, and Adrian L. Burke, pp. 189–218. Paléo Québec 34. Recherches amérindiennes au Québec, Montréal.

Richard, Pierre J. H.
1995   Le couvert végétal du Québec-Labrador il y a 6000 ans BP: essai. *Géographie physique et Quaternaire* 49(1):117–140.

Ritchie, William A.
1980 [1969]   *The Archaeology of New York State*. 2nd ed. Natural History Press, Garden City, New York.

Ritchie, William A., and Richard S. MacNeish
1949   The Pre-Iroquoian Pottery of New York State. *American Antiquity* 15(2):97–124.

Ritchie, William A., and Robert E. Funk
1973   *Aboriginal Settlement Patterns in the Northeast.* Memoir 20, New York State Museum, Albany.
Skibo, James M.
2013   *Understanding Pottery Function.* Springer Press, New York.
Taché, Karine
2011   *Structure and Regional Diversity of the Meadowood Interaction Sphere.* University of Michigan. Museum of Anthropology Memoir 48, Ann Arbor.
Tessier, David
2017   Le site EkCw-4, Moyenne Côte-Nord, Québec: paysage sonore et occupation humaine près d'un *ninimissiu pakatakan* entre 6650 et 3400 ans cal AA. In *L'Archaïque au Québec, six millénaires d'histoire amérindienne,* edited by Adrian L. Burke and Claude Chapdelaine, pp. 209–236. Paléo-Québec 36. Recherches amérindiennes au Québec, Montréal.
Tilley, Christopher
1994   *A Phenomenology of Landscape.* Routledge, London.
Tremblay, Roland
1995   L'île aux Corneilles: deux occupations du Sylvicole supérieur entre la province de Canada et le Saguenay. In *Archéologies québécoises,* edited by Anne-Marie Balac, Claude Chapdelaine, Norman Clermont, and Françoise Duguay, pp. 271–306. Paléo-Québec No. 23. Recherches amérindiennes au Québec.
1997   La connexion abénaquise: quelques éléments de recherche sur la dispersion des Iroquoiens du Saint-Laurent orientaux. *Archéologiques* 10:77–86.
2005   Un petit soupçon dans la Petite Nation: la découverte d'une pierre aviforme en Outaouais. *Archéologiques* 18:59–70.
Transit Analyse
1990   Inventaire archéologique réalisé sur le territoire de la ville de Lennoxville en octobre 1989. Manuscript on file, Ministère des Affaires culturelles du Québec, Quebec.
1991   Inventaire archéologique des lots 154-155, évaluation archéologique du site Bishop (BiEx-2) et fouilles archéologiques sur le site BiEx-3, ville de Lennoxville. Manuscript on file, Ministère des Affaires culturelles du Québec, Quebec.
1992   Évaluation finale du site BiEx-3, île aux Massacres et fouilles ponctuelles sur le site Bishop, BiEx-2. Manuscript on file, Ministère des Affaires culturelles du Québec, Quebec.
1993   Inventaire et évaluation du site BkEu-2 et analyse des collections 64 et 64a, Domaine Aylmer. Manuscript on file, Ministère des Affaires culturelles du Québec, Quebec.
1995   Analyse des collections de vestiges archéologiques des sites préhistoriques BiEx-2 et BiEx-3, Lennoxville. Manuscript on file, Ministère des Affaires culturelles du Québec, Quebec.
Verity, Barbara, and Gilles Péloquin
2011   Even the Owl Is Not Heard: David Thompson's 1834 Journals in the Eastern Townships of Quebec. Townships Cantons Publications, Sherbrooke, Quebec.

Vidal, Violette

2007   Palethnographie du site Nebessis (BiEr-3), une occupation préhistorique sur la berge du lac aux Araignées. In *Entre lacs et montagnes au Méganticois, 12 000 ans d'histoire amérindienne*, edited by Claude Chapdelaine, pp. 219–48. Paléo Québec 32. Recherches amérindiennes au Québec, Montréal.

Wintemberg, William J.

1937   Artifacts from Presumed Ancient Graves in Eastern New Brunswick. *Transactions of the Royal Society of Canada*, section II:205–209.

14

NDAKINA
The Impact of Colonization on Knowledge Systems and Ancestral Knowledge

GENEVIÈVE TREYVAUD

Abstract

The arrival of Europeans in the sixteenth century, European and territorial wars of the seventeenth and eighteenth centuries, colonization, and the rapid privatization of W8banaki traditional territory has had a direct effect on the acquisition of natural resources like ash, shellfish, and sturgeon, and on the sustainability of traditional knowledge about these resources. This chapter presents recent advances in archaeological research on Ndakina and uses case studies from three archaeological projects: the Fort Abénakis (Odanak mission) site, the land-use and occupancy project, and the Abaznodali8wdi project. These recent archaeological surveys and excavations have both unearthed colonization and helped map Ndakina territory.

Résumé

L'arrivée des Européens au 16ᵉ siècle, les guerres territoriales du 17ᵉ et 18ᵉ siècles, la colonisation et la privatisation rapide du territoire W8banaki ont créé un impact sur l'acquisition des ressources naturelles comme le frêne, les coquillages et l'esturgeon et la pérennité des savoirs traditionnels. Cette communication présente l'avancée de la recherche archéologique sur le Ndakina en prenant l'exemple de trois sites archéologiques : Fort Abénakis (Mission d'Odanak), projet UOT et sites de potentiel archéologique, et projet Abazodali8wdi. Le mobilier archéologique issu des campagnes de fouilles témoigne de l'impact de la colonisation et de l'aménagement du territoire.

Affiliation
– Grand Council of the Waban-Aki Nation /Institut National de la Recherche Scientifique-Eau Terre Environnement

Ndakina—Our Land in the W8banaki language[1]—is the ancestral territory of the W8banakiak (Abenaki). Ndakina is not limited to its geographical dimension, but it also encompasses land occupancy, resource exploitation, and culture. We unfortunately have little information on the ancient presence of the W8banakiak in Quebec, and how they lived on and used Ndakina. According to historical sources, the W8banakiak, "the people of the dawn land" or "those who dwell in the east," are the northernmost First Nation on the North American Atlantic seaboard. Archaeologists generally agree that they are descended from the ancient groups (6000 BP to 500 BP) who inhabited the region at the time of European contact in the mid-sixteenth century (Clermont 2001) (figure 14.1).

Archaeological interventions, in the field or on cultural material, disturb places and contexts in which the spiritual, material, and sacred memories of Indigenous ancestors reside. First Nations today can see the possibilities that archaeology brings to furthering their knowledge of their history and territory. Archaeological research focusing on ancient Indigenous cultures has traditionally followed the ideological and aesthetic codes of the dominant colonial society, without giving much thought to the knowledge and beliefs held by the modern descendants of those cultures (Yellowhorn 2019). The Ndakina Office of the Grand Council of the Waban-Aki Nation is trying to bring balance to this situation by insisting on the importance of developing a management, communications, and collaboration plan from the onset of any research project or archaeological intervention on their territory. Projects can only proceed with the assent of the W8banaki research coordination board. The board can enforce fairer research standards to (1) allow the W8banaki Nation to work together with researchers in defining research objectives and methodology; (2) give opportunity to community youth to work as research assistants; (3) ensure that data is returned to the nation and its organizations as the participants see fit; (4) ensure that the nation can be involved in data-analysis processes; (5) ensure that those involved in a project have a say over researchers' interpretations; and (6) ensure that researchers diffuse their results within the nation through various means (presentations, articles, exhibits, graphic media, etc.).

This proactive strategy aims to ensure that research first and foremost benefits the W8banaki Nation's interests. Only by taking back control of the research initiatives will the W8banakiak enjoy true collaborations and build strong partnerships with universities, government branches, and other organizations. Research must no longer be made on the W8banakiak, but with, by, and for the W8banakiak.

Based on three examples of archaeological research projects carried out by the Ndakina office—namely, (1) Fort Abénakis (Odanak mission and village) and the Man8gemasak, (2) the creation of archaeological assessment protocols

---

1. This etymology is derived from one of the oldest Indigenous linguistic forms, where the symbol "8" would express a nasal "o."

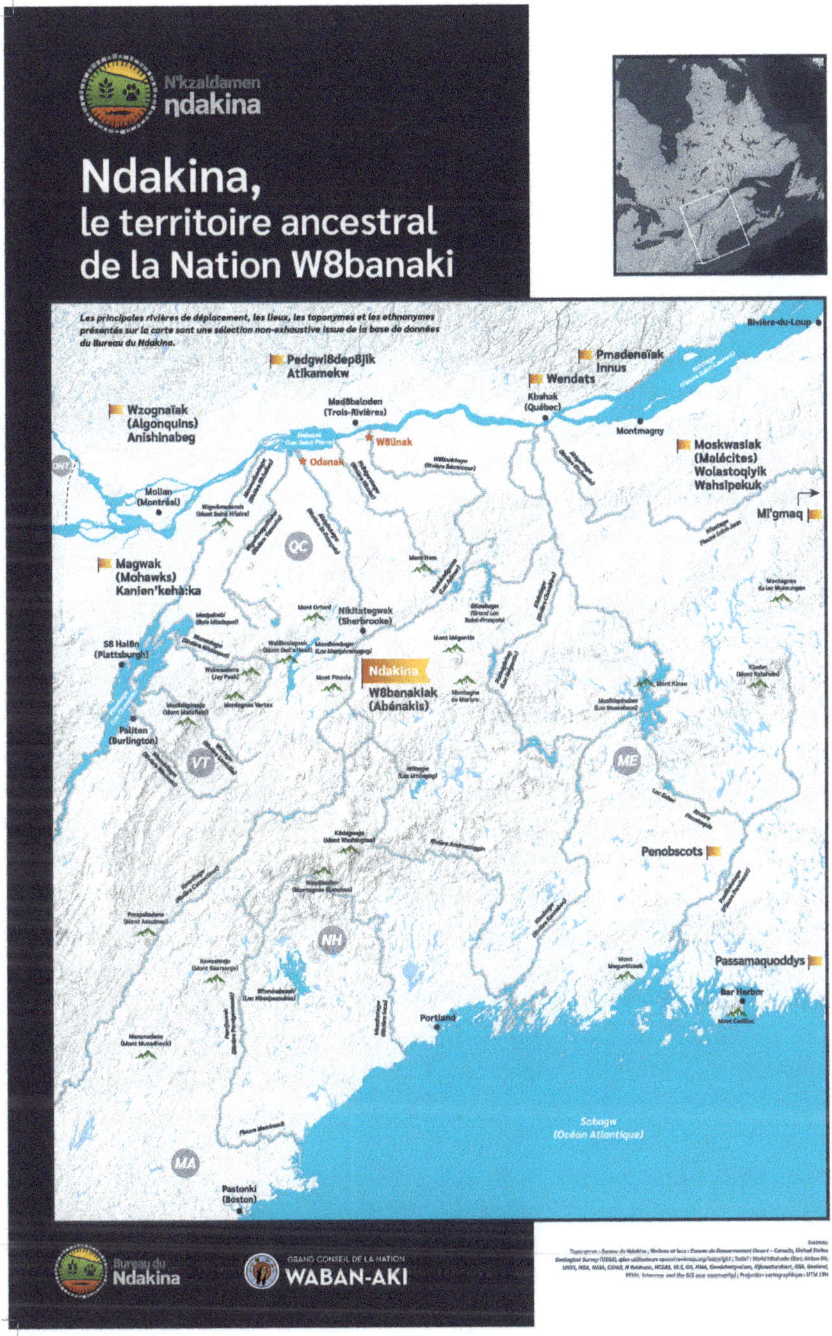

Figure 14.1. Ndakina, the ancestral territory of the W8banaki Nation.
Source: Ndakina Office, Grand Council of the Waban-Aki Nation.

used in land-management consultations, and (3) the Abaznodali8wdi project—this chapter aims to demonstrate the pertinence, on both the scientific and community levels, of the Indigenous archaeology approach on Ndakina (Atalay 2012; Atalay et al. 2016; Bruchac et al. 2010; Nicholas and Andrews 1997).

The W8banaki Nation, Past and Present

The Historical Period

The W8banakiak are part of the Eastern Algonquian family. Until the colonial period, their subsistence mode depended on the resources available on Ndakina (Treyvaud and Plourde 2017). The W8banakiak lived in semi-permanent villages and seasonal fishing and hunting encampments. The main waterways fostered W8banaki mobility, and through their many connections allowed access to the interior of Ndakina. The introduction of maize between 2300 and 1500 BP in the St. Lawrence River Valley and New England transformed the W8banaki way of life (Boyd and Surette 2010; Crawford et al. 2006; Gates St-Pierre and Thompson 2015; Hart et al. 2007). Their settlement strategies turned to a form of semi-nomadism in which their sustenance from hunting, fishing, trapping, and gathering was complemented by growing maize, squash, and pulses. Agriculture was not practised over the whole of Ndakina, however, due to variations in the physical landscape and climate. The W8banakiak, therefore, alternated between the interior and water-adjacent areas along the main watercourses, the St. Lawrence River and the Atlantic coast, following seasonal changes in subsistence strategies tied to the harvesting schedule of the crops, as well as the distribution of the hunting territories (GCWAN 2015; Treyvaud and Plourde 2017; Bourque 1989).

During the Contact and colonial periods, the expansion of Indigenous-European trade amplified the development of horticulture. The involvement of W8banakiak hunters in the fur and game trades changed their habits, leading them to leave their families and villages for longer periods. The W8banakiak had to compensate for the scarcity of certain foodstuffs such as large game with maize and squash, as well as ginseng, wild berries, and nut gathering (Snow 1978; Calloway 1990; Treyvaud and Plourde 2017).

Indigenous-European contacts in the seventeenth and eighteenth centuries had a major impact on the lives of the W8banakiak groups, especially on the Atlantic coast of the United States. The W8banaki Nation soon found itself trapped in the middle of French and English hostilities. All armed confrontations between New France and New England can be grouped as one long event: the "border wars." This expression englobes a series of confrontations that arose from the territorial claims of France and Great Britain, which had both given royal charters to their respective agents in the early seventeenth century to initiate the colonization of North America and the exploitation of its natural resources (Calloway 1990; Lahaise 2006).

While the French and British land claims largely overlapped between the 40th and 45th parallels, from New Jersey to the Gulf of St. Lawrence, it was east of the Kennebec River that colonial competition was the fiercest. This competition was tied to the abundant fishing grounds whose exploitation was central to the economy of the colonies of the Acadian Peninsula (Daugherty 1983). These territorial conflicts escalated until they stretched from the Atlantic coast to the Great Lakes. In this context of uncertainty and violence, many of the W8banakiak groups living close to British colonial settlements began spending more time in the safer parts of their territory, including Kchitegw (the St. Lawrence River Valley). They would temporarily leave the New England coast, only to return in times of relative peace. These W8banakiak eventually settled in the Jesuit missions of the St. Lawrence River Valley, including the Saint-Joseph mission, in Sillery, and the Saint-François-de-Sales mission on the Kik8ntegw (Chaudière River).

Overpopulation problems at the Sillery mission and soil depletion around Saint-François-de-Sales forced the Jesuits to open new missions. As early as the mid-seventeenth century, W8banikiak families started permanently settling along Alsig8ntegw (Saint-François River) and W8linaktegw (Bécancour River) (Treyvaud and Plourde 2017; T.-M. Charland 1964; Sévigny 1976; Day 1981). The new missions at Saint-François (Odanak) and Saint-François-Xavier (Bécancour) had a significant impact on their surrounding landscapes, since the newly sedentarized W8banakiak still relied on the land for their subsistence activities; the Eastern Townships of Quebec, before the conquest, were the hunting grounds of tribes belonging to the Algonquin Nation, as the Abenaquis, or St. Francis Indians (Day 1981). The W8banakiak living along Alsig8ntegw and W8linaktegw would still travel up their respective rivers to the New England coast, living off the resources of Ndakina.

Odanak and W8linak Today

Evidence of W8banakiak presence can be found in toponymy. The works of geographer and W8banaki-language instructor Philippe Charland have demonstrated the abundance of W8banaki place names on Ndakina and in the surrounding regions. These toponyms endure to this day, which illustrates the continuous presence of the W8banakiak in these spaces and their influence over the place names chosen by the descendants of European settlers (P. Charland 2005).

The W8banaki Nation currently regroups 3,000 members, split between two communities, Odanak and W8linak. The former is located on Alsig8ntegw, next to the village of Pierreville. The latter is located within the town of Bécancour, on W8linaktegw. Nowadays, most of the two communities' population speaks French, with a few English speakers in Odanak. The Grand Conseil de la Nation Waban-Aki (Grand Council of the Waban-Aki Nation), the nation's tribal council, has since 1979 served as the administrative body mandated by the Abenaki Councils of Odanak and W8linak to manage a number of services and resources shared by the two communities.

Since Ndakina straddles the Canadian-American border, several W8banakiak have chosen to stay in the United States. They are nevertheless recognized as members by one or the other of the two communities, and maintain contacts and ties with the nation and the residents of those two communities. The historical portrait of W8banaki presence presented above demonstrates that the progressive land dispossession of the W8banakiak began in the early seventeenth century. Their territory is indeed nowadays densely populated and fragmented into private lots, with little remaining as public land. This privatization process has made access to the land difficult for the nation's members who wish to engage in their traditional practices. The W8banakiak have had to adapt their ancestral practices to the many forms of pressure exerted by colonization and land development. For example, a hunting and trapping agreement between the Quebec government and the Abenaki Councils of Odanak and W8linak grants special arrangements to the members of the W8banaki Nation, such as an extension of the big-game hunting season and the distribution of community hunting licenses to be used on a small, designated fraction of Ndakina.

The Ndakina Office

The Ndakina Office of the Grand Council of the Waban-Aki Nation represents and supports the Abenaki Councils of Odanak and W8linak in matters of affirmation, land consultations and claims, and environmental and climate-change adaptation. Thanks to its privileged, respectful relationship with the members of the nation, the office acts as a keeper of W8banakiak knowledge and practices and promotes sustainable development in accordance with the nation's values and knowledge. Furthermore, the office team provides positive exposure for the nation by offering out its expertise in the fields of climate-change preparedness, environmental consulting, geographic information systems (or GIS), archaeology, as well as historical and anthropological research.

The Ndakina office works, in collaborations and partnerships with universities, on research projects concerning traditional knowledge. These projects stem from requests received from W8banakiak or other First Nation communities, or from entities and governmental bodies involved in infrastructure development on Ndakina. Furthermore, the Ndakina office regularly consults with members of the W8banaki Nation to validate and obtain information on traditional activities (hunting, trapping, gathering, cultural practices, etc.) on Ndakina. This data is used, among other things, to map out the geographical locations of these activities and monitor their persistence.

Archaeology at the Ndakina Office

The Ndakina office team follows the Indigenous archaeology approach. This theoretical and methodological approach is founded on the decisional and organizational power of Indigenous peoples, and it empowers them to create archaeological research projects focused on their ancestral and modern cultural heritage (Atalay 2012; Atalay et al. 2016; Bruchac et al. 2010; Nicholas and Andrews 1997). This movement arose in the early 2000s from the efforts of American First Nations to address the issue of researchers of European descent studying Indigenous heritage without consulting Indigenous peoples. This lack of consultation has resulted in projects tainted with colonialism, favouring European perspectives, often to the exclusion of traditional knowledge, knowledge of the land, and Indigenous perspectives on time and space (Watkins 2000; L. T. Smith 2013; C. Smith and Wobst 2004). Indigenous archaeology is also defined by the resolve of First Nations to take charge of the research projects which concern them and build partnerships and collaborations with academic researchers and governmental bodies that share their vision of Indigenous research (Atalay 2012).

Taking Nature Out of Archaeological Research: A Colonialist Perspective

The W8banakiak do not conceive of the land simply as a place, nor as a set of physical components and natural resources. Their idea of land is broader and includes what many have defined as a "sense of place" (William and Stewart 1998). This sense of place involves individual and shared experiences, as well as human-environment interactions. It is defined as "the complex web of lifestyles, meanings and social relations endemic to a place" (Williams and Stewart 1998). Places have physical and structural attributes, as well as a form of social unity; their value extends to their guiding function as points of reference. Places also connote a sense of permanence, stability, continuity, and consistency through time (Piveteau 2010). Places are part of interactive spatial systems and play specific parts that define the territory. Ndakina is made up of such spatial systems, themselves organized around the mobility and knowledge of its actors, as well as the symbolic mechanisms between the W8banakiak and the places where they live.

Archaeology, geography, and ecology have different understandings of the nature of landscapes. Archaeologists see landscapes as places modified by human actions. They will therefore seek tangible evidence of human occupation, as archaeological material or structures. The specificities of the natural environment are not systematically considered in the archaeological process. Conversely, natural sciences will offer theoretical concepts from which humans, fundamental agents of environmental change, are removed. In the words of archaeologist

François Duceppe-Lamarre (1999), "only by blurring the lines between historical and natural sciences can we better understand landscapes."

The Ndakina office promotes a composite definition of heritage and follows a landscape archaeology approach, which emphasizes the importance of the interactions between humans and their environment. Our understanding of these interactions is informed by the works of Charles L. Redman (1999) and Tim Ingold (2000), whose theoretical ecological models articulate the interactions between four spheres: (1) the natural community, (2) the climate and geographical context, (3) the human social system, and (4) the cultural environment. These models foster a deeper understanding of the impact that humans have on nature and how it relates to the use and occupancy of ancestral Indigenous lands. They also reflect First Nation notions of land and environment, in which humans belong to the land and do not own it (Marchand 2012; Bousquet 1999; Treyvaud 2013).

Integrating the concepts of Indigenous archaeology and landscape archaeology has allowed us to broaden our understanding of land use and occupancy, the landscape transformations brought upon by human presence, and the impacts of colonization and anthropization on the land, from ancient times to the present day. This perspective is in keeping with the current broader trend toward the decolonization of research, toward control by First Nations of archaeological material and data, as well as a right to monitor the research and discussions which concern them (L. T. Smith 2013; Treyvaud et al. 2018). However, the decolonization of research can only begin with a reassessment of the precedence of scientific interests over Indigenous values and epistemologies (Raines 1992). This is why the W8banaki Nation created the W8banaki research coordination board, as discussed above.

The Uninterrupted Occupancy of Ndakina
and the Archaeological Chronology of the Northeast

Archaeologists working in the Far Northeast around the 1950s developed a culture-historical framework for the prehistoric or pre-Contact period based on evolutive and adaptative traits. The sequence of periods in this framework (Palaeoindian, Archaic, Woodland, Contact, and colonial, with their respective subperiods) reflects the general technological evolution of the human groups. These units are not consistent with First Nations specificities and values (table 14.1). The Ndakina office prefers using a time-based chronology. In the same spirit, for the pre-Columbian period (before Christopher Columbus's third trip in 1498), we favour the expressions "ancient times" or "ancient period" over "prehistoric" or "paleohistoric," which stem from European archaeological notions, using the possession of writing to discriminate against non-Western human groups (Atalay 2012; Atalay et al. 2016; Watkins 2000).

Table 14.1. Chronology of the uninterrupted occupancy of Ndakina.

Pre-Columbian archaeological periods in the Northeast	Years BP (Before Present)	Archaeological periods favoured by the Ndakina Office for the pre-Columbian period in the Northeast	Years BP (Before Present)
Palaeoindian	12 000 to 8 000		12 000 to 8 000
Archaic	8000 to 3000	Ancient times or Ancient period	8000 to 3000
Woodland	3000 BP to AD 1534		3000 BP to AD 1498
Contact period	AD 1534 to 1608	1498 to first contact (varies between regions – **1524 for the W8banakiak** [Giovanni Verrazzano])	

Research and Land Documentation Projects

Our stated approach has shaped the development of our operating procedures regarding archaeological research and W8banaki archaeological heritage management in the process of land consultations. We present here three examples of the operating procedure developed by the Ndakina office as concerns (1) the Odanak mission, village, and Man8gemasak; (2) the creation of potential assessment protocols as part of archaeological consultation and research work on Ndakina (figure 14.2); (3) Abaznodali8wdi, the basket trail. For each project, we describe the challenges, limitations, and successes we met on the administrative, scientific, political, and community levels.

The Odanak Mission, Village, and Man8gemasak

A team of archaeologists[2] conducting fieldwork in the historical centre of Odanak since 2010 has uncovered elements of a palisade in the form of large, telltale 20–25 cm post moulds. The excavations also revealed the existence of dozens of traditional house-floor pits associated with multiple smaller post moulds, indicating the presence of domestic structures such as storage and sleeping platforms, cooking stands, etc. The sandy pits contained large amounts of well-preserved faunal remains, including fish and terrestrial mammals such as muskrat, beaver, and deer. Preliminary faunal analyses reveal a concentration of

---

2. From 2010 to 2014, field interventions were led by the Musée des Abénakis and the Abenaki Council of Odanak as part of the project Fort Odanak: Le passé revisité (Fort Odanak: The Past Revisited). Since 2015, the Ndakina Office of the Grand Council of the Waban-Aki Nation ensures the protection of the CaFe-7 site and intervenes in matters of development and infrastructure maintenance. The archaeological field school of the Kiuna Institute took place in the north-east sector of the historical village (2019–2021).

wild-animal remains in the southwestern sector of the fortified village, where the traditional houses were located. In contrast, the faunal assemblage of the midden associated with the chapel and the Jesuit missionary's house is comprised of farm animals, including cow, pig, sheep, and chicken (Dupont-Hébert and Noel 2013). The house-floor pits also produced copper ornaments, as well as glass, bone, and argillite beads. Gravers made from modified gun flints and slate body ornaments bearing W8banaki symbols were also found. These objects demonstrate a continuity in the use of traditional tools and symbols by the W8banakiak during the eighteenth century (figures 14.3–14.5).

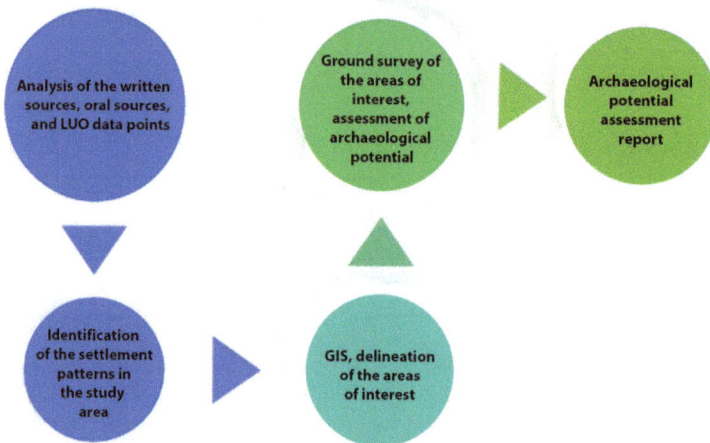

Figure 14.2. Flowchart, archaeological potential assessment process.
Source: Ndakina Office of the Grand Council of the Waban-Aki Nation.

Figure 14.3a. French gun flint modified as a graver (CaFe-7-6B3-2).

Figure 14.3b. Body ornaments made from black slate, bone, and lead, some inscribed with W8banakiak symbols.

Source: © a gill, Société historique d'Odanak.

Figure 14.4. A) Tinkling cones and projectile point (CaFe-7); (B) set of needles and gravers (CaFe-7). *Source:* © a gill, Société historique d'Odanak.

Fragments of carbonized ears of corn of the Indigenous, eight-row Northern Flint variety, were collected, along with charcoal samples from hearths located inside the traditional houses (figures 14.6–14.7). These samples obtained from Contact-period contexts were submitted for radiocarbon dating (table 14.2). The dates, along with the habitation structures associated with wild-animal remains and European materials modified in the W8banaki fashion, clearly testify to the presence of a W8banaki village since the sixteenth century (Treyvaud and Plourde 2017).

Figure 14.5. (A) Wampum beads (CaFe-7); (B) glass beads (CaFe-7).
Source: © a gill, Société historique d'Odanak.

Figure 14.6. Pit and post mould exposed on site CaFe-7.
Source: Société historique d'Odanak.

Table 14.2. Radiocarbon dates from the Odanak mission and village site (CaFe-7).

Université Laval #	Sample #	Radiocarbon years (uncal BP)	Range (±)	Calibrated years AD	Range (±)
ULA-4347	CaFe-7-6R62 (charcoal)	290	15	1583	53
ULA-4348	CaFe-7-6P52-1 (charcoal)	205	15	1727	66
ULA-4349	CaFe-7-6L70 (charcoal)	105	15	1803	92
ULA-4351	CaFe-7-6A92 (charcoal)	290	20	1583	53
ULA-4346	CaFe-7-6A58 (charred maize)	170	20	1803	122
ULA-4350	CaFe-7-6B52 (charcoal)	315	20	1571	49
ULA-4174	CaFe-7-1F16-6 (charred maize)	200	15	1730	66
ULA-4175	CaFe-7-3A-1 (charred maize)	125	15	1813	97

Ndakina and the Man8gemasak of the Odanak site

Anthropomorphic and zoomorphic figurines carved on clay concretions were found at the bottom of pits located both inside and outside of the traditional houses of the Odanak mission and village. The W8banakiak associate the manufacture of these objects with the Man8gemasak, small, forest-dwelling beings. The anthropomorphic or zoomorphic nature of the figures speaks of a symbolic value. The material from which they are made also ties them to the W8banaki creation story (Treyvaud and Bernard 2018).

According to members of the W8banaki Nation and written sources, the Man8gemasak are little beings existing at the edges of rivers and forests. What they look like is unknown as they are never seen; they can make themselves invisible by staying still when humans approach. The Man8gemasak have been given the task of shaping and carving river pebbles. These pebbles bear messages advising the W8banakiak how to behave in certain locations, which places they should avoid, and which paths they should choose.

According to the W8banaki creation story, the Man8gemasak were created when stone giants were shrunk down. Their mission is to protect their surrounding environment. They are known to play tricks on humans when they want them to change their behaviours toward nature. The eventuality of finding a pebble carved by the Man8gemasak forced people to proceed with more caution when entering certain areas. The messages left by the little beings were therefore very important. These pebbles were meant to be left in place, so that they could give information to any W8banakiak travelling in the area. According to oral tradition, the pebbles carved by the Man8gemasak are used for educational and knowledge-transmission purposes. They show children how one should or should not behave on Ndakina. They embody the forest and river beings, who are knowledge holders and protectors (figure 14.8).

Figure 14.7. Sample of Northern Flint maize (*Zea mays* var. *indurata*) collected at site CaFe-7. *Source:* © a gill, Société historique d'Odanak.

Several archaeological sites on Ndakina have produced Man8gemasak, including Wapanucket and Titicut, at the southwestern limit of Ndakina (Massachusetts); Brattleboro and Bellows Falls, Vermont; and Machias and Bingham, Maine. Archaeologists working on Ndakina have referred to these symbolic objects as "pictographs" or "portable petroglyphs" (Robbins 1959; Scothorne 1968; Fowler 1974; Hallaren 1988; figure 14.8 here). They are interpreted as representing a communication system in which the figurative characters and animals possess—and transmit—supernatural properties. While these objects remain poorly studied, a few archaeological reports mention them being found in every chronological context (Fowler 1974; Hallaren 1988). Their existence is first attested around 5000 BP, and endures until the Contact period, at which point Christian symbols (such as the cross or a pictogram representing Jesuit missions) start appearing alongside traditional motifs on incised pebbles.

Perspectives and Developments

W8banakiak ancestors left a legacy of inscriptions, stories, knowledge, and objects. They gave names to places and marked the land with traces of their presence that can still be found in the landscapes and in the Earth. These shreds of ancient human experiences have been passed on to their successors through oral tradition, archaeological evidence, and what remains of the ancient lifeways. The clayey pebbles carved by the Man8gemasak are one of the tools of knowledge transmission on Ndakina. This knowledge informs orally transmitted educational principles, artistic creation, innovation, and the preservation of the social references that are crucial to W8banakiak identity building. Kinship with the ancestors also carries geographical knowledge on land use and occupancy. It facilitates the transmission of culture and identity, and promotes a feeling of perenniality within the group. This heritage provides an impression of continuity to which individuals can contribute but which also transcends them, which is an essential element of identity building. Tracing back this filiation can also help one measure the impact of anthropization on ancestral lands.

Creating a Geomatics Tool for Archaeological Potential Assessments

Landscapes are palimpsests upon which stories are constantly being written and erased. The landscapes of Ndakina are nowadays characterized by urban areas, recreational areas, road infrastructures, agricultural land, and natural or publicly managed forest habitats. Most are defined by human intervention. While all these landscapes have stories to tell, their tales seldom are readily decipherable. Unlike parchment documents, which have rarely been erased and rewritten more than once or twice, the landscapes of Ndakina have been subjected to continuous change through time (Turner 2011; Ingold 2000). Archaeologists conceive of landscapes as places transformed by human agency. They constantly strive to understand how the landscapes in which we live have evolved, and they use archaeological evidence to explain the chain of events that have made the landscapes what they are today. These transformations, coupled with colonial policies of assimilation, have greatly disrupted W8banakiak knowledge transmission on Ndakina. It is with this in mind that the Ndakina office has created archaeological potential assessment protocols that do not rely solely on archaeological data but consider the whole body of knowledge on the territory.

In the context of territorial consultations emanating from developers or governmental bodies, archaeologists must produce an archaeological assessment outlining the potential for ancient occupations and heritage resources requiring protection within the pertinent area. These assessments are prepared using historical, topographical, and archaeological data, as well as data concerning present-day land occupancy. These studies are also used to identify focus zones for the nation and map geographic landmarks (such as rapids, portage routes, and rocky promontories) that are mentioned in the literature and have endured in the ever-changing landscape (figure 14.2).

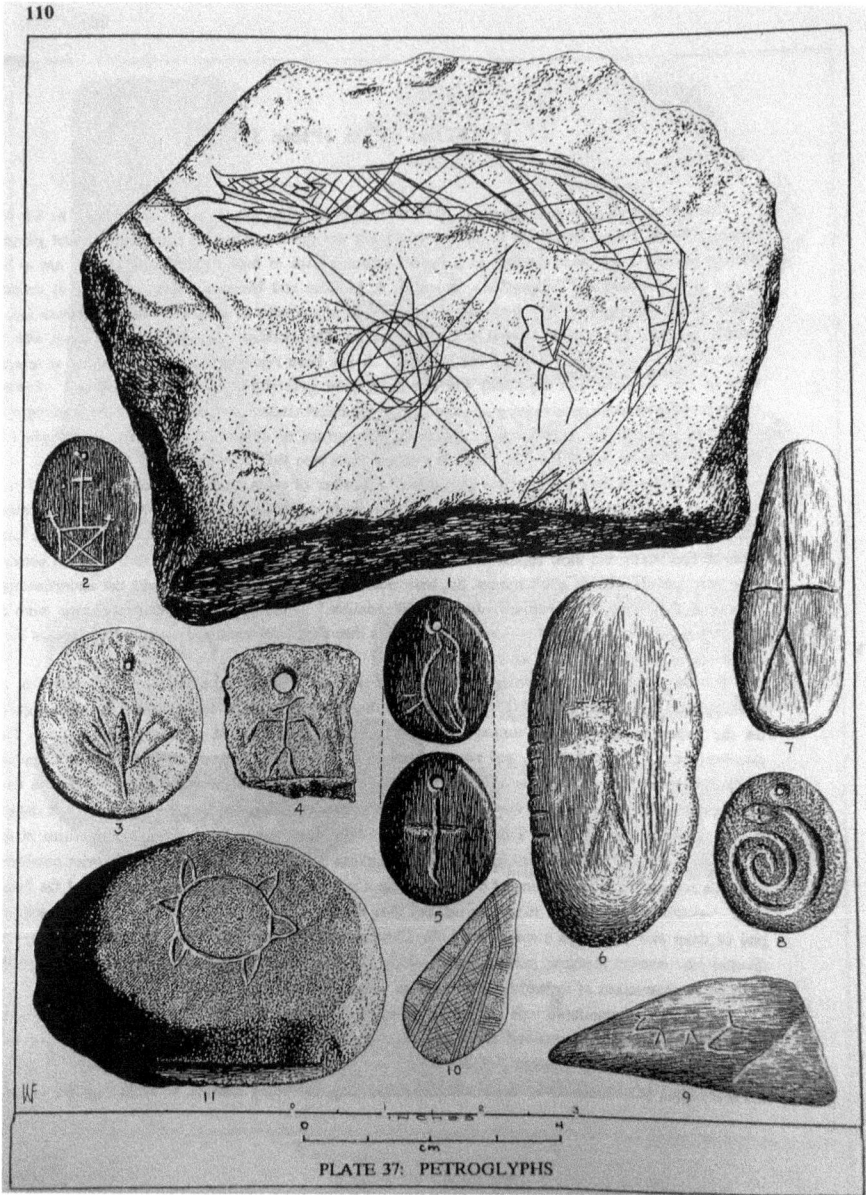

PLATE 37: PETROGLYPHS

Figure 14.8. (A) and (B), group of clay concretions incised with Mang8gemasak figures from the Odanak mission and village site (CaFe-7), Société historique d'Odanak; (C) plate 37 from Hoffman's (1991) revision of *A Handbook of Indian Artifacts from Southern New England from the Original Text of William S. Fowler*.

Land Use and Occupancy as Markers for Archaeological Assessments

The Ndakina office performed an extensive study of W8banakiak land use and occupancy (LUO) on their ancestral territory. The methodology involved conducting "carto-biographical" semi-structured interviews detailing the activities of land users (Tobias 2000). The Ndakina office has so far conducted interviews with around fifty informants, which have generated over 2,000 land-use data points on Ndakina. These semi-structured interviews have also produced a large number of observations by members of the nation—whose active presence on the land often goes back several decades—concerning climate change and weather events, flooding and erosion, invasive exotic species, deforestation, etc. This information, combined with historical sources and archaeological data, demonstrates the continuity of W8banaki LUO on Ndakina. These locations are mapped using GIS, and are delineated to address W8banakiak concerns on land access and preservation.

Geomatics to Identify Zones of Archaeological Interest

The lives of the first peoples of Ndakina were guided by the seasons, the availability of game, and the proximity of the natural resources important to their lifeways. It is on these premises that our geomatics tool was built. Settlement patterns are inferred from these variables, to which we add the network of waterways, the presence of terrace landforms suitable for encampments or villages, and the availability of specific resources, such as tool stone, ash trees, etc. This tool was designed to be evolutive and flexible to adapt to the various challenges of locating zones of high archaeological potential.

The tool is designed to help identify zones of high archaeological potential based on W8banaki settlement patterns. It enables the Ndakina office archaeology team to answer quickly to consultations on development projects on Ndakina, so that the archaeological heritage can be adequately protected. The tool tests different hypotheses and archaeological concepts against W8banaki settlement patterns, geographic landmarks, LUO data points, and geomorphological, geological, and hydrographic data on the impacted area. This tool also serves as a visual aid to understand LUO at different points in time. It is used to plan the field components of research projects.

The tool is an algorithm combining around a hundred separate functions of QGIS, an open-source GIS software. It identifies areas with a low-slope gradient and groups them based on their (rounded-up) gradient value. It then categorizes these areas according to their elevation and proximity to bodies of water and wetlands, and generates a visual overview which the Ndakina office archaeology team can use to identify zones of high archaeological interest.

The geographical map generated by the algorithm is an indispensable tool when surveying or assessing the archaeological potential of a site. It allows archaeologists to instantly visualize the spatial data that they need to quickly respond to issues pertaining to land development and the protection of archaeological resources (figure 14.9).

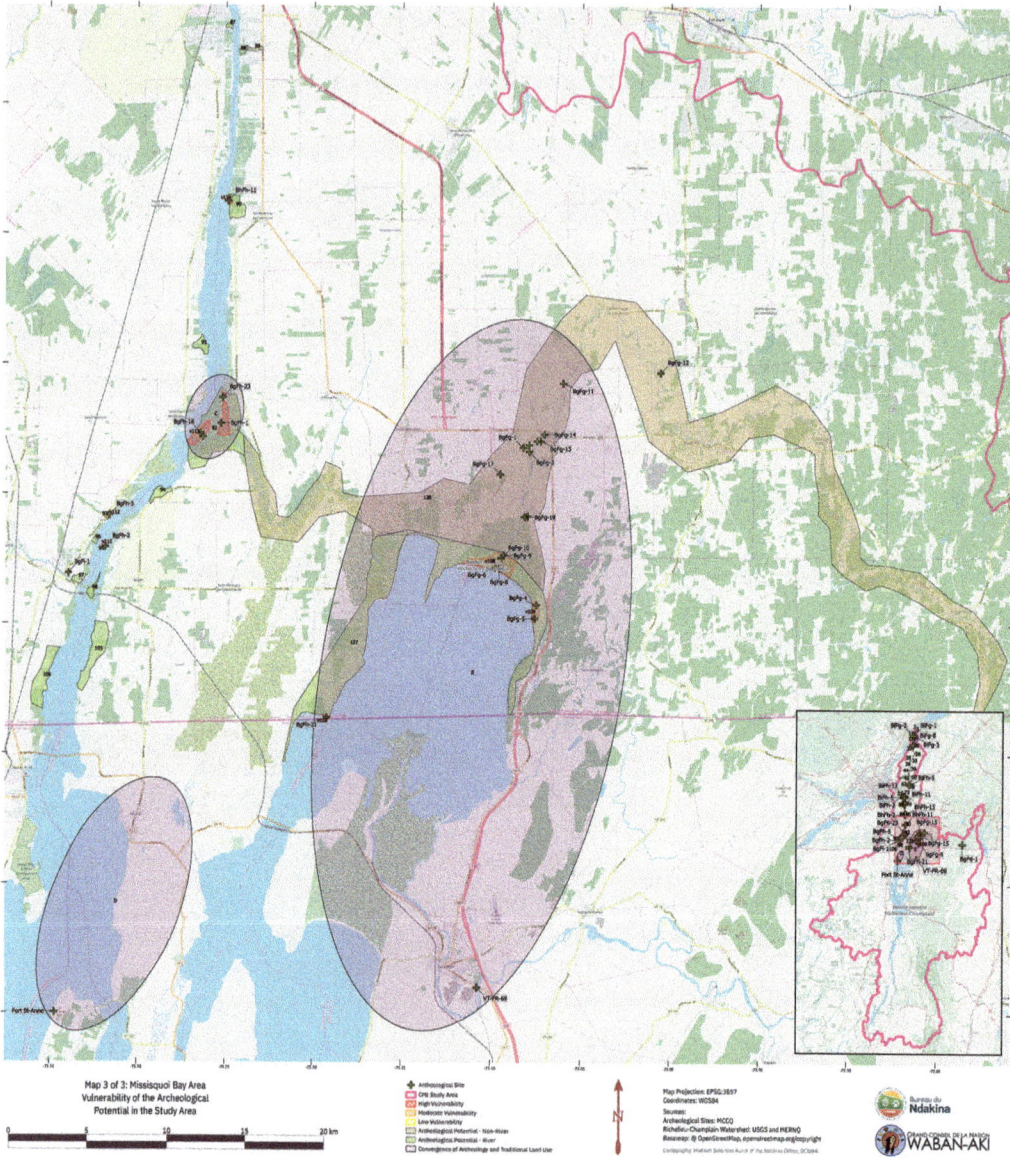

Figure 14.9. Archaeological potential map of an area of interest.
Source: The Ndakina Office of the Grand Council of the Waban-Aki Nation.

Perspectives and Developments

There currently are several active archaeological research projects in the sector comprised between the Alsig8ntegw and Kik8tegw Rivers. These projects are either the Ndakina office's initiatives or are tied to infrastructure construction and forest-industry development projects. The Appalachian section of Ndakina, which straddles the Canada-United States border, is comprised of spatial systems made up of locations that are symbolically important to the W8banakiak. This territory is dotted with landmarks, such as Mount Ktaden (Katahdin) and Namag8ntegw (Lake Mégantic). Its major waterways, including Alsig8ntegw (St. Francis), Wlastegw (Saint John), Koategw (Coaticook), Kweniteg (Connecticut), and Kinebagw (Kennebec), were part of the well-travelled north-south portage routes connecting the Atlantic Coast to the Kchitegw (St. Lawrence River). The forests of this central part of Ndakina hold high archaeological potential, especially since they can be difficult to access. Archaeological prospection is complicated by the largely private tenure of the land, however. Property access must be negotiated plot by plot, and is often denied due to a lack of awareness of W8banakiak or First Nations issues on the part of the owners. New remote-sensing methods can circumvent some of these constraints and limitations. LIDAR (light detection and ranging), or laser remote sensing, allows for a non-invasive exploration of the territory, and has been used to assess archaeological contexts in forested areas in many jurisdictions, notably in Norway and the state of Michigan (Georges-Leroy et al. 2011; Chase et al. 2017; Gallagher and Josephs 2008).

The Ndakina office has been working since 2019 toward the integration of LIDAR remote sensing into its archaeological potential assessments. Our first objective is to map every known archaeological site, geographic landmark, and cultural feature on Ndakina. The end goal of the project is to combine this map with our data on W8banakiak settlement patterns, our ecological data, and our LUO data points. From this data set, we will be able to analyze the natural and anthropic transformations of the territory, observe the workings of forest ecosystems, and monitor erosion on Ndakina.

Abaznodali8wdi, the Basket Trail

Basket making is an ancestral W8banaki practice, of great importance culturally and identity-wise. As the W8banakiak gradually lost access to their land in Quebec at the end of the nineteenth/beginning of the twentieth century, the black-ash basket industry became central to the economy of their communities. By the 1880s, Abaznodal (black-ash baskets) manufacture had become the primary means of subsistence for many families. This industry was central to the social, familial, and cultural cohesion of the nation. Today still, black-ash basket making is a distinctive practice among the W8banakiak. The anthropization of the territory, climate change, and the emerald ash borer (an invasive insect species) all contributed to making the black-ash supply increasingly difficult for the communities. It is therefore crucial to research, document, and analyze basketry in its environmental dimension (figure 14.10).

Figure 14.10. Louis Tahamont's basket display, United States.
Source: Musée des Abénakis archives, p2013.215.

The main goal of this project is to analyze the history and evolution of black ash, sweetgrass, and birchbark basket-manufacturing methods among the W8banakiak, from the sixteenth century to now, in relation with W8banakiak land occupancy on Ndakina. Other questions we seek to answer include: Along what routes was basket-making know-how transmitted? What technology was used in basket making? How has land anthropization affected the W8banaki economy? To what extent have climate change and the advent of the emerald ash borer affected the practice? All of these questions have shaped our research project, which is being carried out in collaboration with the Centre Eau Terre Environnement of the Institut national de la recherche scientifique (INRS-ETE) in Québec City. The impetus for this project came with the discovery of tools and organic materials (ash and birchbark) within a crafting area in one of the traditional houses at the Odanak mission and village site (CaFe-7) in 2013 (Treyvaud and Plourde 2017).

Objectives and Methods

Our specific objective is to document the manufacturing methods of Abaznodal through interviews and specialized analyses (SEM,[3] CT scan,[4] XRF[5]). This project will also help develop expertise and employability for the Ndakina office, the nation, and youth in the NIONA group.[6] The expected outcomes of the project include the creation of a database and a communication medium to ensure the sustainability of basket making among the W8banakiak.

The project is divided along three main lines of research: (1) an archaeological study of basket manufacturing methods and raw-material procurement between 1500 and 1880 CE, (2) a historical and anthropological study of the basket-making industry from 1880 to the present day, and (3) an assessment of the impacts of climate change and the emerald ash borer on basket-making activities among the W8banakiak.

We are integrating into this project the notions of human-environment interactions, cultural landscape, and technology by connecting the dots between the natural resource, the ash tree, and the finished product: the basket. Land occupancy and human-environment interactions are crucial factors in the development of basket making throughout the sequence of raw-material collection, preparation, and transformation. From this viewpoint, it becomes possible to assess the impact that the development of basket making, and the adaptation of the basket makers, had during the transitional (Contact), colonial, modern, and present-day periods. Two key ideas emerge: that of a continuously developing landscape, and that of the W8banaki cultural landscape, with its technology represented here by the basket makers. Our understanding of the interactions

---

3. The Zeiss EVO 50 scanning electron microscope (SEM) offers magnifications levels of 100 to 60,000 times.
4. Our facility is equipped with a Siemens SOMATOM Definition AS 128-slice CT (computerized tomography) scanner, a data-storage and—processing unit, a sedimentology laboratory, and hydraulics, bio-sedimentology, and hydrology equipment.
5. The Itrax XRF (X-ray fluorescence) core scanner collects geochemical data and high-resolution radiographic imagery from marine or lacustrine sediments, in a loss-less, non-destructive process. It uses micro X-ray fluorescence and micro radiography to analyze samples (halved sediment cores, U-channels, etc.) in a continuous and relatively fast operation, so that changes in the geochemical profiles of the samples can be recorded and visualized.
6. Niona is a youth team focused on inter-generational intervention with regard to W8banaki culture. Team members aged 12–17 are mandated with disseminating the culture and positive initiatives of the nation through technological means: radio, video, blogs, and social media. Team members have the opportunity to deepen their knowledge and understanding of the culture through exchanges with adult resources (including Elders sharing their cultural heritage), with professionals sharing specific skills, and with the facilitators, who accompany them throughout the project.

between the evolving landscape and the cultural landscape is based on the works of Redman (1999), Ingold (2000), and Leroi-Gourhan (1974).

Archaeology in the Abaznodali8wdi Project

Technology-based approaches focusing on the materials and techniques involved in the manufacture of an object must also consider the socio-cultural diversity at play in the context of production. Therefore, when approaching a specific technology such as basket making, we must define it as the way in which W8banakiak artisans, as actors of a technological system, are implementing a manufacturing process. In this case, the concept of *chaîne opératoire*, as defined by Leroi-Gourhan (Leroi-Gourhan 1974), can be used as an analytic tool to recreate the manufacturing sequence and re-situate the artifact in its context of fabrication and use. Using the *chaîne opératoire* as the key concept of the archaeological aspect of our project allows us to understand the technological processes of basket making by focusing on the actions and gestures of the basket makers at different stages of the manufacturing process (Leroi-Gourhan 1974; Gaucher 2005).

The *chaîne opératoire* can also serve as a tool to understand how material culture and know-how are transmitted from one generation to the next as part of collective and familial traditions. Our technological data, through the prism of Redman and Ingold's theoretical approach, confirms the influence of the environment on the technological decisions made by W8banakiak artisans regarding raw-material procurement, in this case black ash, sweetgrass, and birchbark (Redman 1999; Ingold 2000; N. N. Smith 1989; C. Smith and Wobst 2004).

In addition to material culture and technology, it is essential that our research also documents the locations where raw materials (black ash and sweetgrass) were procured. This part of our research involves the analysis of core samples of forest sediments, collected through a testing program of known archaeological and historic sites. The cores are analyzed at the geochemistry laboratory of the INRS-ETE, under the supervision of Professor Pierre Francus. Having identified harvesting sites, we can outline a chronological portrait of raw-material procurement and measure the impacts of land anthropization on the resources. This data is combined to a literature review to measure the persistence of basket-making practices among the W8banakiak. Archaeological, historical, and environmental data are georeferenced using QGIS, analyzed, and referenced temporally and spatially, and stored in the Ndakina office's geomatics database.

Originality and Significance of the Project

The originality of this project rests upon the interest expressed by the W8banaki Nation in the scientific and technological analysis of ancestral W8banaki knowledge pertaining to Ndakina. The project thus contributes to the transmission of cultural and natural heritage to the W8banakiak communities, other First Nations, and people of European descent.

This project also marks the first partnership between the W8banaki Nation and the INRS-ETE. Our inclusion of the Grand Council of the Waban-Aki and the Niona youth group in the project is in line with the community-based approach (Atalay et al. 2016). This approach is a powerful tool to help develop programs and policies that reflect the priorities of the community, foster a greater sense of ownership for the nation toward the project, and build knowledge and capacity in the communities in the fields of research, planning and communications.

Conclusion

In this chapter we presented a few examples of the responses that the Ndakina office can offer to issues arising in the process of documenting ancestral knowledge. Numerous issues dealing with approximate data, difficulties in data acquisition, and Eurocentric bias are handled by the office on a daily basis. The combined efforts of the team nevertheless have revealed general trends in the evolution of LUO on Ndakina. Thematic and chronological maps display W8banakiak cultural markers that paint an increasingly clearer picture of W8banakiak settlement patterns and their adaptation to changing spatial systems on the Ndakina landscape.

Research has for too long been done on or about First Nations, and too rarely by, with, and for First Nations. A lot of projects involving "helicopter research" (flyover or fly in, fly out) are completed without considering and integrating Indigenous knowledge (Bernard 2021). Such projects have few positive outcomes for Indigenous peoples, yet they often enjoy greater scientific recognition and funding than initiatives created, managed, and disseminated by Indigenous communities. The research protocol of the Assembly of First Nations Quebec-Labrador as well as their second edition of the Tri-Council Policy Statement: Ethical Conduct for Research Involving Humans both assert the necessity to reorient research projects in accordance with the needs of Indigenous communities, and urge researchers to work in conjunction with these communities before, during, and after the projects. From now on, research initiatives must therefore be part of long-term collaborations with Indigenous communities, and researchers must fully immerse themselves in the milieu rather than make observations from a distance (Bernard 2021).

With these guidelines, research becomes more than just an exercise in data collection; it also fosters contacts and knowledge transmission between generations and families. This approach also prevents a type of rescue archaeology/ anthropology or oral history whose only aim is to document practices considered to be endangered, with no attempt at promoting their transmission or reappropriation by the group. In summary, the concept of direct transmission is central to the partnerships between the Ndakina Office of the Grand Council of the Waban-Aki Nation and its academic and governmental partners.

Acknowledgements

The professional work of the Ndakina office team was intrinsic to the success of the research and consultation projects presented here. I want to thank the whole team; many archaeological projects could not have been completed without them. My thanks also go to Suzie O'Bomsawin, director of the Ndakina office, and Denys Bernard, executive director of the Grand Council of the Waban-Aki Nation, who have agreed to support the Far Northeast: 3000 BP to Contact session at the 52nd annual meeting of the Canadian Archaeological Association, in Québec City.

References Cited

Atalay, Sonya
2012   *Community-Based Archaeology: Research with, by, and for Indigenous and Local Communities*. University of California Press, Berkeley.
Atalay, Sonya, Lee Rains Clauss, Randall H. McGuire, and John R. Welch
2016   *Transforming Archaeology: Activist Practices and Prospects*. Routledge, London.
Bourque, Bruce J.
1989   Ethnicity on the Maritime Peninsula, 1600–1759. *Ethnohistory* 36(3):257–284.
Bousquet, Marie-Pierre
1999   Sites ancestraux et territoire chez les Amérindiens du Québec. *Études Canadiennes/Canadian Studies* 47:29–40.
Boyd, Matthew, and Clarence Surette
2010   Northernmost Precontact Maize in North America. *American Antiquity* 75(1): 117–133.
Bruchac, Margaret, Siobhan Hart, and H. Martin Wobst
2010   *Indigenous Archaeologies: A Reader on Decolonization*. Routledge, London.
Calloway, Colin G.
1990   *The Western Abenakis of Vermont, 1600–1800: War, Migration, and the Survival of an Indian People*. University of Oklahoma Press, Norman.
Charland, Philippe
2005   Définition et reconstitution de l'espace territorial du nord-est amériquain: la reconstruction de la carte du W8banaki par la toponymie abénakise au Québec Aln8baïwi Kdakina – Notre monde à la manière abénakise. PhD dissertation, McGill University, Montréal.
Charland, Thomas-Marie
1964   *Les Abénakis d'Odanak*. Les Éditions du Lévrier, Montréal.
Chase, Adrian S. Z., Diane Z. Chase, and Arlen F. Chase
2017   LiDAR for Archaeological Research and the Study of Historical Landscapes. In *Sensing the Past*, edited by Nicola Masini and Francesco Soldovieri, pp. 89–100. Springer International Publishing, Cham, Switzerland.

Clermont, Norman

2001   *Enquêtes archéologiques dans le Méganticois : l'école de fouilles d'août 2001.* Université de Montréal, Montréal.

Crawford, Gary W., Della Saunders, and David G. Smith

2006   Pre-Contact Maize from Ontario, Canada: Context, Chronology, Variation, and Plant Association. In *Histories of Maize: Multidisciplinary Approaches to the Prehistory, Biogeography, Domestication, and Evolution of Maize (Zea mays L.),* edited by John E. Staller, Robert H. Tykot and Bruce F. Benz, pp. 549–559. Academic Press, New York.

Daugherty, Wayne

1983   *Historique des traitées avec les Indiens des Maritimes.* Affaires indiennes et du Nord Canada, Ottawa.

Duceppe-Lamarre, François

1999   L'archéologie du paysage à la conquête des milieux forestiers, ou l'objet paysage vu par l'archéologue de l'environnement. *Hypothèses* 1(2):85–94.

Dupont-Hébert, Céline, and Stéphane Noël

2013   *Analysis of the Zooarchaeological Assemblages of the CaFe-7 Site: Interventions of 2011 and 2012 in the Historic Quadrangle of Odanak.* Report submitted to the Musée des Abénakis, Odanak, Quebec.

Fowler, Williams S.

1974   Abodes of Four Aboriginal Periods. *Bulletin of the Massachusetts Archaeological Society* 34(34):15–22.

Gallagher, Julie M., and Richard L. Josephs

2008   Using LiDAR to Detect Cultural Resources in a Forested Environment: An Example from Isle Royale National Park, Michigan, USA. *Archaeological Prospection* 15(3):187–206.

Gates St-Pierre, Christian, and Robert G. Thompson

2015   Phytolith Evidence for the Early Presence of Maize in Southern Quebec. *American Antiquity* 80(2):408–415.

Gaucher, Gilles

2005   Comment travaillent les préhistoriens: Initiation aux méthodes de l'archéologie préhistorique. *Bulletin de la Société préhistorique française* 104(1):180–181.

GCWAN (Grand Council of the Waban-Aki Nation)

2015   *Historical study on the presence of the W8banakiak in Quebec.* Ndakina Office of the Grand Council of the Waban-Aki Nation, Ndakina.

Georges-Leroy, Murielle, Jérôme Bock, Étienne Dambrine, and Jean-Luc Dupouey

2011   Apport du lidar à la connaissance de l'histoire de l'occupation du sol en forêt de Haye. *Archeosciences revue d'archéométrie* 35(April):117–129.

Hallaren, William D.

1988   *Prehistoric Indicators from Southeastern Massachusetts, 10,500-8,000 Years B. P.* Scituate Historical Society, Scituate.

Hart, John P., Hetty J. Brumbach, and Robert Lusteck

2007   Extending the Phytolith Evidence for Early Maize (Zea Mays Ssp. Mays) and Squash (Cucurbita Sp.) in Central New York. *American Antiquity* 72(3): 563–583.

Ingold, Tim

2000   *The Perception of the Environment: Essays on Livelihood, Dwelling and Skill.* Routledge, London.

Lahaise, Robert

2006   *Nouvelle-France. English colonies.* Éditions Septentrion, Québec.

Leroi-Gourhan, André

1974   *L'homme et la matière.* Albin Michel, Paris.

Marchand, Mario

2012   La représentation sociale de l'espace traditionnel des autochtones par rapport à celle du territoire des allochtones: l'exemple de la forêt mauricienne, 1534-1934. *Cahiers de géographie du Québec* 56(159):567–582.

Nicholas, George, and Thomas Andrews

1997   Indigenous Archaeology in the Postmodern World. In *At a Crossroads: Archaeology and First Peoples in Canada,* edited by George Nicholas and Thomas Andrews, pp. 1–18. Archaeology Press, Burnaby.

Piveteau, Jean-Luc

2010   Lieu et territoire: une consanguinité dialectique? *Communications* 87(1):149–159.

Raines, June Camille Bush

1992   One Is Missing: Native American Graves Protection and Repatriation Act – An Overview and Analysis. *American Indian Law Review* 17:639.

Redman, Charles L.

1999   *Human Impacts on Ancient Environments.* University of Arizona Press, Tucson.

Robbins, Maurice

1959   Wapanucket No. 6. An Archaic Village in Middleboro, Massachusetts. *Cohannet Chapter of the Massachusetts Archaeological Society.* Massachusetts Archaeological Society, Middleborough.

Scothorne, Donald G.

1968   Oak Island Site: The Archaic Defined. *M.A.S. Bulletin* 28(3 and 4):37–53.

Sévigny, Paul-André

1976   *Les Abénaquis: habitat et migrations, 17ᵉ et 18ᵉ siècles.* Bellarmin, Montréal.

Smith, Claire, and H. Martin Wobst

2004   *Indigenous Archaeologies: Decolonising Theory and Practice.* Routledge, London.

Smith, Linda Tuhiwai

2013   *Decolonizing Methodologies: Research and Indigenous Peoples.* Zed Books, London.

Smith, Nicholas N.

1989   *The Economics of the Wabanaki Basket Industry.* Carleton University, Ottawa.

Snow, Dean R.

1978   Eastern Abenaki. In *Northeast,* edited by Bruce G. Trigger, pp. 137–147. Handbook of North American Indians, Vol. 15, William C. Sturtevant, general editor, Smithsonian Institution, Washington, DC.

Tobias, Terry N.

2009   *Living Proof: The Essential Data-Collection Guide for Indigenous Use-and-Occupancy Map Surveys.* Union of BC Indian Chiefs and Ecotrust Canada, Vancouver.

Treyvaud, Geneviève
2013 Reconstruction des technologies de production métallique employées par les artisans européens et amérindiens du XVIe au XVIIIe siècle au Canada. PhD dissertation, History Department, Université Laval, Québec.
Treyvaud, Geneviève, Suzie O'Bomsawin, and David Bernard
2018 L'expertise archéologique au sein des processus de gestion et d'affirmation territoriale du Grand Conseil de la Nation Waban-Aki. *Recherches amérindiennes au Québec* 48(3):81–90.
Treyvaud, Geneviève, and Michel Plourde
2017 *Les Abénakis d'Odanak, un voyage archéologique.* Musée des Abénakis, Odanak.
Turner, Sam
2011 Paysages et relations: archéologie, géographie, archéogéographie. *Études rurales* 188(February):143–154.
Watkins, Joe
2000 *Indigenous Archeology: American Indian Values and Scientific Practice.* Alta Mira Press, Oxford.
Williams, Daniel R., and Susan I. Stewart
1998 Sense of Place: An Elusive Concept That Is Finding a Home in Ecosystem Management. *Journal of Forestry* 96(5):18–23.
Yellowhorn, Eldon
2019 America Was Great Even Before America: How Eldon Yellowhorn Is Reclaiming Indigenous History. *School Library Journal.* https://www.slj.com?detailStory=america-was-great-even-before-america-eldon-yellowhorn-op-ed, accessed June 15, 2021.

15

THE VILLAGE OF CHOUACOËT AND THE CERAMIC AND PROTOHISTORIC PERIODS ON SACO BAY, MAINE

ARTHUR W. ANDERSON

Abstract

In 1605, Champlain described an Almouchiquois village along the Saco River estuary in Maine, which he named *Chouacoët*, in his account and chart. Recent work at the site has complicated archaeological narratives of the site as a contained, Protohistoric village, instead suggesting more varied settlement over several thousand years. This chapter highlights that equivalencies drawn between the archaeological record of the Protohistoric and European accounts can be tenuous. This work will be presented alongside a reassessment of the later Ceramic and Protohistoric period of coastal southern Maine, an area in which cultural associations with areas to the north and south are only tentatively understood, both ethnohistorically and archaeologically.

Résumé

Champlain décrit, en 1605, un village Almouchiquois au bord de l'estuaire de la rivière Saco, au Maine, qu'il nomme *Chouacoët* dans son récit et sur sa carte. De récents travaux archéologiques sur le site révèlent un historique plus complexe allant au-delà du village protohistorique décrit par Champlain, avec des occupations variées couvrant plusieurs milliers d'années. Ces fouilles illustrent bien la difficulté que peuvent avoir les archéologues à établir plus que des parallèles ténus entre leurs résultats et les sources protohistoriques et européennes. Ces résultats sont présentés en association avec une réévaluation des périodes Céramique tardive et protohistorique dans la partie sud de la côte du Maine, une région dont les liens culturels vers le nord et le sud demeurent mal définis, tant par l'ethnohistoire que par l'archéologie.

Affiliation

– Department of Society, Culture, and Languages, University of New England, Maine, United States

The supposed village site of Chouacoët at the mouth of the Saco River in southern Maine is known primarily from Champlain's famed chart of the area (Champlain 1907; figure 15.1 here) and description of his encounter with the Almouchiquois people (see Baker 2004; Spiess 1995:2) in the summer of 1605. In his narrative of the visit, he wrote that the people at Chouacoët "till and cultivate the soil, something which we have not hitherto observed," and that inhabitants "dwell permanently in this place, and have a large cabin surrounded by palisades made of rather large trees placed by the side of each other, in which they take refuge when their enemies make war upon them. They cover their cabins with oak bark" (Champlain 1907:62, 63). This description, especially its depiction of architecture and horticulture, has been interpreted in much of the subsequent literature as signifying not only a true "village" but as marking the northernmost boundary of horticultural villages on the Atlantic coast in pre- and protohistory (Mack and Will 1999, 2000; Lore 2004, 2006; Will and Mack 1998; Snow 1980: 70). Recent excavations at the site and assessment of Champlain's records suggest that this view may oversimplify the economy and settlement on the Saco River, and overemphasize the starkness of cultural and economic boundaries.

Today, the area described by Champlain is in part on the campus of the University of New England (UNE). The coast around the mouth of the Saco has been much changed by both erosion and accretion caused by large jetties constructed in the late nineteenth century, but the area remains recognizable as that depicted by Champlain. Archaeological investigation of the south bank of the river mouth has an extensive history, beginning at least in the twentieth century, due to the notoriety of Champlain's record. Work at the site has ranged from reports of investigations by "traveling archaeologists" in the late 1950s (Biddeford-Saco Journal 1959) through occasional, opportunistic testing by professional archaeologists in the 1980s and 1990s to large-scale cultural resource management (CRM) work and field schools (Mack and Will 1999, 2000; Will and Mack 1998; Will and Cole-Will, n.d.) associated with the construction of university buildings in the late 1990s and early 2000s.

Unfortunately, little record has survived of the mid-twentieth-century fieldwork. Starting in the late twentieth century, though, CRM work has established Indigenous occupation on the south bank of the Saco dating back to the Susquehanna tradition (ca. 3800 BP) and extending into the first half of the seventeenth century. This major period of work on the site involved phase I, II, and III work conducted as part of the construction of the UNE Marine Science Center and subsequent field schools held in conjunction with the Abbe Museum, in Bar Harbor, Maine (Will and Cole-Will, n.d.). In addition to disturbed patches of shell that had been previously recorded in other areas of the campus, this work identified several concentrations of archaeological material along the south bank of the river. Portions of sites 5.06 (the area at the river mouth) and 5.16, further upriver, were also excavated. Site 5.06 provided radiocarbon dates of 1430–1155 BP on a possible hearth (Lore 2004:69) and 1080–925 BP on ceramic residue (Lore 2004:72), and was interpreted as being the village described by Champlain (Will and Cole-Will, n.d.:1; Mack and Will 1999:45). This asser-tion was based in part on lead shot and potential European flint recovered from the site. Will and co-authors also concluded that the narrative of the raid on the site by Membertou in 1607 (see Morrison and Goetz 1974) constituted destruc-tion of the site and provided a *terminus post quem* for artifacts found there (Will and Cole-Will, n.d.:3). This implies that later-seventeenth-century artifacts at site 5.16 are reoccupation.

Re-excavation and reinterpretation of previous work by UNE began in the summer of 2017, returning to the area of site 5.06. The field schools associated with the various phases of CRM work at the site focused on excavating large areas, ultimately to variable depths of around between 1 m and 1.5 m. These produced a large assemblage of artifacts (well over 1,000 in the 2005 field school). Re-excavations commencing in 2017 focused instead on understanding chronology and site-formation processes. Fourteen mostly discontiguous units were excavated between 2017 and 2019, 12 of them to sterile subsoil, glacial till, or ledge (figure 15.2). This approach highlighted the potential complexity of site-formation processes and challenged the idea that this was a discrete, well-stratified, multi-component habitation site.

The area of archaeological preservation known as site 5.06 lies in a back-beach area facing east in a shallow bowl surrounded by ledge and beach. As noted by previous excavators, this area consisted of a deep sandy matrix containing artifactually rich, stratified Middle to Late Woodland deposits topped by a layer of fairly clean sand with occasional modern debris. Mid-twentieth-century excavations do not seem to have located, or disturbed, the area now recognized as site 5.06 (Mack and Will 1999:45).

The site is deeply stratified, with seemingly alternating layers of lighter and darker sand (figure 15.3) of significantly varying depths sitting atop glacial till in an area bounded by bedrock and beach. Across the site, glacial till is at a depth of 1.2 m near the storm berm in the southeast of the archaeologically sensitive area in N491E504/5 and exceeds 2.1 m depth in the northwest, in unit N510E484 (see figure 15.2). The archaeological strata have relatively little horizontal struc-ture save for the occasional possible disturbed hearth or lens of shell, which effectively preserved other non-calcined faunal remains, including fish and mammal bone and sturgeon (*Acipenser spp.*) scute. Areas in the surrounding forest which had produced no stratigraphy but positive shovel tests in previous phase I excavations were also investigated and confirmed to contain prehistoric artifacts intermixed with modern debris and historic artifacts in shallow topsoil sitting directly on ledge.

Figure 15.1. Samuel Champlain's 1605 chart of Saco Bay.
Source: Courtesy of the John Carter Brown Library.

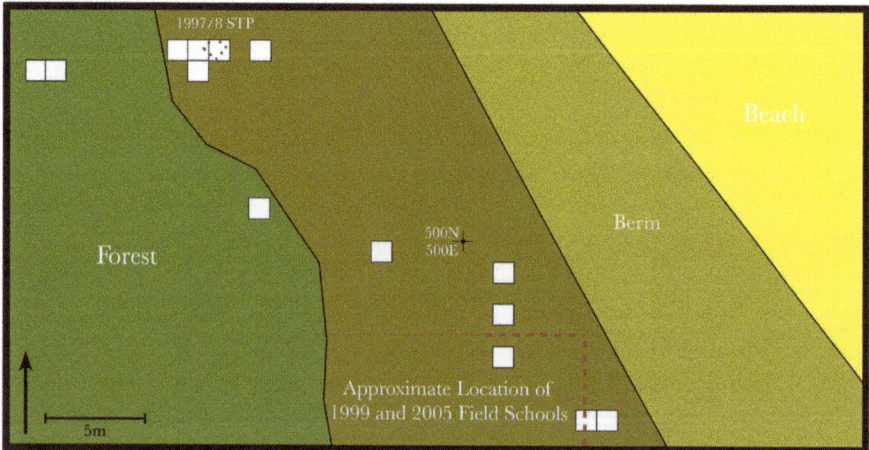

Figure 15.2. Map of 2017–2019 excavations at site 5.06.

Figure 15.3. Example of stratigraphy at site 5.06. Note the cap of clean sand above archaeological layers and the remnants of field-school excavations in profile.

Searching for Villages

Despite Champlain's clear account of horticulture on the site and portrayal of fields or gardens in his depiction of the area, excavations have produced no direct evidence of horticulture such as carbonized maize or evidence of fields such as those from Sandy's Point on Cape Cod (Mrozowski 1994). The lack of architectural remains and paucity of comparable sites in the area are an additional challenge in considering other aspects of Late Woodland settlement distribution, form, and architecture, which have been considered in relation to the introduction of maize horticulture (McBride and Dewar 1987; Chilton 2008; Farley et al. 2019). It is possible that, in time, analysis of starch and residue from the artifactual assemblage may provide more direct evidence (Chilton 2008).

Will and Cole-Will (n.d.:2) consider a large pit to be evidence of horticultural food production based on analogy with storage pits described by Champlain, but no direct evidence in the form of carbonized kernels was found within it. Such direct evidence of maize is known from the Saco River Basin further inland, potentially in quantities that suggest it was of some significance to subsistence bases (Asch Sidell 1999). Additionally, Robert Lore's detailed analysis of the faunal remains from the 1999 field-school season did not identify any significant changes in diet or economic focus in the Middle to Late Woodland period (Lore 2004, 2006), which could be attributable to a major shift in resource base. Architectural remains have not been identified, save for possible hearths.

Overall, the lack of direct evidence for horticulture in the area excavated may be evidence for task-specific use of this area (see below), and may indeed be evidence for a limited impact of horticulture on Woodland subsistence in this region, as potentially implied by Lore's results.

However, this period of excavation concluded (based in large part on Champlain's account) that this area was indeed a village (Will and Cole-Will, n.d.:1; Mack and Will 1999:45), in the sense of a year-round, concentrated area of dwellings reliant in part on horticulture in the mode of John White's depictions of the mid-Atlantic. This provided a northern boundary to the village phenomenon, as described by European visitors, while concurrently the village phenomenon was being questioned, and definition sought, in southern New England (Hart and Means 2002; Leveillee 2006; Kerber 1988; Waller 2000). Definitions of archaeological villages in the northeast vary, but do not range widely. Hart and Means (2002:346) summarize previous definitions and propose that a village is a settlement of more than two households with larger-scale social ties than a hamlet, and often at least one communal structure. Farley et al. (2019:275) suggest "the appearance of multiple multi-seasonally occupied, coterminous domestic features would be broadly interpreted to be a 'village' by most archaeologists."

By these definitions, Champlain's account may provide a village, but the archaeology has not yet provided evidence of domestic architecture or direct evidence of horticulture. It is important to critique the idea that the site represents a northernmost outpost of the "classic" New England horticultural village, especially in light of the reminder from Leveillee et al. (2006:76) that "no agreed upon [pre-Contact] village has been identified archaeologically in southern New England" since the issue of the *Bulletin of the Massachusetts Archaeological Society* publishing the results of a 1987 conference addressing the question "Where Are the Woodland Villages?," a phenomenon further noted by Farley et al. (2019:276), who note that this has "eluded confident explanation" and summarize updates on potential explanations since Kerber's (1988) summary of the phenomenon.

Searching for Champlain

Excavations starting in 2017 spurred re-evaluation of the Euro-American artifacts previously recovered and suggested to be associated with Champlain's visit (Abbe Museum, n.d.). Upon examination, this is a difficult assertion to support with the data presently available. The small lead shot recovered is not morphologically distinct. It lacks either casting sprues or the clear mould lines seen on early-seventeenth-century examples from Popham (Brain 2007:145), or the distinctive teardrop morphology of the later-seventeenth-century "Rupert's shot" (see Dewhurst 1963:371-372) as has been suggested (Abbe Museum, n.d.). Additionally, the horizontal strati-graphic integrity of lead shot in sand is readily questioned. Similar shot was recovered in the 2018 season in a context disturbed by tree roots and other bioturbation. Lead musket balls are also found regularly by UNE students along the beach and riverbanks.

Fragments of European flint shatter are also present. Extant records from the 2005 field school report the material as deep as 80 cm below surface, but as the cap of clean, potentially aeolian sand topping archaeological strata is up to 1-m deep, this may still be high in the archaeological strata (Mack and Will 1999:3). Additionally, significant penetration of historic artifacts into even Palaeoindian strata has been noted on New England sites with comparable sandy matrices such as "Dummer Dry" in New Hampshire (27-CO-149) and the Taxiway site in Maine (site ME 23.39; Gemma-Jayne Hudgell, pers. comm. 2020).

These are catalogued as ballast flint, presumably since gunflints (though clearly known to Champlain, as he draws a comparison with thumbnail scrapers seen in Massachusetts) were uncommon this early in the seventeenth century (Anderson 2020). However, unmentioned retrieval and trade of ballast flint seems incompatible with Champlain's short and well-documented visit. A scraper of potential European flint is also known from phase I investigation of the south bank of the river (Mack and Will 1998:15) in areas which produced later-seventeenth-century material, and gunflints have been recovered from disturbed or clearly historic contexts. It is most parsimonious to suggest that the fragments of flint recovered from 5.06 do not have a direct connection with Champlain's historically documented visit to the area.

Site Formation and Function

Attempts at understanding the site-formation processes suggest that this area was the seaward margin of a Middle and Late Woodland occupation site, a sort of "working waterfront" where initial processing of animal resources, terrestrial and marine, arriving at the site by canoe may have been initially processed (skinned, gutted, etc.) and tools repaired. This human activity was occasionally intermixed with some combination of hillwash, alluvium, or storm deposits, leading to artifactually rich sandy layers with little internal structure. These processes, which may have occasionally disrupted human activity, laid down the sands which produced this apparently unique instance of well-stratified preservation in what appears to be a large-scale prehistoric landscape along the south bank of the Saco.

No architectural remains have been uncovered at the site by any excavators. Initial analysis of the artifactual assemblage reinforces this "working waterfront" idea, with a predominance of broken or exhausted projectile points (figure 15.4), which may have been discarded after breakage. Some very small fragments of biface tip or edge leave open the possibility that the biface could be reworked or resharpened, and the debitage is more consistent with this sort of activity. Biface-thinning flakes and evidence of production are rare, and small (<2 cm) flakes from finishing or reworking dominate the large assemblage. Debitage to tool ratios are in the range of 80:1 to 105:1 in the units fully analyzed to date. The 2017–2019 excavations produced only three clear scrapers, compared to approximately 10 damaged projectile points or bifaces. This supports the idea that higher-level, perhaps domestic, processing tasks such as hide scraping were not carried out in this area.

Faunal remains such as calcined sturgeon scute and bone are widely distributed across the site. Occasional lenses of *Mya arenaria* shell also preserve fragments of spirally fractured cervid long bone (presumably to extract marrow), large cod (*Gadus morhua*) vertebra and sturgeon (*Acipenser oxyrinchus*) scutes, and one cut-marked deer (*Odocoileus virginianus*) sacrum. This assemblage suggests that this may be a site of initial skinning and butchering of animal remains arriving at the site.

Figure 15.4. Broken and exhausted projectile points from site 5.06.

Map or Chart?

This is at odds with the interpretation of the area as an example of the yet unrealized nucleated village in the literature, and prompts a critical reading of Champlain's narrative and depiction of the region. Despite reference to horticulture and a palisaded structure, Champlain does not use words such as "town" or "village" to describe the landscape he visited, and suggests that Chouacoët is the Indigenous name for the river or region that he visited rather than attaching it to a habitation that he thought of as a contiguous and well-defined whole.

Modern commentators often refer to Champlain's "map" as *showing* the village, and earlier excavators have even gone so far as to suggest that the palisaded structure shown on his image is directly equivalent to that described in the narrative and is, in fact, site 5.16, upriver from 5.06 (Mack and Will 1999:46). I would suggest that this is an over-interpretation of Champlain's depiction of the area, which has led to the stretching of the available evidence into a definitive (however defined) horticultural village. The landscape depicted—one of dispersed forest, ponds, individual wigwams, and clusters around longhouses, cornfields, and individuals and groups moving about—is spread across the whole of Saco Bay and several miles inland. Even a conservative estimate of the area depicted measured from modern maps is well over 100 km^2. This map should be more properly considered a nautical chart, in which the chief details are hydrographical and the out-of-scale images of people and flora, and buildings on the land are more properly seen as broad indications of the character of the landscape than as a modern map of the area in question, from which precise locations can be sought. This idea is reinforced by the commonalities in depictions of Wabanaki architecture and landscapes across the area surveyed by Champlain, suggesting even that the engravers in France were working from a repertoire of iconic, simplified depictions of Wabanaki architecture that cannot be seen as literal depictions of what is on the ground, much in the way that discrepancies between John White's original watercolours and subsequent engravings are notable.

Searching for Boundaries

It seems, then, that neither the archaeology nor the records of Champlain truly indicate that 5.06 is the site of a long-sought, archetypal Late Woodland Village. The archaeology, along with the generalized depiction of the landscape in Champlain's chart, is a better match for the idea of dispersed villages as explored by Leveillee et al. (2006). Though the lack of architectural evidence renders this merely a best-fit suggestion, based on the archaeology and ethnohistorical reports, this is the model that most effectively bridges the gap between the ethnohistorical and archaeological records. It provides a model which accepts that the social formation which European visitors may have seen as a village could take a more dispersed and less archaeologically visible form. This is a potential solution to the problem of the missing villages, first broadly explored by Luedtke (1988).

Leveillee et al. (2006:85) arrive at the idea of large but diffuse agricultural settlements covering large areas by suggesting that "rather than having a pre-conceived mould and looking for something that fits into it, let's consider what we do have." At 5.06, what we do have is a large-scale archaeological landscape with significant but varied Middle and Late Woodland activity, and horticulture practised to some degree, at least by the turn of the seventeenth century.

Part of the usefulness of the dispersed village concept is its scalability in a region which appears to be a fluid zone of interaction between different social and economic traditions in the Late Woodland. Champlain does speak of Saco Bay as a boundary, not one of horticulture, architectural tradition, or community forms but one of language, stating that their interpreter "could understand only a few words, as the language of the Almouchiquois (for that is the name of this nation) differs entirely from that of the Souriquois and Etechemins" (Champlain 1907:61). This coincides with a geographical change from the rocky and heavily indented shorelines of the Maine coast to north, and the series of broad, arcing sandy bays which stretch to Cape Cod to the south (see Kelley 1987).

Though changes of environment may align with differing subsistence strategies which provide different context for horticulture, and though this linguistic boundary fits neatly with the idea of the northernmost horticultural village, Champlain records instances of engagement with horticulture or the idea of horticulture along the Maine coast which belie this. At the Kennebec, Champlain (1907:60) recounts that "[t]he people live like those in the neighbourhood of our settlement; and they told us that the savages, who plant the Indian corn, dwelt very far in the interior, and that they had given up planting it on the coasts on account of the war they had with others, who came and took it away." This passage suggests that horticulture was a well-known phenomenon on the coast that had come and gone from more northerly communities. Even if the dispersed-village model requires maize horticulture, it may have ranged far more widely north than hitherto suggested. If Verrazano had made more detailed records along the Kennebec a century earlier, would it be the most northerly outpost of prehistoric village horticulture rather than the Saco? This is an example of the ossification of dynamic prehistoric practices in the archaeological conventional wisdom caused by over-reliance on European records as the Late Woodland springs into the early Protohistoric.

This apparent fluidity demonstrates that horticulture may have been a useful practice in certain social or economic contexts but did not drive the type of social change along the Maine coast that has been posited for southern New England. The impact of maize horticulture in New England has been heavily debated (see Farley et al. 2019 for a recent summary), and some have gone so far as to qualify the introduction of horticulture as a "non-event" (McBride and Dewar 1987:316). In interpretation of site 5.06, this fits with Lore's faunal analysis (2004, 2006), which suggests no major dietary shifts that could be related to the advent of horticulture. This line of evidence minimizes the importance of horticulture but does not rule out social and economic intensification that is characteristic of the Woodland in eastern North America.

Recent faunal analysis in the Canadian Quoddy Region has demonstrated exploitation of tomcod at unprecedented levels in the Late Woodland (Webb 2018). At Port Joli, Nova Scotia, evidence for shifts toward larger, more permanent settlements during the Late Maritime Woodland have been proposed through detailed examination of faunal evidence (Betts et al. 2017). This is in line with the "significant reconfiguration" in the Late Maritime Woodland in the Quoddy Region proposed by David Black (2002:313), and potential evidence for large, late-prehistoric weir structures has recently been uncovered closer to 5.06 at Cape Porpoise, Maine (Spahr 2019), indicating the scale of the exploitation of marine resources in this period.

It seems increasingly likely that the broad intensification of Late Woodland communities is a wider set of phenomena than horticulture. This critical assessment of the idea of a terminal "boundary" of horticulture constrained by technology and climate supports this idea.

The idea that technologies, social and practical, were moving across this linguistic and geographic boundary fits with the preliminary analysis of artifacts, particularly lithics, from recent excavations at 5.06.

Society and Economy

The material cultural assemblage from site 5.06 further demonstrates wide-ranging social and economic networks. Though few of the fragmented projectile points can be identified confidently to type, at least one Fox Creek-style point suggests the influence of southern New England, a phenomenon also noted by Will and Cole-Will (n.d.) in preliminary analysis of earlier finds. The range of lithic materials shows broad connections, however, especially when compared with assemblages to the north or south. The artifacts clearly demonstrate the typical Woodland focus on high-quality and well-travelled lithics (Hrynick et al. 2017:100; Black 2004; Bourque 2004:100) such as yellow jasper (some a microscopic match for Vera Cruz jasper but other examples ambiguous; see Luedtke 1987), Onondaga chert, and Ramah quartzite. However, the assemblage is dominated by rhyolites likely from the Lynn volcanic complex, while also demonstrating trading links both up the Saco and northwards along the Gulf of Maine. Ossipiee hornfels and probably crystal quartz are likely travelling down the river. Materials from the north and east, which are rare to absent on coastal

Massachusetts site like Run Hill (Strauss 1999), are represented—Munsungan chert, Minas Basin chert, and Vinalhaven rhyolite are notably present. Kineo–Traveler rhyolite is common, and Normanskill cherts appear to be present as well.

The ethnohistoric record further illuminates the breadth of this web of social and economic connections from Chouacoët, as Champlain's and Lescarbot's later accounts of Membertou's raid on Chouacoët in 1607 (Morrison and Goetz 1974) demonstrate social networks stretching across the entirety of the Gulf of Maine in the Late Woodland and Protohistoric that are at least close enough to create considerable animosity and violence.

Conclusions

Archaeology on the rest of Saco Bay is notably sparse, save for fragmentary records on early maps and whispers from collectors of another "Indian Village" at Pine Point, across the bay from 5.06. This could suggest that more ephemeral previous occupation coalesced into fairly regular dispersed villages in the Middle to Late Woodland, similar to the pattern suggested by Hart et al. (2005) as an effect of maize horticulture among the Monongahela. These may have been minimally *reliant* on horticulture but still have a socio-economic context for horticulture, a phenomenon which might be coming and going up and down the coast in the centuries prior to European arrival. That said, the area is under-explored compared to much of the rest of the Maine coast due to development and a complex interplay of accretion and erosion, in part caused by human structures designed to control such processes, such as at Camp Ellis across the river from the site.

In conclusion, examination of the porousness of the geographic and linguistic boundary of Saco Bay contradicts the idea of a climate-constrained limit of horticulture and villages, which is then, by necessity, a boundary to increasing social complexity, sedentism, and intensification of resource exploitation in the Late Woodland. It reinforces the suggestion that the broader background of intensification and sedentism in the Late Woodland had multiple instigators beyond maize horticulture (Farley et al. 2019:288). In addition to maize horticulture in southern New England, we see an increase in the scale of resource exploitation in the Maritimes and Quoddy Region (Betts 2017; Black 2002; Webb 2018). Closer to the Saco, late prehistoric intertidal fish weirs have recently been identified, which speak to the scale of the harvesting of marine resources at that time (Spahr 2019). This complicates the idea of a division between New England and the Maritime Peninsula (*sensu* Farley et al. 2019). Intensification is increasingly visible as a phenomenon throughout the Far Northeast and does not have a "border" at the edges of horticulture. Better understanding the fluidity of this boundary is an opportunity to explore the variable manifestations and effects of late Woodland intensification throughout time and space.

Acknowledgements
Huge thanks to Gabe Hrynick and Ken Holyoke for inviting me to this session (and much besides) and to all the other participants for a fascinating couple of days. Thanks also to Art Spiess, Rick Will, and the Abbe Museum for access to unpublished data; to Katherine Patton, Tim Spahr, and Dick Doyle for field assistance and wisdom; and to Delaney Collins for editing and formatting. Work at the Chouacoët site has been supported by the University of New England Office of Research and Scholarship and by FutureReadyNB.

References Cited

Abbe Museum
n.d.   Featured Items from the Abbe's Collections: Lead Shot. Electronic document, http://www.abbemuseum.org/research/collections/curator-features/lead-shot.html, accessed December 15, 2017.

Anderson, Arthur W.
2020   Exploring Economic Priorities of Protohistoric Communities: Case Studies from Northeastern New England and Northern Britannia. Paper presented at the 2020 Society for Historical Archaeology Conference on Historical and Underwater Archaeology, Boston.

Asch Sidell, Nancy
1999   Prehistoric Plant Use in Maine: Palaeoindian to Contact Period. In *Current Northeast Paleobotany*, edited by John P. Hart, pp. 191–224. New York State Museum, Albany.

Baker, Emerson W.
2004   Finding the Almouchiquois: Native American Families, Territories, and Land Sales in Southern Maine. *Ethnohistory* 51(1):73–100.

Betts, Matthew W., Meghan Burchell, and Bernd R. Schöne
2017   An Economic History of the Maritime Woodland Period in Port Joli Harbour, Nova Scotia. *Journal of the North Atlantic* (Special Issue) 10:18–41.

Biddeford-Saco Journal
1959   Indian Relics Uncovered Here. *Biddeford-Saco Journal*, 26 May. Saco, Maine.

Black, David W.
2002   Out of the Blue and Into the Black: The Middle-Late Maritime Woodland Transition in the Quoddy Region, New Brunswick, Canada. In *Northeast Subsistence-Settlement Change: A.D. 700–1300*, edited by John P. Hart and Christina B. Reith, pp. 345–358. New York State Museum, Albany.
2004   *Living Close to the Ledge: Prehistoric Human Ecology of the Bliss Islands, Quoddy Region, New Brunswick, Canada.* 2nd ed. Copetown Press, Saint John.

Bourque, Bruce
2004   *Twelve Thousand Years: American Indians in Maine.* Bison Books, Lincoln, Nebraska.

Brain, Jeffery Phipps
2007   *Fort St. George: Archaeological Investigation of the 1607–1608 Popham Colony.* Occasional Publications in Maine Archaeology 12. The Maine Historic Preservation Commission and the Maine Archaeological Society, Augusta.

Champlain, Samuel
1907   *Voyages of Samuel De Champlain*. Edited by W. L. Grant. Charles Scribner's Sons, New York.

Chilton, Elizabeth S.
2008   So Little Maize, So Much Time: Understanding Maize Adoption in New England. In *Current Northeast Paleoethnobotany II*, edited by John P. Hart, pp. 53–60. New York State Museum, Albany.

Dewhurst, Kenneth
1963   Prince Rupert as a Scientist. *British Journal for the History of Science* 1(4): 365–373.

Farley, William A., Amy N. Fox, and M. Gabriel Hrynick
2019   A Quantitative Dwelling-Scale Approach to the Social Implications of Maize Horticulture in New England. *American Antiquity* 84(2):274–291.

Hart, John P., and Bernard K. Means
2002   Maize and Villages: A Summary and Critical Assessment of Current Northeast Early Late Prehistoric Evidence. In *Northeast Subsistence-Settlement Change: A.D. 700–1300*, edited by John P. Hart and Christina B. Reith, pp. 345–358. New York State Museum, Albany.

Hart, John P., John P. Nass, and Bernard K. Means
2005   Monongahela Subsistence-settlement Change? *Midcontinental Journal of Archaeology* 30(2):327–365.

Hrynick, M. Gabriel, W. Jesse Webb, Christopher E. Shaw, and Taylor Testa
2017   Late Maritime Woodland to Protohistoric Culture Change and Continuity at the Devil's Head Site, Calais, Maine. *Archaeology of Eastern North America* 45:85–108.

Kelley, Joseph T.
1987   An Inventory of Coastal Environments and Classification of Maine's Glaciated Shoreline. In *Glaciated Coastlines*, edited by Peter S. Rosen and Duncan M. Fitzgerald, pp. 151–176. Academic Press, San Diego.

Kerber, Jordan E.
1988   Where Are the Woodland Villages? Preface. *Bulletin of the Massachusetts Archaeological Society* 49(2):44–45.

Leveillee, Alan, Joseph Waller Jr., and Donna Ingham
2006   Dispersed Villages in Late Woodland Period South-Coastal Rhode Island. *Archaeology of Eastern North America* 34:71–89.

Lore, Robert J.
2004   Ceramic Period Adaptations in the Gulf of Maine. Master's thesis, University of Maine, Orono.
2006   Adaptations in the Edge Environment: Faunal Analysis of an Armouchiquois Indian Village. In *Maine Archaeological Society Bulletin* 46(1):1–22.

Luedtke, Barbara E.
1987   The Pennsylvania Connection: Jasper at Massachusetts Sites. *Bulletin of the Massachusetts Archaeological Society* 48(2):37–47.
1988   Where Are the Late Woodland Villages in Eastern Massachusetts? *Bulletin of the Massachusetts Archaeological Society* 49(2):67–75.

Mack, Karen, and Richard Will

1999   Additional Phase I Archaeological Survey of the Proposed University of New England Marine Center, Biddeford, York County, Maine. Manuscript on file at the Maine Historic Preservation Commission, Augusta, Maine.

2000   Results of Phase III Archaeological Testing of the Proposed University of New England's Marine Studies Center, Biddeford, York County, Maine. Manuscript on file at the Maine Historic Preservation Commission, Augusta, Maine.

McBride, Kevin A., and Robert E. Dewar

1987   Agriculture and Cultural Evolution: Causes and Effects in the Lower Connecticut River Valley. In *Emergent Horticultural Economies of the Eastern Woodlands*, edited by William F. Keegan, pp. 205–238. University of Illinois, Carbondale.

Morrison, Alvin H, and Thomas H. Goetz

1974   Membertou's Raid on the Chouacoët "Alamouchiquois"—The Micmac Sack of Saco in 1607; English Translation of Marc Lescarbot. In *6th Algonquian Conference Papers*, pp. 141–79. University of Ottawa Press, Ottawa.

Mrozowski, Stephen A.

1994   The Discovery of a Native American Cornfield on Cape Cod. *Archaeology of Eastern North America* 22:47–62.

Snow, Dean R.

1980   *The Archaeology of New England.* Academic Press, San Diego.

Spahr, Tim

2019   Northeast Algonquian Weir Remains at Redin Island: Comparing Local Features to Historic Illustrations. *Maine Archaeological Society Bulletin* 59(1):1–20.

Spiess, Arthur E.

1995   Early Contact Period Context. *Maine Archaeological Society Bulletin* 35(1):1–20.

Strauss, Alan E.

2019   The Importance of Pond-side Sites During the Late Woodland Period on Cape Cod: The View from Run Hill. *Archaeology of Eastern North America* 47:87–110.

Waller, Joseph N.

2000   Late Woodland Settlement and Subsistence in Southern New England Revisited. *North American Archaeologist* 21(2):139–153.

Webb, W. Jesse.

2018   In a Late Maritime Woodland Peskotomuhkati Fishery from the Mainland Quoddy Region, Southwestern New Brunswick, Canada. Master's thesis, University of New Brunswick, Fredericton.

Will, Richard, and Karen Mack

1998   Phase I Archaeological Survey of the Proposed University of New England's Marine Studies Center, Biddeford, York County, Maine. Manuscript on file at the Maine Historic Preservation Commission, no. 3016, Augusta, Maine.

Will, Richard, and Rebecca Cole-Will

n.d.   The Chouacoët Site: 2005 Investigations. Manuscript on file, Abbe Museum, Bar Harbor, Maine.

16

THE ORIGIN OF ST. LAWRENCE IROQUOIAN POTTERY IN NORTHERN NEW ENGLAND

New Data on an Old Question

ROLAND TREMBLAY,[1] CLAUDE CHAPDELAINE,[2] AND GREG KENNEDY[3]

Abstract

A recurring theme in the study of cultural dynamics during the late pre-Contact period in the Far Northeast is the relation between Iroquoian populations and their surrounding Algonquian neighbours. In northern New England, sites where typical St. Lawrence Iroquoian pottery was found offer the opportunity to address this question in chemically analyzing the clay of vessels. Samples were taken from 11 vessels of typical St. Lawrence Iroquoian style from Vermont and Maine and submitted to neutron-activation analysis. The results are compared with archaeological and natural data from different areas in the St. Lawrence Valley, and are discussed within the wider scope of research on the St. Lawrence Iroquoian and their relation to the ancestors of the Abenaki people of northern New England.

Résumé

L'un des thèmes récurrents de l'étude des dynamiques culturelles au cours de la période tardive précédant le Contact dans le Nord-Est est la relation entre les populations iroquoiennes et leurs voisins algonquiens. Quelques sites, situés dans le nord de la Nouvelle Angleterre et où fut trouvée de la poterie caractéristique des Iroquoiens du Saint-Laurent, offrent une occasion d'aborder cette question par l'entremise d'une comparaison chimique des argiles de la poterie. Des échantillons ont été prélevés sur 11 vases d'un style typiquement iroquoien du Saint-Laurent retrouvés sur des sites du Vermont et du Maine et soumis à des analyses d'activation neutronique. Nous comparons les résultats avec des échantillons de poteries et d'argiles naturelles provenant de différents endroits le long de la vallée du Saint-Laurent et discutons de leurs implications sur la recherche en cours à propos des Iroquoiens du Saint-Laurent et de leurs liens avec les populations ancestrales des Abénaquis du nord de la Nouvelle-Angleterre.

Affiliations

1. Senior Archaeologist, Ethnoscop Inc., Quebec, Canada
2. Département d'anthropologie, Université de Montréal, Quebec, Canada
3. Département de génie physique, Polytechnique Montréal, Quebec, Canada

In the study of late pre–Contact societies of northeastern North America, archaeologists have often relied on the ceramic record to build a cultural framework through space and time. The emphasis on this type of data is certainly disproportional to the importance pottery played in the societies studied, and often hides our poor knowledge of the subsistence portion of material culture. Nevertheless, the particular nature of ceramic production is still of great value for uncovering past human cultural identities and relationships. One area of ceramic studies that has particular potential in that regard concerns the chemical composition of clay. Chemical components will vary according to the source of clay that was used to make pottery, and this variation in the data may be interpreted to represent different cultural phenomena, such as procurement, movement, exchange, stylistic borrowing, etc., in which groups were involved. In northern New England, some late prehistoric archaeological sites have produced pottery identical in style and technology to vessels fabricated by the St. Lawrence Iroquoians during the period between 1400 and 1600 CE. These vessels have generated discussion among Iroquoian and northern New England archaeologists over the years, especially concerning the cultural identity of those who made it (Boisvert et al. 1995; Chapdelaine et al. 1995; Cowie and Petersen 1999; Haviland and Power 1994; Jamieson 2005, 2007; Pendergast 1990; Perkins 1871; Petersen 1990, 1993; Petersen and Sanger 1991; Petersen and Toney 2000; Tremblay 1999, Willoughby 1909, 1935: Wiseman 2000).

Specific examples of this shared style include three complete vessels found in the nineteenth century in Vermont: the Colchester jar and the Bolton Falls jars (Petersen and Toney, 2000). These vessels, as well as other finds in the same general area of the eastern Lake Champlain lowlands, have led some researchers to examine the St. Lawrence Iroquoian connection that seemed to lie behind these vessels. Jim Pendergast even proposed that there was maybe a resident population of St. Lawrence Iroquoians in the region, forming an independent cluster in the same manner that we have identified over the years in the

St. Lawrence River Valley (Abel 2019; Chapdelaine 2015; Pendergast 1990; Petersen 1990; Petersen et al. 2004; Tremblay 2006; Tremblay et al. 2015).

In the 1990s, archaeological work in northern New England uncovered further examples of pottery typical of the St. Lawrence Iroquoian ceramic tradition in Vermont, in and around the Alburg Peninsula on Lake Champlain, at the Bohannon site (VT-GI-26/32), as well as a few others (Gates St-Pierre 2007; Jamieson 2005, 2007; Petersen et al. 2004). The same was true in New Hampshire, at the Ingalls site on the Connecticut River in the Cowas area (Boisvert 1994). In Maine, in the Norridgewock area on the Kennebec River, the Tracy Farm, Moore, and Sandy River sites also revealed pottery that was associated with the St. Lawrence Iroquoian tradition (Cowie and Petersen 1992, 1999; Cowie et al. 2000).

During the same decade, Late Woodland–period archaeology on the Quebec side of the border was uncovering clues that the St. Lawrence Iroquoians had links with the northern New England region. In the area of Brome-Missisquoi, a municipality in the Eastern Townships, north of Lake Champlain, St. Lawrence Iroquoian sites were discovered in the Pike River drainage. The Bilodeau (BgFg-1), Gasser (BgFg-2), and Florent-Gosselin (BgFg-6) sites represent seasonal fishing encampments, just north of the Alburg Peninsula cluster of sites (Blais 1993; Blais et al. 1996; Chapdelaine 1996).

East of the Hudson/Champlain/Richelieu axis, some form of cultural interaction was being hypothesized in more subtle links in the area between the northern Maine rivers (Kennebec, Penobscot, Saint John) and the St. Lawrence lowlands between the Chaudière River/Québec City area and the Madawaska River/Lake Témiscouata area to the east. Here, the northern counterparts of the Norridgewock sites are mirrored by eastern St. Lawrence Iroquoian sites, where clues of interactions across the Appalachian divide occur. Down the St. Lawrence Valley, a few examples of shell-tempered ceramics have been found, mixed in contexts where St. Lawrence Iroquoian pottery (the Place Royale site in Québec City, the Turcotte-Lévesque site on île Verte), were interpreted as clues of northern New England connections with the St. Lawrence Iroquoians. Shell-tempered pottery is not present in the ceramic traditions of the St. Lawrence Valley but exists in the Late Ceramic tradition sequence of northern New England and the Maritime Peninsula (Petersen and Sanger 1991). In the same general eastern area of the St. Lawrence Valley, northern New England lithics are often found in St. Lawrence Iroquoian contexts (Tremblay 1997). As an example, the general use/presence of Kineo rhyolite on Late Woodland sites of the Québec City area and along the St. Lawrence Estuary is a good indicator of relationships between both areas (see Chapdelaine, this volume). At the Norridgewock sites, different elements other than the presence of St. Lawrence Iroquoian pottery, such as the easternmost manifestation of maize horticulture and longhouse architecture on the Atlantic side of the Maritime Peninsula, might be explained by sustained interactions with St. Lawrence Iroquoians (Tremblay and Petersen 2004).

To begin to understand the nature of St. Lawrence Iroquoian pottery in New England, an initial investigation was done by means of instrumental neutron-activation analysis (INAA) on a decorated rim sherd with the corn-ear motif from the Ingalls site that was compared to natural clays and pottery samples from the Pike River area north of Lake Champlain, and to natural clay samples from the Pointe-du-Buisson site near Montréal (Chapdelaine et al. 1995). While the results remain preliminary, some links could be tentatively drawn with the pottery of the Pike River sites.

This work follows up on this initial attempt by broadening the data sample of ceramics sherds analyzed using INAA. Our objective is to determine the origin of the St. Lawrence pottery found in two regions of New England. On the western axis, the selected rim sherds from the Alburg Peninsula in Vermont offer a sample of a hypothetical resident St. Lawrence Iroquoian population at the Bohannon site. For the eastern axis, the rim sherds identified as St. Lawrence Iroquoian from the Norridgewock sites in Maine offer a sample in the context of cultural interactions between Iroquoians of the Québec City region and local Algonquian populations. In both cases, the ceramic samples are compared to known data from the St. Lawrence Valley (figure 16.1). Our goal is to evaluate whether the New England samples were being made locally, by resident populations, or fabricated in the St. Lawrence Valley and obtained through exchange.

The Samples

The Vermont sample comes from the Bohannon site. Located on the Alburg Peninsula on the north end of Lake Champlain, it was found and eventually excavated before the construction of a new highway bridge. Extensive fieldwork revealed a single St. Lawrence Iroquoian-component occupation, dated to the sixteenth century (Petersen et al. 2004). Features included pits with charcoal, pottery, fauna, and organic material under the plow zone.

Five vessels were selected for our study and they all clearly show St. Lawrence Iroquoian characteristics (figure 16.2). Two of them (1264.1 and 1284.1) come from pit feature no. 6, while samples 1343.1 and 538.2 come from pit feature no. 1, and the last vessel (14039.1), a typical low collar vessel, was found in pit feature no. 49 (Petersen et al. 2004:109-115). These three pits, which may have been used for processing or roasting, provided a total of seven radiocarbon dates, of which six support the chronological position of the selected vessels during the last two centuries of the prehistoric sequence, including the three latest ones, obtained on maize.

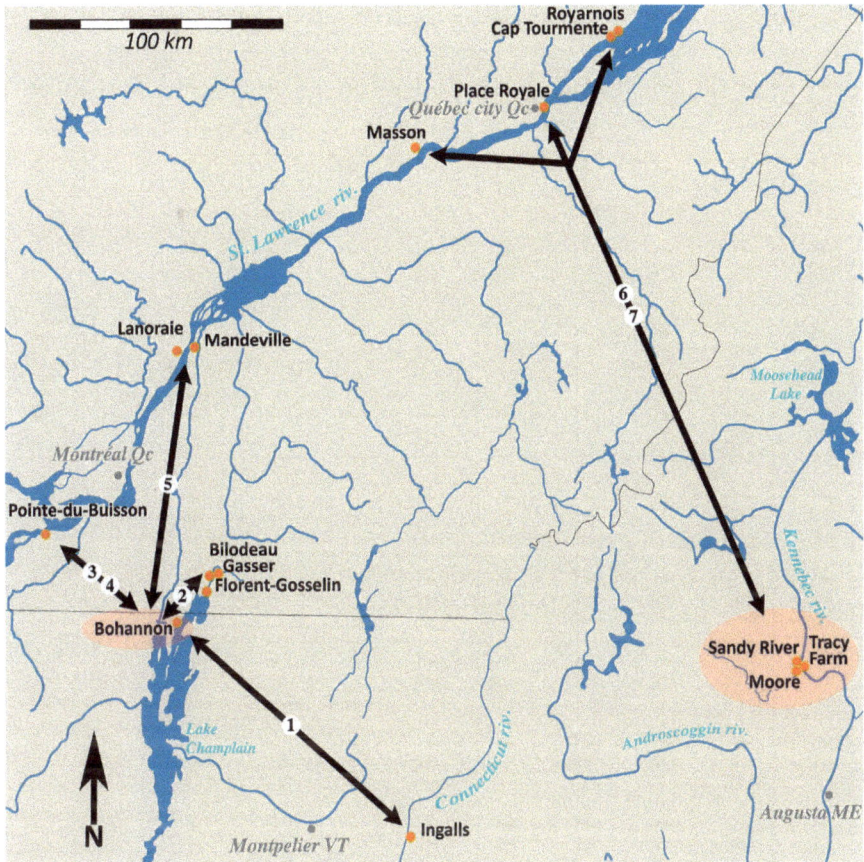

Figure 16.1. Geographical location of the sites discussed in this chapter, with axes of pottery and clay relationships that are examined. The numbers indicated on the axes correspond to the dendrograms appearing in figure 16.4 (dendrogram 1), figure 16.6 (dendrogram 2), and figures 16.8 to 16.12 (dendrograms 3 to 7).

Our Maine sample comes from three sites of the Norridgewock area: the Tracy Farm site on the right bank just upstream from the Sandy River, the Moore site on the left bank, and the Sandy River site on the right bank at the mouth of the Sandy River. These sites are located on the banks of the Kennebec River. The Tracy Farm site is a large late prehistoric/Contact-period site from which a small sample of St. Lawrence Iroquoian pottery was found. Notably, a longhouse structure measuring roughly 5 m wide by nearly 25 m long was found at the site. This is still the unique archaeological occurrence of this type of late pre-Contact house structure in northern New England (Cowie and Petersen 1992:229). Six vessels were sampled, two from each site (figure 16.3). Radiocarbon dates associated with the SLI pottery at the Sandy River site support the possibility of two occupations, both of which from the late prehistoric period. The latest one was originally reported uncalibrated and considered to date around 1650 CE, which is well over the common date of circa 1580 that is usually used to mark the end of the occupation of the St. Lawrence Valley by the St. Lawrence Iroquoians, but once calibrated it is very similar to the latest Bohannon dates on maize and could very well point to a late-1500s occupation (Petersen et al. 2004:102–106).

Table 16.1. Description of Vermont and Maine samples.

# INAA code	site code	site name	catalog number	context	description	associated radiocarbon age BP (uncalibrated)	calibrated date AD (2 sigma, IntCal13)
1014	VT-GI-26	Bohannon	1284-1	pit feature 6	corn ear motif collar	Beta-154528: 700 ± 60 (charcoal)	1219–1333; 1336–1398
1015	VT-GI-26	Bohannon	1264-1	pit feature 6	complex motif with circular punctates on low crestellated collar	Beta-168017: 330 ± 40 (maize)	1466–1645
						Beta-168020: 490 ± 60 (charcoal)	1301–1367; 1382–1516; 1595–1618
						Beta-168021: 380 ± 60 (charcoal)	1437–1641
1016	VT-GI-26	Bohannon	538-2	pit feature 1	complex motif with circular punctate on high collar	Beta-168019: 460 ± 60 (charcoal)	1319–1350; 1391–1525; 1556–1632
						Beta-168016: 330 ± 40 (maize)	1456–1637
1017	VT-GI-26	Bohannon	1343-1	pit feature 1	complex motif with circular punctates on low crestellated collar	Beta-168018: 450 ± 60 (charcoal)	1325–1344; 1394–1528; 1516–1634
1018	VT-GI-26	Bohannon	14039-1	pit feature 49	simple motif on low collar	Beta-23228x: 320 ± 40 (maize)	1470–1648
1019	ME-69-24	Sandy River	778	buried soil feature 9	simple motif on castellated collar	Beta-43975: 500 ± 110 (charcoal)	1300–1369; 1381–1491; 1602–1612
1020	ME-69-24	Sandy River	407	roasting pit feature 5	circular punctates on low collar	Beta-43974: 300 ± 80 (charcoal)	1484–1661
1021	ME-69-20	Moore	316	plow zone	complex motif on low collar	context not dated	
1022	ME-69-20	Moore	444	plow zone	simple motif on low collar	context not dated	
1023	ME-69-11	Tracy Farm	6252	plow zone	circular punctates	context not dated	
1024	ME-69-11	Tracy Farm	1152	plow zone	complex motif with circular punctates on crestellated collar	context not dated	

Figure 16.2. Sampled rim sherds of the Bohannon site, Vermont.

Figure 16.3. Sampled rim sherds of Norridgewock sites, Maine.

Methodology

Neutron-Activation Analysis

Neutron–activation analysis (NAA) relies on the physical properties of the atomic nucleus (see Glascock 1992 for more information on the physical and chemical principles of the method; Chapdelaine et al. 2001). It consists of the introduction of a sample into a nuclear reactor, following which the sample is bombarded with neutrons, producing a nuclear reaction. The absorption of a neutron by an atom of the sample produces a radioisotope. Later, at a time that depends on its half-life, the atom will emit its excess energy in the form of beta and gamma rays. The latter are measured using a semiconductor detector made of germanium (Ge). The gamma-ray spectrum obtained from the analysis of a sample allows the identification of the chemical elements present in the sample on the basis of their gamma-ray energy and the determination of the concentration from the number of gamma rays detected. The chemical elements detected and analyzed in the following study are Na (sodium), Mg (magnesium), Al (aluminum), K (potassium), Ca (calcium), Sc (scandium), Ti (titanium), V (vanadium), Mn (manganese), Fe (iron), Rb (rubidium), Cs (cesium), Ba (barium), La (lanthanum), Eu (europium), Lu (lutetium), Hf (hafnium), Ta (tantalum), Th (thorium), and U (uranium). The analyses were carried out using a Canadian SLOWPOKE nuclear reactor of the École Polytechnique of Montréal under the supervision of Greg Kennedy. This reactor produces a flux of 10^{12} neutrons/cm ^{2}/s.

Sample Preparation

In this process, it is very important to prepare all the samples following the same method. This standardization starts with the preparation of the artifacts. When working with natural clay, it is dried and cleaned of coarse organic and mineral inclusions. The preparation of a clay sample consists of weighing the cleaned clay powder and placing it in a polyethylene vial.

When dealing with baked-clay objects, one needs to choose a clean (and if possible internal) area where no more than 200 mg of clay powder is removed with an electric drill and tungsten steel bit. It is assumed that the sample is representative of the vessel since the baked-clay objects may have a value in a museum setting (e.g., as display items) and the area to extract clay is limited. During this process, the coarser mineral inclusions from the temper are also removed from the artifacts. These are removed from the sample to leave mostly the clay material. This method is slightly destructive, but it allows the extraction of a small quantity of clay without reducing its museum value.

It is important to note that the metal bits used for the clay extraction have been analyzed so that we know their exact chemical composition relative to tungsten. During the analysis process, the chemical elements from the bit are removed from the results based on the observed amount of tungsten. In this case, the bit used was rich in chromium (Cr), antimony (Sb), and cobalt (Co), which were not included in the calculations.

Irradiation and Counting Schemes

Once prepared, the samples are sent to the École Polytechnique de Montréal. Three different irradiation and counting schemes are used depending on the half-lives of the expected elements: Na, Mg, Al, Ca, Ti, V, Mn, and Ba are analyzed with a short irradiation time (1 min.), a decay time of 13 minutes, and a counting time of 10 minutes. For the other elements, the samples are irradiated in batches of 10, with an irradiation time of eight hours. For K, La, and U the decay time is five days and the counting time two hours, and for Sc, Fe, Rb, Cs, Eu, Lu, Hf, Ta, and Th the decay time is 21 days and the counting time three hours. For the three schemes, the decay time (the waiting time between irradiation and gamma-ray counting) has been optimized to improve the quality of the results (Crépeau and Kennedy 1990:68). The three measurements are completed in 25 days, which is mostly waiting time.

Data Normalization

Data from INAA are first expressed in relation to the weight of the sample, the raw data (table 16.2A), and later normalized to remove errors due to dilution (table 16.2B). Indeed, the samples contain non-measured components such as water (H_2O), silica (SiO_2), and organic material whose diluting properties can reduce the concentrations of the elements studied. The method used here consists of dividing the concentration of each chemical element by the sum of all the concentrations considered. Normalized data are expressed in parts per million following this formula

$$N_i = \frac{1,000,000\,C_i}{\sum_{j=1}^{20} C_j}\,,$$

where the C_i is the measured concentration. Once normalized, the data are used to compare samples. This requires the calculation of the distance matrix, using a standardized unit that places all the chemical elements on the same scale. For each element, the unit corresponds to the standard deviation of the normalized concentrations in the clay samples.

The distance between two samples (a and b), which may be referred to as city-block distance (as opposed to Euclidean distance), is calculated with the following formula:

$$Da - b = \sum_{i=1}^{n} \frac{|Na_i - Nb_i|}{u_i}$$

The distance calculation for pairs of artifacts creates a bivariate distance matrix useful for identifying the closest neighbours. A small distance between two samples means that the chemical composition of the two artifacts is very similar. The distance matrix is then easily converted into a dendrogram showing the structure of the data.

In the dendrogram, where each sample is linked to its nearest neighbour, chemically similar artifacts are grouped into ever more inclusive clusters until all samples are part of a single, undifferentiated group. Here, the researcher may choose which distance represents the threshold between similarity and dissimilarity. In these and previous analyses (Clermont el al. 1995:9), a distance of 1 to 19.9 has been considered as a close proximity between two artifacts. A distance of 20 to 29.9 was considered as a relative proximity and a result of 30 and over as a significant difference between two objects.

The method used to calculate distances and to construct a dendrogram is not unique. In order to verify if another clustering method might give different results from the single-link clustering with the city-block distances, we tried single-link clustering with Euclidian distances and the centroid linkage method with Euclidian distances. Both methods gave dendrograms quite similar to figure 16.5, which confirms the validity of our method.

Results and Discussion

The dendrograms presented here are based on distances between the compared samples. For the interested reader, these tables for figures 16.5–16.11 are available on demand, as is the whole matrix of raw data for all the samples used in the comparisons made for this chapter. The reproduction of these eight tables of raw data is not possible here and only the dendrograms are offered to illustrate the results.

The Vermont Sample

The dendrogram of figure 16.4 shows that the five vessels of the Bohannon do cluster well together with distances ranging from 20 to 30, a range that is expected within samples taken from a single component site. This shows some coherence in the clay sourcing used for the vessels from the Bohannon site.

Our first comparison for the Vermont group is with samples from the Cowas area in New Hampshire. It consists of seven pottery samples (N617-N622) from the Ingalls site (27-GR-112) as well as one clay sample (N616) from Pool Brook in North Haverhill, on the Connecticut River (figure 16.5). Three of the pottery samples present typical St. Lawrence Iroquoian

Table 16.2. Raw and normalized data of the Vermont and Maine samples.

A - Raw Data

Vessel ID	INAA #	Na	Mg	Al	K	Ca	Sc	Ti	V	Mn	Fe	Rb	Cs	Ba	La	Ce	Sm	Eu	Tb	Dy	Yb	Lu	Hf	Ta	Th	U
VT 1284-1	1014	17020	11070	69981	26330	10218	9,75	4380	44,3	835	40120	102,1	3,31	836	45,4	107,6	7,39	1,54	0,81	4,78	2,15	0,33	3,71	0,96	9,30	2,13
VT 1264-1	1015	15556	11941	77376	26347	11268	11,80	4694	93,8	1490	45274	116,3	4,11	1130	58,4	203,4	10,99	2,03	1,16	7,01	2,79	0,42	3,57	1,95	11,91	2,05
VT 538-2	1016	17840	12746	79508	22569	14993	11,87	7326	98,2	1251	60457	101,2	3,29	944	68,4	163,4	11,78	2,53	1,30	7,09	3,13	0,43	4,83	3,68	11,41	1,72
VT-1343-1	1017	12990	8362	69190	22823	8744	11,89	5453	82,2	869	46400	104,6	2,67	822	35,2	88,9	6,80	1,45	0,85	5,69	2,52	0,41	7,88	0,76	9,13	1,52
VT-14039-1	1018	19319	8332	73601	26872	6815	10,03	3986	66,9	610	38265	104,8	3,02	626	49,0	116,9	7,67	1,49	0,98	5,48	2,73	0,41	5,78	1,66	10,35	2,00
SR-778	1019	7752	12611	85183	20279	7126	21,75	4488	134,8	545	73263	125,7	8,35	561	33,5	59,6	9,18	1,91	1,35	8,37	3,36	0,54	2,90	0,93	16,16	23,10
SR-407	1020	10384	6732	82776	21712	5471	16,44	3897	78,4	338	24373	124,2	5,75	810	37,5	73,5	7,69	1,36	0,83	5,14	2,14	0,41	4,50	0,89	14,78	45,56
MO-316	1021	9768	5448	84821	29241	3933	15,02	3781	68,6	331	22923	142,6	6,08	567	33,5	68,9	7,38	1,20	0,86	5,09	2,14	0,38	3,92	1,00	13,42	41,54
MO-444	1022	8669	6822	84029	21910	4761	18,65	3638	71,4	394	26026	154,7	6,11	656	40,3	77,3	8,54	1,70	1,09	6,66	2,49	0,40	3,85	0,95	15,75	42,18
TF-6252	1023	9165	3205	89289	23611	4284	17,12	3373	45,2	262	20785	150,5	8,84	563	36,0	71,3	7,08	1,13	0,83	5,37	2,40	0,40	3,90	1,27	15,96	32,98
TF-1152	1024	12533	7525	69181	21888	5202	13,19	3774	40,0	375	31083	91,0	4,25	681	34,2	70,4	7,67	1,42	0,96	6,17	3,17	0,49	5,60	0,85	9,39	15,01

B - Normalized Data

Vessel ID	INAA #	Na	Mg	Al	K	Ca	Sc	Ti	V	Mn	Fe	Rb	Cs	Ba	La	Ce	Sm	Eu	Tb	Dy	Yb	Lu	Hf	Ta	Th	U
VT 1284-1	1014	93962	61113	386346	145361	56411	53,83	24181	244,8	4607	221492	563,7	18,29	4618	250,7	593,8	40,78	8,52	4,48	26,39	11,85	1,83	20,48	5,32	51,34	11,77
VT 1264-1	1015	79526	61047	395565	134693	57604	60,35	23997	479,6	7619	231453	594,4	21,01	5778	298,4	1040,1	56,21	10,36	5,92	35,82	14,27	2,14	18,28	9,98	60,88	10,47
VT 538-2	1016	81788	58433	364501	103465	68735	54,43	33585	450,0	5736	277162	464,0	15,09	4329	313,8	749,0	53,99	11,58	5,97	32,50	14,35	1,97	22,15	16,89	52,29	7,88
VT-1343-1	1017	73801	47505	393094	129668	49679	67,56	30978	467,0	4935	263613	594,3	15,16	4669	199,7	505,3	38,65	8,23	4,82	32,32	14,30	2,34	44,79	4,31	51,86	8,65
VT-14039-1	1018	108037	46596	411605	150281	38110	56,07	22292	374,2	3412	213991	586,2	16,91	3498	273,9	653,8	42,89	8,32	5,47	30,65	15,25	2,30	32,35	9,29	57,86	11,18
SR-778	1019	36520	59413	401316	95540	33574	102,48	21145	634,9	2566	345158	592,3	39,35	2641	157,8	280,8	43,26	8,98	6,38	39,44	15,83	2,54	13,65	4,37	76,15	108,82
SR-407	1020	66177	42902	527533	138373	34864	104,76	24835	499,5	2156	155326	791,7	36,67	5164	239,2	468,5	49,03	8,66	5,31	32,78	13,61	2,63	28,70	5,66	94,21	290,33
MO-316	1021	60584	33793	526104	181368	24392	93,17	23452	425,2	2053	142183	884,5	37,71	3518	207,8	427,2	45,77	7,43	5,34	31,54	13,25	2,36	24,34	6,23	83,27	257,63
MO-444	1022	55089	43356	533999	139237	30257	118,53	23120	454,0	2505	165395	983,4	38,85	4169	255,9	491,2	54,24	10,79	6,94	42,32	15,84	2,83	24,48	6,04	100,09	268,05
TF-6252	1023	55907	19551	544649	198921	26132	104,44	20576	275,5	1600	126786	918,1	53,90	3436	219,8	435,0	43,17	6,89	5,09	32,78	14,66	2,42	23,80	7,72	97,35	201,17
TF-1152	1024	82160	49331	453510	143487	34103	86,50	24740	262,2	2456	203759	596,5	27,84	4462	224,3	461,2	50,29	9,28	6,30	40,45	20,76	3,22	36,70	5,56	61,56	98,43

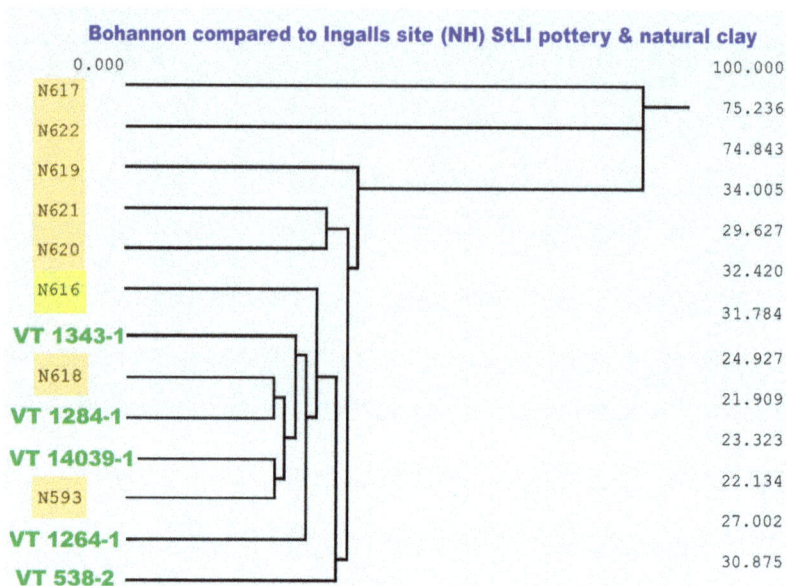

Figure 16.4. Dendrogram 1—Comparison between Bohannon, Ingall (NH), St. Lawrence Iroquoian pottery, and natural clay samples (yellow: natural clay; orange: pottery).

attributes (corn-ear motifs as well as reed punctate impressions suggesting a human figure under a castellation (N593, N617, N618), while the other four are earlier Late Woodland productions. Sample N593 had already been compared, using the same method, with clays from the Pointe-du-Buisson site near Montréal as well as clays and pottery from the Brome-Missisquoi area in Quebec, and the only links that could be drawn were with clays and pottery of the latter area (Chapdelaine et al. 1995:54-58). The distances show some degree of affinity between the Bohannon sherds and two of the St. Lawrence Iroquoian sherds (N593 and N618) as well as the local clay from the Connecticut River (N616). Samples N620, N621, and N619 are at distances not far from the Vermont samples. However, it is very clear that samples N617 and N622 belong to a totally different group. Sample N617 is a collar fragment decorated with a corn-ear motif that is not well done compared with sample N593. Regarding sample N622, it is a rim fragment with a castellation with no special motif, and the geometric design is incomplete but may date from the fourteenth or early fifteenth centuries. These two samples are best explained by proposing that they were made locally from a source near the Ingalls site but not at North Haverhill.

The second comparison between the Bohannon samples is with a group from the Brome-Missisquoi area in Quebec. It consists of three local clay samples from the Pike River and 19 ceramic elements (figure 16.6). The

Figure 16.5. Sampled rim sherds of the Ingalls site, New Hampshire.

ceramics come from three sites: Bilodeau (BgFg-1), with 11 pottery sherds, mostly St. Lawrence Iroquoian (figure 16.7) but also Early Middle Woodland, two clay wastes, and one pipe fragment; Gasser (BgFg-2), with two St. Lawrence Iroquoian pottery sherds; and the Florent-Gosselin site (BgFg-6), with three pottery sherds from different periods (Late Woodland, Late Middle Woodland, and Early Middle Woodland). Results show that the Vermont sample blends well within the Brome-Missiquoi sample, which is, by itself, already quite tight. Clearly, the Bohannon and Brome-Missisquoi St-Lawrence Iroquoian pottery have been fabricated within the same range of natural clays, pointing to local production in the Northern Lake Champlain region. The principal Late Woodland occupation of the Brome-Missisquoi area is at the Bilodeau site, and it has been interpreted as a small fishing camp, occupied by St. Lawrence Iroquoians more related to the Hochelaga province (Montréal area) than to the Maisouna province (Lake Saint-Pierre area) on the basis of ceramic attributes (Blais et al. 1996:114-117). These attributes, which include corn-ear motifs, place the Bilodeau-site occupation between 1400 and 1500 CE.

The third and fourth comparisons of the Bohannon group were made, respectively, with clays and pottery from Pointe-du-Buisson (BhFl-1), a major site on the St. Lawrence River, west of Montréal. We have treated, based on previous studies that have shown that the local clays were not used for the ceramics found at the site, the pottery and natural clay from Pointe-du-Buisson as two different comparison groups (Clermont et al. 1995). The eleven natural clays from Pointe-du-Buisson cluster very tightly together and differ significantly

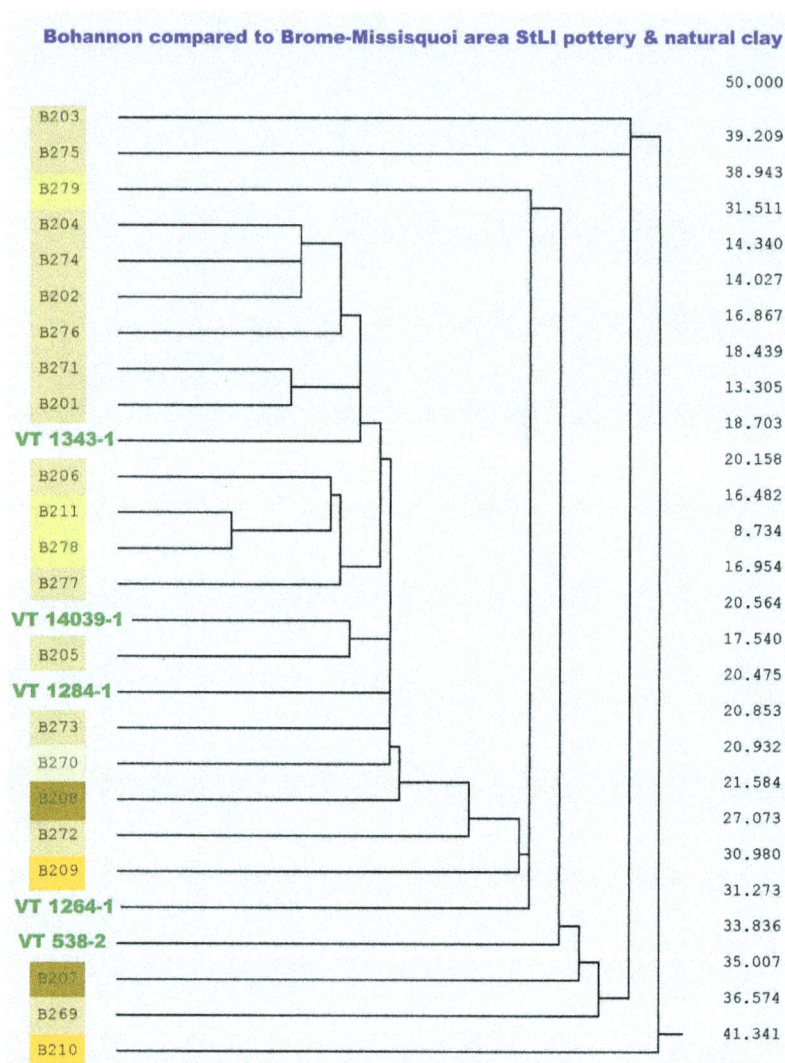

Figure 16.6. Dendrogram 2—Comparison between Bohannon and Brome-Missisquoi St. Lawrence Iroquoian pottery and natural clay samples (yellow: natural clays; beige: Bilodeau-site pottery; orange: Florent-Gosselin-site pottery; brown: Gasser-site pottery).

from the Vermont sample (figure 16.8). The pottery group from the Pointe-du-Buisson site near Montréal consists of sixteen different St. Lawrence Iroquoian vessels taken from station 2 (figure 16.9). The St. Lawrence Iroquoian pottery from this site is also, with one exception, very coherent, and it distinguishes itself from the Vermont sample. There is definitively no common clay sourcing between the St. Lawrence Iroquoians of the Pointe-du-Buisson area and those of the Northern Lake Champlain area.

Figure 16.7. Two of the sampled rim sherds of the Bilodeau site, Quebec.

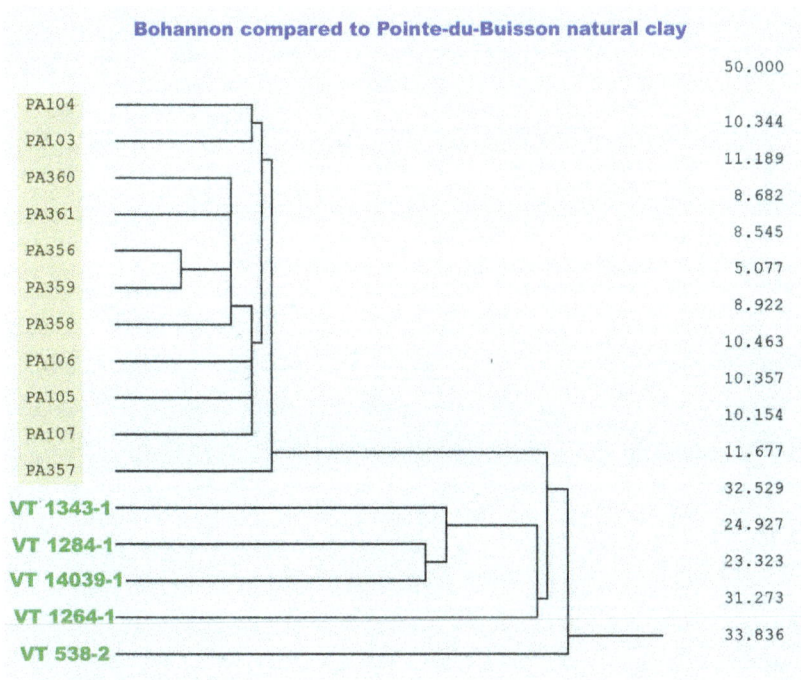

Figure 16.8. Dendrogram 3—Comparison between Bohannon and Pointe-du-Buisson natural clay samples.

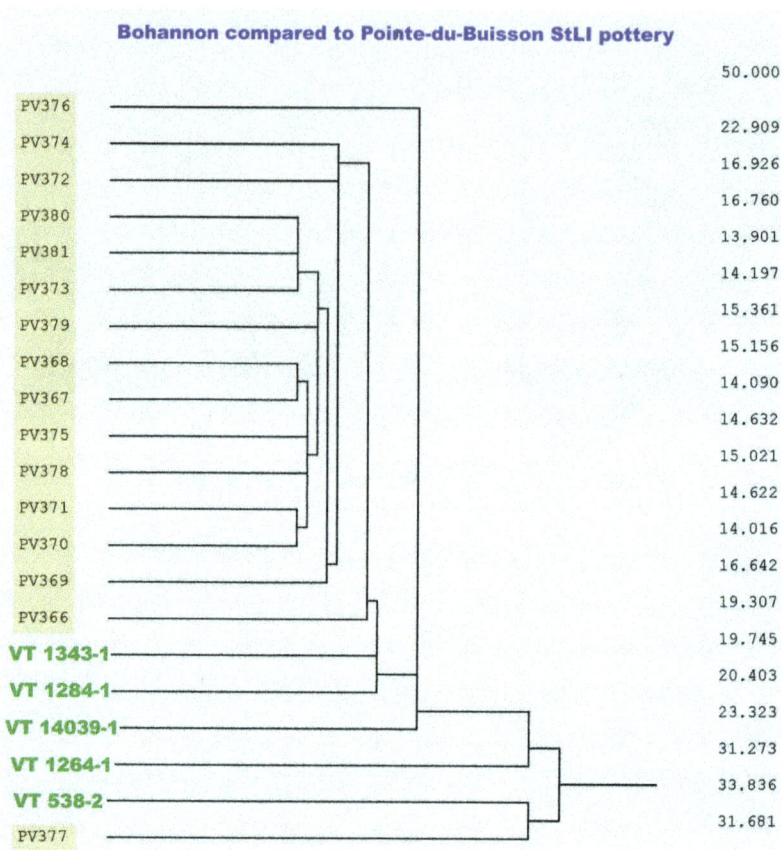

Figure 16.9. Dendrogram 4—Comparison between Bohannon and Pointe-du-Buisson St. Lawrence Iroquoian pottery samples.

Finally, the Bohannon group was compared to a group located farther down the St. Lawrence River, in the Lake Saint-Pierre area where the Richelieu River flows in from the south, carrying the waters of the Lake Champlain Basin. Two sites from this area contributed sixteen pottery samples from St. Lawrence Iroquoian village sites: the Lanoraie site (BlFh-1), with 12 sherds, and the Mandeville site (CaFg-1), with six sherds (figure 16.10). This comparison shows that three of the five sherds of the Bohannon site in Vermont mingle well within the variability of the ceramics of both these sites, while two samples are at a good distance. The results seem to suggest a relative proximity. This proximity follows the Lake Champlain/Richelieu River axis that connects these areas. From a chronological standpoint, the two village sites of the Lake Saint-Pierre area date from different periods: Lanoraie is considered a fifteenth-century occupation (Clermont et al. 1983) and Mandeville is early sixteenth century (Chapdelaine 1989).

The most probable date from the Bohannon site (accelerator mass spectrometry [AMS] on maize) places it later, at mid-sixteenth century (Petersen et al. 2004:110). If a cultural link is to be considered, this might represent a temporal lineage, in which a community gradually moves from the north shore of the St. Lawrence River to the lower Richelieu River area, and eventually up to Northern Lake Champlain, during the troublesome era of the St. Lawrence Iroquoian cultural dismantling during the second half of the sixteenth century. On the other hand, the ceramics from the Bohannon site seem to have some attribute affinities with the Brome-Missisquoi-area ceramics. The extent of this stylistic similarity has never been studied in detail, and this would certainly contribute crucial data to this question, especially to unite these sites into the same cluster.

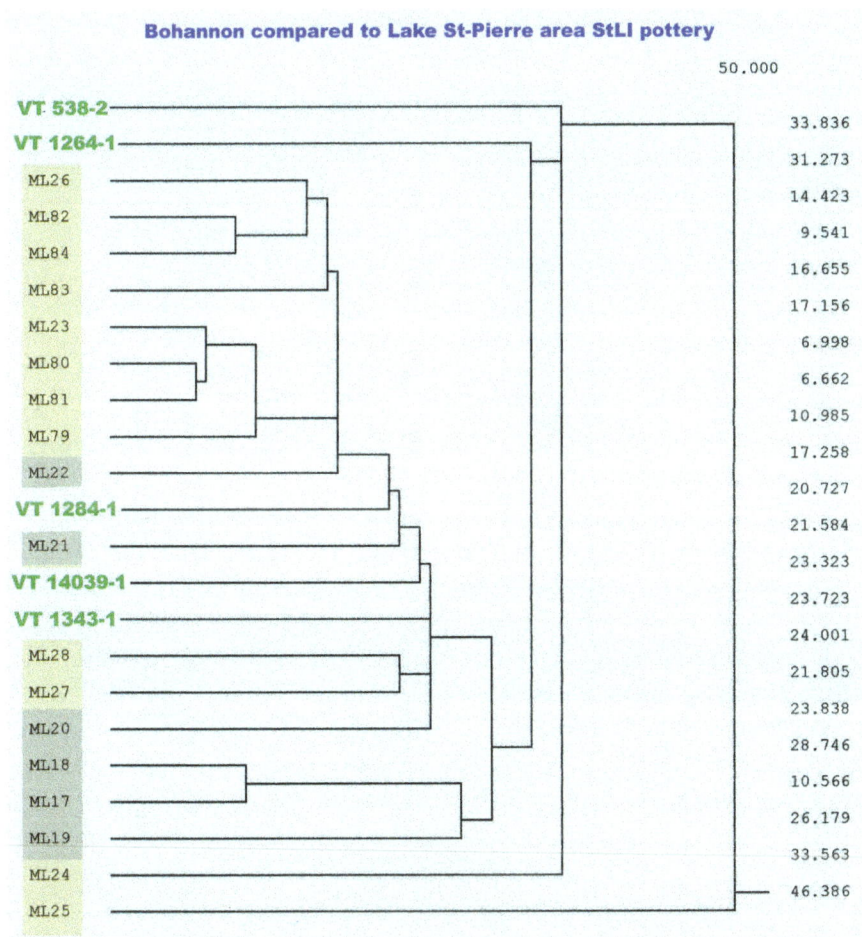

Figure 16.10. Dendrogram 5—Comparison between Bohannon and Lake Saint-Pierre-area St. Lawrence Iroquoian pottery samples (yellow: Lanoraie site; grey: Mandeville site).

The Maine Sample

The pottery samples from the Norridgewock area come from three sites and the selected criteria was the resemblance with the St. Lawrence Iroquoian tradition. The distances between the five samples are not close enough to consider a single chemical grouping among the objects from Maine (the ranges are from 27 to 93). Nevertheless, it represents the reality of an otherwise stylistically coherent group, which strongly suggests the St. Lawrence Iroquoian pottery from the Norridgewock cluster of sites were made from different clays. Unfortunately, we did not have any local clay samples to test the possibility of a local source, but we did have the opportunity to look at the closest St. Lawrence Iroquoian sites to the north, on the other side of the Appalachian range. Two groups were selected for that exercise.

The first group consists of nineteen natural clay samples taken from the Québec City region, mostly on the north shore and downstream (Cap-Tourmente and Côte-de-Beaupré areas), but three come from Québec City itself, one from upstream (Cap-Rouge) and the last one comes from the south shore, in front of Québec City (Saint-Romuald) (figure 16.11). The results clearly show that natural clays from the Québec City region form a very coherent group, with distances all below 30, and that the Maine pottery sample from Norridgewock is totally alien to it. There can be no doubt that the Maine vessels used clays that did not originate from the Québec City region.

The second comparison was made between the Maine samples and 20 St. Lawrence Iroquoian pottery samples from the Canada province (Québec City region) from St. Lawrence Iroquoian sites. Four are from the Masson village site (CdEx-3) west of Québec City, five are from the Place Royale site (CeEt-9) in Québec City, six are from the Royarnois hamlet site (CgEq-19), and five are from two Cap-Tourmente fishing sites (CgEq-4 and CgEq-6), east of Québec City (figure 16.12). As we have seen with the group of local clays, the pottery from this regional cluster also present has a very tight grouping (although a little less than the clays), except for one Royarnois site vessel (PR459). This seems to reflect that the St. Lawrence Iroquoians of the Canada province used clays from the same chemically coherent area, most certainly local. Therefore, the Maine group is again alien to these and did not seem to originate from the same area. The Norridgewock pottery, looking very similar to St. Lawrence Iroquoian pottery, may have been made by St. Lawrence Iroquoian hands, but it was not imported from the St. Lawrence Valley. This opens the possibility that this pottery was made locally in Maine, which in turn would support the hypothesis that some St. Lawrence Iroquoians were living there, maybe as a result of population displacement around the end of the sixteenth century (Petersen et al. 2004:105, 116–117).

Norridgewock compared to Québec City area natural clays

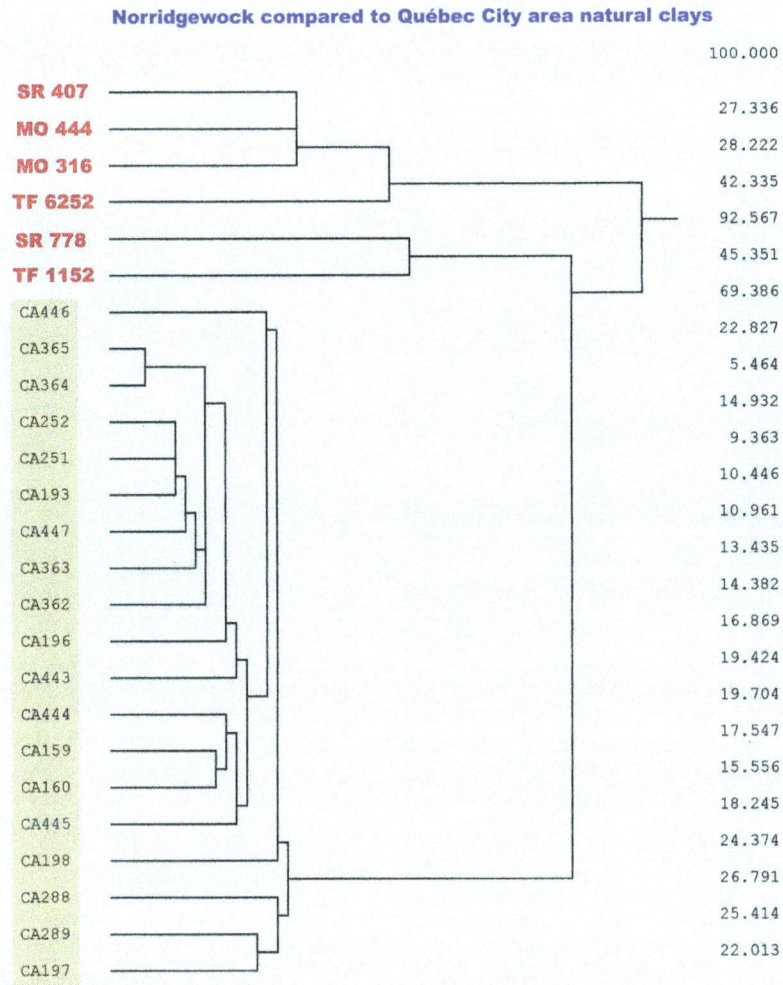

Figure 16.11. Dendrogram 6—Comparison between Norridgewock sites (Me) and Québec City-area natural clay samples.

Conclusion

The presence of possible St. Lawrence Iroquoian pottery in Vermont and Maine, as well as in New Hampshire, remains a fascinating but unresolved quandary. With the help of NAA applied on pottery and natural clays, we have contributed some data that may serve as clues to some aspects of this question, in the form of the chemical relationships of the clays used in the fabrication of this pottery (figure 16.13). The distances between samples, based on the comparison of 25 chemical elements, are used to produce a dendrogram with the single-link cluster analysis to illustrate the relations between selected

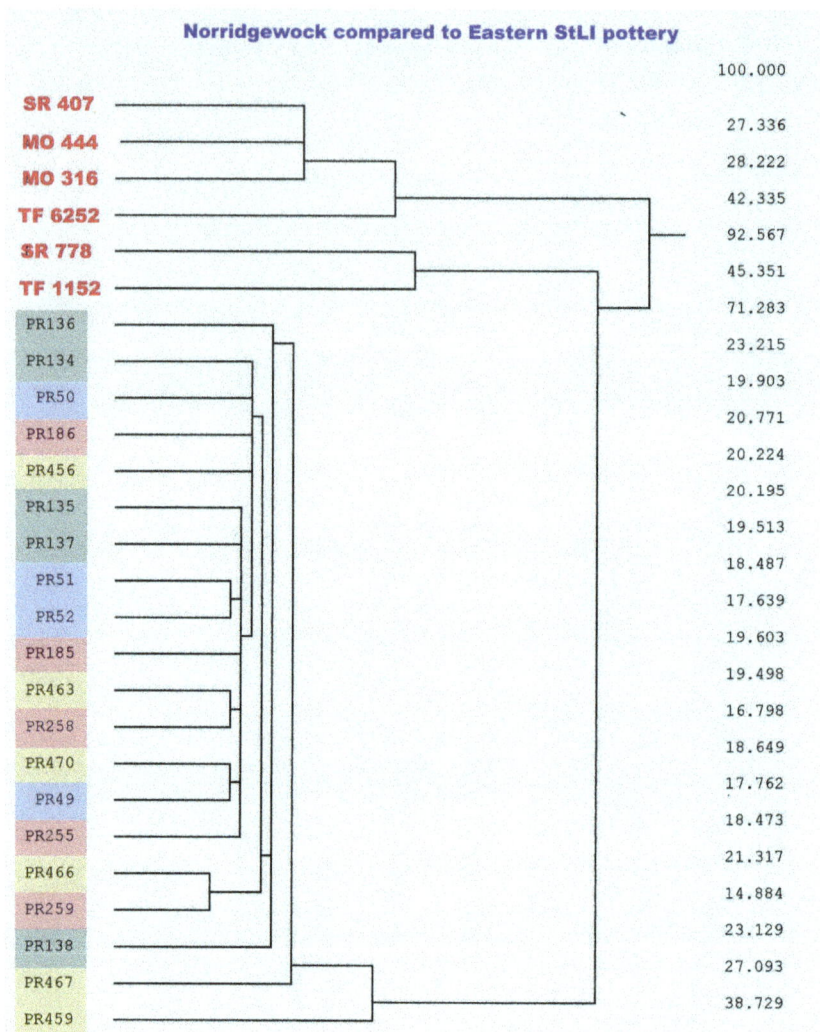

Figure 16.12. Dendrogram 7—Comparison between Norridgewock sites (Me) and eastern St. Lawrence Iroquoian-pottery samples (blue: Masson site; green: Place Royale site; pink: Cap-Tourmente fishing sites; yellow: Royamois site).

samples. The explanation of these results is complex, but we tried to concentrate on the most obvious pattern: that some samples did not share the expected similarity within a site or a region. It is thus important to look at our interpretations with caution.

The most exciting conclusion is that pottery samples from the Bohannon site in northern Vermont seem to share a common clay source with vessels made in the Brome-Missisquoi region of Quebec. The Vermont group and the Pike River group were probably part of a regional cluster. It remains to be defined

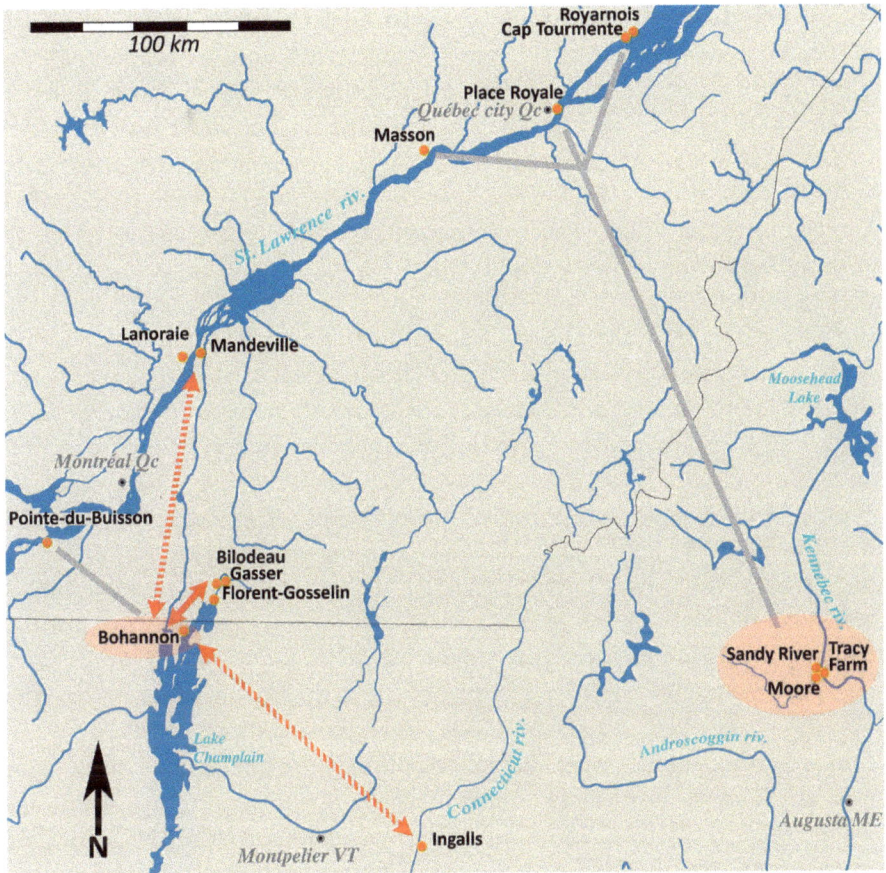

Figure 16.13. Map of the intensity of relationships between the samples (the red arrow represents strong chemical familiarity; red dashed arrows represent a lesser degree of chemical familiarity; grey lines represent no familiarity).

on the basis that Bohannon is indeed a semi-permanent sedentary village. In that context, the Bilodeau site is a fishing camp closer to Bohannon (22 km) than to Mandeville (115 km), and it should be a component of the Northern Lake Champlain cluster.

The comparison with samples from the Ingalls site in the Cowas area of New Hampshire reveals some links with the Vermont-Pike River group, especially two rim sherds typical of the St. Lawrence Iroquoian tradition. The other rim sherds, including a fragment of a less well-made corn-ear motif, show no links with either of the Vermont and Brome-Missisquoi regions. The apparent discrepancies within the Ingalls-site samples could just be the case of a local Abenaki population site in which the St. Lawrence Iroquoian pottery comes in indirectly and irregularly. As was noted before, there does not seem to be any substantial St. Lawrence Iroquoian presence locally (Petersen et al. 2004:108). It should nevertheless be noted that six AMS dates on cultigens (five on maize kernels and one on bean halves) were obtained from this site (Chilton 2006). Only one of them falls in the 1500–1600 CE interval, four of them fall in the 1250–1400 CE range, and one is considered the earliest direct date on maize east of New York state (1019–1159 CE; 2-sigma calibration). This early date contrasts with the other later direct dates on maize from New England, and led Chilton to timidly suggest that there may have been a northern connection with the St. Lawrence Valley implicated in the spread of maize horticulture in New England (Chilton 2006:543-545).

To a lesser degree, the Vermont group share some familiarity with vessels from the Lanoraie and Mandeville village sites. But there seems to be no relationship at all with the Montréal region, either with the pottery or with the local clays. The chemical signature of the Bohannon-site pottery is then part of a coherent local group that encompasses the north of Lake Champlain, the Brome-Missisquoi area, and possibly a portion of the Connecticut River around the Ingalls site. While this does not solve definitely the question of a distinct St. Lawrence Iroquoian cluster in that area, it does reinforce the idea that local St. Lawrence Iroquoians relied on local clays for their pottery production while living in the region on a year-long basis.

The Maine context is totally different from the one in Vermont. There is no new cluster but, rather, the suggestion of a migration of St. Lawrence Iroquoian refugees that were allowed to continue their ceramic tradition with local clay. The results seem to confirm that the Abenakis accepted population segments of St. Lawrence Iroquoian villages abandoned before 1580, probably travelling in from the Canada province. The population movement occurred during the sixteenth century, this based on the decorative style observed on rim sherds attributed to the St. Lawrence Iroquoian ceramic tradition.

The distances between the pottery samples from the Norridgewock sites in central Maine and natural clays and St. Lawrence pottery samples from the Québec City region clearly indicate that they were not fabricated in the St. Lawrence Valley. The Maine vessels were not the result of trade. It is rather argued that they were made locally. This can support the hypothesis that the St. Lawrence Iroquoian presence in the Norridgewock area might in fact be the result of either intermarriage or even refugee populations after the St. Lawrence Iroquoian dispersal during the second half of the sixteenth century. The existing ceramic sample is still, unfortunately, too small and the presumed duration of this hypothetical phenomenon is too short to recognize any changes in style at the very final stage of the sequence.

As a last comment, with few samples from different sites, the chemical approach based on INAA was effective for showing very clearly that there is no relation between the Maine samples and the natural clays and St. Lawrence

Iroquoian pottery from the Québec City region. This result reinforces the idea of a refugee population allowed to produce their ceramic style with local clay.

The results are more ambiguous with the Vermont and New Hampshire samples. They are much more complex because in each group there are some distances that are greater than a score of 30, indicating that different clay sources are involved. However, the Iroquoian population may have been less sedentary, and their summer mobility around the northern end of Lake Champlain allowed the exploitation of different clays beds while fishing and hunting. Finally, if the NAA results are supporting a large geographic cluster with the Bohannon and Brome-Missisquoi sites, the latter must be viewed as satellite fishing camps of a semi-permanent sedentary village. Was this village the Bohannon site or another village site yet to be discovered? As always, any approach to a complex problem such as the origin of the St. Lawrence Iroquoian pottery brings few answers but more questions.

Acknowledgments

This chapter was originally presented as a paper in the James B. Petersen Memorial Session, at the 73rd Annual Meeting of the Eastern States Archeological Federation, held in Fitchburg, Massachusetts, in 2006 (Tremblay et al. 2006). Jim left us much too quickly, in 2005, leaving a void in hearts and minds of colleagues in the archaeological community that had the opportunity to know and work with him. Our updated version is thus dedicated to the memory of this inspiring friend and scholar.

This work was made possible thanks to John G. Crock at the UVM Consulting Archaeology Program and Ellen R. Cowie at the UMF Archaeology Research Center, both of whom opened the doors of their labs to the first author in the summer of 2006 for the sampling of the pottery collections. Their availability for information and discussion throughout the years is greatly appreciated. We also benefited from the help of Kathleen Kenny in Burlington, Vermont, as well as Rosemary Cyr and Robert N. Bartone in Farmington, Maine. Our gratitude also goes to Richard A. Boisvert, who provided us with the various Ingalls-site data, as well as Pierre J. H. Richard for providing the map background we modified in our figures. Finally, our appreciation is also extended to Kenneth Holyoke and Gabriel Hrynick for having this last-minute contribution to the volume.

References Cited

Abel, Timothy J.
2019   The Iroquoian Occupations of Northern New York. In *The Archaeology of New York State, Revisited*, edited by Susan E. Maguire and Lisa Maria Anselmi. NYSM Bulletin. New York State Museum, Albany.

Blais, Judith

1993   The Bilodeau Site Near Missisquoi Bay: Postmolds, Fishbones and Corn Ear Motifs. In *Essays in St. Lawrence Iroquoian Archaeology*, edited by J. F. Pendergast and Claude Chapdelaine, pp. 75–85. Occasional Papers in Northeastern Archaeology no. 8. Copetown Press, Dundas, Ontario.

Blais, Judith, Claude Chapdelaine, and Daniel St-Arnaud

1996   Le Sylvicole supérieur et les Iroquoiens du Saint-Laurent. In *En remontant la rivière aux Brochets, cinq mille ans d'histoire amérindienne dans Brome-Missisquoi*, edited by Claude Chapdelaine, Judith Blais, Jean-Marc Forget, and Daniel St-Arnaud, pp. 101–117. Paléo-Québec 25, Recherches amérindiennes au Québec, Montréal.

Boisvert, Richard A.

1994   1994 SCRAP Field School Ingalls Site, North Haverhill. *New Hampshire Archaeology Society Newsletter* (New Series) 10(2):5–6.

Boisvert, Richard A., Claude Chapdelaine, and Greg Kennedy

1995   Neutron Activation Analysis of Ceramics from the Ingalls Site, North Haverhill, New Hampshire. Paper presented at the 35th Annual Meeting of the Northeastern Anthropological Association, Lake Placid, New York.

Chapdelaine, Claude

1989   *Le site Mandeville à Tracy : variabilité culturelle des Iroquoiens du Saint-Laurent*. Collection Signes des Amériques 7, Recherches amérindiennes au Québec, Montréal.

1996   La place de notre aire d'étude dans les réseaux d'échanges du Nord-Est américain. In *En remontant la rivière aux Brochets, cinq mille ans d'histoire amérindienne dans Brome-Missisquoi*, edited by Claude Chapdelaine, Judith Blais, Jean-Marc Forget, and Daniel St-Arnaud, pp. 119–131. Paléo-Québec 25, Recherches amérindiennes au Québec, Montréal.

2015   Le cadre culturel. In *Mailhot-Curran; un village iroquoien du XVIᵉ siècle*, edited by Claude Chapdelaine, pp 49–68. Paléo-Québec 35, Recherches amérindiennes au Québec, Montréal.

Chapdelaine, Claude, Richard Boisvert, and Greg Kennedy

1995   Les Iroquoiens du Saint-Laurent et le bassin de la rivière Connecticut. In *Étude du réseau d'interactions des Iroquoiens préhistoriques du Québec méridional par les analyses physicochimiques*, edited by Claude Chapdelaine, Norman Clermont, and Robert Marquis, pp. 49–58. Paléo-Québec 24, Recherches amérindiennes au Québec, Montréal.

Chapdelaine, Claude, Jean-François Millaire, and Greg Kennedy

2001   Compositional Analysis and Provenance Study of Spindle Whorls from the Moche Site, North Coast of Peru. *Journal of Archaeological Science* 28:795–806.

Chapdelaine, Claude, Laurier Turgeon, Greg Kennedy, and Dominique Lalande

1992   The Origin of the Iroquoian Rim Sherd from Ile aux Basques. *Canadian Journal of Archaeology* 16:96–101.

Chilton, Elizabeth S.

2006   The Origin and Spread of Maize (*Zea mays*) in New England. In *Histories of Maize: Multidisciplinary Approaches to the Prehistory, Biogeography, Domestication and Evolution of Maize.* edited by John Staller, Robert Tykot, and Bruce Benz, pp. 539–547. Elsevier, Amsterdam.

Clermont, Norman, Claude Chapdelaine, and Georges Barré

1983   *Le site iroquoien de Lanoraie.* Recherches amérindiennes au Québec, Montréal.

Clermont, Norman, Claude Chapdelaine, Greg Kennedy, and Évelyne Cossette

1995   L'activation neutronique et la Pointe-du-Buisson. In *Étude du réseau d'interactions des Iroquoiens préhistoriques du Québec méridional par les analyses physico-chimiques,* edited by Claude Chapdelaine, Norman Clermont, and Robert Marquis, pp. 7–20. Paléo-Québec 24, Recherches amérindiennes au Québec, Montréal.

Cowie, Ellen R., and James B. Petersen

1992   *Archaeological Phase II Testing of the Weston Project, Somerset County, Maine.* Submitted to Central Maine Power Company, Archaeology Research Center, University of Maine at Farmington.

1999   Native American Ceramic Manufacture at the Tracy Farm Site in the Central Kennebec River Valley. *Maine Archaeological Society Bulletin* 39(2):1–42.

Cowie, Ellen R., Robert N. Bartone, and James B. Petersen

2000   Archaeological Investigations at the Tracy Farm Site (69–11 ME) in the Central Kennebec River Drainage, Somerset County, Maine. Archaeology Research Center, University of Maine at Farmington. Submitted to FPL Energy Maine LLC.

Crépeau, Robert and Greg Kennedy

1990   Neutron Activation Analysis of Saint-Lawrence Iroquoian Pottery. *Man in the Northeast* 40:65–74.

Gates St-Pierre, Christian

2007   St. Lawrence Iroquoian Pottery from Plattsburg (NY) in the Collections of the McCord Museum in Montréal. Paper presented at the 74th Annual Meeting of the Eastern States Archaeological Federation, Burlington, Vermont.

Glascock, Michael D.

1992   Characterization of Archaeological Ceramics at MURR by Neutron Activation Analysis and Multivariate Analysis. In *Chemical Characterization of Ceramics Pastes in Archaeology,* edited by H. Neff, pp. 11–26. Madison Monographs in World Archaeology No 7. Prehistory Press, Madison, Wisconsin.

Haviland, William A., and Marjorie W. Power

1994   *The Original Vermonters: Native Inhabitants, Past and Present.* Rev. ed. University Press of New England, Hanover, New Hampshire.

Jamieson, Thomas R.

2005   Filling the Archaeological Void: Saint Lawrence Iroquoians in Alburg, Vermont. *The Journal of Vermont Archaeology* 6:1–12.

2007   Clay to Ceramics: St. Lawrence Iroquoian Sites in Alburgh, Vermont. Paper presented at the 74th Annual Meeting of the Eastern States Archaeological Federation, Burlington, Vermont.

Pendergast, James F.

1990   Native Encounters with Europeans in the Sixteenth Century in the Region Now Known as Vermont. *Vermont History* 58(2):99–124.

Perkins, George H.
1871   Some Relics of the Indians of Vermont. *American Naturalist* 5:11–17.
Petersen, James B.
1990   Evidence of the Saint Lawrence Iroquoians in Northern New England: Population Movement, Trade, or Stylistic Borrowing. *Man in the Northeast* 40: 31–39.
1993   "Iroquoian" Ceramics in New England: A Reconsideration of Ethnicity, Evolution and Interaction. Paper presented at the 57th Annual Meeting of the Society of American Archaeology, Pittsburgh, Pennsylvania.
Petersen, James B., and David Sanger
1991   An Aboriginal Sequence for Maine and the Maritimes Provinces. In *Prehistoric Archaeology in the Maritime Provinces: Past and Present Research*, edited by Michael Deal and Susan Blair, pp. 121–178. Reports in Archaeology 8. The Council of Maritimes Premiers, Maritime Committee on Archaeological Cooperation, Fredericton, New Brunswick.
Petersen, James B., and Joshua R. Toney
2000   Three Native American Ceramic Vessels from Western Vermont: The Colchester and Bolton Jars Revisited. *Journal of Vermont Archaeology* 3:1–16.
Petersen, James B., John G. Crock, Ellen R. Cowie, Richard A. Boisvert, Joshua R. Toney, and Geoffrey Mandel
2004   St. Lawrence Iroquoians in Northern New England: Pendergast Was "Right" and More. In *A Passion for the Past: Papers in Honour of James F. Pendergast*, edited by James V. Wright and Jean-Luc Pilon, pp. 87–123. Mercury Series Archaeology Paper 164. Canadian Museum of Civilization, Gatineau, Quebec.
Tremblay, Roland
1997   La connexion abénaquise : quelques éléments de recherche sur la dispersion des Iroquoiens du Saint-Laurent orientaux. *Archéologiques* 10:77–86.
1999   Regards sur le passé: réflexions sur l'identité des habitants de la vallée du Saint-Laurent au XVI° siècle. *Recherches amérindiennes au Québec* 29(1):41–52.
2006   The St. Lawrence Iroquoians: Corn People. Éditions de l'Homme, Montréal.
Tremblay, Roland, Claude Chapdelaine, and Greg Kennedy
2006   The Origin of Saint Lawrence Iroquoian Pottery in Northern New England: New Data on an Old Question. Paper presented at the James B. Petersen Memorial Session, 73rd Annual Meeting of the Eastern States Archaeological Federation, Fitchburg, Massachusetts.
Tremblay, Roland, Christian Gates St-Pierre, and Michel Plourde
2015   La dispersion des Iroquoiens du Saint-Laurent: synthèse des scénarios existants et nouvelle hypothèse. Paper presented at the joint 42nd Annual Meeting of the Ontario Archaeological Society and the 82nd Annual Meeting of the Eastern States Archaeological Federation, Midland, Ontario.
Tremblay, Roland, and James B. Petersen
2004   Cultural Convergence on the Algonquian / Iroquoian Border: The Case from the Maritime Peninsula. Paper presented at the 69th Annual Meeting of the Society of American Archaeology, Montréal, Quebec.

Willoughby, Charles C.

1909   Pottery of the New England Indians. In *Putnam Anniversary Volume, Anthropological Essays*, pp. 83–101. G. E. Stechert, New York.

1935   *Antiquities of the New England Indians.* Peabody Museum of American Archaeology and Ethnology, Harvard University, Cambridge, Massachusetts.

Wiseman, Fred M.

2000   *The Voice of the Dawn: An Autohistory of the Abenaki Nation.* University Press of New England, Hanover, New Hampshire.

SUBSISTENCE TRENDS DURING THE WOODLAND PERIOD IN NORTHERN VERMONT

A Comparison of Fauna, Flora, and Lipid Data from the Missisquoi River

Ellen Cowie,[1] Gemma-Jayne Hudgell,[2] Robert Bartone,[2] Nancy Asch Sidell,[3] Frances Stewart,[4] Karine Taché,[5] and Aida R. Barbera[6]

Abstract

Archaeological investigations along the Missisquoi River in the Champlain lowlands of northwestern Vermont have provided a wealth of data on Native American lifeways, particularly during the Late Archaic and Woodland periods. Along a stretch of the river in Swanton, archaeological deposits and over 47 radiocarbon dates document trends in subsistence and settlement through virtually the entirety of the Woodland period. Zooarchaeological data from dozens of cultural features suggest a heavy reliance on fish throughout the Woodland period, while complementary paleobotanical evidence documents change in bottomland forest vegetation associated with the adoption of maize agriculture and *Chenopodium berlandieri* (chenopod) as well as harvesting of wild rice and blueberries. Results from lipid analysis by gas chromatography-mass spectrometry combined with carbon and nitrogen bulk isotope analysis of visible and absorbed residues recovered from 27 ceramic pots representing the full span of the Woodland period are compared with the existing subsistence data.

Résumé

Des campagnes de fouilles menées le long de la rivière Missisquoi, dans les basses terres du lac Champlain au nord-ouest du Vermont, nous ont apporté une foule de renseignements sur les modes de vie des peuples autochtones, plus spécialement pour les périodes de l'archaïque supérieur et du Sylvicole. Plus de 47 datations au radiocarbone provenant de deux sites archéologiques bordant la rivière près du village de Swanton nous permettent de documenter les transformations des schèmes d'établissement et des modes de subsistance durant la quasi-totalité de la période Sylvicole. Les données zooarchéologiques provenant de plusieurs dizaines de structures suggèrent une grande importance du poisson durant toute la période Sylvicole. De plus, les données paléobotaniques documentent les changements dans la végétation des forêts de basses terres associées à l'adoption de la culture du maïs et du chénopode (*Chenopodium berlandieri*), et à la cueillette du riz sauvage et des bleuets. Nous comparons aux données existantes sur les modes de subsistance les résultats d'analyses lipidiques par chromatographie en phase gazeuse couplée à la spectrométrie de masse et d'analyses isotopiques de carbone et d'azote obtenus sur des résidus visibles et absorbés prélevés sur plus d'une trentaine de récipients céramiques couvrant la totalité de la période Sylvicole.

Affiliations

1. Independent Consultant, Maine, United States (corresponding author: erc1000@icloud.com)
2. Northeast Archaeology Research Center, Maine, United States
3. Independent Consultant, Maine, United States
4. Independent Consultant, Ontario, Canada
5. Département des sciences historiques, Université Laval, Quebec, Canada
6. Département des sciences historiques, Université Laval, Quebec, Canada

This chapter explores Native American subsistence trends during the Woodland period from the perspective of extensive archaeological deposits located within two sites on the banks of the Missisquoi River in Swanton, northwestern Vermont. Faunal and floral samples are available from numerous archaeological sites across the broad region, and these various data sets illustrate a pattern of varied and complex subsistence strategies. Generally, on the eve of the Woodland period in northern New England, the pattern suggests a reliance on a range of mammals and aquatic resources along with a variety of plant types, followed by a trend of increasing use of non-wood plant resources during the course of the Woodland period (Asch Sidell 2002, 2008; Cowie 2006). This culminates with the adoption of maize agriculture in many areas of northern New England by around 1000–1200 CE, dependent on location. In this chapter, we utilize archaeological data from two sites in Swanton, Vermont, to look at cultural continuity and change in subsistence economies and connected strategies in one place throughout the duration of the Woodland period. These macrofaunal and floral data are compared with organic residue analyses focusing on lipid and isotopic data obtained directly from ceramic vessels.

Vermont sites VT-FR-0318 and VT-FR-0326, the Headquarters and Porcupine sites, respectively, extend over two kilometres in overall length and have provided a wealth of archaeological data on Native American lifeways during the Late Archaic and Woodland periods. Due to the stratified nature of the archaeological deposits, their context and rich content, we are able to examine various subsistence strategies in one place over time. The subsistence data examined here includes macrofaunal and floral remains recovered from over a hundred cultural features, as well as organic residue samples collected from over 30 individual ceramic pots, representing the full range of the Woodland period. These residue samples were analyzed for lipid and bulk isotope signatures.

The combined suite of zooarchaeological and paleobotanical data suggests the site residents were primarily hunters and fisherfolk who also captured turtles and birds and relied heavily on nuts and other plant resources throughout the Woodland period. The zooarchaeological and paleobotanical evidence is clear and suggests a steady continuity in one realm, hunting and fishing, against a backdrop of variability and cultural change in another, horticulture. Native American use of non-wood plant resources, including *Chenopodium berlandieri* (chenopod), squash, sunflower, wild rice, and a variety of fleshy fruits, intensifies concomitant with the adoption of maize at 1040 CE.

The macroscopic subsistence remains, and the results of the ceramic residue analyses correlate well in terms of documenting the reliance on mammal and fish resources, while evidence of plant use as preserved in residues is limited. Nonetheless, the residue analyses do reveal interesting information concerning past foodways, resource-processing techniques, culinary practices, and the possible uses of ceramic vessels. The results of this study suggest sub-regional variability among Native American subsistence strategies, and thus it is important to consider the full suite of site data to best evaluate changes and continuities among past populations with mixed economies.

History of Research and Site Background

Extensive archaeological investigations have been completed in advance of the Vermont Agency of Transportation's planned upgrade of a stretch of Route 78 from the village of Swanton west to the town of Alburgh on Lake Champlain. The University of Maine at Farmington Archaeology Research Center initiated the project in 1999 and conducted phase I and II studies, and the same group of archaeologists, led by the first author, continued with phase III data recovery and mitigation in 2013 with the Northeast Archaeology Research Center, Inc. The information presented in this chapter brings together data from the combined studies completed over the past few decades and detailed in several reports (Corey et al. 2002; Cowie et al. 2012; Hudgell, Cowie, Scharoun, Cyr, and Bartone 2021). While archaeological investigations were focused within the transportation project's relatively narrow purview, the density and exceptional integrity of the archaeological deposits nevertheless provide a substantial data set. The two sites are considered eligible for the National Register of Historic Places (under Criteria C and D), and represent an increasingly recognized pattern in the Northeast of North America of small Archaic-period encampments transitioning to larger and more complex settlements in the later portions of the Middle and Late Woodland periods (Petersen and Cowie 2002).

The Missisquoi Delta region is as rich a habitat today as in the past, and there are over twenty other pre-Contact archaeological sites nearby. Perhaps the best known is the Boucher site (VT-FR-0026), located across the river from the eastern portion of the Headquarters site (VT-FR-0318). The Boucher site is one of the largest Early Woodland–period cemeteries identified in the Northeast and represents the remains of a ritual space used for burial of the dead over an 800-year period (Heckenberger et al. 1990). Boucher and more recent burials and other ritual deposits on the north bank of the Missisquoi River suggest a strong separation of the ritual from the everyday activities evidenced on the southern side of the river at sites VT-FR-0318 and VT-FR-0326.

The Vermont Lake Champlain shoreline is considered the western extent of the ancestral territories of the Wabanaki people and is the ancestral homeland of the Missisquoi band of the Western Abenaki, who live there today. This may have been a fluid border area at least during portions of the Late Woodland period, as evidence of St. Lawrence Iroquoian habitation, possibly related to the Hochelaga community/network centered on the St. Lawrence River in Montréal, which extends to the northern portion of Lake Champlain, as seen at the nearby Bohannan site (VT-GI-0026) in Alburgh, at site VT-CH-0028 on the lower Lamoille River, and in Swanton at site VT-FR-0318 (Chapdelaine 2004: 68; Hudgell, Cowie, Scharoun, Cyr, and Bartone 2021; Hudgell, Beale, Loftus, Cowie, and Bartone 2021; Petersen et al. 2004).

The sites examined herein are located on the main channel of the Missisquoi River within the larger complex of the Missisquoi Delta and Missisquoi Bay of Lake Champlain (figure 17.1). They are essentially contiguous, separated by an infilled creek channel, and cumulatively extend over two kilometres along the floodplain for a total area of around 9.2 hectares. The Missisquoi Delta and floodplain evidence a complex formation and sedimentation/erosional history, in part given the changing levels of postglacial Lake Champlain, and at some point in the past (possibly as recent as 500 years ago) the main channel emptied southwards into Maquam Bay (Fillon 1970). Generally, though, the location and depth of the varied series of occupations at the sites demonstrate a trend of westerly, and then northerly, building landforms. The earliest deposits are located in the eastern portion of site VT-FR-0318, where Late Archaic-period living surfaces and occasional Middle Archaic artifacts are preserved about 1.5 m below the ground surface. The site deposits progress west beginning during the Early Woodland period and grow in intensity and areal extent through the entirety

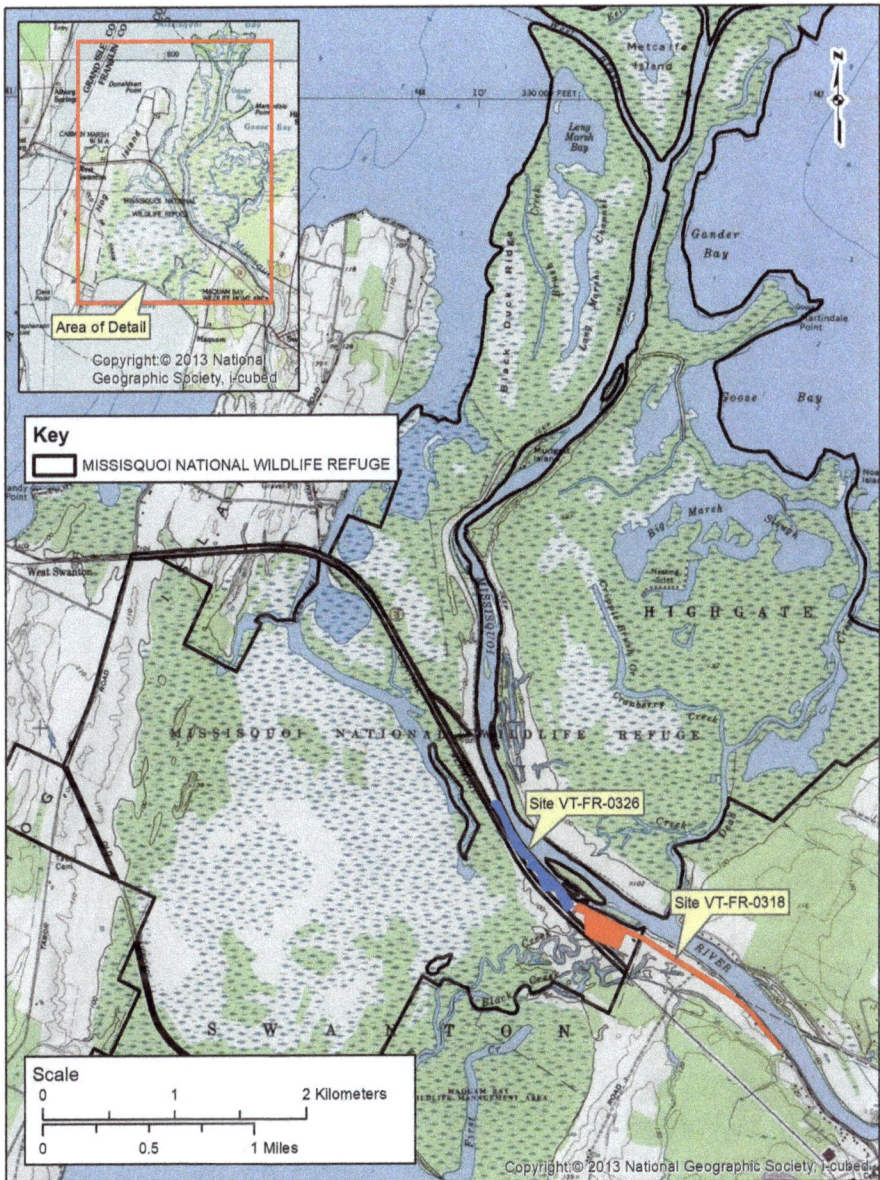

Figure 17.1. Topographic map showing the Missisquoi Delta and location of sites VT-FR-0318 and VT-FR-0326.

of the Woodland period, culminating in extensive Late Woodland-period occupations. Although the stratigraphy is variable given the length of the combined sites, in general the archaeological deposits are sealed in associated anthropogenically enhanced paleosols across the landscape (figure 17.2).

Figure 17.2. Examples of stratigraphy within site VT-FR-0318. The top image shows overbank midden deposits identified in proximity to a Late Woodland period long house structure.

The overall methodology of the various phases of archaeological studies has been consistent and focused on the identification and exploration of cultural features, activity areas, and site structure. All combined, over 390 m^2 were excavated during phase II excavations across the two sites, and phase III data recovery included the areal excavation of 392 m^2 within 3 m x 5 m or larger excavation blocks. Over 270 cultural features were identified, including hearths, pits, living surfaces (enhanced paleosols), activity areas, crushed pots, structural elements, midden features, and burned sediment. Feature recovery included 100% retention for flotation processing in the laboratory, with over nine cubic metres of sediment from the two sites processed. This intensive recovery method has produced a wealth of samples from which to study a broad range of cultural processes.

Recovered artifacts include lithic tools and debitage, fire-cracked rock, and Native American ceramics. Although the lithic tool assemblage is impressive, the ceramic collection is perhaps the most notable. Over 40,000 sherds combine to document the full span of ceramic manufacture in the Northeast. Within this sample are examples of over 340 individual vessels, identified on the basis of rim sherds/fragments or body pieces with distinct attributes: many more vessels are undoubtedly present as represented by less categorical specimens. Not least, the ceramic sample has allowed for the fine-tuning of the stratigraphic sequence and the dating of individual occupations across the landscape.

From the 1,830 carbonized macroscopic plant samples recovered from excavations and cultural features, over 128 samples were analyzed by paleobotanist and co-author Nancy Asch Sidell. Radiocarbon assays were obtained on 39 carbonized floral remains, with an additional eight radiocarbon dates obtained on carbonized organic residue from individual ceramic pots; these document nearly continuous occupation from the Late Archaic through the Late Woodland periods (table 17.1; figure 17.3).

Archaeological Overview: Presentation of Data

Summary data including results from the faunal and floral analyses is provided below for the Woodland-period deposits at sites VT-FR-0318 and -0326. We provide some archaeological data from the Late Archaic period as a backdrop, or starting point, to explore the Late Archaic-Woodland transition. Results of the extensive analyses are presented here as presence/absence (as opposed to minimum number of individuals, MNI, or number of individual specimens, NISP) for the fauna and counts per sample for the floral samples. In addition, we focus on animal classes rather than specific animal species, although we do list identified species, if identified. Given the factors of disposal, preservation, sampling, recovery, and identification, this approach may provide a more

Table 17.1. Radiocarbon dates on carbonized paleobotanical remains and food residue, sites VT-FR-0318 and VT-FR-0326.

Chart Sample # (see Figure 17.3)	Site	Feature # or Vessel	Carbonized Material Dated	Conventional Radiocarbon Age	Calendar Age	2 Sigma Calibrated Age	Beta Analytic #	Cultural Period (Including CP# if Ceramic Specimen)
1	VT-FR-0318	76	Variety of wood	4770±40 BP	2,820 BCE	5600-5460 and 5380-5340 cal BP	203309	Late Archaic
2	VT-FR-0318	75	Wood	4250±40 BP	2,300 BCE	4860-4810 and 4750-4710 cal BP	203308	Late Archaic
3	VT-FR-0318	75	Butternut	4220±40 BP	2,270 BCE	4850-4800 and 4770-4630 cal BP	205049	Late Archaic
4	VT-FR-0318	77	Wood	4030±80 BP	2,080 BCE	4820-4280 cal BP	203310	Late Archaic
5	VT-FR-0318	36	Variety of wood	4020±100 BP	2,070 BCE	4830-4230 cal BP	203380	Late Archaic
6	VT-FR-0318	98	Variety of wood	3960±30 BP	2,010 BCE	4515-4470, 4445-4405, and 4365-4360 cal BP	382953	Late Archaic
7	VT-FR-0318	34	Wood	3870±70 BP	1,920 BCE	4500-4480 and 4440-4090 cal BP	203379	Late Archaic
8	VT-FR-0318	100	Acorn	3750±30	1,800 BCE	4225-4200, 4175-4170, 4160-4070 and 4040-3990 cal BP	382031	Late Archaic
9	VT-FR-0318	152	Variety of wood	3700±30 BP	1,750 BCE	4145-4115, 4100-3970, and 3940-3930 cal BP	395285	Late Archaic
10	VT-FR-0318	N/A	Variety of wood	3650±40 BP	1,700 BCE	4090-3860 cal BP	205050	Late Archaic
11	VT-FR-0318	155	Variety of wood - birch, ash, maple	3650±30 BP	1,700 BE	4080-4030 and 4010-3890 cal BP	395286	Late Archaic
12	VT-FR-0318	N/A	Charred material	3580±30 BP	1,630 BCE	3905-3840 cal BP	426818	Late Archaic
13	VT-FR-0318	149	Hickory nutshell	3180±30 BP	1,230 BCE	3455-3360 cal BP	395284	Late Archaic
14	VT-FR-0318	29	Wood	3000±50 BP	1,050 BCE	3340-3000 cal BP	203302	Early Woodland
15	VT-FR-0318	148	Squash rind	2800±30 BP	850 BCE	2965-2845 cal BP	382034	Early Woodland
16	VT-FR-0326	7	Wood	2410±60 BP	460 BCE	2730-2330 cal BP	156912	Early Woodland
17	VT-FR-0326	V49	Vessel #49 Residue	2340±40 BP	390 BCE	2370-2320 cal BP	156913	Early Woodland (CP1)
18	VT-FR-0326	2	Vessel #19 Residue	2270±40 BP	320 BCE	2350-2290 and 2270-2160 cal BP	156914	Early Woodland (CP1)
19	VT-FR-0318	V180	Vessel #180 Residue	2260±30 BP	310 BCE	2346-2299 and 2258-2158 cal BP	518797	Early Woodland (CP1)
20	VT-FR-0326	29	Butternut	2110±30 BP	160 BCE	2150-1995 cal BP	382038	Early Woodland
21	VT-FR-0326	8	Wood	1890±90 BP	60 CE	2010-1600 cal BP	159808	Middle Woodland
22	VT-FR-0318	V118	Vessel #118 Residue	1850±30 BP	100 CE	1865-1715 cal BP	518793	Middle Woodland (CP2)
23	VT-FR-0318	V171	Vessel #171 Residue	1820±30 BP	130 CE	1860-1850, 1826-1692 and 1654-1630 cal BP	518795	Middle Woodland (CP3)

	Site	Sample	Material	Radiocarbon age BP	CE	Calibrated	Lab number	Period
24	VT-FR-0318	63	Variety of wood	1690±70 BP	260 CE	1740-1420 cal BP	203307	Middle Woodland
25	VT-FR-0318	17	Variety of wood	1590±40 BP	360 CE	1550-1390 cal BP	157549	Middle Woodland
26	VT-FR-0326	35	Wood ash	1580±30 BP	370 CE	1530-1410 cal BP	410909	Middle Woodland
27	VT-FR-0318	136	Beechnut, acorn	1540±30 BP	410 CE	1525-1355 cal BP	382954	Middle Woodland
28	VT-FR-0318	115	Wood	1450±30 BP	500 CE	1390-1300 cal BP	382032	Middle Woodland
29	VT-FR-0326	6	Butternut shell	1160±40 BP	790 CE	1170-970 cal BP	160722	Middle Woodland
30	VT-FR-0318	159	Butternut shell	1100±30 BP	850 CE	1065-955 cal BP	395287	Middle Woodland
31	VT-FR-0318	V8	Vessel #8 Residue	1000±30 BP	950 CE	967-899, 868-822 and 815-798 cal BP	518792	Middle to Late Woodland (CP4-5)
32	VT-FR-0318	39	Variety of wood	910±70 BP	1040 CE	950-680 cal BP	203303	Late Woodland
33	VT-FR-0318	218	Variety of wood - red oak, acer, unidentified	910±30 BP	1040 CE	920-740 cal BP	395288	Late Woodland
34	VT-FR-0318	N/A	Maize	880±30 BP	1070 CE	905-855 and 830-730 cal BP	395289	Late Woodland
35	VT-FR-0318	47	Variety of wood	870±70 BP	1080 CE	930-670 cal BP	203306	Late Woodland
36	VT-FR-0318	175	Maize	870±30 BP		795 to 735 cal BP	428358	Late Woodland
37	VT-FR-0318	9	Maize	840±40 BP	1100 CE	890-860 and 800-680 cal BP	156907	Late Woodland
38	VT-FR-0318	45	Wood	790±50 BP	1160 CE	780-660 cal BP	203305	Late Woodland
39	VT-FR-0318	168	Hickory nut shell	790±30	1160 CE	740-675 cal BP	382036	Late Woodland
40	VT-FR-0318	V312	Vessel #312 Residue	770±30 BP	1180 CE	734-668 cal BP	518796	Late Woodland (CP5-6)
41	VT-FR-0318	220	White pine	730±30 BP	1220 CE	695-660 cal BP	382037	Late Woodland
42	VT-FR-0318	43	Variety of wood	720±60 BP	1230 CE	740-630 and 600-560 cal BP	203304	Late Woodland
43	VT-FR-0318	V155	Vessel #155 Residue	720±30 BP	1230 CE	704-648 and 584-567 cal BP	518794	Late Woodland (CP6)
44	VT-FR-0318	162	Maize	670±30 BP	1280 CE	675-635 and 595-560 cal BP	382955	Late Woodland
45	VT-FR-0318	19	Variety of wood	620±50 BP	1330 CE	670-530 cal BP	156911	Late Woodland
46	VT-FR-0318	16	Variety of wood	580±70 BP	1370 CE	670-510 cal BP	156909	Late Woodland
47	VT-FR-0318	14	Variety of wood	410±40 BP	1540 CE	520-430 and 380-320 cal BP	156908	Contact Period

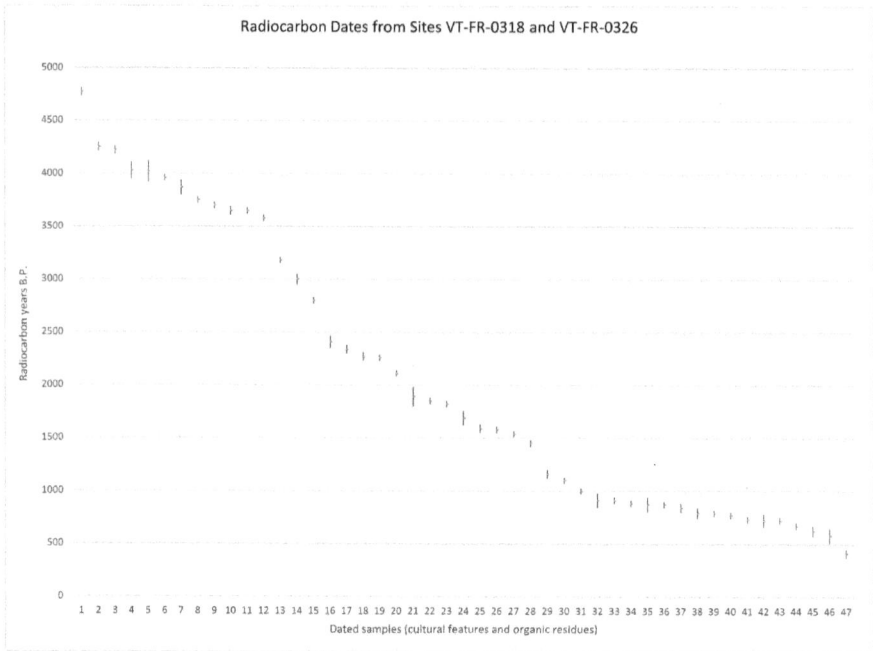

Figure 17.3. Radiocarbon dates obtained on samples from sites VT-FR-0318 and VT-FR-0326.

consistent and robust look at subsistence trends over time. Over 60,000 calcined faunal specimens were analyzed by co-author Dr. Frances Stewart (2005) and represent a subsample from every cultural feature that contained bone. A riffle sampler was employed to acquire a systematic subsample from each provenience within a feature. The same general method was used to prepare and select the 128 floral samples recovered from 92 cultural features and analyzed by Asch Sidell (2016).

Transition to the Early Woodland Period

The VT-FR-0318 and -0326 site data suggest that the transition from the Late Archaic to the Early Woodland period is subtle in terms of available archaeological evidence. Late Archaic material is present at site VT-FR-0318, and 13 radiocarbon dated features suggest repeated occupations dating from 4770+/-40 BP (Beta-203309) to the eve of the Early Woodland period at 3180+/-30 BP (Beta-395284). The overall Late Archaic occupations cover about 200–300 m^2 (figure 17.4). Distinct activity areas, including fire-cracked rock/roasting features, produced quantities of macroscopic floral (21 individual samples analyzed from 15 features) and faunal remains (fauna from 15 features analyzed) and indicate a heavy reliance on nuts: they are present in 14 of the 21 samples (66%), and beechnut and acorn dominate. *Chenopodium* is present in one Late Archaic feature radiocarbon dated to 3750+/-30 BP

(Beta-382031). Faunal remains from these same features indicate an emphasis on fish: 40% of the analyzed features with bone contain fish remains, including catfish (*Ictalurus*), Salmonidae, and Percidae. Other faunal data include unidentifiable mammal remains from 53% of the Late Archaic features and turtle from <1% of the features.

The transition to the Early Woodland period at VT-FR-0318 and -0326 is characterized by a change from settlement focused on the eastern portion of site 0318 to several small encampments scattered along the river and across the landscape. On the basis of ceramic data, overall settlement during the Early Woodland period covers about 1,600 m² in six or seven separate encampments (see figure 17.4). The average size of each individual locus is about 100–400 m². The large rock-roasting areas common in the Late Archaic-period deposits are not present in the Early Woodland period, and instead small activity areas include hearth features associated with lithic tool and debitage scatters lacking notable fire-cracked rock. Radiocarbon dates from three features and three ceramic pots demonstrate occupation spanning nearly the entire Early Woodland period, from 3000+/-50 BP (Beta-203302) to 2110+/-30 BP (Beta-382038).

Early Woodland faunal remains from four cultural features and floral remains from six features constitute the known subsistence remains from this period. Although the faunal sample is small, the data nonetheless suggest a continued reliance on mammal (present in 75% of features with bone) and fish (present in 50%), with bird remains identified in one feature. Identified species include

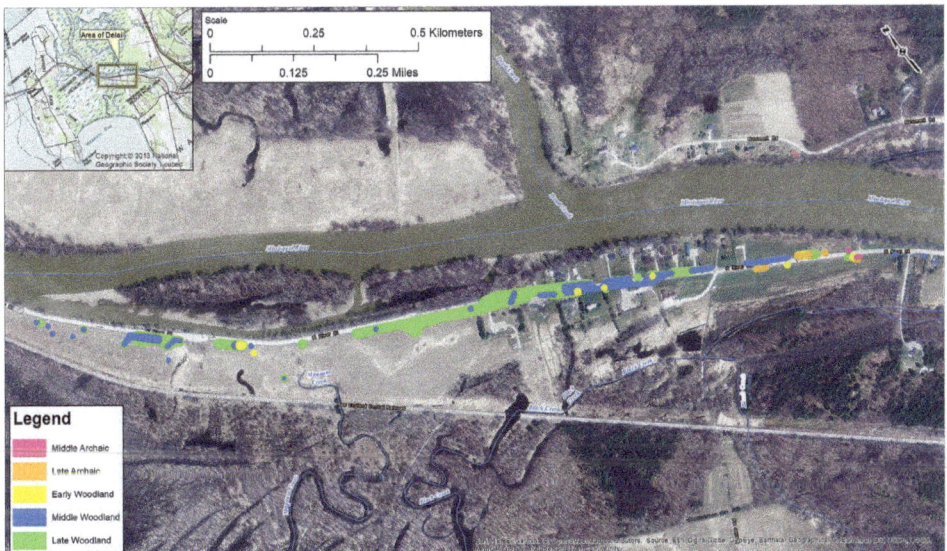

Figure 17.4. Aerial photograph showing the location and extent of settlement through time at sites VT-FR-0318 and VT-FR-0326.

muskrat, mink, and bullhead catfish. The floral remains are more telling and document a definitive increase in use of non-wood plant species. Nuts continue to be the predominant non-wood plant material, with nut remains in half the features analyzed, and butternut is present in all three. Of particular note, 18 fragments of squash rind, identified as *Cucurbita pepo*, are present in one Early Woodland feature (F148). A fragment of this squash rind has been directly dated using accelerator mass spectrometry (AMS) to 2800+/-30 BP (Beta-382034). The thickness of the rind fragments indicates it is an edible squash rather than the pepo gourd variety (Asch Sidell 2016).

The ceramic assemblage from this period includes about 500 sherds, with at least seven unique vessels identified. Carbonized residue from three vessels has been radiocarbon dated: vessel 49 2340+/-40 BP (Beta-156913), vessel 19 2270+/-40 BP (Beta-156914), and vessel 180 2260+/-30 BP (Beta-518797). Among the sample, the majority exhibit interior and exterior fabric paddling, the hallmark of Early Woodland-period (Ceramic period [CP] 1) ceramics in the Northeast (Petersen and Sanger 1991). In general, however, vessels show great variability in terms of overall thickness, presence/absence of visible fabric paddling, and rim forms (figure 17.5). The one example of decoration on vessel 117 and the presence of apparently smoothed surfaces on others indicates the variability of vessel forms and surface treatment and decoration of these Early Woodland–period ceramics. Other rare examples of decorated Early Woodland vessels are known from the Boucher site across the river (Heckenberger et al. 1990). Although the sample size is small at sites VT-FR-0318 and -0326, among the seven designated vessels there appear to be two size categories. Six were sufficiently complete to be measurable for general size, with five measuring 24 cm or more in diameter and one measuring approximately 15 cm, indicating capacities of about 15 litres (3.9 gal.) and 5 litres (1.4 gal.), respectively. Interestingly, the smaller vessel, vessel 117, is the one decorated vessel in the sample.

Middle Woodland Period

The transition from the Early Woodland to the Middle Woodland period is dramatic, with evidence of marked intensification in settlement and subsistence practices. On the basis of ceramic distribution, settlement expands considerably in the early portion of the Middle Woodland period, with an extensive area possibly representing a palimpsest of occupations, but of considerable size (over 300 linear metres along the river and a minimum of over 7,000 combined square metres), as well as three to four other occupations of smaller size (see figure 17.4). Over 35 cultural features assignable to the Middle Woodland period have been identified between the two sites.

Nine radiocarbon dates document the occupational sequence during the Middle Woodland period from 1890+/-30 BP (Beta-159808) to 1100+/-30 BP

Figure 17.5. Early Woodland-period Vinette I vessel 19 directly radiocarbon dated to 2270+/-40 BP Beta-156914).

(Beta-395287). The early portion of the Middle Woodland is evidenced by an extensive series of occupations with ceramics exhibiting pseudo-scallop-shell decoration. This is followed by occupations related to the middle portion of the Middle Woodland period with dentate decorated ceramic forms. On the basis of ceramic data, there is a noticeable lack of ceramic specimens dating to the later portion of the Middle Woodland period, around 500–800 CE. This may well be a sampling issue given the somewhat narrow study area along the roadway and river, especially considering that there are a handful of Jack's Reef-type points and dozens of Levanna points from the sites, as well as a few radiocarbon-dated features, that date to this period.

Faunal remains were recovered from 10 Middle Woodland-period cultural features. Mammal (present in 90% of MW features) and fish remains (present in 80%) predominate, with bird (30%) and reptile (30%) also present. Actual identified species include walleye, bullhead, catfish, wolf/dog, marten, beaver, porcupine, turtle/snapping turtle, and unidentified songbird.

A total of 29 paleobotanical samples dating to the Middle Woodland period were analyzed from 24 cultural features. Evidence of nuts was identified in 18 (75%) of the features, with beechnut, hickory, and acorn predominant, butternut less so. Of particular note among the seed identifications are wild rice (*Zizania spp.*), wild sunflower (*Helianthus spp.*), grape, and elderberry. The wild rice was identified from feature 63, a veritable kitchen midden, radiocarbon dated to 1690+/-70 BP (Beta-203307), the early portion of the Middle Woodland period. Elsewhere, probable wild-rice phytoliths have been identified from organic residues from ceramic pots dated to 1380+/-20 BP in southern Quebec (Gates St-Pierre and Thompson 2015). Feature 63 also contained bird, fish, mammal, turtle, and all varieties of nuts, and taken as a snapshot, demonstrates the range of plants and animals used by the site inhabitants at this time.

Native American ceramics dating to the Middle Woodland period include a large collection of over 12,000 sherds with about half designated as early Middle Woodland (pseudo-scallop-shell decorated) and the other half identified as mid–Middle Woodland (dentate decorated) ceramic forms. The early Middle Woodland (CP2, per Petersen and Sanger 1991) ceramics include at least 49 individual vessels exhibiting exceptionally detailed and intricate pseudo-scallop decorative motifs (figure 17.6) and 62 vessels of dentate-decorated (CP2/3 and CP3) ceramics, but a relative paucity of CP4 types, perhaps suggesting a decline in population. For the CP2 pots, there appears to be one general grouping of vessel size, with capacity ranging from <2 litres (~0.5 gal.) to over 8 litres (~2 gal.). The CP2/3 pots exhibit three size categories, including capacities of <2 litres (~0.5 gal.), between 5 and 9 litres (~1.3–2.3 gal.), and large vessels, ~15 litres (~3.9 gal.).

Figure 17.6. Early Middle Woodland vessel 118 directly radiocarbon dated to 1850+/-30 BP (Beta-518793).

Late Woodland Period

Whatever the factors that affected overall settlement in this area during the latter part of the Middle Woodland period, this trend shifts dramatically in the early portion of the Late Woodland period. Archaeological data from the sites, including location and density of ceramic specimens and cultural features, suggest a significant increase in occupation starting at about 1000 CE with evidence of a growing multi-seasonal settlement. The cumulative Late Woodland-period occupations are extensive, covering over 12,000 m^2 and extending almost two kilometres along the river (see figure 17.4). Most of the identified features are located at site VT-FR-0318; however, site 0326 also possesses a sizable Late Woodland-period occupation. Site structure is more complex than earlier periods, with pronounced differential use of space as reflected in a variety of feature types, including hearths, storage/refuse pits, refuse middens, and structural elements. Exploration of a linear post-mould arrangement led to the identification of a long house, with associated storage/refuse pits, hearths, and a nearby overbank midden (figure 17.7).

Figure 17.7. Aerial view of Late Woodland-period long house at site VT-FR-0318, facing northwest.

Directly dated features and ceramic vessels provide a sequence of 14 radio-carbon dates documenting Late Woodland-period occupation between 910+/-70 BP (Beta-203303) and 580+/-70 BP (Beta-156909). A single radiocarbon date may provide evidence of an early Contact-period occupation at 410+/-40 BP (Beta-156908), although no evidence of typical Contact-period European trade items such as glass beads, copper-kettle scraps, or iron have been recovered. The archaeological and ethnohistoric data both suggest that some or all of the Native American community moved to the north bank of the river on the eve of European contact, and it appears that the bulk of the Late Woodland deposits at the sites date to the first few centuries of the millennia, ca. 1000–1300 CE.

Dozens of Late Woodland cultural features have been identified and sampled from the sites, and the floral and faunal remains collected provide a robust sample to explore potential changes and continuities in Native American subsistence economies. Faunal remains were recovered from 63 cultural features (10 dating to the Middle–Late Woodland period, 53 to Late Woodland), and as in previous times, fish and mammals predominate. Fish was found in 75% of the features with Ictalurus genus catfish as the most prevalent in 21 features. Other fish include northern pike, sturgeon, Salmonidae (possibly including trout, whitefish, graylings, chars, or salmon), and pickerel. Mammal remains were identified in 68% of the features, including beaver, white-tailed deer, marten, and muskrat. Remains of birds and turtle were present in less than 1% of the Late Woodland features.

The most significant change in the Late Woodland-period Native American economies is the adoption of maize agriculture and connected strategies, including the intensification of non-wood plant use. Maize appears at the sites by 1040 CE and is prevalent in the Late Woodland cultural features sampled. Fifty paleobotanical samples recovered from 25 features, along with samples from three living surfaces (paleosols), were analyzed, with maize identified in 21 of the 50 samples (42%) or in 14 of the 27 features (52%). The earliest date associated with maize from the sites is from a large pit, feature 218 (VT-FR-0318), yielding wood radiocarbon dated to 910+/-30 BP (Beta-395288). Direct dates on maize are available from the Late Woodland-period living surface located near the structural remains and nearby midden deposit at 880+/-30 BP (Beta-395289) and 870+/-30 BP (Beta-428358), at 840+/-40 BP on maize from feature 9 (Beta-156907), and 670+/-30 BP (Beta-382955) on maize from feature 162. Given the presence of kernels, glume, and cupule fragments among the samples, it is likely that it was grown and processed near the site.

The adoption of maize did not lessen the reliance on the mast-forest nut resources available in the area. As with all previous occupations, the reliance on nuts continues into the Late Woodland period. Nutshell was identified in

23 (85%) of the Late Woodland-period features analyzed, with shagbark hickory nutshell the most ubiquitous, followed by butternut, acorn, and beechnut.

The number and variety of identified seeds are notable from the Late Woodland features. Wild rice is present in 10 (20%) of the features and *Chenopodium* in 14 features (52%). The *Chenopodium berlandieri* (pitseed goosefoot) found at the site falls mostly in the range (based on seed-coat thickness) of a non-domesticated form of *C. berlandieri*, either wild or a companion weed. Given the presence of this type of *Chenopodium* in association with maize in eight features, it seems likely that the plants were an encouraged weed in the maize fields. There is also an overall increase in the abundance and ubiquity of fleshy fruits such as blueberry, elderberry, huckleberry, and grape. The presence of grasses, field weeds, brambles, and fruit-bearing shrubs provides evidence for local field clearing as these are considered "edge dweller" or "camp follower" species that propagate in open-field settings. Finally, the other notable plant in the Late Woodland-period floral sample is tobacco (*Nicotiana rustica*) from feature 168, radiocarbon dated on associated hickory-nutshell fragments to 790+/-30 BP (Beta-382036). Tobacco, which was a sacred plant grown for ceremonial use, is seldom recovered from archaeological sites in New England (Asch Sidell 2008). Interestingly, nicotine residues have been identified on a tobacco pipe dating to 300 BCE from the nearby Boucher site (Rafferty 2006).

The Late Woodland-period Native American ceramic assemblage recovered from the sites is an impressive collection, with over 13,000 sherds and at least 186 individual vessels identified (figures 17.8–17.9). The early portion of the Late Woodland period (CP5) sees a change from the relatively straight-sided conoidal forms prevalent in the Middle Woodland period to flared rim/body forms, and then, in CP6, the addition of globular-shaped vessels with distinctive collars, pronounced neck, and shoulders. At sites VT-FR-0318 and -0326, this transition likely occurs a little earlier than previously thought given several radiocarbon dated examples of very thin-walled, collared pots at around 1200 CE. Decoration becomes confined to the upper rim or collar area, with cord-wrapped stick (typically tiny cordage elements), incision, and punctate decoration being the most prevalent decorative forms. Small dentate decoration reappears, which is somewhat unique to the St. Lawrence River Valley and Vermont. Among the Late Woodland period ceramics are those typical of local Abenaki manufacture as well as those with characteristics that place them within Iroquoian or proto-Iroquoian typologies. Some specimens fit well within ceramic assemblages from nearby southern Quebec dating to the Late Middle Woodland/Early Late Woodland period. Additional examples from sites VT-FR-0318 and -0326 are reminiscent of the Iroquoian Owasco Tradition reflecting the borrowing and reproduction of styles by local groups along the

St. Lawrence River Valley (Claude Chapdelaine and Roland Tremblay, personal communication, 2021). At site VT-FR-0318, these ceramics are found in the same contexts as those more typical of non-Iroquoian, Abenaki manufacture, namely, cord-wrapped stick decorated pots of the Early Late Woodland period designated as CP5. The association between these types is quite interesting and bears further study. Actual St. Lawrence Iroquoian pots are present in the Late Woodland ceramic assemblage along with non-Iroquoian Abenaki pots, although in far fewer numbers.

Other typical attributes of these Late Woodland-period pots are exterior fabric paddling over much of the body, which is sometimes heavily smoothed, particularly after about 1200 CE. There appear to be three general size categories among the measurable vessels, including an increase in the number of the very smallest vessels. The preliminary size categories include large pots with capacities of 15 litres (3.9 gal.), medium-sized vessels in the 8–12 litres (2–3 gal.) range, and small vessels with capacities of less than 2 litres (~0.5 gal.). Smoking pipes are also present in the Late Woodland ceramic collection, with at least 20 individual pipes recovered (see figure 17.8).

Figure 17.8. Late Woodland vessels and pipes from site VT-FR-0318. *Top left*, vessel 268; *top right*, vessel 183; *bottom*, from left to right, pipes V311, V309, V315, V314, and V340.

Figure 17.9. Late Woodland vessel 312 directly radiocarbon dated to 770 +/-30 BP (Beta-518796).

Organic Residue Analysis

Material and Methods

In archaeology, residues are amorphous and invisible organic remains deriving from foodstuffs and other types of natural products such as resins, waxes, adhesives, pigments and binders. While organic residues have been extracted from a wide range of archaeological materials (e.g., anthropic soils, features, groundstone tools, steatite vessels, metal artifacts, and smoking pipes), it is the study of organic residues associated with archaeological ceramic vessels that has seen the most significant developments in recent decades. Of all the organic compounds in the natural world (including carbohydrates, proteins, and DNA), lipids are the most likely to survive over long timescales, due in part to their hydrophobic nature. The association of lipids and ancient pottery can occur in the form of carbonized deposits adhering to vessel walls and deriving from foodstuff, soot, sealants, or adhesives. Lipids also preserve, invisible to the eye, within porous ceramic matrices. Absorbed residues typically represent a range of resources placed in a pot over its use-life, while visible charred surface deposits tend to result from a smaller number of cooking episodes that led to overheating and carbonization of the vessel's contents.

In this study, twenty-four foodcrust and three absorbed ceramic samples were submitted to lipid analysis (Taché 2020). These samples were assigned to different chronological subdivisions of the Woodland period based on radiocarbon dates and attribute analysis: four were attributed to CP1, four to CP2, four to CP2/3, one to CP4/5, four to CP5, five to CP5/6, and five to CP6

(Petersen and Sanger 1991). The objective of this pilot research is to combine bulk carbon and nitrogen isotope data with lipid analysis by gas chromatography-mass spectrometry (GC-MS) to identify the organic content and determine the use of ceramic containers attributed to different time periods and recovered from sites VT-FR-0318 and VT-FR-0326 (Taché 2020).

For elemental analysis-isotope ratio mass spectrometry (EA-IRMS), no pre-treatment of the samples was undertaken prior to analysis (for a discussion, see Craig et al. 2007; Morton and Schwartz 2004). Each sample was weighed in duplicate (ca. 700 ug) into tin capsules, which were analyzed using a Flash 2000 Organic Elemental Analyzer linked to a Delta V Plus isotope ratio mass spectrometer (both from Thermo Scientific). Vienna Pee Dee Belemnite (VPDB) and atmospheric nitrogen (AIR) were used as international standard for $\delta^{13}C$ and $\delta^{15}N$ measurements, respectively. Carbon and nitrogen isotopes were analyzed in the same analytical run. Samples yielding less than 1% nitrogen were discarded and instrument precision on repeated measurements was always better than 1‰ (and most of the time better than 0.5‰) for both elements, as determined by duplicate measurements.

For GC-MS analysis, foodcrust (ca. 10–20 mg scraped from the potsherd surface) and ceramic samples (ca. 1–2 g drilled from the interior wall) were first weighed before lipids were extracted and methylated by direct acid-catalyzed transesterification to maximize recovery and according to established protocol (Correa-Ascencio and Evershed 2014). GC-MS analysis allows the separation of complex mixtures and the identification of plant- and animal-derived lipids (e.g., sterols, n-alkanoic acids). Lipid extracts analyzed by GC-MS can be tentatively associated with food sources using two major techniques: the biomarker and the relative-abundance approaches. Through the identification of chemical compounds that are unique to a certain resource or class of resources, the biomarker approach allows us to link directly and with confidence a residue with a specific resource, or at the very least with a group of resources. The relative-abundance approach employs the ratios of various common compounds to propose, albeit with a high degree of uncertainty,[1] the general overall composition of a residue (e.g., plant vs. animal). In this chapter, we use a combination of both approaches.

Bulk Carbon and Nitrogen Analysis

Twenty carbonized deposits were analyzed by EA-IRMS to determine their bulk carbon ($\delta^{13}C$) and nitrogen ($\delta^{15}N$) stable isotope values, along with carbon-to-nitrogen ratios (C:N). The $\delta^{15}N$ value increases with trophic level and can be

---

1. This uncertainty is due in large part to the fact that fatty acids and other compounds degrade (through oxidation and/or microbial breakdown) or leach out of pots at different rates in different environments.

used to estimate the proportion of plant and animal protein in terrestrial diets, although variability in $\delta^{15}N$ values can also be due to a number of external factors, including aridity or soil type. In this study, $\delta^{15}N$ values ranging between 4.8‰ and 10.6‰ suggest the preparation of a diversity of resources in pots, including terrestrial plant and/or animal foods but also aquatic, most likely freshwater, organisms (figure 17.10). The atomic C:N ratio is indicative of the amount of protein versus other macromolecules (carbohydrates and lipids). Generally animal tissues, enriched in protein, have lower C:N ratios compared to plant tissues, enriched in carbohydrates such as starch and cellulose. Here, the C:N ratios of most samples analyzed range between 5.17 and 11.4, suggesting the contribution of protein-rich foods rather than plants (Kunikita et al. 2013). Two samples (V117-F and V212-F) with higher C:N ratios may have been mainly derived from plant products; an interpretation supported by their low $\delta^{15}N$ values. In the absence of marine resources, as is likely the case here, the degree of enrichment of ^{13}C over ^{12}C (expressed as $\delta^{13}C$) allows a distinction between C_3 and C_4 plants, which use different mechanisms to take in carbon dioxide from the atmosphere during photosynthesis. Ninety-five percent of plants in the world, including those

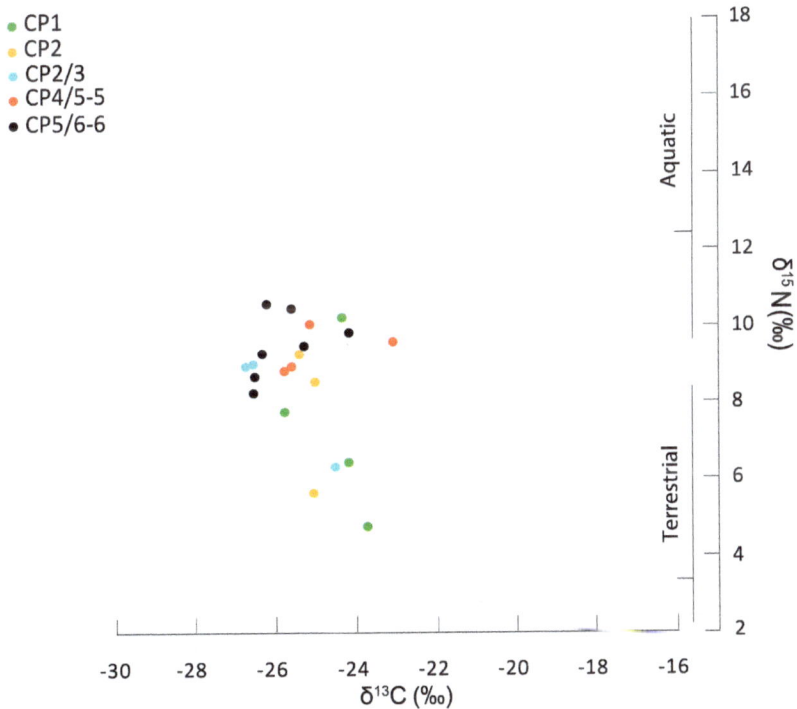

Figure 17.10. Plot of $\delta^{15}N$ versus $\delta^{13}C$ values for foodcrusts adhering to the interior walls of pottery sherds from sites VT-FR-0318 and VT-FR-0326.

consumed as food by humans and animals, are characterized by the C_3 photosynthetic pathway. C_4 plants, on the other hand, comprise mainly tropical grasses, among which some are important food crops (e.g., millets, maize, sugarcane and sorghum). Since maize is the only plant with a C_4 photosynthetic pathway in (pre)historic northeastern North America, these values are often used to estimate the importance of this cereal crop among groups of various cultural and chronological affiliations. The twenty charred deposits included in this study yielded $\delta^{13}C$ values ranging from -23.7‰ to -26.7‰, indicating no or very little input from ^{13}C-enriched C_4 plants, such as maize, in these vessel units.

GC-MS Analysis of Lipids

Fourteen of the 24 foodcrust samples (58%) and all three absorbed samples (100%) contained enough lipids to be interpretable (>100 ug/g for foodcrust samples and >5 ug/g for absorbed samples; Craig et al. 2013; Evershed 2008b) (tables 17.2–17.3). The reason for this discrepancy is not well understood but it has been observed in other northeastern contexts, notably in a study involving Vinette 1 pottery (Taché and Craig 2015). Among the 17 samples yielding lipids, four are characterized by the presence of at least one of three isoprenoid alkanoic acids (phytanic, pristanic, or 4,8,12-TMTD), which are at high concentration in freshwater and marine organisms, and by a range of position alisomers of ω-(o-alkylphenyl)alkanoic acids containing a minimum of 20 carbon atoms (figure 17.11). These suites of compounds can only be produced by the protracted heating of polyunsaturated fatty acids present in aquatic organisms (Craig et al. 2007; Evershed et al. 2008; Hansel et al. 2004). The presence of ω-(o-alkylphenyl)alkanoic acids also implies that the vessels were subjected to prolonged heating (typically temperatures exceeding 270 °C for at least 17 hours), conditions that can be achieved through boiling or roasting of their contents (Evershed et al. 2008; Lucquin et al. 2018). When including the samples containing a partial set of aquatic biomarkers—that is, iω-(o-alkylphenyl) alkanoic acids containing 18 carbon atoms and at least one of the three isoprenoid alkanoic acids mentioned above—the number of vessels likely involved in the processing of aquatic resources rises to 10 (although the abundance of $C_{18:0}$ in sample V155-F also suggests a contribution from degraded animal fats).

Among the samples yielding lipids, V268-I has a chromatographic markedly distinct from all others, characterized by a high $C_{18:0}/C_{16:0}$ ratio and an abundance of $C_{18:1}$, typical of degraded plant oils. Samples V282-F and V173-I are also characterized by a high $C_{18:0}/C_{16:0}$ ratio (>3.0) and may have originated from degraded plant oils, while samples V118-F and V216-F have low $C_{18:0}/C_{16:0}$ ratios (<0.4) typical of animal fats (figure 17.12). However, interpretation based on fatty-acid ratios alone as opposed to the presence of biomarkers should be treated with caution. Pentacyclic triterpenoids with

Table 17.2. Results of organic residue analysis of 24 foodcrust and 3 ceramic samples from sites VT-FR-0318 and VT-FR-0326, Vermont. FA (Cx:y) = fatty acids with carbon length x and number of unsaturations, br=branched chain acids, DCx = α,ω-dicarboxylic acids with carbon length x, TMTD = 4,8,12- trimethyltridecanoic acid, phy = phytanic acid, tri = unidentified triterpene; APAA (C$_{18}$) = ω-(o-alkylphenyl) alkanoic acids with 18 carbon atoms. I = ceramic samples (absorbed residues); F = foodcrust samples (visible residues).

Site: VT-FR-xxx	Laboratory Code (CP Period)	Lipid conc (µg g⁻¹)	Lipid composition	δ¹⁵N	δ¹³C	C:N	Interpretation
326	V19-F (1)	52	Below interpretable threshold	7.8	−25.8	8.1	Ind
326	V49-F (1)	6	Below interpretable threshold	10.2	−24.3	7.9	Ind
318	V180-F (1)	1127	FA(C$_{14-24}$:0 C$_{18:1}$ C$_{17br}$), DC(C$_{7-11}$), APAA(C$_{18,20}$), phy, tri	4.8	−23.7	7.8	Aquatic resources, non-tree resin
318	V117-F (1)	30	Below interpretable threshold	6.5	−24.2	21.4	Ind
318	V158-F (2)	987	FA(C$_{14-24:0}$ C$_{16:1-18:1}$ C$_{15-17br}$), DC(C$_{8-11}$), APAA(C$_{16-20}$), TMTD, phy	9.3	−25.4	7.8	Aquatic resources
318	V118-F (2)	371	FA(C$_{14-20:0}$ C$_{18:1}$ C$_{17br}$), phy	5.7	−25.1	7.0	Terrestrial animal
318	V166/168-F (2)	186	FA(C$_{14-20:0}$ C$_{18:1}$ C$_{17br}$)	8.6	−25.0	5.7	Ind
318	V171-F (2/3)	510	FA(C$_{14-24:0}$ C$_{16:1-18:1}$ C$_{17br}$), DC(C$_{7-13}$), APAA(C$_{16-20}$), phy, tri	9.0	−26.5	8.6	Aquatic resources, non-tree resin
318	V212-F (2/3)	126	FA(C$_{16-18:0}$)	6.4	−24.5	15.5	Ind
318	V216-F (2/3)	299	FA(C$_{16-18:0}$)	9.0	−26.7	11.4	Terrestrial animal
318	V8-F (4/5)	65	Below interpretable threshold	8.9	−25.7	9.2	Ind
318	V235-F (5)	3034	FA(C$_{14-19:0}$ C$_{16:1-18:1}$ C$_{15-17br}$), APAA(C$_{18}$), TMTD, phy	10.1	−25.2	7.1	Aquatic resources
318	V264-F (5)	1709	FA(C$_{14-23:0}$ C$_{18:1}$ C$_{15-17br}$), DC(C$_9$), APAA(C$_{16-18}$), TMTD, phy	9.6	−23.1	7.4	Aquatic resources
318	V241-F (5)	900	FA(C$_{14-19:0}$ C$_{18:1}$ C$_{15-17br}$), DC(C$_{12}$), APAA(C$_{18}$), phy	8.9	−25.6	9.3	Aquatic resources

318	V323-F (5/6)	0	Below interpretable threshold	10.6	−26.2	6.9	Ind
318	V247-F (5/6)	13	Below interpretable threshold				
318	V155-F (6)	5589	FA($C_{14-19:0}$ $C_{18:1}$ $C_{15-17br}$), DC(C_{13}), APAA(C_{18}), phy				Aquatic resources
318	V183-F (6)	1030	FA($C_{14-19:0}$ $C_{18:1}$ C_{17br}), APAA(C_{18}), phy	9.4	−25.3	9.5	Aquatic resources
318	V184-F (6)	546	FA($C_{14-28:0}$ $C_{18:1}$ $C_{15-17br}$), APAA(C_{18})	10.5	−25.6	7.3	Aquatic resources
318	V312-F (5/6)	5	Below interpretable threshold				
318	V311-F (5/6)	27	Below interpretable threshold	9.8	−24.2	7.4	Ind
318	V282-F (6)	269	FA($C_{14-24:0}$ $C_{18:1}$ C_{17br})	8.2	−26.6	11.0	Plant
318	V309-F (5/6)	66	Below interpretable threshold	9.3	−26.3	9.4	Ind
318	V335-F (6)	5	Below interpretable threshold				
318	V145-I (2)	1173	FA(C_{14-24} $C_{18:1}$ $C_{15-17br}$), DC($C_{9,11}$), APAA(C_{18-20}), phy				Aquatic resources
318	V173-I (2/3)	77	FA(C_{14-28} $C_{18:1}$)				Plant
318	V268-I (5)	20	FA(C_{14-18} $C_{16:1-18:1}$)				Plant

Δ12-ursene and Δ12-oleanene structures (possibly α-amyrin), common among angiosperm resins, have been identified in two samples (V180-F and V171-F). These compounds are found in a wide range of plants and conceivably present in the sedimentary environment. However, their presence in these residues may also derive from plant processing, the use of plants as flavouring agents, or the presence of angiosperm resin in pots. There is a possibility that the source could be from the processing of sunflower seeds as well. Finally, the low lipid yields and the absence of distinctive compounds traceable to a specific source in samples V166/168-F and V212-F prevent interpretations.

Table 17.3. Lipid content and proportions of fatty acids from samples yielding interpretable lipid yields through GC-MS analysis. FA (Cx:y)=fatty acids with carbon length x and number of unsaturations; br=branched chain acids; DCx=α,ω-dicarboxylic acids with carbon length x; TMTD=4,8,12- trimethyltridecanoic acid; phy=phytanic acid; tri=unidentified triterpene; APAA18=ω-(o-alkylphenyl) alkanoic acids with 18 carbon atoms; I=ceramic samples (absorbed residues); F=foodcrust samples (visible residues).

		SAMPLE IDENTIFICATION								
		HEADQUARTER SITE								
		V180_F	V158_F	V118_F	V166/168_F	V171_F	V212_F	V216_F	V235_F	V264_F
WEIGHT (mg)		20	30	30	25	30	30	33	25	25
LIPID YIELD (ug/g)		1127	987	371	186	510	126	299	3034	1709
FATTY ACIDS (relative %)	C14:0	0.35	2.71	0.96	1.53	1.47	0.00	0.00	2.01	1.60
	C15br	0.00	0.35	0.00	0.00	0.00	0.00	0.00	tr	tr
	C15:0	0.00	0.59	0.55	1.03	0.56	0.00	0.00	1.13	tr
	C16:1	0.00	2.11	0.00	0.00	0.41	0.00	0.00	1.59	0.00
	C16:0	37.32	52.42	25.69	54.72	60.07	64.96	15.23	52.19	47.46
	C17br	0.26	3.17	0.50	Tr	2.14	0.00	0.00	3.86	2.86
	C17:0	0.50	1.19	1.79	2.05	1.43	0.00	0.00	1.99	2.22
	C18:1	8.93	0.00	1.19	1.67	2.22	0.00	0.00	8.03	8.33
	C18:0	44.53	31.50	68.55	37.87	29.06	35.04	84.77	27.34	36.18
	C19:0	0.00	0.00	0.00	0.00	0.35	0.00	0.00	1.86	1.35
	C20:0	5.89	4.45	0.77	1.14	1.74	0.00	0.00	0.00	0.00
	C21:0	0.00	0.00	0.00	0.00	0.00	0.00	0.00	0.00	tr
	C22:0	1.61	1.16	0.00	0.00	0.48	0.00	0.00	0.00	0.00
	C23:0	0.00	0.00	0.00	0.00	0.00	0.00	0.00	0.00	tr
	C24:0	0.61	0.35	0.00	0.00	0.08	0.00	0.00	0.00	0.00
	C26:0	0.00	0.00	0.00	0.00	0.00	0.00	0.00	0.00	0.00
	C28:0	0.00	0.00	0.00	0.00	0.00	0.00	0.00	0.00	0.00
DICARBOXYLIC ACIDS		DC7-11	DC8-11			DC7-13				DC9
BIOMARKERS		AAPA18-20, phy, unid. triterpene	AAPA16-18-20, TMTD, phy			AAPA16-18-20, phy, unid. triterpene			AAPA18, TMTD, phy	AAPA16-18, TMTD, phy

		SAMPLE IDENTIFICATION							
		HEADQUARTER SITE							
		V241_F	V155_F	V183_F	V184_F	V282_F	V145_I	V173_I	V268_I
WEIGHT (g)		30	23	20	25	20	1.1	0.85	0.85
LIPID YIELD (ug/g)		900	5589	1030	546	269	1173	77	20
	C14:0	1.55	1.09	1.68	2.02	1.38	0.47	0.72	3.81
	C15br	tr	tr	0.00	tr	0.00	0.09	0.00	0.00
	C15:0	1.31	0.63	0.80	tr	0.76	0.26	0.00	1.51
	C16:1	0.00	0.00	0.00	0.00	0.00	0.00	0.00	5.99
	C16:0	58.93	43.92	64.34	63.43	69.83	51.26	77.03	64.27
FATTY ACIDS (relative %)	C17br	4.34	1.76	2.82	3.77	Tr	1.76	0.00	0.00
	C17:0	2.77	2.17	1.66	2.08	1.24	1.96	tr	0.00
	C18:1	3.90	2.25	6.11	3.72	2.78	1.42	1.38	20.20
	C18:0	25.27	46.95	21.13	tr	21.99	38.34	16.38	4.22
	C19:0	1.93	1.24	1.47	23.55	2.02	0.52	0.00	0.00
	C20:0	0.00	0.00	0.00	1.42	0.00	3.04	1.33	0.00
	C21:0	0.00	0.00	0.00	tr	0.00	0.12	0.00	0.00
	C22:0	0.00	0.00	0.00	0.00	0.00	0.59	1.70	0.00
	C23:0	0.00	0.00	0.00	tr	0.00	0.04	tr	0.00
	C24:0	0.00	0.00	0.00	0.00	0.00	0.11	1.44	0.00
	C26:0	0.00	0.00	0.00	0.00	0.00	0.00	tr	0.00
	C28:0	0.00	0.00	0.00	0.00	0.00	0.00	tr	0.00
DICARBOXYLIC ACIDS		DC12	DC13				DC9,11		
BIOMARKERS		AAPA18, phy	AAPA18, phy	AAPA18, phy	AAPA18tr		AAPA18-20, phy		

Discussion

In recapping the archaeological data from the VT-FR-0318 and -0326 sites, we look on a broad scale at both the subtle and substantial changes and continuities related to Native American subsistence strategies during the Woodland period. Against the backdrop of the rich microenvironment of the Missisquoi Delta region, what changes and what stays the same among the series of archaeological occupations present at the sites over this period? In terms of generalized settlement data, we see a pattern of small household encampments during the Early Woodland-period transition to larger, likely multi-family, multi-season habitations during the Middle Woodland period. Finally, this settlement trend continues with large, village-based, year-round settlement and pronounced differential use of space during the Late Woodland period (Petersen and Cowie 2002).

In one realm of subsistence (hunting/fishing/trapping), the zooarchaeological evidence shows a persistent strategy with the reliance on mammals and fish throughout the Woodland period, while in another realm (plant use)

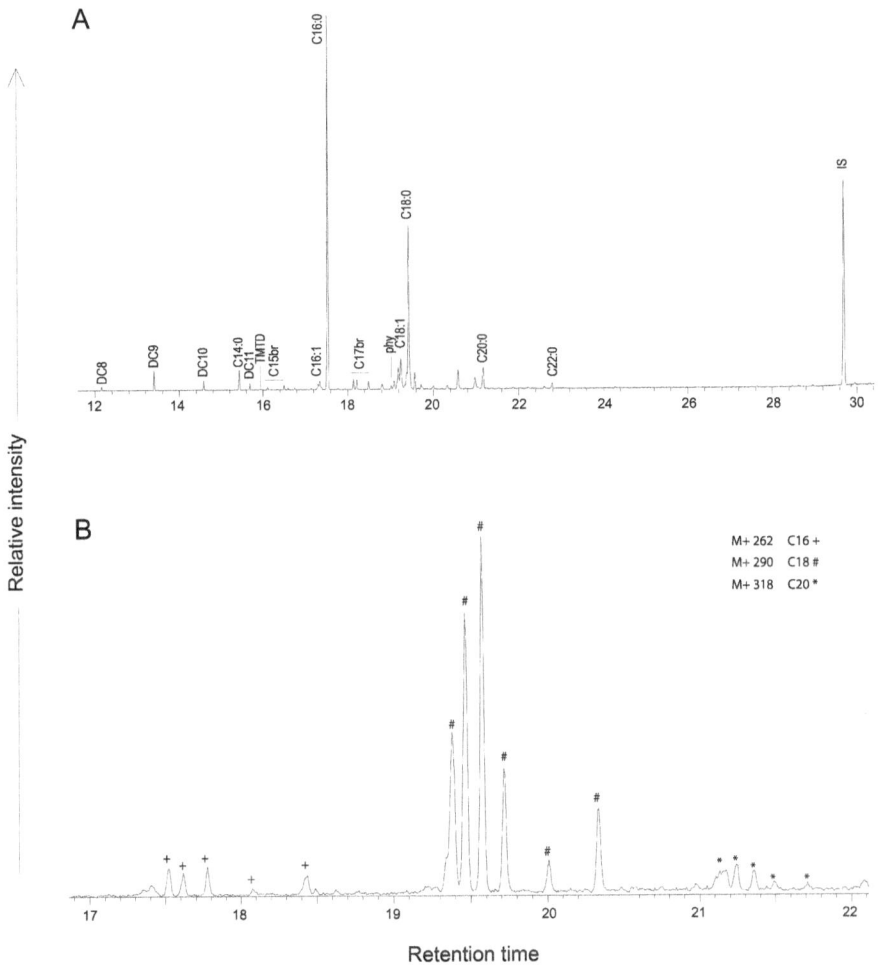

Figure 17.11. A. Partial gas chromatogram of lipid extract from foodcrust sample V158 exhibiting a profile typical of degraded aquatic oil. Cnx are fatty acids with carbon length n and number of unsaturations x; DCx are α,ω-dicarboxylic acids with carbon length x; br are branched-chain acids; TMTD is 4,8,12- trimethyltridecanoic acid; phy is phytanic acid; IS is internal standard (n-hexatriacontane). B. Partial m/z 105 ion chromatogram (inset) shows ω-(o-alkylphenyl)alkanoic acids with 16 (+), 18 (#) and 20 (*) carbon atoms.

paleobotanical evidence shows a similar, long-term, consistent reliance on nut resources but a marked intensification of other plant resources over time. Early and Middle Woodland-period plant-collecting strategies intensify in the Late Woodland with the incorporation of maize agriculture in conjunction with the intensive use and propagation of starchy seeds, fleshy fruits, and other economically important plants. The rich animal resources in the area kept them there and kept them coming back, but the possibilities of horticulture allowed for evolving subsistence strategies and change in the larger cultural dynamic.

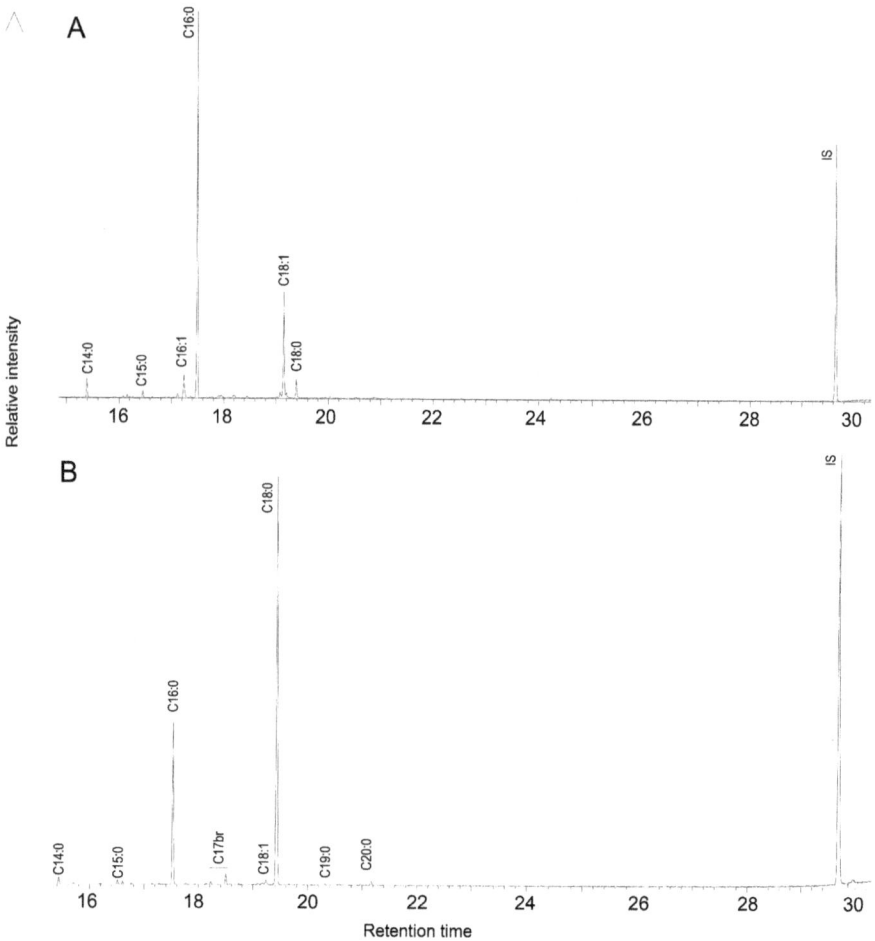

Figure 17.12. Partial gas chromatograms of lipid extracts from A. ceramic sample V268 exhibiting a profile typical of degraded plant oil and B. foodcrust sample VI I8 exhibiting a profile typical of degraded animal fat. Cn:x are fatty acids with carbon length n and number of unsaturations x; br are branched-chain acids; IS is internal standard (n-hexatriacontane).

The zooarchaeological data is represented by a large, calcined bone sample from over 100 features. Among the over 60,000 faunal specimens analyzed, over 87% were unidentifiable, given the calcined nature of the sample. Bird and turtle are underrepresented, particularly given the presence of a major avian flyway passing over the Missisquoi Delta region, as well as the extensive wetlands. Of particular note, throughout the Woodland period fish is a close second to mammal in terms of presence in the cultural features but, given disposal, preservation, recovery and identification factors, fish remains are likely underrepresented. Furthermore, among the primary fish species identified, catfish is likely overrepresented given the distinctive attribute of the species' dorsal spine. Nonetheless, the overall fish-species list—catfish, walleye, whitefish, sturgeon, and Salmonidae—includes some high-fat-content varieties and suggests a range of cultural practices for their collection from weirs, net fishing, spearing, and angling. Some of these species are best caught during spring spawning runs, suggesting collective group activities. Comparatively, the mammal species represented are typical of a terrestrial and riverine setting.

Considering the zooarchaeological remains over time from the Late Archaic to the Early Woodland period, and again throughout the Woodland period, this pattern persists. Mammals and fish predominate, with an overall emphasis on aquatic resources (see Spiess and Mosher 2006).

Against the backdrop of a relatively constant pattern of hunting/fishing strategies focused on aquatic resources, the trends we see in plant use over this same time period are not constant but intensify over time. While the use of nut resources remains fairly constant, the increasing prevalence of non-wood (and non-nut) plant resources from the Late Archaic through the Woodland period is dramatic. This view does not focus on any specific plant types, but rather on the number of species utilized over time. From the paleobotanical samples analyzed, non-wood plant species during the Late Archaic period include three plants (*Chenopodium*, hawthorn, and vervain), two during the Early Woodland period (*Cucurbita pepo*, and *Andropogon gerardii* [big bluestem]), 10 in the Middle Woodland samples, and over 30 during the Late Woodland period (figure 17.13).

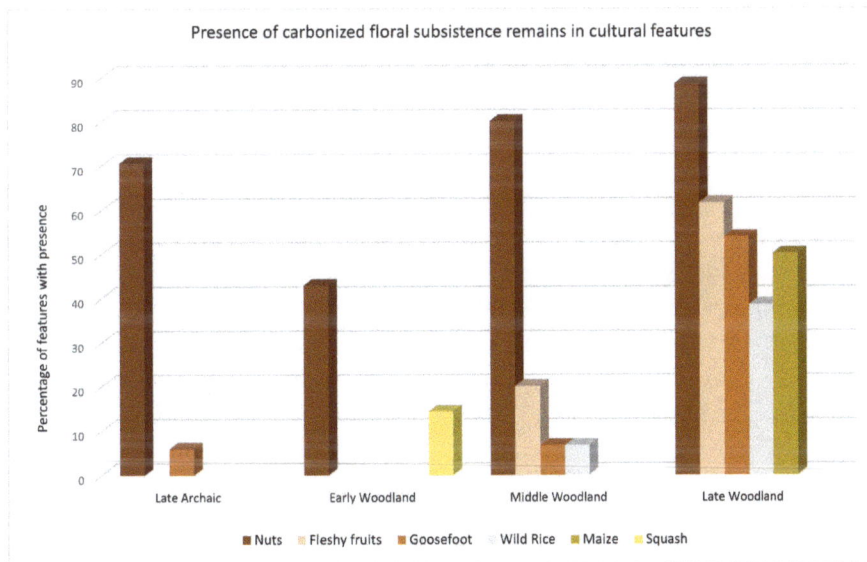

Figure 17.13. Chart showing increase in plant use over time, as expressed by presence of floral subsistence categories in percentage of features from sites VT-FR-0318 and VT-FR-0326.

The details are clear as well. The people living along the river during the Middle Woodland period took advantage of the local plant resources with the use of wild rice, *Chenopodium*, and sunflower; then, in the Late Woodland period, we see a significant increase in plant use with maize as the primary plant resource, along with *Chenopodium* and wild rice, among others. The correlation of maize and increase in seed density has been established from data across the Northeast, and the paleobotanical data from sites VT-FR-0318 and -0326 further confirms this regional pattern (Asch Sidell 2002). As noted, maize was identified in 21 of the 50 paleobotanical samples dating to the Late Woodland period, and the presence of cob fragments indicates that the maize was likely grown on site. The quantity and variety of plant resources reflect collection for food, medicine, and perhaps special technological purposes.

Consideration of wood identifications can shed additional light on this transition. The data set reflects a mosaic of plant communities, including bottomland forest (maple, ash, butternut, elm), white pine–northern hardwoods (beech, sugar maple, yellow birch, red pine, hemlock, fir, hornbeam, hop hornbeam), oak–hickory, and disturbed woods/thicket (cherry, poplar, pitch pine, hawthorn). The Late Archaic–period deposits at site VT-FR-0318 and the Early Woodland–period at site VT-FR-0326 yielded more wood from bottomland forest and less oak–hickory forest than did the later occupations, which may have cleared some of the bottomlands. The high incidence and variety of fleshy fruits present in the Late Woodland period samples may reflect disturbance by fire or other field-clearing activities.

A review of an archaeological database compiled by the State of Vermont (Robinson and Ostrum 2016), containing subsistence data and radiocarbon dates from over 75 Native American sites in the state, provides a useful comparison to better understand patterning seen at sites VT-FR-0318 and -0326. In general, given the large sample size available from sites VT-FR-0318 and -0326, especially for occupations dating to the Middle and Late Woodland periods, the comparative data is patchy; however, a few sites in the database are worthy of mention in that they offer similar evidence. For example, for the Early Woodland period, the Canaan Bridge site (VT-ES-0002) yielded *Chenopodium* in four of the analyzed features, and although from ritual contexts, both acorn and butternut are included in two of the burials from the Boucher site (VT-FR-0026), situated across the river from VT-FR-0318. Sites of note dating to the Middle Woodland period include the Winooski site (VT-CH-0046) and Swanton Water District site (VT-FR-0012), where butternut dominates the samples, while the Late Woodland–period features from the Skitchewaug site (VT-WN-0041) suggest a roughly even use of acorn, beechnut, butternut, hickory, and bitternut.

However, it is in comparison to other Late Woodland–period sites found in alluvial settings that a similar pattern to that seen at sites VT-FR-0318 and -0326 is most evident. Plant resources, including maize and assorted other species such as varying combinations of *Chenopodium*, squash, and sunflower, along with a suite of fleshy fruits (blueberry, elderberry, grape, bramble), seems to be relatively common at Late Woodland sites located in riverine settings. Supporting data from the aforementioned Vermont database includes that from Skitchewaug (VT-WN-0041) (maize, bean, squash, and grape), Swanton Water District (VT-FR-0012) (elderberry, vervain), and Donahue (maize, grape) (Robinson and Ostrum 2016).

In addition, recent work at several Late Woodland sites on the Otter Creek also provide important comparative material. For instance, at the Wales site (VT-AD-0496), directly dated maize fragments suggest an occupation dating to 1300–1410 CE, with site occupants also making use of *Chenopodium*, sunflower, bean, blueberry, and elderberry, as well as bullhead catfish (Hudgell et al. 2019). At the Wyman Island site (VT-AD-0044), dated to ca. 1300–1550 CE, maize was recovered from nearly 75% of the 14 floral samples, along with evidence of *Chenopodium*, vervain, blueberry, grape, elderberry, and bramble (Hudgell et al. 2018). Site VT-RU-0627 is a small Late Woodland-period hamlet with a direct AMS date on maize of 1360 CE, and identified blueberry and bramble seeds (Grindle et al. 2017). Lastly, site VT-FR-0030, located on the Missisquoi directly across from site VT-FR-0318, includes a Late Woodland/Contact–period occupation dated to 1670–1780 CE, with features yielding maize, grape, bramble, huckleberry, and pin cherry; acorn and hickory nut; and fauna including mammal and fish, specifically sucker (Hudgell et al. 2015). As a group of Late Woodland sites situated in riverine/alluvial settings, they conform well with the pattern evident from the sites detailed in this study, VT-FR-0318 and -0326. Together, the paleobotanical data reflects changes in bottomland forest make-up, open-field cultivation, and horticulture. Furthermore, the paleobotanical data from sites VT-FR-0318 and -0326, along with information from these other archaeological sites, can be considered as part of the so-called Eastern Agricultural Complex; in particular, the cultivation of squash, goosefoot (*Chenopodium*), and sunflower prior to the adoption of maize (Asch Sidell 2002, 2008).

Turning to the biomolecular and isotopic data, it is useful to review what we know about the source of these samples, the ceramic pots. As noted, the ceramic sample from the sites includes over 40,000 sherds, reflecting nearly the entire sequence of ceramic manufacture by Native Americans in the Northeast, with ceramics from all but the last century at most (CP7) represented. In terms of ceramic use over time, it is certainly the case that during the Early Woodland period pots were not ubiquitous, and among the small Early Woodland–period encampments known from the sites we see a single pot generally per habitation area. Contrast that with ceramic manufacture during the Middle Woodland period, when we see a dramatic rise in the numbers of pots (>100), and again in the Late Woodland period (>180).

Although this ceramic analysis is not yet finalized, during the Early Woodland period there are two general sizes of pots; then, among the Middle Woodland–period ceramic assemblage, we see three general size categories, with the addition of the largest vessel size of over 15+ litres (~3.9+ gal.). Finally, three vessel-size categories are also evident in the Late Woodland period.

In general terms, the results of the organic residue analyses correlate well with the zooarchaeological and paleobotanical data, in that all suggest a diversity of resources (a mix of aquatic [fish], animal foods, and plants) were cooked/processed in the ceramic pots. This data comes from the actual lipid signatures as identified from 12 of the samples as well as the bulk isotopic values obtained including $\delta^{15}N$ values, C:N ratios, and $\delta^{13}C$ value (see table 17.2). From the 24 ceramic pots which produced interpretable results, 10 pots suggest the presence of aquatic resources, 10 show evidence of protein-rich resources, and four suggest evidence of plant remains. It should be noted that the protein-rich resource could be fish and that the lipid signatures indicating aquatic resources does not include aquatic mammals. Further, the low values returned from some of the pots (uninterpretable) could reflect evidence of plants.

Looking at the results through time, there is a similar result from the Early to the Late Woodland period, with an emphasis on protein-rich and aquatic resources in the residue from the pots and less so for plant resources. Although residue from four pots suggests evidence of plant remains (two from the C:N ratio—V180 and V171, and two from lipid signatures V173 and V268), there is little evidence for maize in the analyzed foodcrust samples. Such evidence would show as a degree of enrichment of ^{13}C over ^{12}C that distinguishes C_3 and C_4 plants. As mentioned above, the $\delta^{13}C$ values obtained from the 20 foodcrust samples ranged from -23.7‰ to -26.7‰. Analysis of reference plant species from eastern United States and Canada establish that the $\delta^{13}C$ values of C_3 plants range between -22‰ and -33‰, compared to a range between -10‰ and -20‰ for C_4 plants including maize (Morton and Schwartz 2004). While it is possible that some of the samples included in this study reflect a mixing of C_4 and C_3 plant resources (or C_3-fed animals), generally speaking, it seems that maize was not a major contributor to the residues.

Even though we see continuous reliance on the mast forest-nut resources throughout the Woodland period, and intensification of plant use during the Middle–Late Woodland period based on the macro-paleobotanical remains, this is not really reflected in the foodcrusts that have been sampled. Of the 24 vessels with interpretable results, eleven are Late Woodland pots and just one showed evidence of plant remains (V268—plant oil). There is the possibility that the samples with non-interpretable results (low lipid yields) contained plants. Several scenarios suggest themselves in light of these results: for whatever reason (and likely several factors are at play), the culinary practices during the Late Woodland period did not result in evidence of plant remains showing up in the lipid or bulk isotopic results from the carbonized foodcrust. It is understood that food-crusts carbonized and adhered to the interior of vessels likely represent the result of one or two cooking episodes, in contrast to the "absorbed residue" samples, which likely represent the combined suite of resources used in a pot over its use life. It appears likely that evidence of plant remains including nuts and C_3/C_4 plants are being masked in processing, preparation, and cooking activities in terms of the content of carbonized foodcrust. Other analyses have detected maize, rice, and squash using phytoliths evidence from ceramic foodcrusts (e.g., Hart et al. 2007; Gates St-Pierre et al. 2015), so we know that these resources were processed in the ceramics, but, for various reasons, their detection using lipids and bulk isotope data has not been as productive. This study has certainly highlighted these limitations and complexities.

Regarding vessel size and the results from the organic residue analyses, there is no discernable pattern. Small and big pots appear to have been used for the same range of resources (aquatic, protein rich, and plant resources), although our sample of varied-sized pots is small. It has been suggested that Early Woodland–period potters may have initially used pots for processing aquatic resources high in fat in order to extract oil. This may have occurred during periods of high resource abundance, such as fish spawning and/or fall nut processing, and asso-ciated social gatherings (Taché and Craig 2015). This may have been an initial impetus for the early adoption and use of ceramic pots in the northeast, and the evidence from sites VT-FR-0318 and VT-FR-0326 does not preclude such a scenario. The apparent low numbers of ceramic pots in use during the Early Woodland period fits well with this interpretation. The lack of the large rock-roasting areas during the Early Woodland period, but common in the preceding Late Archaic period, creates additional questions for the early use of ceramic pots. In contrast, the Middle and Late Woodland periods show an increase in the numbers of vessels and a greater size variance, suggesting a changing role for ceramic vessels over time. Additional research is needed to further explore this assertion.

Conclusions

Given their exceptional context and content, the Missisquoi River archeological deposits from sites VT-FR-0318 and -0326 discussed herein provide us with an exceptional glimpse of cultural processes and changes during the Woodland period. Visible trends include continuity in hunting and fishing alongside a significant increase in the use of plant resources over the duration of the Woodland period. This broad view of subsistence strategies provides a perspective of various cultural processes through time and in one place; the results suggest a strong sense of place and continuity over the Late Archaic–Woodland transition and a persistent intensification during the Woodland-period transition to agricultural economies. Sub-regional subsistence patterns and strategies are apparent, and thus it is important to consider the full suite of site data—site structure, range of subsistence remains, and functional aspects—to best evaluate the significance of variable subsistence practices through time. It is likely that there is considerable variation across the region within broadly recognized patterns and trends.

The biomolecular data provides an important comparative base and, in general terms, the overall $\delta^{15}N$ values correlate well with the macro floral and faunal data in suggesting that a diversity of resources was prepared in ceramic pots. The lack of specific evidence of plant remains in the available foodcrust samples, in particular, from the Late Woodland pots is striking given the prevalence of maize in the sampled cultural features. For as yet fully understood reasons, the intensification of plant use including maize in the Late Woodland period is not reflected in the biomolecular data, suggesting that processing and culinary practices, among other processes and mechanisms, are masking their presence. From a methodological standpoint, it suggests that a lack of C_4 plants in Late Woodland ceramic-vessel foodcrust data does not preclude the presence of maize in other related contexts.

Finally, the full complement of archaeological data suggests increasing plant use is associated with increased population, settlement nucleation, and sedentism during the Middle Woodland period, culminating in the Late Woodland period with the fishing/hunting/farming, village-based communities.

Acknowledgements

There are many people and organizations to thank given the scope and duration of the archaeology work involved with the Vermont Agency of Transportation's Route 78 improvement project. We began the work back in 1999, and over the course of several years of field work there were many people who participated and supported the work. First we would like to thank the Vermont Agency of Transportation and, in particular, Jeannine Russell, for her assistance and support. At the Vermont Division for Historic Preservation, Giovanna Peebles, Scott Dillon, and Jess Robinson provided critical support for our work, and we thank Jess for providing critical comments to an earlier draft of this chapter. We would also like to thank the Abenaki Nation of Missisquoi for their support and assistance over the years. The Swanton community and the individual landowners were generous in allowing access and, in most cases, have deeded ownership of the archaeological collections to the State of Vermont. As a primary landowner, the Missisquoi National Wildlife Refuge and its staff were always helpful and supportive of the archaeological investigations. Dozens and dozens of archaeological technicians worked at the sites over the years and are here thanked en masse for their hard work and attention to detail. Rosemary Cyr and Hutch McPheters at the Northeast Archaeology Research Center are thanked for their expertise and assistance with countless details relating to the project and this study. We also thank Brian Giebel (Advanced Laboratory for Chemical and Isotopic Signatures, CUNY Advanced Research Science Center) for undertaking the bulk stable isotope analyses. Finally, Claude Chapdelaine and Roland Tremblay are thanked for looking at select ceramic pots and giving their input and expertise. Any errors or omissions are the responsibility of the authors.

References Cited

Asch Sidell, Nancy

2002   Paleobotanical Indicators of Subsistence and Settlement Change in the Northeast. In *Northeast Subsistence-Settlement Change A.D. 700–1300*, edited by John P. Hart and Christina Rieth, pp. 241–263. New York State Museum Bulletin, 496. The University of the State of New York, Albany.

2008   The Impact of Maize-based Agriculture on Prehistoric Plant Communities in the Northeast. In *Current Northeast Paleobotany II*, edited by John P. Hart, pp. 29–52. New York State Museum Bulletin 512. The University of the State of New York, Albany.

2016   *Headquarters (VT-FR-318) & Porcupine (VT-FR-326) Floral Remains.* Submitted to the Northeast Archaeology Research Center, Farmington, Maine.

Chapdelaine, Claude

2004   A Review of the Latest Developments in St. Lawrence Iroquoian Archaeology. In, *A Passion for the Past; Papers in Honour of James B. Pendergast*, edited by James V. Wright and Jean-Luc Pilon; pp. 63–75. Mercury Series Archaeology Paper 164, Canadian Museum of Civilization, Gatineau, Quebec.

Corey, Richard, Edward C. Kitson, Stephen R. Scharoun, Jessica A. Reed, Robert N. Bartone, and Ellen R. Cowie

2002   *Archaeological Phase I Survey and Archaeological Phase II Testing of the Shift/Off Alignment and the On-Alignment Portions of the Vermont Route 78 Swanton Project NH 036-1(9), Swanton, Franklin County, Vermont.* University of Maine at Farmington Archaeology Research Center. Submitted to the Vermont Agency of Transportation, Montpelier.

Correa-Ascencio, Marisol, and Richard P. Evershed

2014   High Throughput Screening of Organic Residues in Archaeological Potsherds Using Direct Acidified Methanol Extraction. *Analytical Methods* 6:1330–1340.

Cowie, Ellen R.

2006   Early to Late Woodland Period Plant Use along the Missisquoi River and Missisquoi Bay in Northern Vermont. Paper presented at the 71st Annual Meeting of the Society for American Archaeology, San Juan, Puerto Rico.

Cowie, Ellen R., Gemma-Jayne Hudgell, Michael Brigham, Stephen R. Scharoun, Rosemary A. Cyr, Edward C. Kitson, Hutch M. McPheters and Robert N. Bartone
2012   *Archaeological Phase II Testing of the Headquarters Site (VT-FR-318) in the Vermont Route 78 Swanton Project NH 036-1(9), Swanton, Franklin County, Vermont.* University of Maine at Farmington Archaeology Research Center. Submitted to the Vermont Agency of Transportation, Montpelier.

Craig, Oliver E., M. Forster, Soren H. Andersen, Eva Koch, P. Crombé, N. J. Milner, B. Stern, G. N. Bailey, and Carl P. Heron
2007   Molecular and Isotopic Demonstration of the Processing of Aquatic Products in Northern European Prehistoric Pottery. *Archaeometry* 49(1):135–152.

Craig, Oliver E., H. Saul, Alexandre Lucquin, Yastami Nishida, Karine Taché, L. Clarke, A. Thompson, D. T. Altoft, J. Uchiyama, M. Ajimoto, Kevin Gibbs, Sven Isaksson, Carl P. Heron, and Peter Jordan
2013   Earliest Evidence for the Use of Pottery. *Nature* 496(7445):351–354.

Evershed, Richard P.
2008   Experimental Approaches to the Interpretation of Absorbed Organic Residues in Archaeological Ceramics. *World Archaeology* 40(1):26–47.

Fillon, Richard Henry
1970   The Sedimentation and Recent Geological History of the Missisquoi Delta. Master's thesis, Geology Department, University of Vermont, Burlington.

Gates St-Pierre, Christian, and Robert G. Thompson
2015   Phytolith Evidence for the Early Presence of Maize in Southern Quebec. *American Antiquity* 80(2):408–415.

Grindle, Jacob E., Gemma-Jayne Hudgell, Stephen R. Scharoun, Rosemary A. Cyr, Robert N. Bartone, and Ellen R. Cowie
2017   *Archaeological Phase I Survey and Phase II Testing within the Otter Creek Hydroelectric Project, FERC # 2558, Rutland and Addison Counties, Vermont.* Northeast Archaeology Research Center, Farmington, Maine. Submitted to Green Mountain Power, Rutland.

Hansel, Fabricio A., Mark S. Copley, Luiz A. S. Madureira, and Richard P. Evershed
2004   Thermally Produced ω-(o-alkylphenyl)Alkanoic Acids Provide Evidence for the Processing of Marine Products in Archaeological Pottery Vessels. *Tetrahedron Letters* 45(14):2999–3002.

Hart, John, Hetty Jo Brumbach, and Robert Lusteck
2007   Extending Phytolith Evidence for Early Maize (Zea mays) and Squash (Cucurbit sp.) in Central New York. *American Antiquity* 72(3):563–583.

Heckenberger, Michael J., James B. Petersen, Louise A. Basa, Ellen R. Cowie, Arthur E. Spiess and Robert E. Stuckenrath
1990   Early Woodland Period Mortuary Ceremonialism in the Far Northeast: A View from the Boucher Cemetery. *Archaeology of Eastern North America* 18:109–144.

Hudgell, Gemma-Jayne, Ellen R. Cowie, and Robert N. Bartone
2015   *Archaeological Phase III Data Recovery at Site VT-FR-30 for the Streambank Stabilization Project, Missisquoi National Wildlife Refuge, Highgate, Franklin County, Vermont.* Northeast Archaeology Research Center, Farmington, Maine. Submitted to Panamerican Consultants, Buffalo.

Hudgell, Gemma-Jayne, Robert N. Bartone, and Ellen R. Cowie

2018   *Archaeological Phase III Data Recovery at Native American Site VT-AD-44 within the Weybridge Hydroelectric Project (FERC No. 2731), Weybridge, Addison County, Vermont.* Northeast Archaeology Research Center, Farmington, Maine. Submitted to Green Mountain Power, Rutland.

2019   *Archaeological Phase III Data Recovery at the Native American Wales Site VT-AD-496 within the Vergennes Hydroelectric Project (FERC No. 2674), Weybridge, Addison County, Vermont.* Northeast Archaeology Research Center, Farmington, Maine. Submitted to Green Mountain Power, Rutland.

Hudgell, Gemma-Jayne, Ellen R. Cowie, Stephen R. Scharoun, Rosemary A. Cyr, and Robert N. Bartone

2021   *Archaeological Phase III Data Recovery of the Headquarters and Porcupine Sites (VT-FR-318 and VT-FR-326) in the Vermont Route 78 Swanton Project NH036-1(9), Swanton, Franklin County, Vermont.* Northeast Archaeology Research Center, Farmington, Maine. Submitted to the Vermont Agency of Transportation, Montpelier.

Hudgell, Gemma-Jayne, David W. Beale, Sarah E. Loftus, Ellen R. Cowie, and Robert N. Bartone

2021   *Archaeological Phase III Data Recovery at Native American Site VT-CH-28, within the Lamoille Hydroelectric Project (FERC No. 2205), Milton, Chittenden County,* Northeast Archaeology Research Center, Farmington, Maine. Submitted to Green Mountain Power, Rutland.

Kunikita, Dai, Igor Shevkomud, Kunio Yoshida, Shizuo Onuki, Toshiro Yamahara, and Hiroyuki Matsuzaki

2013   Dating Charred Remains on Pottery and Analyzing Food Habits in the Early Neolithic Period in Northeast Asia. *Radiocarbon* 55(3):1334–1340.

Lucquin, Alexandre, Harry K. Robson, Yvette Eley, Shinya Shoda, Dessislava Veltcheva, Kevin Gibbs, Carl P. Heron, Sven Isaksson, Yastami Nishida, Yasuhiro Taniguchi, Shōta Nakajima, Kenichi Kobayashi, Peter Jordan, Simon Kaner, and Oliver E. Craig

2018   The Impact of Environmental Change on the Use of Early Pottery by East Asian Hunter-Gatherers. *Proceedings of the National Academy of Sciences* 115(31): 7931–7936.

Morton, June D., and Henry P. Schwartz

2004   Palaeodietary Implications from Stable Isotopic Analysis of Residues on Prehistoric Ontario Ceramics. *Journal of Archaeological Science* 31(5):503–517.

Petersen, James B., and Ellen R. Cowie

2002   From Hunter-Gatherer Camp to Horticultural Village: Late Prehistoric Indigenous Subsistence and Settlement in New England. In *Northeast Subsistence-Settlement Change A.D. 700–1300*, edited by John P. Hart and Christina Rieth, pp. 265–287. New York State Museum Bulletin, 496. The University of the State of New York, Albany.

Petersen, James B., and David Sanger

1991   An Aboriginal Ceramic Sequence for Maine and the Maritime Provinces. In *Prehistoric Archaeology in the Maritimes, Reports in Archaeology No. 8*, edited by

Michael Deal and Susan Blair, pp. 121–178. Council of Maritime Premiers, Fredericton.

Petersen, James B., John G. Crock, Ellen R. Cowie, Richard A. Boisvert, Joshua R. Toney, and Geoffrey Mandel

2004   St. Lawrence Iroquoians in Northern New England: Pendergast Was "Right" and More. In, *A Passion for the Past: Papers in Honour of James B. Pendergast*, edited by James V. Wright and Jean-Luc Pilon, pp. 87–123. Mercury Series Archaeology Paper 164, Canadian Museum of Civilization, Gatineau, Quebec.

Rafferty, Sean M.

2006   Evidence of Early Tobacco in Northeast North America. *Journal of Archaeological Science* 33(4):453–458.

Robinson, Francis "Jess," and Brett Ostrum

2016   *Database of Vermont Radiocarbon Dates and Directly Associated Diagnostic Artifact.* A Publication of the Vermont Division for Historic Preservation, Montpelier.

Spiess, Arthur, and John Mosher

2006   Archaic Period Hunting and Fishing around the Gulf of Maine. In *The Archaic of the Far Northeast*, edited by David Sanger and M. A. P. Renouf, pp. 383–408. University of Maine Press, Orono.

Stewart, Frances

2005   *Zooarchaeological Remains from Excavations in 2003 at the Headquarters Site (VT-FR-318), Vermont.* Submitted to the University of Maine at Farmington Archaeology Research Center.

Taché, Karine

2020   *Testing Variation: Lipid Analysis of Ceramic Residues from the Headquarter and Porcupine Sites, Vermont.* Submitted to the Northeast Archaeology Research Center, Farmington.

Taché, Karine, and Oliver E. Craig

2015   Cooperative Harvesting of Aquatic Resources and the Beginning of Pottery Production in North-Eastern North America. *Antiquity* 89(343):177–190.

Index

MERCURY SERIES / LA COLLECTION MERCURE

**The best resource on the history, archaeology, and culture of Canada
is proudly published by the University of Ottawa Press and the Canadian
Museum of History**

**Les Presses de l'Université d'Ottawa et le Musée canadien de l'histoire
publient avec fierté la meilleure ressource en ce qui a trait à l'histoire,
à l'archéologie et à la culture canadiennes**

Series Editor/Direction de la collection: Pierre M. Desrosiers
Editorial Committee/Comité éditorial: Laura Sanchini, Janet Young
Managing Editor/Responsable de l'édition: Robyn Jeffrey
Coordination: Pascal Scallon-Chouinard

Strikingly Canadian and highly specialized, the *Mercury Series* presents works in the research domain of the Canadian Museum of History and benefits from the publishing expertise of the University of Ottawa Press. Created in 1972, the series is in line with the Canadian Museum of History's strategic directions. The *Mercury Series* consists of peer-reviewed academic research, and includes numerous landmark contributions in the disciplines of Canadian history, archaeology, culture, and ethnology. Books in the series are published in at least one of Canada's official languages, and may appear in other languages.

Remarquablement canadienne et hautement spécialisée, la *collection Mercure* réunit des ouvrages portant sur les domaines de recherches du Musée canadien de l'histoire et s'appuie sur le savoir-faire des Presses de l'Université d'Ottawa. Fondée en 1972, elle répond aux orientations stratégiques du Musée canadien de l'histoire. La *collection Mercure* propose des recherches scientifiques évaluées par les pairs et regroupe de nombreuses contributions majeures à l'histoire, à l'archéologie, à la culture et à l'ethnologie canadiennes. Les ouvrages sont publiés dans au moins une des langues officielles du Canada, avec possibilité de parution dans d'autres langues.

Recent Titles/Titres récents

Stacey J. Barker, Krista Cooke, and Molly McCullough, *Material Traces of War: Stories of Canadian Women and Conflict, 1914–1945*, 2021.

Michael K. Hawes, Andrew C. Holman, and Christopher Kirkey, eds., *1968 in Canada: A Year and Its Legacies*, 2021.

Steven Schwinghamer and Jan Raska, *Pier 21: A History*, 2020.

Robert Sweeny, ed., *Sharing Spaces: Essays in Honour of Sherry Olson*, 2020.

Matthew Betts, *Place-Making in the Pretty Harbour: The Archaeology of Port Joli, Nova Scotia*, 2019.

Lauriane Bourgeon, *Préhistoire béringienne: étude archéologique des Grottes du Poisson-Bleu (Yukon)*, 2018.

Jenny Ellison and Jennifer Anderson, eds., *Hockey: Challenging Canada's Game – au-delà du sport national*, 2018.

Myron Momryk, *Mike Starr of Oshawa: A Political Biography*, 2018.

John Willis, ed., *Tu sais, mon vieux Jean-Pierre: Essays on the Archaeology and History of New France and Canadian Culture in Honour of Jean-Pierre Chrestien*, 2017.

Anna Kearney Guigné, *The Forgotten Songs of the Newfoundland Outports: As Taken from Kenneth Peacock's Newfoundland Field Collection, 1951–1961*, 2016.

For a complete list of the University of Ottawa Press titles, visit:
Pour une liste complète des titres des Presses de l'Université d'Ottawa, voir :
press.uOttawa.ca